CEDU(쎄듀)는 **A C**omprehensive **E**nglish e**DU**cation(종합적 영어교육)의 약자입니다.

펴낸이	김기훈 I 김진희
펴낸곳	(주)쎄듀 I 서울특별시 강남구 논현로 305 (역삼동)
발행일	2024년 10월 4일 초판 1쇄
내용문의	www.cedubook.com
구입문의	콘텐츠 마케팅 사업본부
	Tel. 02-6241-2007
	Fax. 02-2058-0209
등록번호	제 22-2472호
ISBN	978-89-6806-436-4
	978-89-6806-435-7 (세트)

쎄듀
빈순삽함

빈칸추론
글의순서
문장삽입
함의추론

저자

김기훈
現 ㈜쎄듀 대표이사
現 메가스터디 영어영역 대표강사
前 서울특별시 교육청 외국어 교육정책자문위원회 위원
저서   천일문 / 천일문 Training Book / 천일문 GRAMMAR
      첫단추 BASIC / Grammar Q / ALL씀 서술형 / Reading Relay
      어휘끝 / 어법끝 / 쎄듀 본영어 / 절대평가 PLAN A
      The 리딩플레이어 / 빈칸백서 / 오답백서
      첫단추 / 파워업 / 쎈쓰업 / 수능영어 절대유형 / 수능실감 등

쎄듀 영어교육연구센터
쎄듀 영어교육센터는 영어 콘텐츠에 대한 전문지식과 경험을 바탕으로
최고의 교육 콘텐츠를 만들고자 최선의 노력을 다하는 전문가 집단입니다.
김진경 전임연구원   **남현화** 연구원

마케팅	콘텐츠 마케팅 사업본부
제작	정승호
영업	문병구
인디자인 편집	한서기획
디자인	윤혜영, 정지은
일러스트	오렌.J
영문교열	James Clayton Sharp

Preface

빈칸 추론은 수능 영어에서 가장 높은 오답률을 기록하는 대표적인 유형입니다. 절대평가가 도입된 이후에는 글의 순서와 문장 삽입 유형도 빈칸 추론만큼이나 높은 오답률을 보이고 있습니다. 또한 함의 추론 유형은 2018학년도 6월 모의평가에 처음 등장한 이후 매년 한 문항씩 출제되고 있으며, 평균 정답률이 약 50%로 매우 어려운 유형에 속합니다.

수능 영어 독해 28문항 중 위 고난도 유형들이 총 9문항을 차지하며, 대부분 3점짜리 문항이어서 총점으로는 22~25점에 해당합니다. 따라서 이것들을 모두 틀리게 되면 3등급 이하의 성적을 받게 됩니다.

이러한 고난도 유형은 상위권 학생들의 변별력을 높이기 위해 고도의 논리 추론 능력을 요구하는 문제들로 구성되어 있어 오답률이 높을 수밖에 없습니다. 단순히 일부 문장을 정확히 해석하는 것만으로는 해결되지 않으며, 정답과 오답의 근거를 논리를 바탕으로 명확하게 추론해 내는 것이 중요합니다. 이 논리 추론력은 단순히 많은 문제를 푼다고 해서 자동으로 길러지지 않습니다. 출제자가 의도한 정답의 단서를 찾아내고 오답을 피하는 전략을 깊이 있게 이해한 후, 이를 실전에서 자연스럽게 활용할 수 있도록 체화하는 과정이 필요합니다.

이에 따라 본 교재는 이 네 가지 주요 유형에 집중하여 체계적으로 전략 학습과 적용 훈련을 할 수 있도록 구성되었습니다.

❶ 유형별 기출 Point와 전략

최신 기출 지문을 통해 문제 풀이의 핵심 포인트를 유형별로 점검하며, 출제자가 의도한 함정을 피할 수 있는 해결 전략을 제시합니다.

❷ 단계별 적용 및 문제 해결

기출 문제에서 핵심 전략 포인트를 학습한 후, 해당 내용을 기출 지문 전체에 적용해 보고, 이어서 실전 문제에 전략을 적용하여 실전 감각을 키울 수 있도록 구성했습니다.

절대평가는 본인이 학습한 만큼 성과가 나타나는 시험입니다. 본 교재의 체계적인 학습과 훈련을 통해 목표하는 등급에 도달할 수 있기를 바랍니다. 끝까지 최선을 다해 여러분의 목표를 이루시길 응원합니다!

저자

Preview

1 기출 Preview

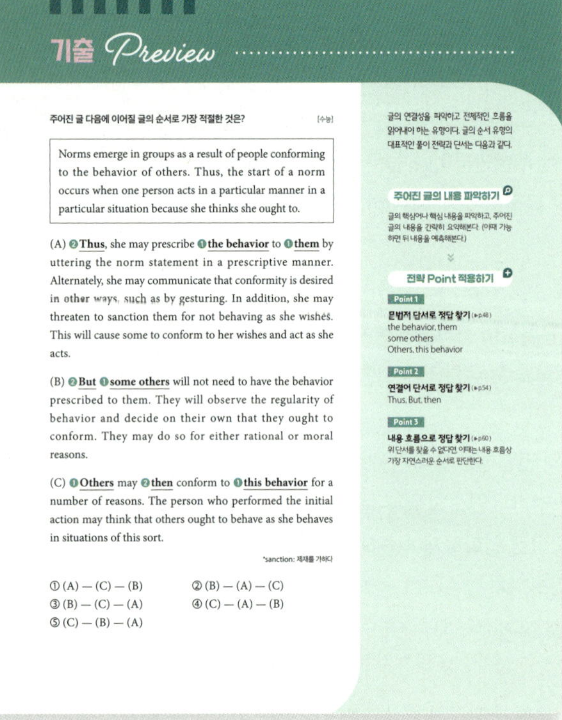

기출 *Preview*

주어진 글 다음에 이어질 글의 순서로 가장 적절한 것은? [수능]

Norms emerge in groups as a result of people conforming to the behavior of others. Thus, the start of a norm occurs when one person acts in a particular manner in a particular situation because she thinks she ought to.

(A) ❷**Thus**, she may prescribe ❶**the behavior** to ❶**them** by uttering the norm statement in a prescriptive manner. Alternately, she may communicate that conformity is desired in other ways, such as by gesturing. In addition, she may threaten to sanction them for not behaving as she wishes. This will cause some to conform to her wishes and act as she acts.

(B) ❷**But** ❶**some others** will not need to have the behavior prescribed to them. They will observe the regularity of behavior and decide on their own that they ought to conform. They may do so for either rational or moral reasons.

(C) ❶**Others** may ❷**then** conform to ❶**this behavior** for a number of reasons. The person who performed the initial action may think that others ought to behave as she behaves in situations of this sort.

*sanction: 제재를 가하다

① (A) — (C) — (B)   ② (B) — (A) — (C)
③ (B) — (C) — (A)   ④ (C) — (A) — (B)
⑤ (C) — (B) — (A)

글의 연결성을 파악하고 전체적인 흐름을 읽어내야 하는 유형이다. 글의 순서 유형의 대표적인 풀이 전략과 단서는 다음과 같다.

주어진 글의 내용 파악하기

글의 핵심어나 핵심 내용을 파악하고, 주어진 글의 내용을 간략히 요약해본다. (이때 가능하면 뒤 내용을 예측해본다.)

전략 Point 적용하기

Point 1
문법적 단서로 정답 찾기 (▶p.48)
the behavior, them
some others
Others, this behavior

Point 2
연결어 단서로 정답 찾기 (▶p.54)
Thus, But, then

Point 3
내용 흐름으로 정답 찾기 (▶p.60)
위 단서를 찾을 수 없다면 이때는 내용 흐름상 가장 자연스러운 순서로 판단한다.

빈칸 추론, 글의 순서, 문장 삽입, 함의 추론 유형별로 최신 기출 문항을 먼저 풀어 보고, 각 유형에서 학습할 전략 포인트를 항목별로 미리 확인할 수 있다.

2 Point Zoom

Point 1 문법적 단서로 정답 찾기

글의 선후 관계를 판단하는 데 있어 가장 강력한 단서는 지시사/대명사, 정관사 the 등이다. 이들이 가지고 있는 문법적 특성이 글의 선후 관계를 분명하게 드러내준다. 따라서 글의 순서를 판단할 때 가장 우선적으로 고려해야 할 단서들이다.

1 지시사/대명사

우선 지시사/대명사가 포함된 글의 내용을 이해한 뒤, 그 수를 감안하여 받고 있는 내용을 찾는다.
this[these], that[those], it, such는 앞에 나온 단어나 구뿐만 아니라 절, 문장을 받을 수도 있으므로 주의해야 한다.

Zoom ①

Notation(악보 표기법) was more than a practical method for preserving an expanding repertoire of music.
→ **It** changed the nature of the art itself. To write something down means .... [모평]

Zoom ②

Tell your family and friends **stories of how you are inspired by the passion and how it makes a difference not only to you but also to others.**
→ **These stories** will make them realise that you are meant to follow your passion.

◆ 지시사/대명사의 수는 이들이 무엇을 받는지를 알려주는 중요한 단서이다. 하지만, 그 후보가 여럿인 경우에는 혼동하지 않도록 주의해야 한다. 아래를 보고, 이어질 글의 순서로 가장 적절한 것을 골라보자.

Wilderness dining has two extremes: gourmet eaters and survival eaters. The first bake cakes and bread and cook multi-course dinners. [수능 응용]

(A) **They** walk only a few miles each day and may use the same campsite for several nights. Survival eaters are up and walking within minutes of waking.
(B) **They** walk dozens of miles every day; lunch is a series of cold snacks eaten on the move.

① (A) — (B)   ② (B) — (A)

Zoom ①

각 전략 포인트를 포함한 기출 지문을 발췌하여, 실제 출제 경향을 확인하고 익힐 수 있다.

함정 주의

'함정 주의' 코너에서 특별히 주의해야 할 부분을 간단한 기출 문제의 풀이나 예시로 학습할 수 있다.

3 Focus & Practice

발췌된 핵심 부분으로 효율적인 전략 적용 학습을 할 수 있다.

4 Read & Apply

최신 기출 문제의 전체 지문과 선택지로 학습한 전략을 적용하여 풀어볼 수 있다.

5 Actual Test

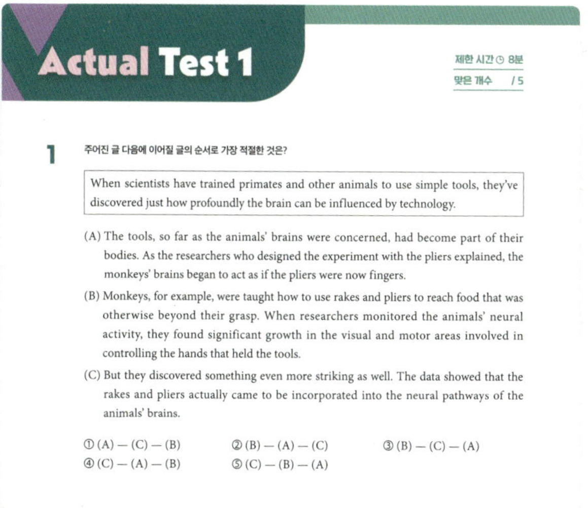

각 유형 학습을 마무리한 뒤, 실전 문제 5문항으로 구성된 2회분의 테스트로 실전 감각을 키우는 훈련을 할 수 있다.

6 Final Check

네 개 유형의 전략 학습과 적용 훈련을 마치고 나서, 각 유형을 한 문항씩 총 4문항을 풀어보며 마무리로 점검해 볼 수 있다.

Preview

7 유형별 맞춤 해설

유형별 전략 적용 & 정답 해설 코너는 각 유형의 전략 Point에 따라 빈칸/함의는 추론 근거,
순서/삽입은 글의 흐름을 파악할 수 있도록 제시했다.

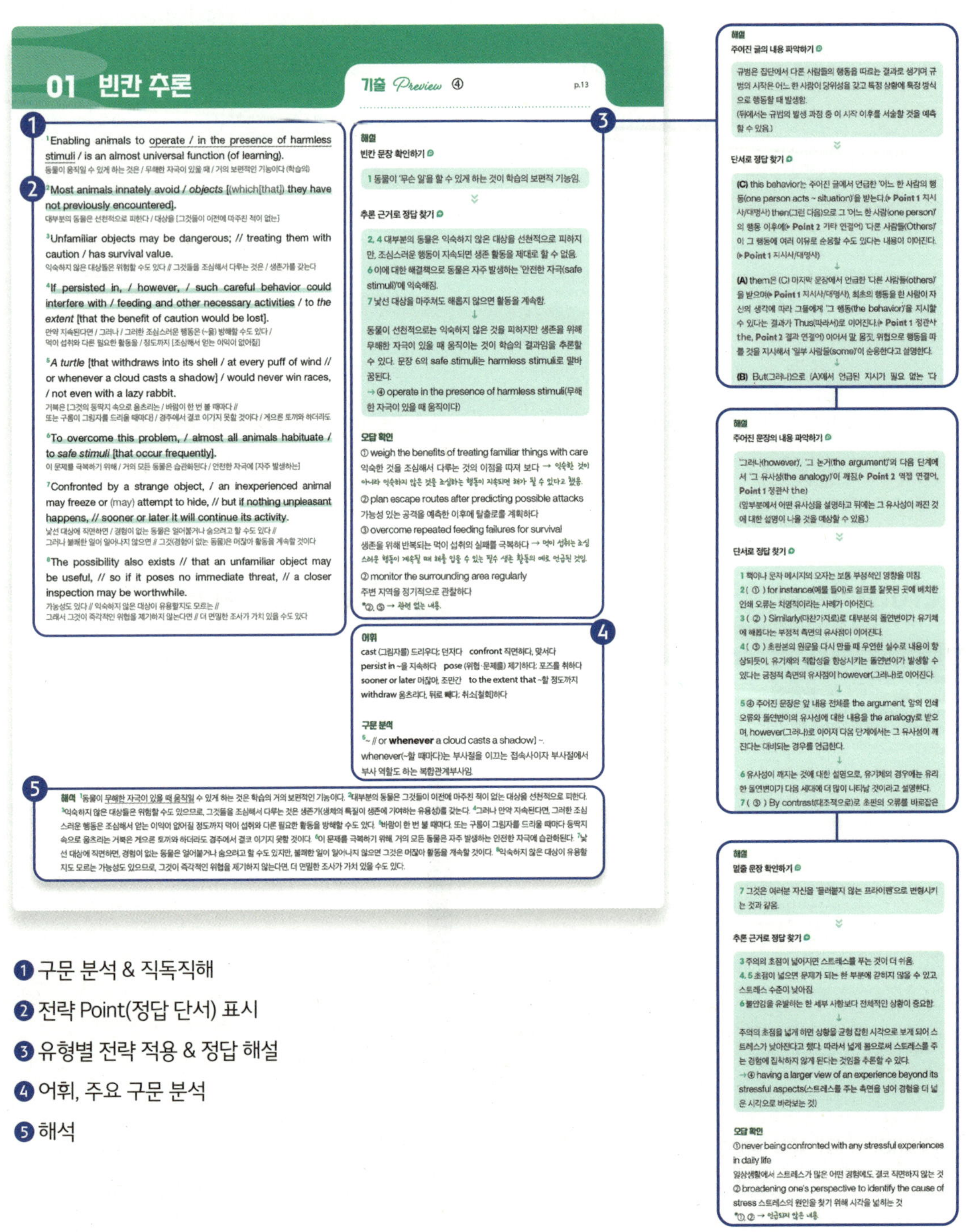

❶ 구문 분석 & 직독직해

❷ 전략 Point(정답 단서) 표시

❸ 유형별 전략 적용 & 정답 해설

❹ 어휘, 주요 구문 분석

❺ 해석

Contents

◆ 킬러문항 배제 이후의 출제 경향

킬러문항의 배제란 영어를 해석하고도 내용이 이해가 안 되는 추상적인 소재, 공교육에서 다루는 일반적인 수준보다 어려운 어휘와 복잡한 문장 구조가 사용된 긴 문장의 배제를 뜻합니다. 이에 따라 변별력 확보를 위해 선택지의 표현이 까다로워지고, 문장 간의 논리적 관계 및 흐름 파악이 중요해졌습니다.

정답 선택지에는 글의 주제나 핵심 키워드의 단순 말바꿈이 아닌 추상적/간접적으로 암시하는 표현이 제시되는 경향이 있습니다.

> What is striking about them is that <u>any number of them could be substituted for one another without loss.</u> [24학년도 대수능 33번]
>
> 그것들(다양한 감정을 보여주는 얼굴 그림)에 관해 놀라운 점은 그것들(얼굴 그림)이 얼마든지 손실 없이 서로 대체될 수 있었다는 것이다. → 다양한 감정을 나타내는 얼굴 그림이 서로 비슷하게 보여서 구분되지 않았다는 것을 '손실 없이 서로 대체될 수 있었다'는 표현으로 암시함.

오답 선택지 또한 소재와 키워드, 지문에서 나온 단어나 유사한 어구로 쉽게 혼동되는 것들을 제시하여 오답률을 높였습니다.

> There have been psychological studies in which subjects were shown **photographs of people's faces** and asked to identify the expression or state of mind evinced.
>
> [오답 선택지] every one of them was illustrated with photographic precision.
> (모든 얼굴 그림들이 사진과 같이 정밀하게 그려졌다.) → 얼굴 사진과 얼굴 그림을 비교하여 둘 다 얼굴의 감정을 알아내기는 어려웠다는 내용에 대해서 '얼굴 사진'에 관련한 키워드를 사용함.

글의 흐름을 파악해야 하는 글의 순서와 문장 삽입 유형은 추상적이고 전문적인 소재의 지문 외에도 문장 간의 연결이 논리적으로 치밀하지 않아서 논리적 흐름 파악을 방해하거나, 논리적 흐름을 파악할 수 있는 단서들이 부족한 문항들이 킬러문항으로 선정되어 배제되었습니다. 따라서 논리적 흐름을 나타내는 명확한 단서가 있는 글이 출제될 것으로 보입니다.

If learning were simply a matter of accumulating lists of facts, then it shouldn't make any difference if we are presented with information that is just a little bit beyond what we already know or totally new information. [25학년도 9월 모평 36번]
(→ 학습이 단순히 사실들의 목록을 축적하는 것이라면 우리가 아는 것과 약간 다르거나 아예 새로운 정보를 받아도 별로 영향이 없을 것임.)

(C) Each fact would simply be stored separately. According to connectionist theory, **however**, our knowledge is organized into patterns of activity, and … we have to modify the old patterns so as to keep the old material while adding the new information. (→ 각 사실이 개별적으로 저장될 것인데(주어진 글에 대한 이유로 부연 설명), 그러나(however) connectionist theory에 의하면 우리의 지식은 활동의 패턴들로 정리되고, 새로운 정보를 추가하면서 오래된 것도 유지하기 위해 옛 패턴은 수정됨.)

(A) The adjustments are clearly smallest when **the new information is only slightly new** …. (→ 새로운 정보가 약간만 새로운 경우에는 조정이 확실히 작음.)

(B) If we are trying to understand **something totally new**, however, we need to make larger adjustments …. (→ 그러나(however) 완전히 새로운 것을 이해하려는 경우에는 더 큰 조정을 해야 함. (약간만 새로운 정보에 이어 완전히 새로운 정보에 따른 조정의 대비))

◆ 새로운 출제 경향에 어떻게 대비해야 할까?

대의 파악 유형과 빈칸 추론 유형 모두 선택지의 매력도가 높아짐에 따라, 지문의 내용을 대략적으로 파악하여 핵심 키워드나 글의 성격을 일반적으로 나타내는 선택지를 고르는 기술보다는, 글의 구조에 따라 핵심이 되는 내용들을 짚어가며 글의 전체적인 내용을 파악하는 것이 중요합니다. 오답 선택지의 매력도도 높아졌으므로, 핵심 키워드만 가지고 섣불리 선택지를 소거하기보다는 지문의 내용과 흐름을 풀어서 표현하는 선택지를 찾도록 해야 합니다.

글의 흐름을 파악하는 글의 순서와 문장 삽입 유형은 논리적 흐름이 명확하게 출제될 것이므로 문장 간의 논리적 관계, 글의 논리적 흐름을 나타내는 단서를 파악하는 것이 중요합니다. 논리적 흐름 파악의 단서로 중요한 연결어들은 뒤의 준비편 2에 정리되어 있으니 미리 확인하고 숙지하도록 합니다.

연결어는 글의 앞뒤가 논리적으로 어떻게 이어지는지를 나타내줍니다. 특히, 글의 순서와 문장 넣기 유형에서 중요한 단서로 작용하는 경우가 많으므로 의미와 기능을 잘 정리해두도록 합시다.

구분	연결어	기능
역접	1. 그러나, 그럼에도 불구하고: but, however, still, yet, nevertheless, nonetheless 2. 반대로, 대신에: conversely, instead[alternatively] 3. 반면에, 대조적으로: in[by] contrast, on the other hand, on the contrary 4. 오히려: rather	앞과 반대, 대조되는 내용을 연결한다. 앞의 초점과 대비되는 놀라운 사실이나 정보를 덧붙이기도 한다.
예시	예를 들면 : for example, by way of example, for instance, as an illustration	구체적인 예를 제시할 때 쓰인다.
첨가	게다가, 더군다나, 또한 : also, furthermore, in addition, additionally, moreover, besides, what is more	앞 내용과 연결되는, 또 다른 내용을 추가할 때 쓰인다.
비교	마찬가지로, 같은 방식으로 : similarly, likewise, in the same way	둘 이상의 사물이나 개념의 유사성을 제시할 때 쓰인다.
결과	그래서, 따라서, 결과적으로 : thus, so, therefore, hence, consequently, accordingly, as a result, in turn, in consequence	앞선 내용에 의거하여 내릴 수 있는 '결론'의 내용을 이끌기도 한다.

강조	사실은, 실제로는 : in (actual) fact, actually, in particular, in effect, indeed, specifically, clearly, as a matter of fact, obviously, certainly, above all, (it is) needless to say (that), it goes without saying that, definitely * in (actual) fact, actually는 첨가와 강조(역접) 두 가지 기능이 있음. 　1. 사실은[실은]: 자세한 내용을 덧붙임 (첨가의 기능) 　2. 사실은[실제로는]: 반대되는 내용을 강조 (역접의 기능)	앞과 반대되는 내용을 강조하거나 자세한 내용을 덧붙일 때 쓰인다.
요약	요약하면, 간단히 말해서 : in short, in brief, in sum(mary), in conclusion, to sum up, to summarize, to put it simply	글의 요지뿐만 아니라, 앞서 언급된 세부 사항에 대한 요약이나 부분적인 결론을 이끌 수도 있다.
환언	즉, 다시 말해서 : in other words, that is (to say), namely, to put it another way, so to speak, as it were	앞 내용과 같은 내용을 다른 어구로 표현할 때 쓰인다.
화제 전환	한편, 그런데 한편에서는 : meanwhile, in the meantime	화제를 바꿀 때 쓰인다.
기타	then(그다음에), at the same time(동시에), unfortunately[unluckily](불행히도)	

01

빈칸 추론

기출 *Preview*

Enabling animals to ____
is an almost universal function of learning. **Most animals innately avoid objects they have not previously encountered.** Unfamiliar objects may be dangerous; treating them with caution has survival value. **If persisted in, however, such careful behavior could interfere with feeding and other necessary activities** to the extent that the benefit of caution would be lost. A turtle that withdraws into its shell at every puff of wind or whenever a cloud casts a shadow would never win races, not even with a lazy rabbit. **To overcome this problem, almost all animals habituate to safe stimuli that occur frequently.** Confronted by a strange object, an inexperienced animal may freeze or attempt to hide, but **if nothing unpleasant happens, sooner or later it will continue its activity.** The possibility also exists that an unfamiliar object may be useful, so if it poses no immediate threat, a closer inspection may be worthwhile.

*innately: 선천적으로

① weigh the benefits of treating familiar things with care
② plan escape routes after predicting possible attacks
③ overcome repeated feeding failures for survival
④ operate in the presence of harmless stimuli
⑤ monitor the surrounding area regularly

글에서 근거를 찾아 빈칸에 들어가야 할 말을 추론해야 하는 유형이다. 정답 선택지는 근거에 해당하는 글의 내용을 다른 말로 바꾸어 표현하는 경우가 많다. 빈칸 추론 유형의 대표적인 풀이 전략은 다음과 같다.

빈칸 문장의 내용 파악하기 

우리말로 간략히 요약하여, '무엇'을 추론해야 하는지를 파악한다.

전략 Point 적용하기 

빈칸의 위치에 따라 적절한 방식으로 빈칸의 추론 근거를 찾는다.

Point 1
빈칸이 초반에 있을 때 정답 찾기
(▶p.14)

Point 2
빈칸이 중반에 있을 때 정답 찾기
(▶p.20)

Point 3
빈칸이 후반에 있을 때 정답 찾기
(▶p.26)

Point 4
빈칸이 마지막에 있을 때 정답 찾기
(▶p.32)

빈칸이 초반에 있을 때 정답 찾기

빈칸 문장에서 찾아야 할 것을 파악한 뒤에 다음과 같은 사항에 유의하여 단서를 찾는다.

빈칸이 첫 문장에 있을 때는 빈칸 문장이 주제문인 경우가 많다. 마지막 문장이 주제문을 재진술하는 양괄식 단락의 가능성도 있기 때문에, 먼저 마지막 문장을 살펴보는 것이 좋다.

Zoom 1

It is not hard to see that a strong economy, where opportunities are plentiful and jobs go begging, _________________________.

빈칸 문장: 튼튼한 경제가 '무엇을 함'.

↓

(중간 생략) In the American construction boom of the late 1990s, for example, **even the carpenters' union — long known as a "traditional bastion**(요새) **of white men**, a world where a coveted(부러움을 사는) union card was handed down from father to son" — **began openly encouraging women, blacks, and Hispanics to join its internship program.** (주제문 재진술) At least in the workplace, **jobs chasing people obviously does more to promote a fluid society** than people chasing jobs. [모평]

→ 빈칸: helps break down social barriers

+ 일자리가 많으면 더 좋은 일자리로 사람들이 많이 옮겨가므로 사회가 보다 유동적으로 된다는 내용을 말바꿈하여 표현했다.

마지막 문장에 단서가 없을 때는 단서가 나올 때까지 차례대로 읽어 내려간다. 단서가 구체적이고 세부적으로 제시될 것이므로, 주제문에 어울리도록 종합해서 일반화해야 한다.

Zoom 2

News, especially in its televised form, is constituted not only by its choice of topics and stories but by its _________________________.

빈칸 문장: TV 뉴스는 주제 선정 외에 '무엇'으로도 구성됨.

↓

(중간 생략) Indeed, **contemporary news construction has come to rely on an increased use of faster editing tempos and 'flashier' presentational styles including the use of logos, sound-bites, rapid visual cuts and the 'star quality' of news readers.** (이하 생략) [수능]

→ 빈칸: verbal and visual idioms or modes of address

+ 현대의 뉴스 구성이 여러 표현 방식을 사용한다고 구체적으로 부연 설명하는 내용을 말바꿈하여 표현했다.

◆ 빈칸 문장이 주제문일 때, 이를 뒷받침하는 세부 사항은 예시, 상술, 논거 등으로 다양할 수 있다. 이때 세부 사항의 내용을 포괄하지 않고, 일부 내용만 말바꿈한 선택지를 고르지 않도록 주의해야 한다. 아래를 보고, 빈칸에 들어갈 말로 가장 적절한 것을 골라보자.

The future of our high-tech goods may lie not in the limitations of our minds, but in ________________________.

↓

Our ingenuity will soon outpace our material supplies. Fortunately, rare metals are key ingredients in green technologies such as electric cars, wind turbines, and solar panels. They help to convert free natural resources like the sun and wind into the power that fuels our lives. But without increasing today's limited supplies, we have no chance of developing the alternative green technologies we need to slow climate change. [수능 응용]

*ingenuity: 창의력

① our ability to secure the ingredients to produce them
② our effort to make them as eco-friendly as possible

빈칸 문장 앞에 한두 문장이 있는 경우에는 그 앞부분을 빈칸 문장에 포함시켜서 찾아야 할 단서를 파악하는 것이 좋다. 대부분, 앞 내용을 통해 무엇에 대한 글인지를 알 수 있기 때문이다. 빈칸 문장이 앞 내용을 뒷받침하는 경우에는 앞뒤 내용을 종합하여 잘 뒷받침하는 것을 고른다.

Zoom ③

Everyone who drives, walks, or swipes(판독기에 통과시키다) **a transit card in a city views herself as a transportation expert** from the moment she walks out the front door. And how she views the street ________________________.

빈칸 문장: 모두가 자신을 교통 전문가로 여기고 그녀(교통 전문가)의 도로를 바라보는 방식은 '어떠함.'

↓

(중간 생략) And like **all politics, all transportation is local and intensely personal.** [수능]

➡ 빈칸: tracks pretty closely with how she gets around

✦ 지역적이고 개인적인 문제라는 내용을 말바꿈하여 표현했다.

Focus & Practice

[1~4] 다음 빈칸에 들어갈 말로 가장 적절한 것을 고르시오.

1

One unspoken truth about creativity — it isn't about wild talent so much as it is about ______________. To find a few ideas that work, you need to try a lot that don't. It's a pure numbers game. Geniuses don't necessarily have a higher success rate than other creators; they simply do more — and they do a range of different things. They have more successes *and* more failures. That goes for teams and companies too. It's impossible to generate a lot of good ideas without also generating a lot of bad ideas. ... [모평]

① superiority
② productivity
③ achievement

2

Even when we do something as apparently simple as picking up a screwdriver, our brain automatically ______________________________. We can literally feel things with the end of the screwdriver. When we extend a hand, holding the screwdriver, we automatically take the length of the latter into account. ... We do the same with the much more complex tools we use, in much more complex situations. The cars we pilot instantaneously and automatically become ourselves. ... Without the extension of self into machine, it would be impossible to drive. [모평 응용]

① recalls past experiences of utilizing the tool
② judges which part of our body can best be used
③ adjusts what it considers body to include the tool

3 Prior to photography, _________________________. While painters have always lifted particular places out of their 'dwelling' and transported them elsewhere, paintings were time-consuming to produce, relatively difficult to transport and one-of-a-kind. ... Photography became coupled to consumer capitalism and the globe was now offered 'in limitless quantities, figures, landscapes, events which had not previously been utilised either at all, or only as pictures for one customer'. ... Gradually photographs became cheap mass-produced objects that made the world visible, aesthetic and desirable. ... Light, small and mass-produced photographs became dynamic vehicles for the spatiotemporal circulation of places. [모평 응용]

*aesthetic: 미적인

① painting was the major form of art
② art held up a mirror to the world
③ places did not travel well

4 Although prices in most retail outlets are set by the retailer, this does not mean that these prices _________________________. On any particular day we find that all products have a specific price ticket on them. However, this price may be different from day to day or week to week. ... If, for example, bad weather leads to a poor potato crop, then the price that supermarkets have to pay to their wholesalers for potatoes will go up and this will be reflected in the prices they mark on potatoes in their stores. Thus, these prices do reflect the interaction of demand and supply in the wider marketplace for potatoes. Although they do not change in the supermarket from hour to hour to reflect local variations in demand and supply, they do change over time to reflect the underlying conditions of the overall production of and demand for the goods in question. [모평 응용]

① reflect the principle of demand and supply
② may not change from hour to hour
③ do not adjust to market forces over time

Read & Apply

정답 및 해설 p. 5

1 다음 빈칸에 들어갈 말로 가장 적절한 것은? [모평]

"What's in a name? That which we call a rose, by any other name would smell as sweet." This thought of Shakespeare's points up a difference between roses and, say, paintings. Natural objects, such as roses, are not ______________. They are not taken as vehicles of meanings and messages. They belong to no tradition, strictly speaking have no style, and are not understood within a framework of culture and convention. Rather, they are sensed and savored relatively directly, without intellectual mediation, and so what they are called, either individually or collectively, has little bearing on our experience of them. What a work of art is titled, on the other hand, has a significant effect on the aesthetic face it presents and on the qualities we correctly perceive in it. A painting of a rose, by a name other than the one it has, might very well smell different, aesthetically speaking. The painting titled *Rose of Summer* and an indiscernible painting titled *Vermillion Womanhood* are physically, but also semantically and aesthetically, distinct objects of art.

*savor: 음미하다 **indiscernible: 식별하기 어려운 ***semantically: 의미적으로

① changed   ② classified   ③ preserved
④ controlled   ⑤ interpreted

2 다음 빈칸에 들어갈 말로 가장 적절한 것은? [수능]

Elinor Ostrom found that there are several factors critical to bringing about stable institutional solutions to the problem of the commons. She pointed out, for instance, that the actors affected by the rules for the use and care of resources must have the right to ______________________________. For that reason, the people who monitor and control the behavior of users should also be users and/or have been given a mandate by all users. This is a significant insight, as it shows that prospects are poor for a centrally directed solution to the problem of the commons coming from a state power in comparison with a local solution for which users assume personal responsibility. Ostrom also emphasizes the importance of democratic decision processes and that all users must be given access to local forums for solving problems and conflicts among themselves. Political institutions at central, regional, and local levels must allow users to devise their own regulations and independently ensure observance.

*commons: 공유지 **mandate: 위임

① participate in decisions to change the rules
② claim individual ownership of the resources
③ use those resources to maximize their profits
④ demand free access to the communal resources
⑤ request proper distribution based on their merits

3 다음 빈칸에 들어갈 말로 가장 적절한 것은? [모평]

Research with human runners challenged conventional wisdom and found that the ground-reaction forces at the foot and the shock transmitted up the leg and through the body after impact with the ground _______________ as runners moved from extremely compliant to extremely hard running surfaces. As a result, researchers gradually began to believe that runners are subconsciously able to adjust leg stiffness prior to foot strike based on their perceptions of the hardness or stiffness of the surface on which they are running. This view suggests that runners create soft legs that soak up impact forces when they are running on very hard surfaces and stiff legs when they are moving along on yielding terrain. As a result, impact forces passing through the legs are strikingly similar over a wide range of running surface types. Contrary to popular belief, running on concrete is not more damaging to the legs than running on soft sand.

*compliant: 말랑말랑한 **terrain: 지형

① varied little
② decreased a lot
③ suddenly peaked
④ gradually appeared
⑤ were hardly generated

Point 2 — 빈칸이 중반에 있을 때 정답 찾기

빈칸이 중반에 있을 때는 이를 뒷받침하는 내용이 뒤에 이어지는 경우가 대부분이다(도입-빈칸 문장(주제문)-세부 사항/결론 구조). 뒤에서 뒷받침하는 내용을 중점적으로 읽으며 추론 근거를 찾는 것이 좋다.

Zoom 1

(이전 생략) The discovery of administrative tablets from the temple complexes at Uruk suggests that token use and consequently writing evolved as a tool of centralized economic governance. Given the lack of archaeological(고고학적인) evidence from Uruk-period domestic sites, it is not clear whether individuals also used the system for ___________________.

빈칸 문장: 가정집 터의 고고학적 증거가 없어서 개인들도 '무엇'을 위해 그 체계(= 토큰과 문자)를 사용했는지는 불명확함.

↓

(중간 생략) The use of identifiable symbols and pictograms on the early tablets is **consistent with administrators needing a lexicon**(어휘 목록) **that was mutually intelligible** by literate and nonliterate parties. As cuneiform script(쐐기 문자) became more abstract, **literacy must have become increasingly important to ensure one understood what he or she had agreed to.** [수능]

➜ 빈칸: personal agreements

✚ 상호 간의 이해, 서로의 합의를 이해하기 위해 읽고 쓰는 능력이 중요해졌을 것이라는 내용을 말바꿈하여 표현했다.

특히 빈칸 문장이 역접 연결어(but, however, instead 등)를 포함하는 경우에는 뒤에 이어지는 내용에 집중한다.

Zoom 2

Many people create and share pictures and videos on the Internet. The difficulty is finding what you want. Typically, people want to search using words (rather than, say, example sketches). (중간 생략) We apply image classification and object detection methods and tag the image with the output words. **But** tags aren't ___________________.

빈칸 문장: 하지만 태그는 '무엇'이 아님.

↓

It matters who is doing what, and tags don't capture this. For example, tagging a picture of a cat in the street with the object categories "cat", "street", "trash can" and "fish bones" **leaves out the information that the cat is pulling the fish bones out of an open trash can on the street.** [모평]

➜ 빈칸: a comprehensive description of what is happening in an image

✚ 태그는 누가 무엇을 하고 있는지에 대한 정보를 포착하지 못한다는 내용을 말바꿈하여 표현했다.

빈칸 문장이 앞의 내용을 뒷받침하는 세부 사항인 경우도 있다(도입-주제문-빈칸 문장(세부 사항) 구조). 특히 앞에 역접 연결어가 있는 경우, 역접 연결어가 주제문을 이끌고 빈칸 문장이 이를 뒷받침하는 주요 세부 사항일 수 있다. 빈칸 문장을 뒷받침하는 부 세부 사항이 이어진다면 이를 통해 추론하는 것도 가능하다.

Zoom ③

(이전 생략) **But**, more often, **individual experiences are embedded**(끼워 넣어진다) **in social contexts where other people with shared attachments socialize around the object of their affections**. Much of the pleasure of fandom ___________________________________.

빈칸 문장: 팬덤의 많은 즐거움이 '어떠함'.

↓

In their diaries, Bostonians of the 1800s described being part of the crowds at concerts as part of the pleasure of attendance. A compelling(강력한) argument can be made that **what fans love is less the object of their fandom than the attachments to (and differentiations from) one another that those affections afford**. [모평]

➜ 빈칸: comes from being connected to other fans

✚ 개인적 경험은 같은 팬덤의 타인과 어울리는 사회적 상황에서 형성된다는 앞의 내용을 세부적으로 설명했다. 팬들이 스타와 같은 팬덤의 대상보다 팬들 간 애착과 차이를 더 사랑한다는 내용으로 뒷받침된다.

◆ 글의 중반에 있는 빈칸 문장에는 지시사/대명사가 포함되는 경우가 많다. 이때는 지칭하는 대상이 무엇인지 문맥을 보고 우선 파악해야 한다. 이에 유의하여, 빈칸에 들어갈 말로 적절한 것을 골라보자.

함정 주의

There have been psychological studies in which subjects were shown photographs of people's faces and asked to identify the expression or state of mind evinced. The results are invariably very mixed. In the 17th century the French painter and theorist Charles Le Brun drew a series of faces illustrating the various emotions that painters could be called upon to represent.

↓

What is striking about **them** is that ___________________________________.
What is missing in all this is any setting or context to make the emotion determinate. ...
In real life as well as in painting we do not come across just faces. ... [수능]

*evince: (감정 따위를) 분명히 나타내다

① all of them could be matched consistently with their intended emotions
② any number of them could be substituted for one another without loss

Focus & Practice

정답 및 해설 p. 8

[1~4] 다음 빈칸에 들어갈 말로 가장 적절한 것을 고르시오.

1

Choosing similar friends can have a rationale. Assessing the survivability of an environment can be risky ... so humans have evolved the desire to associate with similar individuals as a way to perform this function efficiently. This is especially useful to a species that lives in so many different sorts of environments. However, the carrying capacity of a given environment _______________________. If resources are very limited, the individuals who live in a particular place cannot all do the exact same thing .... A rational strategy would therefore sometimes be to *avoid* similar members of one's species. [수능]

① exceeds the expected demands of a community
② is decreased by diverse means of survival
③ places a limit on this strategy

2

... People who have a high sense of self-efficacy tend to pursue challenging goals that may be outside the reach of the average person. People with a strong sense of self-efficacy, therefore, may be more willing to step outside the culturally prescribed behaviors to attempt tasks or goals for which success is viewed as improbable by the majority of social actors in a setting. For these individuals, _______________________.
For example, Australians tend to endorse the "Tall Poppy Syndrome." This saying suggests that any "poppy" that outgrows the others in a field will get "cut down;" in other words, any overachiever will eventually fail. Interviews and observations suggest that it is the high self-efficacy Australians who step outside this culturally prescribed behavior to actually achieve beyond average. [모평]

*self-efficacy: 자기 효능감 **endorse: 지지하다

① self-efficacy is not easy to define
② culture will have little or no impact on behavior
③ setting a goal is important before starting a task

3

Among the most fascinating natural temperature-regulating behaviors are those of social insects such as bees and ants. These insects are able to maintain a nearly constant temperature in their hives or mounds throughout the year. The constancy of these microclimates depends not just on the location and insulation of the habitat, but on ________________________________. When the surrounding temperature increases, the activity in the hive decreases, which decreases the amount of heat generated by insect metabolism. In fact, many animals decrease their activity in the heat and increase it in the cold, and people who are allowed to choose levels of physical activity in hot or cold environments adjust their workload precisely to body temperature. ...

*insulation: 단열

① the activity of the insects in the colony
② the building materials of the habitat
③ the physical development of the inhabitants

4

... The typical scenario in the less developed world is one in which a very few commercial agriculturalists are technologically advanced while the vast majority are incapable of competing. Indeed, this vast majority ________________________________ because of larger global causes. As an example, in Kenya, farmers are actively encouraged to grow export crops such as tea and coffee at the expense of basic food production. The result is that a staple crop, such as maize, is not being produced in a sufficient amount. The essential argument here is that the capitalist mode of production is affecting peasant production in the less developed world in such a way as to limit the production of staple foods, thus causing a food problem.

*staple: 주요한 **maize: 옥수수 ***peasant: 소농(小農)

① have lost control over their own production
② have challenged the capitalist mode of production
③ have reduced their involvement in growing cash crops

Read & Apply

정답 및 해설 p. 10

1 다음 빈칸에 들어갈 말로 가장 적절한 것은? [모평]

In the post-World War II years after 1945, unparalleled economic growth fueled a building boom and a massive migration from the central cities to the new suburban areas. The suburbs were far more dependent on the automobile, signaling the shift from primary dependence on public transportation to private cars. Soon this led to the construction of better highways and freeways and the decline and even loss of public transportation. With all of these changes came a _______________ of leisure. As more people owned their own homes, with more space inside and lovely yards outside, their recreation and leisure time was increasingly centered around the home or, at most, the neighborhood. One major activity of this home-based leisure was watching television. No longer did one have to ride the trolly to the theater to watch a movie; similar entertainment was available for free and more conveniently from television.

*unparalleled: 유례없는

① downfall　　　　② uniformity　　　　③ restoration
④ privatization　　⑤ customization

2 다음 빈칸에 들어갈 말로 가장 적절한 것은? [모평]

People have always needed to eat, and they always will. Rising emphasis on self-expression values does not put an end to material desires. But prevailing economic orientations are gradually being reshaped. People who work in the knowledge sector continue to seek high salaries, but they place equal or greater emphasis on doing stimulating work and being able to follow their own time schedules. Consumption is becoming progressively less determined by the need for sustenance and the practical use of the goods consumed. People still eat, but a growing component of food's value is determined by its _______________ aspects. People pay a premium to eat exotic cuisines that provide an interesting experience or that symbolize a distinctive lifestyle. The publics of postindustrial societies place growing emphasis on "political consumerism," such as boycotting goods whose production violates ecological or ethical standards. Consumption is less and less a matter of sustenance and more and more a question of lifestyle — and choice.

*prevail: 우세하다 **cuisine: 요리

① quantitative　　② nonmaterial　　③ nutritional
④ invariable　　　⑤ economic

3 다음 빈칸에 들어갈 말로 가장 적절한 것은?

In labor-sharing groups, people contribute labor to other people on a regular basis (for seasonal agricultural work such as harvesting) or on an irregular basis (in the event of a crisis such as the need to rebuild a barn damaged by fire). Labor sharing groups are part of what has been called a "moral economy" since no one keeps formal records on how much any family puts in or takes out. Instead, accounting is ________________. The group has a sense of moral community based on years of trust and sharing. In a certain community of North America, labor sharing is a major economic factor of social cohesion. When a family needs a new barn or faces repair work that requires group labor, a barn-raising party is called. Many families show up to help. Adult men provide manual labor, and adult women provide food for the event. Later, when another family needs help, they call on the same people.

*cohesion: 응집성

① legally established   ② regularly reported
③ socially regulated   ④ manually calculated
⑤ carefully documented

빈칸 문장 뒤에 한두 문장 정도가 더 있는 경우이다. 그 문장들이 빈칸 문장에 대한 부연 설명일 경우에는 단서가 되므로 우선적으로 읽는 것이 좋다. 최근에는 단순히 글의 맺음말인 경우도 많기 때문에 단서가 없다면 바로 앞부분부터 읽어 내려가야 한다.

Zoom 1

Long before Walt Whitman wrote *Leaves of Grass*, poets had addressed themselves to fame. (중간 생략) But to this ancient desire to live forever on the page, he **added a new sense of fame**. Readers would not simply attend to the poet's work; they would be attracted to **thc greatness of his personality**. (중간 생략) Whitman defined poetic fame **in relation to the crowd**. Other poets might look for their inspiration from the goddess of poetry. Whitman's poet sought ________________________________.

빈칸 문장: Whitman의 시인상은 '무엇'을 추구했음.

↓

In the instability of American democracy, **fame would be dependent on celebrity, on the degree to which the people rejoiced in the poet and his work**. [수능]

→ 빈칸: the approval of his contemporaries

+ 명성이 지명도, 즉 사람들이 시인과 그의 작품을 얼마나 좋아하는지에 달렸다는 내용을 말바꿈하여 표현했다.

빈칸 문장이 앞 내용과 논리적으로 더 긴밀히 연결되어 있을 수도 있다. 이때는 앞에서부터 읽어 내려가며 추론할 수 있다.

Zoom 2

An invention or discovery that is too far ahead of its time is worthless; no one can follow. Ideally, **an innovation opens up only the next step from what is known** and invites the culture to move forward one hop. (중간 생략) Gregor Mendel's 1865 theories of genetic heredity were correct but ignored for 35 years. (중간 생략) Decades later science faced the urgent questions that Mendel's discoveries could answer. Now his insights ________________________________.

빈칸 문장: 이제(Mendel의 발견이 질문에 답할 수 있었을 때) 그의 통찰력은 '어떠했음'.

↓

Within a few years of one another, three different scientists each independently rediscovered Mendel's forgotten work, which of course had been there all along. [모평]

(뒤 문장 요약: Mendel의 연구는 다른 과학자들에 의해 세 번이나 재발견됨.)

→ 빈칸: were only one step away

+ Mendel의 발견이 질문에 대한 답이 되고 다른 과학자들에 의해 재발견되었다는 것은 그의 통찰력(발견)이 이제 단 한 걸음만 떨어져 있는 이상적 혁신이 되었다는 것을 의미한다.

(이전 생략) Most of us **assign separate functions to separate rooms**, but even if you look at a one-room house you will find the same internal specialization. In a cabin or a mud hut, or even a Mesolithic cave from 30,000 years ago, **this part is for cooking, that part is for sleeping; this part is for making tools and weaving, that part is for waste.** We keep ___________________________.

빈칸 문장: 우리는 '무엇'을 유지함.

↓

To a varying extent, other animals do **the same. A part of an animal's territory is for eating, a part for sleeping, a part for swimming or wallowing, a part may be set aside for waste, depending on the species of animal.** [모평]

➜ 빈칸: a neat functional organization

✚ 다른 동물들도 (우리와) 똑같이 영역을 각기 기능에 따라 분리한다는 내용을 말바꿈하여 표현했다.

(이전 생략) 'Reading' now applies to a greater number of representational forms than at any time in the past: pictures, maps, screens, design graphics and photographs are all regarded as text. (중간 생략) Thus, **reading becomes a more complicated kind of interpretation than it was when children's attention was focused on the printed text**, with sketches or pictures as an adjunct(부속물). Children now learn from a picture book that words and illustrations complement and enhance each other. Reading is not simply ___________________________.

↓

빈칸 문장: 읽기는 단순히 '무엇'이 아님

Even in the easiest texts, **what a sentence 'says' is often not what it means.** [수능]

➜ 빈칸: word recognition

✚ 읽기가 텍스트만을 해석하는 것이 아니라는 내용을 말바꿈하여 표현했다.

Focus & Practice

정답 및 해설 p. 13

1

... Ecological relationships certainly have their own logic and in this sense 'nature' can be seen to have a self-regulating but not necessarily stable dynamic independent of human intervention. But the context for ecological interactions ______________________.
We may not determine how or what a lion eats but we certainly can regulate where the lion feeds. [모평]

*ecological: 생태학의

① has increasingly been set by humanity
② changes too frequently to be regulated
③ has been affected by various natural conditions

2

The role of science can sometimes be overstated, with its advocates slipping into scientism. Scientism is the view that the scientific description of reality is the only truth there is. With the advance of science, there has been a tendency to slip into scientism, and assume that any factual claim can be authenticated if and only if the term 'scientific' can correctly be ascribed to it. The consequence is that non-scientific approaches to reality ... may become labelled as merely subjective, and therefore of little ______________________
in terms of describing the way the world is. The philosophy of science seeks to avoid crude scientism and get a balanced view on what the scientific method can and cannot achieve.

*ascribe: 속하는 것으로 생각하다 **crude: 투박한

① question
② account
③ bias

3

... Often externalizing conversations involve tracing the influence of the problem in a child's life over time and how the problem has disempowered the child by limiting his ability to see things in a different light. The counsellor helps the child to change by deconstructing old stories and reconstructing preferred stories about himself and his life. To help the child to develop a new story, the counsellor and child search for times when the problem has not influenced the child or the child's life and focus on the different ways the child thought, felt and behaved. These _______________________ help the child create a new and preferred story. As a new and preferred story begins to emerge, it is important to assist the child to hold on to, or stay connected to, the new story.

① distances from the alternative story
② methods of linking the child's stories to another's
③ exceptions to the problem story

4

Digital technology accelerates dematerialization by hastening the migration from products to services. ... But dematerialization is not just about digital goods. The reason even solid physical goods — like a soda can — can deliver more benefits while inhabiting less material is because their heavy atoms are substituted by weightless bits. The tangible is replaced by intangibles — intangibles like better design, innovative processes, smart chips, and eventually online connectivity — that do the work that more aluminum atoms used to do. Soft things, like intelligence, are thus embedded into hard things, like aluminum, that make hard things behave more like software. Material goods infused with bits increasingly act as if _______________________. Nouns morph to verbs. Hardware behaves like software. In Silicon Valley they say it like this: "Software eats everything." [모평]

*morph: 변화하다

① they were intangible services
② they replaced all digital goods
③ hardware could survive software

Read & Apply

정답 및 해설 p. 15

1 다음 빈칸에 들어갈 말로 가장 적절한 것은? [수능]

How many of the lunches that you ate over the last week can you recall? Do you remember what you ate today? I hope so. Yesterday? I bet it takes a moment's effort. And what about the day before yesterday? What about a week ago? It's not so much that your memory of last week's lunch has disappeared; if provided with the right cue, like where you ate it, or whom you ate it with, you would likely recall what had been on your plate. Rather, it's difficult to remember last week's lunch because your brain has filed it away with all the other lunches you've ever eaten as *just another lunch*. When we try to recall something from a category that includes as many instances as "lunch" or "wine," many memories compete for our attention. The memory of last Wednesday's lunch isn't necessarily gone; it's that you lack ______________________________. But a wine that talks: That's unique. It's a memory without rivals.

① the channel to let it flow into the pool of ordinary memories
② the right hook to pull it out of a sea of lunchtime memories
③ the glue to attach it to just another lunch memory
④ the memory capacity to keep a box of sleeping memories
⑤ the sufficient number of competitors in a battle for attention

2 다음 빈칸에 들어갈 말로 가장 적절한 것은? [모평]

Through recent decades academic archaeologists have been urged to conduct their research and excavations according to hypothesis-testing procedures. It has been argued that we should construct our general theories, deduce testable propositions and prove or disprove them against the sampled data. In fact, the application of this 'scientific method' often ran into difficulties. The data have a tendency to lead to unexpected questions, problems and issues. Thus, archaeologists claiming to follow hypothesis-testing procedures found themselves having to create a fiction. In practice, their work and theoretical conclusions partly developed ______________________________. In other words, they already knew the data when they decided upon an interpretation. But in presenting their work they rewrote the script, placing the theory first and claiming to have tested it against data which they discovered, as in an experiment under laboratory conditions.

*excavation: 발굴 **deduce: 추론하다

① from the data which they had discovered

② from comparisons of data in other fields

③ to explore more sites for their future studies

④ by supposing possible theoretical frameworks

⑤ by observing the hypothesis-testing procedures

3 다음 빈칸에 들어갈 말로 가장 적절한 것은? [수능]

People have always wanted to be around other people and to learn from them. Cities have long been dynamos of social possibility, foundries of art, music, and fashion. Slang, or, if you prefer, "lexical innovation," has always started in cities — an outgrowth of all those different people so frequently exposed to one another. It spreads outward, in a manner not unlike transmissible disease, which itself typically "takes off" in cities. If, as the noted linguist Leonard Bloomfield argued, the way a person talks is a "composite result of what he has heard before," then language innovation would happen where the most people heard and talked to the most other people. Cities drive taste change because they ____, who not surprisingly are often the creative people cities seem to attract. Media, ever more global, ever more far-reaching, spread language faster to more people.

*foundry: 주물 공장 **lexical: 어휘의

① provide rich source materials for artists

② offer the greatest exposure to other people

③ cause cultural conflicts among users of slang

④ present ideal research environments to linguists

⑤ reduce the social mobility of ambitious outsiders

빈칸 문장을 직전 문장과 함께 확인하는 것이 도움이 되는 경우가 많다. 특히 빈칸 문장에 대명사, 연결사 등이 포함되는 경우 직전 문장을 통해 찾아야 할 것을 좀 더 정확히 판단할 수 있다. 직전 문장에 직접적인 단서가 있을 가능성도 있기 때문이다.

Zoom ①

(이전 생략) Conversely, the renewed interest in genetics has led to **a growing awareness that there are many wild plants and animals with interesting or useful genetic properties that could be used for a variety of as-yet-unknown purposes. This** has led in turn to a realization that ________________________ **because they may harbor tomorrow's drugs against cancer, malaria, or obesity.** [모평]

직전 문장+빈칸 문장: 빈칸 문장의 This는 아직 알려지지 않은 다양한 목적으로 이용될 수 있는 많은 야생 동식물이 있다는 증가하는 인식을 지칭하며, they가 질병 치료제를 가지고 있을 수도 있기 때문에 이는 '어떤' 깨달음으로 이어짐.

→ 빈칸: we should avoid destroying natural ecosystems

+ 야생 동식물이 가지고 있을지 모르는 유용함에 대한 인식은 자연 생태계(natural ecosystems[they])를 보존해야겠다는 깨달음을 주었을 것이다.

Zoom ②

There was nothing modern about the idea of men making women's clothes .... In the old days, however, **the client was always primary and her tailor was an obscure**(무명의) **craftsman** .... (중간 생략) Beginning in the late nineteenth century, **with the hugely successful rise of the artistic male couturier**(고급 여성복 디자이너)**, it was the designer who became celebrated,** and the client elevated by his inspired attention.

↓

In a climate of admiration for male artists and their female creations, the dress-designer first flourished as the same sort of creator. Instead of the old rule that dressmaking is a craft, ________________________ was invented that had not been there before. [모평]

직전 문장+빈칸 문장: 의상 제작자는 처음으로 창작자로서 성공했으며, 의상 제작이 기술이라는 옛 규칙 대신에 지금은 이전에 없던 '무엇'이 만들어짐.

→ 빈칸: a modern connection between dress-design and art

+ 앞에서 의상 제작이 고객 위주로 이루어졌던 과거의 재단사와 19세기 후반에 성공적으로 부상한 예술적인 남성 고급 여성복 디자이너가 대조되었다. 또한 직전 문장과 빈칸 문장의 '창작'과 '기술'의 대조를 말바꿈하여 표현했다.

빈칸 문장이 대명사나 연결사 없이 길고 복잡할 때는 빈칸 문장을 중심으로 유추해 보고 글 초반의 내용으로 확인한다.

Zoom ③

Young contemporary artists who employ digital technologies in their practice rarely make reference to computers. For example, Wade Guyton, an abstractionist who uses a word processing program and inkjet printers, **does not call himself a computer artist**. (중간 생략)

↓

For the present generation of artists, the computer, or more appropriately, the laptop, is one in a collection of integrated, portable digital technologies that link their social and working life. **With tablets and cell phones surpassing personal computers in Internet usage**, and as **slim digital devices resemble nothing like the room-sized mainframes and bulky desktop computers of previous decades**, it now appears that the computer artist is finally ______________________. [모평]

빈칸 문장: 인터넷 사용에 있어 태블릿과 핸드폰이 개인 컴퓨터를 능가하고 얇은 기기들이 커다란 컴퓨터와 닮지 않아서 이제 컴퓨터 예술가는 결국 '어떠한' 것으로 보임.

➜ 빈칸: extinct

✚ 빈칸 문장의 의미는 예전의 컴퓨터들이 성능이나 크기 문제로 사라지고 오늘날의 디지털 기기가 이들을 대체하고 있다는 것이다. 따라서 컴퓨터 예술가도 결국 '사라진' 상태라는 의미가 되어야 한다. 이는 지문 초반에 디지털 기술을 사용하는 현대 예술가가 컴퓨터를 언급하지 않는다는 설명과도 연결된다.

직전 문장이 대명사 등으로 인해 내용 파악이 어려운 경우에는 글을 처음부터 읽어 내려가며 단서를 파악하도록 한다.

Zoom ④

Heritage is concerned with the ways in which very selective material artefacts, mythologies, memories and traditions become resources for the present. **The contents, interpretations and representations of the resource are selected according to the demands of the present** .... It follows too that **the meanings and functions of memory and tradition are defined in the present**. Further, heritage is more concerned with meanings than material artefacts. (중간 생략) In turn, **they may later be discarded as the demands of present societies change**, or even, as is presently occurring in the former Eastern Europe, when pasts have to be reinvented to reflect new presents.

↓

Thus heritage is ______________________. [수능]

빈칸 문장: 따라서 유산은 '어떠한 것'임.

➜ 빈칸: as much about forgetting as remembering the past

✚ 현재의 요구에 따라 유산이 선택되고, 현재의 요구 변화에 따라 버려질 수도 있다고 했다. 이는 유산이 현재의 가치와 의미를 반영하기 위해 과거의 것을 잊는 것과도 관련된다는 결론으로 말바꿈된다.

Focus & Practice

1

... The Oxford definition focuses on "what" post-truth is: the idea that feelings sometimes matter more than facts. But just as important is the next question, which is why this ever occurs. Someone does not argue against an obvious or easily confirmable fact for no reason; he or she does so when it is to his or her advantage. When a person's beliefs are threatened by an "inconvenient fact," sometimes it is preferable to challenge the fact. This can happen at either a conscious or unconscious level (since sometimes the person we are seeking to convince is ourselves), but the point is that this sort of post-truth relationship to facts occurs only when we are seeking to assert something _______________________________. [모평]

① to hold back our mixed feelings
② to carry the constant value of absolute truth
③ that is more important to us than the truth itself

2

... Psychology seeks to make patterns, find regularity, and ultimately impose order on human experience and behavior. Writers, by contrast, dive into the unruly, untamed depths of human experiences. ... If we psychologists are too bent on identifying the orderly pattern, the regularities of children's minds, we may miss an essential and pervasive characteristic of our topic: the child's more unruly and imaginative ways of talking and thinking. It is not only the developed writer or literary scholar who seems drawn toward a somewhat wild and idiosyncratic way of thinking; young children are as well. The psychologist interested in young children may have to _______________________ _______________________ in order to get a good picture of how children think. [모평]

*unruly: 제멋대로 구는 **pervasive: 널리 퍼져 있는 ***idiosyncratic: 색다른

① venture a little more often into the wilderness
② help them recall their most precious memories
③ disregard the key characteristics of children's fiction

3 Successful integration of an educational technology is marked by that technology being regarded by users as an unobtrusive facilitator of learning, instruction, or performance. When the focus shifts from the technology being used to the educational purpose that technology serves, then that technology is becoming a comfortable and trusted element, and can be regarded as being successfully integrated. Few people give a second thought to the use of a ball-point pen although the mechanisms involved vary — some use a twist mechanism and some use a push button on top, and there are other variations as well. ... New and emerging technologies often introduce both fascination and frustration with users. As long as ____ in promoting learning, instruction, or performance, then one ought not to conclude that the technology has been successfully integrated — at least for that user. [수능]

*unobtrusive: 눈에 띄지 않는

① the user successfully achieves familiarity with the technology
② the user's focus is on the technology itself rather than its use
③ the user continues to employ outdated educational techniques

4 Some people have defined wildlife damage management as the science and management of overabundant species, but this definition is too narrow. All wildlife species act in ways that harm human interests. Thus, all species cause wildlife damage, not just overabundant ones. One interesting example of this involves endangered peregrine falcons in California, which prey on another endangered species, the California least tern. Certainly, we would not consider peregrine falcons as being overabundant, but we wish that they would not feed on an endangered species. ... The goal of wildlife damage management in this case would be to stop the falcons from eating the terns without __________ the falcons. [모평]

*peregrine falcon: 송골매 **least tern: 작은 제비갈매기

① harming
② training
③ overfeeding

Read & Apply

정답 및 해설 p. 20

1 다음 빈칸에 들어갈 말로 가장 적절한 것은? [수능]

There is something deeply paradoxical about the professional status of sports journalism, especially in the medium of print. In discharging their usual responsibilities of description and commentary, reporters' accounts of sports events are eagerly consulted by sports fans, while in their broader journalistic role of covering sport in its many forms, sports journalists are among the most visible of all contemporary writers. The ruminations of the elite class of 'celebrity' sports journalists are much sought after by the major newspapers, their lucrative contracts being the envy of colleagues in other 'disciplines' of journalism. Yet sports journalists do not have a standing in their profession that corresponds to the size of their readerships or of their pay packets, with the old saying (now reaching the status of cliché) that sport is the 'toy department of the news media' still readily to hand as a dismissal of the worth of what sports journalists do. This reluctance to take sports journalism seriously produces the paradoxical outcome that sports newspaper writers are much read but little ________________.

*discharge: 이행하다 **rumination: 숙고 ***lucrative: 돈을 많이 버는

① paid   ② admired
③ censored   ④ challenged
⑤ discussed

2 다음 빈칸에 들어갈 말로 가장 적절한 것은? [모평]

A large part of what we see is what we expect to see. This explains why we "see" faces and figures in a flickering campfire, or in moving clouds. This is why Leonardo da Vinci advised artists to discover their motifs by staring at patches on a blank wall. A fire provides a constant flickering change in visual information that never integrates into anything solid and thereby allows the brain to engage in a play of hypotheses. On the other hand, the wall does not present us with very much in the way of visual clues, and so the brain begins to make more and more hypotheses and desperately searches for confirmation. A crack in the wall looks a little like the profile of a nose and suddenly a whole face appears, or a leaping horse, or a dancing figure. In cases like these the brain's visual strategies are ______________ ________________________________.

*flicker: 흔들리다

① ignoring distracting information unrelated to visual clues
② projecting images from within the mind out onto the world
③ categorizing objects into groups either real or imagined
④ strengthening connections between objects in the real world
⑤ removing the broken or missing parts of an original image

3 다음 빈칸에 들어갈 말로 가장 적절한 것은? [모평]

The debates between social and cultural anthropologists concern not the differences between the concepts but the analytical priority: which should come first, the social chicken or the cultural egg? British anthropology emphasizes the social. It assumes that social institutions determine culture and that universal domains of society (such as kinship, economy, politics, and religion) are represented by specific institutions (such as the family, subsistence farming, the British Parliament, and the Church of England) which can be compared cross-culturally. American anthropology emphasizes the cultural. It assumes that culture shapes social institutions by providing the shared beliefs, the core values, the communicative tools, and so on that make social life possible. It does not assume that there are universal social domains, preferring instead to discover domains empirically as aspects of each society's own classificatory schemes — in other words, its culture. And it rejects the notion that any social institution can be understood _________________________.

*anthropology: 인류학 **subsistence farming: 자급 농업 ***empirically: 경험적으로

① in relation to its cultural origin
② in isolation from its own context
③ regardless of personal preferences
④ without considering its economic roots
⑤ on the basis of British-American relations

Actual Test 1

1 다음 빈칸에 들어갈 말로 가장 적절한 것은?

In today's world we have come to neglect the habit of writing because so many other forms of communication have taken its place. Telephones, tape recorders, computers, and fax machines are more efficient in conveying news. If the only goal is to transmit information, then writing deserves to become obsolete. But writing is for ______________ ______________________. In the past, educated persons used journals and personal correspondence to put their experiences into words, which allowed them to reflect on what had happened during the day. The incredibly detailed letters many Victorians wrote are an example of how people used writing to establish order from the random events they experienced. The kind of material we write in diaries and letters does not exist before it is written down. It is the slow, organically growing process of thought involved in writing that lets the ideas emerge in the first place.

① recording historic events
② enjoying one's free time
③ creating new information
④ drawing inspiration from the world
⑤ communicating effectively with others

2 다음 빈칸에 들어갈 말로 가장 적절한 것은?

One of Napoleon Bonaparte's most important insights was that ___________________.
As a child of the middle classes, he wasn't about to elevate noble lords above their ability.
"Bonaparte judged men by what they could do, and not by their genealogy. He looked not
at the decorations that adorned the breast, but at the exploits that stamped the warrior;
not at the learning that made the perfect tactician, but at the real practical force that
brought out great achievement," wrote J. T. Headley. Napoleon's surest colleagues had
risen from the ranks or were plucked from obscurity. One was the son of a grocer,
another of a mechanic, and so on. This gave Napoleon a crucial advantage in battle,
because his opponents inevitably based their selection strategies on nobility, and their
armies were led by dukes and lords rather than by talented professional soldiers.

*the ranks: 《군대》 사병, 졸병

① talent is no respecter of birth
② the age of nobility was about to end
③ a great leader is also a great follower
④ a competent strategist is also a strong warrior
⑤ success depends not only on ability, but also on effort

다음 빈칸에 들어갈 말로 가장 적절한 것은?

In 1978, economist Richard Easterlin conducted a survey among adults. He asked them to pick items from a list that they "would like to own," and then, from that same list, items they "currently own." Sixteen years later, he corralled the same group and asked them the same questions with the same list. While nearly everyone had acquired all of the items on their respective "wish lists," instead of being satisfied they chose new items from the list which were not desired during the initial survey. Termed the "hedonic treadmill," it has become clear to economists and "happiness experts" alike that ________________________. In turn, this has led to the concern that a focus on GDP — gross domestic product — as the primary indicator of a country's well-being has sidetracked us from what we really want, while taxing the environment along the way in our incessant push to produce.

*corral: (한곳으로) 모으다 **hedonic: 쾌락의, 향락적인

① desires vary as we grow older
② "more" does not necessitate "better"
③ happiness is not as "intangible" as we expect
④ the premise of the experiment was erroneous
⑤ an economic approach to well-being is desirable

4

다음 빈칸에 들어갈 말로 가장 적절한 것은?

Our tendency to focus only on outcomes narrows our self-image. When we envy other people for their assets, accomplishments, or characteristics, it is often because we are making a faulty comparison. We look at the fruits of their efforts instead of at the efforts themselves. For example, imagine that while talking to a professor in her office, you hear her use a word that you do not understand. You may feel intimidated and stupid. Now imagine that the same professor is sitting at her desk with an open dictionary. You would probably conclude that she knows that unfamiliar word because she spends time looking up words, looking for them in the books she reads, or learning them in some other simple manner. You, too, could do this. Focusing on the process, on the steps one must take to develop knowledge and skills, will ________________________.

① help us implement our plans realistically

② give us the confidence to make the best choice

③ be the best place to start if we want a quick result

④ keep us from forming a belittling view of ourselves

⑤ allow us to compare our current situation with others'

5 다음 빈칸에 들어갈 말로 가장 적절한 것은?

A social network is a social structure, which is connected by one or more specific types of interdependency, such as friendship, kinship, common interest, or financial exchange. Ideas flow and move within the social networks we create, and these networks ________________ ________________. Similar to the way an ant colony is "intelligent" even if individual ants are not, or the way flocks of birds determine where to fly by combining the desires of each bird, social networks can capture and contain information that is transmitted across people and time, like oral histories, and can aggregate millions of decisions to set market prices or select candidates in an election. The human social network does what no person could do alone. And the ability of networks to create, sustain, and strengthen our collective goals helps us to achieve much more than the building of towers or the destruction of walls as the scale of interactions increases.

① are revolutionizing how we view our world

② will increase the size of human social groups

③ have a tendency to intrude on one's privacy

④ complement and augment individual competence

⑤ block face-to-face communication between individuals

1　다음 빈칸에 들어갈 말로 가장 적절한 것은?

When reading poems, in general, readers feel that they must know more about the poets and their times than they really have to. We put much faith in commentaries, critiques, biographies — but this may be only because we doubt our own ability to read. Almost anyone can read any poem, if he is willing to go to work on it. Anything you discover about a poet's life or times is valid and may be helpful. But a vast knowledge of the context of a poem is no guarantee that the poem itself will be understood. To be understood, it must be ___________________________. Reading any great poem is a lifetime job — not, of course, in the sense that it should go on and on throughout a lifetime, but rather that as a great poem, it deserves many return visits. We may learn more about a poem than we realize when we are free from it for a while.

① read over and over with breaks
② interpreted in a variety of ways
③ viewed in a historical context
④ appreciated at one sitting
⑤ evaluated from your own perspective

2 다음 빈칸에 들어갈 말로 가장 적절한 것은?

People who support the "law of averages" buy lottery tickets over and over because they mistakenly believe that something is more likely to occur in the future because it hasn't occurred yet. The attraction of this law is due in part to its similarity to a genuine statistical law — the law of large numbers. According to this, if you toss an unbiased coin a small number of times, say 10 times, the occurrence of heads may deviate considerably from the mean (average), which is 5; but if you toss it a large number of times — say 1000 times — the occurrence of heads is likely to be much closer to the mean (500). So, in a series of random events of equal probability, it is true that things will even themselves out if the series is extended far enough. However, this statistical law has no bearing on the probability of any single event occurring; in particular, a current event has no recollection of any previous deviation from the mean and cannot _______________________________.
So there is no comfort here for the habitual lottery ticket buyer.

*mean: 《수학》 평균

① increase your wealth if you're fortunate
② tell us anything about the ideal number of trials
③ alter its outcome to correct an earlier imbalance
④ serve as motivation for choosing which bet to place
⑤ help us to calculate the standard deviation

 다음 빈칸에 들어갈 말로 가장 적절한 것은?

To live means to experience — through doing, feeling, thinking. Experience takes place in time, so time is the ultimate scarce resource we have. The content of our experience determines our quality of life, and beyond the unavoidable demands of daily life, there is still room for personal choice that makes control over time, to a certain extent, in our hands. Of course, it is not our decision alone to make — stringent constraints dictate what we should do, not only as members of the human race but also as members of a certain society and culture. However, as the historian E. P. Thompson noted, even in the most oppressive decades of the Industrial Revolution, when workers slaved away for more than eighty hours a week in mines and factories, there were some who spent their few precious free hours in literary pursuits or political action instead of following the majority into the pubs. To make a long story short, one of the most essential decisions in life is about how we ________________________.

① try to attain wealth and honor
② allocate or invest our time
③ find our true career
④ behave as members of society
⑤ bear the difficulties of life

4 다음 빈칸에 들어갈 말로 가장 적절한 것은?

Color is a ubiquitous feature of the environment, though we rarely notice colors unless they're particularly bright or deviate dramatically from our expectations. Nonetheless, they can shape a range of outcomes: A recent study conducted by University of Rochester psychologists Andrew Elliott and Daniela Niesta, for example, showed that men are slightly more attractive to women when they wear red shirts rather than shirts of another color. The same effect applies to women, who seem more attractive to men when their pictures are bordered in red. Red signals both romantic intent and dominance among lower-order species, and this applies to both males and females. This relationship between red and dominance explains findings by the evolutionary anthropologists Russell Hill and Robert Barton of the University of Durham that, "across a range of sports," contestants who wear red tend to ________________________.

① account for less than half of competitors
② suffer from careless mistakes and inattention
③ bring out the competitiveness in others
④ outperform those wearing other colors
⑤ play aggressively and disregard rules

5 다음 빈칸에 들어갈 말로 가장 적절한 것은?

The great paradox of capitalism is that destruction brings creation. Companies trying to put each other out of business in fact put many more businesses into existence and people into jobs, as they strive for better technology, more efficient ways of operating, smarter ways of pricing their product — for anything that will win them more customers and give them an edge over the competition. But this only works if _______________________________________. Consumers do not benefit when companies are free to do whatever they want to get a competitive edge. Competition has to be based on agreed norms and within set boundaries, rather than on aiming to win at any cost. The quality of football would not improve if teams could use any means necessary to score a goal. Similarly, capitalism produces benefits when there is fair competition over products and pricing, within the law, so that the most efficient business wins.

① consumers support the competition
② the goal of the business is obvious
③ companies have better technical competency
④ certain rules of the game are observed
⑤ we understand the dark side of capitalism

02

글의 순서

주어진 글 다음에 이어질 글의 순서로 가장 적절한 것은?　[수능]

> Norms emerge in groups as a result of people conforming to the behavior of others. Thus, the start of a norm occurs when one person acts in a particular manner in a particular situation because she thinks she ought to.

(A) **❷Thus**, she may prescribe **❶the behavior** to **❶them** by uttering the norm statement in a prescriptive manner. Alternately, she may communicate that conformity is desired in other ways, such as by gesturing. In addition, she may threaten to sanction them for not behaving as she wishes. This will cause some to conform to her wishes and act as she acts.

(B) **❷But ❶some others** will not need to have the behavior prescribed to them. They will observe the regularity of behavior and decide on their own that they ought to conform. They may do so for either rational or moral reasons.

(C) **❶Others** may **❷then** conform to **❶this behavior** for a number of reasons. The person who performed the initial action may think that others ought to behave as she behaves in situations of this sort.

*sanction: 제재를 가하다

① (A) — (C) — (B)　　② (B) — (A) — (C)
③ (B) — (C) — (A)　　④ (C) — (A) — (B)
⑤ (C) — (B) — (A)

글의 연결성을 파악하고 전체적인 흐름을 읽어내야 하는 유형이다. 글의 순서 유형의 대표적인 풀이 전략과 단서는 다음과 같다.

주어진 글의 내용 파악하기 

글의 핵심어나 핵심 내용을 파악하고, 주어진 글의 내용을 간략히 요약해본다. (이때 가능하면 뒤 내용을 예측해본다.)

⌄

전략 Point 적용하기 

Point 1

문법적 단서로 정답 찾기 (▶ p.48)
the behavior, them
some others
Others, this behavior

Point 2

연결어 단서로 정답 찾기 (▶ p.54)
Thus, But, then

Point 3

내용 흐름으로 정답 찾기 (▶ p.60)
위 단서를 찾을 수 없다면, 이때는 내용 흐름상 가장 자연스러운 순서로 판단한다.

Point 1 문법적 단서로 정답 찾기

글의 선후 관계를 판단하는 데 있어 가장 강력한 단서는 지시사/대명사, 정관사 the 등이다. 이들이 가지고 있는 문법적 특성이 글의 선후 관계를 분명하게 드러내준다. 따라서 글의 순서를 판단할 때 가장 우선적으로 고려해야 할 단서들이다.

1 지시사/대명사

우선 지시사/대명사가 포함된 글의 내용을 이해한 뒤, 그 수를 감안하여 받고 있는 내용을 찾는다.

this[these], that[those], it, such는 앞에 나온 단어나 구뿐만 아니라 절, 문장을 받을 수도 있으므로 주의해야 한다.

Zoom 1

Notation(악보 표기법) was more than a practical method for preserving an expanding repertoire of music.

→ **It** changed the nature of the art itself. To write something down means .... [모평]

Zoom 2

Tell your family and friends **stories of how you are inspired by the passion and how it makes a difference not only to you but also to others**.

→ **These stories** will make them realise that you are meant to follow your passion.

◆ 지시사/대명사의 수는 이들이 무엇을 받는지를 알려주는 중요한 단서이다. 하지만, 그 후보가 여럿인 경우에는 혼동하지 않도록 주의해야 한다. 아래를 보고, 이어질 글의 순서로 가장 적절한 것을 골라보자.

함정 주의

> Wilderness dining has two extremes: gourmet eaters and survival eaters. The first bake cakes and bread and cook multi-course dinners. [수능 응용]

(A) **They** walk only a few miles each day and may use the same campsite for several nights. Survival eaters are up and walking within minutes of waking.

(B) **They** walk dozens of miles every day; lunch is a series of cold snacks eaten on the move.

① (A) — (B)   ② (B) — (A)

2 정관사 the

<the+명사>는 앞서 언급된 불특정한 의미의 <(a/an)+명사>를 받는 것인지를 확인할 필요가 있다.

Zoom 3

It takes time to develop and launch products. Consequently, many companies know 6–12 months ahead of time that they will be launching **a new product**.
→ In order to create interest in **the product**, companies will often launch pre-market advertising campaigns. [모평]

단, 관사의 쓰임은 이 외에도 매우 다양하다는 것에 주의해야 한다. 문맥상 이미 특정할 경우, 아래와 같이 <the+명사>가 바로 나올 수도 있다. 즉 앞에 <(a/an)+명사>가 있어야만 하는 것은 아니므로, 이를 찾느라 시간을 허비하지 않도록 한다.

Zoom 4

Movies also tell stories that, in the end, we find satisfying. **The bad guys** are usually punished; **the romantic couple** almost always find each other despite the obstacles ....

[수능]

+ The bad guys, the romantic couple은 앞의 '영화가 말하는 이야기(stories that, in the end, we find satisfying)'의 내용으로 특정된 것이다. 따라서 bad guys, a romantic couple을 앞에서 찾으려 하지 말아야 한다.

3 대용어

영어는 같은 말을 반복하여 사용하는 것을 매우 꺼리기 때문에 대명사가 우리말보다 아주 많이 쓰인다. 또한, 대용어도 많이 쓰이는데, 대용어란 앞선 말을 다른 단어로 바꾸어 표현하는 것이다. 흔히 유의어가 이에 해당한다.

Zoom 5

Today the term artist is used to refer to **a broad range of** creative individuals across the globe from both past and present. ...
→ In contrast to **the diversity** it is applied to, the meaning of this term continues to be mostly based on Western views and values. [모평]

Focus & Practice

정답 및 해설 p. 34

1

Its mass of plants and other organic material absorb and store tons of carbon. ... Since the Industrial Revolution began in the eighteenth century, CO_2 released during industrial processes has greatly increased the proportion of carbon in the atmosphere.

(A) Carbon sinks have been able to absorb about half of this excess CO_2, and the world's oceans have done the major part of that job.

(B) The value of carbon sinks is that they can help create equilibrium in the atmosphere by removing excess CO_2. One example of a carbon sink is a large forest. [모평]

① (A)   ② (B)

2

In crying out, the squirrel draws attention to itself, which may well attract the predator.

(A) When a ground squirrel sees a predator in the distance, it will sound an alarm call that alerts other squirrels to run for cover. It's a risky move.

(B) New evidence suggests that squirrels also sound alarm calls for former playmates, not genetically related. [모평 응용]

① (A)   ② (B)

3

In some countries they are then sprayed with ethylene before sale to the consumer to induce ripening. However, fruit picked before it is ripe has less flavour than fruit picked ripe from the plant.

(A) The problem for growers and retailers is that ripening is followed sometimes quite rapidly by deterioration and decay and the product becomes worthless. Tomatoes and other fruits are, therefore, usually picked and transported when they are unripe.

(B) The fruit ripening process brings about the softening of cell walls, sweetening and the production of chemicals that give colour and flavour. The process is induced by the production of a plant hormone called ethylene. [모평]

① (A)   ② (B)

4 Any reliance on schematic knowledge will be shaped by this information about what's "normal."

(A) Bear in mind that schemata summarize the broad pattern of your experience, and so they tell you, in essence, what's typical or ordinary in a given situation.

(B) Schematic knowledge helps you — guiding your understanding and enabling you to reconstruct things you cannot remember. [수능 응용]

① (A)　　　　　　　　　　② (B)

[5~6] 주어진 글 다음에 이어질 글의 순서로 가장 적절한 것을 고르시오.

5 Researchers in psychology follow the scientific method to perform studies that help explain and may predict human behavior. This is a much more challenging task than studying snails or sound waves.

(A) For all of these difficulties for psychology, the payoff of the scientific method is that the findings are replicable; that is, if you run the same study again following the same procedures, you will be very likely to get the same results.

(B) It often requires compromises, such as testing behavior within laboratories rather than natural settings, and asking those readily available to participate rather than collecting data from a true cross-section of the population. [수능 응용]

① (A) — (B)　　　　　　　　② (B) — (A)

6 According to one traditional definition, *aesthetics* is the branch of philosophy that deals with beauty, especially beauty in the arts. Examining the pleasing features of the *Mona Lisa* or a snow-capped mountain, for example, would come under aesthetics.

(A) Picasso's *Guernica* is widely admired but not for being beautiful. So a better definition of aesthetics would be that it is the branch of philosophy that deals with the ways things please people in being experienced.

(B) That definition seems too narrow, since works of art and natural objects may interest us in other ways than by being beautiful. Instead of evoking admiration of beauty, artists may evoke puzzlement, shock, and even disgust. [모평 응용]

① (A) — (B)　　　　　　　　② (B) — (A)

Read & Apply

정답 및 해설 p. 36

1 주어진 글 다음에 이어질 글의 순서로 가장 적절한 것은? [수능]

> Negotiation can be defined as an attempt to explore and reconcile conflicting positions in order to reach an acceptable outcome.

(A) Areas of difference can and do frequently remain, and will perhaps be the subject of future negotiations, or indeed remain irreconcilable. In those instances in which the parties have highly antagonistic or polarised relations, the process is likely to be dominated by the exposition, very often in public, of the areas of conflict.

(B) In these and sometimes other forms of negotiation, negotiation serves functions other than reconciling conflicting interests. These will include delay, publicity, diverting attention or seeking intelligence about the other party and its negotiating position.

(C) Whatever the nature of the outcome, which may actually favour one party more than another, the purpose of negotiation is the identification of areas of common interest and conflict. In this sense, depending on the intentions of the parties, the areas of common interest may be clarified, refined and given negotiated form and substance.

*reconcile: 화해시키다 **antagonistic: 적대적인 ***exposition: 설명

① (A) — (C) — (B) ② (B) — (A) — (C) ③ (B) — (C) — (A)
④ (C) — (A) — (B) ⑤ (C) — (B) — (A)

2 주어진 글 다음에 이어질 글의 순서로 가장 적절한 것은? [수능]

> In spite of the likeness between the fictional and real world, the fictional world deviates from the real one in one important respect.

(A) The author has selected the content according to his own worldview and his own conception of relevance, in an attempt to be neutral and objective or convey a subjective view on the world. Whatever the motives, the author's subjective conception of the world stands between the reader and the original, untouched world on which the story is based.

(B) Because of the inner qualities with which the individual is endowed through heritage and environment, the mind functions as a filter; every outside impression that passes through it is filtered and interpreted. However, the world the reader encounters in literature is already processed and filtered by another consciousness.

(C) The existing world faced by the individual is in principle an infinite chaos of events and details before it is organized by a human mind. This chaos only gets processed and modified when perceived by a human mind.

*deviate: 벗어나다 **endow: 부여하다 ***heritage: 유산

① (A) — (C) — (B) ② (B) — (A) — (C) ③ (B) — (C) — (A)
④ (C) — (A) — (B) ⑤ (C) — (B) — (A)

3 주어진 글 다음에 이어질 글의 순서로 가장 적절한 것은? [모평]

> The growing complexity of computer software has direct implications for our global safety and security, particularly as the physical objects upon which we depend — things like cars, airplanes, bridges, tunnels, and implantable medical devices — transform themselves into computer code.

(A) As all this code grows in size and complexity, so too does the number of errors and software bugs. According to a study by Carnegie Mellon University, commercial software typically has twenty to thirty bugs for every thousand lines of code — 50 million lines of code means 1 million to 1.5 million potential errors to be exploited.

(B) This is the basis for all malware attacks that take advantage of these computer bugs to get the code to do something it was not originally intended to do. As computer code grows more elaborate, software bugs flourish and security suffers, with increasing consequences for society at large.

(C) Physical things are increasingly becoming information technologies. Cars are "computers we ride in," and airplanes are nothing more than "flying Solaris boxes attached to bucketfuls of industrial control systems."

*exploit: 활용하다

① (A) — (C) — (B) ② (B) — (A) — (C) ③ (B) — (C) — (A)
④ (C) — (A) — (B) ⑤ (C) — (B) — (A)

Point 2 · 연결어 단서로 정답 찾기

앞서 준비편 2(☞ p.10)에서 연결어의 의미와 기능을 학습한 바 있다. 이중, 순서 유형에서 특히 중요한 연결어에 대해 알아본다.

1 역접 연결어

However, But 외에도 다양한 연결어가 출제되며 가장 빈출된다. 앞의 흐름이나 초점에 반대, 대조되는 내용을 이끈다.

Zoom 1

Wildfire is a natural phenomenon in many Australian environments. The intentional setting of fire to manage the landscape was practised by Aboriginal people for millennia.

→ **However**, the pattern of burning that stockmen introduced was unlike previous regimes(양식). When conditions allowed, they would set fire to the landscape as they moved their animals out for the winter.

▶ <u>오스트레일리아 원주민들</u>은 수천 년 동안 경관을 관리하기 위해 의도적으로 불을 질렀다.
　→ **역접 연결어 However** → <u>목축업자들</u>이 불태우는 패턴은 이전의 양식(오스트레일리아 원주민들의 양식)과 달랐다.

2 환언 vs. 첨가 연결어

의미와 기능을 서로 혼동할 수 있으므로 주의한다. 환언은 앞서 말한 것과 같은 내용을 다른 말로 바꿔 말하는 것이고, 첨언은 다른 내용을 덧붙이는 것이다.

Zoom 2

Stressful events sometimes force people to develop new skills, reevaluate priorities, learn new insights, and acquire new strengths.

→ **In other words**, the adaptation process initiated by stress can lead to personal changes for the better. [모평]

▶ <u>스트레스를 주는 사건들</u>이 개발시켜주는 장점들이 있다.
　→ **환언 연결어 In other words** → <u>스트레스</u>는 더 나은 쪽으로의 변화로 이어질 수 있다.

Zoom 3

A student who is only exposed to extracts of literary works will never have the satisfaction of knowing the overall pattern of a book.

→ **Moreover**, there are some literary features that cannot be adequately illustrated by a short excerpt(발췌).

▶ 문학 작품의 발췌 글만 본다면 전반적인 양상을 아는 <u>만족감을 가질 수 없음</u>. (발췌 글만 보는 것의 단점 1)
　→ **첨가 연결어 Moreover** → 짧은 발췌로는 <u>설명될 수 없는 문학적 특징</u>도 있음. (발췌 글만 보는 것의 단점 2)

3 ▶ 결과 연결어

'원인-결과'의 논리 관계에서 '결과'를 이끈다. 하지만, 순서 유형에서는 앞선 글의 내용에 의거하여 내릴 수 있는 '결론'이나 '판단'을 이끄는 경우가 많다.

Zoom 4

If one is doing something new or for the first time, then being observed while doing it decreases performance. On the other hand, being observed while doing some task or engaging in some activity that is well known or well practiced tends to enhance performance.

→ **So**, if you are learning to play a new sport, it is better to begin it alone, but when you become skilled at it, then you will probably perform better with an audience. [수능]

▶ 새로운 일은 지켜보아지면 수행력이 저하되지만, 잘 아는 일은 지켜보아지면 수행력이 향상된다.
　→ **결과 연결어 So** → 새로운 스포츠를 배운다면 혼자 시작하는 것이 낫지만, 숙련되면 관중이 있을 때 더 잘할 것이다.

◆ 예를 이끄는 연결어는 글의 중반부, 결과[결론]를 이끄는 연결어는 글의 후반부에 자주 등장한다. 그러나 이런 위치가 연결어의 종류에 따라 글에서 반드시 정해져 있는 것은 아니다. 연결어가 자주 등장하는 위치가 아니라, 오로지 앞뒤 글의 논리적 관계에 따라 순서를 판단해야 한다.

함정 주의 ⸙

> Cultural characteristics are not only passed from parents to children, but may be passed on from any one individual to another by word of mouth or by writing.
>
> ↓
>
> **So** some cultural changes may be adopted quite quickly by a whole population. Transmission of culture is rather like transmission of an infection. ...
>
> ↓
>
> Like flu and colds, cultural habits such as pop music preferences and clothing fashions may spread very quickly nowadays, especially through the media of radio and television. [모의 응용]
>
> ▶ 여기서 연결어 So(따라서)는 문화적인 특징이 구전이나 글로 전파될 수 있다는 앞 내용에 의거한 결론을 이끈다. 그다음에는 문화의 전파를 전염병에 비유하고, 마지막으로 예를 들어 설명하는 글이 이어진다. 이처럼 연결어 So를 포함한 글은 글의 중반부에 얼마든지 위치할 수 있다.

Focus & Practice

정답 및 해설 p. 39

1

A traditional goal of science historians was 'to clarify and deepen an understanding of *contemporary* scientific methods or concepts by displaying their evolution'. This entailed relating the progressive accumulation of breakthroughs and discoveries.

(A) In the mid-1950s, however, a number of faults in this view of history became apparent. Closer analysis of scientific discoveries, for instance, led historians to ask whether the dates of discoveries and their discoverers can be identified precisely.

(B) Furthermore, the evaluation of past discoveries and discoverers according to present-day standards does not allow us to see how significant they may have been in their own day.

[수능 응용]

① (A)　　　　　　　　　　② (B)

2

Although personal robotic assistants provide services similar to those of smart-home assistants, their social presence offers an opportunity that is unique to social robots.

(A) Instead, personal robotic assistants have a distinct social presence and have visual features suggestive of their ability to interact socially, such as eyes, ears, or a mouth.

(B) For instance, in addition to playing music, a social personal assistant robot would express its engagement with the music so that users would feel like they are listening to the music together with the robot. [모평 응용]

① (A)　　　　　　　　　　② (B)

3

In one survey, 61 percent of Americans supported the government spending more on 'assistance to the poor'. But when the same population was asked whether they supported spending more government money on 'welfare', only 21 percent were in favour.

(A) But the word 'welfare' has negative connotations, perhaps because of the way many politicians and newspapers portray it.

(B) Therefore, the framing of a question can heavily influence the answer in many ways, which matters if your aim is to obtain a 'true measure' of what people think.

① (A)　　　　　　　　　　② (B)

4

> Most of us have a general, rational sense of what to eat and when — there is no shortage of information on the subject.

(A) Yet there is often a disconnect between what we know and what we do. We may have the facts, but decisions also involve our feelings. Many people who struggle with difficult emotions also struggle with eating problems.

(B) However, people who eat for emotional reasons are not necessarily overweight. People of any size may try to escape an emotional experience by preoccupying themselves with eating or by obsessing over their shape and weight. [모평]

① (A)   ② (B)

5 주어진 글 다음에 이어질 글의 적절한 순서대로 기호를 쓰시오.

> Most consumer magazines depend on subscriptions and advertising. Subscriptions account for almost 90 percent of total magazine circulation. Single-copy, or newsstand, sales account for the rest.

(A) For example, the *Columbia Journalism Review* is marketed toward professional journalists and its few advertisements are news organizations, book publishers, and others.

(B) However, single-copy sales are important: they bring in more revenue per magazine, because subscription prices are typically at least 50 percent less than the price of buying single issues.

(C) Further, potential readers explore a new magazine by buying a single issue; .... Professional or trade magazines are specialized magazines and are often published by professional associations. They usually feature highly targeted advertising. [수능]

*revenue: 수입

___________ — ___________ — ___________

Read & Apply

정답 및 해설 p. 41

1 주어진 글 다음에 이어질 글의 순서로 가장 적절한 것은?　　　　[모평]

> Plants show finely tuned adaptive responses when nutrients are limiting. Gardeners may recognize yellow leaves as a sign of poor nutrition and the need for fertilizer.

(A) In contrast, plants with a history of nutrient abundance are risk averse and save energy. At all developmental stages, plants respond to environmental changes or unevenness so as to be able to use their energy for growth, survival, and reproduction, while limiting damage and nonproductive uses of their valuable energy.

(B) Research in this area has shown that plants are constantly aware of their position in the environment, in terms of both space and time. Plants that have experienced variable nutrient availability in the past tend to exhibit risk-taking behaviors, such as spending energy on root lengthening instead of leaf production.

(C) But if a plant does not have a caretaker to provide supplemental minerals, it can proliferate or lengthen its roots and develop root hairs to allow foraging in more distant soil patches. Plants can also use their memory to respond to histories of temporal or spatial variation in nutrient or resource availability.

*nutrient: 영양소 **fertilizer: 비료 ***forage: 구하러 다니다

① (A) — (C) — (B)　　　② (B) — (A) — (C)　　　③ (B) — (C) — (A)
④ (C) — (A) — (B)　　　⑤ (C) — (B) — (A)

2 주어진 글 다음에 이어질 글의 순서로 가장 적절한 것은?　　　　[모평]

> Green products involve, in many cases, higher ingredient costs than those of mainstream products.

(A) They'd rather put money and time into known, profitable, high-volume products that serve populous customer segments than into risky, less-profitable, low-volume products that may serve current noncustomers. Given that choice, these companies may choose to leave the green segment of the market to small niche competitors.

(B) Even if the green product succeeds, it may cannibalize the company's higher-profit mainstream offerings. Given such downsides, companies serving mainstream consumers with successful mainstream products face what seems like an obvious investment decision.

(C) Furthermore, the restrictive ingredient lists and design criteria that are typical of such products may make green products inferior to mainstream products on core performance dimensions (e.g., less effective cleansers). In turn, the higher costs and lower performance of some products attract only a small portion of the customer base, leading to lower economies of scale in procurement, manufacturing, and distribution.

*segment: 조각 **cannibalize: 잡아먹다 ***procurement: 조달

① (A) — (C) — (B)   ② (B) — (A) — (C)   ③ (B) — (C) — (A)
④ (C) — (A) — (B)   ⑤ (C) — (B) — (A)

3 주어진 글 다음에 이어질 글의 순서로 가장 적절한 것은? [모평]

> Ever since the first scientific opinion polls revealed that most Americans are at best poorly informed about politics, analysts have asked whether citizens are equipped to play the role democracy assigns them.

(A) Such factors, however, can explain only the misinformation that has always been with us. The sharp rise in misinformation in recent years has a different source: our media. "They are making us dumb," says one observer. When fact bends to fiction, the predictable result is political distrust and polarization.

(B) It's the difference between ignorance and irrationality. Whatever else one might conclude about self-government, it's at risk when citizens don't know what they're talking about. Our misinformation owes partly to psychological factors, including our tendency to see the world in ways that suit our desires.

(C) However, there is something worse than an inadequately informed public, and that's a misinformed public. It's one thing when citizens don't know something, and realize it, which has always been a problem. It's another thing when citizens don't know something, but think they know it, which is the new problem.

*poll: 여론 조사

① (A) — (C) — (B)   ② (B) — (A) — (C)   ③ (B) — (C) — (A)
④ (C) — (A) — (B)   ⑤ (C) — (B) — (A)

Point 3 내용 흐름으로 정답 찾기

최근 문제들은 문법적 단서나 연결어 단서가 잘 보이지 않는 경우가 많다. 이때는 내용 흐름이 가장 자연스럽게 순서를 정하면 된다. 대표적인 경우를 알아보자.

1 일반적/추상적 진술 → 구체적/세부적 진술

글이 일반적/추상적 진술로 끝날 때, 이를 설명하는 구체적/세부적 진술이 뒤따르는 것이 자연스럽다.

Zoom 1

... In addition, **the human resource development function may be dramatically changed to keep the emphasis on continuous learning.**
→ In a learning organization, every employee must take the responsibility for acquiring and transferring knowledge. Formal training programs ... are insufficient to address shifting training needs and encourage timely information sharing. [모평]

글이 생소한 어구로 끝을 맺으면, 이를 구체적으로 설명하는 정의/예시가 이어지는 흐름이 자연스럽다.

Zoom 2

A fascinating species of water flea exhibits a kind of flexibility that evolutionary biologists call ***adaptive plasticity***.
→ If the baby water flea is developing into an adult in water that includes the chemical signatures of creatures that prey on water fleas, it develops a helmet and spines. If the water around it doesn't include the chemical signatures of predators, the water flea doesn't develop these protective devices. [수능]

만약 일반적/추상적 진술이 두 개(A, B)가 등장한 경우에는 글을 좀 더 폭넓게 보아야 한다. A와 B가 나열된 순서대로 각각에 대한 구체적/세부적 진술이 이어지는 것이 보통이다.

Zoom 3

The ancient Greeks used to describe two very different ways of thinking — (A) ***logos*** and (B) ___mythos___. **Logos roughly referred to the world of the logical, the empirical, the scientific.**
→ ***Mythos*** **referred to the world of dreams, storytelling and symbols.**

✦ 주어진 글에서 고대 그리스인들이 'logos'(A)와 'mythos'(B)라는 두 가지의 매우 다른 사고의 방식을 서술하곤 했다고 하고 logos(A)를 구체적으로 설명하므로, 그 뒤에는 mythos(B)에 대한 설명이 이어지는 것이 자연스럽다.

2 질문 → 답변 / 문제 → 해결

질문 뒤에 답변이 이어지고, 문제 뒤에 해결이 이어지는 흐름이 자연스럽다.

Zoom 4

Some people wear their hair the same way, buy the same brand of shoes and eat the same breakfast for no reason other than the ease of a comfortable, predictable life. Yet many others train for marathons, quit smoking and switch fields. **What is the difference between these two groups of people?**
→ **It's their perspective.** People who change do not question whether change is possible or look for reasons they cannot change. [수능 응용]

Zoom 5

In economics, there is a principle known as the *sunk cost fallacy*. … **This leads people to continue on paths or pursuits that should clearly be abandoned.**
→ Sometimes, **the smartest thing a person can do is quit.** [모평]

3 원인 → 결과

원인이 있고 나서 그에 대한 결과가 따르는 것이므로, 다른 단서가 없을 때는 원인 뒤에 결과가 이어지는 흐름이 자연스럽다.

Zoom 6

Some cities have required households to dispose of all waste in special trash bags, purchased by consumers themselves, and often costing a dollar or more each.
→ **The results** have been greatly increased recycling and more careful attention by consumers to packaging and waste. [수능]

※ 이 외에도 **시간순**(e.g. 과거 → 현재 등), **과정순**(e.g. 실험이 진행되는 과정), **근거 없는 믿음**(myth) → **사실**(truth) 등으로 이어져야 글의 흐름이 자연스럽다.

Focus & Practice

정답 및 해설 p. 44

[1~3] 주어진 글 다음에 이어질 글로 가장 적절한 것을 고르시오.

1

The fossil record supports the prediction that single-celled organisms evolved before multicelled organisms — multicelled organisms are found in layers of earth millions of years after the first appearance of single-celled organisms. Note that the possibility always remains that the opposite could be found.

(A) If multicelled organisms were indeed found to have evolved before single-celled organisms, then the theory of evolution would be rejected.

(B) Sequential changes are found in many fossils showing the change of certain features over time from a common ancestor, as in the case of the horse. [모평 응용]

① (A)   ② (B)

2

Crossing the street in Los Angeles is tricky business, but luckily, at the press of a button, we can stop traffic. Or can we?

(A) The button's real purpose is to make us believe we have an influence on the traffic lights, and thus we're better able to endure the wait for the signal to change.

(B) The same goes for "door-open" and "door-close" buttons in elevators. Such tricks are called "placebo buttons" and they are being used in all sorts of contexts.

① (A)   ② (B)

3

The QWERTY keyboard in the 19th century was designed to keep frequently used keys (like E and O) physically separated in order to prevent them from jamming. By the time the technology for electronic typing evolved, millions of people had already learned to type on millions of QWERTY typewriters.

(A) You might wonder why this particular configuration of keys, with its awkward placement of the letters, became the standard.

(B) Replacing the QWERTY keyboard with a more efficient design would have been both expensive and difficult to coordinate.

① (A)   ② (B)

4

> Culture operates in ways we can consciously consider and discuss but also in ways of which we are far less cognizant.

(A) In some cases, however, we are far less aware of why we believe a certain claim to be true, or how we are to explain why certain social realities exist.

(B) When we have to offer an account of our actions, we consciously understand which excuses might prove acceptable, given the particular circumstances we find ourselves in. In such situations, we use cultural ideas as we would use a particular tool.

(C) We select the cultural notion as we would select a screwdriver: certain jobs call for a Phillips head while others require an Allen wrench. [모평]

_________ — _________ — _________

5

> Imitation seems to be a key to the transmission of valuable practices among nonhumans. The most famous example is that of the macaque monkeys on the island of Koshima in Japan.

(A) A few years later, Imo introduced another innovation. Researchers on the island occasionally gave the monkeys wheat on the beach, where it quickly became mixed with sand.

(B) Imo, though, realized that if you threw a handful of wheat and sand into the ocean, the sand would sink and the wheat would float. Again, within a few years most of her fellow macaques were throwing wheat and sand into the sea and obtaining the benefits.

(C) In the early 1950s, Imo, a one-year-old female macaque, somehow hit upon the idea of washing her sweet potatoes in a stream before eating them. Soon it was hard to find a Koshima macaque who wasn't careful to wash off her sweet potato before eating it.

[모평 응용]

_________ — _________ — _________

Read & Apply

1 주어진 글 다음에 이어질 글의 순서로 가장 적절한 것은? [모평]

> When two natural bodies of water stand at different levels, building a canal between them presents a complicated engineering problem.

(A) Then the upper gates open and the ship passes through. For downstream passage, the process works the opposite way. The ship enters the lock from the upper level, and water is pumped from the lock until the ship is in line with the lower level.

(B) When a vessel is going upstream, the upper gates stay closed as the ship enters the lock at the lower water level. The downstream gates are then closed and more water is pumped into the basin. The rising water lifts the vessel to the level of the upper body of water.

(C) To make up for the difference in level, engineers build one or more water "steps," called locks, that carry ships or boats up or down between the two levels. A lock is an artificial water basin. It has a long rectangular shape with concrete walls and a pair of gates at each end.

*rectangular: 직사각형의

① (A) — (C) — (B)　　　② (B) — (A) — (C)　　　③ (B) — (C) — (A)
④ (C) — (A) — (B)　　　⑤ (C) — (B) — (A)

2 주어진 글 다음에 이어질 글의 순서로 가장 적절한 것은? [수능]

> The objective of battle, to "throw" the enemy and to make him defenseless, may temporarily blind commanders and even strategists to the larger purpose of war. War is never an isolated act, nor is it ever only one decision.

(A) To be political, a political entity or a representative of a political entity, whatever its constitutional form, has to have an intention, a will. That intention has to be clearly expressed.

(B) In the real world, war's larger purpose is always a political purpose. It transcends the use of force. This insight was famously captured by Clausewitz's most famous phrase, "War is a mere continuation of politics by other means."

(C) And one side's will has to be transmitted to the enemy at some point during the confrontation (it does not have to be publicly communicated). A violent act and its larger political intention must also be attributed to one side at some point during the confrontation. History does not know of acts of war without eventual attribution.

*entity: 실체 **transcend: 초월하다

① (A) — (C) — (B) ② (B) — (A) — (C) ③ (B) — (C) — (A)
④ (C) — (A) — (B) ⑤ (C) — (B) — (A)

3 주어진 글 다음에 이어질 글의 순서로 가장 적절한 것은?

[모평]

> Darwin saw blushing as uniquely human, representing an involuntary physical reaction caused by embarrassment and self-consciousness in a social environment.

(A) Maybe our brief loss of face benefits the long-term cohesion of the group. Interestingly, if someone blushes after making a social mistake, they are viewed in a more favourable light than those who don't blush.

(B) If we feel awkward, embarrassed or ashamed when we are alone, we don't blush; it seems to be caused by our concern about what others are thinking of us. Studies have confirmed that simply being told you are blushing brings it on. We feel as though others can see through our skin and into our mind.

(C) However, while we sometimes want to disappear when we involuntarily go bright red, psychologists argue that blushing actually serves a positive social purpose. When we blush, it's a signal to others that we recognize that a social norm has been broken; it is an apology for a faux pas.

*faux pas: 실수

① (A) — (C) — (B) ② (B) — (A) — (C) ③ (B) — (C) — (A)
④ (C) — (A) — (B) ⑤ (C) — (B) — (A)

Actual Test 1

1　주어진 글 다음에 이어질 글의 순서로 가장 적절한 것은?

> When scientists have trained primates and other animals to use simple tools, they've discovered just how profoundly the brain can be influenced by technology.

(A) The tools, so far as the animals' brains were concerned, had become part of their bodies. As the researchers who designed the experiment with the pliers explained, the monkeys' brains began to act as if the pliers were now fingers.

(B) Monkeys, for example, were taught how to use rakes and pliers to reach food that was otherwise beyond their grasp. When researchers monitored the animals' neural activity, they found significant growth in the visual and motor areas involved in controlling the hands that held the tools.

(C) But they discovered something even more striking as well. The data showed that the rakes and pliers actually came to be incorporated into the neural pathways of the animals' brains.

① (A) — (C) — (B)　　② (B) — (A) — (C)　　③ (B) — (C) — (A)
④ (C) — (A) — (B)　　⑤ (C) — (B) — (A)

2 주어진 글 다음에 이어질 글의 순서로 가장 적절한 것은?

> In the field of financial planning there is a universally accepted principle that it's critical to pay yourself first before you pay your other bills — to think of yourself as a creditor.

(A) The identical principle is also critical to implement any program of spiritual practice. If you don't start implementing your program right away, but instead you wait till you finish all your other chores, then you will probably never start.

(B) The reason for this financial wisdom is that if you delay putting money into a savings account until after everybody else is paid, there will be nothing left for you to save!

(C) The result is that you'll keep postponing your savings plan until it's too late to do anything about it. This cycle of delayed saving can leave you feeling frustrated and financially unprepared. But if you pay yourself first, somehow there will be just enough to pay everyone else as well.

① (A) — (C) — (B) ② (B) — (A) — (C) ③ (B) — (C) — (A)
④ (C) — (A) — (B) ⑤ (C) — (B) — (A)

주어진 글 다음에 이어질 글의 순서로 가장 적절한 것은?

> When an animal is having a chronically difficult time filling its belly, something intriguing happens in its body at a molecular level.

(A) Its aging slows down, and cells don't die as quickly as they do when food is available. Contrary to what you might think, a cell's health in this situation doesn't deteriorate. The body, sensing deprivation, seems to call all hands on deck to conserve energy and prepare for the worst.

(B) Numerous studies back up this assumption. Reducing the normal diets of creatures such as fruit flies, rats, and monkeys by 35 to 40 percent has shown similar outcomes, with lifespans increasing by as much as 30 percent.

(C) In other words, each cell grows tougher and more cautious. This is thanks largely to a class of proteins called sirtuins, which some scientists suspect reduce the rate of cell growth.

① (A) — (C) — (B)　　② (B) — (A) — (C)　　③ (B) — (C) — (A)

④ (C) — (A) — (B)　　⑤ (C) — (B) — (A)

주어진 글 다음에 이어질 글의 순서로 가장 적절한 것은?

> There are many non-linear interactions in ecology and, as in the weather and the stock market, a small disturbance can lead to a sudden and unpredictable change in state.

(A) Each of those habitats is filled with a chance group of ecologically equivalent creatures, each of which arrived by accident. Not only do such examples reveal our ignorance of the laws behind ecosystems, but they hint that chaos and complexity may be the rule rather than the exception.

(B) An attempt to shoot foxes to increase the number of red grouse prey, for instance, might have an undesirable effect, for the predators normally catch only the birds most filled with parasites, and once they are removed, disease will spread and kill many more birds than before.

(C) Such unforeseeable consequences emphasize that many of the connections among species within a community are far from simple. In the intricate world beneath the soil, as a case in point, organisms differ wildly from place to place but somehow generate roughly the same mix of nutrients.

*red grouse: 《조류》 붉은 뇌조

① (A) — (C) — (B)   ② (B) — (A) — (C)   ③ (B) — (C) — (A)
④ (C) — (A) — (B)   ⑤ (C) — (B) — (A)

5 주어진 글 다음에 이어질 글의 순서로 가장 적절한 것은?

> When people try to control situations that are essentially uncontrollable, they are inclined to experience high levels of stress.

(A) Like stress, these negative emotions can damage the immune response. We can see from this that health is not linearly related to control. For optimum health, people should be encouraged to take control to a point but to recognize when further control is impossible.

(B) And that's because sometimes the only way to get what you want is to take active control. This matters because research has shown that when people who feel helpless fail to take control, they experience negative emotional states such as anxiety and depression.

(C) Thus, suggesting that they need to take active control is bad advice in those situations. Better advice would be to try to accept that some things are beyond control. Similarly, teaching people to accept a situation that could readily be changed could be bad advice.

① (A) — (C) — (B)   ② (B) — (A) — (C)   ③ (B) — (C) — (A)
④ (C) — (A) — (B)   ⑤ (C) — (B) — (A)

Actual Test 2

1 주어진 글 다음에 이어질 글의 순서로 가장 적절한 것은?

> In a series of experimental studies with young children, feeding practices commonly employed by parents were shown to accidentally encourage behaviors counter to their intentions.

(A) This reinforces the idea that using a variety of rewards, including healthy options alongside occasional treats like sweets, can be an effective strategy for encouraging positive behavior in children.

(B) On the other hand, if children are given both sweet and non-sweet foods as rewards for encouraged behavior, the preference for those foods is enhanced.

(C) For example, limiting access to tasty foods promotes children's preference for and intake of these "forbidden foods." Forcing or pressuring children to eat certain foods decreases the preference for those foods. Rewarding children for eating a disliked food resulted in a decline in the preference for that food.

① (A) — (C) — (B)　　② (B) — (A) — (C)　　③ (B) — (C) — (A)
④ (C) — (A) — (B)　　⑤ (C) — (B) — (A)

2 주어진 글 다음에 이어질 글의 순서로 가장 적절한 것은?

> Most Americans firmly believe in the general goal of equal opportunity for rich and poor children.

(A) In fact, none of these policies has eliminated poverty or closed the gap between rich and poor children's prospects for success. This suggests that addressing the complex and multifaceted challenges of poverty requires a comprehensive effort that goes beyond mere policy changes.

(B) They also agree that poor children should not suffer from hunger, homelessness, or lack of medical care. However, there are differing opinions on how to accomplish these goals.

(C) This is nothing new: Americans have always disagreed about how to help their poorest citizens. Every generation of reformers believes that it can solve the problems of poor children by implementing new and improved policies.

① (A) — (C) — (B) ② (B) — (A) — (C) ③ (B) — (C) — (A)
④ (C) — (A) — (B) ⑤ (C) — (B) — (A)

주어진 글 다음에 이어질 글의 순서로 가장 적절한 것은?

In the early 1980s, when personal computers were first made available, software publishers were worried that hackers might copy what they considered to be their intellectual property: the core code of their programs.

(A) This way, if the core code was stolen and adapted for another application, the undocumented feature would also be incorporated into the new program. And that would constitute proof of the theft.

(B) The practice continued to take off later in the 1980s when programmers were not always given official credit for their work. To prove their involvement, they'd bury a little something in the code, just to prove they were there in the beginning.

(C) It was quite simple to access the core code of a program, and the laws against it weren't all that clear at the time. So little undocumented features were added before applications were released.

① (A) — (C) — (B)   ② (B) — (A) — (C)   ③ (B) — (C) — (A)
④ (C) — (A) — (B)   ⑤ (C) — (B) — (A)

4 주어진 글 다음에 이어질 글의 순서로 가장 적절한 것은?

One of the dangers of not choosing to spend a portion of your time deliberately pursuing pleasure is that you may allow yourself to simply drift through the day, unwittingly contenting yourself by offsetting any negativity with periods of time that are just ordinary.

(A) Taking affirmative action is the best solution to creating a positive lifestyle structure, one that creates pockets of time to spend doing whatever makes you happy. The moment you stop doing everything else and focus on doing whatever makes you happy, you will feel yourself start to relax.

(B) The short-term effects of this are minimal, but long term it can have a significant detrimental impact, since ordinary routines are in themselves insufficient to properly counter any negativity you may experience.

(C) Continued application will result in a sustained increase in happiness, and that will grow over time. So make sure that you don't simply wander aimlessly without ever giving sufficient pause to actively engage in making yourself happy.

① (A) — (C) — (B)　　② (B) — (A) — (C)　　③ (B) — (C) — (A)
④ (C) — (A) — (B)　　⑤ (C) — (B) — (A)

5 주어진 글 다음에 이어질 글의 순서로 가장 적절한 것은?

> Quite frequently, we make mistakes in our observations. For example, what was your instructor wearing on the first day of class? If you have to guess, it's because most of our daily observations are casual and semiconscious.

(A) Moreover, they add a degree of precision well beyond the capacity of the unassisted human senses. Suppose, for example, that you'd taken color photographs of your instructor that day.

(B) If you'd gone to the first class with a conscious plan to observe and record what your instructor was wearing, you'd be far more likely to be accurate. In many cases, both simple and complex measurement devices help guard against inaccurate observations.

(C) In contrast to casual human inquiry, scientific observation methods like this one constitute a conscious activity. They require you to focus all of your attention on a given subject.

① (A) — (C) — (B)　　② (B) — (A) — (C)　　③ (B) — (C) — (A)
④ (C) — (A) — (B)　　⑤ (C) — (B) — (A)

03

문장 삽입

글의 흐름으로 보아, 주어진 문장이 들어가기에 가장 적절한 곳은?　[수능]

> At the next step in ❶the argument, ❷however, ❶the analogy breaks down.

Misprints in a book or in any written message usually have a negative impact on the content, sometimes (literally) fatally. (　①　) The displacement of a comma, for instance, may be a matter of life and death. (　②　) Similarly most mutations have harmful consequences for the organism in which they occur, meaning that they reduce its reproductive fitness. (　③　) Occasionally, however, a mutation may occur that increases the fitness of the organism, just as an accidental failure to reproduce the text of the first edition might provide more accurate or updated information. (　④　) A favorable mutation is going to be more heavily represented in the next generation, since the organism in which it occurred will have more offspring and mutations are transmitted to the offspring. (　⑤　) By contrast, there is no mechanism by which a book that accidentally corrects the mistakes of the first edition will tend to sell better.

*analogy: 유사　**mutation: 돌연변이

주어진 문장의 단서와 문장 간의 논리적 의미 관계를 따져 각 문장 간의 연결성을 파악해야 하는 유형이다. 문장 삽입 유형의 대표적인 풀이 전략과 단서는 다음과 같다.

주어진 문장의 내용 파악하기

핵심어나 핵심 소재를 파악하고, 주어진 문장에 단서가 있다면 앞뒤에 위치할 내용을 예측해본다. 선택지 번호가 시작되기 전의 글 초반 내용은 예측에 도움이 될 수 있다.

전략 Point 적용하기

Point 1

문법적 단서로 정답 찾기 (▶p.76)
the argument, the analogy

Point 2

연결어 단서로 정답 찾기 (▶p.82)
however

Point 3

내용 흐름으로 정답 찾기 (▶p.88)
주어진 문장에 위 단서가 없다면, 이때는 글을 읽어 내려가며 내용 흐름을 파악한다.

Point 1   문법적 단서로 정답 찾기

주어진 문장에 있는 문법적 단서(지시사/대명사, 정관사 the)는 주어진 문장이 어떤 내용의 사이에 들어가야 하는지를 판단하는 데 도움이 되므로 중요하다. 주어진 문장의 문법적 단서가 가리키는 대상은 바로 앞 문장뿐만 아니라 그보다 더 앞부분에 등장하기도 한다.

1 지시사/대명사

우선 지시사/대명사가 포함된 주어진 문장의 내용을 파악하고, 받고 있는 내용을 찾는다.

Zoom 1

The apparent universality of sleep, and the observation that mammals have developed such highly complex mechanisms to preserve sleep on at least one side of the brain at a time, suggests that **sleep provides some vital service(s) for the organism**.

↓

This is particularly true since one aspect of sleep is **decreased responsiveness to the environment**.

↓

If sleep is universal even when **this potential price** must be paid, the implication may be that it has important functions that cannot be obtained just by quiet, wakeful resting. [모평 응용]

▶ sleep provides ~ the organism → This, decreased responsiveness ~ environment → this potential price

Zoom 2

Suppose you are conducting a meeting and you want **to ensure that everyone there has a copy of the agenda**. You can deal with this by **labelling each copy of the handout in turn with the initials of each of those present**.

↓

As long as you do not run out of copies before completing **this process**, you will know that you have a sufficient number to go around.

↓

You have then solved **this problem** without resorting to arithmetic(산수) and without explicit counting. [모평]

✚ 주어진 문장 다음의 this problem은 바로 앞 문장이 아니라 그보다 더 앞에 등장한 어구(to ensure ~ agenda)를 가리킨다.

▶ labelling each copy ~ present → this process, to ensure that everyone ~ the agenda → this problem

Zoom ③

Control over direct discharge of mercury from industrial operations is clearly needed for prevention of Minamata disease. However, it is now recognized that **traces of mercury can appear in lakes far removed from any such industrial discharge**.

↓

It is postulated(가정되다) that **such contamination** may result from airborne transport from **remote power plants or municipal incinerators**(소각로).

↓

Strictly controlled emission standards for **such sources** are needed to minimize **this problem**. [수능]

▶ traces of mercury can appear ~ industrial discharge → such contamination, this problem,
  remote power plants or municipal incinerators → such sources

2 정관사 the

주어진 문장에 <the+명사>가 있다면, 앞서 언급된 불특정한 명사를 받는 것인지를 확인할 필요가 있다.
특히 문장 삽입 유형에서는 <the+대용어>의 형태로, 다른 말로 바꾸어 받는 경우가 많다.

Zoom ④

Some creative companies are making it possible for their clients to share ownership and access to just about everything; by joining **a yacht sharing service**, members can live the Portuguese dream by sharing **a yacht** with up to seven other people.

↓

In describing **the service**, a recent newspaper article warned consumers that sharing **the yacht** means "there is no guarantee you will always be able to use it when you want."

↓

This apparent limitation is precisely what helps consumers make it a treat.

▶ a yacht sharing service → the service, a yacht → the yacht

Focus & Practice

[1~6] 주어진 문장이 들어가기에 가장 적절한 곳을 고르시오.

1

> This allows the solids to carry the waves more easily and efficiently, resulting in a louder sound.

Sound waves are capable of traveling through many solid materials as well as through air. (①) Solids, like wood for example, transfer the sound waves much better than air typically does because the molecules in a solid substance are much closer and more tightly packed together than they are in air. (②) The density of the air itself also plays a determining factor in the loudness of sound waves passing through it.

2

> Surprised by the vision of an unfamiliar silhouette pushing into the house, these dogs were using their eyes instead of their noses.

Because dogs are so good at using their noses, we assume that they can smell anything, anytime. But dogs use other senses, too, and the brains of both humans and dogs tend to intensify one sense at a time. (①) Many owners have been snapped at by their dogs when they returned home with a new hairdo or a new coat. (②) Their noses may be remarkable, but they're not always switched on. [수능 응용]

3

> They also rated how generally extroverted those fake extroverts appeared, based on their recorded voices and body language.

Some years ago, a psychologist named Richard Lippa called a group of introverts to his lab and asked them to act like extroverts while pretending to teach a math class. Then he and his team, with video cameras in hand, measured the length of their strides, the amount of eye contact they made with their "students," the percentage of time they spent talking, and the volume of their speech. (①) Then Lippa did the same thing with actual extroverts and compared the results. (②) He found that although the latter group came across as more extroverted, some of the fake extroverts were surprisingly convincing. [수능]

4 | Human beings discovered this art thousands of years ago, and they have invented several devices to make it easier and faster.

One kind of 'spinning' in fiber processing is the formation of individual fibers by squeezing a liquid through one or more small openings in a nozzle and letting it harden. (①) Spiders and silkworms have been spinning fibers in this way for millions of years, but chemists and engineers learned the procedure from them only about a century ago. In the another kind of spinning two or more fibers are twisted together to form a thread. (②) The ancient distaff and spindle are examples that were replaced by the spinning wheel in the Middle Ages. [모평 응용]

*distaff and spindle: 실을 감는 막대와 추

5 | That is why people experience jet lag when traveling across time zones.

Biological rhythms in humans facilitate physiological and behavioral changes on a roughly twenty-four-hour cycle no matter what is happening outside, whether a cold front moves in or clouds block the light of the sun. (①) Their internal clocks continue to run in accordance with the place they left behind, not the one to which they have come, and it can take some time to realign the two. (②) The most remarkable thing is that our internal body clocks can be readjusted by environmental cues. (③) We may get jet lag for a few days when we ask our body clocks to adapt to a vastly different schedule of day and night cycles on the other side of the Earth, but they can do it. [모평 응용]

6 | The net effect of this was that, although customers benefited, the banks lost out as their costs increased but the total number of customers stayed the same.

Where the degree of competition is particularly intense a zero sum game can quickly become a negative sum game, in that everyone in the market is faced with additional costs. (①) As an example of this, when one of the major high street banks in Britain tried to gain a competitive advantage by opening on Saturday mornings, it attracted a number of new customers who found the traditional Monday-Friday bank opening hours to be a constraint. (②) However, faced with a loss of customers, the competition responded by opening on Saturdays as well. (③) In essence, this proved to be a negative sum game.

[모평]

Read & Apply

정답 및 해설 p. 62

1 글의 흐름으로 보아, 주어진 문장이 들어가기에 가장 적절한 곳은? [모평]

> This makes sense from the perspective of information reliability.

The dynamics of collective detection have an interesting feature. Which cue(s) do individuals use as evidence of predator attack? In some cases, when an individual detects a predator, its best response is to seek shelter. (①) Departure from the group may signal danger to nonvigilant animals and cause what appears to be a coordinated flushing of prey from the area. (②) Studies on dark-eyed juncos (a type of bird) support the view that nonvigilant animals attend to departures of individual group mates but that the departure of multiple individuals causes a greater escape response in the nonvigilant individuals. (③) If one group member departs, it might have done so for a number of reasons that have little to do with predation threat. (④) If nonvigilant animals escaped each time a single member left the group, they would frequently respond when there was no predator (a false alarm). (⑤) On the other hand, when several individuals depart the group at the same time, a true threat is much more likely to be present.

*predator: 포식자 **vigilant: 경계하는 ***flushing: 날아오름

2 글의 흐름으로 보아, 주어진 문장이 들어가기에 가장 적절한 곳은?

> Grazing animals have different kinds of adaptations that overcome these deterrents.

Coevolution is the concept that two or more species of organisms can reciprocally influence the evolutionary direction of the other. In other words, organisms affect the evolution of other organisms. Since all organisms are influenced by other organisms, this is a common pattern. (①) For example, grazing animals and the grasses they consume have coevolved. (②) Grasses that are eaten by grazing animals grow from the base of the plant near the ground rather than from the tips of the branches as many plants do. (③) Furthermore, grasses have hard materials in their cell walls that make it difficult for animals to crush the cell walls and digest them. (④) Many grazers have teeth that are very long or grow continuously to compensate for the wear associated with grinding hard cell walls. (⑤) Others, such as cattle, have complicated digestive tracts that allow microorganisms to do most of the work of digestion.

*digestive tract: 소화관

> There's a reason for that: traditionally, park designers attempted to create such a feeling by planting tall trees at park boundaries, building stone walls, and constructing other means of partition.

Parks take the shape demanded by the cultural concerns of their time. Once parks are in place, they are no inert stage — their purposes and meanings are made and remade by planners and by park users. Moments of park creation are particularly telling, however, for they reveal and actualize ideas about nature and its relationship to urban society. (①) Indeed, what distinguishes a park from the broader category of public space is the representation of nature that parks are meant to embody. (②) Public spaces include parks, concrete plazas, sidewalks, even indoor atriums. (③) Parks typically have trees, grass, and other plants as their central features. (④) When entering a city park, people often imagine a sharp separation from streets, cars, and buildings. (⑤) What's behind this idea is not only landscape architects' desire to design aesthetically suggestive park spaces, but a much longer history of Western thought that envisions cities and nature as antithetical spaces and oppositional forces.

*aesthetically: 미적으로 **antithetical: 대조적인

Point 2   연결어 단서로 정답 찾기

앞서 준비편 2(☞ p.10)에서 연결어의 의미와 기능을 학습했다. 각 연결어와 맞지 않는 흐름상 단절이 있는 곳에 주어진 문장을 넣고 뒤 문장과 자연스럽게 연결되는지 확인한다. 문장 삽입 유형에서 특히 많이 출제되는 연결어를 확인해 본다.

1 역접 연결어

however, instead, rather, still 등 다양한 연결어가 출제되며 가장 빈출된다. 글의 흐름이 반대, 대조되는 부분을 찾는다.

> **Zoom ①**
>
> Although scientists are trained in the substantive content of their discipline, they are not formally instructed in 'how to be a good scientist'.
>
> ↓
>
> **Instead**, the apprentice scientist gains his or her understanding of the moral values inherent in the role by absorption from their colleagues — socialization.
>
> ↓
>
> We think that these values are under threat, just as the value of the professions themselves is under threat. [모평]

▶ 과학자들은 '좋은 과학자가 되는 방법(도덕적 가치)'에 대한 공식적인 교육은 받지 않는다.
　→ 역접 연결어 Instead → 도덕적 가치에 대한 이해는 사회화를 통해 얻는다.
　→ 이러한 가치(these values = 도덕적 가치)가 위협받고 있다고 여겨진다.

2 결과 연결어

> **Zoom ②**
>
> In some cases, the habitat that provides the best opportunity for survival may not be the same habitat as the one that provides for highest reproductive capacity.
>
> ↓
>
> **Thus**, individuals of many resident species may be forced to balance costs in the form of lower nonbreeding survivorship by remaining in the specific habitat where highest breeding success occurs.
>
> ↓
>
> Migrants, however, are free to choose the optimal habitat for survival during the nonbreeding season and for reproduction during the breeding season. [수능]

▶ 생존을 위한 최고의 서식지가 최고의 번식 능력을 가능하게 하는 서식지와 같지 않을 수 있다.
　→ 결과 연결어 Thus → 많은 텃새들은 번식 성공률이 높은 서식지에 머무르는 대신 낮은 비번식기 생존율이라는 대가를 치를 수 있다.
　→ 그러나(however) 철새들은 번식기, 비번식기에 따라 서식지를 자유롭게 선택한다.

3 첨가 vs. 강조 연결어

첨가 연결어가 있는 경우에는 앞에 나온 내용에 대하여 새로운 내용을 추가로 제시한다. 강조 연결어의 경우에는 앞 내용에 대한 자세한 내용을 덧붙이며, in fact, actually는 앞과 반대되는 내용을 강조하기도 한다.

Zoom 3

It has become apparent that broadly effective pesticides can have harmful effects on beneficial insects ....

↓

Also, it has become difficult for companies to develop new pesticides, even those that can have major beneficial effects and few negative effects.

↓

Very high costs are involved in following all of the procedures needed to gain government approval for new pesticides. [모평]

▶ 살충제가 유익한 곤충을 해칠 수 있다. (살충제의 단점 1)
　→ **첨가 연결어 Also** → 성능이 좋은 새로운 살충제의 개발이 어려워졌다. (살충제의 단점 2)
　→ 새로운 살충제에 대한 정부의 승인을 얻는 데 많은 비용이 든다. (개발 어려움에 대한 구체적 설명)

Zoom 4

The importance of Babylonian astronomers' detailed celestial(천체의) records, the seed of what we now call the scientific method, did not develop smoothly.

↓

Indeed, in the Middle Ages in Europe, calculating by hand and eye was seen as producing rather shabby knowledge, inferior to that of abstract thought.

↓

The suspicion was due to the influence of ancient Greeks in the era's scholasticism.

▶ 관측하고 기록하는 측정의 중요성이 순조롭게 발전하지는 않았다.
　→ **강조 연결어 Indeed** → 유럽 중세 시대에 손과 눈으로 계산하는 것은 조잡하다고 여겨졌다. (순조롭게 발전하지 않았다는 것의 상세한 내용)
　→ 그 불신은 스콜라 철학에의 고대 그리스인들의 영향에 기인했다.

4 예시 연결어

Zoom 5

Literature is not the only socialising agent in the life of children, even among the media.

↓

For example, today, the influence of books is overshadowed by that of television.

↓

There is, however, a considerable degree of interaction between the two media.

▶ 문학은 매체들 가운데서도, 아이들의 삶에서 유일한 사회화 요인은 아니다.
　→ **예시 연결어 for example** → 책의 영향력은 TV의 영향력에 의해 빛을 잃었다.
　→ 하지만(however) 그 두 매체 사이에는 상당한 정도의 상호 작용이 있다.

Focus & Practice

정답 및 해설 p. 65

[1~6] 주어진 문장이 들어가기에 가장 적절한 곳을 고르시오.

1

> Still, many believe we will eventually reach a point at which conflict with the finite nature of resources is inevitable.

It's possible that innovations and cultural changes can expand Earth's human capacity. (①) We are already seeing this as the world economies are increasingly looking at "green," renewable industries like solar and hydrogen energy. (②) That means survival could ultimately depend on getting the human population below its capacity. [모평 응용]

2

> For example, the first step in servicing or installing equipment is talking with the clients to understand how they used the equipment.

To service representatives in an electronics firm, learning to sell was a very different game from what they had been playing. (①) But it turned out they already knew a lot more about sales than they thought. (②) The same is true in selling. [모평 응용]

3

> Even so, research confirms the finding that nonverbal cues are more credible than verbal cues, especially when verbal and nonverbal cues conflict.

Researchers have reported various nonverbal features of sarcasm. Most disagree as to whether nonverbal cues are essential to the perception of sarcasm or the emotion that prompts it. (①) Also, nonverbal cues are better indicators of speaker intent. (②) As the nature of sarcasm implies a contradiction between intent and message, nonverbal cues may "leak" and reveal the speaker's true mood as they do in deception. (③) Ostensibly, sarcasm is the opposite of deception in that a sarcastic speaker typically intends the receiver to recognize the sarcastic intent; whereas, in deception the speaker typically intends that the receiver not recognize the deceptive intent. [모평]

*sarcasm: 비꼼 **ostensibly: 표면상

4

> Actually, it does, but there is more room for the moisture to be absorbed in these less densely packed areas before it shows.

Why does the skin on the extremities wrinkle after a bath? Despite its appearance, your skin is actually expanding. The stratum corneum — the thick, dead, rough layer of the skin that protects us from the environment and that makes the skin on our hands and feet tougher and thicker than that on our stomachs or faces — expands when it soaks up water. (①) This expansion causes the wrinkling effect. (②) So why doesn't the skin on other parts of the body also wrinkle when soaked? (③) One doctor said that soldiers whose feet are submerged in wet boots for a long period will exhibit wrinkling all over the covered area.

*extremities: 손발 **submerge: (물에) 잠그다

5

> A problem, however, is that supervisors often work in locations apart from their employees and therefore are not able to observe their subordinates' performance.

In most organizations, the employee's immediate supervisor evaluates the employee's performance. (①) This is because the supervisor is responsible for the employee's performance, providing supervision, handing out assignments, and developing the employee. (②) Should supervisors rate employees on performance dimensions they cannot observe? (③) To eliminate this dilemma, more and more organizations are implementing assessments referred to as *360-degree evaluations*. [모평]

6

> A round hill rising above a plain, therefore, would appear on the map as a set of concentric circles, the largest at the base and the smallest near the top.

A major challenge for map-makers is the depiction of hills and valleys, slopes and flatlands collectively called the *topography*. This can be done in various ways. One is to create an image of sunlight and shadow, creating a visual representation of the shape of the land. (①) Another, technically more accurate way is to draw contour lines. (②) A contour line connects all points that lie at the same elevation. (③) When the contour lines are positioned closely together, the hill's slope is steep; if they lie farther apart, the slope is gentler. [수능]

*concentric: 중심이 같은

Read & Apply

정답 및 해설 p. 67

1 글의 흐름으로 보아, 주어진 문장이 들어가기에 가장 적절한 곳은? [모평]

> Moreover, more than half of Americans age 18 and older derive benefits from various transfer programs, while paying little or no personal income tax.

Both the budget deficit and federal debt have soared during the recent financial crisis and recession. (①) During 2009–2010, nearly 40 percent of federal expenditures were financed by borrowing. (②) The huge recent federal deficits have pushed the federal debt to levels not seen since the years immediately following World War Ⅱ. (③) The rapid growth of baby-boomer retirees in the decade immediately ahead will mean higher spending levels and larger and larger deficits for both Social Security and Medicare. (④) All of these factors are going to make it extremely difficult to slow the growth of federal spending and keep the debt from ballooning out of control. (⑤) Projections indicate that the net federal debt will rise to 90 percent of GDP by 2019, and many believe it will be even higher unless constructive action is taken soon.

*deficit: 부족, 결손 **federal: 연방의 ***soar: 급등하다, 치솟다

> As a result, they are fit and grow better, but they aren't particularly long-lived.

When trees grow together, nutrients and water can be optimally divided among them all so that each tree can grow into the best tree it can be. If you "help" individual trees by getting rid of their supposed competition, the remaining trees are bereft. They send messages out to their neighbors unsuccessfully, because nothing remains but stumps. Every tree now grows on its own, giving rise to great differences in productivity. (①) Some individuals photosynthesize like mad until sugar positively bubbles along their trunk. (②) This is because a tree can be only as strong as the forest that surrounds it. (③) And there are now a lot of losers in the forest. (④) Weaker members, who would once have been supported by the stronger ones, suddenly fall behind. (⑤) Whether the reason for their decline is their location and lack of nutrients, a passing sickness, or genetic makeup, they now fall prey to insects and fungi.

*bereft: 잃은 **stump: 그루터기 ***photosynthesize: 광합성하다

3 글의 흐름으로 보아, 주어진 문장이 들어가기에 가장 적절한 곳은? [모평]

> Rather, it evolved naturally as certain devices were found in practice to be both workable and useful.

Film has no grammar. (①) There are, however, some vaguely defined rules of usage in cinematic language, and the syntax of film — its systematic arrangement — orders these rules and indicates relationships among them. (②) As with written and spoken languages, it is important to remember that the syntax of film is a result of its usage, not a determinant of it. (③) There is nothing preordained about film syntax. (④) Like the syntax of written and spoken language, the syntax of film is an organic development, descriptive rather than prescriptive, and it has changed considerably over the years. (⑤) "Hollywood Grammar" may sound laughable now, but during the thirties, forties, and early fifties it was an accurate model of the way Hollywood films were constructed.

*preordained: 미리 정해진

Point 3 내용 흐름으로 정답 찾기

주어진 문장에 문법적 단서나 연결어 단서가 없을 때는 주어진 문장과 앞 문장의 관계를 크게 구체적/세부적 진술, 또는 일반적/추상적 진술의 관계로 나누어 의미 관계로 위치를 판단할 수 있다. 단, 정답 위치에 주어진 문장을 넣고 나서, 뒤 문장과의 연결이 자연스러운지 확인하는 것을 잊지 말아야 한다.

1 일반적/추상적 진술

주어진 문장이 일반적/추상적 진술인 경우는 대부분 첫 번째 '일반적/추상적 진술(A)(+(A)의 부연 설명)'이 먼저 나오고, 주어진 문장이 두 번째 '일반적/추상적 진술(B)'이다. 앞의 (A)에 대한 내용이 끝나고, 주어진 문장의 부연 설명이나 글의 마무리 또는 다음 진술이 이어지는 위치를 파악해야 한다.

Zoom 1

Scientists who have observed plants growing in the dark have found that they are vastly different in appearance, form, and function from those grown in the light.
(A) Seedlings grown in the dark limit the amount of energy going to organs that do not function at full capacity in the dark, like cotyledons(떡잎) and roots, and instead initiate elongation(연장) of the seedling stem to propel the plant out of darkness.

↓

> (B) In full light, seedlings reduce the amount of energy they allocate to stem elongation.

↓

(B의 부연 설명) The energy is directed to expanding their leaves and developing extensive root systems.

✦ 주어진 문장은 앞에서 언급한 (A) 어둠 속에서 자라는 실생 식물의 에너지 사용과 대비되는 (B) 아주 밝은 곳에서 자라는 실생 식물의 에너지 사용에 대한 내용을 제시한다. 그다음 문장은 아주 밝은 곳에서 자라는 실생 식물의 에너지 사용에 대해 구체적으로 부연 설명한다.

주어진 문장이 예시 등의 구체적/세부적 진술로 앞 내용을 부연 설명하는 경우이다.

Zoom 2

In contrast to literature or **film**, tourism leads to 'real', tangible worlds, while nevertheless remaining tied to **the sphere of fantasies, dreams, wishes — and myth**. It thereby allows the ritual **enactment** of mythological ideas.

↓

> There is a considerable difference as to whether **people** watch **a film about the Himalayas on television** and **become excited** by the 'untouched nature' of the majestic mountain peaks, or **whether they get up and go on a trek to Nepal**.

↓

Even in the latter case, they remain, at least partly, in an imaginary world. [모평 응용]

＋ 주어진 문장은 앞 문장은 대한 예로서, 앞 내용(film, the sphere ~ myth, enactment)을 부연 설명한다. 다음 문장의 the latter case, they가 각각 주어진 문장의 whether they ~ Nepal, people과 연결되는 흐름이 자연스럽다.

일반적/추상적 진술이 두 개(A, B) 등장하여 비교, 대조, 나열될 때 주어진 문장이 부연 설명에 해당하는 경우, A 뒤에 들어가야 할지 아니면 B 뒤에 들어가야 할지를 주의해서 판단해야 한다.

Zoom 3

(A) Both humans and rats have evolved **taste preferences for *sweet* foods**, which provide rich sources of calories. **(A의 부연 설명)** A study of food preferences among the Hadza hunter-gatherers of Tanzania found that honey was the most highly preferred food item, an item that has the highest caloric value. Human newborn infants also show **a strong preference for sweet liquids**. Both humans and rats dislike *bitter* and *sour* foods, which tend to contain toxins.
(B) They also **adaptively adjust their eating behavior in response to deficits in water, calories, and salt**.

↓

> **(B의 부연 설명)** Experiments show that rats display an immediate liking for salt the first time they experience **a salt deficiency**.

↓

They likewise increase their intake of sweets and water when their energy and fluids become depleted. [수능]

＋ 주어진 문장은 소금 결핍에 대응하는 섭식 행동 조정의 예로 부족에 대응하여 적응하도록 섭식 행동을 조정한다는 B의 내용을 부연 설명한다. 다음 문장에서 에너지, 체액의 고갈에도 마찬가지로(likewise) 조정한다는 유사한 예가 자연스럽게 이어진다.

※ 이 외에도 **원인 → 결과**, **질문 → 답변**, **문제 → 해결** 등 자연스러운 흐름이 되도록 문장의 적절한 위치를 판단한다.

Focus & Practice

정답 및 해설 p. 70

[1~6] 주어진 문장이 들어가기에 가장 적절한 곳을 고르시오.

1

> Most readers of reports and papers are reading the documents because they are interested in, and know something about, the subject.

Too many writers interpret the term *logical* to mean chronological, and it has become habitual to begin reports and papers with careful reviews of previous work. (①) Usually, this is tactically weak. (②) Therefore, to rehearse to them the findings of previous work is simply to bore them with unnecessary reminders. [수능]

*chronological: 연대순의

2

> Note that copyright covers the expression of an idea and not the idea itself.

The expression of an idea is protected by copyright, and people who infringe on that copyright can be taken to court and prosecuted. (①) This means, for example, that while there are numerous smartphones all with similar functionality, this does not represent an infringement of copyright as the idea has been expressed in different ways and it is the expression that has been copyrighted. (②) Copyright is free and is automatically invested in the author, for instance, the writer of a book or a programmer who develops a program, unless they sign the copyright over to someone else. [수능]

*infringe: 침해하다 **prosecute: 기소하다

3

> The result was that we don't always buy what we like best, but when things have to happen quickly, we tend to go for the product that catches our eye the most.

Milica Milosavljevic and his coworkers conducted an experiment looking at the relationship between visual salience and the decision to purchase. They showed subjects 15 different food items on fMRI, such as candy bars, chips, fruity items, etc. (①) These were rated by the subjects on a scale of 1–15 according to "favorite snack" to "don't like at all." (②) They were then presented in varying brightness and time, with subjects always having to make a choice between two products. (③) If we are also distracted because we are talking to someone, on the phone, or our thoughts are elsewhere at the moment, our actual preference for a product falls further into the background and visual conspicuousness comes to the fore.

*salience: 두드러짐 **fMRI: 기능적 자기 공명 영상 ***conspicuousness: 눈에 잘 띔

4 | You don't sit back and speculate about the meaning of life when you are stressed. |

The brain is a high-energy consumer of glucose, which is its fuel. Your brain can't store fuel, however, so it has to "pay as it goes." Since your brain is incredibly adaptive, it economizes its fuel resources. (①) Thus, during a period of high stress, it shifts away from the analysis of the nuances of a situation to a singular and fixed focus on the stressful situation at hand. (②) Instead, you devote all your energy to trying to figure out what action to take. (③) Sometimes, however, this shift from the higher-thinking parts of the brain to the automatic and reflexive parts of the brain can lead you to do something too quickly, without thinking.

*glucose: 포도당

5 | Personal stories connect with larger narratives to generate new identities. |

The growing complexity of the social dynamics determining food choices makes the job of marketers and advertisers increasingly more difficult. In the past, mass production allowed for accessibility and affordability of products, and was accepted as a sign of progress. (①) Nowadays it is increasingly replaced by the fragmentation of consumers among smaller and smaller segments that are supposed to reflect personal preferences. (②) In reality, these supposedly individual preferences end up overlapping with emerging, temporary, always changing, almost tribal formations solidifying around cultural sensibilities, social identifications, political sensibilities, and dietary and health concerns. (③) These consumer communities go beyond national boundaries, feeding on global and widely shared repositories of ideas, images, and practices. [모평 응용]

*fragmentation: 파편화 **repository: 저장소

Read & Apply

1 글의 흐름으로 보아, 주어진 문장이 들어가기에 가장 적절한 곳은? [수능]

> It may be easier to reach an agreement when settlement terms don't have to be implemented until months in the future.

Negotiators should try to find ways to slice a large issue into smaller pieces, known as using *salami tactics*. (①) Issues that can be expressed in quantitative, measurable units are easy to slice. (②) For example, compensation demands can be divided into cents-per-hour increments or lease rates can be quoted as dollars per square foot. (③) When working to fractionate issues of principle or precedent, parties may use the time horizon (when the principle goes into effect or how long it will last) as a way to fractionate the issue. (④) Another approach is to vary the number of ways that the principle may be applied. (⑤) For example, a company may devise a family emergency leave plan that allows employees the opportunity to be away from the company for a period of no longer than three hours, and no more than once a month, for illness in the employee's immediate family.

*increment: 증가 **fractionate: 세분하다

2 글의 흐름으로 보아, 주어진 문장이 들어가기에 가장 적절한 곳은? [모평]

> In the case of specialists such as art critics, a deeper familiarity with materials and techniques is often useful in reaching an informed judgement about a work.

Acknowledging the making of artworks does not require a detailed, technical knowledge of, say, how painters mix different kinds of paint, or how an image editing tool works. (①) All that is required is a general sense of a significant difference between working with paints and working with an imaging application. (②) This sense might involve a basic familiarity with paints and paintbrushes as well as a basic familiarity with how we use computers, perhaps including how we use consumer imaging apps. (③) This is because every kind of artistic material or tool comes with its own challenges and affordances for artistic creation. (④) Critics are often interested in the ways artists exploit different kinds of materials and tools for particular artistic effect. (⑤) They are also interested in the success of an artist's attempt — embodied in the artwork itself — to push the limits of what can be achieved with certain materials and tools.

*affordance: 행위 유발성 **exploit: 활용하다

3 글의 흐름으로 보아, 주어진 문장이 들어가기에 가장 적절한 곳은? [모평]

> We become entrusted to teach culturally appropriate behaviors, values, attitudes, skills, and information about the world.

Erikson believes that when we reach the adult years, several physical, social, and psychological stimuli trigger a sense of *generativity*. A central component of this attitude is the desire to care for others. (①) For the majority of people, parenthood is perhaps the most obvious and convenient opportunity to fulfill this desire. (②) Erikson believes that another distinguishing feature of adulthood is the emergence of an inborn desire to teach. (③) We become aware of this desire when the event of being physically capable of reproducing is joined with the events of participating in a committed relationship, the establishment of an adult pattern of living, and the assumption of job responsibilities. (④) According to Erikson, by becoming parents we learn that we have the need to be needed by others who depend on our knowledge, protection, and guidance. (⑤) By assuming the responsibilities of being primary caregivers to children through their long years of physical and social growth, we concretely express what Erikson believes to be an inborn desire to teach.

1 글의 흐름으로 보아, 주어진 문장이 들어가기에 가장 적절한 곳은?

> For example, when the body gears up to combat infectious agents, it creates a burst of oxygen free radicals to destroy the invaders very efficiently.

The true force behind life lies in tiny cellular factories of energy, called mitochondria, which burn almost all the oxygen we breathe in. But breathing has a price. (①) The burning of oxygen that keeps us alive and active generates by-products called oxygen free radicals. (②) They serve as both guardians and destroyers in our system. (③) On the one hand, they help ensure our survival. (④) On the other hand, oxygen free radicals bounce randomly through the body, attacking cells, turning their fats rancid, rusting their proteins, piercing their membranes and corrupting their genetic code until the cells become dysfunctional or just give up and die. (⑤) These fierce radicals are also the potent agents of aging.

*rancid: (기름기가 든 음식이) 산패(酸敗)한[맛이 변한]　**membrane: (얇은) 막; 세포막

2 글의 흐름으로 보아, 주어진 문장이 들어가기에 가장 적절한 곳은?

> But this may not always be possible.

By teaching people to identify their negative thoughts and replace them with more positive ones, cognitive therapists hope to help patients overcome dysfunctional thinking by becoming masters of their own emotions. (①) By training ourselves to eliminate thoughts that provoke bad moods and to encourage thoughts that foster pleasant emotions, we may be able to gain some measure of control over our emotional state and lift ourselves out of the blues by willpower alone. (②) Sometimes, the intensity of the emotion may not permit alternative thoughts to be entertained, which is why cognitive therapy does not always work. (③) For someone who is slightly blue, it may help to suggest alternative ways of looking at his situation. (④) But for someone in the grip of a severe depression, such suggestions may appear rather insensitive. (⑤) Telling a severely discouraged person to think positively is not a very effective way to cheer him up.

*dysfunctional: 역기능적인, 제대로 기능하지 않는

글의 흐름으로 보아, 주어진 문장이 들어가기에 가장 적절한 곳은?

> Of course, the "naughty" puppet, who had been on the left, had it taken away.

Consider how a four-year-old boy takes justice into his own hands. The boy has just seen a puppet show in which one puppet played with a ball while interacting with two other puppets. (①) The center puppet would slide the ball to the puppet on the right, who would always pass it back. (②) And the center puppet would slide the ball to the puppet on the left, who would always run away with it. (③) After the play the two puppets on the ends were brought down from the stage and set before the boy. (④) Each was placed next to a pile of treats, and the boy was asked to take one away from one puppet. (⑤) But this wasn't enough — he then leaned over and hit the puppet!

4 글의 흐름으로 보아, 주어진 문장이 들어가기에 가장 적절한 곳은?

> To account for situations like these, W. D. Ross argued that moral duties are not universal constraints.

Deontologists are often criticized for arguing that moral rules are absolute and cannot conflict. Consider the case of Dutch fishermen smuggling Jewish refugees to England during World War II. (①) They were sometimes stopped by Nazis, who inquired as to who was on board and where the boat was headed. (②) The fishermen had a choice: lie or allow the passengers (and themselves) to be captured. (③) Here two absolute rules ("it is wrong to lie" and "it is wrong to let innocent people be captured") conflict. (④) Rather, they are conditional obligations to act that result from the specifics of a situation. (⑤) One must judge in a given case which duties apply and which duties are of more importance.

*deontologist: 《철학》 의무론자 **smuggle: 밀입국[출국]시키다

As it is far more convenient to carry and to use, modern money has largely replaced the *rai* as everyday currency.

Instead of metal coinage or paper money, the natives of the Pacific island of Yap traditionally traded huge, doughnut-shaped, limestone discs. (①) These are called *rai*, and their value is based on size and weight. (②) *Rai* stones may be used for social transactions such as marriages, inheritances, and political deals, or just in exchange for food. (③) Of course, carrying a large stone around instead of money is not always possible. (④) Instead, many of them are placed in front of meeting houses or specific pathways, so though the ownership of a particular stone changes, the stone itself is rarely moved. (⑤) It is true, though, that it is still a unit of exchange for the islanders, according to their tradition.

1 글의 흐름으로 보아, 주어진 문장이 들어가기에 가장 적절한 곳은?

> Due to the uncertainty whether cars are supposed to stop — or if they will — pedestrians act more cautiously.

Studies demonstrate that motorists are more likely to yield to pedestrians in marked crosswalks. But as researchers have discovered, that does not necessarily make things safer. (①) When they compared the way pedestrians crossed streets, they found that people at unmarked crosswalks tended to look both ways more often and cross the road more quickly. (②) Researchers suspect that both drivers and pedestrians are more aware that drivers are supposed to yield in marked crosswalks. (③) But neither are aware of this fact when it comes to unmarked crosswalks. (④) Marked crosswalks, by contrast, may give pedestrians a false sense of security. (⑤) It turns out the lack of clear traffic expectations is actually a good thing for pedestrians.

2 글의 흐름으로 보아, 주어진 문장이 들어가기에 가장 적절한 곳은?

> Also, like the fish, coral at those depths grows extremely slowly, and may never recover from damage from trawling.

Fishing vessels are trawling thousands of feet below the ocean surface. (①) They may be wiping out life at the ocean depths even faster than scientists can discover it. (②) Recently, stronger nets, cable, and engines have allowed fishing companies to extend their reach to depths of 3,000 feet and beyond. (③) At those depths, growth is so slow that harvested fish can take decades to be replaced. (④) A recent study found that 95 percent of the trawled ocean bottom in deep water off Tasmania is bare rock. (⑤) In contrast, coral covers almost 100 percent of untrawled areas, which also contain many sponges and sea fans.

*trawl: 저인망 어업을 하다 **sponge: 해면동물 ***sea fan: 산호충, 부채꼴 산호

> If water lacked its extraordinary qualities, ice would sink, and lakes and oceans would freeze from the bottom up.

Most liquids, when chilled, contract by about 10 percent, and water does too, but only down to a point. Once it nears its freezing point, it begins to expand in an unexpected manner. (①) By the time it is solid, it is almost a tenth more voluminous than it was before. (②) Because it expands, ice floats on water — "an utterly bizarre property," according to John Gribbin. (③) Without surface ice to hold heat in, the water's warmth would radiate away, which would leave it even chillier and create yet more ice. (④) Soon even the oceans would freeze and almost certainly stay that way for a very long time, probably forever — hardly the conditions to nurture life. (⑤) Thankfully for us, water seems unaware of the rules of chemistry or laws of physics.

> The precise proportions of the ingredients and the way in which the drink is served depend on the person who makes it.

Espresso is strong coffee made by forcing high-pressure steam through finely ground coffee beans; it is served in a tiny cup. (①) When steamed milk is added to espresso, it becomes caffe latte — Italian for "milk coffee." (②) But when an espresso is mixed with steamed milk and foamed milk, it's called a cappuccino. (③) For instance, some people think that an authentic Italian cappuccino should be about one part espresso, one part steamed milk, and two parts foamed milk. (④) However, others say it should be made with equal parts espresso, steamed milk, and foamed milk. (⑤) There are many non-traditional variations of these drinks, including mocha latte and cappuccino sprinkled with chocolate powder.

*foamed milk: 우유 거품

> So they built airstrips out of straw and coconuts, and dressed themselves to resemble the military personnel they'd encountered.

The "cargo cult" is an example of observed patterns that have no basis in an underlying cause. The phrase originally described practices developed by the native inhabitants of islands in the South West Pacific after the Second World War. (①) They'd observed first the Japanese and then the Allied soldiers building airstrips, marching, directing landing aircraft, and wearing certain styles of dress. (②) Associated with these curious behaviors was the arrival of giant flying machines carrying vast quantities of exotic material goods — canned food, clothes, vehicles, guns, radios, and so on — called "cargo" by the newcomers. (③) When the war ended and the visitors left, the natives reasoned that if they carried out the same sort of activities, the planes would return. (④) They reproduced the waved landing signals from their "runways." (⑤) They'd observed a pattern — the curious behavior of the visitors followed by the arrival of rich rewards — and concluded that there was a connection. But the inferred relationship was not actually a causal one.

*airstrip: 임시 활주로 **Allied: (제2차 세계 대전 시의) 연합군의

04

함의 추론

밑줄 친 <u>a nonstick frying pan</u>이 다음 글에서 의미하는 바로 가장 적절한 것은?

[수능]

How you focus your attention plays a critical role in how you deal with stress. Scattered attention harms your ability to let go of stress, because even though your attention is scattered, it is narrowly focused, for you are able to fixate only on the stressful parts of your experience. When your attentional spotlight is widened, you can more easily let go of stress. You can put in perspective many more aspects of any situation and not get locked into one part that ties you down to superficial and anxiety-provoking levels of attention. A narrow focus heightens the stress level of each experience, but a widened focus turns down the stress level because you're better able to put each situation into a broader perspective. One anxiety-provoking detail is less important than the bigger picture. It's like transforming yourself into <u>a nonstick frying pan</u>. You can still fry an egg, but the egg won't stick to the pan.

*provoke: 유발시키다

① never being confronted with any stressful experiences in daily life
② broadening one's perspective to identify the cause of stress
③ rarely confining one's attention to positive aspects of an experience
④ having a larger view of an experience beyond its stressful aspects
⑤ taking stress into account as the source of developing a wide view

글의 맥락을 파악하여, 밑줄 친 부분이 함축하는 의미를 추론하는 유형이다. 함의 추론 유형의 대표적인 풀이 전략과 단서는 다음과 같다.

밑줄 문장의 내용 파악하기 

밑줄 친 부분을 포함한 문장을 먼저 읽고, 밑줄 문장과 앞뒤에서 단서를 찾을 수 있는지 확인한다.

전략 Point 적용하기

Point 1
밑줄 문장과 앞뒤의 맥락으로 정답 찾기 (▶p.104)
밑줄 문장에 연결어, 대시(—), 세미콜론(;) 등으로 부연 설명이 이어지거나 밑줄 친 부분에 대한 소재나 내용에 대한 단서가 있어서 바로 앞뒤의 내용으로 유추할 수 있는 경우이다.

Point 2
글의 주제로 정답 찾기 (▶p.110)
밑줄 문장과 바로 앞뒤에 밑줄 문장의 소재에 대한 단서가 없는 경우이다. 글을 읽어 내려가며 글의 대의를 파악하고, 이를 나타내는 선택지를 고른다.

함의 추론 유형은 빈칸 추론과 마찬가지로 어떤 내용을 유추해야 하는지를 확인하기 위해 밑줄 친 부분이 있는 문장을 먼저 확인한다. 밑줄 문장이나 바로 앞뒤에 밑줄 친 부분의 내용을 유추할 수 있는 부연 설명이나 소재에 대한 언급이 있을 수 있다. 단서로 유추한 이후에는 글 전반의 내용으로 확인하는 것이 좋다.

밑줄 문장에 연결어, 대시(—), 세미콜론(;) 등으로 부연 설명이 이어지는 경우에는 확실한 단서를 찾을 수도 있다.

Zoom 1

(이전 생략) We can see the world only as it appears to us, not "as it truly is," because **there is no "as it truly is"** without a perspective to give it form. Philosopher Thomas Nagel argued that there is no "<u>view from nowhere</u>," **since we cannot see the world except from a particular perspective**, and that perspective influences what we see.

밑줄 문장: 철학자 Thomas Nagel에 의하면 '아무것도 아닌 곳에서 나온 관점'은 없는데, 우리는 특정 관점에서 보는 것 외에는 세계를 볼 수 없고, 그 관점이 우리가 보는 것에 영향을 미치기 때문임.

We can experience the world only through the human lenses that make it intelligible to us. [모평]

→ 밑줄 의미 = <u>unbiased and objective view of the world</u>

+ 밑줄 문장에서 연결어 since로 우리가 특정 관점(주관적 관점)으로만 세계를 본다는 이유를 덧붙였다. 따라서 '특정 관점 없이 보는 관점'은 없다는 것을 뜻하는 것이며, 바로 앞 문장에서도 '정말 있는 그대로'의 세계는 없다고 했다.

밑줄 문장으로 소재는 파악했지만 명확한 설명이 없다면 바로 앞뒤의 내용을 먼저 확인한다. 특히 밑줄 문장 뒤에 한두 문장만 있다면, 밑줄 문장을 직접적으로 바꿔 말하거나 부연 설명하는 경우가 많으므로 중요하다.

Zoom 2

Humans are omnivorous, meaning that they can consume and digest a wide selection of plants and animals found in their surroundings. (중간 생략) **This dilemma, the need to experiment combined with the need for conservatism**, is known as <u>the omnivore's paradox</u>.

밑줄 문장: 보수성에 대한 필요와 실험의 필요가 결합된 이 딜레마는 <u>잡식성의 역설</u>로 알려져 있음.

It results in **two contradictory psychological impulses regarding diet. The first is an attraction to new foods; the second is a preference for familiar foods.**

→ 밑줄 의미 = <u>need to be both flexible and cautious about foods</u>

+ 밑줄 문장에서 보수성과 실험의 필요가 결합된 딜레마라고 언급하고, 뒤 문장에서 새로운 음식에 대한 끌림과 익숙한 음식에 대한 선호의 모순되는 충동이라고 설명했다. 따라서 음식에 대해 융통성 있으면서도 조심해야 하는 것과 관련 있음을 알 수 있다.

밑줄 문장이 글 초반에 위치한 경우에는 밑줄 문장과 앞뒤의 내용으로 글의 소재와 흐름을 유추한 후에 이를 설명하는 부분을 찾아서 글을 읽어 내려간다.

Zoom ③

Many ancillary(보조의) **businesses that today seem almost core** at one time started out as <u>journey edges</u>.

밑줄 문장: 오늘날 거의 핵심인 것처럼 보이는 많은 보조 사업들이 한때는 <u>여정의 가장자리</u>로서 시작했음.

For example, retailers often boost sales with **accompanying support such as assembly or installation services**. Think of a home goods retailer selling an unassembled outdoor grill as a box of parts and leaving its customer's mission incomplete. When that retailer also sells assembly and delivery, it takes another step in the journey to the customer's true mission of cooking in his backyard. (중간 생략) Maintenance, installation, training, delivery, anything at all that **turns do-it-yourself into a do-it-for-me solution originally resulted from exploring the edge** of where core products intersect(교차하다) with customer journeys. [모평]

→ 밑줄 의미 = <u>providing extra services beyond customers' primary purchase</u>

✛ 오늘날 거의 핵심으로 보이는 많은 보조 사업들이 여정의 가장자리로서 시작했다고 했으므로 보조 사업의 발전 과정에 대한 내용을 찾는다. 이어서 소매상이 제품 판매(journey) 이외에 조립이나 설치 서비스 등의 지원을 제공하는 것(journey edges)을 예로 들었다. 마지막 문장에서도 고객의 일을 대신 해주는 해결책이 가장자리를 탐구하는 것에서 왔다고 말바꿈하여 표현했다. 따라서 핵심이고 기본적인 것(제품 판매)이 아니었던 것(조립이나 설치 서비스 등)을 제공하는 것과 관련됨을 알 수 있다.

Focus & Practice

정답 및 해설 p. 86

1

... Tourism can mean progress, but most often also means the loss of traditions and cultural uniqueness. And, of course, there are examples of 'cultural pollution', 'vulgarization' and 'phony-folk-cultures'. The background for such characteristics is often more or less romantic and the normative ideas of a former or prevailing authenticity. Ideally (to some) there should exist ancient cultures for modern consumers to gaze at, or even step into for a while, while travelling or on holiday. This is a cage model that is difficult to defend in a global world where we all, indigenous or not, are part of the same social fabric. [모평]

*indigenous: 토착의 **vulgarization: 상스럽게 함

① preserving a past culture in its original form for consumption
② limiting public access to prehistoric sites for conservation
③ maintaining a budget for cultural policies and regulations

2

I suspect fungi are a little more forward "thinking" than their larger partners. Among trees, each species fights other species. Let's assume the beeches native to Central Europe could emerge victorious in most forests there. ... What would happen if a new pathogen came along that infected most of the beeches and killed them? In that case, wouldn't it be more advantageous if there were a certain number of other species around ... that would continue to grow and provide the shade needed for a new generation of young beeches to sprout and grow up? Diversity provides security for ancient forests. Because fungi are also very dependent on stable conditions, they support other species underground and protect them from complete collapse to ensure that one species of tree doesn't manage to dominate.

*beech: 너도밤나무 **pathogen: 병원균

① eager to support the dominance of one species
② aware that diversity leads to the stability of forests
③ indifferent to helping forests regenerate after collapse

3 The arts and aesthetics offer emotional connection to the full range of human experience. "The arts can <u>be more than just sugar on the tongue</u>," Anjan Chatterjee, a professor at the University of Pennsylvania, says. "In art, when there's something challenging, which can also be uncomfortable, this discomfort, if we're willing to engage with it, offers the possibility of some change, some transformation. That can also be a powerful aesthetic experience." The arts, in this way, become vehicles to contend with ideas and concepts that are difficult and uncomfortable otherwise. When Picasso painted his masterpiece *Guernica* in 1937, he captured the heartbreaking and cruel nature of war, and offered the world a way to consider the universal suffering caused by the Spanish Civil War. ...

① play a role in relieving psychological anxiety
② enlighten us about the absoluteness of beauty
③ embrace a variety of experiences beyond pleasure

4 ... Although a customer-centered firm seeks to deliver high customer satisfaction relative to competitors, it does not attempt to *maximize* customer satisfaction. A company can always increase customer satisfaction by lowering its price or increasing its services. But this may result in lower profits. Thus, the purpose of marketing is to generate customer value profitably. This requires a very delicate balance: the marketer must continue to generate more customer value and satisfaction but not '<u>give away the house</u>'.

① overlook a competitor's strengths
② hurt the reputation of the company
③ risk the company's profitability

Read & Apply

1 밑줄 친 make oneself public to oneself가 다음 글에서 의미하는 바로 가장 적절한 것은? [수능]

Coming of age in the 18th and 19th centuries, the personal diary became a centerpiece in the construction of a modern subjectivity, at the heart of which is the application of reason and critique to the understanding of world and self, which allowed the creation of a new kind of knowledge. Diaries were central media through which enlightened and free subjects could be constructed. They provided a space where one could write daily about her whereabouts, feelings, and thoughts. Over time and with rereading, disparate entries, events, and happenstances could be rendered into insights and narratives about the self, and allowed for the formation of subjectivity. It is in that context that the idea of "the self [as] both made and explored with words" emerges. Diaries were personal and private; one would write for oneself, or, in Habermas's formulation, one would make oneself public to oneself. By making the self public in a private sphere, the self also became an object for self-inspection and self-critique.

*disparate: 이질적인 **render: 만들다

① use writing as a means of reflecting on oneself
② build one's identity by reading others' diaries
③ exchange feedback in the process of writing
④ create an alternate ego to present to others
⑤ develop topics for writing about selfhood

2 밑줄 친 an empty inbox가 다음 글에서 의미하는 바로 가장 적절한 것은? [모평]

The single most important change you can make in your working habits is to switch to creative work first, reactive work second. This means blocking off a large chunk of time every day for creative work on your own priorities, with the phone and e-mail off. I used to be a frustrated writer. Making this switch turned me into a productive writer. Yet there wasn't a single day when I sat down to write an article, blog post, or book chapter without a string of people waiting for me to get back to them. It wasn't easy, and it still isn't, particularly when I get phone messages beginning "I sent you an e-mail *two hours ago* ...!" By definition, this approach goes against the grain of others' expectations and the pressures they put on you. It takes willpower to switch off the world, even for an hour. It feels uncomfortable, and sometimes people get upset. But it's better to disappoint a few people over small things, than to abandon your dreams for an empty inbox. Otherwise, you're sacrificing your potential for the illusion of professionalism.

① following an innovative course of action
② attempting to satisfy other people's demands
③ completing challenging work without mistakes
④ removing social ties to maintain a mental balance
⑤ securing enough opportunities for social networking

3 밑줄 친 refining ignorance가 다음 글에서 의미하는 바로 가장 적절한 것은? [수능]

Although not the explicit goal, the best science can really be seen as <u>refining ignorance</u>. Scientists, especially young ones, can get too obsessed with results. Society helps them along in this mad chase. Big discoveries are covered in the press, show up on the university's home page, help get grants, and make the case for promotions. But it's wrong. Great scientists, the pioneers that we admire, are not concerned with results but with the next questions. The highly respected physicist Enrico Fermi told his students that an experiment that successfully proves a hypothesis is a measurement; one that doesn't is a discovery. A discovery, an uncovering — of new ignorance. The Nobel Prize, the pinnacle of scientific accomplishment, is awarded, not for a lifetime of scientific achievement, but for a single discovery, a result. Even the Nobel committee realizes in some way that this is not really in the scientific spirit, and their award citations commonly honor the discovery for having "opened a field up," "transformed a field," or "taken a field in new and unexpected directions."

*pinnacle: 정점

① looking beyond what is known towards what is left unknown
② offering an ultimate account of what has been discovered
③ analyzing existing knowledge with an objective mindset
④ inspiring scientists to publicize significant discoveries
⑤ informing students of a new field of science

최근에는 밑줄 문장에서 내용이나 소재에 대한 단서를 찾을 수 없는 경우가 많다. 이때는 밑줄 문장의 앞뒤에 단서가 있는지 먼저 확인하고, 글을 앞에서부터 읽어 내려가며 글의 주제, 대의를 파악하여 의미를 유추해야 한다. 밑줄 친 부분은 글의 대의를 효과적으로 드러내는 것이다.

밑줄 문장에는 주로 비유적 표현이나 지문의 문맥으로만 알 수 있는 어구가 포함되어 있다. 이러한 표현들은 주목을 끄는 효과가 있으므로, 글쓴이의 주장과 관련이 깊다.

Zoom 1

(이전 생략) It's therefore not a surprise when a restaurant server offers you a menu. When she brings you a glass with a clear fluid in it, you don't have to ask if it's water. After you eat, you don't have to figure out why you aren't hungry anymore. **All these things are expected and are therefore not problems to solve.** (중간 생략) On a daily basis, **functional fixedness is a relief**, not a curse. That's why **you shouldn't even attempt to consider all your options and possibilities.** You can't. **If you tried to, then you'd never get anything done.** So don't knock the box. Ironically, **although it limits your thinking, it also makes you smart.** It helps you to stay one step ahead of reality. [모평]

밑줄 문장: 그러므로 상자를 부수지 마라.

→ 밑줄 의미 = Deal with a matter based on your habitual expectations.

✚ 밑줄 문장 뒤에서 그것이 사고를 제한하기는 하지만 똑똑하게 만들어 주기도 한다고 했으므로, 글쓴이가 무엇을 긍정적으로 주장하는지를 확인해야 한다. 글 전반에서 예상 가능한 것들(functional fixedness, 즉 the box)은 '안도가 된다'고 했으며, 모든 선택지와 가능성을 고려하지 말라고도 주장하고 있다. 따라서 늘 하는 예상을 바탕으로 문제를 처리하라는 것과 연결된다.

밑줄 친 부분이나 밑줄 문장에 지시사/대명사가 있는 경우도 있다. 이때는 지시사/대명사가 가리키는 것도 확인해야 한다.

Zoom ②

A job search is not a passive task. (중간 생략) If you are acting with purpose, ... then you need to be direct, focused and whenever possible, clever. Everyone else searching for a job has the same goal, competing for the same jobs. **You must do more than the rest of the herd.** Regardless of how long it may take you to find and get the job you want, **being proactive will logically get you results faster than if you rely only on browsing online job boards and emailing an occasional resume.** <u>Leave those activities to the rest of the sheep.</u>

밑줄 문장: <u>그러한 활동들은 나머지 양들에게 남겨라.</u>

→ 밑줄 의미 = <u>Be more active to stand out from other job-seekers.</u>

+ 밑줄의 those activities는 앞 문장에 나온 '온라인 구인란을 훑어보고 가끔 이력서를 이메일로 보내는 구직 활동(browsing ~ resume)' 을 지칭한다. 그것에만 의존하는 것보다 적극적(proactive)인 것이 더 빠른 결과를 가져올 것이라고 했으므로 그러한 수동적인 활동을 비판하는 것이다. 글 전반을 보면 구직 활동은 수동적인 일이 아니며, 다른 구직자들보다 '더 많은 것을 해야만 한다(must do more)'고 했다. 따라서 수동적 구직 활동은 나머지 다른 구직자들(the rest of the sheep)에게 맡기고, 두드러지기 위해 더 적극적으로 행동하라는 것과 연결된다.

Zoom ③

Author Elizabeth Gilbert tells the fable of a great saint who would lead his followers in meditation. Just as the followers were dropping into their zen((불교) 선(禪)) moment, they would be disrupted by a cat that would walk through the temple meowing and bothering everyone. The saint came up with a simple solution: He began to tie the cat to a pole during meditation sessions. **This solution quickly developed into a ritual: Tie the cat to the pole first, meditate second. When the cat eventually died of natural causes, a religious crisis followed.** What were the followers supposed to do? How could they possibly meditate without tying the cat to the pole? This story illustrates what I call invisible rules. These are habits and behaviors that have unnecessarily rigidified(굳어진) into rules. **Although written rules can be resistant to change, invisible ones are more stubborn.** They're <u>the silent killers.</u>

밑줄 문장: 그들은 <u>조용한 살인자임.</u>

→ 밑줄 의미 = <u>hidden rules that govern our actions unconsciously</u>

+ 밑줄 문장의 They는 직전 문장에 언급된 '보이지 않는 것들(규칙들)(invisible ones)'이다. 직전 문장에서 문서화된 규칙들보다 보이지 않는 규칙들이 더 완강하다고 했으므로, '변화에 완강하게 저항하는 성격과 관련됨을 알 수 있다. 글 전반을 보면 사원에서 명상 전에 고양이를 묶어두는 것이 의례로 굳어졌는데, 고양이가 죽어서 없어지자 종교적 위기가 생겼다는 내용으로, 습관과 행동으로 굳어진 보이지 않는 규칙들이 우리의 행동에 더 큰 영향력이 있다는 내용임을 알 수 있다.

Focus & Practice

정답 및 해설 p. 91

[1~4] 밑줄 친 부분이 의미하는 바로 가장 적절한 것을 고르시오.

1

Our language helps to reveal our deeper assumptions. Think of these revealing phrases: When we accomplish something important, we say it took "blood, sweat, and tears." We say important achievements are "hard-earned." ... When we talk of "easy money," we are implying it was obtained through illegal or questionable means. We use the phrase "That's easy for you to say" as a criticism, usually when we are seeking to invalidate someone's opinion. It's like we all automatically accept that the "right" way is, inevitably, the harder one. In my experience this is hardly ever questioned. What would happen if you do <u>challenge this sacred cow</u>? We don't even pause to consider that something important and valuable could be made easy. What if the biggest thing keeping us from doing what matters is the false assumption that it has to take huge effort?

*invalidate: 틀렸음을 입증하다

① resist the tendency to avoid any hardship
② escape from the pressure of using formal language
③ doubt the solid belief that only hard work is worthy

2

To balance the need for breadth (everyone feels a bit burned out) and depth (some are so burned out, they can no longer do their jobs), we ought to think of burnout not as a *state* but as a *spectrum*. In most public discussion of burnout, we talk about workers who "are burned out," as if that status were black and white. ... If there is a clear line between burned out and not, as there is with a lightbulb, then we have no good way to categorize people who say they are burned out but still manage to do their work competently. Thinking about burnout as a spectrum solves this problem; those who claim burnout but are not debilitated by it are simply dealing with a partial or less-severe form of it. They are experiencing burnout without *being* burned out. <u>Burnout hasn't had the last word.</u>

*debilitate: 쇠약하게 하다

① Public discussion of burnout has not reached an end.
② There still exists room for a greater degree of exhaustion.
③ Degrees of exhaustion are shaped by individuals' perceptions.

3

If you had wanted to create a "self-driving" car in the 1950s, your best option might have been to strap a brick to the accelerator. Yes, the vehicle would have been able to move forward on its own, but it could not slow down, stop, or turn to avoid barriers. ... But does that mean the entire concept of the self-driving car is not worth pursuing? No, it only means that at the time we did not yet have the tools we now possess to help enable vehicles to operate both autonomously and safely. This once-distant dream now seems within our reach. It is much the same story in medicine. Two decades ago, we were still taping bricks to accelerators. Today, we are approaching the point where we can begin to bring some appropriate technology to bear in ways that advance our understanding of patients as unique individuals. In fact, many patients are already wearing devices that monitor their conditions in real time ....

*autonomously: 자율적으로

① the importance of medical education was overlooked

② the devices for safe driving were unavailable at that time

③ lack of advanced tools posed a challenge in understanding patients

4

Research in the science of peak performance and motivation points to the fact that different tasks should ideally be matched to our energy level. For example, analytical tasks are best accomplished when our energy is high and we are free from distractions and able to focus. I generally wake up energized. Over the years, I have consistently stuck to the habit of "eating my problems for breakfast." I'm someone who tends to overthink different scenarios and conversations that haven't happened yet. When I procrastinate on talking with an unhappy client or dealing with an unpleasant email, I find I waste too much emotional energy during the day. ... So for me, it'll always be the first thing I get done. If you know you are not a morning person, be strategic about scheduling your difficult work later in the day.

*procrastinate: 미루다

① trying to reflect on pleasant events from yesterday

② handling the most demanding tasks while full of energy

③ preparing at night to avoid decision making in the morning

Read & Apply

정답 및 해설 p. 93

1   밑줄 친 <u>a stick in the bundle</u>이 다음 글에서 의미하는 바로 가장 적절한 것은?   [모평]

Lawyers sometimes describe ownership as a *bundle of sticks*. This metaphor was introduced about a century ago, and it has dramatically transformed the teaching and practice of law. The metaphor is useful because it helps us see ownership as a grouping of interpersonal rights that can be separated and put back together. When you say *It's mine* in reference to a resource, often that means you own a lot of the sticks that make up the full bundle: the sell stick, the rent stick, the right to mortgage, license, give away, even destroy the thing. Often, though, we split the sticks up, as for a piece of land: there may be a landowner, a bank with a mortgage, a tenant with a lease, a plumber with a license to enter the land, an oil company with mineral rights. Each of these parties owns <u>a stick in the bundle</u>.

*mortgage: 저당 잡히다 **tenant: 임차인

① a legal obligation to develop the resource
② a priority to legally claim the real estate
③ a right to use one aspect of the property
④ a building to be shared equally by tenants
⑤ a piece of land nobody can claim as their own

2   밑줄 친 <u>playing intellectual air guitar</u>가 다음 글에서 의미하는 바로 가장 적절한 것은?   [수능]

Any learning environment that deals with only the database instincts or only the improvisatory instincts ignores one half of our ability. It is bound to fail. It makes me think of jazz guitarists: They're not going to make it if they know a lot about music theory but don't know how to jam in a live concert. Some schools and workplaces emphasize a stable, rote-learned database. They ignore the improvisatory instincts drilled into us for millions of years. Creativity suffers. Others emphasize creative usage of a database, without installing a fund of knowledge in the first place. They ignore our need to obtain a deep understanding of a subject, which includes memorizing and storing a richly structured database. You get people who are great improvisers but don't have depth of knowledge. You may know someone like this where you work. They may look like jazz musicians and have the appearance of jamming, but in the end they know nothing. They're <u>playing intellectual air guitar</u>.

*rote-learned: 기계적으로 암기한

① acquiring necessary experience to enhance their creativity
② exhibiting artistic talent coupled with solid knowledge of music
③ posing as experts by demonstrating their in-depth knowledge
④ performing musical pieces to attract a highly educated audience
⑤ displaying seemingly creative ability not rooted in firm knowledge

3

밑줄 친 "The best is the enemy of the good."이 다음 글에서 의미하는 바로 가장 적절한 것은? [모평]

Gold plating in the project means needlessly enhancing the expected results, namely, adding characteristics that are costly, not required, and that have low added value with respect to the targets — in other words, giving more with no real justification other than to demonstrate one's own talent. Gold plating is especially interesting for project team members, as it is typical of projects with a marked professional component — in other words, projects that involve specialists with proven experience and extensive professional autonomy. In these environments specialists often see the project as an opportunity to test and enrich their skill sets. There is therefore a strong temptation, in all good faith, to engage in gold plating, namely, to achieve more or higher-quality work that gratifies the professional but does not add value to the client's requests, and at the same time removes valuable resources from the project. As the saying goes, "The best is the enemy of the good."

*autonomy: 자율성 **gratify: 만족시키다

① Pursuing perfection at work causes conflicts among team members.
② Raising work quality only to prove oneself is not desirable.
③ Inviting overqualified specialists to a project leads to bad ends.
④ Responding to the changing needs of clients is unnecessary.
⑤ Acquiring a range of skills for a project does not ensure success.

Actual Test 1

1 밑줄 친 "funeral societies"가 다음 글에서 의미하는 바로 가장 적절한 것은?

The practice of risk-sharing is one of the most widespread and well-established activities in human societies all over the world, and for evidence of just how important a practice it is, one need look no further than our highly institutionalized insurance industry. People pay for insurance, because it offers them a means to protect against unexpected and rare events that they would otherwise be unable to prepare for. This concept dates as far back as ancient Greece, when people teamed up in funeral societies to make small annual contributions to pay for the funeral of any member who happened to die. As a means of insuring individuals against the financial risk of untimely death, the forward-thinking Athenians embraced the concept of cooperative protection. Building upon the ancient concept of shared security, the principle of risk-sharing is not only preserved but has also evolved into diverse forms. Investors and entrepreneurs have crafted numerous "funeral societies" to address a wide range of challenges.

① balances between high risk and high reward
② adaptations for inevitable personal challenges
③ strategic risk distributions based on virtue
④ step-by-step plans for unforeseen circumstances
⑤ collaborative networks for mutual risk mitigation

2 밑줄 친 <u>a few misplaced items</u>가 다음 글에서 의미하는 바로 가장 적절한 것은?

Indecision is one of the most damaging of all time-wasters. Don't get caught in the endless loop of "Should I wash the dishes first or tidy the living room?" or "Is it more important to call a client or finish this report?" This internal struggle can leave you immobilized, consuming precious moments and hindering productivity. Breaking free from this cycle is crucial, as when you're involved or in motion, you travel on momentum — you'll get something done. I believe that most procrastination is due to the fear of making a wrong decision, but you're far better off making mistakes than not making decisions. Think of it like organizing a messy desk. Your goal is to create a clear and functional work environment. Avoid investing excessive time picturing an ideal layout. Once you start and clear the chaos, <u>a few misplaced items</u> won't bother you. Remember, progress holds far greater power than perfection.

① unnecessary stress from dwelling on past mistakes
② issues exerting little effect on the overall situation
③ the time wasted in the process of trial and error
④ internal conflicts that lead to resistance to change
⑤ discouraging comments from anonymous sources

3 밑줄 친 "The only journey is the one within."이 다음 글에서 의미하는 바로 가장 적절한 것은?

In today's interconnected world, we frequently shift from one trend to another and effortlessly explore the world around us. Exposure to diverse experiences keeps us mentally stimulated, broadening our horizons and prompting us to acquire new skills and knowledge. Yet, while external experiences enrich our lives, it is within our own thoughts, emotions, and reflections that we discover the true essence of who we are. Just as we follow the outside world, we need to carve out time to decipher the underlying patterns shaping our perspectives. Through contemplation and self-analysis, we chart the contours of our inner world, which enables us to move through life with intention and deliberation. In essence, the process of understanding and extracting meaning from external experiences through internal exploration is what molds the fundamental structure of our being, defining who we are and who we aspire to be. As it is often said, "The only journey is the one within."

① The society one belongs influences one's self-perception.
② External influences tend to amplify personal vulnerability.
③ Internal reflection empowers conscious choices.
④ The true self emerges from a lifetime's experiences.
⑤ Following inner voice earns the respect of others.

4 밑줄 친 the true constellations above가 다음 글에서 의미하는 바로 가장 적절한 것은?

Scores of Hollywood horror movies portray full-moon nights as peak times of creepy occurrences such as murders and psychotic behaviors. With regard to this lunar effect, some researchers have argued that people generally fall prey to a phenomenon called "illusory correlation" — the perception of an association when one does not in fact exist. Such illusory correlations result in part from our mind's inclination to recall unusual events better than ordinary ones. When there is a full moon and something decidedly odd happens, we usually notice it, tell others about it, and remember it. We do so because such co-occurrences are rare and thus memorable. In contrast, when there is a full moon and nothing odd happens, this night without incident quickly fades from our memory. Due to selective recall, links between mutually unrelated events are made. Only by stepping out of the moon's shadow can we see the true constellations above.

① the hidden truth beyond our current knowledge

② a sound decision uninfluenced by past experiences

③ a diverse perspective that defeat a singular viewpoint

④ an objective and unbiased understanding of reality

⑤ an independence from commonly held beliefs

5 밑줄 친 a never-ending state of jet lag가 다음 글에서 의미하는 바로 가장 적절한 것은?

A researcher at a sleep clinic in Boston wondered whether drinking coffee may not, in the long run, make people sleepier. He did a survey and found that people who drank coffee generally described themselves as sleepy in the mornings. Ordinarily, people who give up coffee say that the clear stimulus they used to feel is no longer there, but that the average productivity of their day improves. Some people who drink coffee to "reset" their body clocks each morning end up having difficulty going to bed on time, which in turn makes the need for coffee greater. Continual consumption of caffeine causes a biochemical imbalance in the body by boosting production of counter-caffeine chemicals. This may also lead to side effects such as headaches. Ultimately, coffee drinkers become like perpetual travelers, constantly seeking alertness while in <u>a never-ending state of jet lag</u>.

① an imbalance between emotions and surroundings

② a mismatch of personal commitments and sleep cycles

③ an irregular work schedule due to fluctuating deadlines

④ an ongoing conflict of managing sleep and work demands

⑤ a chronic disruption to the body's natural sleep rhythm

1　밑줄 친 the canvas devoid of color가 다음 글에서 의미하는 바로 가장 적절한 것은?

Language has two interrelated benefits: one is that it is social, and the other is that it supplies expressions to make thoughts public that would otherwise remain private. When we see or hear something that a companion is not looking at or listening to, we can usually make him or her aware of it by saying, "look," or "listen," or even by a simple gesture. But if we saw a fox, for example, "yesterday," it wouldn't be possible without language to communicate this fact to anyone who wasn't present with us at that moment. This depends upon the fact that the word "fox" applies equally to a fox seen or a fox remembered, so that we can make a memory or thought known to others. Language unlocks the past experience, transforming "yesterday's fox" into a story others can see. Without its unique ability, we can only see the canvas devoid of color.

① distorted reality constructed by individual bias
② a limited amount of nuance in emotional depth
③ direct experience independent from past interpretations
④ preexisting notions within the public consciousness
⑤ a loss of connection with personal authenticity

2　밑줄 친 <u>matching uniforms of team sports</u>가 다음 글에서 의미하는 바로 가장 적절한 것은?

Many political scientists used to assume that people vote selfishly, choosing the candidate that will benefit them the most. But research on public opinion has led to the conclusion that self-interest is a weak indicator of policy preferences. In fact, political opinions function as <u>matching uniforms of team sports</u>. Parents of children in public school are not more supportive of government aid to schools than other citizens; people who lack health insurance are not more likely to support government-issued health insurance than people already covered by insurance. Rather, people care about their *groups*, whether those be racial, regional, political, or religious. In matters of public opinion, citizens seem to be asking themselves not "What's in it for me?" but rather "What's in it for us?" In essence, political beliefs act as a way to identify with and represent the groups we belong to.

① expressions of universal moral values
② reflections of prevailing cultural norms
③ personal connections to a larger group
④ significant divisions between different groups
⑤ competitive advantages against current regulations

3 밑줄 친 a solid fortress around himself가 다음 글에서 의미하는 바로 가장 적절한 것은?

The adage "practice makes perfect" needs qualification. It would indeed be more correct to say that "practice makes permanent," for it is practice that is of the right kind which leads to the highest levels of skilled performance. To give an example from tennis, imagine a tennis player who had poured countless hours into mastering the two-handed backhand for increased power and consistency on the court. While it served him well early on, this technique revealed its weaknesses as he progressed against more skilled opponents. Recognizing the necessity of altering the old approach, the player attempted to switch his swinging pattern to a one-handed backhand. However, despite the awareness of the need for change, ingrained muscle memory and the comforting familiarity of the old swing kept creeping back. Even when he managed to execute that stroke, his performance became even worse than it was with his well-established backhand. Brick by brick, the player had built a solid fortress around himself.

① a strong desire to acquire new knowledge
② a mental stability achieved through persistence
③ a conviction that goes beyond mere imitation
④ a defensive stance blocking meaningful competition
⑤ a suboptimal habit cemented by blind repetition

4 밑줄 친 conducting a symphony guided only by a vague rhythm이 다음 글에서 의미하는 바로 가장 적절한 것은?

Unlike the Mesopotamian cultures, the early Greeks paid less attention to astronomy and more to cosmology. Their gaze was not on the precise steps of the stars, but on the grand stage upon which Earth and its cosmic companions performed. Because of this, their astronomical observations were not accurate. Time was not marked by the strict notes of astronomical precision. In fact, during the Greek times, most dates were given in terms of the rhythmic beats of the Olympiads, the four-year intervals between Olympic Games. If something happened during the 10th Olympiad, it meant the event occurred within a four-year span. Pinpointing the exact year within those four years proved difficult due to this broad time frame. Such notations created headaches for historians, who ended up conducting a symphony guided only by a vague rhythm. A common practice was to make educated guesses as to the actual dates of Greek events.

① focusing more on the cultural impact of events on society
② interpreting events without specific chronological markers
③ documenting only significant events based on personal judgment
④ struggling with identifying biases from factual information
⑤ taking an excessively long time to make any progress

5 밑줄 친 <u>a set of night vision binoculars</u>가 다음 글에서 의미하는 바로 가장 적절한 것은?

If you went on an African safari but traveled around only during daylight hours to see animals, you would miss out on a whole lot of action in the bush. This is due to the fact that a significant percentage of wildlife is active at night, fostering a dynamic ecosystem after sunset. By way of analogy, we can see a similar problem in the business world when managers are only attuned to the strongest, brightest signals such as highly-promoted big-ticket projects that carry little risk. They fail to perceive the weaker signals, the bolder experiments led by individuals or small teams who prefer to stay out of the corporate spotlight. Yet, as these hidden innovators may hold the key to unlocking unforeseen opportunities and breakthroughs, the manager who can pick up the "weaker signals" will reap big rewards. What managers need is not just a sharper eye, but <u>a set of night vision binoculars</u>.

① decreasing reliance on established methods
② applying information verified by specialized experts
③ identifying the personal weaknesses of individuals
④ looking more closely at details of challenging situations
⑤ directing attention to where it matters the most

Final Check 1

1 다음 빈칸에 들어갈 말로 가장 적절한 것은?

Surprisingly, caffeine is not a typical stimulant; it does not push brain cells to become alert and perform better. Caffeine, rather, ___________________. Instead of triggering the release of "up" chemicals, it blocks the action of the neurotransmitter, adenosine, that ordinarily tells the brain to quiet down and go to sleep. Since the caffeine molecule chemically resembles adenosine, it can occupy brain cell receptor sites, displacing adenosine. This prevents adenosine from suppressing the alertness caused by "upper" neurotransmitters, such as dopamine. Thus, caffeine, by disguising itself as adenosine, fools brain cells into remaining in a persistent state of excitability. A little caffeine goes a long way. Experts say that the caffeine in a couple of cups of coffee can knock out half the brain's adenosine receptors for a couple of hours, keeping your brain on high alert.

*neurotransmitter: 《생물》 신경 전달 물질

① works in a roundabout way
② performs with other stimulants
③ takes part in many brain functions
④ fosters various effects of chemicals
⑤ functions differently according to its type

2 주어진 글 다음에 이어질 글의 순서로 가장 적절한 것은?

> Throughout history, auroral displays in the skies at high latitudes have been a source of wonder, but not until the twentieth century were they understood to be caused by particles emitted from the sun.

(A) Such events exert various impacts on the earth's environment, which are generally called space weather. At the surface they cause changes in the earth's magnetic field, which brings about variations in the direction of compass needles.

(B) The electrically charged particles form the solar wind that constantly bathes the earth and that, due to interaction with the earth's magnetic field, reaches further into the atmosphere near the poles. Variations in the solar wind are produced by solar storms and particle ejections, which tend to be more frequent when the sun approaches the peak of its 11-year sunspot cycle.

(C) The shifts in the magnetic field also influence electrical currents flowing in the upper atmosphere and thereby impact on the transmission of long-distance radio signals. Pilots and astronauts are subject to enhanced radiation hazard while variations in solar heating affect atmospheric drag and thus spacecraft orbits.

*auroral: 오로라[극광]의 **ejection: 방출 ***atmospheric drag: 대기 장애물

① (A) — (C) — (B)　　　　② (B) — (A) — (C)
③ (B) — (C) — (A)　　　　④ (C) — (A) — (B)
⑤ (C) — (B) — (A)

3 글의 흐름으로 보아, 주어진 문장이 들어가기에 가장 적절한 곳은?

> The potential applications for such artificial intelligence systems extend well beyond the high-security confines of U.S. state penitentiaries.

In the yard of a Tennessee prison, every movement of the inmates is tracked by six hidden cameras whose software recognizes facial expressions, physical gestures, and group behavior patterns. (①) Unlike prison guards, who are subject to distractions and fatigue, the computer-vision system is continuously alert to potentially dangerous incidents and instantly warns prison officers when danger is detected. (②) Computer-vision systems in hospitals can remind staff to wash their hands before and after touching patients, or send alerts when a restless patient is at the risk of falling out of bed. (③) They can analyze the faces of people watching pilot TV shows or movie trailers, and studios can tailor their offerings according to the data. (④) Computers are definitely getting better at observing and understanding human behavior and emotions. (⑤) Where the proliferation of such watchful artificial intelligence will lead us remains to be seen.

*penitentiary: 교도소

4 밑줄 친 the symphony of staccatos가 다음 글에서 의미하는 바로 가장 적절한 것은?

Stephen Bertman, in *Hyperculture: The Human Cost of Speed*, contends that America's addiction to speed has transformed its values. More and more information is presented in shorter and shorter statements, which are broadcast on radio or TV. A typical hour of prime-time television has as many as thirty-six commercials, and individual images seldom remain on screen long. At prime-time hours, viewers face the dilemma of whether they should wait for the commercials to end or start flipping the channels. This extends to other forms of media as well. Social media posts often have limited word counts and news is delivered in short, attention-grabbing headlines. Such short-lived impressions lead people to expect impermanence in all aspects of their lives, even important principles and beliefs — persistence to be replaced by the temporary, memory by sensation, and intellect by impulse. The "power of now" has immersed us in the symphony of staccatos.

① an intense real-world engagement
② a deepening connection with the past
③ an ongoing chase for fleeting stimuli
④ a constant change for personal advancement
⑤ an ambition to achieve more and push boundaries

Final Check 2

1 다음 빈칸에 들어갈 말로 가장 적절한 것은?

It is common for those who have glimpsed something beautiful to express regret at not having been able to photograph it. So successful has been the camera's role in defining beauty that photographs, rather than the real world, have ______________________ ____________. Except for those situations in which the camera is used to document commemorative events, what moves people to take photographs is finding something beautiful. Just to demonstrate how truly beautiful their dwelling is, house-proud hosts may well pull out home photographs instead of showing someone around the house itself. We, too, regard ourselves as attractive at precisely those times that we believe we would look good in a photograph. After all, nobody exclaims, "Isn't that ugly! I must take a photograph of it." And even if someone did say that, all it would mean is: "I find that ugly thing ... beautiful."

① inspired us to create beauty in our lives
② changed our impressions of the beautiful
③ allowed us to remember the very moment
④ led us to search for beauty in nature
⑤ become the standard of the beautiful

2 주어진 글 다음에 이어질 글의 순서로 가장 적절한 것은?

> Most researchers agree that short-term memory is anchored and translated into long-term memory when we sleep.

(A) Neuroscientist Mayank Mehta likened it to erasing the chalkboard so new messages do not overlap and get confused with old ones. Giulio Tononi and his colleague propose that the large, slow brain waves that dominate deep sleep wash the board clean by reducing the number of active connections, while the brief bursts of faster activity inscribe new learning.

(B) The process, called memory consolidation, appears to involve two simultaneous procedures: weakening rarely used neural connections and strengthening the patterns of newly formed memories by replaying them.

(C) The wonderful result of this brain-wave activity is that new memories are allowed to stand out clearly. It seems that we forget in order to remember, and we do this best when we are deeply asleep, all is quiet, our breathing is slow, and the slate is clean.

① (A) — (C) — (B)　　　　② (B) — (A) — (C)
③ (B) — (C) — (A)　　　　④ (C) — (A) — (B)
⑤ (C) — (B) — (A)

Final Check 2

3 글의 흐름으로 보아, 주어진 문장이 들어가기에 가장 적절한 곳은?

> What is more, even when the ritual is somewhat forced, it can send a powerful political message.

It's instructive to compare and contrast two greeting rituals: the *handshake*, currently the predominant greeting ritual in Western countries, and the *handkiss*, which was popular among European aristocrats in the 18th and 19th centuries (but which has since fallen out of fashion). Both are gestures of trust and friendship, but they differ in their political implications. (①) Shaking hands is symmetric and fundamentally represents equality; it's a ritual between supposed equals. (②) Hand-kissing, however, is inherently asymmetric, setting the kisser apart from, and subordinate to, the recipient of the kiss. (③) The kisser must press his lips on another person's (potentially germ-ridden) hands, while simultaneously lowering his head and possibly kneeling. (④) This gesture is submissive, and when it's performed freely, it's an implicit promise of loyalty. (⑤) Kings and popes, for example, would often "invite" their subjects to line up for public kiss-the-ring ceremonies, putting everyone's loyalty and submission on conspicuous display and thereby creating common knowledge of the leader's dominance.

*aristocrat: 귀족 **symmetric: 균형이 잡힌, 대칭적인

밑줄 친 <u>flip the light switch</u>가 다음 글에서 의미하는 바로 가장 적절한 것은?

Imagine a company asking customers what features they want to see in their product. Unfortunately for the company, it is a fatal mistake to change the product to deliver those requested features. What is crucial is the forethought to reinvent its product and make the product better in a way that customers could never have imagined until they saw the product. Customers can only talk about the things that are broken and how they want them to be fixed. An entrepreneur needs to keep in mind that while fulfilling customers' needs is a part of the job description, there are other goals. Part of the entrepreneur's job is to invent the future. Successful entrepreneurs understand that the greatest satisfaction comes not from fixing the present, but from inventing the future. When customers seek a brighter candle, entrepreneurs don't just pour more wax. They <u>flip the light switch</u>.

① challenge the status quo to go beyond desires
② adapt to changing demands and market conditions
③ build loyal customer base through active communication
④ determine customer preferences based on data
⑤ gather information to navigate uncertainties

1 다음 빈칸에 들어갈 말로 가장 적절한 것은?

Once upon a time, status was bestowed upon people by their class and birth. Nowadays, immersed in a consumer culture of overwhelming choice, we define our social circle by style and aesthetics. As Virginia Postrel explains in *The Substance of Style*, our surface is our entire identity. Before we say anything with words, we declare ourselves through look and feel. *Here I am. I'm like this. I'm not like that.* Aesthetic identity is an expression of ________________________________. Do you want to be thought of as a practical, frugal person who sees fashion accessories as foolish and vain? Or do you prefer to seem like those who pay attention to every detail, including personal appearance? No matter what, you'll tend to attract the like-minded while alienating those who disagree. Because others make similar selections, for similar reasons, *I like this* becomes *I'm like this.*

① why style has become more significant than before
② with whom we want, or expect, to be grouped
③ how you dress and act in the way you like most
④ why you judge others more harshly than yourself
⑤ how you have been influenced by the media

2 주어진 글 다음에 이어질 글의 순서로 가장 적절한 것은?

In Madagascar, botanists have discovered a species of tree so big that it can be identified in satellite images. The species is unique to Madagascar; nothing like this tree has ever been seen before.

(A) Those who witnessed the flowering were amazed. They reported that initially one very long shoot emerged alone from the treetop. Then, a few weeks later, this single shoot began to change and spread. They said that in the end the thing resembled a Christmas tree.

(B) Hundreds of tiny flowers then blossomed on the branches. After pollination, the tiny flowers turn into fruit, but since a massive amount of energy is spent on this reproductive cycle, the tree cannot but collapse and die after flowering.

(C) Madagascar islanders knew of its existence, but none had seen it flower until recently, when it flowered in an extraordinary way. Botanists from England's Kew Gardens, hearing of the event, traveled to the island to see it for themselves.

① (A) — (C) — (B)　　　　② (B) — (A) — (C)
③ (B) — (C) — (A)　　　　④ (C) — (A) — (B)
⑤ (C) — (B) — (A)

3 글의 흐름으로 보아, 주어진 문장이 들어가기에 가장 적절한 곳은?

> Deductive reasoning, on the other hand, starts with broad generalizations and gradually focuses in on a specific statement of assumed truth.

Scientists construct their understanding of nature through logical reasoning, in which they follow a sequence of statements that are true to their conclusion. There are two types of logical reasoning: inductive and deductive. (①) Inductive reasoning begins with a detailed truth about something at first. (②) Then it uses that truth to construct a generalized understanding of how the greater system or phenomenon functions. (③) Using this approach to understand complex systems can be tricky because a few small details may not accurately represent the entirety of the system. (④) The approach is most useful when you don't properly understand the details of something, but you can observe some of its outcomes. (⑤) A scientist rules out one option after another, by means of it, until he or she has narrowed the field of truth down to just one or a few reasonable explanations.

밑줄 친 <u>step into the role of the architect</u>가 다음 글에서 의미하는 바로 가장 적절한 것은?

We turn to our surroundings to mirror and remind us of the moods and ideas we respect. Wallpaper, benches, paintings, and streets help us combat the feeling that our true selves are disappearing. In this way, we honor that place whose outlook most matches our own with the word *home*. To speak of a building as a home is simply to recognize that it's in harmony with our hearts. Our love of a home is an acknowledgement that our identity is not entirely self-determined. Just as our moods and ideas are reflected in our environment, so too are they shaped by it. In a sense, our homes become physical manifestations of our inner selves, sculpted from the very essence of who we are. Yet, as our inner selves shift over time, our homes often become outdated versions. This is when we <u>step into the role of the architect</u>. In the process of reconstruction, we bridge the gap between the old and the new.

① reorganize our places to discover our potential
② transform ourselves to break free from old habits
③ explore new experiences to broaden our perspective
④ harmonize our environments with our evolving identities
⑤ give weight to long-lasting consequences and sustainability

더 빨리, 더 많이,
더 오래 남는 어휘

나만의 스마트 단어장 P 보카 ^{on 쎄듀런}

내게 맞춰 암기하니까, 외워질 수밖에!

 **1** '나'에게 딱! 맞는 암기&문제모드만 골라서 학습!

5가지 암기모드

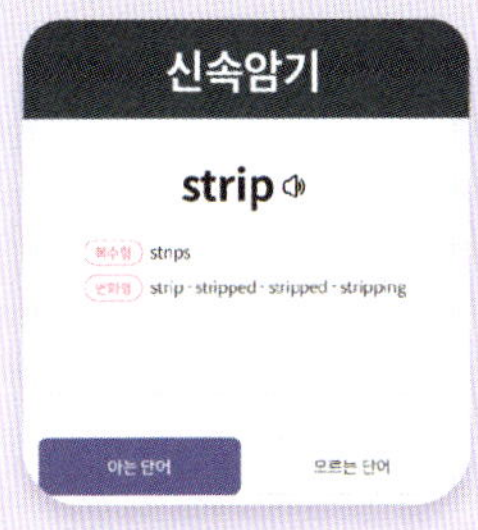

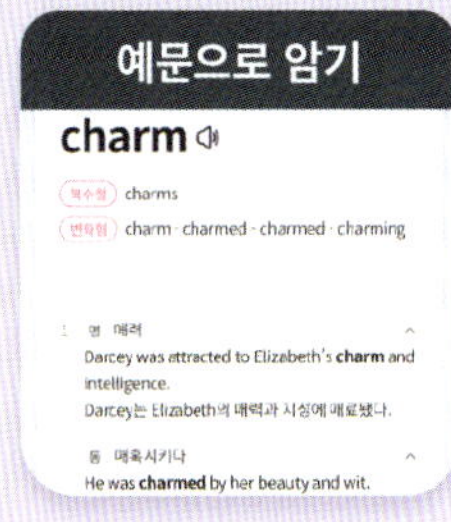

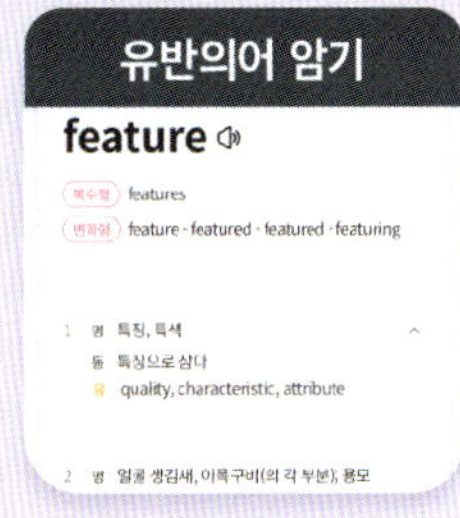

8가지 문제모드

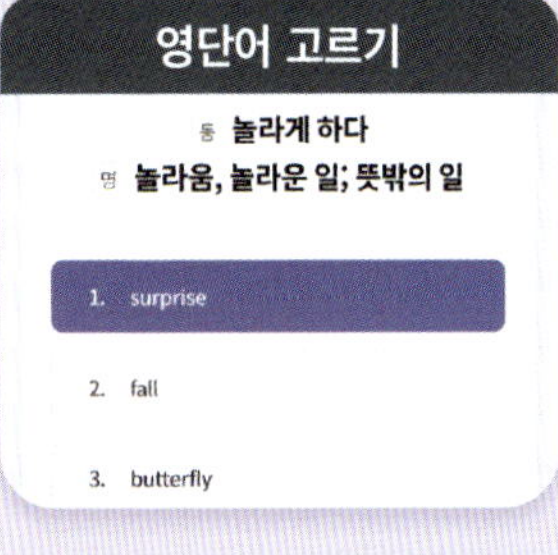

 암기모드를 선택하면, 최적의 문제 모드를 자동 추천!

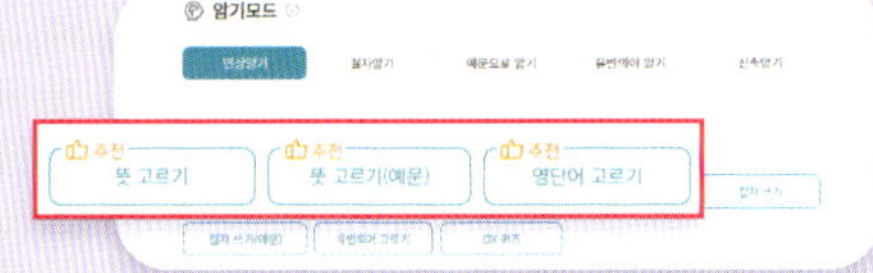

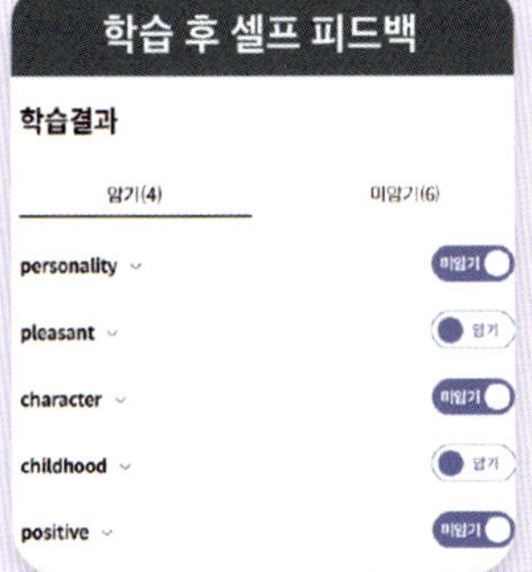

2 자동 생성 단어장! 단어장만 복습하는 다양한 액티비티!

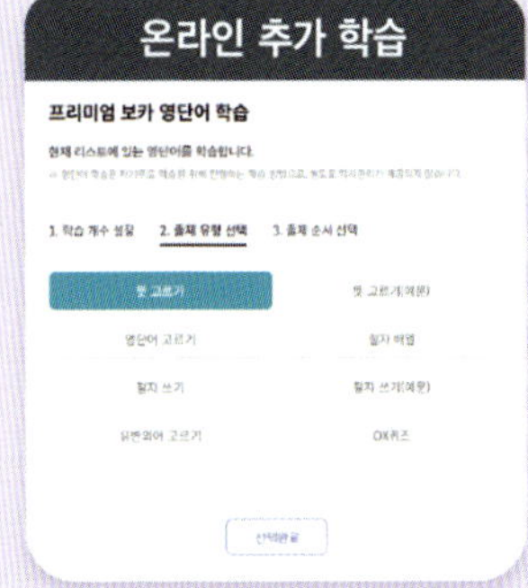

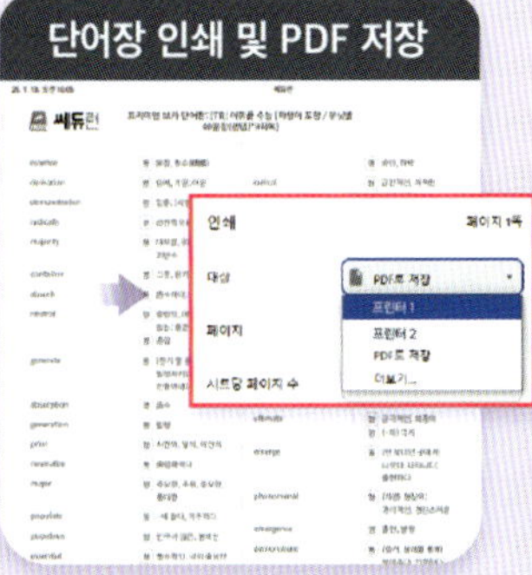

수능 영어 고난도 어휘까지 한번에 끝!
어휘끝 블랙
WORD COMPLETE BLACK
수능 고난도 어휘까지 해결하는 진정한 어휘력
어휘끝 블랙
All New 최신 개정
어휘끝 블랙
How to learn and work with unfamiliar vocabulary
BLACK
휴대용 단어 암기장
어휘끝 블랙 BLACK
영단어 암기장
접사
어근
다의어
구동사
테마
어휘 특성별 학습 전략에 맞춘 체계적 학습
수능 필수 어휘 총정리를 넘어 고난도 어휘까지!
최신 수능 및 기출 반영
2,770여개 표제어
3가지 버전 MP3
쎄듀런 7단계 온라인 암기
< 유료 서비스 >

쎄듀 빈순삽함

빈칸추론

글의순서

문장삽입

함의추론

정답 및 해설

전략편

[1] Enabling animals to <u>operate / in the presence of harmless stimuli</u> / is an almost universal function (of learning).
동물이 움직일 수 있게 하는 것은 / 무해한 자극이 있을 때 / 거의 보편적인 기능이다 (학습의)

[2] Most animals innately avoid / *objects* [(which[that]) they have not previously encountered].
대부분의 동물은 선천적으로 피한다 / 대상을 [그것들이 이전에 마주친 적이 없는]

[3] Unfamiliar objects may be dangerous; // treating them with caution / has survival value.
익숙하지 않은 대상들은 위험할 수도 있다 // 그것들을 조심해서 다루는 것은 / 생존가를 갖는다

[4] If persisted in, / however, / such careful behavior could interfere with / feeding and other necessary activities / to *the extent* [that the benefit of caution would be lost].
만약 지속된다면 / 그러나 / 그러한 조심스러운 행동은 (~을) 방해할 수도 있다 /
먹이 섭취와 다른 필요한 활동을 / 정도까지 [조심해서 얻는 이익이 없어질]

[5] *A turtle* [that withdraws into its shell / at every puff of wind // or whenever a cloud casts a shadow] / would never win races, / not even with a lazy rabbit.
거북은 [그것의 등딱지 속으로 움츠리는 / 바람이 한 번 불 때마다 //
또는 구름이 그림자를 드리울 때마다] / 경주에서 결코 이기지 못할 것이다 / 게으른 토끼와 하더라도

[6] To overcome this problem, / almost all animals habituate / to *safe stimuli* [that occur frequently].
이 문제를 극복하기 위해 / 거의 모든 동물은 습관화된다 / 안전한 자극에 [자주 발생하는]

[7] Confronted by a strange object, / an inexperienced animal may freeze or (may) attempt to hide, // but if nothing unpleasant happens, // sooner or later it will continue its activity.
낯선 대상에 직면하면 / 경험이 없는 동물은 얼어붙거나 숨으려고 할 수도 있다 //
그러나 불쾌한 일이 일어나지 않으면 // 그것(경험이 없는 동물)은 머잖아 활동을 계속할 것이다

[8] The possibility also exists // that an unfamiliar object may be useful, // so if it poses no immediate threat, // a closer inspection may be worthwhile.
가능성도 있다 // 익숙하지 않은 대상이 유용할지도 모르는 //
그래서 그것이 즉각적인 위험을 제기하지 않는다면 // 더 면밀한 조사가 가치 있을 수도 있다

해설

빈칸 문장 확인하기

1 동물이 '무슨 일'을 할 수 있게 하는 것이 학습의 보편적 기능임.

추론 근거로 정답 찾기

2, 4 대부분의 동물은 익숙하지 않은 대상을 선천적으로 피하지만, 조심스러운 행동이 지속되면 생존 활동을 제대로 할 수 없음.
6 이에 대한 해결책으로 동물은 자주 발생하는 '안전한 자극(safe stimuli)'에 익숙해짐.
7 낯선 대상을 마주쳐도 해롭지 않으면 활동을 계속함.
↓
동물이 선천적으로는 익숙하지 않은 것을 피하지만 생존을 위해 무해한 자극이 있을 때 움직이는 것이 학습의 결과임을 추론할 수 있다. 문장 6의 safe stimuli는 harmless stimuli로 말바꿈됨.
→ ④ operate in the presence of harmless stimuli(무해한 자극이 있을 때 움직이다)

오답 확인

① weigh the benefits of treating familiar things with care
익숙한 것을 조심해서 다루는 것의 이점을 따져 보다 → 익숙한 것이 아니라 익숙하지 않은 것을 조심하는 행동이 지속되면 해가 될 수 있다고 했음.
② plan escape routes after predicting possible attacks
가능성 있는 공격을 예측한 이후에 탈출로를 계획하다
③ overcome repeated feeding failures for survival
생존을 위해 반복되는 먹이 섭취의 실패를 극복하다 → 먹이 섭취는 조심스러운 행동이 계속될 때 해를 입을 수 있는 필수 생존 활동의 예로 언급된 것임.
⑤ monitor the surrounding area regularly
주변 지역을 정기적으로 관찰하다
*②, ⑤ → 관련 없는 내용.

어휘

cast (그림자를) 드리우다; 던지다   confront 직면하다, 맞서다
persist in ~을 지속하다   pose (위협·문제를) 제기하다; 포즈를 취하다
sooner or later 머잖아, 조만간   to the extent that ~할 정도까지
withdraw 움츠리다, 뒤로 빼다; 취소[철회]하다

구문 분석

[5] ~ // or **whenever** a cloud casts a shadow] ~.
whenever(~할 때마다)는 부사절을 이끄는 접속사이자 부사절에서 부사 역할도 하는 복합관계부사임.

해석 [1] 동물이 무해한 자극이 있을 때 움직일 수 있게 하는 것은 학습의 거의 보편적인 기능이다. [2] 대부분의 동물은 그것들이 이전에 마주친 적이 없는 대상을 선천적으로 피한다. [3] 익숙하지 않은 대상들은 위험할 수도 있으므로, 그것들을 조심해서 다루는 것은 생존가(생체의 특질이 생존에 기여하는 유용성)를 갖는다. [4] 그러나 만약 지속된다면, 그러한 조심스러운 행동은 조심해서 얻는 이익이 없어질 정도까지 먹이 섭취와 다른 필요한 활동을 방해할 수도 있다. [5] 바람이 한 번 불 때마다, 또는 구름이 그림자를 드리울 때마다 등딱지 속으로 움츠리는 거북은 게으른 토끼와 하더라도 경주에서 결코 이기지 못할 것이다. [6] 이 문제를 극복하기 위해, 거의 모든 동물은 자주 발생하는 안전한 자극에 습관화된다. [7] 낯선 대상에 직면하면, 경험이 없는 동물은 얼어붙거나 숨으려고 할 수도 있지만, 불쾌한 일이 일어나지 않으면 그것은 머잖아 활동을 계속할 것이다. [8] 익숙하지 않은 대상이 유용할지도 모르는 가능성도 있으므로, 그것이 즉각적인 위험을 제기하지 않는다면, 더 면밀한 조사가 가치 있을 수도 있다.

Point 1   빈칸이 초반에 있을 때 정답 찾기

Zoom 1

해석 기회가 풍부하고 일자리를 원하는 사람이 없는 튼튼한 경제가 __________ (라)는 것을 이해하기는 어렵지 않다.

- **plentiful** 풍부한   **go begging** (물건 등을) 원하는 사람이 없다

→ (중간 생략) 예를 들면, 1990년대 후반 미국의 건설 호황기에 '백인 남성들의 전통적 요새, 즉 부러움을 사는 (노동조합의) 조합원증이 아버지에게서 아들에게로 물려졌던 세계'로 오랫동안 알려진 목수 노동조합조차도 그것의 인턴 프로그램에 참가하라고 여성과 흑인 그리고 히스패닉계에게 공개적으로 권장하기 시작했다. 최소한 일터에서는 일자리가 사람을 쫓는 것이 사람이 일자리를 쫓는 것보다 유동적인 사회를 조성하기 위해 분명히 더 많은 것을 한다.

- **boom** 호황, 붐   **carpenter** 목수   **union** 노동조합; 연합
  hand down ~을 물려주다   **openly** 공개적으로   **promote** 조성[조장]하다; 촉진하다   **fluid** 유동적인; 유(동)체

→ 빈칸: 사회적 장벽을 무너뜨리는 데 도움이 된다

- **break down** ~을 무너뜨리다[부수다]   **barrier** 장벽, 장애물

Zoom 2

해석 뉴스, 특히 텔레비전으로 방송되는 형태는 그것의 주제와 이야기 선정뿐만 아니라 그것의 __________ 에 의해서도 구성된다.

- **constitute** 구성하다; (법률을) 제정하다

→ (중간 생략) 실제로, 현대의 뉴스 구성은 로고, 짧은 어록, 빠른 시각적 컷(장면), 그리고 뉴스 프로 진행자의 '스타 기질'의 이용을 포함하여 더 빠른 편집 속도와 '더 현란한' 표현 방식의 증가된 사용에 의존하게 되었다. (이하 생략)

- **contemporary** 현대의, 당대의; 동시대의   **construction** 구성; 건설, 건축
  flashy 현란한; 호화스러운   **sound-bite** (방송용으로 발췌한) 짧은 어록

→ 빈칸: 언어적, 시각적 표현 양식이나 보도 방식

- **idiom** 표현 양식; 관용구, 숙어   **address** 보도, 전달; 연설

함정 주의 ①

해석 우리 첨단 기술 제품의 미래는 우리 생각의 한계가 아니라, __________ 에 있을지도 모른다. • **high-tech** 첨단 기술의   **limitation** 한계; 제한

→ 우리의 창의력은 곧 우리의 물질적인 공급을 앞지를 것이다. 다행히, 희귀 금속들이 전기 자동차, 풍력 발전용 터빈, 태양 전지판과 같은 친환경 기술의 핵심 재료이다. 그것들(친환경 기술들)은 태양과 바람과 같은 무료 천연 자원을 우리의 생활에 연료를 공급하는 동력으로 전환하는 데 도움을 준다. 하지만 오늘날의 제한된 공급을 늘리지 않고는, 우리는 기후 변화를 늦추기 위해 우리가 필요로 하는 친환경 대체 기술을 개발할 가망이 없다.

- **outpace** 앞지르다   **wind turbine** 풍력 발전용 터빈   **solar panel** 태양 전지판
  convert 전환하다, 변하게 하다   **alternative** 대체의

① 그것을 생산하기 위한 재료를 확보하는 우리의 능력
② 그것을 가능한 한 친환경적이게 만들려고 하는 우리의 노력

- **eco-friendly** 친환경적인

해설 빈칸 문장은 첨단 기술 제품의 미래가 우리 생각의 한계가 아니라 '무엇'에 있을지도 모른다는 내용이다. 우리의 창의력이 곧 물질적인 공급을 앞지를 것이라고 했고, 친환경 기술을 통해 천연 자원으로 동력을 만들 수 있지만 재료 공급을 늘려야 친환경 대체 기술을 개발할 수 있다고 했다. 이는 첨단 기술 실현을 위한 자원, 즉 재료의 공급을 늘려야 한다는 내용이므로, 빈칸에 들어갈 말로 가장 적절한 것은 ① 'our ability to secure the ingredients to produce them(그것을 생산하기 위한 재료를 확보하는 우리의 능력)'이다. 친환경적인

미래 기술을 만들어야 한다는 내용이 아니므로 ②는 적절하지 않다. 친환경 대체 기술은 미래 첨단 기술의 예로 언급된 것임에 유의해야 한다.

Zoom 3

해석 도시에서 운전하거나 걷거나 교통 카드를 단말기에 대는 모든 사람은 현관문을 나서는 순간부터 자신을 교통 전문가로 여긴다. 그리고 그녀(그 사람)가 도로를 바라보는 방식은 __________. • **transit** 교통 (체계); 운송

→ (중간 생략) 그리고 모든 정치와 마찬가지로, 모든 교통은 지역적이고 몹시 개인적이다. • **intensely** 몹시, 극도로; 열심히

→ 빈칸: 그 사람이 돌아다니는 방식(이용하는 교통수단)과 매우 밀접하게 일치한다

- **track with** ~와 일치하다   **get around** 돌아다니다

Focus & Practice

1 ②   **2** ③   **3** ③   **4** ③

1 ②

해석 창의성에 대한 한 가지 무언의 사실은 그것이 자연 그대로의(천부적인) 재능에 관한 것이라기보다는 생산성에 관한 것이라는 점이다. 효과 있는 몇몇 아이디어를 발견하기 위하여, 여러분은 그렇지 않은(효과가 없는) 많은 것들을 시도할 필요가 있다. 그것은 순전한 숫자 놀음이다. 천재들은 다른 창작자들보다 반드시 더 높은 성공률을 가지고 있지 않으며, 그들은 그저 더 많이 하고 다양한 여러 가지의 것들을 한다. 그들은 더 많은 성공 '그리고' 더 많은 실패를 한다. 그것은 단체와 회사에도 해당된다. 많은 나쁜 아이디어도 만들어 내지 않으면서 많은 좋은 아이디어를 만들어 내는 것은 불가능하다. …

- **wild** 자연 그대로의; 야생의   **go for** ~에 해당되다; ~을 좋아하다

① 우월성   ② 생산성   ③ 성취

해설 빈칸 문장은 창의성이 천부적인 재능이 아닌 '무엇'에 관한 것이라는 내용이다. 이어서 '효과 있는 몇몇 아이디어'로 창의성을 달리 표현하여, 이를 위해 효과 없는 많은 것들을 시도해야 한다고 했다. 또한 더 많이 하는 것, 많은 아이디어를 만들어 내는 것이 중요하다고 설명했다. 일단 많은 아이디어를 생산해 내야 창의적인 좋은 아이디어로 나온다는 내용이므로, 빈칸에 들어갈 말로 가장 적절한 것은 ② 'productivity(생산성)'이다. 천부적인 재능이 아닌 창의성이 얼마나 우월한지와 관련된다는 언급은 없으므로 ①은 적절하지 않으며, 천재들의 성공률이 반드시 더 높은 것은 아니라고 언급했으므로 ③도 적절하지 않다.

2 ③

해석 우리가 나사돌리개를 집는 것만큼 겉보기에는 간단한 무언가를 할 때조차도, 우리의 뇌는 무의식적으로 그것이 신체로 여기는 것을 도구를 포함하도록 조정한다. 우리는 말 그대로 나사돌리개의 끝부분으로 사물을 느낄 수 있다. 나사돌리개를 들고 손을 뻗을 때 우리는 무의식적으로 후자(나사돌리개)의 길이를 계산에 넣는다. … 우리는 훨씬 더 복잡한 상황에서 우리가 사용하는 훨씬 더 복잡한 도구에도 똑같이 한다. 우리가 조종하는 자동차는 순간적이면서도 무의식적으로 우리 자신이 된다. … 기계로까지 자신을 확장하지 않는다면 운전하는 것은 불가능할 것이다.

•apparently 겉보기에는; 명백히, 분명하게   screwdriver 나사돌리개   automatically 무의식적으로; 자동으로   literally 말 그대로, 문자 그대로   extend (손·발 등을) 뻗다; 확장하다 *cf.* extension 확장   take A into account A를 계산에 넣다[고려하다]   latter 후자(의)   pilot 조종하다; 조종사, 파일럿   instantaneously 순간적으로; 즉각적으로

① 그 도구를 활용했던 지난 경험을 상기한다
② 우리 신체의 어느 부분이 가장 잘 활용될 수 있는지를 판단한다
③ 그것이 신체로 여기는 것을 도구를 포함하도록 조정한다

해설 빈칸 문장은 나사돌리개를 집는 것만큼 겉보기에 간단한 일을 할 때조차도, 뇌가 무의식적으로 '어떻게 한다'는 내용이다. 이어서 우리가 나사돌리개를 들고 손을 뻗을 때 손이 닿을 수 있는 거리에 나사돌리개의 길이도 계산에 넣으며, 더 복잡한 상황과 더 복잡한 도구의 경우에도 똑같이 한다고 했다. 이는 우리가 사용하는 도구와 우리의 몸을 하나로 여긴다는 것을 보여주므로, 빈칸에 들어갈 말로 가장 적절한 것은 ③ 'adjusts what it considers body to include the tool(그것이 신체로 여기는 것을 도구를 포함하도록 조정한다)'이다. 어떤 도구를 활용했던 경험을 떠올린다는 내용은 없으므로 ①은 적절하지 않고, 신체가 아니라 도구를 활용하는 내용이므로 ②도 적절하지 않다.

3 ③

해석 사진이 나오기 전에 장소들은 잘 이동하지 않았다. 화가들이 항상 특정한 장소를 그것의 '거주지'에서 들어내서 다른 곳으로 옮겨왔지만, 그림은 제작하는 데 많은 시간이 걸렸고, 상대적으로 운반하기 어려웠고, 유일무이했다. … 사진은 소비 자본주의와 결합하게 되었고 이제 세계는 '이전에는 전혀 이용되지 않았거나 오직 한 명의 고객을 위한 그림으로만 이용되었던 인물, 풍경, 사건들을 무제한의 양으로' 제공받았다. … 점차 사진은 세계를 가시적이고, 미적이며, 매력적이게 만드는 값싼 대량 생산품이 되었다. … 가볍고 작고 대량 생산된 사진은 장소의 시공간적 이동을 위한 역동적인 수단이 되었다.

•dwelling 거주(지), 사는 집   time-consuming (많은) 시간이 걸리는   one-of-a-kind 유일한; 특별한   couple 결합[연결]하다; 두 사람[개]   capitalism 자본주의   utilise[utilize] 이용[활용]하다   vehicle (전달) 수단, 매개체; 차량, 탈것   spatiotemporal 시공간적인   circulation (장소에서 장소로의) 이동; 유통; 순환

① 그림은 예술의 주요한 형식이었다
② 예술이 세상을 여실히 보여주었다
③ 장소들은 잘 이동하지 않았다

•hold up a mirror to A A를 여실히 보여주다, A를 그대로 반영하다

해설 빈칸 문장은 사진이 나오기 전인 과거에는 '어떠했다'는 내용이다. 이어서 그림은 제작하는 데 시간이 오래 걸리고, 운반이 어렵고, 하나뿐이라는 제약을 제시한 다음, 값싼 대량 생산품이 된 사진은 장소의 시공간적 이동을 위한 수단이 되었다고 설명했다. 따라서 사진이 나오기 전에는 반대로 장소의 이동이 어려웠을 것이므로, 빈칸에 들어갈 말로 가장 적절한 것은 ③ 'places did not travel well(장소들은 잘 이동하지 않았다)'이다. travel은 여기서 '그림에 담겨 다른 곳으로 이동하다'를 의미한다. 그림이 예술의 주요 형식이었는지 언급되지 않았으므로 ①은 적절하지 않다. 또, 사진에 비해 그림에 제약이 있다고는 했으나, 사진이 나오기 전에도 예술이 세상을 보여주었는지 아닌지는 언급되지 않았으므로 ②도 적절하지 않다.

4 ③

해석 비록 대부분의 소매점에서 가격은 소매상에 의해 정해지긴 하지만, 이는 이 가격이 시간이 지나면서 시장의 힘에 조정되지 않는다는 것을 의미하는 것은 아니다. 그 어느 특정한 날에도 우리는 모든 상품은 그것에 명확한 가격표가 있다는 것을 안다. 그러나 이 가격은 날마다 또는 주마다 다를 수도 있다. … 예를 들어, 만약에 악천후가 부족한 감자 수확량을 초래한다면, 슈퍼마켓이 감자에 대해 그들의 도매상에게 지불해야 하는 가격은 상승할 것이고, 이는 그들(슈퍼마켓)이 자신의 가게에 있는 감자에 매기는 가격에 반영될 것이다. 따라서 이 가격들은 더 넓은 감자 시장에서의 수요와 공급의 상호 작용을 정말로 반영한다. 비록 가격들이 수요와 공급에서의 지역적 변동을 반영하기 위해 슈퍼마켓에서 시간마다 바뀌지는 않지만, 그것들은 문제의 상품에 대한 전반적인 생산과 수요의 기저에 놓인 상황을 반영하기 위해 시간이 지나면서 정말로 바뀐다.

•retail outlet 소매점   retailer 소매상   crop (한 철에 거둔) 수확량; (농)작물   marketplace 시장   variation 변동, 변화; 차이   underlying 기저의; 근원적인, 기초를 이루는   condition ((복수형)) 상황, 환경   overall 전반적인, 전체의   in question 문제의, 논의가 되고 있는

① 수요와 공급의 원리를 반영한다
② 시간마다 바뀌지 않을 수도 있다
③ 시간이 지나면서 시장의 힘에 조정되지 않는다

해설 빈칸 문장은 소매상에 의해 정해진 가격이 '무엇'을 의미하는 것은 아니라는 내용이다. 이어지는 내용에서는 소매점의 가격은 더 넓은 시장에서의 수요와 공급의 상호 작용을 반영하기 위해 변동될 수 있다고 설명했다. 따라서 소매상의 가격은 '시장의 상황을 반영하지 않는 것'이 아니므로, 빈칸에 들어갈 말로 가장 적절한 것은 ③ 'do not adjust to market forces over time(시간이 지나면서 시장의 힘에 조정되지 않는다)'이다. 빈칸 문장이 부정어를 포함해(does not mean) ①은 정반대 의미가 되어 적절하지 않으며, 가격이 시간마다 바뀌는 것은 아니라고 했으므로 마찬가지로 반대 의미가 되는 ②도 적절하지 않다. 빈칸 문장이 부정어(not, no, never, seldom, neither, little, rarely 등)를 포함한 경우, 빈칸에서 그것을 다시 부정하면 이중 부정이 되어 긍정의 의미가 된다는 점에 주의해야 한다.

1 ⑤

[1] "What's in a name? // *That* [which we call a rose], /
by any other name / would smell as sweet."
"이름이 뭐가 중요한가? // 그것은 [우리가 장미라고 부르는] /
다른 어떤 이름으로든 / 똑같이 향기로울 것이다"

[2] This thought (of Shakespeare's) / points up a difference
(between roses and, say, paintings).
이 생각은 (Shakespeare의) / 차이를 강조한다 (장미와 이를테면 그림 사이의)

[3] Natural objects, / (such as roses), / are not <u>interpreted</u>.
자연물은 / (장미와 같은) / 해석되지 않는다

[4] They are not taken / as vehicles (of meanings and messages).
그것들(자연물)은 받아들여지지 않는다 / 매개체로 (의미와 메시지의)

[5] They belong to no tradition, / strictly speaking have no style /
and <u>are not understood</u> / within a framework (of culture and
convention).
그것들(자연물)은 어떤 전통에도 속하지 않는다 / 엄밀히 말하면 양식이 없다 /
그리고 이해되지 않는다 / 틀 안에서 (문화와 관습의)

[6] Rather, / they are sensed and (are) savored relatively directly, /
without intellectual mediation, //
좀 더 정확하게 말하면 / 그것들(자연물)은 비교적 직접적으로 감지되고 음미된다 /
지성을 필요로 하는 매개 없이 //

and so what they are called, / either individually or collectively,
/ has little bearing / on our experience of them.
그리고 따라서 그것들이 불리는 것은 / 개별적으로든 집합적으로든 /
관련이 거의 없다 / 그것들(자연물)에 대한 우리의 경험과는

[7] What a work of art is titled, / on the other hand, / has a significant
effect / on *the aesthetic face* [(which[that]) it presents] / and on
the qualities [(which[that]) we correctly perceive in it].
미술 작품이 무엇이라고 제목이 붙는지는 / 반면에 / 상당한 영향을 미친다 /
미학적 면에 [그것(미술 작품)이 나타내는] / 그리고 특징에 [그것에서 우리가 올바르게 인지하는]

[8] A painting of a rose, / (by a name other than *the one* [(that) it
has]), / might very well smell different, / aesthetically speaking.
장미 한 송이의 그림은 / ((~인) 것(이름)과는 다른 이름으로 불리는 [그것(장미 한 송이의 그림)이
가지고 있는]) / 아마 정말로 향기가 다를 것이다 / 미학적으로 말해

[9] *The painting* (titled *Rose of Summer*) / and *an indiscernible
painting* (titled *Vermillion Womanhood*) / are physically, but
also semantically and aesthetically, / distinct objects of art.
그림 ('Rose of Summer'라고 제목 붙여진) / 그리고 식별하기 어려운 그림은 ('Vermillion
Womanhood'라고 제목 붙여진) / 물리적으로, 또한 의미적으로나 미학적으로도 ~이다 / 별개의
미술품

해설

빈칸 문장 확인하기 

3 장미와 같은 자연물은 '어떻지' 않음.

추론 근거로 정답 찾기 ⊕

1, 2 이름의 중요성에 대하여 장미와 그림 간의 차이를 대조함.
4 자연물은 의미와 메시지를 전달하지 않음.
5, 6 자연물은 문화와 관습의 틀 안에서 이해되지 않고, 지적 매개
없이 비교적 직접적으로 감상됨.

자연물은 지적 매개 없이 직접적으로 감지되고 음미되므로, 그것
이 무엇이라고 불리든 그것에 대한 감상(경험)은 변하지 않는다
는 내용이다. 제목이 이해에 영향을 미치는 미술 작품과는 달리,
자연물은 직접적으로 이해되는 것이므로 '해석되지' 않음을 추론
할 수 있다.

→ ⑤ interpreted(해석되는)

오답 확인

① changed 변하는 → 미술품은 제목에 따라 의미와 특징이 변하는 반면
자연물은 그렇지 않다고는 했지만, 자연물 자체가 변하지 않는다는 내용이 아님.
② classified 분류되는 → 자연물이 문화와 관습의 틀에 속하지 않는다고
는 했지만 이는 비교적 직접적으로 음미된다는 의미이며, 자연물이 분류되지 않는다
는 내용은 아님.
③ preserved 보존되는
④ controlled 통제되는
＊③, ④ → 언급되지 않은 내용.

어휘

convention 관습, 관례   distinct 별개의, 다른; 뚜렷한, 분명한
face 면; 직면하다   framework 틀, 뼈대
have a bearing on ~와 관련이 있다   intellectual 지성을 필요로 하는,
지적인   interpret 해석하다, 이해하다   mediation 매개; (말·정보의)
전달; 중재, 조정   might (very) well 아마 (정말로) ~일 것이다;
(~하는 것도) 당연하다   point up ~을 강조하다[두드러지게 하다]

구문 분석

[1] ~ // *That* [which we **call a rose**], / by any other name /
would smell as sweet."
관계사절 내의 <call+O+C>에서 빠져 있는 목적어가 선행사 That임.

해석 [1] "이름이 뭐가 중요한가? 우리가 장미라고 부르는 그것은 다른 어떤 이름으로든 똑같이 향기로울 것이다." [2] Shakespeare의 이 생각은 장미와 이를테면 그림 사이의 차
이를 강조한다. [3] 장미와 같은 자연물은 <u>해석되지</u> 않는다. [4] 그것들은 의미와 메시지의 매개체로 받아들여지지 않는다. [5] 그것들은 어떤 전통에도 속하지 않고, 엄밀히 말하면 양식
이 없으며, 문화와 관습의 틀 안에서 이해되지 않는다. [6] 좀 더 정확하게 말하면, 그것들은 지성을 필요로 하는 매개 없이 비교적 직접적으로 감지되고 음미되며, 따라서 개별적으
로든 집합적으로든, 그것들이 불리는 것은 그것들에 대한 우리의 경험과는 관련이 거의 없다. [7] 반면에 미술 작품이 무엇이라고 제목이 붙는지는 그것이 나타내는 미학적 면과 그
것에서 우리가 올바르게 인지하는 특징에 상당한 영향을 미친다. [8] 그것이 가지고 있는 것과는 다른 이름으로 불리는 장미 한 송이의 그림은, 미학적으로 말해, 아마 정말로 향기
가 다를 것이다. [9] 'Rose of Summer'라고 제목 붙여진 그림과 'Vermillion Womanhood'라고 제목 붙여진 식별하기 어려운 그림은 물리적으로, 또한 의미적으로나 미학적으로
도 별개의 미술품이다.

2 ①

1 Elinor Ostrom found // that there are *several factors* (critical to bringing about stable institutional solutions / to the problem of the commons).
Elinor Ostrom은 알게 되었다 // 몇몇 요인이 있다는 것을 (안정적인 제도적 해결책을 가져오는 데 중대한 / 공유지 문제에 대한)

2 She pointed out, / for instance, // that *the actors* (affected by the rules (for the use and care of resources)) / must have the right (to participate in decisions (to change the rules)).
그녀는 지적했다 / 예를 들어 // 행위자들이 (규칙의 영향을 받는 (자원의 이용 및 관리에 대한)) / 권리를 가져야 한다고 (결정에 참여할 (규칙을 변경하는))

3 For that reason, / *the people* [who monitor and control the behavior of users] / should also be users / and/or (should) have been given a mandate / by all users.
그러한 이유로, / 사람들은 [이용자들의 행동을 감시하고 통제하는] / 또한 이용자들이어야 한다 / 그리고/또는 위임을 받았어야 한다 / 모든 이용자들에 의해

4 This is a significant insight, // as it shows //
이것은 중요한 통찰이다 // 그것이 보여주기 때문이다 //

that prospects are poor (for *a centrally directed solution* (to the problem of the commons) (coming from a state power)) /
전망이 좋지 않다는 것을 (중앙 통제된 해결책의 (공유지 문제에 대한) (국가 권력에서 나오는)) /

in comparison with *a local solution* [for which users assume personal responsibility].
지역적인 해결책에 비해서 [이용자들이 개인적인 책임을 지는]

5 Ostrom also emphasizes / the importance (of democratic decision processes) /
Ostrom은 또한 강조한다 / 중요성을 (민주적 의사 결정 과정의) /

and that all users must be given access / to local forums (for solving problems and conflicts (among themselves)).
그리고 모든 이용자에게 참가할 권리가 주어져야 한다는 것을 / 지역 포럼에 (문제와 갈등을 해결하기 위한 (그들 사이의))

6 Political institutions (at central, regional, and local levels) / must allow users / to devise their own regulations / and (to) independently ensure observance.
정치 기관들은 (중앙, 지방 및 지역 차원의) / 이용자들이 (~하도록) 해야 한다 / 자체 규정을 고안하도록 / 그리고 독립적으로 준수할 수 있도록

해설

빈칸 문장 확인하기 

2 예를 들어, 자원의 이용 및 관리에 대한 규칙의 영향을 받는 행위자들이 '어떤' 권리를 가져야 한다고 지적함.

⌄

추론 근거로 정답 찾기

1 Elinor Ostrom은 공유지 문제의 제도적 해결책에 중요한 몇몇 요인이 있음을 알게 됨.
3 공유지 이용자들을 감시 및 통제하는 사람들도 이용자이거나 모든 이용자에게 위임받은 사람이어야 함.
5, 6 민주적 의사 결정 과정과 이용자 모두의 참가권이 중요하며, 이용자들이 자체 규정을 고안하고 준수하도록 해야 함.

↓

이용자의 직접적 감시 및 통제, 민주적 의사 결정과 모두의 참가권, 자체 규정의 고안과 준수는 모두 규칙을 변경하는 결정에 참여할 이용자의 권리에 대한 것임을 추론할 수 있다.

→ ① participate in decisions to change the rules(규칙을 변경하는 결정에 참여하다)

오답 확인

② claim individual ownership of the resources
자원에 대한 개인의 소유권을 주장하다 → 이용자이거나 모든 이용자에 의해 위임받은 사람이 직접 이용자를 감시, 통제해야 한다고 했을 뿐, 이용자들이 스스로의 개인적 소유권을 주장해야 한다는 내용이 아님.

③ use those resources to maximize their profits
자신의 이익을 최대화하기 위해 그 자원을 이용하다

④ demand free access to the communal resources
공동 자원에 대한 자유로운 접근권을 요구하다 → 규칙을 만들고 준수하도록 해야 한다고 했으므로 자유로운 접근권이 아님.

⑤ request proper distribution based on their merits
자신의 공로를 바탕으로 적당한 분배를 요청하다
*③, ⑤ → 언급되지 않은 내용.

어휘

assume (책임 등을) 지다; 추정하다　bring about ~을 가져오다[초래하다]
devise 고안하다, 발명하다　directed 통제된, 규제된
observance (법률·관례의) 준수; 관찰　prospect 전망; 가망, 가능성
regional 지방[지역]의

구문 분석

2 ~ must have **the right (to participate in decisions (to change the rules))**.
the right와 to participate 이하, decisions와 to change 이하는 각각 동격 관계임.

해석 **1** Elinor Ostrom은 공유지(특정한 개인의 소유가 아닌, 국가 또는 공공단체에 의하여 소유되는 토지) 문제에 대한 안정적인 제도적 해결책을 가져오는 데 중대한 몇몇 요인이 있다는 것을 알게 되었다. **2** 예를 들어, 그녀는 자원의 이용 및 관리에 대한 규칙의 영향을 받는 행위자들이 <u>규칙을 변경하는 결정에 참여할</u> 권리를 가져야 한다고 지적했다. **3** 그러한 이유로 이용자들의 행동을 감시하고 통제하는 사람들은 또한 이용자들이고/이용자이거나 모든 이용자에 의해 위임을 받았어야 한다. **4** 이것은 중요한 통찰인데, 이용자들이 개인적인 책임을 지는 지역적인 해결책에 비해서 국가 권력에서 나오는 공유지 문제에 대한 중앙 통제된 해결책의 전망이 좋지 않다는 것을 그것이 보여주기 때문이다. **5** Ostrom은 또한 민주적 의사 결정 과정의 중요성과 모든 이용자에게 그들 사이의 문제와 갈등을 해결하기 위한 지역 포럼에 참가할 권리가 주어져야 한다는 것을 강조한다. **6** 중앙, 지방 및 지역 차원의 정치 기관들은 이용자들이 자체 규정을 고안하고 독립적으로 준수할 수 있도록 해야 한다.

3 ①

1 Research (with human runners) / challenged conventional wisdom / and found //
연구는 (달리는 사람에 관한) / 사회적 통념에 이의를 제기했다 / 그리고 알아냈다 //

that the ground-reaction forces at the foot / and *the shock* (transmitted up the leg and through the body / after impact with the ground) / varied little //
발에서 일어나는 지면 반발력 / 그리고 충격은
(다리 위로 몸을 관통하여 전달되는 / 지면과의 충돌 후에) / 거의 달라지지 않았다는 것을 //

as runners moved / from extremely compliant / to extremely hard running surfaces.
달리는 사람이 이동했을 때 / 매우 말랑말랑한 활주면에서 / 매우 단단한 활주면으로

2 As a result, / researchers gradually began to believe // that runners are subconsciously able to adjust leg stiffness /
그 결과 / 연구자들은 점차 믿기 시작했다 //
달리는 사람이 다리의 강직도를 잠재의식적으로 조정할 수 있다고 /

prior to foot strike / based on their perceptions (of the hardness or stiffness of *the surface* [on which they are running]).
발이 (지면을) 치기 전에 / 자신의 인식에 근거하여 (지표면의 견고함이나 단단함에 대한 [자신이 달리고 있는])

3 This view suggests // that runners create / *soft legs* [that soak up impact forces] // when they are running on very hard surfaces /
이 견해는 시사한다 // 달리는 사람이 만든다는 것을 / 푹신한 다리를 [충격력을 흡수하는] // 그들이 매우 단단한 지표면에서 달리고 있을 때 /

and (runners create) stiff legs // when they are moving along on yielding terrain.
그리고 단단한 다리를 (만든다) // 그들이 물렁한 지형에서 움직이고 있을 때

4 As a result, / *impact forces* (passing through the legs) / are strikingly similar / over a wide range of running surface types.
그 결과 / 충격력은 (다리를 통해 전해지는) / 눈에 띄게 비슷하다 / 다양한 활주면 유형에 걸쳐서

5 Contrary to popular belief, / running on concrete is not more damaging to the legs / than running on soft sand.
일반적인 생각과는 반대로, / 콘크리트 위를 달리는 것은 다리에 더 해롭지 않다 / 푹신한 모래 위를 달리는 것보다

해설

빈칸 문장 확인하기 🔎

1 사회적 통념과 달리 말랑한 활주면에서 단단한 활주면으로 달리는 사람이 이동했을 때, 발에서 일어나는 지면 반발력과 지면과의 충돌 후 몸으로 전해지는 충격은 '어떠하다'는 것을 연구로 알아냄.

추론 근거로 정답 찾기 ➕

4 다양한 활주면에서 다리를 통해 전해지는 충격력은 매우 비슷함.
5 일반적인 생각(= 사회적 통념)과 반대로 콘크리트 위를 달리는 것이 모래 위를 달리는 것보다 다리에 더 해롭지 않음.

활주면 유형과 상관없이 충격력이 유사하다는 것이므로 충격에는 변화가 거의 없음을 추론할 수 있다.
*준부정어 little(거의 ~없는)이 쓰여 '거의 달라지지 않았다'를 의미함에 유의한다.

→ ① varied little(거의 달라지지 않았다)

오답 확인

② decreased a lot 많이 감소했다
③ suddenly peaked 갑자기 최고조에 달했다
*②, ③ → 다양한 활주면 유형에서의 충격력이 비슷하다고 했으므로 충격이 감소하거나 증가했다는 내용은 틀림.
④ gradually appeared 점차 나타났다
⑤ were hardly generated 거의 발생되지 않았다
*④, ⑤ → 활주면의 유형에 따른 충격력의 정도를 비교했으므로 충격이 없다거나 나타나거나 발생하지 않는 것이 아님.

어휘

conventional wisdom 사회적 통념   ground-reaction force 지면 반발력   perception 인식; 지각, 자각   soak up 흡수하다, 빨아들이다   strikingly 눈에 띄게, 두드러지게   subconsciously 잠재의식적으로   transmit 전달하다; 나르다, 운송하다   yielding 물렁한, 유연한

구문 분석

3 This view suggests // that runners **create** / *soft legs* [that soak up impact forces] // when they are running on very hard surfaces / and (runners create) **stiff legs** // when they are moving along on yielding terrain.
create의 목적어로 soft legs가 이끄는 명사구와 stiff legs가 이끄는 명사구가 and로 병렬 연결된 구조.
5 ~ / running on concrete is **not more** damaging to the legs / **than** running on soft sand.
<A not more ~ than B>: A가 B보다 더 ~한 것은 아니다

해석 **1** 달리는 사람에 관한 연구는 사회적 통념에 이의를 제기하고, 발에서 일어나는 지면 반발력과 지면과의 충돌 후에 다리 위로 몸을 관통하여 전달되는 충격은 달리는 사람이 매우 말랑말랑한 활주면에서 매우 단단한 활주면으로 이동했을 때 거의 달라지지 않았다는 것을 알아냈다. **2** 그 결과, 연구자들은 달리는 사람이 자신이 달리고 있는 지표면의 견고함이나 단단함에 대한 자신의 인식에 근거하여 발이 (지면을) 치기 전에 다리의 강직도를 잠재의식적으로 조정할 수 있다고 점차 믿기 시작했다. **3** 이 견해는 달리는 사람이 매우 단단한 지표면에서 달리고 있을 때 충격력을 흡수하는 푹신한 다리를 만들고 물렁한 지형에서 움직이고 있을 때 단단한 다리를 만든다는 것을 시사한다. **4** 그 결과, 다리를 통해 전해지는 충격력은 다양한 활주면 유형에 걸쳐서 눈에 띄게 비슷하다. **5** 일반적인 생각과는 반대로, 콘크리트 위를 달리는 것은 푹신한 모래 위를 달리는 것보다 다리에 더 해롭지 않다.

Zoom 1

해석 (이전 생략) 우루크에 있는 사원 단지에서 나온 행정 (점토)판의 발견은 토큰 사용과 결과적으로 문자가 중앙 집권화된 경제 지배의 도구로 발달했다는 것을 시사한다. 우루크 시대 가정집 터에서 나온 고고학적 증거가 없음을 고려하면, 개인들도 ___________ 을(를) 위해 그 체계를 사용했는지는 명확하지 않다.

• administrative 행정[관리]의　tablet (점토)판　complex (건물) 단지; 복잡한
token (화폐 대용으로 쓰는) 토큰; 상징, 표시　centralize 중앙 집권화하다
domestic 가정의; 국내의

→ (중간 생략) 초기의 (점토)판에서의 인식 가능한 기호와 그림 문자의 사용은 행정가들이 읽고 쓸 줄 아는 측과 읽고 쓸 수 없는 측이 서로 이해할 수 있는 어휘 목록을 필요로 했던 것과 일치한다. 쐐기 문자가 더욱 추상적이게 되면서, 한 사람이 자신이 합의했던 것을 이해했다는 것을 확실히 하기 위해 읽고 쓰는 능력이 점점 더 중요해졌음이 틀림없다. • abstract 추상적인　literacy (글을) 읽고 쓰는 능력

→ 빈칸: 사적인 합의 • agreement 합의

Zoom 2

해석 많은 사람이 인터넷에서 사진과 비디오를 만들고 공유한다. 어려운 점은 여러분이 원하는 것을 찾는 것이다. 일반적으로 사람들은 (이를테면, 예시 스케치보다는) 단어를 사용하여 검색하기를 원한다. (중간 생략) 우리는 이미지 분류와 객체 감지 방법을 적용하여 출력 단어로 이미지를 태그한다. 하지만 태그는 ___________ 이(가) 아니다.

• typically 일반적으로; 전형적으로　classification 분류; 유형, 범주
detection 감지, 발견　output 출력(하다); 생산[산출](량)

→ 누가 무엇을 하고 있는지가 중요한데, 태그는 이것을 포착하지 못한다. 예를 들어, 거리에 있는 고양이의 사진을 '고양이', '거리', '쓰레기통', '생선 뼈'의 객체 범주로 태그하는 것은 그 고양이가 거리에 있는 뚜껑이 없는 쓰레기통에서 생선 뼈를 꺼내고 있다는 정보를 빠뜨린다.

• capture 포착[표현]하다; 붙잡다, 포획하다　category 범주
leave out ~을 빠뜨리다[제외하다]

→ 빈칸: 이미지에서 일어나고 있는 일에 대한 포괄적인 설명
• comprehensive 포괄적인, 종합적인

Zoom 3

해석 (이전 생략) 그러나 더 흔히 개인적인 경험은 공유된 애착을 가진 다른 사람들이 그들 애정의 대상을 중심으로 어울리는 사회적인 상황에 끼워 넣어진다(깊이 새겨진다). 팬덤의 많은 즐거움은 ___________.

• context 상황; 문맥　attachment 애착; 붙이기; 부착; 부착[부가]물
socialize 어울리다, 교제하다; 사회화하다　affection 애정
fandom 팬덤 ((유명인이나 특정 분야를 열성적으로 좋아하는 사람이나 그 무리))

→ 1800년대의 보스턴 사람들은 콘서트에서 군중의 일부가 되는 것을 참석하는 즐거움의 일환으로 그들의 일기에 묘사했다. 팬들이 사랑하는 것은 그들 팬덤의 대상이라기보다는 그 애정이 제공하는 서로에 대한 애착이라는 (그리고 서로 간의 차이라는) 강력한 주장이 제기될 수 있다.

• attendance 참석, 출석　differentiation 차이(의 인정)
afford 제공하다; ~할 여유가 되다, ~할 수 있다

→ 빈칸: 다른 팬들과 연결되는 데서 온다

함정 주의　 ②

해석 피실험자들이 사람들의 얼굴 사진을 보고 분명히 나타나는 표정이나 마음 상태를 식별하도록 요청받은 심리학 연구가 있어 왔다. 그 결과는 언제나 매우 엇갈린다. 17세기에 프랑스의 화가이자 이론가인 Charles Le Brun은 화가들이 표현해 달라고 요청받을 수 있는 다양한 감정을 분명히 보여주는 일련의 얼굴을 그렸다.

• subject 피실험자; 주제; 학과, 과목　invariably 언제나, 변함없이
mixed (의견·생각 등이) 엇갈리는; 혼합된　illustrate 분명히 보여주다
call (up)on ~에게 요청하다, 부탁하다

→ 그것들에 관해 놀라운 점은 ___________ (라)는 것이다. 이 모든 것에서 빠진 것은 감정을 확실하게 만들어 주는 어떤 배경이나 맥락이다. … 그림에서뿐만 아니라 실생활에서도 우리는 단지 얼굴만 우연히 마주치는 것이 아니다.

• striking 놀라운, 주목할 만한　determinate 확실한, 확정적인
come across ~을 우연히 마주치다[발견하다]

① 그것들 모두가 의도된 감정과 일관되게 일치할 수 있었다

② 그것들이 얼마든지 손실 없이 서로 대체될 수 있었다
• substitute for ~을 대체[대신]하다

해설 빈칸 문장은 them을 포함하여 그것들에 관해 놀라운 점이 '무엇'이라는 내용이다. 앞에서는 얼굴 사진을 보고 표정이나 마음 상태를 식별하도록 하면 결과가 언제나 엇갈린다는 연구 결과를 설명하고, Charles Le Brun이 다양한 감정을 분명히 보여주는 일련의 얼굴을 그렸다고 했다. 뒤에서는 이 모든 것에서 감정을 확실히 알 수 있게 하는 배경이나 맥락이 빠졌다고 하고, 그림에서뿐만 아니라 실생활에서도 우리가 얼굴만 마주치는 것이 아니라고 했다. 이는 배경이나 맥락 없이는 감정을 제대로 이해할 수 없다는 내용으로, 얼굴 사진에 기반을 둔 실험 결과와 마찬가지로 얼굴 그림에 대한 식별도 명확히 구분되지 않았음을 알 수 있다. 따라서 빈칸 문장의 them은 'Charles Le Brun이 그린 다양한 감정을 분명히 보여주는 일련의 얼굴(얼굴 그림)'을 받으며, 빈칸에 들어갈 말로 가장 적절한 것은 ② 'any number of them could be substituted for one another without loss(그것들이 얼마든지 손실 없이 서로 대체될 수 있었다)'이다. 배경과 맥락이 빠져 있는 얼굴 그림을 보고서는 의도된 감정을 맞출 수 없을 것이므로, 반대되는 내용인 ①은 적절하지 않다.

Focus & Practice　　p.22

1 ③　　**2** ②　　**3** ①　　**4** ①

1 ③

해석 비슷한 친구를 선택하는 것은 논리적 근거가 있을 수 있다. 어떤 환경의 생존 가능성을 판단하는 것은 위험할 수 있는데 … 그래서 인간은 이 기능을 효율적으로 수행하기 위한 한 가지 방법으로 비슷한 사람들과 어울리려는 욕구를 발달시켜 왔다. 이것(비슷한 사람들과 어울리려는 욕구)은 매우 다양한 유형의 환경에 사는 종에게 특히 유용하다. 그러나 주어진 환경의 수용력은 이 전략(비슷한 사람과 어울리려는 생존 전략)에 제한을 둔다. 자원이 매우 한정되어 있다면, 특정 장소에 사는 사람들은 모두 똑같은 것을 할 수는 없다.… 그러므로 합리적인 전략은 때로는 자기 종의 비슷한 구성원들을 '피하는' 것일 것이다.

• rationale 논리적 근거[이유] *cf.* rational 합리적인, 이성적인
assess 판단[평가]하다   survivability 생존 가능성   associate 어울리다; 연상하다,
연관 짓다   species ((생물)) 종(種)   carrying capacity (환경) 수용력; 적재량
① 공동체의 예상 수요를 초과한다
② 다양한 생존 수단에 의해 줄어든다
③ 이 전략에 제한을 둔다
• exceed 초과하다, ~보다 많다   means 수단, 방법

해설 빈칸 문장은 주어진 환경의 수용력이 '어떠하다'는 내용이다. 역접 연결어
However가 이끌고 있으므로 앞과 반대되는 내용이 이어질 것이다. 빈칸 문
장 앞에서는 인간이 생존 가능성을 높이기 위해 비슷한 사람들과 어울리려는
욕구를 발달시켜 왔다고 했고, 뒤에서는 자원이 한정된 환경에서는 비슷한 구
성원들을 피하는 것이 합리적이라고 했다. 이를 달리 표현하면 주어진 환경의
수용력에 따라 비슷한 사람들과 어울리는 전략은 적절하지 않을 수도 있다는
것이다. 따라서 빈칸에 들어갈 말로 가장 적절한 것은 ③ 'places a limit on
this strategy(이 전략에 제한을 둔다)'이다. 공동체의 동일한 수요를 충족하
기에 환경 수용력이 부족한 경우를 설명하므로 ①은 적절하지 않고, 환경 수용
력이 사람들의 생존 전략에 영향을 미치는 것이지 영향을 받아 줄어드는 것이
아니므로 ②도 적절하지 않다.

2 ②

해석 … 높은 자기 효능감을 가진 사람들은 보통 사람들의 범위 밖에 있을 수도
있는 도전적인 목표를 추구하는 경향이 있다. 그러므로 강한 자기 효능감을 가
진 사람들은 어떤 환경의 사회적인 행위자들 대다수에 의해 성공이 있을 법하
지 않다고 여겨지는 일이나 목표를 시도하기 위해 더 기꺼이 문화적으로 규정
된 행동 밖으로 나아가려 할 수도 있다. 이런 사람들에게 문화는 행동에 거의 혹
은 전혀 영향을 주지 않을 것이다. 예를 들어, 호주 사람들은 '키 큰 양귀비 증후
군'을 지지하는 경향이 있다. 이 말은 들판에서 다른 것들보다 더 크게 자라는
어떤 '양귀비'라도 '베이게' 될 것임을, 다시 말해 표준 이상의 성공을 거두는 사
람은 누구든지 결국 실패할 것임을 시사한다. 면접과 관찰은 실제로 평균 이상
을 성취하기 위해 이 문화적으로 규정된 행동 밖으로 나아가는 사람은 바로 높
은 자기 효능감을 가진 호주 사람들이라는 것을 나타낸다.
• pursue 추구하다, 해나가다   prescribe (규칙·방침을) 규정하다; (약·치료법을)
처방하다   improbable 있을 법하지 않은   syndrome 증후군   saying 말;
속담, 격언   outgrow ~보다 더 커지다
① 자기 효능감은 정의를 내리기 쉽지 않다
② 문화는 행동에 거의 혹은 전혀 영향을 주지 않을 것이다
③ 일을 시작하기 전에 목표를 설정하는 것이 중요하다
• define 정의를 내리다, 뜻을 명확히 하다

해설 빈칸 문장은 '이런 사람들(these individuals)'에게 '무엇이 어떠하다'는
내용이다. 앞 내용을 보면, 자기 효능감이 높은 사람들에 대한 서술이 이어지는
것이므로, these individuals는 자기 효능감이 높은 사람들을 가리킴을 알 수
있다. 이어지는 예에서, 호주인들은 보통 표준 이상의 성공을 거두는 사람은 결
국 실패한다는 '키 큰 양귀비 증후군'을 지지하는데, 자기 효능감이 높은 호주인
들은 평균 이상을 성취하고자 문화적으로 규정된 행동 밖으로 나아간다고 했
다. 따라서 빈칸에 들어갈 말로 가장 적절한 것은 ② 'culture will have little
or no impact on behavior(문화는 행동에 거의 혹은 전혀 영향을 주지 않
을 것이다)'이다. 자기 효능감을 정의하려는 내용이 아니므로 ①은 적절하지 않
고, 목표 설정에 관한 내용이 아니므로 ③도 적절하지 않다.

3 ①

해석 가장 흥미진진한 자연의 체온 조절 행동 중에는 벌과 개미와 같은 사회적
곤충들의 행동이 있다. 이 곤충들은 일 년 내내 자신들의 벌집이나 개밋둑에서
거의 일정한 온도를 유지할 수 있다. 이러한 미기후의 항상성은 서식지의 위치
와 단열뿐만 아니라, 군집 내 곤충들의 활동에도 달려 있다. 주변 온도가 올라가
면, 벌집 내 활동은 줄어드는데, 이는 곤충의 신진대사에 의해 발생하는 열의 양
을 감소시킨다. 사실, 많은 동물은 더위 속에서는 활동을 줄이고 추위 속에서는
활동을 늘리는데, 덥거나 추운 환경에서 신체 활동의 수준을 선택할 수 있는 인
간은 자신들의 작업량을 정확히 체온에 맞춰 조절한다. …
• constant 일정한, 변함없는; 끊임없는 *cf.* constancy 항상성, 불변(성)   hive 벌집
mound 개밋둑; 흙더미   microclimate 미기후 ((특정 좁은 지역의 기후))
metabolism 신진[물질]대사   workload 작업[업무]량
precisely 정확히, 바로, 꼭; 정확하게
① 군집 내 곤충들의 활동
② 서식지의 건축 재료
③ 서식 동물의 신체 발달
• colony 군집[집단]; 식민지   inhabitant 서식 동물; 주민, 거주자

해설 빈칸 문장은 '이러한 미기후(벌집이나 개밋둑의 온도)'의 항상성이 서식
지의 위치와 단열뿐만 아니라 '무엇'에도 달려 있다는 내용이다. 빈칸 문장 뒤에
서 벌은 주변 온도가 올라가면 벌집 내 활동을 줄여 신진대사로 발생하는 열의
양을 감소시킨다는 예를 들었다. 또한 많은 동물이 온도에 따라 활동을 조절한
다고 설명했다. 이는 모두 어떤 환경에서의 활동에 관한 것이므로 빈칸에 들어
갈 말로 가장 적절한 것은 ① 'the activity of the insects in the colony
(군집 내 곤충들의 활동)'이다. 서식지 온도에 영향을 주는 요소로는 서식지의
위치와 단열만 언급되었으므로 ②는 적절하지 않으며, 동물의 신체 발달 정도
가 온도에 영향을 미친다는 내용은 언급되지 않았으므로 ③도 적절하지 않다.

4 ①

해석 … 저개발 세계에서의 전형적인 시나리오는 아주 소수의 상업 농장주들
이 기술적으로 앞서 있는 반면에 대다수는 경쟁할 수 없다는 것이다. 사실, 이
대다수는 더 큰 세계적인 원인 때문에 자신들의 생산에 대한 통제력을 잃었다.
한 예로, 케냐에서 농부들은 기초식품 생산을 희생하면서 차와 커피와 같은 수
출 작물을 재배하도록 적극적으로 장려된다. 그 결과는 옥수수와 같은 주요 작
물이 충분한 양으로 생산되고 있지 않다는 것이다. 여기에서 본질적인 논점은
자본주의적 생산 방식이 주요 식품의 생산을 제한하는 방식으로 저개발 세계
의 소농의 생산에 영향을 미쳐 식량 문제를 일으키고 있다는 것이다.
• commercial 상업의   agriculturalist 농장주, 농업 전문가
incapable of ~할 수 없는   actively 적극적으로   crop (농)작물
at the expense of ~을 희생하면서   sufficient 충분한
capitalist 자본주의적인; 자본주의자
① 자신들의 생산에 대한 통제력을 잃었다
② 자본주의적 생산 방식에 이의를 제기했다
③ 환금 작물을 재배하는 것에 대한 개입을 줄였다
• cash crop 환금 작물 ((팔기 위해 재배하는 농작물))

해설 빈칸 문장은 사실 '이 대다수(this vast majority)'가 더 큰 세계적인 원
인 때문에 '어떠했다'는 내용이다. 빈칸 문장 뒤에서 케냐에서 기초식품 대신
수출 작물의 재배가 장려되어 주요 작물이 충분히 생산되지 못하는 문제를 예
로 들었다. 그리고 본질적인 논점은 자본주의적 생산 방식이 저개발 국가의 주
요 식품의 생산을 제한하는 것이라고 설명했다. 따라서 빈칸 문장의 this vast
majority, 즉 기술적으로 뒤처진 대다수의 농업 종사 인구는 이러한 원인(자
본주의적 생산)에 영향을 받아서 생산에 대한 통제력을 잃은 것이므로, 빈칸
에 들어갈 말로 가장 적절한 것은 ① 'have lost control over their own
production(자신들의 생산에 대한 통제력을 잃었다)'이다. 자본주의적 생산
방식을 따라서 식량 부족 문제가 생겼으므로 이의를 제기했다는 ②는 적절하
지 않다. 또한 수출 작물 재배가 장려된다고 했으므로 개입을 줄였다는 ③도 적
절하지 않다.

1 ④

[1] In the post-World War Ⅱ years after 1945, / unparalleled economic growth fueled / a building boom / and a massive migration (from the central cities to the new suburban areas).
1945년 이후 제2차 세계 대전 다음 시기에 / 유례없는 경제 성장은 부채질했다 /
건축 붐을 / 그리고 대규모 이주를 (중심 도시에서 새로운 교외 지역으로의)

[2] The suburbs were far more dependent on the automobile, / signaling the shift (from primary dependence on public transportation to private cars).
교외는 자동차에 훨씬 더 많이 의존했다 /
그리고 이는 전환을 시사했다 (대중교통에의 주된 의존에서 자가용으로의)

[3] Soon / this led / to the construction (of better highways and freeways) / and the decline and even loss (of public transportation).
곧 / 이것은 이어졌다 / 건설로 (더 나은 고속도로와 초고속도로의) /
그리고 감소, 심지어 상실로까지 (대중교통의)

[4] With all of these changes / came a <u>privatization</u> (of leisure).
이러한 모든 변화와 함께 / 사유화가 이루어졌다 (여가의)

[5] As more people owned their own homes, / (with more space inside and lovely yards outside), // their recreation and leisure time was increasingly centered / around the home or, at most, the neighborhood.
더 많은 사람이 자신의 집을 소유함에 따라 / (내부에는 더 많은 공간이 있고 외부에는 아름다운 마당이 있는) // 그들의 휴양과 여가 시간은 점점 더 집중되었다 / 집이나 기껏해야 이웃에

[6] One major activity (of this home-based leisure) / was watching television.
한 가지 주요 활동은 (이러한 가정에 기반을 둔 여가의) / 텔레비전을 시청하는 것이었다

[7] No longer did one have to ride the trolly to the theater / to watch a movie; // similar entertainment was available / for free and more conveniently / from television.
더 이상 사람들은 전차를 타고 극장까지 갈 필요가 없었다 /
영화를 보기 위해 // 유사한 오락물이 이용 가능했다 / 무료로 그리고 더 편리하게 / 텔레비전에서

해설

빈칸 문장 확인하기

> **4** 이러한 모든 변화와 함께 여가의 '무엇'이 이루어짐.

추론 근거로 정답 찾기

> **5** 많은 사람이 집을 소유하게 되면서 휴양과 여가 시간이 점점 더 집이나 이웃에 집중됨.
> **6** 가정에 기반을 둔 주요 여가 활동 중 하나는 텔레비전 시청이었음.
>
> 사람들이 집을 소유하면서 집과 이웃에 여가 시간을 집중하게 되었고, 텔레비전 시청 같은 가정에 기반을 둔 여가 활동을 하게 되었다는 내용이다. 즉 자신의 집에서 개인적으로 여가를 즐기게 되었다는 것이므로 여가의 사유화가 이루어졌음을 추론할 수 있다.
> → ④ privatization(사유화)

오답 확인

① downfall 몰락
② uniformity 획일성
→ 텔레비전 시청은 집을 기반으로 한 여가 활동의 한 예로 언급되었을 뿐, 여가가 획일화되었다는 내용이 아님.
③ restoration 부활
⑤ customization 맞춤화
*①, ③, ⑤ → 언급되지 않음.

어휘

at (the) most 기껏해야　center around ~에 집중하다
freeway 초고속도로 ((교차, 건널목 그 밖의 장애물이 없는 고속 자동차 도로))
fuel 부채질하다; 연료(를 공급하다)　migration 이주, 이동
signal 시사[암시]하다; 신호(를 보내다)　suburban 교외의
cf. suburb 교외　trolly[trolley] 전차; 손수레
[선택지] privatization 사유화

구문 분석

[4] With all of these changes / came a privatization (of leisure).
부사구(With ~ changes)가 문장 앞에 나와 <V+S> 어순으로 도치가 일어남.
[7] No longer did one have to ride the trolly to the theater / ~.
부정어 포함 어구(No longer)가 문장 앞에 나와 <조동사+S+V> 어순으로 도치가 일어남.

해석 **[1]** 1945년 이후 제2차 세계 대전 다음 시기에 유례없는 경제 성장은 건축 붐과 중심 도시에서 새로운 교외 지역으로의 대규모 이주를 부채질했다. **[2]** 교외는 자동차에 훨씬 더 많이 의존했고, 이는 대중교통에의 주된 의존에서 자가용으로의 전환을 시사했다. **[3]** 곧 이것은 더 나은 고속도로와 초고속도로의 건설과 대중교통의 감소, 심지어 상실로까지 이어졌다. **[4]** 이러한 모든 변화와 함께 여가의 <u>사유화</u>가 이루어졌다. **[5]** 더 많은 사람이 내부에는 더 많은 공간이 있고 외부에는 아름다운 마당이 있는 자신의 집을 소유함에 따라 그들의 휴양과 여가 시간은 점점 더 집이나 기껏해야 이웃에 집중되었다. **[6]** 이러한 가정에 기반을 둔 여가의 한 가지 주요 활동은 텔레비전을 시청하는 것이었다. **[7]** 더 이상 사람들은 영화를 보기 위해 전차를 타고 극장까지 갈 필요가 없었고, 텔레비전에서 유사한 오락물이 무료로, 그리고 더 편리하게 이용 가능했다.

2 ②

[1] People have always needed to eat, // and they always will (need to eat).
사람들은 항상 먹을 필요가 있었다 // 그리고 그들은 항상 그럴(먹을 필요가 있을) 것이다

[2] Rising emphasis (on self-expression values) / does not put an end to material desires.
커지는 강조가 (자기표현 가치에 관한) / 물질적 욕구를 끝내지는 않는다

[3] But / prevailing economic orientations are gradually being reshaped.
하지만 / 우세한 경제적 방향성들이 차츰 다시 형성되고 있다

[4] *People* [who work in the knowledge sector] / continue to seek high salaries, //
사람들은 [지식 분야에서 일하는] / 계속 높은 임금을 추구한다 //
but they place equal or greater emphasis / on doing stimulating work / and being able to follow their own time schedules.
하지만 그들은 동등하거나 더 큰 중점을 둔다 / 자극이 되는 일을 하는 것에 /
그리고 그들 자신의 시간 일정을 따를 수 있는 것에

[5] Consumption is becoming progressively less determined / by the need (for sustenance) / and the practical use (of *the goods* (consumed)).
소비는 점차 덜 결정된다 / 필요에 의해 (생명을 유지하는 것의) /
그리고 실질적인 사용에 의해 (상품의 (소비되는))

[6] People still eat, // but a growing component (of food's value) / is determined / by its nonmaterial aspects.
사람들은 여전히 먹는다 // 하지만 증가하는 구성 요소가 (음식 가치의) /
결정된다 / 그것의 비물질적인 측면에 의해

[7] People pay a premium / to eat *exotic cuisines* [that provide an interesting experience / or that symbolize a distinctive lifestyle].
사람들은 추가금을 낸다 / 이국적인 요리를 먹기 위해 [흥미로운 경험을 제공하는 /
또는 독특한 생활 방식을 상징하는]

[8] The publics (of postindustrial societies) / place growing emphasis / on "political consumerism," / (such as boycotting *goods* [whose production violates ecological or ethical standards]).
대중은 (후기 산업 사회의) / 점점 더 많은 중점을 둔다 /
'정치적 소비주의'에 / (상품의 구매를 거부하는 것과 같은 [생산이 생태학적 또는 윤리적 기준을 위반하는])

[9] Consumption is less and less a matter (of sustenance) / and more and more a question (of lifestyle — and choice).
소비는 점점 덜 문제이다 (생명을 유지하는 것의) / 그리고 점점 더 문제이다 (생활 방식 그리고 선택의)

해설

빈칸 문장 확인하기 ◉

[6] 사람들이 먹는 음식 가치의 증가하는 구성 요소가 '어떤' 측면에 의해 결정됨.

추론 근거로 정답 찾기 ◉

[5] 생명 유지나 실질적 사용은 소비 결정에 점차 덜 중요함.
[7] 사람들은 흥미롭거나 독특한 생활 방식을 나타내는 음식을 먹기 위해 돈을 더 냄.
[9] 소비는 점점 더 생활 방식이나 선택에 따른 문제가 됨.

생존보다는 생활 방식이나 선택에 따른 소비가 증가한다는 내용이다. 빈칸 문장 앞에서는 소비가 점차 생명 유지보다는 실질적 사용에 따라 결정된다고 했고, 뒤에서는 흥미롭거나 독특한 생활 방식을 나타내는 음식을 위해 돈을 더 낸다고 했다. 따라서 음식 가치의 구성 요소가 점점 비물질적인 측면으로 결정됨을 추론할 수 있다.
→ ② nonmaterial(비물질적인)

오답 확인

① quantitative 양적인
③ nutritional 영양의
→ 생명 유지 필요에 의한 결정이 덜해진다고 했으므로 영양이 음식 가치의 구성 요소를 결정한다고 볼 수 없음.
④ invariable 불변의
*①, ④ → 언급되지 않음.
⑤ economic 경제적인
→ 이국적인 요리를 먹기 위해 추가금을 낸다고 했으므로 경제적인 측면이 음식의 가치를 구성하는 요소를 결정한다고 볼 수 없음.

어휘

boycott 구매를 거부하다; 불매 운동   component (구성) 요소; 부품
consumerism 소비주의 ((소비에 가치의 중심을 두는 사고방식))
distinctive 독특한; 뚜렷이 구별되는   exotic 이국적인; 외국의
orientation 방향(성), 지향; 예비 교육   postindustrial 후기 산업의,
탈공업화의   premium 추가금, 할증료; (상품이) 값비싼, 고급의
sector 분야, 부문   sustenance 생명을 유지하는 것; 생계
[선택지] invariable 불변의   quantitative 양적인

구문 분석

[7] People pay a premium / to eat *exotic cuisines* [**that** provide an interesting experience / or **that** symbolize a distinctive lifestyle].
선행사 exotic cuisines를 수식하는 두 개의 관계사절이 or로 병렬 연결됨.

해석 **[1]** 사람들은 항상 먹을 필요가 있었고, 항상 그럴 것이다. **[2]** 자기표현 가치에 관한 커지는 강조가 물질적 욕구를 끝내지는 않는다. **[3]** 하지만 우세한 경제적 방향성들이 차츰 다시 형성되고 있다. **[4]** 지식 분야에서 일하는 사람들은 계속 높은 임금을 추구하지만, 그들은 자극이 되는 일을 하는 것과 그들 자신의 시간 일정을 따를 수 있는 것에 동등하거나 더 큰 중점을 둔다. **[5]** 소비는 생명을 유지하는 것의 필요와 소비되는 상품의 실질적인 사용에 의해 점차 덜 결정된다. **[6]** 사람들은 여전히 먹지만, 음식 가치의 증가하는 구성 요소가 그것의 비물질적인 측면에 의해 결정된다. **[7]** 사람들은 흥미로운 경험을 제공하거나 독특한 생활 방식을 상징하는 이국적인 요리를 먹기 위해 추가금을 낸다. **[8]** 후기 산업 사회의 대중은 생산이 생태학적 또는 윤리적 기준을 위반하는 상품의 구매를 거부하는 것과 같은 '정치적 소비주의'에 점점 더 많은 중점을 둔다. **[9]** 소비는 점점 덜 생명을 유지하는 것의 문제이며 점점 더 생활 방식, 그리고 선택의 문제이다.

3 ③

[1] In labor-sharing groups, / people contribute labor / to other people /
노동 공유 집단에서 / 사람들은 노동을 제공한다 / 다른 사람들에게 /

on a regular basis (for seasonal agricultural work (such as harvesting)) / or on an irregular basis (in the event of a crisis (such as *the need* (to rebuild *a barn* (damaged by fire)))).
정기적으로 (계절에 따른 농사일을 위해 (수확과 같은)) / 혹은 비정기적으로 (위기가 발생할 경우 (필요성과 같은 (헛간을 다시 지을 (화재로 손상된)))))

[2] Labor sharing groups are part (of what has been called a "moral economy") // since no one keeps formal records (on how much any family puts in or takes out).
노동 공유 집단은 일부이다 ('도덕 경제'라고 불려온 것의) // 아무도 공식적인 기록을 해두지 않기 때문에 (어떤 가족이 얼마나 많은 것을 쏟고 얼마나 많은 것을 가져가는지에 대한)

[3] Instead, / accounting is socially regulated.
대신에 / 계산은 사회적으로 규제된다

[4] The group has / *a sense of moral community* (based on years of trust and sharing).
그 집단은 가지고 있다 / 도덕적 공동체 의식을 (다년간의 신뢰와 나눔에 기반을 둔)

[5] In a certain community (of North America), / labor sharing is a major economic factor (of social cohesion).
특정 지역 사회에서 (북미의) / 노동 공유는 주요 경제적 요소이다 (사회적 응집성의)

[6] When a family needs a new barn / or faces *repair work* [that requires group labor], // a barn-raising party is called.
한 가족이 새 헛간을 필요로 할 때 / 또는 수리 작업에 직면할 때 [집단 노동을 필요로 하는] // 헛간을 세우는 모임이 소집된다

[7] Many families show up / to help.
여러 가족이 나온다 / 돕기 위해

[8] Adult men provide manual labor, // and adult women provide food (for the event).
성인 남성은 육체노동을 제공한다 // 그리고 성인 여성은 음식을 제공한다 (그 일을 위한)

[9] Later, / when another family needs help, // they call on the same people.
나중에 / 다른 가족이 도움을 필요로 할 때 // 그들은 같은 사람들에게 요청한다

해설

빈칸 문장 확인하기 

3 '대신에(Instead)', 계산은 '어떠함'.

추론 근거로 정답 찾기

2 노동 공유 집단은 그들이 주고받은 노동에 대해 공식적으로 기록하지 않음.
4 도덕적 공동체 의식이 신뢰와 나눔에 기반하고 있음.

역접 연결어 Instead가 빈칸 문장을 이끌고 있으므로, 앞 내용과 반대되는 내용이 뒷받침하며 이어질 것이다. 앞에서는 노동을 주고받는 것을 공식적으로 기록하지 않는다고 하고, 뒤에서는 노동 공유 집단이 신뢰와 나눔을 기반으로 한 도덕적 공동체 의식을 가진다고 했다. 따라서 노동 공유의 계산은 기록에 의해 공식적으로 규제되는 것이 아니라 사회적으로 규제된다는 것을 추론할 수 있다.
→ ③ socially regulated(사회적으로 규제되는)

오답 확인

① legally established 법률적으로 확립되는
② regularly reported 정기적으로 보고되는
④ manually calculated 수동으로 계산되는
*①, ②, ④ → 언급되지 않음.
⑤ carefully documented 신중하게 기록되는
→ 공유한 노동에 대한 공식적인 기록을 하지 않는다고 했으므로 틀림.

어휘

accounting 계산; 회계   agricultural 농사[농업]의   barn 헛간; 외양간   call on ~에게 요청[요구]하다   in the event of ~할 경우, 만약 ~하면   manual 육체를 쓰는; 수동의; 손의, 손을 쓰는 *cf.* manually 수동으로; 손으로   moral 도덕(상)의; 도덕적인   on a regular basis 정기적으로   [선택지] document 기록하다; 서류, 문서   legally 법률적[합법적]으로   regulate 규제하다; 조절하다

구문 분석

[2] Labor sharing groups are part (of what **has been called a "moral economy"**) // ~.
<call+O+C(O를 C라고 부르다)>의 수동형.

해석 **[1]** 노동 공유 집단에서 사람들은 정기적으로 (수확과 같은 계절에 따른 농사일을 위해) 혹은 비정기적으로 (화재로 손상된 헛간을 다시 지을 필요성과 같은 위기가 발생할 경우) 다른 사람들에게 노동을 제공한다. **[2]** 아무도 어떤 가족이 얼마나 많은 것을 쏟고 얼마나 많은 것을 가져가는지에 대한 공식적인 기록을 해두지 않기 때문에, 노동 공유 집단은 '도덕 경제'라고 불려온 것의 일부이다. **[3]** 대신에, 계산은 사회적으로 규제된다. **[4]** 그 집단은 다년간의 신뢰와 나눔에 기반을 둔 도덕적 공동체 의식을 가지고 있다. **[5]** 북미의 특정 지역 사회에서 노동 공유는 사회적 응집성의 주요 경제적 요소이다. **[6]** 한 가족이 새 헛간을 필요로 하거나 집단 노동을 필요로 하는 수리 작업에 직면할 때, 헛간을 세우는 모임이 소집된다. **[7]** 여러 가족이 돕기 위해 나온다. **[8]** 성인 남성은 육체노동을 제공하고, 성인 여성은 그 일을 위한 음식을 제공한다. **[9]** 나중에, 다른 가족이 도움을 필요로 할 때, 그들은 같은 사람들에게 요청한다.

Zoom 1

해석 Walt Whitman이 <Leaves of Grass>를 쓰기 오래 전, 시인들은 명성에 초점을 맞추었다. (중간 생략) 그러나 페이지 위에서 영원히 살고 싶다는 아주 오래된 이 갈망에 그는 명성의 새로운 의미를 더했다. 독자들은 시인의 작품에만 주의를 기울이지 않으며, 그들은 시인의 인격적 위대함에 매료되리라는 것이었다. (중간 생략) Whitman은 시적 명성을 군중과 관련하여 정의했다. 다른 시인들은 그들의 영감을 시의 여신으로부터 찾을지도 모른다. Whitman의 시인상은 ___________을(를) 추구했다.

•**address** ~에 초점을 맞추다; 연설(하다); 주소　**sense** (어구의) 의미, 뜻; 감각
attend to A A에 주의를 기울이다　**inspiration** 영감(을 주는 것)
seek 추구하다; 찾다
→ 미국 민주주의의 불안정 속에서, 명성은 지명도, 즉 사람들이 시인과 그의 작품을 얼마나 좋아하는지에 달려 있었을 것이다.

•**instability** 불안정　**dependent** (~에) 달려 있는; 의지하는; 의존적인
celebrity 지명도, 명성; 유명 인사　**rejoice** 좋아하다, 기뻐하다
➜ 빈칸: 그의 동시대인들의 기호
•**approval** 기호, 좋아함; 승인　**contemporary** 동시대인; 동시대의; 현대의

Zoom 2

해석 시대를 너무 앞선 발명이나 발견은 가치가 없는데, 누구도 따라갈 수 없기 때문이다. 이상적으로, 혁신은 이미 아는 것으로부터 단지 다음 단계만을 가능하게 하고, 그 문화에 한 번의 짧은 도약을 촉구한다. (중간 생략) Gregor Mendel의 1865년 유전자 유전 이론은 옳았지만 35년 동안 무시되었다. (중간 생략) 수십 년 후 과학은 Mendel의 발견이 답할 수 있는 긴급한 질문에 직면했다. 이제 그의 통찰력은 ___________.

•**worthless** 가치 없는　**ideally** 이상적으로　**open up** ~을 가능하게 하다; ~을 열다
genetic 유전자의; 유전(학)의　**heredity** 유전(적 특징)　**urgent** 긴박한, 시급한
insight 통찰력
→ 서로 몇 년 이내로, 세 명의 다른 과학자들이 각각 따로 Mendel의 잊힌 이론을 재발견했는데, 물론 그 이론은 내내 그곳에 있었다.

•**independently** 따로, 독립적으로; ~와 관계없이　**all along** 내내, 줄곧
➜ 빈칸: 단 한 걸음만 떨어져 있었다

Zoom 3

해석 (이전 생략) 우리 대부분은 서로 다른 방에 서로 다른 기능을 할당하지만, 여러분이 원룸 주택을 살펴봐도 같은 내부의 특수화를 발견할 것이다. 오두막이나 진흙 오두막 안, 혹은 심지어 3만 년 전의 중석기 시대의 동굴 안에도, 이 부분은 요리를 위한 곳이고, 저 부분은 잠을 자기 위한 곳이며, 이 부분은 도구 제작과 옷감 짜기를 위한 곳이고, 저 부분은 배설물을 위한 곳이다. 우리는 ___________을(를) 유지한다.

•**assign** 할당하다, 배정하다; 선임[임명]하다　**specialization** 특수[전문]화
cabin (보통 나무로 된) 오두막; (비행기) 객실　**Mesolithic** 중석기 시대의
weave (옷감 등을) 짜다
→ 다양한 정도로, 다른 동물들도 똑같은 것을 한다. 동물의 종에 따라, 동물의 영역 중 일부는 먹기 위한 것이고, 일부는 잠을 자기 위한 것이며, 일부는 헤엄치거나 뒹굴기 위한 것이고, 일부는 배설물을 위해 따로 남겨질 수도 있다.

•**extent** 정도, 규모　**wallow** 뒹굴다　**set aside** ~을 따로 남겨 두다
➜ 빈칸: 정돈된 기능적 구조
•**neat** 정돈된, 단정한; 깔끔한

Zoom 4

해석 (이전 생략) 이제 '읽기'는 과거 그 어느 때보다 더 많은 표현 형식에 적용되는데, 그림, 지도, 화면, 디자인 그래픽, 사진이 모두 텍스트로 여겨진다. (중간 생략) 그러므로, 읽는 아이들의 주의가 인쇄된 텍스트에 집중되고 스케치나 그림이 부속물이었던 때 그랬던 것보다 더 복잡한 종류의 해석이 된다. 이제 아이들은 그림책으로부터 글과 삽화가 서로를 보완하여 향상시킨다는 것을 알게 된다. 읽기는 단순히 ___________이(가) 아니다.

•**apply** 적용되다[하다]; 신청하다; (약 등을) 바르다　**representational** 표현의, 묘사의　**interpretation** 해석, 이해; 해설, 설명　**illustration** 삽화; 실례
complement 보완[보충]하다　**enhance** (질·능력을) 향상시키다, 높이다
→ 가장 쉬운 텍스트에서조차도 문장이 '말하는 것'이 흔히 그 문장이 의미하는 것은 아니다.
➜ 빈칸: 단어 인식
•**recognition** 인식; 인정

Focus & Practice　　　　　　　　　p.28

1 ①　　　**2** ②　　　**3** ③　　　**4** ①

1 ①

해석 ... 생태학적 관계는 확실히 그것 나름의 논리를 가지고 있고, 이런 의미에서 '자연'은 인간의 개입과 무관한 자율적이지만 반드시 안정적이지는 않은 역동성을 가지고 있는 것으로 보일 수 있다. 그러나 생태학적 상호 작용의 환경은 점점 더 인류에 의해 설정되어 왔다. 우리는 사자가 어떻게 또는 무엇을 먹는지를 정하지 못할 수도 있지만, 사자가 어디에서 먹이를 먹는지를 확실히 통제할 수 있다.

•**self-regulating** 자율적인　**dynamic** 역동성, 역학　**intervention** 개입; 중재
context 환경, 배경; 문맥
① 점점 더 인류에 의해 설정되어 왔다
② 너무 자주 바뀌어 통제될 수 없다
③ 다양한 자연조건에 의해 영향을 받아 왔다

해설 빈칸 문장은 생태학적 상호 작용의 환경이 '어떠하다'는 내용이다. 빈칸 문장과 But으로 연결되는 앞 문장은 인간의 개입과 '무관한' 역동성을 말하고 있다. 또한 빈칸 문장 뒤에서 우리는 사자가 무엇을 어떻게 먹을지 결정할 가능성이 없을지 몰라도 어디서 먹는지는 확실히 통제할 수 있다고 했다. 이는 곧 인간이 개입할 수 있다는 것, 즉 인간이 자연을 통제할 수 있다는 것이므로, 빈칸에 들어갈 말로 가장 적절한 것은 ① 'has increasingly been set by humanity(점점 더 인류에 의해 설정되어 왔다)'이다. 환경이 자주 바뀐다는 언급은 없고 통제를 받는다는 내용이므로 ②는 적절하지 않고, 환경이 인간의 통제를 받는 것이지 자연조건의 영향을 받는 것이 아니므로 ③도 적절하지 않다.

2 ②

해석 과학의 역할은 그것의 옹호자들이 과학만능주의에 빠지면서 때때로 과장될 수 있다. 과학만능주의는 현실에 대한 과학적 서술이 존재하는 유일한 진실이라는 견해이다. 과학의 발전과 함께, 과학만능주의에 빠져 사실에 입각한

어떠한 주장도 '과학적'이라는 용어가 정확하게 그것에 속하는 것으로 생각될 수 있는 경우에 그리고 오직 그런 경우에만 입증될 수 있다고 간주하는 경향이 있어 왔다. 그 결과, 현실에 대한 비과학적 접근 방식은 … 그저 주관적일 뿐이고, 따라서 세상이 존재하는 방식을 서술하는 면에서 거의 중요하지 <u>않</u>다고 꼬리표가 붙여질지도 모른다. 과학 철학은 투박한 과학만능주의를 피하고 과학적 방법이 성취할 수 있는 것과 성취할 수 없는 것에 관한 균형 잡힌 생각을 가지려고 노력한다.
• **overstate** 과장하다, 허풍을 떨다 **advocate** 옹호자, 지지자; 옹호[지지]하다
slip (좋지 못한 상황에) 빠지다; 미끄러지다 **scientism** 과학만능주의
assume 간주하다, 가정하다 **factual** 사실에 입각한; 실제의
claim 주장; (권리·사실을) 주장하다 **authenticate** 입증하다; 인증하다
label 꼬리표를 붙이다; 분류하다
① 의문
② 중요성
③ 편견
• **account** 중요성, 가치; 설명; 계좌

해설 빈칸 문장은 비과학적 접근 방식은 주관적인 것에 불과하여 세상이 존재하는 방식을 서술하는 면에서 거의 '~하지' 않는다는 꼬리표가 붙여질 수 있다는 것이 결과라는 내용이다. <of+추상명사>는 형용사로 쓰이는데, of와 빈칸 사이에 준부정어 little(거의 ~않는)이 있어 빈칸 내용을 부정하는 의미가 됨에 주의한다. 빈칸 문장 앞에서는 과학이 발전하며 과학만능주의에 의해 '과학적'이라는 용어가 들어가야만 사실에 입각한 주장이 입증될 수 있다고 여기는 경향이 있어 왔다고 했다. 뒤에서는 과학 철학은 과학만능주의를 지양하고 균형 잡힌 생각을 가지려 노력한다고 했다. 그러므로 앞 문장의 결과를 설명하는 빈칸 문장은 이러한 균형 잡힌 생각과 대조되며 과학만능주의의 시각에서 본 비과학적 접근 방식에 대한 부정적인 내용일 것을 추론할 수 있다. 따라서 빈칸에 들어갈 말로 가장 적절한 것은 ② 'account(중요성)'이다. 과학만능주의적 시각에서 비과학적 접근 방식에 의문이나 편견이 거의 없다는 설명은 글의 내용과 반대되므로 ①과 ③은 적절하지 않다.

3 ③

해설 … 외재화하는 대화는 오랜 시간 동안 아동의 삶에 미친 문제의 영향과 어떻게 그 문제가 다른 관점에서 상황을 보는 아동의 능력을 제한함으로써 아동으로부터 힘을 빼앗아 왔는지를 추적하는 것을 흔히 포함한다. 상담사는 아동 자신과 아동의 삶에 관한 옛 이야기를 해체하고 선호하는 이야기를 재구성함으로써 아동이 변화하도록 돕는다. 아동이 새로운 이야기를 전개하도록 돕기 위해, 상담사와 아동은 그 문제가 아동이나 아동의 삶에 영향을 미치지 않았던 때를 찾아 아동이 생각하고, 느끼고, 행동했던 다른 방식들에 초점을 둔다. 이러한 <u>그 문제 이야기에 대한 예외들</u>(그 문제 이야기에 해당되지 않는 것들)은 아동이 새롭고 선호하는 이야기를 만들어 내도록 돕는다. 새롭고 선호하는 이야기가 나오기 시작할 때, 아동이 그 새로운 이야기에 매달리도록, 즉 그 새로운 이야기와 연결된 상태를 유지하도록 돕는 것이 중요하다.
• **externalize** 외재[표면]화하다 **trace** 추적하다; 자국, 흔적
disempower ~으로부터 힘[영향력]을 빼앗다 **counsellor** 상담사, 상담 전문가
deconstruct 해체[분해]하다 **reconstruct** 재구성하다; 재건하다
emerge 나오다, 나타나다 **hold on to A** A에 매달리다, A를 고수하다[지키다]
① 대안적 이야기로부터의 거리
② 아동의 이야기를 다른 사람의 이야기와 연결하는 방법들
③ 그 문제 이야기에 대한 예외들

해설 빈칸 문장은 이러한 '무엇'이 아동이 새롭고 선호하는 이야기를 만들어 내도록 돕는다는 내용으로 앞 문장을 부연 설명한다. 따라서 '이러한(These)'이 지칭하는 내용을 중심으로 하는 단서를 앞부분에서 찾아야 한다. 빈칸 문장 앞에서는 아동이 새로운 이야기를 전개하도록 돕기 위해 상담사와 아동은 문제

가 없던 때를 찾고 그때의 사고와 행동 방식에 초점을 둔다고 했다. 이는 문제의 영향이 없던 때, 즉 문제에 대한 예외에 주목하는 것이므로, 빈칸에 들어갈 말로 가장 적절한 것은 ③ 'exceptions to the problem story(그 문제 이야기에 대한 예외들)'이다. 대안적 이야기는 문제에서 벗어난, 즉 새로운 선호되는 이야기를 의미하는데 이와 거리를 두는 것은 글의 내용과 반대되므로 ①은 적절하지 않다. 또한 타인의 이야기가 아니라 아동이 만든 새로운 선호하는 이야기에 집중하도록 해야 한다고 했으므로 ②도 적절하지 않다.

4 ①

해설 디지털 기술은 제품에서 서비스로의 이동을 촉진함으로써 비물질화를 가속화한다. … 그러나 비물질화는 단지 디지털 상품에 관한 것만은 아니다. 탄산음료 캔과 같은 고체의 물리적 상품조차도 더 적은 양의 물질을 가지고 있으면서 더 많은 이익을 내놓을 수 있는 이유는 그것들의 무거운 원자가 무게가 없는 비트로 대체되기 때문이다. 유형의 것들은 더 많은 알루미늄 원자들이 하곤 했던 일을 하는 무형의 것들, 즉 더 나은 설계, 혁신적인 과정, 스마트 칩, 그리고 궁극적으로 온라인 연결성과 같은 무형의 것들에 의해 대체된다. 따라서 딱딱한 물건들이 더 소프트웨어같이 작동하도록 만드는, 지능과 같이 부드러운 것들이 알루미늄과 같은 딱딱한 물건에 내장된다. 비트가 주입된 물질적 상품들은 점점 마치 <u>그것들이 무형의 서비스</u>인 것처럼 행동한다. 명사가 동사로 변화한다. 하드웨어가 소프트웨어처럼 작동한다. 실리콘 밸리에서 사람들은 그것을 이렇게 말한다. "소프트웨어가 모든 것을 씹어 삼킨다."
• **accelerate** 가속화하다 **dematerialization** 비물질화 **hasten** 촉진하다, 재촉하다 **migration** 이동, 이주 **tangible** 유형의 (것)(↔ intangible 무형의 (것))
innovative 혁신적인 **connectivity** 연결성, 접속 가능성 **embed** 내장하다, 끼워 넣다[박다] **infuse** (사상 등을) 주입하다, 불어넣다
① 그것들이 무형의 서비스이다
② 그것들이 모든 디지털 상품들을 대체한다
③ 하드웨어가 소프트웨어보다 더 오래 존속할 수 있다

해설 빈칸 문장은 비트가 주입된 물질적 상품들이 점점 마치 '무엇인' 것처럼 행동한다는 내용이다. 빈칸을 as if가 이끌고 선택지의 동사가 모두 과거형이므로 '실제로는 그렇지 않은' 행동임을 의미한다. 특히 뒤 빈칸 문장 다음의 하드웨어(물질적 상품)가 소프트웨어(무형의 것)처럼 작동한다는 내용에 주목할 필요가 있다. 앞에서는 디지털 기술이 비물질화를 가속화하는데, 단지 디지털 상품뿐만 아니라 고체인 물리적 상품도 비트로 대체되어 '비물질화'가 이루어진다고 했다. 또 유형의 것들이 무형의 것들로 대체된다고 했으므로, 빈칸에 들어갈 말로 가장 적절한 것은 ① 'they were intangible services(그것들이 무형의 서비스이다)'이다. 물질적 상품이 디지털 상품을 대체하는 것이 아니라 물질적 상품이 무형의 것으로 서비스화된다는 내용이므로 ②는 적절하지 않고, 하드웨어와 소프트웨어의 유지 기간을 비교하는 내용이 아니므로 ③도 적절하지 않다.

1 ②

1 How many of *the lunches* [that you ate / over the last week] /
can you recall?
점심 중 얼마나 많이 [여러분이 먹은 / 지난주 동안] / 여러분은 기억해 낼 수 있는가

2 Do you remember what you ate today? // I hope so.
여러분은 오늘 먹은 것을 기억하는가 // 나는 그러길 바란다

3 Yesterday? // I bet // (that) it takes a moment's effort. //
And what about the day before yesterday? // What about a
week ago?
어제는? // 틀림없이 // (기억해 내는 데) 잠깐의 노력이 필요할 것이다 //
그리고 그저께는 어떤가 // 일주일 전은 어떤가

4 It's not so much // that your memory (of last week's lunch) /
has disappeared; //
(~인) 것은 아니다 // 여러분의 기억이 (지난주 점심에 대한) / 사라진 //

if provided with the right cue, / (like where you ate it, or whom
you ate it with), // you would likely recall // what had been on
your plate.
만약 적절한 단서가 제공된다면 / (여러분이 어디에서 그것을 먹었는지, 혹은 그것을 누구와 함께 먹었
는지와 같은) / 여러분은 아마 기억해 낼 것이다 // 여러분의 접시에 무엇이 담겨 있었는지를

5 Rather, / it's difficult to remember last week's lunch //
because your brain has filed it away / with *all the other lunches*
[(which[that]) you've ever eaten] / as *just another lunch*.
오히려 / 지난주의 점심을 기억하는 것이 어렵다 //
여러분의 뇌가 그것을(지난주의 점심을) 정리해 두었기 때문에 / 다른 모든 점심들과 함께
[여러분이 먹어 본 적이 있는] / '흔해 빠진 점심'으로

6 When we try to recall something / from *a category*
[that includes as many instances / as "lunch" or "wine,"] //
many memories compete / for our attention.
우리가 어떤 것을 기억해 내려고 할 때 / 범주로부터
[많은 사례를 포함하는 / '점심'이나 '와인'과 같은] / 많은 기억이 경쟁한다 / 우리의 주목을 위해

7 The memory (of last Wednesday's lunch) / isn't necessarily
gone; // it's // that you lack *the right hook* (to pull it / out of
a sea of lunchtime memories).
기억이 (지난 수요일 점심에 대한) / 반드시 사라진 것은 아니다 //
~이다 // 여러분은 적절한 낚싯바늘이 없는 것 (그것을(지난 수요일 점심에 대한 기억)을 끄집어 낼 / 점
심시간의 기억이라는 바다 밖으로)

8 But / *a wine* [that talks]: // That's unique. // It's a memory
(without rivals).
하지만 / 와인 [말하는] // 그것은 유일무이하다 // 그것은 기억이다 (경쟁 상대가 없는)

해석 **1** 여러분은 지난주 동안 여러분이 먹은 점심 중 얼마나 많이 기억해 낼 수 있는가? **2** 여러분은 오늘 먹은 것을 기억하는가? 나는 그러길 바란다. **3** 어제는? 틀림없이 (기억해
내는 데) 잠깐의 노력이 필요할 것이다. 그리고 그저께는 어떤가? 일주일 전은 어떤가? **4** 지난주 점심에 대한 여러분의 기억이 사라진 것은 아닌데, 만약 어디에서 그것을 먹었는
지, 혹은 그것을 누구와 함께 먹었는지와 같은 적절한 단서가 제공된다면, 여러분은 아마 접시에 무엇이 담겨 있었는지를 기억해 낼 것이다. **5** 오히려, 여러분의 뇌가 그것을(지난주
의 점심을) 여러분이 먹어 본 적이 있는 다른 모든 점심들과 함께 '흔해 빠진 점심'으로 정리해 두었기 때문에 지난주의 점심을 기억하는 것이 어렵다. **6** 우리가 '점심'이나 '와인'과
같은 많은 사례를 포함하는 범주로부터 어떤 것을 기억해 내려고 할 때, 많은 기억이 우리의 주목을 위해 경쟁한다. **7** 지난 수요일 점심에 대한 기억이 반드시 사라진 것은 아니며,
여러분은 점심시간의 기억이라는 바다 밖으로 그것을(지난 수요일 점심에 대한 기억)을 끄집어 낼 적절한 낚싯바늘이 없는 것이다. **8** 하지만 말하는 와인, 그것은 유일무이하다. 그
것은 경쟁 상대가 없는 기억이다.

2 ①

¹Through recent decades / academic archaeologists have been urged / to conduct their research and excavations / according to hypothesis-testing procedures.
최근 몇십 년 동안 내내 / 학계의 고고학자들은 촉구되어 왔다 / 그들의 연구와 발굴을 수행하도록 / 가설 검증 절차에 따라

²It has been argued // that we should construct our general theories, / (should) deduce testable propositions / and (should) prove or disprove them / against the sampled data.
(~라고) 주장되어 왔다 // 우리가 일반적인 이론을 구축해야 한다고 / 검증할 수 있는 명제를 추론(해야 한다고) / 그리고 그것들을 증명하거나 (그것들이) 틀렸음을 증명(해야 한다고) / 샘플로 추출된 자료와 비교하여

³In fact, / the application (of this 'scientific method') / often ran into difficulties.
사실 / 적용은 (이런 '과학적 방법'의) / 자주 어려움을 겪었다

⁴The data have a tendency (to lead to unexpected questions, problems and issues).
자료는 경향이 있다 (예기치 않은 질문, 문제 그리고 쟁점으로 이어지는)

⁵Thus, *archaeologists* (claiming / to follow hypothesis-testing procedures) / found themselves having to create a fiction.
따라서 / 고고학자들은 (사실임을 주장하는 / 가설 검증 절차를 따른 것이) / 깨닫고 보니 꾸며낸 이야기를 쓰고 있었다

⁶In practice, / their work and theoretical conclusions partly developed / from *the data* [which they had discovered].
실제로 / 그들의 연구물과 이론적 결론이 부분적으로 발전했다 / 자료에서 [그들이 발견했던]

⁷In other words, / they already knew the data // when they decided upon an interpretation.
다시 말해서 / 그들은 이미 그 자료를 알고 있었다 // 그들이 어떤 해석으로 결정지을 때

⁸But / in presenting their work / they rewrote the script, /
그러나 / 그들의 연구물을 발표할 때 / 그들은 대본을 다시 썼다 /
placing the theory first / and claiming to have tested it / against *data* [which they discovered], / as in an experiment (under laboratory conditions).
이론을 앞세우면서 / 그리고 그것(이론)을 검증했다고 주장하면서 / 자료와 비교하여 [자신들이 발견한] / 실험에서와 같이 (실험실 조건 하의)

해석 **¹**최근 몇십 년 동안 내내 학계의 고고학자들은 가설 검증 절차에 따라 연구와 발굴을 수행하도록 촉구되어 왔다. **²**우리가 일반적인 이론을 구축하고, 검증할 수 있는 명제를 추론해서, 그것들을 샘플로 추출된 자료와 비교하여 증명하거나 그것들이 틀렸음을 증명해야 한다고 주장되어 왔다. **³**사실 이런 '과학적 방법'의 적용은 자주 어려움을 겪었다. **⁴**자료는 예기치 않은 질문, 문제 그리고 쟁점으로 이어지는 경향이 있다. **⁵**따라서 가설 검증 절차를 따른 것이 사실임을 주장하는 고고학자들은 깨닫고 보니 꾸며낸 이야기를 쓰고 있었다. **⁶**실제로, 그들의 연구물과 이론적 결론이 부분적으로 그들이 발견했던 자료에서 발전했다. **⁷**다시 말해서, 그들이 어떤 해석으로 결정지을 때 그들은 이미 그 자료를 알고 있었다. **⁸**그러나 연구물을 발표할 때, 그들은 실험실 조건 하의 실험에서와 같이 이론을 앞세우고 그것(이론)을 자신들이 발견한 자료와 비교하여 검증했다고 주장하면서 대본을 다시 썼다.

3 ②

1 People have always wanted / to be around other people and to learn from them.
사람들은 항상 원해 왔다 / 다른 사람들 주위에 머무르며 그들로부터 배우기를

2 Cities have long been dynamos (of social possibility), / foundries (of art, music, and fashion).
도시는 오랫동안 발전기였다 (사회적 가능성의) / 즉 주물 공장 (예술, 음악, 패션의)

3 Slang, / or, (if you prefer), / "lexical innovation," / has always started in cities — / an outgrowth (of *all those different people* (so frequently exposed / to one another)).
속어 / 또는 (여러분이 선호한다면) / '어휘의 혁신'은 / 항상 도시에서 시작되었다 /
결과물 (그 모든 각양각색의 사람들의 (매우 빈번히 노출된 / 서로에게))

4 It spreads outward, / in a manner (not unlike *transmissible disease*), // which itself typically "takes off" in cities.
그것(속어)은 밖으로 퍼져나간다 / 방식으로 (전염성 질병과 다르지 않은) //
그리고 그것(전염성 질병) 자체는 보통 도시에서 '시작한다'

5 If, / (as the noted linguist Leonard Bloomfield argued), // *the way* [(that) a person talks] / is a "composite result (of what he has heard before)," //
만약에 ~라면 / (저명한 언어학자 Leonard Bloomfield가 주장하듯) //
방식이 [한 사람이 말하는] / '합성 결과물'이(라면) (그가 전에 들었던 것의) //

then language innovation would happen // where the most people / heard and talked to the most other people.
그렇다면 언어 혁신은 일어날 것이다 // 가장 많은 사람들이 (~한) 곳에서 / 가장 많은 다른 사람들이 하는 말을 듣고 가장 많은 다른 사람들에게 말한

6 Cities drive taste change // because they offer / the greatest exposure (to *other people*), //
도시는 취향 변화를 이끈다 // 그곳이 제공하기 때문에 / 가장 많은 노출을 (다른 사람들에게의) //

who not surprisingly are often *the creative people* [(who(m) [that]) cities seem to attract].
그리고 그들(다른 사람들)은 놀랄 것도 없이 흔히 창의적인 사람이다 [도시가 끌어들이는 듯 보이는]

7 *Media*, / (ever more global, ever more far-reaching), / spread language faster / to more people.
미디어는 / (그 어느 때보다 더 세계적이고, 그 어느 때보다 더 멀리까지 미치는) /
언어를 더 빨리 퍼뜨린다 / 더 많은 사람에게

해설

빈칸 문장 확인하기 ♤

6 도시는 '무엇을 하기' 때문에 취향 변화를 이끌며, 빈칸에 언급된 누군가는 흔히 도시가 끌어들이는 듯 보이는 창의적인 사람들임.
(뒤 내용 요약: 미디어는 언어를 매우 빨리 퍼뜨림.)

추론 근거로 정답 찾기 ♁

3, 4 속어는 다양한 사람들이 서로에게 빈번히 노출되는 도시에서 시작되어 전염성 질병처럼 퍼져나감.
5 언어 혁신은 가장 많은 사람들이 소통하는 곳에서 일어남.

도시에서는 다양한 사람들이 서로에게 노출되어, 속어나 언어 혁신은 도시에서 시작되어 밖으로 퍼진다고 했다. 따라서 도시가 취향 변화를 이끄는 것은 다른 사람들에게 노출이 많이 되기 때문이며, 그 다른 사람들이 도시가 끌어들이는 창의적인 사람들이라고 설명하고 있음을 추론할 수 있다.

→ ② offer the greatest exposure to other people(다른 사람들에게의 가장 많은 노출을 제공하다)

오답 확인

① provide rich source materials for artists
예술가들에게 풍부한 원재료를 공급하다 → art, music, fashion은 도시에서 발전되어 온 것의 예시이며, 빈칸 문장의 the creative people도 예술가에 대한 내용이 아님.

③ cause cultural conflicts among users of slang
속어 사용자들 사이에서 문화 갈등을 초래하다

④ present ideal research environments to linguists
언어학자들에게 이상적인 연구 환경을 제공하다 → 언어학자의 말을 인용한 것은 사람들끼리의 노출이 많은 도시에서 언어 혁신이 일어난다는 설명이며, 언어학자의 환경에 대한 내용이 아님.

⑤ reduce the social mobility of ambitious outsiders
야심 있는 외부인의 사회 이동을 줄이다
* ③, ⑤ → 언급되지 않은 내용.

어휘

composite 합성의; 합성물   drive 이끌다, 추진하다
dynamo 발전기   far-reaching (영향이) 멀리까지 미치는
linguist 언어학자   noted 저명한, 유명한   outgrowth 결과물
slang 속어, 은어   transmissible 전염성의; 보낼[전할] 수 있는

구문 분석

4 It spreads outward, / in a manner (**not unlike** *transmissible disease*), // ~.
이중부정은 긍정을 의미함.

해석 **1** 사람들은 항상 다른 사람들 주위에 머무르며 그들로부터 배우기를 원해 왔다. **2** 도시는 오랫동안 사회적 가능성의 발전기, 즉 예술, 음악, 패션의 주물 공장이었다. **3** 속어, 또는 여러분이 선호한다면 '어휘의 혁신'은 항상 도시에서 시작되었는데, 서로에게 매우 빈번히 노출된 그 모든 각양각색의 사람들의 결과물이다. **4** 그것(속어)은 전염성 질병과 다르지 않은 방식으로 밖으로 퍼져나가는데, 그것(전염성 질병) 자체는 보통 도시에서 '시작한다'. **5** 저명한 언어학자 Leonard Bloomfield가 주장하듯, 만약에 한 사람이 말하는 방식이 '그가 전에 들었던 것의 합성 결과물'이라면, 언어 혁신은 가장 많은 사람들이 가장 많은 다른 사람들이 하는 말을 듣고 가장 많은 다른 사람들에게 말한 곳에서 일어날 것이다. **6** 도시는 그곳이 다른 사람들에게의 가장 많은 노출을 제공하기 때문에 취향 변화를 이끄는데, 그들(다른 사람들)은 놀랄 것도 없이 흔히 도시가 끌어들이는 듯 보이는 창의적인 사람들이다. **7** 그 어느 때보다 더 세계적이고, 그 어느 때보다 더 멀리까지 미치는 미디어는 언어를 더 빨리 더 많은 사람에게 퍼뜨린다.

Zoom 1

해석 (이전 생략) 반대로, 유전학에 대한 새로워진 관심은 아직 알려지지 않은 다양한 목적을 위해서 이용될 수 있는 흥미롭거나 유용한 유전적 특성을 가진 많은 야생 동식물이 있다는 증가하는 인식으로 이어졌다. 이는 결국 그것들(자연 생태계)이 암, 말라리아 또는 비만에 맞서는 미래의 약의 거처가 될 수도 있기 때문에 ___________ (라)는 깨달음으로 이어졌다.
• **renewed** 새로워진, 재개된 **genetics** 유전학 **awareness** 인식, 자각; 의식 **property** 특성, 속성; 재산; 부동산 **harbor** (동물 등의) 거처가 되다; 항구 **obesity** 비만
➔ 빈칸: 우리가 자연 생태계를 파괴하는 것을 피해야 한다

Zoom 2

해석 남자가 여자 옷을 만든다는 생각에는 현대적인 것이 전혀 없었다.... 하지만 옛날에는 고객이 항상 가장 중요했고 그녀의 재단사는 무명의 장인이었다.... (중간 생략) 예술적인 남성 고급 여성복 디자이너의 매우 성공적인 부상과 함께 19세기 후반을 시작으로, 유명해진 사람은 바로 디자이너였고, 고객은 그의 영감 어린 관심에 의해 (격이) 높아졌다.
• **primary** 가장 중요한, 주된; 최초의 **tailor** 재단사 **craftsman** 장인; 공예가 **celebrated** 유명한, 저명한 **elevated** (지위 등이) 높아진, 높은 **inspired** 영감 어린, 영감을 받은
→ 남성 예술가와 그들의 여성을 위한 창작물(여성복)에 대한 감탄의 분위기 속에서, 의상 디자이너는 처음으로 같은 종류의 창작자로서 성공했다. 의상 제작은 기술이라는 옛 규칙 대신에, 이전에는 없던 ___________ 이(가) 만들어졌다.
• **climate** 분위기; 기후 **admiration** 감탄, 존경 **flourish** 성공하다; 번영[번창]하다 **craft** 기술; (수)공예
➔ 빈칸: 의상 디자인과 예술 사이의 현대적 연결

Zoom 3

해석 자신들의 작업에 디지털 기술을 이용하는 젊은 현대 예술가들은 컴퓨터를 거의 언급하지 않는다. 예를 들어, 워드 프로세싱 프로그램과 잉크젯식 프린터를 사용하는 추상파 화가인 Wade Guyton은 스스로를 컴퓨터 예술가라고 부르지 않는다. (중간 생략)
• **contemporary** 현대의; 동시대의 **employ** 이용[사용]하다; 고용하다 **make reference to A** A를 언급하다 **abstractionist** 추상파 화가
→ 현세대의 예술가들에게 컴퓨터, 혹은 더 적절히는 휴대용 컴퓨터는, 그들의 사회생활과 직업 생활을 연결하는 통합된, 휴대용 디지털 기술의 모음 중 하나이다. 인터넷 사용에 있어 태블릿과 핸드폰이 개인 컴퓨터를 능가하면서, 그리고 얇은 디지털 기기들이 수십 년 전의 방 크기의 중앙 컴퓨터 그리고 부피가 큰 탁상용 컴퓨터와 전혀 닮지 않았기 때문에 이제 컴퓨터 예술가는 결국 ___________ 것으로 보인다.
• **generation** 세대 ((비슷한 연령층)) **integrate** 통합하다, 전체로 합치다 **portable** 휴대용의, 들고 다닐 수 있는 **surpass** 능가하다, 뛰어넘다 **device** 기기, 장치 **mainframe** 중앙 컴퓨터 **bulky** 부피가 큰
➔ 빈칸: 사라진
• **extinct** 사라진; (동식물 등이) 멸종된

Zoom 4

해석 유산은 매우 선별적인 물질적 인공물, 신화, 기억, 그리고 전통이 현재를 위한 자원이 되는 방식과 관련이 있다. 그 자원의 내용, 해석, 표현은 현재의 요구에 따라 선택된다.... 또한 기억과 전통의 의미와 기능들이 현재에서 정의된다는 결론이 된다. 게다가, 유산은 물질적 인공물보다 의미와 더 관련 있다. (중간 생략) 결국, 현재 사회의 요구가 변화함에 따라, 혹은 심지어, 구 동유럽에서 현재 일어나고 있듯이, 새로운 현재를 반영하기 위해서 과거가 다시 만들어져야 할 때, 그것들은 나중에 버려질지도 모른다.
• **heritage** (국가, 사회의) 유산, 전통; 세습 재산 **be concerned with** ~와 관련이 있다 **artefact** (특히 역사적·문화적 의미가 있는) 인공물, 가공품 **mythology** 신화 **representation** 표현, 묘사; 대표(자) **discard** 버리다, 폐기하다
→ 따라서 유산은 ___________ (이)다.
➔ 빈칸: 과거를 기억하는 것만큼 과거를 잊는 것에 관한 것

Focus & Practice
p.34

1 ③ **2** ① **3** ② **4** ①

1 ③

해석 ... Oxford 사전의 정의는 탈진실이란 '무엇'인가에 초점을 두는데, 이는 때로는 감정이 사실보다 더 중요하다는 생각이다. 하지만 그다음 질문이 그만큼 중요한데, 이는 도대체 '왜' 이것이 발생하는가이다. 어떤 사람은 아무런 이유 없이 명백하거나 쉽게 확인할 수 있는 사실에 반론을 펴지 않고, 그 사람은 그것이 자신에게 이익이 될 때 그렇게 한다. 어떤 사람의 믿음이 '불편한 사실'에 의해 위협받을 때, 때때로 그 사실에 이의를 제기하는 것이 선호된다. 이것은 의식적인 수준이나 무의식적인 수준에서 일어날 수 있지만 (왜냐하면 때때로 우리가 납득시키려고 시도하고 있는 사람이 우리 자신이기 때문에), 핵심은 사실에 대한 이러한 종류의 탈진실 관계가 우리가 진실 그 자체보다 우리에게 더 중요한 어떤 것을 주장하려고 시도하고 있을 때만 발생한다는 것이다.
• **definition** 정의 **post-truth** 탈진실 ((객관적 사실보다 개인의 감정이 여론 형성에 더 큰 영향을 미치는 현상)) **confirmable** 확인할 수 있는 **threaten** 위협[협박]하다 **inconvenient** 불편한, 곤란한 **preferable** 선호되는; 더 좋은 **conscious** 의식적인; 의식[자각]이 있는(↔ unconscious 무의식적인; 의식을 잃은) **seek to-v** v하려고 (시도)하다 **convince** 납득시키다; 설득하다 **assert** 주장하다, 단언하다
① 우리의 뒤섞인 감정들을 억제하는
② 절대적 진실의 변함없는 가치를 지니기 위한
③ 진실 그 자체보다 우리에게 더 중요한
• **hold back** 억제[저지]하다 **constant** 변함없는; 끊임없는

해설 빈칸 문장이 This를 포함하고 있으므로 직전 문장과 함께 보면, 불편한 사실에 의해 믿음이 위협받을 때 이의를 제기하는 것이 의식적, 무의식적으로 모두 일어나지만, 이런 탈진실 관계가 우리가 '어떤' 것을 주장하려고 시도하고 있을 때만 발생한다는 내용이다. 앞에서부터 살펴보면, 탈진실의 발생 이유는 사람이 자신에게 이익이 될 때 사실에 반대하여 의견을 주장하기 때문이라고 했다. 이를 앞서 파악한 내용과 종합하여 보면, 빈칸 문장의 This는 이익이 될 때, 혹은 불편한 사실에 의해 믿음이 위협받을 때 사실에 대한 반대 주장을 하

거나 이의를 제기하는 것, 즉 탈진실 관계의 발생임을 알 수 있다. 따라서 사실보다 우리에게 더 중요한 것이 있을 때 탈진실이 일어난다는 것을 추론할 수 있으므로, 빈칸에 들어갈 말로 가장 적절한 것은 ③ 'that is more important to us than the truth itself(진실 그 자체보다 우리에게 더 중요한)'이다. 감정을 억제하기보다 중시할 때 탈진실이 일어난다고 했으므로 ①은 적절하지 않다. 또한 탈진실은 절대적인 진실보다 감정과 신념을 중시하므로 ②는 글의 내용과 반대된다.

2 ①

해석 … 심리학은 패턴을 만들고, 규칙성을 발견하고, 궁극적으로 인간의 경험과 행동에 질서를 부과하려고 한다. 반면에, 작가는 인간 경험의 제멋대로 굴고, 길들여지지 않은 깊이에 몰두한다. … 만약 우리 심리학자들이 질서 있는 패턴, 즉 아이 마음의 규칙성을 찾는 데 너무 열심이라면, 우리는 우리 주제의 근본적이고 널리 퍼져 있는 특성, 즉 아이의 더욱 제멋대로이고 상상력이 풍부한 대화와 사고의 방식을 놓칠 수도 있다. 다소 제멋대로이고 색다른 사고방식에 끌리는 것처럼 보이는 사람은 재능이 발달한 작가나 문학 학자뿐만 아니라, 어린아이도 또한 그러하다. 어린 아이에게 관심이 있는 심리학자는 아이가 어떻게 생각하는지를 잘 이해하기 위해 <u>조금 더 자주 위험을 무릅쓰고 황무지로 들어가야 할지도 모른다</u>.

• **regularity** 규칙성   **dive into** ~에 몰두하다; ~에 뛰어들다
untamed 길들여지지 않은   **bent on** ~에 열심인   **identify** 찾다, 발견하다; 알아보다   **orderly** 질서 있는; 정돈된
① 조금 더 자주 위험을 무릅쓰고 황무지로 들어간다
② 그들이 자신의 가장 소중한 기억을 생각해 내도록 돕다
③ 아동 소설의 핵심적인 특징을 무시한다
• **venture into** 위험을 무릅쓰고 ~으로 들어가다   **wilderness** 황무지
disregard 무시[경시](하다)

해설 빈칸 문장은 아이가 어떻게 생각하는지를 잘 이해하기 위해서는 심리학자가 '무엇을 해야 할지도 모른다'는 내용이다. 직전 문장을 보면, 아이들이 작가나 문학 학자처럼 제멋대로이고 색다른 사고방식에 끌린다고 했다. 앞에서부터 읽어보면, 심리학과 문학의 다른 특성이 대조되고 있고 심리학자들이 심리학의 특성대로 아이 마음의 규칙성을 찾으려고 하면 아이를 제대로 파악하지 못할 수도 있다고 했다. 따라서 아동의 사고방식을 이해하기 위해서는 이처럼 제멋대로인 측면, 즉 심리학이 아닌 문학적 측면에 초점을 두어야 함을 추론할 수 있으므로, 빈칸에 들어갈 말로 가장 적절한 것은 ① 'venture a little more often into the wilderness(조금 더 자주 위험을 무릅쓰고 황무지로 들어간다)'이다. 여기서 wilderness는 앞에서 언급한 아이의 특성을 비유적으로 표현한 것이다. 소중한 기억은 언급되지 않았으므로 ②는 적절하지 않으며, 아동 소설에 대한 내용이 아니므로 ③도 적절하지 않다.

3 ②

해석 교육 기술의 성공적인 통합은 그 기술이 사용자에 의해 학습이나 교육, 또는 수행의 눈에 띄지 않는 촉진제로 여겨지는 것으로 특징지어진다. 사용되고 있는 기술에서 기술이 도움이 되는 교육적 목적으로 초점이 옮겨가면, 그 다음에 그 기술은 편하고 신뢰받는 요소가 되어 가며, 성공적으로 통합되는 것으로 여겨질 수 있다. 어떤 것들은 돌리는 방법을 사용하고, 어떤 것들은 위에 달린 누르는 버튼을 사용하며, 또한 다른 변형(된 방법)들도 있듯이 관련된 방법이 가지각색이지만, 볼펜 사용에 대해 다시 생각하는 사람은 거의 없다. … 새롭고 최근에 만들어진 기술은 흔히 사용자들에게 매력과 좌절감 둘 다를 접하게 한다. 학습, 교육 또는 수행을 촉진하는 데 있어서 <u>사용자의 초점이 기술의 사용이 아니라 기술 그 자체에 맞춰져 있는</u> 한, 그러면 적어도 그 사용자에게는 그 기술이 성공적으로 통합되었다고 결론을 내려서는 안 된다.

• **integration** 통합   **mark** 특징짓다; 표시(하다)   **facilitator** 촉진제
instruction 교육; 설명; 지시   **serve** 도움이 되다; 봉사하다, 섬기다
second thought 다시 생각함, 재고(再考)   **mechanism** 방법, 메커니즘; 기계 장치; 구조   **emerging** 최근에 만들어진, 신흥의, 신생의
promote 촉진하다; 홍보하다; 승진시키다
① 사용자가 성공적으로 그 기술에 대한 친숙함을 얻는다
② 사용자의 초점이 기술의 사용이 아니라 기술 그 자체에 맞춰져 있다
③ 사용자가 계속해서 시대에 뒤진 교육 기술을 사용한다
• **outdated** 시대에 뒤진, 구식인

해설 빈칸 문장은 학습, 교육, 수행의 촉진에 있어 '어떤 조건 하에서는' 그 기술이 성공적으로 통합된 것이 아니라는 내용이다. 빈칸 직전 문장에서는 새롭고 최근에 만들어진 기술은 매력과 좌절감을 모두 접하게 한다고 했는데, 이는 기술이 완전히 통합되지 않은 경우, 즉 성공적인 통합이 아닌 경우에 해당한다. 앞에서부터 살펴보면, 첫 문장에서 성공적인 교육 기술의 통합은 그 기술이 눈에 띄지 않는 촉진제로 여겨진다고 했다. 이어서 기술 자체에서 그 기술의 교육적 목적으로 초점이 옮겨가야 성공적 통합이라고 설명하며 볼펜을 예로 들었다. 따라서 기술이 성공적으로 통합되었다고 볼 수 없는 조건으로 적절한 것은 사용자의 초점이 기술 자체에 있는 것임을 추론할 수 있으므로, 빈칸에 들어갈 말로 가장 적절한 것은 ② 'the user's focus is on the technology itself rather than its use(사용자의 초점이 기술의 사용이 아니라 기술 그 자체에 맞춰져 있다)'이다. 사용자가 기술에 친숙해진 것은 교육 기술이 성공적으로 통합된 경우에 해당하므로 글의 내용과 반대되어 ①은 적절하지 않다. 또한 통합 여부가 교육 기술이 구식인지 신식인지에 영향을 받는다는 내용은 없으므로 ③도 적절하지 않다.

4 ①

해석 어떤 사람들은 야생 동물 피해 관리를 (개체 수가) 과다한 종들에 대한 과학과 관리로 정의했지만, 이 정의는 너무 한정적이다. 모든 야생 동물 종들은 인간의 이익에 해를 끼치는 방식으로 행동한다. 따라서 단지 과다한 종뿐만 아니라 모든 종이 야생 동물 피해를 일으킨다. 이것의 흥미로운 한 사례는 캘리포니아의 멸종 위기에 처한 송골매를 포함하는데, 이것들은 캘리포니아 작은 제비갈매기라는 또 다른 멸종 위기에 처한 종을 먹이로 삼는다. 틀림없이 우리는 송골매를 과다한 상태라고 여기지는 않겠지만, 우리는 그것들이 멸종 위기에 처한 종을 먹지 않기를 바란다. … 이런 경우에 야생 동물 피해 관리의 목표는 송골매에 <u>해를 끼치지</u> 않으면서 송골매가 작은 제비갈매기를 먹지 못하게 하는 것일 것이다.

• **wildlife** 야생 동물   **overabundant** 과다한, 과잉의   **endangered** 멸종 위기에 처한   **prey on** ~을 먹이로 삼다   **management** 관리; 경영(진)
① 해를 끼치는 것
② 훈련시키는 것
③ 먹이를 너무 많이 주는 것

해설 빈칸 문장은 '이런 경우(in this case)'에 야생 동물 피해 관리의 목표가 송골매에 '무엇을 하지' 않으면서 송골매가 작은 제비갈매기를 먹지 못하게 하는 것이라는 내용이다. 첫 문장에서 모든 종의 야생 동물이 피해를 일으킨다고 언급한 다음, 멸종 위기종인 송골매와 캘리포니아 작은 제비갈매기를 예로 들었다. 송골매도 보호해야 하지만 그것이 다른 멸종 위기종(캘리포니아 작은 제비갈매기)을 먹기를 바라지 않는다는 내용으로, 빈칸 문장의 in this case는 이 사례를 가리킨다. 따라서 빈칸에 들어갈 말로 가장 적절한 것은 ① 'harming(해를 끼치는 것)'이다. 송골매의 훈련은 언급되지 않았으므로 ②는 적절하지 않다. 또한 얼마나 많은 먹이를 줘야 하는지에 대한 내용이 아니므로 ③도 적절하지 않다.

1②

¹**There** is *something* (deeply paradoxical) / about the professional status of sports journalism, / especially in the medium of print.
(~한) 것이 있다 (몹시 역설적인) / 스포츠 저널리즘의 직업적 지위에 관해 / 특히 인쇄 매체에서

²**In** discharging their usual responsibilities (of description and commentary), / reporters' accounts of sports events are eagerly consulted / by sports fans, //
그들(기자)의 일상적인 책무를 이행함에 있어서 (설명과 해설인) /
기자들의 스포츠 경기에 관한 설명은 열심히 찾아진다 / 스포츠 팬들에 의해 //
while in their broader journalistic role (of covering sport in its many forms), / sports journalists are among the most visible (of all contemporary writers).
한편 그들의 더 폭넓은 기자의 역할에서 (여러 형식으로 스포츠를 취재하는) /
스포츠 기자들은 가장 눈에 띄는 사람들 중 하나이다 (모든 현대의 저술가들 중에서)

³**The** ruminations (of the elite class of 'celebrity' sports journalists) / are much sought after / by the major newspapers, /
숙고는 ('유명 인사' 스포츠 기자들로 이루어진 엘리트 등급의) / 많이 찾아진다 / 주요 신문사에 의해 /
their lucrative contracts being the envy (of colleagues (in other 'disciplines' of journalism)).
그들('유명 인사' 엘리트급의 스포츠 기자들)의 수익성이 좋은 계약은 부러움의 대상이다 (동료들의 (저널리즘의 다른 '분야'에 있는))

⁴**Yet** / sports journalists do not have *a standing* (in their profession) [that corresponds to the size (of their readerships or of their pay packets)], /
하지만 / 스포츠 기자들은 지위를 갖지 않는다 (자신들의 직업에서)
[크기와 일치하는 (그들의 독자 수나 급여 액수의)] /
with *the old saying* (now reaching the status of cliché) // that sport is the 'toy department of the news media' / still (being) readily to hand / as a dismissal of the worth (of what sports journalists do).
옛말이 ~한 채로 (이제는 상투적인 문구의 지위에 도달한) // 스포츠는 '뉴스 매체의 장난감 부서'라는 /
여전히 손쉽게 접할 수 있는 / 가치에 대한 묵살로서 (스포츠 기자들이 하는 일의)

⁵**This** reluctance (to take sports journalism seriously) / produces the paradoxical outcome // that sports newspaper writers are much read but little admired.
이러한 꺼림은 (스포츠 저널리즘을 진지하게 받아들이는 데 대한) / 역설적인 결과를 만들어 낸다 //
스포츠 신문 기자들이 많이 읽히지만 거의 존경받지 못하는

해설

빈칸 문장 확인하기 

5 스포츠 저널리즘을 진지하게 받아들이지 않는 것은 스포츠 신문 기자들이 많이 읽히지만 거의 '무엇'하지 못하는 역설적인 결과를 만듦.

⌄⌄

추론 근거로 정답 찾기 

4 스포츠 기자들은 독자나 급여 규모에 맞는 지위를 가지지 못하며, 그들의 업무 가치에 대한 묵살이 존재함.
↓
스포츠 기사가 많이 읽히고 수익이 큰 것에 비해 스포츠 기자의 직업 지위는 이에 맞지 않고 업무 가치를 묵살당한다고 했다. 따라서 많이 읽히지만 존경받지 못하는 역설이 있음을 추론할 수 있다.
*앞에 준부정어 little(거의 ~ 않는)이 있어 빈칸을 부정하는 의미가 됨에 유의해야 한다.
→ ② admired(존경받는)

오답 확인

① paid 돈을 받는
→ 수익성이 좋다고 했으므로 글의 내용과 반대됨.
③ censored 검열되는
→ 검열에 관한 내용은 없음.
④ challenged 도전받는
→ 직업적 위상이 높지 않다고 했으므로 글의 내용과 반대됨.
⑤ discussed 논의되는
→ 논의가 없다는 내용은 없으며, 오히려 눈에 띈다고 했음.

어휘

cliché 상투적인 문구[생각] consult 찾아보다, 참고하다; 상담하다
discipline 분야, 부문; 규율, 훈육; 학문 dismissal 묵살, 일축; 해고
medium (*pl.* media) 매체, 수단; 중간의 pay packet 급여 액수
readership 독자 수[층] reluctance 꺼림, 마지못해 함
to hand (쉽게) 접할[사용할] 수 있는

구문 분석

³The ruminations ~ / are much sought after / by the major newspapers, / **their lucrative contracts being the envy** ~.
분사구문의 의미상의 주어(their lucrative contracts)와 문장의 주어(The ruminations)가 달라 분사 앞에 의미상의 주어를 남김.

2 ②

1 A large part (of what we see) / is what we expect to see.
많은 부분은 (우리가 보는 것의) / 우리가 보기를 기대하는 것이다

2 This explains // why we "see" faces and figures / in a flickering campfire, or in moving clouds.
이것은 설명한다 // 우리가 얼굴과 형상을 '보는' 이유를 / 흔들리는 모닥불 속이나 움직이는 구름 속에서

3 This is // why Leonardo da Vinci advised artists to discover their motifs / by staring at patches (on a blank wall).
이것이 ~이다 // Leonardo da Vinci가 화가들에게 그들의 주제를 발견하라고 조언한 이유 / 부분들을 응시함으로써 (빈 벽의)

4 A fire provides a constant flickering change / in *visual information* [that never integrates into anything solid] /
불은 끊임없이 흔들리는 변화를 제공한다 / 시각 정보에 [한결같은 어떤 것에도 절대 통합되지 않는] /
and thereby allows the brain to engage in a play of hypotheses.
그리고 그렇게 함으로써 뇌가 가설 놀이에 참여하게 한다

5 On the other hand, / the wall does not present us / with very much / in the way of visual clues, //
반면에 / 벽은 우리에게 주지 않는다 / 그리 많은 것을 / 시각적인 단서의 형태로 //
and so the brain begins to make more and more hypotheses / and desperately searches for confirmation.
그래서 뇌는 점점 더 많은 가설을 세우기 시작한다 / 그리고 필사적으로 확인을 구한다

6 A crack in the wall looks / a little like the profile (of a nose) // and suddenly a whole face appears, / or a leaping horse (appears), or a dancing figure (appears).
벽의 갈라진 틈은 보인다 / 약간 옆모습처럼 (코의) //
그리고 갑자기 얼굴 전체가 나타난다 / 또는 뛰는 말이나 춤추는 형상이 (나타난다)

7 In cases like these / the brain's visual strategies are projecting images / from within the mind out onto the world.
이와 같은 경우에 / 뇌의 시각적 전략은 이미지를 투영하는 것이다 / 마음속에서 바깥세상으로

해설

빈칸 문장 확인하기 

7 '이러한 경우(In cases like these)', 뇌의 시각적 전략은 '무엇'임.

⌄

추론 근거로 정답 찾기 

1 우리는 우리가 보길 기대하는 것을 봄.
4, 5 불, 벽을 보고 뇌는 가설을 세우는데, 시각적 단서가 부족할수록 가설을 더 많이 만들고 확인함.
6 벽의 갈라진 틈에서 다양한 형상을 보게 됨.

↓

우리는 우리가 보기를 기대하는 것을 보며, 뇌는 가설(마음속으로 보길 기대한 이미지)을 만들고 확인한다고 했다. 따라서 벽의 갈라진 틈에서 나타나는 다양한 형상은 우리가 보길 기대한 이미지가 투영된 것임을 알 수 있다. 빈칸 문장의 these는 벽의 틈에서 다양한 형상이 나타나는 경우를 가리키며, 이 경우 뇌의 시각적 전략은 뇌가 마음속 이미지를 밖으로 투영하는 것임을 추론할 수 있다.
→ ② projecting images from within the mind out onto the world(마음속에서 바깥세상으로 이미지를 투영하는 것)

오답 확인

① ignoring distracting information unrelated to visual clues
시각적 단서와 관련 없는 정신을 산만하게 하는 정보를 무시하는 것
③ categorizing objects into groups either real or imagined 사물을 실제이거나 상상한 그룹 중 하나로 분류하는 것
*①, ③ → 시각적 단서와 관련 없는 정보나 사물 분류에 관한 내용은 없음.
④ strengthening connections between objects in the real world 현실 세계에서 사물들 사이의 관련성을 강화하는 것
→ 뇌가 이미지의 가설을 세우는 것을 실제 사물 간의 관련성을 강화하는 것으로 볼 수 없음.
⑤ removing the broken or missing parts of an original image 원래의 이미지에서 부서지거나 없어진 부분을 제거하는 것
→ a crack in the wall(벽의 갈라진 틈)을 활용한 오답. 이미지의 일부를 제거하는 것은 유추할 수 없음.

어휘

confirmation 확인; 확정   integrate into ~에 통합되다
patch (다른 것과 달라 보이는) 부분; (헝겊) 조각
profile 옆모습, 옆얼굴   solid 한결같은, 고른; 단단한; 고체(의)
[선택지] distract 산만하게 하다   project 투영하다, 비추다

구문 분석

3 This is // why Leonardo da Vinci **advised** artists **to discover** their motifs / by staring at patches ~.
<advise+O+to-v>: O가 v하도록 조언하다

해석 **1** 우리가 보는 것의 많은 부분은 우리가 보기를 기대하는 것이다. **2** 이것은 우리가 흔들리는 모닥불 속이나 움직이는 구름 속에서 얼굴과 형상을 '보는' 이유를 설명한다. **3** 이것이 Leonardo da Vinci가 화가들에게 빈 벽의 부분들을 응시함으로써 그들의 주제를 발견하라고 조언한 이유다. **4** 불은 한결같은 어떤 것에도 절대 통합되지 않는 시각 정보에 끊임없이 흔들리는 변화를 제공하고, 그렇게 함으로써 뇌가 가설 놀이에 참여하게 한다. **5** 반면에, 벽은 우리에게 시각적인 단서의 형태로 그리 많은 것을 주지 않고, 그래서 뇌는 점점 더 많은 가설을 세우기 시작하고 필사적으로 확인을 구한다. **6** 벽의 갈라진 틈은 약간 코의 옆모습처럼 보이고 갑자기 얼굴 전체가 나타나거나 뛰는 말이나 춤추는 형상이 나타난다. **7** 이와 같은 경우에 뇌의 시각적 전략은 마음속에서 바깥세상으로 이미지를 투영하는 것이다.

3 ②

¹The debates (between social and cultural anthropologists) /
concern / not the differences between the concepts but the
analytical priority: //

논쟁은 (사회 인류학자와 문화 인류학자 사이의) /
~에 관한 것이다 / 개념들 간의 차이가 아니라 분석적 우선사항 //

which should come first, / the social chicken or the cultural
egg?

즉 어느 것이 먼저인가 / 사회적 닭 혹은 문화적 달걀

²British anthropology emphasizes the social.

영국의 인류학은 사회적인 것을 강조한다

³It assumes // that social institutions determine culture //

그것(영국의 인류학)은 추정한다 // 사회 제도가 문화를 결정한다고 //

and that universal domains of society (such as kinship,
economy, politics, and religion) / are represented /

그리고 사회의 보편적인 영역이 (친척 관계, 경제, 정치, 그리고 종교와 같은) / 나타난다고 /

by *specific institutions* (such as the family, subsistence farming,
the British Parliament, and the Church of England) [which can
be compared cross-culturally].

구체적인 제도에 의해 (가족, 자급 농업, 영국 의회, 그리고 영국 국교회와 같은)
[비교 문화적으로 비교될 수 있는]

⁴American anthropology emphasizes the cultural.

미국의 인류학은 문화적인 것을 강조한다

⁵It assumes // that culture shapes social institutions /
by providing *the shared beliefs, the core values, the
communicative tools, and so on* [that make social life possible].

그것(미국의 인류학)은 추정한다 // 문화가 사회 제도를 형성한다고 /
공유된 믿음, 핵심적 가치관, 의사소통 도구 등을 제공함으로써 [사회생활을 가능하게 만드는]

⁶It does not assume // that there are universal social domains, /

그것(미국의 인류학)은 추정하지 않는다 // 보편적인 사회적 영역이 있다고 /

preferring instead to discover domains empirically /
as aspects (of each society's own classificatory schemes — /
in other words, its culture).

그리고 대신에 영역들을 경험적으로 발견하는 것을 선호한다 /
측면으로서 (각 사회 자체의 분류 체계의 / 다른 말로, 그것의 문화(의))

⁷And / it rejects the notion // that any social institution can be
understood / in isolation from its own context.

그리고 / 그것은 개념을 거부한다 // 어떤 사회 제도든 이해될 수 있다는 /
그것 자체의 맥락에서 분리되어

해설

빈칸 문장 확인하기 

> **7** '그것(it)'은 어떤 사회 제도든 '어떻게' 이해될 수 있다는 개념을 거부함.

추론 근거로 정답 찾기 

> **5, 6** 미국 인류학에서는 문화가 사회 제도를 형성하며, 사회 영역을 각각의 문화 측면에서 경험적으로 발견하는 것을 선호함.
>
> ↓
>
> 미국의 인류학은 영국과 반대로 사회 제도가 문화에 의해 만들어진다고 보고, 사회 영역을 문화의 측면에서 발견한다고 했다. 빈칸 문장의 it은 미국의 인류학을 받아서 사회 제도가 문화와 별개로 이해될 수 있다는 개념을 거부한다는 내용이 이어질 것을 추론할 수 있다.
> *거부하는 개념이므로 미국의 인류학의 관점과 반대되는 것을 찾아야 함에 주의한다.
>
> → ② in isolation from its own context(그것 자체의 맥락에서 분리되어)

오답 확인

① in relation to its cultural origin
그것의 문화적 기원과 관련하여 → 미국의 인류학은 문화적 기원과 관련해 사회 제도를 이해하므로 글의 내용과 반대됨.

③ regardless of personal preferences
개인적인 선호에 상관없이

④ without considering its economic roots
그것의 경제적인 뿌리를 고려하지 않은 채로
*③, ④ → 언급되지 않은 내용.

⑤ on the basis of British-American relations
영국과 미국 사이의 관계를 기반으로 → 영국과 미국의 인류학을 대조하는 내용으로, 두 나라의 관계에 대한 내용이 아님.

어휘

analytical 분석적인   anthropologist 인류학자
classificatory 분류(상)의   concern ~에 관한 것이다; 우려[걱정](하다)
cross-culturally 비교 문화적으로   domain 영역, 분야; 영토
kinship 친척 관계; 유사, 근사   parliament 의회, 국회
scheme 체계; 계획, 설계; 개요

구문 분석

²British anthropology emphasizes **the social**.
<the+형용사>: ~한 것[사람들]

해석 ¹사회 인류학자와 문화 인류학자 사이의 논쟁은 개념들 간의 차이가 아니라 분석적 우선 사항에 관한 것인데, 즉 사회적 닭 혹은 문화적 달걀, 어느 것이 먼저냐는 것이다. ²영국의 인류학은 사회적인 것을 강조한다. ³그것은 사회 제도가 문화를 결정하고 (친척 관계, 경제, 정치, 그리고 종교와 같은) 사회의 보편적인 영역이 (가족, 자급 농업, 영국 의회, 그리고 영국 국교회와 같은) 비교 문화적으로 비교될 수 있는 구체적인 제도에 의해 나타난다고 추정한다. ⁴미국의 인류학은 문화적인 것을 강조한다. ⁵그것은 문화가 사회생활을 가능하게 만드는 공유된 믿음, 핵심적 가치관, 의사소통 도구 등을 제공함으로써 사회 제도를 형성한다고 추정한다. ⁶그것은 보편적인 사회적 영역이 있다고 추정하지 않고 대신에 각 사회 자체의 분류 체계, 다른 말로, 그것의 문화의 측면으로서 영역들을 경험적으로 발견하는 것을 선호한다. ⁷그리고 그것은 어떤 사회 제도든 그것 자체의 맥락에서 분리되어 이해될 수 있다는 개념을 거부한다.

1 ③

[1] In today's world / we have come to neglect the habit of writing // because so many other forms (of communication) / have taken its place.
오늘날의 세계에서 / 우리는 글 쓰는 습관을 소홀히 하게 되었다 // 왜냐하면 정말 많은 다른 형태들이 (의사소통의) / 그것의 자리를 차지했기 때문이다

[2] Telephones, tape recorders, computers, and fax machines / are more efficient / in conveying news.
전화, 테이프 녹음기, 컴퓨터, 팩스 기계는 / 더 효율적이다 / 소식을 전하는 데

[3] If the only goal is to transmit information, // then writing deserves to become obsolete.
유일한 목적이 정보를 전달하는 것이라면 // 글쓰기는 구식이 되어도 마땅하다

[4] But / writing is for creating new information.
그러나 / 글쓰기는 새로운 정보를 창조하기 위한 것이다

[5] In the past, / educated persons *used journals and personal correspondence* / *to put their experiences into words*, // which allowed them to reflect / on what had happened during the day.
과거에는 / 교육받은 사람들이 일기와 개인적인 서신 왕래를 이용했다 / 자신의 경험을 말로 표현하기 위해 // 그리고 그것이 그들이 곰곰이 생각하게 했다 / 그날 있었던 일에 대해

[6] *The incredibly detailed letters* [(which[that]) many Victorians wrote] / are an example (of how people used writing / to establish order / from *the random events* [(which[that]) they experienced]).
믿기 어려울 만큼 상세한 편지들은 [많은 빅토리아 시대 사람들이 쓴] / 예이다 (사람들이 어떻게 글쓰기를 사용했는지에 대한 / 질서를 세우기 위해 / 임의의 사건들에서 [그들이 경험한])

[7] *The kind of material* [(which[that]) we write in diaries and letters] / does not exist // before it is written down.
소재의 종류는 [우리가 일기장과 편지에 쓰는] / 존재하지 않는다 // 그것이 글로 적히기 전에는

[8] It is *the slow, organically growing process of thought* (involved in writing) // that lets the ideas emerge / in the first place.
바로 느리고도 유기적으로 커가는 생각의 과정이다 (글쓰기에 수반되는) // 생각(정보)을 나타나게 하는 것은 / 최초로

해설

빈칸 문장 확인하기 

> 4 그러나 글쓰기는 '무엇'을 위한 것임.

추론 근거로 정답 찾기 

> 3 글쓰기의 목적은 정보 전달뿐만이 아님.
> 5 글을 씀으로써 경험을 언어로 표현하고 깊이 생각함.
> 7,8 글로 적고 나서야 비로소 소재가 존재하며, 글을 쓰는 과정에서 정보가 처음 만들어짐.
>
> ↓
>
> 글쓰기는 정보를 전달하는 목적만 가진 것이 아니라고 했다. 글을 통해 경험을 언어로 표현하고, 소재는 글로 적고 나서야 존재하며, 정보는 글을 쓸 때 커지는 생각의 과정에서 처음 만들어진다고 했으므로, 글쓰기는 새로운 정보를 창조하기 위한 것임을 추론할 수 있다.
>
> → ③ creating new information(새로운 정보를 창조하기)

오답 확인

① recording historic events
역사적으로 중요한 사건을 기록하기
② enjoying one's free time
개인의 여가시간을 즐기기
④ drawing inspiration from the world
세상으로부터 영감을 이끌어내기
＊①, ②, ④ → 언급되지 않은 내용.
⑤ communicating effectively with others
다른 사람과 효과적으로 의사소통하기 → 다른 효율적인 의사소통 형태들이 글쓰기의 자리를 차지했다고 했음.

어휘

convey 전하다, 전달하다(= transmit); 나르다, 운송하다
correspondence 서신 왕래, 통신; 상응, 대응　emerge 나타나다, 나오다
neglect (의무 등을) 소홀히 하다; 태만, 방치　obsolete 구식의, 쓸모없게 된
organically 유기적으로; 조직적으로; 유기농으로

구문 분석

[8] **It is** *the slow, organically growing process of thought* (involved in writing) // **that** lets the ideas emerge / in the first place.
<It is ~ that> 강조구문으로 the slow ~ in writing이 강조됨.

해석 [1]오늘날의 세계에서 정말 많은 다른 의사소통의 형태들이 그것의 자리를 차지했기 때문에 우리는 글 쓰는 습관을 소홀히 하게 되었다. [2]전화, 테이프 녹음기, 컴퓨터, 팩스 기계는 소식을 전하는 데 더 효율적이다. [3]유일한 목적이 정보를 전달하는 것이라면, 글쓰기는 구식이 되어도 마땅하다. [4]그러나 글쓰기는 새로운 정보를 창조하기 위한 것이다. [5]과거에는, 교육받은 사람들이 자신의 경험을 말로 표현하기 위해 일기와 개인적인 서신왕래를 이용했고, 그것은 그날 있었던 일에 대해 그들이 곰곰이 생각하게 했다. [6]많은 빅토리아 시대 사람들이 쓴 믿기 어려울 만큼 상세한 편지들은 사람들이 그들이 경험한 임의의 사건들에서 질서를 세우기 위해 어떻게 글쓰기를 사용했는지에 대한 예이다. [7]우리가 일기장과 편지에 쓰는 소재의 종류는 그것이 글로 적히기 전에는 존재하지 않는다. [8]최초로 생각(정보)을 나타나게 하는 것은 바로 글쓰기에 수반되는 느리고도 유기적으로 커가는 생각의 과정이다.

2 ①

1 One of Napoleon Bonaparte's most important insights was //
that <u>talent is no respecter of birth</u>.
Napoleon Bonaparte의 가장 중요한 통찰 가운데 하나는 ~이었다 //
재능은 태생을 가리지 않는다는 것

2 As a child of the middle classes, / he wasn't about to elevate
noble lords / above their ability.
중류 계급의 자손으로서 / 그는 신분 높은 귀족들을 등용하려고 하지 않았다 / 그들의 능력 이상으로

3 "Bonaparte judged men / by what they could do, / and not by
their genealogy.
"Bonaparte는 사람들을 판단했다 / 그들이 무엇을 할 수 있느냐로 / 그들의 혈통이 아니라

4 He looked / not at *the decorations* [that adorned the breast], /
but at *the exploits* [that stamped the warrior]; /
그는 보았다 / 장식물이 아니라 [가슴을 꾸민] / 공적을 [전사임을 보여주는] /

not at *the learning* [that made the perfect tactician], / but at
the real practical force [that brought out great achievement]," /
wrote J. T. Headley.
배움이 아니라 [완벽한 전술가를 만든] / 참되고 실질적인 힘을 [위대한 성취를 이끌어 낸]" /
(~라고) J. T. Headley는 기록했다

5 Napoleon's surest colleagues / had risen from the ranks / or
were plucked from obscurity.
Napoleon의 가장 신뢰할 수 있는 동료들은 / 사병에서 진급했다 / 또는 미천한 신분에서 뽑혔다

6 One was the son of a grocer, another of a mechanic, and so
on.
한 사람은 식료품 장수의 아들이었고, 또 다른 사람은 기계공의 아들 등이었다

7 This gave Napoleon a crucial advantage in battle, //
이것(이렇게 발탁한 것)이 전투에서 Napoleon에게 결정적인 이점을 주었다 //

because his opponents inevitably based their selection
strategies on nobility, // and their armies were led by dukes
and lords / rather than by talented professional soldiers.
그의 적수들은 필연적으로 자신들의 선발 전략을 고귀한 태생에 기반을 두었기 때문이다 //
그리고 그들의 군대는 공작과 영주에 의해 이끌어졌기 (때문이다) / 유능한 전문 병사들이 아니라

오답 확인

② the age of nobility was about to end
귀족의 시대가 막 끝나가고 있었다 → 귀족 신분만으로 등용하지 않을 뿐, 귀족의 시대가 끝나간 것은 아님.
③ a great leader is also a great follower
위대한 리더는 훌륭한 부하이기도 하다
④ a competent strategist is also a strong warrior
유능한 전략가는 강력한 전사이기도 하다
⑤ success depends not only on ability, but also on effort
성공은 능력뿐 아니라 노력에도 달려 있다
*③, ④, ⑤ → 언급되지 않은 내용.

어휘

adorn 꾸미다, 장식하다   **elevate** 등용하다, 승진시키다; (들어) 올리다
exploit 공적, 공훈; 개척[개발]하다; (부당하게) 이용하다
genealogy 혈통, 가계   **lord** 귀족; 영주
noble 신분 높은, 고귀한; 귀족의 *cf.* **nobility** 고귀한 태생, 고귀함; 귀족
obscurity 미천한 신분; 불분명, 흐릿함   **opponent** 적수, 반대자, 상대
pluck 뽑다, 잡아 뜯다; (현악기를) 퉁기다, 뜯다   **stamp** ~임을 보여주다; 도장을 찍다; 짓밟다   **tactician** 전술가, 책략가
[선택지] be no respecter of ~을 가리지[차별하지] 않다

구문 분석

4 He looked / **not** at *the decorations* [that adorned the breast], / **but** at *the exploits* [that stamped the warrior]; / **not** at *the learning* [that made the perfect tactician], / **but** at *the real practical force* ~.
<not A but B(A가 아니라 B)> 구조가 세미콜론(;)으로 병렬 연결됨.

해석 **1** Napoleon Bonaparte의 가장 중요한 통찰 가운데 하나는 <u>재능은 태생을 가리지 않는다</u>는 것이었다. **2** 중류 계급의 자손으로서, 그는 신분 높은 귀족들을 그들의 능력 이상으로 등용하려고 하지 않았다. **3** "Bonaparte는 사람들을 그들의 혈통이 아니라 그들이 무엇을 할 수 있느냐로 판단했다. **4** 그는 가슴을 꾸민 장식물이 아니라 전사임을 보여주는 공적을 보았다, 즉 완벽한 전술가를 만든 배움이 아니라 위대한 성취를 이끌어 낸 참되고 실질적인 힘을 보았다."고 J. T. Headley는 기록했다. **5** Napoleon의 가장 신뢰할 수 있는 동료들은 사병에서 진급했거나, 미천한 신분에서 뽑혔다. **6** 한 사람은 식료품 장수의 아들이었고, 또 다른 사람은 기계공의 아들 등이었다. **7** 이것이 전투에서 Napoleon에게 결정적인 이점을 주었는데, 그의 적수들은 필연적으로 자신들의 선발 전략을 고귀한 태생에 기반을 두었고, 그들의 군대는 유능한 전문 병사들이 아니라 공작과 영주에 의해 이끌어졌기 때문이다.

3 ②

¹In 1978, / economist Richard Easterlin conducted a survey / among adults.
1978년에 / 경제학자인 Richard Easterlin이 조사를 실시했다 / 성인들에게

²He asked them / to pick *items* (from a list) [that they "would like to own,"] / and then, / from that same list, / *items* [(which[that]) they "currently own]."
그는 그들에게 요청했다 / 물품들을 선택하도록 (목록에서) [그들이 '소유하고 싶은'] / 그리고 다음으로 / 그 동일한 목록에서 / 물품들을 (선택하도록) [그들이 '현재 소유하고 있는']

³Sixteen years later, / he corralled the same group / and asked them the same questions / with the same list.
16년 후에 / 그는 동일한 집단을 모았다 / 그리고 그들에게 동일한 질문을 던졌다 / 동일한 목록으로

⁴While nearly everyone had acquired all of the items (on their respective "wish lists)," //
거의 모두가 물품들을 전부 얻었지만 (각자의 '희망 사항 목록'에 있는) //

instead of being satisfied / they chose *new items* (from the list) [which were not desired / during the initial survey].
(그것에) 만족하는 대신 / 그들은 새로운 물품들을 선택했다 (목록에서) [바라지 않았던 / 첫 조사 동안에는]

⁵Termed the "hedonic treadmill," / it has become clear / to economists and "happiness experts" alike // that "more" does not necessitate "better."
'쾌락의 쳇바퀴'라고 불리며 / (~이) 분명해졌다 / 경제학자와 '행복 전문가' 모두에게 // '더 많은 것'이 '더 나은 것'을 수반하지 않는다는 것이

⁶In turn, / this has led to the concern // that a focus on GDP — / (gross domestic product) — / as the primary indicator (of a country's well-being) / has sidetracked us / from what we really want, /
결과적으로 / 이것은 우려로 이어졌다 // GDP에 대한 주목이 / (즉 국내 총생산) / 주요 지표로서의 (한 국가의 안녕에 관한) / 우리로 하여금 벗어나게 했다는 / 우리가 진정으로 원하는 것에서 /

while taxing the environment along the way / in our incessant push to produce.
그 과정에서 환경에 무거운 부담을 지우는 동시에 / 생산하려는 끊임없는 노력을 기울이며

오답 확인

① desires vary as we grow older
우리가 나이가 들면서 욕망이 달라진다 → 나이에 따른 욕망의 변화가 아닌 물질적 욕망이 충족되지 않음을 시사함.

③ happiness is not as "intangible" as we expect
행복은 우리가 예상하는 만큼 '무형의' 것이 아니다

④ the premise of the experiment was erroneous
실험의 전제가 잘못되었다

*③, ④ → 언급되지 않은 내용.

⑤ an economic approach to well-being is desirable
안녕에 대한 경제적 접근이 바람직하다 → 안녕에 대한 물질적 추구가 바람직하지 않다는 글의 내용과 반대됨.

어휘

gross 총, 전체의; 중대한   incessant 끊임없는, 쉴 새 없는
respective 각자의, 각각의   sidetrack (주제에서) 벗어나다; 곁길로 새게 하다; (철도의) 측선   treadmill 쳇바퀴; 트레드밀 ((회전식 벨트 위를 달리는 운동 기구))
[선택지] intangible 무형의; 만질 수 없는   premise (주장의) 전제

구문 분석

⁶In turn, / this has led to **the concern** // **that** a focus on GDP ~ / **while** taxing the environment along the way / in our incessant push to produce.
the concern과 that 이하는 동격 관계이며, while taxing ~ to produce는 의미를 분명히 하기 위해 접속사를 남긴 분사구문임.

해석 ¹1978년에 경제학자인 Richard Easterlin이 성인들에게 조사를 실시했다. ²그는 그들에게 '소유하고 싶은' 물품들을 목록에서 선택한 다음, 그 동일한 목록에서 그들이 '현재 소유하고 있는' 물품들을 선택하도록 요청했다. ³16년 후에 그는 동일한 집단을 모아 동일한 목록으로 동일한 질문을 던졌다. ⁴거의 모두가 각자의 '희망 사항 목록'에 있는 물품들을 전부 얻었지만, (그것에) 만족하는 대신, 그들은 첫 조사 동안에는 원하지 않았던 새로운 물품들을 목록에서 선택했다. ⁵'쾌락의 쳇바퀴'라고 불리며, '더 많은 것'이 '더 나은 것'을 수반하지 않는다는 것이 경제학자와 '행복 전문가' 모두에게 분명해졌다. ⁶결과적으로, 이것은 한 국가의 안녕에 관한 주요 지표로서의 GDP, 즉 국내 총생산에 대한 주목이, 생산하려는 끊임없는 노력을 기울이며 그 과정에서 환경에 무거운 부담을 지우는 동시에, 우리로 하여금 우리가 진정으로 원하는 것에서 벗어나게 했다는 우려로 이어졌다.

4 ④

1 Our tendency (to focus only on outcomes) / narrows our self-image.
우리의 성향은 (오직 결과에만 집중하는) / 우리의 자아상을 협소하게 만든다

2 When we envy other people / for their assets, accomplishments, or characteristics, // it is often because we are making a faulty comparison.
우리가 다른 사람들을 부러워할 때 / 그들의 자산, 성취, 혹은 특징으로 //
그것은 종종 우리가 잘못된 비교를 하고 있기 때문이다

3 We look at the fruits of their efforts / instead of at the efforts themselves.
우리는 그들 노력의 결과를 본다 / 노력 그 자체가 아니라

4 For example, / imagine // that / while talking to a professor in her office, // you hear her use *a word* [that you do not understand].
예를 들어 / 상상해 보라 // ~라고 / 한 교수님의 연구실에서 그녀와 이야기를 나누고 있는 동안 //
당신이 그녀가 단어를 쓰는 것을 듣는다(고) [당신이 이해하지 못하는]

5 You may feel intimidated and stupid.
당신은 자신감을 잃고 바보 같다고 느낄지 모른다

6 Now imagine // that the same professor is sitting at her desk / with an open dictionary.
이제 상상해보라 // 그 교수가 자신의 책상에 앉아 있다고 / 펼쳐진 사전과 함께

7 You would probably conclude // that she knows that unfamiliar word //
당신은 아마도 결론지을 것이다 // 그녀가 그 생소한 단어를 안다고 //
because she spends time / looking up words, / looking for them in *the books* [(which[that]) she reads], / or learning them in some other simple manner.
그녀가 시간을 보내기 때문에 / 단어들을 찾아보는 데 / 책에서 그것(단어)들을 찾는 데 [그녀가 읽는]
/ 혹은 다른 몇 가지 간단한 방식으로 그것들(단어)을 배우는 데

8 You, too, could do this.
당신 역시 이렇게 할 수 있다

9 Focusing on the process, / (on *the steps* [(which[that]) one must take / to develop knowledge and skills]), / will <u>keep us from forming a belittling view of ourselves</u>.
과정에 집중하는 것은 / (즉 단계들에 [반드시 밟아야 하는 /
지식과 기술을 키우기 위해]) / 우리가 우리 자신을 과소평가하는 견해를 형성하는 것을 막아줄 것이다

빈칸 문장 확인하기 ◎

9 지식과 기술을 키우기 위해 필요한 단계들인 과정에 집중하는 것이 '어떠할' 것임.

추론 근거로 정답 찾기 ◎

1 우리가 결과에만 집중하면 자아상이 작아짐.
2, 3 우리는 노력이 아닌 노력의 결과만 보는 잘못된 비교를 하여 다른 사람들을 부러워함.

↓

결과에만 집중하는 성향은 자아상을 협소하게 만들고, 노력이 아닌 노력의 결과만 보고 타인을 부러워하는 것은 잘못된 비교라고 했다. 이어서 자신에게 없는 지식이 타인에게만 있다는 결과만 보면 부정적인 자아를 가질 수 있지만, 그 지식을 얻는 과정을 생각하면 자신도 그렇게 할 수 있다는 결론을 내린다는 것을 예로 든다. 따라서 과정을 봄으로써 자신을 과소평가하는 견해를 형성하는 것을 막을 수 있음을 추론할 수 있다.

→ ④ keep us from forming a belittling view of ourselves(우리가 우리 자신을 과소평가하는 견해를 형성하는 것을 막다)

오답 확인

① help us implement our plans realistically
우리의 계획을 현실적으로 시행하는 데 도움을 주다
② give us the confidence to make the best choice
최선의 선택을 내릴 수 있는 자신감을 우리에게 주다
*①, ② → 관련 없는 내용.
③ be the best place to start if we want a quick result
우리가 빠른 결과를 원한다면 가장 좋은 출발점이 되다 → 빠른 결과는 언급되지 않음.
⑤ allow us to compare our current situation with others'
우리의 현재 상황을 다른 사람들의 현재 상황과 비교하게 하다
→ 과정에 집중하기 때문에 남과 자신을 비교하는 것은 아니므로 틀림.

어휘

asset 자산, 재산   faulty 잘못된; 흠이 있는   fruit 결과, 성과; 열매
intimidated 자신감을 잃은; 겁을 내는
[선택지] belittle 과소평가[경시]하다, 얕보다; 하찮게 만들다
current 현재의; 통용되는; 흐름   implement 시행하다; 도구, 기구

구문 분석

9 Focusing on the process, / ~ will **keep** us **from forming** a belittling view of ourselves.
<keep A from v-ing>: A가 v하는 것을 막다

해석 **1** 오직 결과에만 집중하는 우리의 성향은 우리의 자아상을 협소하게 만든다. **2** 우리가 다른 사람들의 자산, 성취, 혹은 특징으로 그들을 부러워할 때, 그것은 종종 우리가 잘못된 비교를 하고 있기 때문이다. **3** 우리는 노력 그 자체가 아니라 그들 노력의 결과를 본다. **4** 예를 들어, 한 교수님의 연구실에서 그녀와 이야기를 나누고 있는 동안, 그녀가 당신이 이해하지 못하는 단어를 쓰는 것을 듣는다고 상상해 보라. **5** 당신은 자신감을 잃고 바보 같다고 느낄지 모른다. **6** 이제 그 교수가 펼쳐진 사전과 함께 자신의 책상에 앉아 있다고 상상해보라. **7** 당신은 아마도 그녀가 단어들을 찾아보는 데, 그녀가 읽는 책에서 그 단어들을 찾는 데, 혹은 다른 몇 가지 간단한 방식으로 그것들을 배우는 데 시간을 보내기 때문에 그 생소한 단어를 안다고 결론지을 것이다. **8** 당신 역시 이렇게 할 수 있다. **9** 과정에, 즉 지식과 기술을 키우기 위해 밟아야 하는 단계들에 집중하는 것은 <u>우리가 우리 자신을 과소평가하는 견해를 형성하는 것을 막아줄</u> 것이다.

5 ④

¹A social network is *a social structure*, // which is connected by one or more specific types of interdependency, (such as friendship, kinship, common interest, or financial exchange).
소셜 네트워크는 사회 구조이다 // 한 가지 또는 그 이상의 특정 상호 의존 유형에 의해 연결된 (우정, 친족 관계, 공통 관심사 혹은 금전적 거래와 같은)

²Ideas flow and move / within *the social networks* [(which[that]) we create], // and these networks <u>complement and augment individual competence</u>.
생각은 흐르고 움직인다 / 소셜 네트워크 안에서 [우리가 만든] // 그리고 이러한 네트워크는 개인의 능력을 보완하고 증대시킨다

³Similar to *the way* [(that) an ant colony is "intelligent" // even if individual ants are not], / or *the way* [(that) flocks of birds determine where to fly / by combining the desires of each bird], /
방식처럼 [개미 집단은 '똑똑한' // 각각의 개미들이 똑똑하지 않더라도] / 혹은 방식 [새 떼가 어디로 날아갈지 결정하는 / 각각의 새들이 원하는 바를 결합하여] /

social networks can capture and contain *information* [that is transmitted across people and time], / (like oral histories), / and can aggregate millions of decisions / to set market prices or select candidates in an election.
소셜 네트워크는 정보를 포착하여 담을 수 있다 [사람과 시간을 통해 전달되는] / (구술 역사처럼) / 그리고 수백만 개의 결정들을 모을 수 있다 / 시장 가격을 정하거나 선거에서 후보자를 선출하기 위해

⁴The human social network does // what no person could do alone.
인간의 소셜 네트워크는 한다 // 그 누구도 혼자서는 할 수 없는 것을

⁵And / the ability of networks (to create, sustain, and strengthen our collective goals) / helps us to achieve much more /
그리고 / 네트워크의 능력은 (우리의 집단적인 목표를 창조, 유지, 강화하는) / 우리가 훨씬 더 많은 것을 성취하는 데 도움을 준다 /

than the building of towers or the destruction of walls // as the scale of interactions increases.
고층 빌딩을 짓거나 벽을 허무는 것보다 // 상호 작용의 규모가 커지면서

해설

빈칸 문장 확인하기 🔎

² 생각은 소셜 네트워크 안에서 흐르고 움직이며, 이 네트워크는 '어떠함'.

⌄

추론 근거로 정답 찾기 ➕

⁴ 인간은 소셜 네트워크를 통해 혼자서 할 수 없는 것을 함.
⁵ 집단적인 네트워크로 우리는 더 많은 것을 성취함.

↓

소셜 네트워크는 집단적 상호 작용을 통하여 개인적으로는 할 수 없는 일을 가능하게 하고 더 많은 것을 성취하게 한다고 했다. 따라서 소셜 네트워크를 통해 개인의 능력을 보완하고 증대시키는 것이 가능함을 추론할 수 있다.
→ ④ complement and augment individual competence (개인의 능력을 보완하고 증대시키다)

오답 확인

① are revolutionizing how we view our world
우리가 세상을 바라보는 방식에 혁신을 일으키고 있다
② will increase the size of human social groups
인간 사회 집단의 크기를 증가시킬 것이다
*①, ② → 언급되지 않은 내용.
③ have a tendency to intrude on one's privacy
개인의 사생활을 침해하는 경향이 있다
⑤ block face-to-face communication between individuals
개인 간의 면대면 의사소통을 막다
*③, ⑤ → 소셜 네트워크의 부정적 측면이 아닌 긍정적 측면을 다루는 내용이므로 틀림.

어휘

aggregate 모으다, 결집하다; 총계(의)　flock (동물·사람의) 떼, 무리
interdependency 상호 의존　kinship 친족 관계
[선택지] augment 증대시키다, 증가시키다　competence 능력, 역량
complement 보완[보충]하다; 보완[보충]하는 것
intrude 침해[침범]하다; 침입하다　revolutionize 혁신을 일으키다

구문 분석

³Similar to **the way** [**(that)** an ant colony is "intelligent" // even if individual ants are not], / or **the way** [**(that)** flocks of birds determine where to fly / by combining the desires of each bird], / ~.
the way (that)는 '~하는 방식'의 의미로, 관계부사의 역할을 하는 that이 생략됨.

해석 ¹소셜 네트워크는 한 가지 또는 그 이상의 우정, 친족 관계, 공통 관심사 혹은 금전적 거래와 같은 특정 상호 의존 유형에 의해 연결된 사회 구조이다. ²생각은 우리가 만든 소셜 네트워크 안에서 흐르고 움직이며, 이러한 네트워크는 <u>개인의 능력을 보완하고 증대시킨다</u>. ³각각의 개미들이 똑똑하지 않더라도 개미 집단은 '똑똑한' 방식처럼, 또는 새 떼가 각각의 새들이 원하는 바를 결합하여 어디로 날아갈지 결정하는 방식처럼, 소셜 네트워크는 구술 역사처럼 사람과 시간을 통해 전달되는 정보를 포착하여 담을 수 있고, 시장 가격을 정하거나 선거에서 후보자를 선출하기 위해 수백만 개의 결정들을 모을 수 있다. ⁴인간의 소셜 네트워크는 그 누구도 혼자서는 할 수 없는 것을 한다. ⁵그리고 우리의 집단적인 목표를 창조, 유지, 강화하는 네트워크의 능력은 상호 작용의 규모가 커지면서 우리가 고층 빌딩을 짓거나 벽을 허무는 것보다 훨씬 더 많은 것을 성취하는 데 도움을 준다.

1 ①

[1] When reading poems, / in general, / readers feel //
that they must know more about the poets and their times //
than they really have to.
시(詩)를 읽을 때 / 일반적으로 / 독자들은 느낀다 //
그들(독자들)이 시인과 그들이 살았던 시대에 관해 더 많이 알아야 한다고 //
그들(독자들)이 실제로 그래야(알아야) 하는 것보다

[2] We put much faith in commentaries, critiques, biographies — //
but this may be // only because we doubt our own ability to
read.
우리는 주석, 평론, (시인의) 일대기를 대단히 신뢰한다 //
그러나 이는 ~일지도 모른다 // 다만 우리가 우리 자신의 독해 능력을 의심하기 때문

[3] Almost anyone can read any poem, // if he is willing to go to
work on it.
거의 누구든지 어떤 시든 읽을 수 있다 // 그가 기꺼이 그것(시 읽기)을 시작하려 한다면

[4] *Anything* [(that) you discover about a poet's life or times] / is
valid / and may be helpful.
어떤 것이라도 [시인의 삶이나 시대에 관해 당신이 발견하는] / 타당하다 /
그리고 도움이 될지도 모른다

[5] But / a vast knowledge (of the context of a poem) /
is no guarantee // that the poem itself will be understood.
그러나 / 방대한 지식이 (시의 배경에 관한) /
보장하는 건 아니다 // 시 자체가 이해될 것이라는 것을

[6] To be understood, / it must be read over and over with breaks.
(시가) 이해되기 위해서는 / 그것(시)은 잠시 쉬어가며 반복적으로 읽혀야 한다

[7] Reading any great poem is a lifetime job — / not, of course, in
the sense // that it should go on and on throughout a lifetime, //
어떤 위대한 시라도 그것을 읽는 것은 평생의 일이다 / 물론 의미에서가 아니라 //
그것(위대한 시를 읽는 일)이 평생에 걸쳐 계속되어야 한다는 //
but rather (in the sense) that as a great poem, / it deserves
many return visits.
오히려 위대한 시로서 / 그것(위대한 시)이 여러 번 다시 읽힐 가치가 있다는 (의미에서)

[8] We may learn more about a poem // than we realize //
when we are free from it for a while.
우리는 시에 대해 더 많이 배울 수 있을지도 모른다 // 우리가 깨닫는 것보다 //
우리가 그것(시)에서 잠시 벗어나 있을 때

빈칸 문장 확인하기 

> **[6]** 이해되기 위해서, '그것(it)'은 '어떻게 되어야 함.

추론 근거로 정답 찾기 ➕

> **[5]** 시의 배경에 관한 지식이 시에 대한 이해를 보장하진 않음.
> **[7]** 위대한 시는 여러 번 다시 읽힐 가치가 있다는 점에서 그것을 읽는 일은 평생의 일임.
> **[8]** 시를 읽지 않고 있을 때 시에 대해 더 많이 배울 수도 있음.

앞에서 시의 배경에 관한 지식이 이해를 보장하진 않는다고 했으므로, 빈칸 문장의 it은 '시'를 가리킨다. 이어서 시를 읽는 것은 여러 번 다시 읽을 가치가 있는 평생의 일이며, 시에서 잠시 벗어나면 시에 대해 더 배울 수도 있다고 했다. 따라서 시가 이해되기 위해서는 잠시 쉬어가며 반복적으로 읽어야 함을 추론할 수 있다.

→ ① read over and over with breaks(잠시 쉬어가며 반복적으로 읽히다)

오답 확인

② interpreted in a variety of ways
다양한 방식으로 해석되다
③ viewed in a historical context
역사적 맥락에서 바라보아지다 → 방대한 배경지식이 시 이해에 필수적이지 않다는 앞 문장의 내용과 반대됨.
④ appreciated at one sitting
(앉은 자리에서) 단숨에 감상되다 → 쉬어가며 여러 번 감상해야 한다는 글의 요지와 반대됨.
⑤ evaluated from your own perspective
자신만의 관점에서 평가되다
*②, ⑤ → 언급되지 않은 내용.

어휘

biography 일대기, 전기   commentary 주석, 논평
critique 평론, 비평   guarantee 보장(하는 것); 보장[약속]하다
valid 타당한; 유효한
[선택지] appreciate 감상하다; ~의 진가를 인정하다; 감사하다

구문 분석

[7] ~ / **not**, of course, in the sense // that it should go on and
on throughout a lifetime, // **but** rather (in the sense) that
as a great poem, / it deserves many return visits.
<not A but B>: A가 아니라 B인

해석 **[1]** 시(詩)를 읽을 때, 일반적으로 독자들은 시인과 그들이 살았던 시대에 관해 실제로 알아야 하는 것보다 더 많이 알아야 한다고 느낀다. **[2]** 우리는 주석, 평론, (시인의) 일대기를 대단히 신뢰하지만, 이는 다만 우리가 우리 자신의 독해 능력을 의심하기 때문일지도 모른다. **[3]** 거의 누구든지 기꺼이 시 읽기를 시작하려 한다면, 어떤 시든 읽을 수 있다. **[4]** 시인의 삶이나 시대에 관해 당신이 발견하는 어떤 것이라도 타당하며 도움이 될지도 모른다. **[5]** 그러나 시의 배경에 관한 방대한 지식이 시 자체가 이해될 것이라는 것을 보장하는 건 아니다. **[6]** (시가) 이해되기 위해서는 시는 잠시 쉬어가며 반복적으로 읽혀야 한다. **[7]** 어떤 위대한 시라도 그것을 읽는 것은 평생의 일인데, 물론 그것(위대한 시를 읽는 일)이 평생에 걸쳐 계속되어야 한다는 의미에서가 아니라, 오히려 위대한 시로서 그것(위대한 시)이 여러 번 다시 읽힐 가치가 있다는 의미에서다. **[8]** 우리가 시에서 잠시 벗어나 있을 때, 우리는 우리가 깨닫는 것보다 그것에 대해 더 많이 배울 수 있을지도 모른다.

2 ③

¹ *People* [who support the "law of averages"] / buy lottery tickets over and over //

사람들은 ['평균의 법칙'을 지지하는] / 계속해서 복권을 구매한다 //

because they mistakenly believe // that something is more likely to occur in the future // because it hasn't occurred yet.

그들이 잘못 믿고 있기 때문에 // 무언가가 미래에 일어날 가능성이 더 높다고 // 그것이 아직 일어나지 않았으므로

² The attraction of this law / is due in part to its similarity to a genuine statistical law — / the law of large numbers.

이 법칙이 가진 매력적 요소는 / 부분적으로 이것의 실제 통계 법칙과의 유사성에 기인한다 / 즉 대수(大數)의 법칙

³ According to this, / if you toss an unbiased coin a small number of times, / (say 10 times), // the occurrence of heads may deviate considerably from *the mean* (average), // which is 5; //

이것(이 법칙)에 따르면 / 여러분이 공평한 동전을 적은 횟수로 던지면 / (예컨대 열 번) // 동전의 앞면이 나타나는 것은 평균에서 상당히 벗어날 수도 있다 // 그리고 그것은 다섯 번이다 //

but if you toss it a large number of times — / (say 1000 times) — // the occurrence of heads is likely to be much closer to the mean (500).

그러나 만약 여러분이 그것(동전)을 아주 많이 던진다면 / (예컨대 천 번) // 앞면이 나타나는 것은 평균(오백 번)에 훨씬 더 근접해질 가능성이 높다

⁴ So, / in a series of random events (of equal probability), / it is true // that things will even themselves out // if the series is extended far enough.

그러므로 / 일련의 임의적 사건들에서 (동일한 확률을 지닌) / (~은) 진실이다 // 상황이 그 스스로를 균등하게 나눌 것이라는 것은 // 연속적 사건이 매우 충분히 연장된다면

⁵ However, / this statistical law has no bearing on the probability (of any single event occurring); //

그러나 / 이 통계 법칙은 확률과 관련이 없다 (어떤 단일 사건이 일어나는 것의) //

in particular, / a current event has no recollection (of any previous deviation from the mean) / and cannot <u>alter its outcome</u> / to correct an earlier imbalance.

특히 / 현재 일어나는 사건은 기억하지 못한다 (이전 평균에서의 어떤 편차도) / 그리고 그것의 결과를 바꿀 수 없다 / 이전의 불균형을 바로잡기 위해

⁶ So / there is no comfort here / for the habitual lottery ticket buyer.

그러므로 / 여기에 위안은 존재하지 않는다 / 습관적 복권 구매자를 위한

해설

빈칸 문장 확인하기 

5 그러나 '이 통계 법칙(this statistical law)'은 단일 사건이 일어날 확률과는 관련이 없으며, 특히 현재 일어나는 사건은 이전의 평균 편차를 기억하지 못하고 '무엇을 할' 수 없음.

추론 근거로 정답 찾기

1 평균의 법칙을 지지하는 사람들은 아직 일어나지 않은 일이 미래에 일어날 가능성이 더 높다고 잘못 믿어 계속 복권을 삼.
6 습관적 복권 구매자를 위한 위안은 없음.

확률이 같은 임의적 사건들이 많이 반복되면 결과가 평균에 근접해진다는 통계 법칙은 단일 사건이 발생하는 확률과는 관련이 없다고 했다. 즉, 복권을 계속 사더라도 이전에 당첨되지 않았다는 사실이 그 다음 결과에 영향을 미치지 않음을 추론할 수 있다.
*빈칸 앞에 부정어 cannot이 있어 빈칸 내용을 부정하는 의미가 됨에 주의한다.

→ ③ alter its outcome to correct an earlier imbalance
(이전의 불균형을 바로잡기 위해 그것의 결과를 바꾸다)

오답 확인

① increase your wealth if you're fortunate
당신이 운이 좋다면 부(富)를 증대하다 → 글의 내용과 반대됨.
② tell us anything about the ideal number of trials
시도의 이상적인 횟수에 대해 우리에게 무엇이든 말하다 → 이상적 시도 횟수에 대한 내용은 없음.
④ serve as motivation for choosing which bet to place
어떤 내기를 할지 고르는 동기로서 기능하다
⑤ help us to calculate the standard deviation
우리가 표준 편차를 계산하는 데 도움을 주다
*④, ⑤ → 관련 없는 내용.

어휘

deviation 편차; 일탈   even out 균등하게 나누다; 안정되다
have no bearing on ~와 관련이 없다   recollection 기억(력)
statistical 통계(학)의, 통계(학)적인

구문 분석

¹ ~ **because** they mistakenly believe // that something is more likely to occur in the future // **because** it hasn't occurred yet.
because가 이끄는 부사절 내의 목적어인 that절에 또 다른 because절이 삽입됨.

해석 **¹** '평균의 법칙'을 지지하는 사람들은, 무언가가 아직 일어나지 않았으므로 그것이 미래에 일어날 가능성이 더 높다고 잘못 믿고 있기 때문에 계속해서 복권을 구매한다. **²** 이 법칙이 가진 매력적 요소는 부분적으로 이것의 실제 통계 법칙, 즉 대수(大數)의 법칙과의 유사성에 기인한다. **³** 이 법칙에 따르면, 여러분이 공평한(앞면이나 뒷면으로 치우치지 않은) 동전을 적은 횟수로, 예컨대 열 번 던지면, 동전의 앞면이 나타나는 것은 평균인 다섯 번에서 상당히 벗어날 수도 있으나, 만약 여러분이 그것을 아주 많이, 예컨대 천 번 던진다면, 앞면이 나타나는 것은 평균(오백 번)에 훨씬 더 근접해질 가능성이 높다. **⁴** 그러므로 동일한 확률을 지닌 일련의 임의적 사건들에서, 연속적 사건이 매우 충분히 연장된다면, 상황이 그 스스로를 균등하게 나눌 것이라는 것은 진실이다. **⁵** 그러나 이 통계 법칙은 어떤 단일 사건이 일어나는 것의 확률과 관련이 없는데, 특히 현재 일어나는 사건은 이전 평균에서의 어떤 편차도 기억하지 못하고, <u>이전의 불균형을 바로잡기 위해 그것의 결과를 바꿀</u> 수 없다. **⁶** 그러므로 여기에 습관적 복권 구매자를 위한 위안은 존재하지 않는다.

3 ②

¹To live means to experience — / through doing, feeling, thinking.
산다는 것은 경험함을 의미한다 / 행동하고, 느끼고, 생각함으로써

²Experience takes place in time, // so time is *the ultimate scarce resource* [(which[that]) we have].
경험이란 시간 속에서 일어난다 // 따라서 시간은 궁극적인 진귀한 자원이다 [우리가 가진]

³The content (of our experience) / determines our quality of life, // and beyond the unavoidable demands of daily life, /
내용이 (우리가 경험하는) / 우리의 삶의 질을 결정한다 // 그리고 일상생활에서 불가피하게 요구되는 것 이상으로 /

there is still room for *personal choice* [that makes control over time, / (to a certain extent), / in our hands].
개인의 선택권에 대한 여지는 여전히 존재한다 [시간을 통제하는 / (어느 정도) / 우리 손으로]

⁴Of course, / it is not our decision alone to make — // stringent constraints dictate // what we should do, /
물론 / 그것은 우리가 홀로 내리는 결정은 아니다 // 즉 엄중한 제한이 좌우한다 // 우리가 무엇을 해야 하는지를 /

not only as members of the human race / but also as members of a certain society and culture.
인류의 구성원으로서뿐만 아니라 / 특정 사회와 문화의 구성원으로서

⁵However, / as the historian E. P. Thompson noted, //
그러나 / 역사학자인 E. P. Thompson이 언급했듯이 //

even in *the most oppressive decades of the Industrial Revolution*, // when workers slaved away / for more than eighty hours a week / in mines and factories, //
산업혁명기의 가장 억압적인 수십 년 동안에도 //
노동자들이 노예처럼 일했던 / 일주일에 80시간 넘게 / 광산과 공장에서 //

there were *some* [who spent their few precious free hours / in literary pursuits or political action / instead of following the majority into the pubs].
일부가 있었다 [자신의 얼마 안 되는 소중한 자유 시간을 쓴 / 문학적 취미나 정치적 행동에 / 대다수를 따라 술집에 가는 대신]

⁶To make a long story short, / one of the most essential decisions in life is / about how we <u>allocate or invest our time</u>.
한마디로 말해 / 인생에서 가장 중요한 결정들 가운데 하나는 ~이다 / 우리가 어떻게 우리의 시간을 할당하거나 투자할 것인가에 관한 것

해설

빈칸 문장 확인하기 

> **6** 한마디로 말해, 인생에서 가장 중요한 결정들 가운데 하나는 우리가 어떻게 '무엇을 할' 것인가에 관한 것임.

추론 근거로 정답 찾기 ⊕

> **2** 시간 속에서 경험이 발생하므로 시간은 귀중한 자원임.
> **3** 경험이 삶의 질을 결정하는데, 개인은 어느 정도 스스로 시간을 통제할 수 있음.
> **5** 억압적인 시대에도 적은 자유 시간을 타인을 따르기보다 자신의 의지에 따라 쓰는 사람들이 있었음.

빈칸 문장 바로 앞에서는 얼마 없는 자유 시간을 자신의 관심사에 쓴 사람들의 예를 들었고, 앞에서부터 살펴보면 경험이 있게 하는 귀중한 시간을 개인이 어느 정도 통제할 수 있다고 했다. 따라서 시간을 어떻게 나누어 쓸 것인지가 중요한 결정임을 추론할 수 있다.
→ ② allocate or invest our time(우리의 시간을 할당하거나 투자하다)

오답 확인

① try to attain wealth and honor
부와 명예를 얻기 위해 노력하다
③ find our true career
우리의 진정한 직업을 찾다
④ behave as members of society
사회 구성원으로서 행동하다 → members of a certain society를 활용한 오답. 사회 구성원으로서 제한은 있지만 개인이 시간을 어떻게 할당할지가 중요한 결정이라는 내용임.
⑤ bear the difficulties of life
인생의 어려움을 견디다
*①, ③, ⑤ → 관련 없는 내용.

어휘

constraint 제한, 제약   dictate 좌우하다, 영향을 주다; 지시하다
oppressive 억압적인, 탄압하는; 답답한   pursuit 취미, 소일거리; 추구
scarce 진귀한; 드문   slave away 노예처럼 일하다   stringent 엄중한; 긴박한, 절박한
[선택지] allocate 할당하다; 배분하다   attain (명성·성공을) 얻다; 달성하다

구문 분석

⁴~ / **not only** as members of the human race / **but also** as members of a certain society and culture.
<not only A but also B>: A뿐만 아니라 B도

해석 ¹산다는 것은 행동하고, 느끼고, 생각함으로써 경험함을 의미한다. ²경험이란 시간 속에서 일어나고, 따라서 시간은 우리가 가진 궁극적인 진귀한 자원이다. ³우리가 경험하는 내용이 우리의 삶의 질을 결정하며, 일상생활에서 불가피하게 요구되는 것 이상으로, 우리 손으로 어느 정도 시간을 통제하는 개인의 선택권에 대한 여지는 여전히 존재한다. ⁴물론, 그것은 우리가 홀로 내리는 결정은 아닌데, 즉 인류의 구성원으로서뿐만 아니라 특정 사회와 문화의 구성원으로서 우리가 무엇을 해야 하는지를 엄중한 제한이 좌우한다. ⁵그러나 역사학자인 E. P. Thompson이 언급했듯이, 노동자들이 일주일에 80시간 넘게 광산과 공장에서 노예처럼 일했던 산업혁명기의 가장 억압적인 수십 년 동안에도, 대다수를 따라 술집에 가는 대신 자신의 얼마 안 되는 소중한 자유 시간을 문학적 취미나 정치적 행동에 쓴 일부가 있었다. ⁶한마디로 말해, 인생에서 가장 중요한 결정들 가운데 하나는 우리가 어떻게 우리의 시간을 할당하거나 투자할 것인가에 관한 것이다.

4 ④

[1] Color is a ubiquitous feature of the environment, // though we rarely notice colors //

색채는 주위 어디에나 있는 특성이다 // 우리가 색채를 주목하는 일이 드물긴 해도 //

unless they're particularly bright or deviate dramatically from our expectations.

그것들(색채)이 특히 밝거나 우리의 예상에서 극적으로 벗어날 때 외에는

[2] Nonetheless, / they can shape a range of outcomes: //

그렇지만 / 그것들(색채)은 다양한 결과를 만들어 낼 수 있다 //

A recent study (conducted by University of Rochester psychologists Andrew Elliott and Daniela Niesta), / for example, / showed //

최근의 연구는 (로체스터 대학교의 심리학자인 Andrew Elliott과 Daniela Niesta에 의해 수행된) / 예를 들어 / 보여주었다 //

that men are slightly more attractive to women // when they wear red shirts / rather than shirts of another color.

남성이 여성에게 조금 더 매력적이라는 것을 // 그들이 붉은 셔츠를 입고 있을 때 / 다른 색상의 셔츠보다는

[3] The same effect applies to *women*, // who seem more attractive to men // when their pictures are bordered in red.

여성에게도 같은 효과가 적용된다 // 그리고 그들(여성)은 남성에게 더 매력적으로 보인다 // 그들의 사진에 붉은색으로 테가 둘러졌을 때

[4] Red signals both romantic intent and dominance / among lower-order species, // and this applies to both males and females.

붉은색은 구애의 의지와 우위 둘 다를 나타낸다 / 하등 종(種) 사이에서는 // 그리고 이것은 수컷과 암컷 모두에 적용된다

[5] This relationship (between red and dominance) / explains findings (by the evolutionary anthropologists Russell Hill and Robert Barton of the University of Durham) //

이러한 관계는 (붉은색과 우월함 사이의) / 연구 결과를 설명해준다 (더럼 대학교의 진화 인류학자 Russell Hill과 Robert Barton의) //

that, / "across a range of sports," / *contestants* [who wear red] / tend to outperform *those* (wearing other colors).

~라는 / '다양한 운동 경기 전반에서' / 참가자들이 [붉은 옷을 입은] / (~한) 사람들(참가자들)보다 더 좋은 결과를 내는 경향이 있다(는) (다른 색의 옷을 입은)

해설

빈칸 문장 확인하기 ✐

[5] 붉은색과 우월함 사이의 '이러한 관계(This relationship)'는 다양한 운동 경기 전반에서 붉은 옷을 입은 참가자들이 '어떤' 경향이 있다는 연구 결과를 설명해 줌.

추론 근거로 정답 찾기 ✚

[2], [3] 사람은 붉은색 옷을 입거나 붉은색 테두리 속 사진에 있을 때 더 매력적으로 보임.
[4] 하등 종은 붉은색으로 구애 의지와 우위를 나타냄.

↓

앞에서 붉은색과 우월함의 관계를 여러 예를 통해 보여주었다. 이를 빈칸 문장에서 This relationship으로 받고 있으므로 경기에서도 붉은색 옷이 가져오는 긍정적인 효과, 즉 붉은 옷을 입은 이들이 다른 색 옷을 입은 참가자보다 좋은 결과를 내는 효과가 있을 것임을 추론할 수 있다.

→ ④ outperform those wearing other colors(다른 색의 옷을 입은 참가자들보다 더 좋은 결과를 내다)

오답 확인

① account for less than half of competitors
참가자의 절반 미만을 차지하다
② suffer from careless mistakes and inattention
부주의한 실수와 태만함으로 고통을 받다
*①, ② → 언급되지 않은 내용.
③ bring out the competitiveness in others
다른 사람들의 경쟁력을 끌어내다 → 붉은 색 옷을 입은 사람들이 더 좋은 결과를 냈다는 글의 내용과 반대됨.
⑤ play aggressively and disregard rules
공격적으로 경기하고 규칙을 무시하다 → 붉은색의 긍정적 영향이라고 볼 수 없음.

어휘

anthropologist 인류학자   border 테를 두르다; 가장자리; 국경, 경계
contestant (경기의) 참가자, 경쟁자   deviate (일상·예상 등을) 벗어나다
dominance 우위, 우월; 지배   intent 의지; 의도; 몰두[열중]하는
signal 나타내다, 표시하다; 신호(하다)   ubiquitous 어디에나 있는, 아주 흔한
[선택지] account for (부분·비율을) 차지하다; ~을 설명하다
disregard 무시(하다)   inattention 태만, 무관심

구문 분석

[5] This relationship ~ / explains **findings** ~ // **that**, / "across a range of sports," / *contestants* [who wear red] / tend to ~.
findings와 that 이하의 절은 동격 관계임.

해석 [1] 특히 밝거나 우리의 예상에서 극적으로 벗어날 때 외에는 주목받는 일이 드물긴 해도, 색채는 주위 어디에나 있는 특성이다. [2] 그렇지만 색채는 다양한 결과를 만들어 낼 수 있다. 예를 들어, 로체스터 대학교의 심리학자인 Andrew Elliott과 Daniela Niesta에 의해 수행된 최근의 연구는 남성이 다른 색상의 셔츠보다는 붉은 셔츠를 입고 있을 때 여성에게 조금 더 매력적이라는 것을 보여주었다. [3] 여성에게도 같은 효과가 적용되는데, 그들의 사진에 붉은색으로 테가 둘러졌을 때 여성은 남성에게 더 매력적으로 보인다. [4] 붉은색은 하등 종(種) 사이에서는 구애의 의지와 우위 둘 다를 나타내고, 이것은 수컷과 암컷 모두에 적용된다. [5] 붉은색과 우월함 사이의 이러한 관계는 '다양한 운동 경기 전반에서' 붉은 옷을 입은 참가자들이 다른 색의 옷을 입은 참가자들보다 더 좋은 결과를 내는 경향이 있다는, 더럼 대학교의 진화 인류학자 Russell Hill과 Robert Barton의 연구 결과를 설명해준다.

5 ④

[1] The great paradox of capitalism is // that destruction brings creation.

자본주의의 커다란 역설은 ~이다 // 파괴가 창조를 불러온다는 것

[2] *Companies* (trying to put each other out of business) / in fact / put many more businesses into existence and people into jobs, //

기업들은 (서로 파산하게 하려고 노력하는) / 사실상 /
더 많은 사업체가 생겨나게 하고 있으며 (더 많은) 사람들을 일하게 하고 있다 //

as they strive / for better technology, more efficient ways of operating, smarter ways (of pricing their product) — / for *anything* [that will win them more customers and give them an edge over the competition].

애를 쓰면서 / 더 나은 기술, 더 효과적인 운영 방식, 더 똑똑한 방법을 위해 (자신들의 제품에 가격을 매기는) / 즉 어떤 것을 위해서든 [더 많은 고객을 확보하고 경쟁사에 대한 우위를 갖게 하는]

[3] But / this only works // if certain rules of the game are observed.

그러나 / 이것(파괴가 창조를 불러온다는 것)은 오직 효과가 있다 // 그 게임의 특정한 규칙들이 지켜지는 경우에만

[4] Consumers do not benefit // when companies are free to do // whatever they want / to get a competitive edge.

소비자는 이익을 얻지 못한다 // 기업들이 자유롭게 할 때 //
자신들이 하고 싶은 무엇이든 / 경쟁 우위를 확보하기 위해

[5] Competition has to be based on agreed norms and within set boundaries, / rather than on aiming to win at any cost.

경쟁은 합의된 규범에 기초해 정해진 한도 내에 있어야 한다 /
어떤 대가를 치르고라도 이기는 것을 목표로 하기보다는

[6] The quality of football would not improve // if teams could use *any means* (necessary to score a goal).

풋볼의 질은 향상되지 않을 것이다 // 풋볼팀들이 어떠한 수단이라도 사용할 수 있다면 (골을 득점하는 데 필요한)

[7] Similarly, / capitalism produces benefits // when there is fair competition (over products and pricing), / within the law // so that the most efficient business wins.

마찬가지로 / 자본주의는 이윤을 낸다 // 공정한 경쟁이 있을 때 (제품과 가격 책정에 대한) / 법 테두리 안에서 // 그 결과 가장 효율적인 기업이 승리하게 된다

해설

빈칸 문장 확인하기 

3 그러나 '이것(this)'은 오직 '어떤' 경우에만 효과가 있음.

추론 근거로 정답 찾기 ➕

1 파괴가 창조를 불러온다는 것이 자본주의의 역설임.

4 기업들이 경쟁 우위를 위해 무엇이든 할 때 소비자는 이익을 얻지 못함.

5 경쟁은 합의된 규범에 따라서만 행해져야 함.

7 법 테두리 안에서 공정한 경쟁이 이루어져야 함.

앞에서 자본주의의 역설이 파괴가 창조를 불러온다는 것이라고 설명했으므로, 빈칸 문장의 this가 가리키는 것은 이 역설의 내용이다. 이어서 뒤에서는 기업의 자유로운 경쟁 행위는 소비자에게 이익이 되지 못하며, 경쟁은 합의된 규범과 정해진 한도 내에 있어야 한다고 했다. 따라서 자본주의에서 파괴가 창조를 불러오려면 경쟁의 규칙이 지켜져야 함을 추론할 수 있다.

→ ④ certain rules of the game are observed(그 게임의 특정한 규칙들이 지켜지다)

오답 확인

① consumers support the competition
소비자들이 경쟁을 지지하다

② the goal of the business is obvious
사업의 목표가 분명하다

③ companies have better technical competency
기업들이 더 나은 기술력을 갖다 → 기업들이 더 나은 기술을 위해 애쓴다고는 했으나 이는 기업이 경쟁하는 사례로서 제시되었을 뿐, 파괴가 창조를 불러오는 조건과는 관련이 없음.

⑤ we understand the dark side of capitalism
우리가 자본주의의 어두운 면을 이해하다

*①, ②, ⑤ → 언급되지 않은 내용.

어휘

boundary 한도, 한계; 경계(선)　capitalism 자본주의 (체제)
edge 우위, 우세; 가장자리, 날　norm 규범; 표준
out of business 파산하여, 폐업하여　strive 애쓰다, 노력하다, 힘쓰다
[선택지] competency 능력; 적성　observe (규칙 등을) 지키다, 준수하다

구문 분석

[7] ~ // **so that** the most efficient business wins.
<~(,) so (that)>: (그 결과) ~하다

해석 **[1]** 자본주의의 커다란 역설은, 파괴가 창조를 불러온다는 것이다. **[2]** 더 나은 기술, 더 효과적인 운영 방식, 자신들의 제품에 가격을 매기는 더 똑똑한 방법, 즉, 더 많은 고객을 확보하고 경쟁사에 대한 우위를 갖게 하는 어떤 것을 위해서든 애를 쓰면서 서로 파산하게 하려고 노력하는 기업들은 사실상 더 많은 사업체가 생겨나게 하고 있으며 (더 많은) 사람들을 일하게 하고 있다. **[3]** 그러나 이것(파괴가 창조를 불러온다는 것)은 오직 그 게임의 특정한 규칙들이 지켜지는 경우에만 효과가 있다. **[4]** 기업들이 경쟁 우위를 확보하기 위해 자신들이 하고 싶은 무엇이든 자유롭게 할 때 소비자는 이익을 얻지 못한다. **[5]** 경쟁은 어떤 대가를 치르고라도 이기는 것을 목표로 하기보다는, 합의된 규범에 기초해 정해진 한도 내에 있어야 한다. **[6]** 풋볼팀들이 골을 득점하는 데 필요한 어떠한 수단이라도 사용할 수 있다면 풋볼의 질은 향상되지 않을 것이다. **[7]** 마찬가지로, 자본주의도 법 테두리 안에서 제품과 가격 책정에 대한 공정한 경쟁이 있을 때 이윤을 내고, 결과적으로 가장 효율적인 기업이 승리하게 된다.

---

¹Norms emerge in groups / as a result of people conforming / to the behavior of others.
규범은 집단에서 생긴다 / 사람들이 순응하는 것의 결과로 / 다른 사람들의 행동에

²Thus, / the start of a norm occurs // when one person acts / in a particular manner / in a particular situation // because she thinks // (that) she ought to.
따라서 / 규범의 시작은 발생한다 // 어느 한 사람이 행동할 때 /
특정 방식으로 / 특정 상황에서 / 그 사람이 생각해서 // 자신이 그래야 한다고

↓

(C) ³Others may then conform / to this behavior / for a number of reasons.
그런 다음 다른 사람들은 순응할 수도 있다 / 이 행동에 / 여러 가지 이유로

⁴*The person* [who performed the initial action] / may think // that others ought to behave // as she behaves / in situations of this sort.
사람은 [최초의 행동을 한] / 생각할 수도 있다 //
다른 사람들이 행동해야 한다고 // 자신이 행동하는 대로 / 이러한 종류의 상황에서

↓

(A) ⁵Thus, / she may prescribe the behavior / to them / by uttering the norm statement / in a prescriptive manner.
따라서 / 그 (최초의 행동을 한) 사람은 그 행동을 지시할 수도 있다 / 그들에게 /
규범 진술을 말함으로써 / 지시하는 방식으로

⁶Alternately, / she may communicate // that conformity is desired / in other ways, / such as by gesturing.
다른 방식으로 / 그 사람은 전달할 수도 있다 // 순응이 요구된다는 것을 / 다른 방식으로 / 몸짓과 같은

⁷In addition, / she may threaten to sanction them / for not behaving // as she wishes.
게다가 / 그 사람은 그들에게 제재를 가하겠다고 위협할 수도 있다 /
행동하지 않은 것에 대해 // 자신이 원하는 대로

⁸This will cause some / to conform to her wishes / and act // as she acts.
이것은 일부 사람들이 (~하게) 할 것이다 / 그 사람의 바람에 순응하게 / 그리고 행동하게 //
그 사람이 행동하는 대로

↓

(B) ⁹But / some others will not need / to have the behavior prescribed / to them.
그러나 / 다른 일부 사람들은 필요가 없을 것이다 / 그 행동이 지시되게 할 / 자신에게

¹⁰They will observe / the regularity of behavior / and decide on their own // that they ought to conform.
그들은 관찰할 것이다 / 행동의 규칙성을 / 그리고 스스로 결정할 것이다 // 자신이 순응해야 한다고

¹¹They may do so / for either rational or moral reasons.
그들은 그렇게 할 수도 있다 / 합리적 또는 도덕적 이유로

해설

주어진 글의 내용 파악하기 ⑫

규범은 집단에서 다른 사람들의 행동을 따르는 결과로 생기며 규범의 시작은 어느 한 사람이 당위성을 갖고 특정 상황에 특정 방식으로 행동할 때 발생함.
(뒤에서는 규범의 발생 과정 중 이 시작 이후를 서술할 것을 예측할 수 있음.)

⋙

단서로 정답 찾기 ⊕

(C) this behavior는 주어진 글에서 언급한 '어느 한 사람의 행동(one person acts ~ situation)'을 받는다.(▶ **Point 1 지시사/대명사**) then(그런 다음)으로 그 '어느 한 사람(one person)'의 행동 이후에(▶ **Point 2 기타 연결어**) '다른 사람들(Others)'이 그 행동에 여러 이유로 순응할 수도 있다는 내용이 이어진다.(▶ **Point 1 지시사/대명사**)

↓

(A) them은 (C) 마지막 문장에서 언급한 '다른 사람들(others)'을 받으며(▶ **Point 1 지시사/대명사**), 최초의 행동을 한 사람이 자신의 생각에 따라 그들에게 '그 행동(the behavior)'을 지시할 수 있다는 결과가 Thus(따라서)로 이어진다.(▶ **Point 1 정관사 the, Point 2 결과 연결어**) 이어서 말, 몸짓, 위협으로 행동을 따를 것을 지시해서 '일부 사람들(some)'이 순응한다고 설명한다.

(B) But(그러나)으로 (A)에서 언급된 지시가 필요 없는 '다른 일부 사람들(some others)'의 상반되는 경우가 이어져(▶ **Point 2 역접 연결어, Point 1 지시사/대명사**), 스스로 순응하기로 결정하는 다른 사람들도 있다고 덧붙이며 글을 맺는다.

어휘

alternately 다른 방식으로; 번갈아　**conform** 순응하다, 따르다; (~에) 일치하다 *cf.* **conformity** 순응, 따름　**emerge** 생기다; 나오다, 나타나다　**norm** 규범; 표준; 기준　**prescribe** 지시하다; 규정하다; 처방을 내리다 *cf.* **prescriptive** 지시하는; 규범적인　**rational** 합리적인, 이성적인　**statement** 진술(서), 성명(서)　**utter** 말하다, 발언하다; 완전한

구문 분석

⁹But / some others will not need / to **have** the behavior **prescribed** / to them.
<사역동사 have+O+p.p.>: O가 ~되도록 하다

해석 ¹규범은 집단에서 사람들이 다른 사람들의 행동에 순응하는 것의 결과로 생긴다. ²따라서 규범의 시작은 어느 한 사람이 자신이 그래야 한다고 생각해서 특정 상황에서 특정 방식으로 행동할 때 발생한다. (C) ³그런 다음 다른 사람들은 여러 가지 이유로 이 행동에 순응할 수도 있다. ⁴최초의 행동을 한 사람은 다른 사람들이 이러한 종류의 상황에서 자신이 행동하는 대로 행동해야 한다고 생각할 수도 있다. (A) ⁵따라서 그 사람은 지시하는 방식으로 규범 진술을 말함으로써 그들에게 그 행동을 지시할 수도 있다. ⁶다른 방식으로, 그 사람은 몸짓과 같은 다른 방식으로 순응이 요구된다는 것을 전달할 수도 있다. ⁷게다가 그 사람은 자신이 원하는 대로 행동하지 않은 것에 대해 그들에게 제재를 가하겠다고 위협할 수도 있다. ⁸이것은 일부 사람들이 그 사람의 바람에 순응하고 그 사람이 행동하는 대로 행동하게 할 것이다. (B) ⁹그러나 다른 일부 사람들은 그 행동이 자신에게 지시되게 할 필요가 없을 것이다. ¹⁰그들은 행동의 규칙성을 관찰하고 자신이 순응해야 한다고 스스로 결정할 것이다. ¹¹그들은 합리적 또는 도덕적 이유로 그렇게 할 수도 있다.

Zoom 1

해석 악보 표기법은 음악의 확장되는 연주곡목을 보존하기 위한 실용적인 방법 이상이었다.
•practical 실용적인; 현실적인   preserve 보존하다; 지키다   expand 확장되다; 확장하다
➜ 그것(악보 표기법)은 예술 그 자체의 본성을 바꾸었다. 무언가를 써 내려가는 것은 의미한다.... •nature 본성, 천성; 자연

Zoom 2

해석 여러분의 가족과 친구들에게 당신이 열정에 어떻게 영감을 받고 그것이 여러분뿐만 아니라 다른 사람들에게도 어떻게 변화를 주는지에 대한 이야기들을 들려줘라.
•inspire 영감을 주다; 고무[격려]하다   passion 열정, 정열; 강렬한 감정
➜ 이 이야기들(당신이 열정에 어떻게 영감을 받고 그것이 여러분뿐만 아니라 다른 사람들에게도 어떻게 변화를 주는지에 대한 이야기들)은 여러분이 열정을 따라야만 한다는 것을 그들이 깨닫게 할 것이다.

함정 주의 ①

해석 야생에서의 식사는 두 가지의 극단적인 것이 있는데, 그것은 미식가와 생존을 위해 먹는 사람이다. 첫 번째는 케이크와 빵을 굽고 여러 단계의 코스 저녁 식사를 요리한다.
•wilderness 야생, 황야   extreme 극단적인 것; 극단; 극도의   gourmet 미식가
(A) 그들은 매일 단지 몇 마일만 걸으며 며칠 밤 동안 같은 야영장을 사용할 수도 있다. 생존을 위해 먹는 사람들은 잠에서 깨고 곧 일어나서 걷는다.
•campsite 야영장, 야영지; 캠프장
(B) 그들은 매일 수십 마일을 걸으며, 점심은 이동하면서 먹는 일련의 데워 먹지 않는 간식으로 이루어진다. •dozens of 수십의, 많은
해설 주어진 글은 야생에서의 식사가 미식가와 생존을 위해 먹는 사람으로 나뉜다고 하며, 그중 미식가에 대해 먼저 설명한다. (A), (B) 모두 They로 시작하고 있으므로, 어느 것이 미식가에 대한 설명에 자연스럽게 이어질지를 찾는다. (A)는 이동을 적게 하는 사람들(미식가들을 지칭하는 것을 알 수 있다. 주어진 글에서 언급된 식사를 하려면 이동을 많이 할 수 없을 것이기 때문이다.)에 대한 것이고, 뒤이어 생존을 위해 먹는 사람들에 대한 설명이 이어진다. (B)는 이동을 많이 하고 데워 먹지 않는 간식을 점심으로 먹는 사람들에 대한 내용이므로 (A)에서 언급한 생존을 위해 먹는 사람들에 대한 설명이 이어지는 것임을 알 수 있다. 따라서 적절한 순서는 (A) — (B)이다.

Zoom 3

해석 제품을 개발하고 출시하는 것은 시간이 걸린다. 결과적으로, 많은 회사들은 자신들이 신제품을 출시할 것을 6~12개월 먼저 안다.
•launch 출시하다; 착수하다
➜ 그 제품(신제품)에 대한 관심을 불러일으키기 위해 회사들은 흔히 출시 전 광고 캠페인에 착수하곤 한다.

Zoom 4

해석 영화는 또한 우리가 결국 만족스럽다고 느끼는 이야기를 한다. (영화의 이야기 속에서) 나쁜 사람들은 보통 벌을 받고, 낭만적인 커플은 장애물에도 불구하고 거의 항상 서로를 만나게 된다.... •obstacle 장애(물)

Zoom 5

해석 오늘날 예술가라는 용어는 과거와 현재 모두의 전 세계의 폭넓은 범위의 창의적인 개인들을 지칭하는 데 사용된다....
•term 용어; 기간; 학기   range 범위, 폭
➜ 그것(예술가라는 용어)이 적용되는 다양성과는 대조적으로, 이 용어의 의미는 대체로 서양의 관점과 가치관에 계속해서 기반을 두고 있다.
•diversity 다양성

Focus & Practice   p.50

1 ②   **2** ①   **3** ①   **4** ①   **5** ②   **6** ②

1 ②

해석 그것의 대량의 식물 및 다른 유기 물질은 아주 많은 탄소를 흡수하고 저장한다. ... 18세기에 산업 혁명이 시작된 이후로, 산업 공정 중에 방출된 이산화탄소는 대기의 탄소 비율을 크게 증가시켰다.
•mass 대량, 다수; 덩어리   organic 유기의; 유기농의   absorb 흡수하다
carbon 탄소   Industrial Revolution 산업 혁명   release 방출하다; 발표, 개봉
process 공정, 제조법; 과정, 절차; 처리[가공]하다   greatly 크게, 대단히
proportion 비율, 부분; 균형   atmosphere 대기; 분위기
(A) 카본 싱크는 이 과잉 이산화탄소 중 대략 절반을 흡수할 수 있었고, 세계의 바다가 그 일의 주된 역할을 해왔다. •excess 과잉의, 초과한; 과잉, 지나침
(B) 카본 싱크의 가치는 그것들이 과잉 이산화탄소를 제거함으로써 대기 내의 평형 상태를 만드는 데 도움을 줄 수 있다는 것이다. 카본 싱크의 한 예는 거대한 숲이다. •equilibrium 평형 상태
해설 주어진 글의 '그것의(Its)'는 뒤의 어구(mass of plants ~ material)로 보아 '식물 및 다른 유기 물질을 가지고 있는 것', 즉 (B)에서 카본 싱크의 한 예로 제시한 '거대한 숲(a large forest)'을 가리키는 것이다.(▶ Zoom 1, 2 지시사/대명사)

2 ①

해석 소리를 지르면서, 그 다람쥐는 자신에게로 주의를 끄는데, 이는 아마도 포식자의 주의를 끌 것이다.
•may well 아마 ~일 것이다   predator 포식자, 포식 동물
(A) 어떤 들다람쥐가 멀리 있는 포식자를 보면, 다른 다람쥐들이 숨을 곳을 찾아 달아나도록 알리는 경고음을 낼 것이다. 이는 위험한 행동이다.
•alert (위험을) 알리다, 경보를 발하다   risky 위험한
(B) 새로운 증거는 다람쥐들이 유전적으로 관련 없는, 옛 놀이 친구를 위해서도 경고음을 낸다는 것을 보여준다.
•former 옛날의, 과거의; 이전의   playmate (어린 시절의) 놀이 친구
해설 주어진 글의 '그 다람쥐(the squirrel)'는 소리를 지르며 주의를 끈다고 했으므로, (A)에서 포식자를 보고 경고음을 낸다고 언급한 '어떤 들다람쥐(a ground squirrel)'를 받는 것이다.(▶ Zoom 3, 4 정관사 the)

3 ①

해석 일부 국가에서는 그다음에 숙성을 유도하기 위해 소비자에게의 판매 전에 그것들에 에틸렌이 뿌려진다. 그러나 익기 전에 수확된 과일은 식물에서 익은 상태로 수확된 과일보다 맛이 덜하다.
• **spray with** ~을 뿌리다　**induce** 유도하다; 유발[초래]하다　**ripening** 숙성
cf. **ripe** 익은
(A) 재배자와 소매업자에게 문제는 숙성에 때로 아주 빠르게 품질 저하와 부패가 뒤따라서 상품이 가치 없게 된다는 것이다. 그러므로 토마토와 다른 과일들은 대개 익지 않았을 때 수확되어 운송된다.
• **deterioration** (품질의) 저하　**decay** 부패(하다)　**worthless** 가치 없는
transport 운송(하다)　**unripe** 익지 않은
(B) 과일 숙성 과정은 세포벽의 연화, 단맛, 그리고 색과 맛을 주는 화학 물질의 생성을 야기한다. 그 과정은 에틸렌이라고 불리는 식물 호르몬의 생성에 의해 유발된다.. • **softening** 연화, 부드럽게 하기
해설 주어진 글의 '그것들(they)'은 소비자에게 판매하기 전에 에틸렌이 뿌려진다고 했으므로, (A) 마지막 문장의 '토마토와 다른 과일들(Tomatoes and other fruits)'을 받는 것이다.(▶ Zoom 1, 2 지시사/대명사)

4 ①

해석 도식적 지식에 대한 어떠한 의존이든 어떤 것이 '정상적인' 것인지에 대한 이러한 정보에 의해 형성될 것이다.
• **reliance** 의존, 의지　**schematic** 도식적인; 도식으로 나타낸
cf. **schema** (*pl.* **schemata**) 도식
(A) 도식이 여러분의 경험의 광범위한 패턴을 요약하며 그래서 그것(도식)이 본질적으로 주어진 상황에서 무엇이 전형적이거나 평범한 것인지 여러분에게 알려 준다는 것을 명심하라.
• **bear in mind** ~을 명심[유념]하다　**in essence** 본질적으로　**typical** 전형적인, 대표적인; 일반적인
(B) 도식적 지식은 여러분의 이해를 이끌고 여러분이 기억할 수 없는 것들을 재구성할 수 있게 하면서 여러분을 돕는다. • **reconstruct** 재구성하다; 재건[복원]하다
해설 주어진 글에서 "정상적인" 것에 대한 이러한 정보(this information ~ "normal")'에 의해 도식적 지식에 대한 의존이 형성될 것이라고 했으므로, 이는 (A)의 '도식이 본질적으로 주어진 상황에서 무엇이 전형적이거나 평범한 것인지 알려 준다는 것(they[schemata] tell you, ~ situation)'을 받는 것이다.(▶ Zoom 1, 2 지시사/대명사)

5 ②

해석 심리학 연구자들은 인간의 행동을 설명하는 데 도움을 주고 예측할 수도 있는 연구를 수행하기 위해 과학적인 방법을 따른다. 이는 달팽이나 음파를 연구하는 것보다 훨씬 더 힘든 일이다. • **challenging** 힘든, 어려운; 도전적인
(A) 심리학에 대한 이러한 모든 어려움에도 불구하고, 과학적인 방법의 이득은 연구 결과가 반복 가능하다는 것이다. 즉 여러분이 같은 절차를 따르면서 같은 연구를 다시 진행한다면, 같은 결과를 얻을 가능성이 매우 클 것이다.
• **payoff** 이득, 이익, 보상; 지불　**finding(s)** 연구 결과　**replicable** 반복 가능한
procedure 절차; 순서
(B) 그것은 종종 자연적인 환경보다 실험실 내에서의 행동을 검사하는 것, 그리고 모집단의 실제 대표적인 예에서 데이터를 모으기보다는 손쉽게 구할 수 있는 사람들에게 참여하도록 요청하는 것과 같은 절충이 필요하다.
• **compromise** 절충[타협](하다)　**readily** 손쉽게　**available** 구합[이용할] 수 있는
cross-section 대표적인 예; (횡)단면　**population** 모집단; 인구; 주민
해설 주어진 글의 '심리학 연구자들이 과학적 방법을 따른다(Researchers ~ the scientific method)'는 것을 (B)에서 '그것(It)'으로 받으며, 심리학에서 과학적 방법을 따르는 것에는 절충이 필요함을 사례를 들어 힘든 일임을 설명한다.(▶ Zoom 1 지시사/대명사) (A)의 '이러한 어려움(these difficulties)'은 (B)에서 언급한 '절충(compromises)'의 내용을 가리킨다.(▶ Zoom 5 대용어)

6 ②

해석 한 전통적 정의에 따르면, '미학'은 아름다움, 특히 예술에서의 아름다움을 다루는 철학의 분야이다. 예를 들어, '모나리자'나 꼭대기가 눈으로 덮인 산이 주는 즐거운 특징들을 고찰하는 것은 미학으로 분류될 것이다.
• **aesthetics** 미학　**branch** 분야; 나뭇가지　**philosophy** 철학
examine 고찰[조사]하다; 검사하다　**pleasing** 즐거운, 기분 좋은
cf. **please** 즐겁게 하다; 만족시키다　**snow-capped** 꼭대기가 눈으로 덮인
come under ~으로 분류되다, ~의 항목에 들다
(A) Picasso의 '게르니카'는 널리 칭송되고 있으나 아름답기 때문이 아니다. 그러므로 미학에 대한 더 나은 정의는, 그것(미학)이 사물이 경험되면서 사람들을 즐겁게 하는 방식을 다루는 철학의 분야라는 것이 될 것이다.
• **admire** 칭송[칭찬]하다, 감탄하다 *cf.* **admiration** 감탄, 칭찬, 존경
(B) 예술 작품들과 자연물들은 아름답다는 것에 의한 것 외에 다른 방식으로 우리의 관심을 끌 수도 있으므로 그러한 정의는 너무 좁아 보인다. 아름다움에 대한 감탄을 불러일으키는 것 대신에, 예술가들은 어리둥절함, 충격, 심지어 혐오감을 일으킬 수도 있다.
• **definition** 정의　**evoke** 불러일으키다; 떠올리게 하다　**puzzlement** 어리둥절함
disgust 혐오감(을 일으키다)
해설 주어진 글의 '한 전통적 정의(one traditional definition)'를 (B)에서 '그러한 정의(That definition)'로 받아 너무 좁다고 한다.(▶ Zoom 1, 2 지시사/대명사) 뒤이어 (A)에서는 Picasso의 '게르니카'를 예로 들어, '더 나은 정의(a better definition)'를 설명한다.

1 ④

> ¹Negotiation can be defined / as an attempt (to explore and reconcile conflicting positions / in order to reach an acceptable outcome).
> 협상은 정의될 수 있다 / 시도로 (상충되는 입장을 탐색하고 조정하려는 /
> 받아들일 수 있는 어떤 결과에 도달하기 위해)

↓

(C) ²Whatever the nature (of *the outcome*) (is), // which may actually favour one party more than another, // the purpose (of negotiation) / is the identification of areas (of common interest and conflict).
속성이 무엇이든 (그 결과의) // 그것(결과)은 실제로 다른 당사자보다 한쪽 당사자에게 더 유리할 수도 있는데 // 목적은 (협상의) / 영역을 확인하는 것이다 (공통의 이익과 갈등의)

³In this sense, / depending on the intentions (of the parties), / the areas of common interest / may be clarified, refined and given negotiated form and substance.
이러한 의미에서 / 의도에 따라 (당사자들의) /
공통의 이익 영역은 / 명확해지고, 정제되며, 협상된 형식과 내용이 주어질 수 있다

↓

(A) ⁴Areas of difference can and do frequently remain, / and will perhaps be the subject (of future negotiations), / or indeed remain irreconcilable.
(의견) 차이가 있는 영역은 남아 있을 수 있고, 실제로 자주 남는다 /
그리고 아마도 주제가 될 것이다 (향후 협상의) / 또는 실제로 조정할 수 없는 상태로 남을 (것이다)

⁵In *those instances* [in which the parties have highly antagonistic or polarised relations], / the process is likely to be dominated by the exposition, / (very often in public), / (of the areas of conflict).
그런 경우에 [당사자들이 매우 적대적이거나 양극화된 관계를 맺고 있는] /
그 과정은 설명에 의해 지배될 가능성이 있다 / (매우 자주 공개적으로) / (갈등 영역에 대한)

↓

(B) ⁶In these and sometimes other forms of negotiation, / negotiation serves functions (other than reconciling conflicting interests).
이러한 방식의 협상과 때로는 다른 방식의 협상에서 /
협상은 기능을 수행한다 (상충되는 이익을 조정하는 것 외의)

⁷These will include delay, publicity, diverting attention / or seeking intelligence (about the other party and its negotiating position).
이러한 것들(상충되는 이익을 조정시키는 것 외의 기능)은 지연, 홍보, 주의를 돌리는 것을 포함하기 마련이다 / 또는 정보를 구하는 것 (상대방과 그쪽의 협상 입장에 관한)

해설

주어진 글의 내용 파악하기 

> 협상은 받아들일 수 있는 어떤 결과에 도달하기 위한 상충되는 입장의 탐색과 조정 시도임.

≫

단서로 정답 찾기 ➕

> **(C)** the outcome은 주어진 글에서 언급한 '받아들일 수 있는 어떤 결과(an acceptable outcome)'를 받는다.(▶ **Zoom 3, 4** 정관사 the) 그 결과가 어떻든 협상의 목적은 공통 이익과 갈등의 영역을 확인하는 것이라고 하고, 공통의 이익 영역을 설명한다.
>
> ↓
>
> **(A)** 또 다른 영역인 갈등의 영역에 대해 당사자들이 매우 적대적이거나 양극화된 경우 갈등 영역에 대한 설명은 공개적으로 될 가능성이 있다고 설명한다.
>
> ↓
>
> **(B)** these는 (A)에서 언급한 '당사자들이 매우 적대적이거나 양극화된 경우(those instances ~ relations)'를 받으며 (▶ **Zoom 1, 2** 지시사/대명사), 이 경우를 포함한 협상의 다른 기능들을 제시하며 글을 맺는다.

어휘

acceptable 받아들일 수 있는; 용인되는   **clarify** 명확하게 하다
conflicting 상충[상반]되는   **divert** (생각·관심을) 다른 데로 돌리다; 전환하다
dominate 지배하다; 우세하다   **favo(u)r** ~에게 유리하다; 선호하다
identification (존재·중요성 등의) 확인, 인지; 신원 확인; 신분증
instance 경우, 사례   **intention** 의도; 목적   **negotiation** 협상, 교섭
party (소송·계약 등의) 당사자; 정당; 파티   **polarise[polarize]** 양극화하다
publicity 홍보, 광고   **refine** 정제하다, 불순물을 없애다
substance 내용; 물질; 실체

구문 분석

²**Whatever** the nature (of *the outcome*) (is), // ~.
whatever(무엇이 ~하더라도)는 부사절 접속사이면서 be동사의 보어 역할을 하는 복합관계대명사로 쓰이며, 이때 be동사는 생략 가능함.
⁴Areas of difference can and do frequently remain, / ~ or indeed **remain irreconcilable**.
<remain+C(형용사)>: C한 상태로 남다

해석 ¹협상은 받아들일 수 있는 어떤 결과에 도달하기 위해 상충되는 입장을 탐색하고 조정하려는 시도로 정의될 수 있다. (C) ²그 결과의 속성이 무엇이든, 그것(결과)은 실제로 다른 당사자보다 한쪽 당사자에게 더 유리할 수도 있는데, 협상의 목적은 공통의 이익과 갈등의 영역을 확인하는 것이다. ³이러한 의미에서 당사자들의 의도에 따라 공통의 이익 영역은 명확해지고, 정제되며, 협상된 형식과 내용이 주어질 수 있다. (A) ⁴의견 차이가 있는 영역은 남아 있을 수 있고, 실제로 자주 남으며, 아마도 향후 협상의 주제가 되거나 실제로 조정할 수 없는 상태로 남을 것이다. ⁵당사자들이 매우 적대적이거나 양극화된 관계를 맺고 있는 그런 경우에, 그 과정은 매우 자주 공개적으로 갈등 영역에 대한 설명에 의해 지배될 가능성이 있다. (B) ⁶이러한 방식의 협상과 때로는 다른 방식의 협상에서, 협상은 상충되는 이익을 조정하는 것 외의 기능을 수행한다. ⁷이러한 것들은 지연, 홍보, 주의를 돌리거나 상대방과 그쪽의 협상 입장에 관한 정보를 구하는 것을 포함하기 마련이다.

2 ⑤

> [1] In spite of the likeness (between the fictional and real world), / the fictional world deviates from the real one / in one important respect.
> 유사성에도 불구하고 (허구와 현실 세계 사이의) /
> 허구의 세계는 현실 세계로부터 벗어난다 / 한 가지 중요한 측면에서

↓

(C) [2] *The existing world* (faced by the individual) / is in principle an infinite chaos (of events and details) // before it is organized / by a human mind.
현재의 세계는 (개인이 직면하는) / 이론상으로는 끝없는 혼돈 상태이다 (사건들과 세부 사항들의) // 그것(현재의 세계)이 체계화되기 전에는 / 인간의 정신에 의해

[3] This chaos only gets processed and modified / when perceived / by a human mind.
이 혼돈 상태는 오직 처리되고 수정된다 / 인식될 때 / 인간의 정신에 의해

↓

(B) [4] Because of *the inner qualities* [with which the individual is endowed / through heritage and environment], / the mind functions as a filter; //
내적 특성으로 인해 [개인이 부여받은 / 유산과 환경을 통해] / 정신은 여과기의 역할을 한다 //
every outside impression [that passes through it] / is filtered and interpreted.
모든 외부의 인상이 [그것(정신)을 거쳐 가는] / 걸러지고 해석된다

[5] However, / *the world* [(which[that]) the reader encounters / in literature] / is already processed and filtered / by another consciousness.
그러나 / 세계는 [독자가 접하는 / 문학에서] / 이미 처리되고 걸러져 있다 / 또 다른 의식에 의해

↓

(A) [6] The author has selected the content / according to his own worldview and his own conception (of relevance), /
작가는 내용을 선정해 왔다 / 자신의 세계관과 자신의 개념에 따라 (적절성에 대한) /
in an attempt (to be neutral and objective / or convey a subjective view (on the world)).
시도에서 (중립적이고 객관적이고자 하는 / 또는 주관적인 견해를 전달하려는 (세계에 대한))

[7] Whatever the motives (are), // the author's subjective conception (of the world) / stands / between the reader and *the original, untouched world* [on which the story is based].
동기가 무엇이든 // 작가의 주관적인 개념은 (세계에 대한) / 있다 / 독자와 원래의 본래 그대로의 세계 사이에 [이야기의 기반이 되는]

해설

주어진 글의 내용 파악하기 🔎

> 허구의 세계는 한 가지 측면에서 현실 세계와 다름.

⌄

단서로 정답 찾기 ➕

(C) The existing world는 주어진 글의 '현실 세계(real world, the real one)'를 다른 말로 받아(▶ **Zoom 5** 대용어), 현재의 세계는 혼돈 상태이며 인간 정신에 의해 인식되고 체계화된다고 설명한다.

↓

(B) the mind는 (C) 마지막 문장의 '인간의 정신(a human mind)'을 받는다.(▶ **Zoom 3, 4** 정관사 the) 인간의 정신이 외부 현실 세계를 거르고 해석하여 처리하는 것을 부연 설명한 다음, 문학을 통해 접하는 허구 세계는 또 다른 의식에 의해 처리되고 걸러져 있다고 현실 세계와 대조한다.
*허구 세계부터 설명하는 순서라고 생각할 수 있으나, (B)에서 설명하는 인간 정신의 역할에 관한 내용은 주어진 글에 없으므로 (B)는 주어진 글 바로 뒤에 올 수 없다.

↓

(A) The author는 (B)에서 언급한 '또 다른 의식(another consciousness)'을 받는다.(▶ **Zoom 5** 대용어) 허구 세계는 작가의 주관적인 세계관이 반영된 세계라는 내용으로 글을 맺고 있다.

어휘

chaos 혼돈(된 상태); 혼란   conception 개념, 생각; 구상
consciousness 의식   encounter 접하다, 마주치다; 만남
fictional 허구의; 소설적인   in principle 이론상으로는
likeness 유사성, 닮음   modify 수정하다, 변경하다   neutral 중립(적인)
perceive 인식[인지]하다; 여기다   relevance 적절[타당]성; 관련성
respect (측)면; 존경(하다); 존중(하다)   untouched 본래 그대로의, 훼손되지 않은; 손을 대지 않은

구문 분석

[3] This chaos only gets processed and modified / **when perceived** / by a human mind.
when perceived 이하는 의미를 명확하게 하기 위해 접속사를 생략하지 않은 분사구문임.

[해석] [1] 허구와 현실 세계 사이의 유사성에도 불구하고 허구의 세계는 한 가지 중요한 측면에서 현실 세계로부터 벗어난다. (C) [2] 개인이 직면하는 현재의 세계는 인간의 정신에 의해 그것이 체계화되기 전에는 이론상으로는 사건들과 세부 사항들의 끝없는 혼돈 상태이다. [3] 이 혼돈 상태는 오직 인간의 정신에 의해 인식될 때 처리되고 수정된다. (B) [4] 개인이 유산과 환경을 통해 부여받은 내적 특성으로 인해 정신은 여과기의 역할을 하는데, 그것(정신)을 거쳐 가는 모든 외부의 인상이 걸러지고 해석된다. [5] 그러나 문학에서 독자가 접하는 세계는 또 다른 의식에 의해 이미 처리되고 걸러져 있다. (A) [6] 작가는 중립적이고 객관적이고자 하는, 또는 세계에 대한 주관적인 견해를 전달하려는 시도에서 자신의 세계관과 적절성에 대한 자신의 개념에 따라 내용을 선정해 왔다. [7] 동기가 무엇이든, 세계에 대한 작가의 주관적인 개념은 독자와 이야기의 기반이 되는 원래의 본래 그대로의 세계 사이에 있다.

3 ④

> ¹The growing complexity (of computer software) / has direct implications / for our global safety and security, //
> 증가하는 복잡성은 (컴퓨터 소프트웨어의) / 직접적인 영향을 미친다 / 우리의 전 세계적 안전과 보안에 //
> particularly as *the physical objects* [upon which we depend] — / things (like cars, airplanes, bridges, tunnels, and implantable medical devices) — / transform themselves into computer code.
> 특히 물리적 사물이 ~하면서 [우리가 의존하는] / 즉 (~한) 것들 (자동차, 비행기, 교량, 터널, 이식할 수 있는 의료 기기와 같은) / 스스로를 컴퓨터 코드로 전환(하면서)

↓

(C) ²Physical things are increasingly becoming information technologies.
물리적 사물들은 점점 더 정보 기술이 되어가고 있다

³Cars are / "*computers* [(which[that]) we ride in]," // and airplanes are nothing more than "*flying Solaris boxes* (attached to bucketfuls of industrial control systems)."
자동차는 ~이다 / '컴퓨터 [우리가 타는]' // 그리고 비행기는 '나는 솔라리스(미국 컴퓨터 회사에서 개발한 운영체제) 박스'에 불과하다 (수많은 산업 제어 시스템에 부착된)

↓

(A) ⁴As all this code grows / in size and complexity, //
so too does / the number (of errors and software bugs).
이 모든 코드가 증가함에 따라 / 크기와 복잡성에서 //
또한 증가한다 / 수도 (오류와 소프트웨어 버그의)

⁵According to a study by Carnegie Mellon University, / commercial software typically has twenty to thirty bugs / for every thousand lines of code — //
카네기 멜런 대학교의 연구에 따르면 / 상업용 소프트웨어에는 보통 20~30개의 버그가 있다 / 코드 1,000줄마다 //
50 million lines of code means / *1 million to 1.5 million potential errors* (to be exploited).
5천만 줄의 코드는 의미한다 / 1백만~150만 개의 잠재적 오류를 ((부적절하게) 활용될 수 있는)

↓

(B) ⁶This is the basis (for *all malware attacks* [that take advantage of these computer bugs / to get the code to do *something* [(that) it was not originally intended to do]]).
이것이 근간이다 (모든 악성 소프트웨어 공격의 [이 컴퓨터 버그를 이용하는 / 코드가 (~한) 것을 하도록 [그것이 원래 하도록 의도되지 않았던]])

⁷As computer code grows more elaborate, // software bugs flourish // and security suffers, / with increasing consequences (for society at large).
컴퓨터 코드가 더 복잡해짐에 따라 // 소프트웨어 버그가 난무한다 //
그리고 보안은 악화된다 / 커지는 영향과 함께 (전반적인 사회에 대한)

해설

주어진 글의 내용 파악하기 🔎

> 물리적 사물이 컴퓨터 코드화되며, 점점 더 복잡해지는 컴퓨터 소프트웨어가 우리의 전 세계적 안전과 보안에 직접적인 영향을 미침.

단서로 정답 찾기 ➕

> (C) Physical things는 주어진 글의 the physical objects를 다른 말로 받은 것이다.(▶ Zoom 5 대용어) 이어서 주어진 글에 나열된 코드화된 물리적 사물인 car, airplanes, ~ medical devices를 부연 설명하고 있다.
>
> (A) all this code는 주어진 글과 (C)에서 언급된 코드화된 물리적 사물들을 받는다.(▶ Zoom 1, 2 지시사/대명사, Zoom 5 대용어) 이어서 한 연구를 예로 들어, 코드가 커지고 복잡해지는 것에 따라 '오류와 소프트웨어 버그도 증가한다는 문제점(so too does the number of errors and software bugs)'을 설명한다.
> *all this code가 주어진 글의 마지막 문장에 언급된 computer code에 바로 이어지지 않음에 유의해야 한다.
>
> (B) (A)에서 언급한 문제점을 This로 받아서(▶ Zoom 1, 2 지시사/대명사) 이것이 악성 소프트웨어 공격의 근간이라고 하며, 코드가 복잡해지는 것에 따른 악영향을 언급하는 것으로 글을 맺고 있다.

어휘

at large 전반적인, 대체적인   bucketfuls of 수많은, 대량의   consequence 영향(력); 결과(= implication)   elaborate 복잡한; 정교한   flourish 난무하다; 번창[번성]하다   implantable 이식할 수 있는   malware 악성 소프트웨어   take advantage of ~을 이용하다

구문 분석

⁴As all this code grows / in size and complexity, //
so too **does** / **the number (of errors and software bugs)**.
<so+V+S(S도 또한 V하다)>의 도치구문으로 여기서 does는 grows를 의미함.

⁵~ 50 million lines of code **means** ~.
50 million lines of code는 한 줄 한 줄의 코드가 아닌 총체적인 개념으로 보아 단수 취급함.

해석 ¹컴퓨터 소프트웨어의 증가하는 복잡성은 우리의 전 세계적 안전과 보안에 직접적인 영향을 미치는데, 우리가 의존하는 물리적 사물, 즉 자동차, 비행기, 교량, 터널, 이식할 수 있는 의료 기기와 같은 것들이 스스로를 컴퓨터 코드로 전환하면서 특히 그렇다. (C) ²물리적 사물들은 점점 더 정보 기술이 되어가고 있다. ³자동차는 '우리가 타는 컴퓨터'이고, 비행기는 '수많은 산업 제어 시스템에 부착된 나는 솔라리스(미국 컴퓨터 회사에서 개발한 운영 체제) 박스'에 불과하다. (A) ⁴이 모든 코드가 크기와 복잡성에서 증가함에 따라, 오류와 소프트웨어 버그의 수도 또한 증가한다. ⁵카네기 멜런 대학교의 연구에 따르면, 상업용 소프트웨어에는 보통 코드 1,000줄마다 20~30개의 버그가 있는데, 5천만 줄의 코드는 (부적절하게) 활용될 수 있는 1백만~150만 개의 잠재적 오류를 의미한다. (B) ⁶이것이 코드가 원래 하도록 의도되지 않았던 것을 하도록 이 컴퓨터 버그를 이용하는 모든 악성 소프트웨어 공격의 근간이다. ⁷컴퓨터 코드가 더 복잡해짐에 따라, 소프트웨어 버그는 난무하고 전반적인 사회에 대한 커지는 영향과 함께 보안은 악화된다.

Zoom 1

해석 들불은 여러 오스트레일리아 환경에서 자연스러운 현상이다. 경관을 관리하기 위한 의도적인 방화는 수천 년 동안 원주민들에 의해 행해졌다.
• **wildfire** 들불, 들에서 난 불   **landscape** 경관, 풍경
Aboriginal (오스트레일리아) 원주민
➜ 그러나, 목축업자들이 시작한 불태우는 패턴은 이전의 양식과는 달랐다. 조건이 맞으면, 그들은 겨울에 대비해 그들의 가축을 이동시켜 가면서 경관에 불을 지르곤 했다.
• **pattern** 패턴, 양상; 무늬   **stockman** (*pl.* stockmen) 목축업자
introduce (생각·유행 등을) 시작하다, 창안하다; 도입하다; 소개하다
previous 이전의, 앞의

Zoom 2

해석 스트레스를 주는 사건들은 때때로 사람들이 새로운 기술을 개발하고, 우선 사항을 재평가하고, 새로운 통찰을 배우고, 새로운 강점을 얻게 만든다.
• **reevaluate** 재평가하다   **priority** 우선 (사항)   **insight** 통찰(력); 이해
acquire 얻다, 습득하다
➜ 다시 말해, 스트레스에 의해 시작된 적응 과정은 더 나은 쪽으로의 개인적인 변화로 이어질 수 있다. • **adaptation** 적응; 각색   **initiate** 시작하다, 일으키다

Zoom 3

해석 문학 작품의 발췌 글에만 노출된 학생은 책의 전반적인 양상을 아는 만족감을 결코 갖지 못할 것이다.
• **expose** 노출시키다; 드러내다   **extract** 발췌(하다); 추출(하다)
overall 전반적인, 전체의; 종합적으로
➜ 게다가 짧은 발췌로는 충분히 설명될 수 없는 몇몇 문학적인 특징이 있다.
• **feature** 특징, 특성; 특징으로 하다   **adequately** 충분히, 적당히
illustrate 설명하다, 예증하다; 삽화를 넣다

Zoom 4

해석 어떤 사람이 새롭거나 처음으로 하는 일을 하고 있다면, 그때는 그 일을 하는 동안 지켜보아지는 것이 수행력을 저하시킨다. 반면에, 잘 알고 있거나 많이 연습한 과제를 하거나 활동에 관여할 때 지켜보아지는 것은 수행력을 향상시키는 경향이 있다.
• **observe** 지켜보다, 관찰하다; (규칙을) 준수하다   **decrease** 저하[감소]시키다, 줄이다
performance 수행[실행](력); (기계의) 성능, 효율; 실적, 성과
engage in ~에 관여[참여]하다   **tend to-v** v하는 경향이 있다
enhance (질·능력을) 향상시키다, 높이다
➜ 따라서, 여러분이 새로운 스포츠를 배운다면 그것을 혼자 시작하는 것이 낫지만, 그것에 숙련되면 그때는 아마 관중이 있을 때 더 잘할 것이다.
• **skilled** 숙련된, 노련한   **audience** 관중, 청중

함정 주의

해석 문화적인 특징은 부모로부터 자식에게 전달될 뿐만 아니라 구전이나 글로 어느 한 사람으로부터 다른 사람에게 전달될 수도 있다.
• **characteristic** 특징, 특질; 특유의   **pass on** 전달하다, 넘겨주다
by word of mouth 구전으로
➜ 따라서 몇몇 문화적인 변화는 인구 전체에 의해 상당히 빠르게 채택될 수 있다. 문화의 전파는 전염병의 전염과 꽤 비슷하다. ...

• **adopt** 채택하다, (자신의 것으로) 받아들이다; 입양하다   **population** 인구; 모집단
transmission 전파, 전달; 전염   **infection** 전염병; 감염
➜ 독감과 감기처럼, 대중음악의 선호와 옷의 유행과 같은 문화적인 관습은 오늘날 특히 라디오와 텔레비전 매체를 통해 매우 빠르게 퍼질 수도 있다.
• **media** 매체

Focus & Practice p.56

1 ① **2** ② **3** ② **4** ① **5** (B) — (C) — (A)

1 ①

해석 과학 사학자의 전통적인 목표는 "당대의" 과학적 방법이나 개념의 점진적인 발전을 보여줌으로써 그것에 대한 이해를 명확하게 하고 깊게 하는 것'이었다. 이것은 획기적인 발전과 발견의 점진적인 축적에 대하여 이야기하는 것을 수반했다.
• **contemporary** 당대의, 현대의; 동시대의   **evolution** (점진적인) 발전; 진화
entail 수반하다   **relate** ~에 대하여 이야기하다; 관련시키다
progressive 점진적인; 진보[혁신]적인   **accumulation** 축적, 누적
breakthrough 획기적 발전; 돌파(구)
(A) 하지만 1950년대 중반에, 역사에 대한 이러한 관점에서 많은 결함이 분명해졌다. 예를 들어, 과학적 발견에 대한 더 면밀한 분석은 사학자들로 하여금 발견 시점과 그것들의 발견자가 정확하게 확인될 수 있는지를 묻도록 했다.
• **identify** 확인하다; 식별하다; 동일시하다   **precisely** 정확하게; 바로
(B) 게다가, 오늘날의 기준에 따라 과거의 발견과 발견자들을 평가하는 것은 우리가 그것들이 당시에 얼마나 중요했을지를 알 수 없게 한다.
• **significant** 중요한; 상당한

해설 주어진 글은 과학 사학자의 전통적인 목표가 과학적 방법이나 개념의 점진적인 발전을 보여주는 것이었다는 내용이다. (A)는 역접 연결어 however(하지만)가 이끌며, '역사에 대한 이러한 관점(this view of history)'에 결함이 있다는 상반되는 내용을 말하므로 주어진 글 다음에 이어질 글로 적절하다. (B)는 첨가 연결어 Furthermore(게다가)가 이끌어 앞 내용에 대한 추가적인 내용을 덧붙여야 하는데, 오늘날의 기준에 따라 과거 발견의 중요도를 판단할 수는 없다는 내용으로 주어진 글에서 언급한 과학 사학자의 전통적인 목표와 반대되므로 뒤에 이어질 수 없다.

2 ②

해석 개인용 로봇 보조가 스마트 홈 보조의 서비스와 유사한 서비스를 제공할지라도, 그것들의 사회적 실재감은 소셜 로봇 특유의 기회를 제공한다.
• **assistant** 보조물, 보조 수단   **unique to A** A 특유의, A 고유의
(A) 대신에, 개인용 로봇 보조에는 뚜렷한 사회적 실재감이 있고 눈, 귀 또는 입과 같은 사회적으로 상호 작용하는 그것들의 능력을 암시하는 시각적 특징을 가지고 있다.
• **distinct** 뚜렷한, 분명한; 별개의   **suggestive of** ~을 암시[시사]하는
(B) 예를 들어, 음악을 틀어주는 것뿐 아니라, 소셜 개인용 보조 로봇은 마치 사용자가 로봇과 함께 그 음악을 듣고 있는 것처럼 느끼도록 음악과의 교감을 표현할 것이다. • **engagement** 교감, 참여; 약속; 약혼

해설 주어진 글에서 개인용 로봇 보조의 사회적 실재감이 소셜 로봇 특유의 기회를 제공한다고 했다. (B)는 예시 연결어 For instance가 이끌어, 사용자가 로봇과 음악을 같이 듣는다는 느낌이 들도록 로봇이 음악적 교감을 표현할 것이라는 내용인데, 이는 주어진 글의 '사회적 실재감'에 대한 구체적인 예에 해당하므로 적절하다. (A)는 역접 연결어 Instead(대신에)가 이끌고 있는데, 개인용 로봇 보조에 사회적 실재감이 있다는 내용이므로 주어진 글과 흐름이 반대되지 않는다.

3 ②

해석 한 조사에서 미국인들의 61%는 정부가 '빈곤층 지원'에 더 많은 돈을 쓰는 것을 지지했다. 그러나 같은 모집단이 그들이 '복지'에 더 많은 정부 예산을 쓰는 것을 지지하는지 질문받았을 때, 단지 21%만이 찬성했다.
• **assistance** 지원, 도움 **welfare** 복지; 안녕, 행복 **in favour** 찬성하는, 지지하는
(A) 그러나 '복지'라는 단어는 아마도 많은 정치인들과 신문들이 그것을 묘사하는 방식 때문에, 부정적인 함축된 의미를 지니고 있다.
• **connotation** (함축된) 의미 **politician** 정치인 **portray** (그림·글로) 묘사하다, 표현하다
(B) 따라서, 질문의 구성은 여러 방식으로 답변에 크게 영향을 미칠 수 있으며, 이는 만약 당신의 목표가 사람들이 생각하는 것에 대한 '진정한 척도'를 얻는 것이라면 중요하다. • **framing** 구성; 구상 **measure** 척도, 기준; 측정하다
해설 주어진 글은 같은 모집단 내에서 빈곤층 지원에 정부 예산을 늘리는 것보다 복지에 늘리는 것을 지지하는 비율이 더 낮다는 내용이다. (B)는 결과 연결어 Therefore(따라서)가 이끌어, 질문의 구성이 답변에 큰 영향을 미칠 수 있다는 결론을 말하므로 적절하다. (A)는 역접 연결어 But(하지만)이 이끄는데, '복지'라는 단어가 부정적인 함축된 의미를 지닌다며 주어진 글 내용의 원인에 해당하는 내용을 말하므로 적절하지 않다.

4 ①

해석 우리 대부분은 무엇을 언제 먹을지에 대한 일반적이고 합리적인 관념을 갖고 있는데, 그 문제에 관한 정보는 부족하지 않다.
• **rational** 합리적인, 이성적인 **shortage** 부족, 결핍 **subject** 문제, 사안, 주제; 과목; (연구) 대상
(A) 하지만 우리가 알고 있는 것과 우리가 행하는 것 사이에는 종종 단절이 존재한다. 우리가 진실을 알고 있을지도 모르지만, 결정은 우리의 감정도 수반한다. 힘겨운 감정과 씨름하는 많은 사람들은 또한 섭식 문제와 씨름한다.
• **disconnect** 단절; 연결을 끊다 **involve** 수반[포함]하다; 관련시키다
struggle with ~와 씨름하다, ~로 고심하다
(B) 그러나 감정적인 이유로 먹는 사람이 반드시 과체중인 것은 아니다. 어떤 몸집의 사람들이라도 스스로를 먹는 것에 몰두하게 하거나 자신의 몸매와 몸무게에 대해 강박감을 가짐으로써 감정적 경험에서 벗어나려고 노력할지도 모른다.
• **overweight** 과체중(의) **preoccupy** 몰두하게 하다, ~의 마음을 빼앗다; 먼저 차지하다 **obsess** 강박감을 갖다
해설 주어진 글은 우리 대부분이 무엇을 언제 먹을지에 대한 합리적 관념을 갖고 있고 정보도 충분하다는 내용이다. (A)는 역접 연결어 Yet(하지만)이 이끌며, 우리가 알고 있는 것(즉 관념)과 행하는 것에는 종종 단절이 있다고 하며 주어진 글에 대조되는 내용을 말하므로 적절하다. (B)도 역접 연결어 However(그러나)가 이끌지만, 감정적인 이유로 먹는 사람이 반드시 과체중인 것은 아니라며 그 이유를 설명하므로 주어진 글에 대조되는 내용이 아니다.

5 (B) — (C) — (A)

해석 대부분의 소비자 잡지는 구독과 광고에 의존한다. 구독은 전체 잡지 판매 부수의 거의 90퍼센트를 차지한다. 낱권, 다시 말해 가판대 판매가 나머지를 차지한다.
• **subscription** 구독(료) **account for** (비율을) 차지하다; 설명하다 **circulation** (신문·잡지의) 판매 부수; 순환; 유통 **single-copy** 낱권 **newsstand** (신문·잡지) 가판대
(A) 예를 들어, <Columbia Journalism Review>는 전문 언론인을 대상으로 판매되며 그 잡지의 몇 안 되는 광고는 언론사, 출판사 등이다.
(B) 하지만, 낱권 판매는 중요한데, 왜냐하면 구독 가격이 호를 하나씩 사는 가격보다 보통 최소 50퍼센트는 더 싸서, 그것이 잡지 한 권당 더 많은 수익을 가져오기 때문이다.
• **bring in** (이익 등을) 가져오다; 도입하다
(C) 게다가, 잠재적 독자들은 하나의 호를 구매함으로써 새로운 잡지를 탐색한다. .... 전문가용 잡지 또는 업계지는 전문화된 잡지이며 흔히 전문가 협회에 의해 출판된다. 그것들은 보통 매우 표적화된 광고를 특징으로 한다.
• **issue** (정기 간행물의) 호; 쟁점, 문제 **trade magazine** 업계지 ((특정 업계나 전문 직업인 상대의 잡지)) **specialized** 전문화된 **association** 협회; 연계; 연관
해설 주어진 글은 소비자 잡지는 구독과 광고에 의존하며 낱권 판매는 판매 부수의 10%에 불과하다는 내용이다. (B)는 역접 연결어 However(하지만)가 이끌어, 낱권 판매가 수익이 더 많아서 중요하다는 내용인데, 이는 주어진 글과 반대되는 내용이므로 주어진 글 뒤에 이어져야 한다. 이어서 (C)에서 첨가 연결어 Further(게다가)가 이끌며 잠재적 독자가 하나의 호를 구매해서 새로운 잡지를 탐색한다는 낱권 판매의 또 다른 중요성을 추가로 제시하고, 전문가용 잡지나 업계지가 매우 표적화된 광고를 특징으로 한다고 언급하는 것이 자연스럽다. 마지막으로 (A)는 예시 연결어 For example이 이끌어 전문 언론인을 대상으로 하는 잡지가 언론사, 출판사의 광고를 담는다는 내용인데, 이는 표적화된 광고의 구체적 예에 해당하므로 자연스럽다.

1 ⑤

> [1] Plants show finely tuned adaptive responses // when nutrients are limiting.
> 식물은 미세하게 조정된 적응 반응을 보인다 // 영양분이 제한적일 때
>
> [2] Gardeners may recognize yellow leaves / as a sign (of poor nutrition and the need for fertilizer).
> 정원사는 노란 잎을 인식할 수도 있다 / 신호로 (부족한 영양과 비료의 필요성에 대한)

↓

(C) [3] But / if a plant does not have / *a caretaker* (to provide supplemental minerals), //
그러나 / 식물에 없다면 / 관리인이 (추가 미네랄을 공급해 줄) //
it can proliferate or lengthen its roots / and (can) develop root hairs / to allow foraging / in more distant soil patches.
그것(식물)은 그것의 뿌리를 증식하거나 늘일 수 있다 / 그리고 뿌리털을 발달시킬 수 있다 / (미네랄을) 구하러 다니도록 / 더 먼 토양에서

[4] Plants can also use their memory / to respond to histories (of temporal or spatial variation (in nutrient or resource availability)).
식물은 또한 자신의 기억을 이용할 수 있다 / 역사에 대응하기 위해 (시간적 또는 공간적 변화의 (영양분 혹은 자원 이용 가능성에 있어))

↓

(B) [5] Research (in this area) / has shown // that plants are constantly aware / of their position (in the environment), / in terms of both space and time.
연구는 (이 분야에서의) / 보여주었다 // 식물이 끊임없이 인식한다는 것을 / 자신의 위치를 (환경에서의) / 공간과 시간 둘 다의 측면에서

[6] *Plants* [that have experienced variable nutrient availability / in the past] / tend to exhibit risk-taking behaviors, / (such as spending energy on root lengthening / instead of leaf production).
식물은 [일정하지 않은 영양분 이용 가능성을 경험한 / 과거에] / 위험을 감수하는 행동을 보이는 경향이 있다 / (뿌리를 늘이는 데 에너지를 쓰는 것과 같은 / 잎 생산 대신)

↓

(A) [7] In contrast, / plants (with a history of nutrient abundance) / are risk averse / and save energy.
반대로 / 식물은 (영양분이 풍족했던 내력을 가진) / 위험을 회피하려 한다 / 그리고 에너지를 절약한다

[8] At all developmental stages, / plants respond / to environmental changes or unevenness /
모든 발달 단계에서 / 식물은 반응한다 / 환경 변화나 불균형에 /
so as to be able to use their energy / for growth, survival, and reproduction, / while limiting / damage and nonproductive uses (of their valuable energy).
에너지를 사용할 수 있도록 / 성장, 생존, 번식에 / 제한하는 동시에 / 손상과 비생산적인 사용을 (그것의 귀중한 에너지의)

해설

주어진 글의 내용 파악하기 

식물은 영양분이 제한적이면 조정된 적응 반응을 보이며, 정원사는 노란 잎을 보고 영양과 비료가 부족하다는 것을 인식함.

⌄

단서로 정답 찾기 ✚

(C) But(그러나)으로 관리인이 없는 경우에는 식물이 뿌리를 발달시켜 미네랄을 구한다는 상반되는 상황에 대한 설명이 이어진다.(▶ **Zoom 1 역접 연결어**) 이어서 식물은 기억으로 영양분 및 자원 관련 시공간적 변화에 대응함을 설명한다.

↓

(B) this area는 (C)에서 언급한 '식물이 기억을 이용해 대응하는 것'에 관한 분야를 받으며(▶ **Point 1 지시사/대명사**), 식물이 환경에서의 위치를 인식한다는 연구 결론을 말한다. 이어서 영양분이 일정하지 않은 것을 경험한 식물의 행동을 예로 든다.

↓

(A) In contrast(반대로)로 이어져, 영양분이 풍족했던 식물의 대조되는 사례를 설명한다.(▶ **Zoom 1 역접 연결어**)

어휘

abundance 풍족, 풍부   adaptive 적응성의, 적응할 수 있는
finely 미세하게; 세밀하게   patch 좁은 땅; 밭   proliferate 증식[번식]하다
reproduction 번식; 복제   risk averse 위험을 회피하려 하는
spatial 공간적인   supplemental 추가[보충]의   temporal 시간적인;
일시적인; 속세의   unevenness 불균형; 고르지 않음   variation 변화,
변동; (~의) 변형 *cf.* variable 일정하지 않은, 변화하기 쉬운

구문 분석

[2] Gardeners may **recognize** yellow leaves / **as** a sign (of poor nutrition and the need for fertilizer).
<recognize A as B>: A를 B로 인식하다
[6] *Plants* [that have experienced variable nutrient availability / in the past] / tend to exhibit risk-taking behaviors, / (such as **spending** energy **on** root lengthening / instead of leaf production).
<spend A on B>: B하는 데 A를 쓰다[들이다]

해석 [1] 식물은 영양분이 제한적일 때 미세하게 조정된 적응 반응을 보인다. [2] 정원사는 노란 잎을 부족한 영양과 비료의 필요성에 대한 신호로 인식할 수도 있다. (C) [3] 그러나 식물에 추가 미네랄을 공급해 줄 관리인이 없다면, 그것(식물)은 더 먼 토양에서 (미네랄을) 구하러 다니도록 뿌리를 증식하거나 늘이고 뿌리털을 발달시킬 수 있다. [4] 식물은 또한 영양분 혹은 자원 이용 가능성에 있어 시간적 또는 공간적 변화의 역사에 대응하기 위해 자신의 기억을 이용할 수 있다. (B) [5] 이 분야에서의 연구는 식물이 공간과 시간 둘 다의 측면에서 환경에서의 자신의 위치를 끊임없이 인식한다는 것을 보여주었다. [6] 과거에 일정하지 않은 영양분 이용 가능성을 경험한 식물은 잎 생산 대신 뿌리를 늘이는 데 에너지를 쓰는 것과 같은 위험을 감수하는 행동을 보이는 경향이 있다. (A) [7] 반대로, 영양분이 풍족했던 내력을 가진 식물은 위험을 회피하려 하고 에너지를 절약한다. [8] 모든 발달 단계에서 식물은 그것의 귀중한 에너지의 손상과 비생산적인 사용을 제한하는 동시에, 성장, 생존, 번식에 에너지를 사용할 수 있도록 환경 변화나 불균형에 반응한다.

2 ⑤

> [1] Green products involve, / (in many cases), / higher ingredient costs / than those (of mainstream products).
> 친환경 제품은 수반한다 / (많은 경우) / 더 높은 원료비를 / 그것(원료비)보다 (주류 제품의)

↓

(C) [2] **Furthermore,** / *the restrictive ingredient lists and design criteria* [that are typical of such products] /

게다가 / 제한 성분 목록과 디자인 기준이 [그러한 제품(친환경 제품)의 전형적인] /

may make green products inferior / to mainstream products / on core performance dimensions (e.g., less effective cleansers).

친환경 제품을 열등하게 만들 수 있다 / 주류 제품보다 /
핵심 성능 면에서 (예를 들어, 덜 효과적인 세척제)

[3] In turn, / the higher costs and lower performance (of some products) / attract only a small portion (of the customer base), /

결과적으로 / 더 높은 비용과 더 낮은 성능은 (일부 제품의) /
오직 적은 부분만 유인한다 (고객층의) /

leading to lower economies of scale / in procurement, manufacturing, and distribution.

그래서 더 낮은 규모의 경제로 이어진다 / 조달, 제조, 유통에서의

↓

(B) [4] Even if the green product succeeds, // it may cannibalize the company's higher-profit mainstream offerings.

친환경 제품이 성공한다 할지라도 // 그것(친환경 제품)은 기업의 수익이 더 높은 주류 제품을 잡아먹을 수 있다

[5] Given such downsides, / *companies* (serving mainstream consumers / with successful mainstream products) / face // what seems like an obvious investment decision.

이런 부정적인 면을 고려해 볼 때 / 기업들은 (주류 소비자에게 공급하는 / 성공적인 주류 제품을) /
직면한다 // 너무 뻔한 투자 결정처럼 보이는 것에

↓

(A) [6] They'd rather put money and time / into *known, profitable, high-volume products* [that serve populous customer segments] /

그들은 차라리 돈과 시간을 투자하고 싶어 한다 / 이미 알려져 있고 수익성이 있는 다량의 제품에 [다수의 고객층을 만족시키는] /

than into *risky, less-profitable, low-volume products* [that may serve current noncustomers].

위험하고 수익성이 더 낮은 소량의 제품보다는 [현재 고객이 아닌 사람들을 만족시킬 수도 있는]

[7] Given that choice, / these companies may choose / to leave the green segment of the market / to small niche competitors.

그런 선택을 고려해 볼 때 / 이 기업들은 선택할 수도 있다 / 시장의 친환경 부문을 맡기기를 /
작은 틈새 경쟁사들에게

어휘

criterion (*pl.* criteria) 기준 dimension 면; 차원 distribution 유통; 분배 downside 부정적인[불리한] 면 ingredient cost 원료비 niche (시장의) 틈새 offering 팔 물건; 제공된 것 populous 다수의; 인구가 많은 portion 부분; (음식의) 1인분; 몫 serve 만족시키다; (서비스를) 제공하다

구문 분석

[5] **Given** such downsides, / *companies* ~.
전치사 Given은 '~을 고려해 볼 때'로 해석함.

[6] They**'d rather** put money and time / **into** *known, profitable, high-volume products* [that serve populous customer segments] / **than into** *risky, less-profitable, low-volume products* [that may serve current noncustomers].
- <would rather A than B>: B 하기보다는 차라리 A 하고 싶다[하겠다]
- into가 이끄는 두 개의 전치사구가 병렬구조를 이룸.

해석 [1]많은 경우 친환경 제품은 주류 제품의 원료비보다 더 높은 원료비를 수반한다. (C) [2]게다가 그런 제품(친환경 제품)의 전형적인 제한 성분 목록과 디자인 기준이 친환경 제품을 주류 제품보다 핵심 성능 면에서 열등하게 만들 수 있다(예를 들어, 덜 효과적인 세척제). [3]결과적으로, 일부 제품의 더 높은 비용과 더 낮은 성능은 고객층의 오직 적은 부분만 유인해서, 조달, 제조, 유통에서의 더 낮은 규모의 경제로 이어진다. (B) [4]친환경 제품이 성공한다 할지라도, 그것(친환경 제품)은 기업의 수익이 더 높은 주류 제품을 잡아먹을 수 있다. [5]이런 부정적인 면을 고려해 볼 때, 성공적인 주류 제품을 주류 소비자에게 공급하는 기업들은 너무 뻔한 투자 결정처럼 보이는 것에 직면한다. (A) [6]그들은 현재 고객이 아닌 사람들을 만족시킬 수도 있는 위험하고 수익성이 더 낮은 소량의 제품보다는, 차라리 다수의 고객층을 만족시키는 이미 알려져 있고 수익성이 있는 다량의 제품에 돈과 시간을 투자하고 싶어 한다. [7]그런 선택을 고려해 볼 때, 이 기업들은 작은 틈새 경쟁사들에게 시장의 친환경 부문을 맡기기를 선택할 수도 있다.

3 ⑤

> ¹Ever since the first scientific opinion polls revealed // that most Americans are at best poorly informed / about politics,
> 첫 번째 과학적 여론 조사가 밝힌 이후로 // 대부분의 미국인이 기껏해야 빈약하게 알고 있다는 것을 / 정치에 대해서
>
> // analysts have asked // whether citizens are equipped to play *the role* [(which[that]) democracy assigns them].
> // 분석가들은 물었다 // 시민들이 역할을 할 능력이 있는지 [민주주의가 그들에게 부여한]

↓

(C) ²However, / there is something worse / than an inadequately informed public, // and that's a misinformed public.
그러나 / 더 나쁜 것이 있다 / 불충분하게 알고 있는 대중보다 // 그리고 그것은 잘못 알고 있는 대중이다

³It's one thing // when citizens don't know something, and realize it, // which has always been a problem.
(~은) 하나의 경우이다 // 시민들이 어떤 것을 모르면서, 그것(모르는 것)을 인식하고 있는 경우는 // 그리고 그것은 늘 문제가 되어 왔다

⁴It's another thing // when citizens don't know something, but think // (that) they know it, // which is the new problem.
(~은) 이와 별개이다 // 시민들이 어떤 것을 모르지만 생각하는 경우는 // 자신들이 알고 있다고 // 그리고 그것은 새로운 문제이다

↓

(B) ⁵It's the difference (between ignorance and irrationality).
차이점이 있다 (무지와 무분별함 사이에는)

⁶Whatever else one might conclude / about self-government, // it's at risk // when citizens don't know // what they're talking about.
다른 어떤 것으로 결론을 내리더라도 / 자치 정부에 관해 // (~은) 위험하다 // 시민들이 알지 못하는 경우는 // 자신들이 무엇을 말하고 있는지

⁷Our misinformation owes partly to psychological factors, / including our tendency (to see the world / in *ways* [that suit our desires]).
우리가 잘못 아는 것은 부분적으로 심리적 요인들의 탓이다 / 우리의 경향을 포함하여 (세상을 바라보는 / 방식으로 [우리의 욕망에 맞는])

↓

(A) ⁸Such factors, / however, / can explain only *the misinformation* [that has always been with us].
그런 요인들은 / 하지만 / 잘못된 정보만 설명할 수 있다 [늘 우리와 함께 있어 온]

⁹The sharp rise (in misinformation) / in recent years / has a different source: / our media.
급격한 증가에는 (잘못된 정보의) / 최근에 / 다른 원인이 있다 / 바로 우리의 미디어

¹⁰"They are making us dumb," // says one observer.
"그것들(우리의 미디어)은 우리를 어리석게 만들고 있습니다." // 한 논평자는 말한다

¹¹When fact bends to fiction, // the predictable result is political distrust and polarization.
사실이 허구에 굴복하면 // 예견할 수 있는 결과는 정치적 불신과 대립이다

해설

주어진 글의 내용 파악하기 

대부분의 미국인이 정치에 대해서 잘 모름.

⌄⌄

단서로 정답 찾기 ⊕

(C) However(그러나)로 시작하여 잘 모르는 대중보다 잘못 아는 대중이 더 나쁘다고 대조되는 내용을 말한다.(▶ **Zoom 1** 역접 연결어) 이어서 정치를 모르는 것도 문제이지만, 모르면서 알고 있다고 생각하는 것도 문제라고 부연 설명한다.

(B) '모르면서 모르는 것을 인식하는 경우(don't know ~ realize it)'를 '무지(ignorance)'로, 모르면서 알고 있다고 생각하는 경우'(don't know ~ know it)'를 '무분별함(irrationality)'으로 받는다.(▶ **Point 1** 대용어) 잘 모르면서 말하는 것은 위험하다고 하며, 잘못 아는 것은 부분적으로 심리적 요인들 때문이라고 설명한다.

↓

(A) Such factors는 (B)의 '심리적 요인들(psychological factors)'을 받으며(▶ **Point 1** 지시사/대명사), 그러한 요인들 외에도 미디어라는 다른 요인이 있다는 내용이 however(하지만)을 통해 이어진다.(▶ **Zoom 1** 역접 연결어)

어휘

at best 기껏해야, 잘해야   **be equipped to-v** v할 능력이 있다
bend 굴복[복종]하다; 구부러지다   **ignorance** 무지, 무식
inadequately 불충분하게   **informed** 알고 있는
(↔ **misinformed** 잘못 알고 있는)   **irrationality** 무분별함; 불합리
misinformation 잘못 아는 것; 잘못된 정보   **observer** 논평자; 관찰자, 관측자   **owe to A** A의 탓[책임]이다   **predictable** 예견[예측]할 수 있는
polarization (의견의) 대립, 분열   **poorly** 빈약[불충분]하게; 형편없이

구문 분석

³,⁴It's **one thing** // when citizens don't know something, and realize it, ~ // It's **another thing** // when citizens don't know something, but think // (that) they know it, ~.
<A is one thing, B is another thing>: A와 B는 (완전) 별개이다
⁶**Whatever** else one might conclude / about self-government, ~.
여기서 whatever(어떤 것이 ~이라도)는 양보 부사절을 이끄는 접속사이면서 부사절의 목적어 역할도 하는 복합관계대명사임.

해석 ¹첫 번째 과학적 여론 조사가 대부분의 미국인이 정치에 대해서 기껏해야 빈약하게 알고 있다는 것을 밝힌 이후로, 분석가들은 시민들이 민주주의가 그들에게 부여한 역할을 할 능력이 있는지 물었다. (C) ²그러나 불충분하게 알고 있는 대중보다 더 나쁜 것이 있는데, 그것은 잘못 알고 있는 대중이다. ³시민들이 어떤 것을 모르면서, 그것(모르는 것)을 인식하고 있는 경우는 늘 문제가 되어 왔다. ⁴이와 별개로, 시민들이 어떤 것을 모르지만 자신들이 알고 있다고 생각하는 경우는 새로운 문제이다. (B) ⁵무지와 무분별함 사이에는 차이점이 있다. ⁶자치 정부에 관해 다른 어떤 것으로 결론을 내리더라도, 시민들이 자신들이 무엇을 말하고 있는지 알지 못하는 경우는 위험하다. ⁷우리가 잘못 아는 것은 우리의 욕망에 맞는 방식으로 세상을 바라보는 우리의 경향을 포함하여, 부분적으로 심리적 요인들의 탓이다. (A) ⁸하지만 그런 요인들은 늘 우리와 함께 있어 온 잘못된 정보만 설명할 수 있다. ⁹최근에 잘못된 정보의 급격한 증가에는 다른 원인이 있는데, (그것은) 바로 우리의 미디어이다. ¹⁰"그것들(우리의 미디어)은 우리를 어리석게 만들고 있습니다."라고 한 논평자는 말한다. ¹¹사실이 허구에 굴복하면, 예견할 수 있는 결과는 정치적 불신과 대립이다.

Zoom 1

해석 … 게다가 인적 자원 개발 기능은 지속적 학습에 대한 강조를 유지하기 위해 극적으로 변화될 수도 있다.

• human resource 인적 자원　emphasis 강조, 중요성

➔ 학습하는 조직에서 모든 직원은 지식을 습득하고 전달하는 책임을 맡아야 한다. 형식적인 훈련 프로그램은 … 변화하는 훈련 요구를 처리하고 시기적절한 정보 공유를 장려하기에 불충분하다.

• acquire 습득하다, 얻다　transfer 전달하다, 전하다　formal 형식적인, 표면적인; 공식적인　insufficient 불충분한　address (문제 등을) 처리하다, 다루다; 연설(하다)　shifting 변화하는, 바뀌는; 이동하는　timely 시기적절한, 적시의

Zoom 2

해석 물벼룩이라는 굉장히 흥미로운 종은 진화 생물학자들이 '적응적 가소성'이라고 부르는 일종의 유연성을 보인다.

• fascinating 굉장히 흥미로운; 매혹적인　water flea 물벼룩　flexibility 유연성　adaptive 적응하는　plasticity 가소성

➔ 만약 새끼 물벼룩이 물벼룩을 잡아먹는 생물의 화학적 특징을 포함하는 물에서 성체로 발달하고 있으면, 그것은 투구와 가시 돌기를 발달시킨다. 만일 그것 (새끼 물벼룩) 주위의 물이 포식자의 화학적 특징을 포함하지 않으면, 그 물벼룩은 이러한 보호 장치를 발달시키지 않는다.

• signature 특징; 서명　prey on ~을 잡아먹다　helmet 투구 (모양의 것); 헬멧　spine 가시 돌기; 척추　predator 포식자　device 장치, 기구; 방법

Zoom 3

해석 고대 그리스인들은 'logos'와 'mythos'라는 두 가지의 매우 다른 사고의 방식을 서술하곤 했다. logos는 개략적으로 논리적인 것, 실증적인 것, 과학적인 것의 세계를 표현했다.

• roughly 개략적으로; 대략; 거칠게　refer to A A를 표현하다[나타내다]; A를 참고하다　logical 논리적인; 타당한　empirical 실증적인, 경험[실험]에 의거한

➔ mythos는 꿈, 스토리텔링, 그리고 상징의 세계를 표현했다.

Zoom 4

해석 몇몇 사람들은 편하고 예측할 수 있는 삶의 편안함 외에는 다른 이유 없이 같은 방식으로 머리를 하고, 같은 브랜드의 신발을 사고, 같은 아침 식사를 먹는다. 그러나 많은 다른 사람들은 마라톤을 대비해 훈련하고, 담배를 끊고, 활동 분야를 바꾼다. 이 두 집단의 사람들 간의 차이점은 무엇일까?

• ease 편안함, 안락함　switch 바꾸다, 전환하다

➔ 그것은 그들의 관점이다. 변화하는 사람들은 변화가 가능한지 의심하거나 그들이 변화할 수 없는 이유를 찾지 않는다.

• perspective 관점, 시각　question 의심하다, 의문을 제기하다; 질문(하다); 문제

Zoom 5

해석 경제학에 '매몰 비용 오류'라고 알려진 원리가 있다. … 이것은 사람들이 분명히 그만두어야 하는 계획이나 일을 계속하게 한다.

• path (행동) 계획; 길; 방향　pursuit 일, 활동; 추구　abandon 그만두다; 버리다

➔ 때로는 한 사람이 할 수 있는 가장 현명한 일은 그만두는 것이다.

Zoom 6

해석 일부 도시는 가구들이 모든 폐기물을 소비자에 의해 직접 구입된, 흔히 각각 1달러 이상이 드는 전용 쓰레기봉투에 담아 처리하도록 요구해 왔다.

• household 가구, 가정[가족](의)　dispose of ~을 처리하다[없애다]

➔ 그 결과는 크게 증가된 재활용과 포장재와 폐기물에 대한 소비자의 더 세심한 주의였다.　• packaging 포장(재)

Focus & Practice　　　　p.62

1 ①　　**2** ①　　**3** ②　　**4** (B) — (C) — (A)
5 (C) — (A) — (B)

1 ①

해석 화석 기록은 다세포 생물 이전에 단세포 생물이 진화했다는 예측을 뒷받침하는데, 다세포 생물은 단세포 생물의 최초 출현 수백만 년 후의 지구 지층에서 발견된다. 그 반대가 발견될 수도 있다는 가능성이 항상 남아 있음에 주목하라.

• fossil 화석　organism 생물(체), 유기체　evolve 진화하다; 발전시키다　layer 지층; (쌓인 것의) 층　note 주목[주의]하다; 언급하다　opposite 반대(의)

(A) 다세포 생물이 단세포 생물 이전에 진화한 것으로 실제로 밝혀진다면, 그러면 진화론은 거부될 것이다.　• reject 거부[거절]하다

(B) 말의 경우에서처럼, 많은 화석에서 시간이 흐름에 따라 공통의 조상으로부터 특정한 특징의 변화를 보여주는 잇따른 변화가 발견된다.

• sequential 잇따른, 순차적인

해설 주어진 글은 단세포 생물이 다세포 생물보다 먼저 진화했다는 예측을 화석 기록이 뒷받침하나, 그 예측과 반대되는 것이 발견될 수도 있다는 내용이다. (A)는 그 반대가 발견될 가능성을 구체적으로 설명하므로 주어진 글 다음에 이어질 글로 적절하다. (B)는 화석이 생물의 잇따른 변화를 보여준다는 내용을 말의 예를 들어 설명하므로 주어진 글과 연결되지 않는다.

2 ①

해석 로스앤젤레스에서 길을 건너는 것은 힘든 일인데, 다행히 버튼을 누르는 것으로, 우리는 차량들을 멈추게 할 수 있다. 아니면 우리가 과연 그럴 수 있을까?

• tricky 힘든, 까다로운; 교묘한　traffic 차량들, 교통(량)

(A) 그 버튼의 진짜 목적은 우리로 하여금 우리가 신호등에 영향력을 가지고 있다고 믿게 만들기 위함이고, 그럼으로써 우리는 신호가 바뀌기를 기다리는 것을 더 잘 견딜 수 있다.

• influence 영향(력); 영향을 주다　endure 견디다, 참다; 오래가다

(B) 엘리베이터의 '문 열림'과 '문 닫힘' 버튼도 마찬가지이다. 그러한 속임수들은 '플라시보 버튼'이라고 불리며, 온갖 종류의 환경에서 사용되고 있다.

• the same goes for ~ ~도 마찬가지이다　placebo 플라시보, (유효 성분이 없는) 위약　context 환경, 정황; 문맥, 맥락

해설 주어진 글은 우리가 길을 건널 때 정말 버튼을 눌러 차량들을 멈추게 할 수 있는지에 대해 의문을 제기한다. (A)는 버튼의 진짜 목적이 우리가 영향력이 있다고 믿게 만들어서 신호를 더 잘 기다리도록 하기 위함이라는 내용으로, 주어진 글의 질문에 대한 답변이 되어 적절하다. (B)는 다른 사례인 엘리베이터 버튼도 마찬가지라고 제시하며 이것들을 곧바로 속임수라고 칭하므로 주어진 글 뒤에 이어지기에 적절하지 않다.

3 ②

해석 19세기의 QWERTY 키보드는 빈번히 사용되는 키들(E와 O같은)이 걸리는 것을 방지하기 위하여 물리적으로 따로 떨어져 있게 설계되었다. 전자 타자 기술이 발전했을 무렵, 수백만의 사람들이 이미 수백만의 QWERTY 타자기로 타자 치기를 배웠다.
•**frequently** 빈번히, 자주   **separate** 따로 떨어지다; 분리된
jam (기계에 무엇이) 걸림, 막힘
(A) 당신은 왜 어색한 글자 배치를 가진 이 특정한 키의 배치 형태가 표준이 되었는지 궁금해 할 수도 있다.
•**configuration** 배치 형태; 배열; 형상   **awkward** 어색한; 곤란한; 불편한
placement 배치, 놓기   **standard** 표준, 규격; 보통
(B) QWERTY 키보드를 더 효율적인 디자인으로 바꾸는 것은 값비싸고 조정하기도 어려웠을 것이다.
•**replace** 바꾸다, 갈다; 대체하다   **efficient** 효율적인; 능률적인
coordinate 조정하다; 조직화하다

해설 주어진 글은 QWERTY 키보드가 빈번히 사용되는 키들이 걸리는 것을 방지하기 위해 떨어져 있도록 설계되었는데, 타자 기술이 발전했을 무렵에는 이미 많은 사람들이 그 타자기로 타자 치는 것을 배운 이후였다는 내용이다. (B)는 QWERTY 타자기를 더 효율적인 디자인으로 바꾸는 것이 값비싸고 조정하기 어려웠을 것이라고 설명하는데, 이는 주어진 글에 제시된 원인(이미 많은 사람들이 QWERTY 타자기로 타자 치는 것을 배움)에 대한 결과에 해당하므로 주어진 글 다음에 이어지기에 적절하다. (A)는 어색한 글자 배치를 가진 키의 배치 형태가 왜 표준이 되었는지 궁금해 할 수 있다고 의문을 소개하는 내용이므로 그 원인을 설명하는 주어진 글 뒤에 올 수 없다.

4 (B) — (C) — (A)

해석 문화는 우리가 의식적으로 고려하고 논의할 수 있는 방식뿐만 아니라 우리가 훨씬 덜 인식하는 방식으로도 작용한다.
•**operate** 작용하다, 영향을 미치다; 작동하다; 수술하다   **consciously** 의식적으로
cognizant 인식하는
(B) 우리의 행동에 대한 설명을 해야 할 때, 우리는 우리가 처해 있는 특정한 상황을 고려해 볼 때 어떤 변명이 받아들일 만하다고 판명될 수 있을지를 의식적으로 이해한다. 그런 상황에서 우리는 특정 도구를 사용하는 것처럼 문화적 관념을 사용한다.
•**account** 설명(하다); 계좌   **excuse** 변명(하다); 용서(하다)
prove (~임이) 판명되다[드러나다]; 입증하다   **acceptable** 받아들일 만한, 용인되는
(C) 우리가 스크루드라이버를 선택하듯이 우리는 문화적 개념을 선택하는데, 어떤 일은 십자 홈이 난 나사못을 필요로 하는 반면에 다른 일은 육각 렌치를 필요로 한다.
•**notion** 개념, 관념   **call for** ~을 필요로 하다; 요구하다
(A) 하지만 어떤 경우, 우리는 왜 우리가 어떤 주장을 사실이라고 믿는지에 대해 또는 왜 어떤 사회적 현실이 존재하는지를 어떻게 우리가 설명해야 할지에 대해 훨씬 덜 알고 있다.
•**aware of** ~을 알고[의식하고] 있는   **claim** 주장(하다); 요구(하다)

해설 주어진 글은 문화는 우리가 의식하는 방식뿐만 아니라 덜 인식하는 방식으로도 작용한다고 설명한다. (B)는 두 방식 중 전자인 '우리가 의식하는 방식'으로 작용하는 것에 대해 구체적으로 설명하므로 가장 먼저 오는 것이 적절하다. 이어서 우리가 상황에 따라 특정한 도구를 선택하듯이 의식적으로 문화적 개념을 선택한다는 내용을 스크루드라이버를 예로 들어 설명하는 (C)가 이어진다. 마지막으로 (A)에서 또 다른 방식인 '덜 인식하는 방식'으로 문화적 관념이 작용하는 경우를 설명하는 흐름이 자연스럽다.

5 (C) — (A) — (B)

해설 모방은 인간이 아닌 것들 사이에서 유익한 관행의 전달에 있어 핵심인 것으로 보인다. 가장 유명한 예는 일본 코시마섬의 마카크 원숭이들의 예이다.
•**transmission** 전달, 전송; 전염   **valuable** 유익한, 귀중한; 값비싼
(C) 1950년대 초, 한 살인 암컷 마카크 Imo는 웬일인지 불현듯 자신의 고구마를 먹기 전에 그것을 개울에 씻는 것을 생각해 냈다. 곧 자신의 고구마를 먹기 전에 주의 깊게 씻지 않는 코시마 마카크를 찾기는 어려웠다.
•**hit upon** 불현듯 ~을 생각해 내다   **stream** 개울, 시내; 줄줄 흐르다
(A) 몇 년 후에, Imo가 또 다른 혁신을 창안했다. 섬의 연구원들은 때때로 해변에서 그 원숭이들에게 밀을 주었는데, 그곳에서는 밀이 금방 모래와 섞였다.
•**introduce** 창안하다, 시작하다; 도입하다   **innovation** 혁신, 쇄신; 획기적인 것
occasionally 때때로, 가끔
(B) 하지만, Imo는 밀과 모래의 한 줌을 바다 속으로 던지면, 모래는 가라앉고 밀은 떠오를 것임을 깨달았다. 또, 몇 년 지나지 않아 그녀(Imo)의 동료 마카크 대부분이 밀과 모래를 바다 속으로 던져서 이익을 얻고 있었다.
•**fellow** 동료; 친구   **obtain** 얻다, 구하다; 획득하다

해설 주어진 글에서 모방이 유익한 관행의 전달에 있어 핵심으로 보인다고 하며 마카크 원숭이의 사례를 들었다. (C)는 Imo라는 마카크 원숭이를 소개한 다음, 이 원숭이의 고구마를 씻어 먹는 행동을 섬의 원숭이 전체가 모방하여 퍼진 사례를 구체적으로 설명하므로 주어진 글 다음에 이어지기에 적절하다. 이어서 (A)는 'A few years later(몇 년 후에)'로 시작하여 시간의 흐름을 나타내고, Imo가 또 다른 혁신을 창안했다고 하며 연구원들이 해변에서 준 밀이 금방 모래와 섞였다는 문제를 언급한다. 마지막으로 (B)에서 Imo가 모래와 섞인 밀을 바다에 던져 분리하는 방법을 깨닫자, 다른 대부분의 원숭이들도 이 행동을 따라 밀과 모래를 분리했다는 해결에 대한 내용이 이어지는 것이 적절하다.

1 ⑤

> ¹When two natural bodies of water stand at different levels, // building a canal (between them) / presents a complicated engineering problem.
> 두 개의 자연 수역(水域)이 서로 다른 높이에 있을 때 //
> 운하를 건설하는 것은 (그것들(두 개의 자연 수역) 사이에) / 복잡한 공학 문제를 야기한다

↓

(C) ²To make up for the difference in level, / engineers build *one or more water "steps,"* / (called locks), [that carry ships or boats / up or down / between the two levels].
높이의 차이를 벌충하기 위해 / 공학자들은 하나 이상의 물 '계단'을 만든다 /
(로크라고 불리는) / [선박이나 보트를 운반하는 / 위 또는 아래로 / 두 높이 사이에서]

³A lock is an artificial water basin.
로크는 인공적인 물웅덩이이다

⁴It has a long rectangular shape (with concrete walls and a pair of gates at each end).
그것(로크)은 긴 직사각형 모양으로 되어 있다 (콘크리트 벽과 양 끝에 한 쌍의 문이 있는)

↓

(B) ⁵When a vessel is going upstream, // the upper gates stay closed // as the ship enters the lock (at the lower water level).
선박이 상류로 가는 경우 // 위쪽 문은 닫혀 있다 // 선박이 로크에 들어가는 동안 (더 낮은 수위에 있는)

⁶The downstream gates are then closed // and more water is pumped into the basin.
그러고 나서 하류의 문이 닫힌다 // 그리고 더 많은 물이 웅덩이 안으로 쏟아 부어진다

⁷The rising water lifts the vessel / to the level (of the upper body of water).
상승하는 물이 선박을 끌어올린다 / 높이까지 (위쪽 수역의)

↓

(A) ⁸Then / the upper gates open // and the ship passes through.
그다음에 / 위쪽 문이 열린다 // 그리고 선박이 빠져나간다

⁹For downstream passage, / the process works the opposite way.
하류 통행의 경우 / 그 과정은 정반대로 작동한다

¹⁰The ship enters the lock (from the upper level), // and water is pumped / from the lock // until the ship is in line with the lower level.
선박이 로크로 들어간다 (위쪽 높이에서) // 그리고 물이 퍼내진다 /
로크에서 // 선박이 더 낮은 높이와 일직선을 이룰 때까지

해설

주어진 글의 내용 파악하기 ❷

> 서로 다른 높이의 수역 사이에 운하를 건설하는 데 복잡한 공학 문제가 있음.
> (뒤 내용은 문제점을 구체적으로 설명하거나 해결책을 제시할 것을 예측할 수 있음.)

≫

단서로 정답 찾기 ➕

> **(C)** 높이 차이의 문제에 대한 해결책으로 '로크'가 제시된다. (▶ Zoom 5 문제 → 해결) 로크는 선박이나 보트를 다른 높이의 수역으로 운반하며, 콘크리트 벽과 양 끝에 문이 있는 긴 직사각형 구조임을 설명한다.
>
> ↓
>
> **(B)** 선박이 상류로 올라갈 때의 경우를 예로 들어 로크의 작동 방식을 순차적으로 설명한다. 먼저 낮은 수위에 있는 선박이 로크에 들어갈 때 위쪽 문은 닫혀 있고, 이후에 하류의 문이 닫히고 물이 채워져 물이 선박을 끌어올린다고 한다.
>
> ↓
>
> **(A)** Then(그다음에)을 통해(▶ Point 2 기타 연결어) 앞에 언급된 과정 이후에 위쪽 문이 열리고 배가 나간다는 설명이 이어진다. 이어서 하류로 내려가는 경우에는 이 과정이 반대로 작동함을 덧붙인다.

어휘

artificial 인공적인   basin (물)웅덩이; 대야; 분지   canal 운하, 수로
in line with ~와 일직선을 이루다; ~와 같은 수준인, ~와 비슷한
make up for ~을 벌충[만회]하다   passage 통행, 통과; 통로
present 야기하다; 제시하다; 출석[참석]하다; 현재의
pump A into[from] B A를 B로[에서] 쏟아 붓다[퍼내다]
upstream 상류로; 상류의(↔ downstream 하류의; 하류로)
vessel (대형) 선박; 그릇

구문 분석

²To make up for the difference in level, / engineers build *one or more water "steps,"* / (called locks), / [that carry ships or boats / up or down / between the two levels].
선행사인 one or more water "steps"와 that이 이끄는 관계대명사절 사이에 water "steps"를 수식하는 과거분사구 called locks가 삽입된 구조임.

해석 ¹두 개의 자연 수역(水域)이 서로 다른 높이에 있을 때, 그것들(두 개의 자연 수역) 사이에 운하를 건설하는 것은 복잡한 공학 문제를 야기한다. (C) ²높이의 차이를 벌충하기 위해 공학자들은 두 높이 사이에서 선박이나 보트를 위 또는 아래로 운반하는, 로크라고 불리는 하나 이상의 물 '계단'을 만든다. ³로크는 인공적인 물웅덩이이다. ⁴그것(로크)은 콘크리트 벽과 양 끝에 한 쌍의 문이 있는 긴 직사각형 모양으로 되어 있다. (B) ⁵선박이 상류로 가는 경우, 선박이 더 낮은 수위에 있는 로크에 들어가는 동안 위쪽 문은 닫혀 있다. ⁶그러고 나서 하류의 문이 닫히고 더 많은 물이 웅덩이 안으로 쏟아 부어진다. ⁷상승하는 물이 선박을 위쪽 수역의 높이까지 끌어올린다. (A) ⁸그다음에 위쪽 문이 열리고 선박이 빠져나간다. ⁹하류 통행의 경우, 그 과정은 정반대로 작동한다. ¹⁰선박이 위쪽 높이에서 로크로 들어가고, 선박이 더 낮은 높이와 일직선을 이룰 때까지 로크에서 물이 퍼내진다.

2 ②

¹The objective of battle, / to "throw" the enemy and to make him defenseless, / may temporarily blind commanders and even strategists / to the larger purpose of war.
전투의 목표는 / 즉 적군을 '맹렬히 쓰러뜨려' 무방비하게 만드는 것 /
일시적으로 지휘관과 심지어 전략가까지도 보지 못하게 만들 수도 있다 / 전쟁의 더 큰 목적을

²War is never an isolated act, // nor is it ever only one decision.
전쟁은 결코 단일 행위가 아니다 // 또한 단 하나의 결정도 결코 아니다

↓

(B) ³In the real world, / war's larger purpose is always a political purpose.
현실 세계에서 / 전쟁의 더 큰 목적은 언제나 정치적 목적이다

⁴It transcends the use of force.
그것은 물리력의 사용을 초월한다

⁵This insight was famously captured / by Clausewitz's most famous phrase, // "War is a mere continuation of politics / by other means."
이 통찰은 훌륭하게 표현되었다 / Clausewitz의 가장 유명한 명언에 의해 //
"전쟁은 단지 정치의 연장에 불과하다 / 다른 수단에 의한"

↓

(A) ⁶To be political, / a political entity or a representative of a political entity, // whatever its constitutional form (is), / has to have an intention, a will.
정치적이려면 / 정치적 실체나 정치적 실체의 대표자는 //
그 조직상의 형태가 무엇이든지 / 의도, 즉 의지가 있어야 한다

⁷That intention has to be clearly expressed.
그 의도는 분명히 표현되어야 한다

↓

(C) ⁸And / one side's will has to be transmitted to the enemy / at some point / during the confrontation // (it does not have to be publicly communicated).
그리고 / 한쪽의 의지는 적에게 전달되어야 할 것이다 /
어느 시점에 / 대치하는 동안 // (그것(한쪽의 의지)이 공개적으로 전달될 필요는 없다)

⁹A violent act and its larger political intention / must also be attributed to one side / at some point / during the confrontation.
폭력적인 행위와 그것의 더 큰 정치적 의도는 / 또한 한쪽의 탓으로 돌려져야 한다 /
어느 시점에 / 대치하는 동안

¹⁰History does not know / of acts of war (without eventual attribution).
역사는 알지 못한다 / 전쟁 행위에 대해 (궁극적인 귀인이 없는)

해설

주어진 글의 내용 파악하기 ◉

전투에는 적군을 쓰러뜨리는 것보다 더 큰 목표가 있으며, 전쟁은 단일 행위도, 단 하나의 결정도 아님.

⌄⌄

단서로 정답 찾기 ➕

(B) 주어진 글에 언급된 '전쟁의 더 큰 목적(the larger purpose of war)'은 정치적 목적이며, 전쟁은 정치의 연장일 뿐이라고 구체적으로 설명한다.(▶ **Zoom 1, 2, 3 일반적/추상적 진술 → 구체적/세부적 진술**)

↓

(A) (B)에서 언급한 전쟁의 '정치적 목적(a political purpose)'의 조건을 이어서 제시하며 부연 설명한다.(▶ **Zoom 1, 2, 3 일반적/추상적 진술 → 구체적/세부적 진술**) 정치적 실체나 대표자는 의도(의지)가 있어야 하고, 그 의도는 분명히 표현되어야 한다는 것이다.

↓

(C) 그리고 한쪽의 의지가 적에게 전달되어야 할 것이라고 (A)의 내용에 덧붙여 부연 설명한다. 이어서 폭력적 행위와 정치적 의도가 한쪽의 탓으로 돌려져야 한다고 정치적 목적의 조건을 추가로 제시하며, 역사에 알려진 모든 전쟁에는 궁극적 귀인이 있다는 결론으로 글을 맺는다.

어휘

attribution 귀인, (원인에) 돌리기; 속성 **blind A to B** A에게 B를 보지 못하게 만들다 **capture** 표현[포착]하다; 붙잡다
commander 지휘관, 사령관 **confrontation** 대치, 대립
constitutional 조직상의; 헌법(상)의; 합법적인 **famously** 훌륭하게, 멋지게 **isolated** 단 하나[한 번]의; 외딴; 고립된
mere 단지 ~에 불과한; 단순한 **phrase** 명언; 간결한 표현; 구(句)
representative 대표(자); 대표하는 **strategist** 전략가
throw 맹렬히 쓰러뜨리다; 던지다 **transmit** 전달하다; 전송하다

구문 분석

²War is never an isolated act, // **nor is it** ever only one decision.
<nor+V+S>는 '~도 (또한) 아니다'의 의미로 부정어 nor 뒤에 도치가 일어남.

⁹A violent act and its larger political intention / must also **be attributed to** one side / ~.
A violent act and its larger political intention이 한쪽의 탓으로 '돌려지는' 수동의 의미이므로 <attribute A to B(A를 B의 탓으로 돌리다)>의 수동형이 쓰임.

---

^{해석} ¹전투의 목표, 즉 적군을 '맹렬히 쓰러뜨려' 무방비하게 만드는 것은 일시적으로 지휘관과 심지어 전략가까지도 전쟁의 더 큰 목적을 보지 못하게 만들 수도 있다. ²전쟁은 결코 단일 행위가 아니며, 또한 단 하나의 결정도 결코 아니다. (B) ³현실 세계에서 전쟁의 더 큰 목적은 언제나 정치적 목적이다. ⁴그것은 물리력의 사용을 초월한다. ⁵이 통찰은 "전쟁은 단지 다른 수단에 의한 정치의 연장에 불과하다."라는 Clausewitz의 가장 유명한 명언에 의해 훌륭하게 표현되었다. (A) ⁶정치적이려면, 정치적 실체나 정치적 실체의 대표자는, 그 조직상의 형태가 무엇이든지, 의도, 즉 의지가 있어야 한다. ⁷그 의도는 분명히 표현되어야 한다. (C) ⁸그리고 한쪽의 의지는 대치하는 동안 어느 시점에 적에게 전달되어야 할 것이다(그것이 공개적으로 전달될 필요는 없다). ⁹또한 폭력적인 행위와 그것의 더 큰 정치적 의도는 대치하는 동안 어느 시점에 한쪽의 탓으로 돌려져야 한다. ¹⁰역사는 궁극적 귀인이 없는 전쟁 행위에 대해 알지 못한다.

3 ③

[1]Darwin saw blushing / as (being) uniquely human, / (as) representing *an involuntary physical reaction* (caused by embarrassment and self-consciousness / in a social environment).

Darwin은 얼굴이 붉어지는 것을 여겼다 / 고유하게 인간적인 것으로 /
즉 비자발적인 신체 반응을 나타내는 것(으로) (당혹감과 남의 시선을 의식하는 것으로 야기되는 / 사회적 환경에서)

↓

(B) [2]If we feel awkward, embarrassed or ashamed // when we are alone, // we don't blush; //

우리가 어색하거나 당혹스럽거나 부끄럽다고 느끼더라도 // 우리가 혼자 있을 때 //
우리는 얼굴이 붉어지지 않는다 //

it seems to be caused / by our concern (about what others are thinking of us).

그것(얼굴이 붉어지는 것)은 야기되는 것처럼 보인다 / 우리의 염려에 의해 (다른 사람들이 우리를 어떻게 생각하고 있는지에 대한)

[3]Studies have confirmed // that simply being told // (that) you are blushing / brings it on.

연구들은 확인해 왔다 // 단지 듣는 것만으로도 // 얼굴이 붉어졌다고 /
그것(얼굴이 붉어지는 것)을 야기한다는 것을

[4]We feel // as though others can see / through our skin and into our mind.

우리는 느낀다 // 마치 다른 사람들이 볼 수 있는 것처럼 / 우리의 피부를 꿰뚫어 우리의 마음을 들여다

↓

(C) [5]However, / while we sometimes want to disappear // when we involuntarily go bright red, // psychologists argue // that blushing actually serves a positive social purpose.

그러나 / 우리가 가끔 사라지고 싶어 하는 반면에 // 자신도 모르게 얼굴이 새빨개질 때 //
심리학자들은 주장한다 // 얼굴이 붉어지는 것이 실제로는 긍정적인 사회적 목적에 도움이 된다고

[6]When we blush, // it's a signal to others // that we recognize // that a social norm has been broken; // it is an apology (for a faux pas).

우리가 얼굴이 붉어질 때 // 그것(얼굴이 붉어지는 것)은 다른 사람들에게 신호이다 // 우리가 인식한다는 // 사회적 규범이 어겨졌음을 // 그리고 그것(얼굴이 붉어지는 것)은 사과이다 (실수에 대한)

↓

(A) [7]Maybe / our brief loss of face benefits / the long-term cohesion (of the group).

어쩌면 / 우리가 잠시 체면을 잃는 것이 도움이 될지도 모른다 / 장기적인 결합에 (집단의)

[8]Interestingly, / if someone blushes / after making a social mistake, // they are viewed / in a more favourable light / than *those* [who don't blush].

흥미롭게도 / 누군가가 얼굴이 붉어지면 / 사회적 실수를 저지른 후 //
그들은 바라봐진다 / 더 호의적인 관점에서 / 사람들보다 [얼굴이 붉어지지 않는]

해석 [1]Darwin은 얼굴이 붉어지는 것을 고유하게 인간적인 것, 즉 사회적 환경에서 당혹감과 남의 시선을 의식하는 것으로 야기되는 비자발적인 신체 반응을 나타내는 것으로 여겼다. (B) [2]우리가 혼자 있을 때 어색하거나 당혹스럽거나 부끄럽다고 느끼더라도 우리는 얼굴이 붉어지지 않는데, 그것(얼굴이 붉어지는 것)은 다른 사람들이 우리를 어떻게 생각하고 있는지에 대한 우리의 염려에 의해 야기되는 것처럼 보인다. [3]연구들은 단지 얼굴이 붉어졌다고 듣는 것만으로도 그것(얼굴이 붉어지는 것)을 야기한다는 것을 확인해 왔다. [4]우리는 마치 다른 사람들이 우리의 피부를 꿰뚫어 우리의 마음을 들여다볼 수 있는 것처럼 느낀다. (C) [5]그러나, 우리가 가끔 자신도 모르게 얼굴이 새빨개질 때 사라지고 싶어 하는 반면에, 심리학자들은 얼굴이 붉어지는 것이 실제로는 긍정적인 사회적 목적에 도움이 된다고 주장한다. [6]우리가 얼굴이 붉어질 때, 그것은 다른 사람들에게 우리가 사회적 규범이 어겨졌음을 인식한다는 신호이며, 실수에 대한 사과이다. (A) [7]어쩌면 우리가 잠시 체면을 잃는 것이 집단의 장기적인 결합에 도움이 될지도 모른다. [8]흥미롭게도 누군가가 사회적 실수를 저지른 후 얼굴이 붉어지면, 그들은 얼굴이 붉어지지 않는 사람들보다 더 호의적인 관점에서 바라봐진다.

1 ③

> [1] When scientists have trained primates and other animals to use simple tools, // they've discovered // just how profoundly the brain can be influenced / by technology.
> 과학자들이 영장류와 다른 동물들이 간단한 도구를 사용하도록 훈련했을 때 // 그들은 발견했다 // 뇌가 얼마나 깊이 영향을 받을 수 있는지를 / 기술에 의해

↓

(B) [2] Monkeys, / for example, / were taught // how to use rakes and pliers / to reach *food* [that was otherwise beyond their grasp].
원숭이들은 / 예를 들어 / 배웠다 // 갈퀴와 집게를 사용하는 법을 / 음식을 손을 뻗어 잡기 위해 [그렇지 않으면(갈퀴와 집게를 사용하지 않으면) 그것들의 손이 닿지 않는 곳에 있는]

[3] When researchers monitored the animals' neural activity, // they found significant growth // in *the visual and motor areas* (involved in controlling *the hands* [that held the tools]).
연구자들이 그 동물들(원숭이들)의 신경 활동을 관찰했을 때 // 그들은 상당한 성장을 발견했다 // 시각령과 운동령에서의 (손을 통제하는 데 관여하는 [도구를 붙잡는])

↓

(C) [4] But / they discovered *something* (even more striking) / as well.
하지만 / 그들(연구자들)은 (~한) 것을 발견했다 (훨씬 더 주목할 만한) / 또한

[5] The data showed // that the rakes and pliers actually came to be incorporated / into the neural pathways of the animals' brains.
그 자료는 보여주었다 // 갈퀴와 집게가 실제로 통합되었다는 것을 / 그 동물들(원숭이들)의 뇌의 신경 경로에

↓

(A) [6] The tools, / (so far as the animals' brains were concerned), // had become part of their bodies.
그 도구들은 / (그 동물들(원숭이들)의 뇌에 관한 한) // 그것들 몸의 일부분이 되었다

[7] As *the researchers* [who designed the experiment with the pliers] / explained, // the monkeys' brains began to act // as if the pliers were now fingers.
연구자들이 ~듯이 [집게를 가지고 실험을 계획한] / 설명했(듯이) // 원숭이들의 뇌는 행동하기 시작했다 // 마치 집게가 이제 손가락인 것처럼

해설

주어진 글의 내용 파악하기 

동물들에게 도구를 사용하도록 훈련시키는 실험을 통해 과학자들은 그것들의 뇌가 기술에 의해 큰 영향을 받는다는 사실을 발견함.

⌄

단서로 정답 찾기

(B) for example(예를 들어)로 원숭이들이 갈퀴와 집게를 사용하는 법을 배우자 시각령과 운동령이 상당히 성장했다는 발견 내용이 이어진다.(▸ Point 2 예시 연결어)

↓

(C) they는 앞 문장의 '연구자들(researchers)'을 받으며 (▸ Point 1 지시사/대명사) 그들이 훨씬 더 주목할 만한 것도 발견했다는, 앞과 대비하여 놀라운 사실이 But(하지만)으로 이어진다.(▸ Point 2 역접 연결어) 이어서 갈퀴와 집게가 실제로 원숭이들의 뇌의 신경 경로에 통합되었다고 설명한다.

↓

(A) The tools는 앞에서 언급한 '갈퀴와 집게(the rakes and pliers)'를 받는다.(▸ Point 1 대용어) 연구자들이 설명한 것처럼, 원숭이들의 뇌는 그 도구들을 자신의 몸의 일부로 받아들였다고 설명한다.

어휘

beyond A's grasp A의 손이 닿지 않는 곳에; A가 이해할 수 없는
incorporate A into B A를 B에 통합하다[집어넣다]　neural 신경(계)의
otherwise (만약) 그렇지 않으면[않았다면]; (~와는) 다르게
primate 영장류　profoundly 깊이; 완전히　plier 집게, 펜치
rake 갈퀴; 갈퀴질을 하다, 갈퀴로 모으다　striking 주목할 만한; 눈에 띄는, 인상적인

구문 분석

[6] The tools, / (**so far as** the animals' brains were concerned), // had become part of their bodies.
부사절 접속사 so far as는 '~하는 한'으로 해석함.
[7] ~, // the monkeys' brains began to act // **as if** the pliers **were** now fingers.
<as if+S´+were ~> 가정법은 '마치 ~인 것처럼'으로 해석함.

해석 [1] 과학자들은 영장류와 다른 동물들이 간단한 도구를 사용하도록 훈련했을 때, 뇌가 기술에 의해 얼마나 깊이 영향을 받을 수 있는지를 발견했다. (B) [2] 예를 들어, 원숭이들은 그렇지 않으면(갈퀴와 집게를 사용하지 않으면) 그것들의 손이 닿지 않는 곳에 있는 음식을 손을 뻗어 잡기 위해 갈퀴와 집게를 사용하는 법을 배웠다. [3] 연구자들이 원숭이들의 신경 활동을 관찰했을 때, 도구를 붙잡는 손을 통제하는 데 관여하는 시각령(대뇌에 있는 시각에 관계된 영역)과 운동령(대뇌에서 운동 발현에 관계된 영역)에서의 상당한 성장을 발견했다. (C) [4] 하지만 연구자들은 훨씬 더 주목할 만한 것 또한 발견했다. [5] 그 자료는 갈퀴와 집게가 실제로 원숭이들의 뇌의 신경 경로에 통합되었다는 것을 보여주었다. (A) [6] 원숭이들의 뇌에 관한 한, 그 도구들은 그것들 몸의 일부분이 되었다. [7] 집게를 가지고 실험을 계획한 연구자들이 설명했듯이, 원숭이들의 뇌는 마치 집게가 이제 손가락인 것처럼 행동하기 시작했다.

2 ③

¹In the field of financial planning / there is a universally accepted principle //
재무 계획 분야에는 / 일반적으로 받아들여지는 원칙이 있다 //
that it's critical / to pay yourself first // before you pay your other bills — / to think of yourself as a creditor.
(~이) 중요하다는 / 먼저 자신에게 돈을 내는 것이 // 다른 청구서에 돈을 내기 전에 /
즉, 자신을 채권자로 생각하는 것

↓

(B) **²The reason for this financial wisdom is // that if you delay putting money into a savings account // until after everybody else is paid, // there will be nothing left for you to save!**
이 재무 지혜의 근거는 ~이다 // 당신이 만약 저축 계좌에 돈을 넣는 것을 미룬다면 //
다른 모든 이들이 돈을 지급받은 이후까지 // 당신에게는 저축할 돈이 하나도 남아 있지 않을 것이라는 점

(C) **³The result is // that you'll keep postponing your savings plan // until it's too late to do anything about it.**
그 결과는 ~이다 // 당신이 계속해서 저축 계획을 연기할 거라는 것 //
너무 늦어서 그것(저축)에 대해 아무것도 하지 못할 때까지

⁴This cycle of delayed saving / can leave you feeling frustrated and financially unprepared.
이러한 지연되는 저축의 반복은 / 당신이 좌절감을 느끼고 재정적으로 준비가 안 된 상태가 되게 할 수 있다

⁵But / if you pay yourself first, // somehow there will be just enough / to pay everyone else as well.
그러나 / 만약 당신이 자기 자신에게 먼저 돈을 내면 // 어떻게든 충분히 있을 것이다 /
다른 모든 사람에게도 돈을 지불할 만큼은

↓

(A) **⁶The identical principle is also critical / to implement any program of spiritual practice.**
동일한 원칙이 또한 중요하다 / 어떤 정신 수행 프로그램을 실행하는 데도

↓

⁷If you don't start implementing your program right away, // but instead you wait // till you finish all your other chores, // then you will probably never start.
만약 당신이 프로그램 실행을 당장 시작하지 않고 //
대신에 당신이 기다린다면 // 당신의 다른 잡다한 모든 일을 끝낼 때까지 //
그렇다면 당신은 아마도 절대 시작하지 않을 것이다

해설

주어진 글의 내용 파악하기 

재무 계획 분야에서의 원칙은 다른 곳에 돈을 내기 전에 본인 몫의 돈을 먼저 배분해 놓는 것임.

⌄

단서로 정답 찾기 ➕

(B) this financial wisdom은 주어진 글에서 언급한 '원칙(a universally ~ as a creditor)'을 받으며(▶ **Point 1** 지시사/대명사, 대용어), 그 근거는 다른 곳에 돈을 내는 것을 우선시하면 저축할 돈이 남지 않기 때문이라고 설명한다.

(C) 앞에서 말한 '저축할 돈이 남지 않은(nothing left ~ to save)' 상황에 대해 '계속해서 저축 계획을 연기할 것(keep postponing ~ plan)'이라는 결과가 이어진다.(▶ **Point 3** 원인 → 결과) 반대로 자신에게 먼저 돈을 내면 다른 곳에도 지불할 돈이 어떻게든 있을 것이라고 설명한다.

↓

(A) The identical principle은 주어진 글에서부터 언급한 재무 계획 분야에서의 원칙을 말하며(▶ **Point 1** 대용어), 그 원칙이 정신적 수행을 하는 데도 중요하다는 내용으로 글을 마무리 짓는다.

어휘

creditor 채권자   **identical** 동일한, 똑같은   **implement** 실행[이행]하다
postpone 연기하다, 미루다   **principle** 원칙, 원리
somehow 어떻게든; 아무래도   **spiritual** 정신의, 정신적인; 영적인

구문 분석

²The reason for this financial wisdom is // that if you delay putting money into a savings account // until after everybody else is paid, // there will be nothing left for you to save!
접속사 that이 이끄는 절이 be동사의 보어이며, if가 이끄는 조건 부사절 내에 until이 이끄는 시간 부사절이 포함된 구조임.

해석 ¹재무 계획 분야에는 다른 청구서에 돈을 내기 전에 먼저 자신에게 돈을 내는 것, 즉 자신을 채권자로 생각하는 것이 중요하다는 일반적으로 받아들여지는 원칙이 있다. (B) ²이 재무 지혜의 근거는 당신이 만약 다른 모든 이들이 돈을 지급받은 이후까지 저축 계좌에 돈을 넣는 것을 미룬다면, 당신에게는 저축할 돈이 하나도 남아 있지 않을 것이라는 점이다! (C) ³그 결과는 당신이 너무 늦어서 저축에 대해 아무것도 하지 못할 때까지 계속해서 저축 계획을 연기할 거라는 것이다. ⁴이러한 지연되는 저축의 반복은 당신이 좌절감을 느끼고 재정적으로 준비가 안 된 상태가 되게 할 수 있다. ⁵그러나 만약 당신이 자기 자신에게 먼저 돈을 내면, 다른 모든 사람에게도 돈을 지불할 만큼은 어떻게든 충분히 있을 것이다. (A) ⁶동일한 원칙이 어떤 정신 수행 프로그램을 실행하는 데도 또한 중요하다. ⁷만약 당신이 프로그램 실행을 당장 시작하지 않고, 대신에 당신의 다른 잡다한 모든 일을 끝낼 때까지 기다린다면, 그렇다면 당신은 아마도 절대 시작하지 않을 것이다.

3 ①

> [1] When an animal is having a chronically difficult time filling its belly, // something intriguing happens / in its body / at a molecular level.
> 어떤 동물이 배를 채우는 데 만성적으로 힘든 시간을 보낼 때 //
> 무언가 아주 흥미로운 일이 벌어진다 / 그것(그 동물)의 몸에서는 / 분자 단위로

↓

(A) [2] Its aging slows down, // and cells don't die as quickly // as they do // when food is available.
그것(그 동물)의 노화 속도는 느려진다 // 그리고 세포는 빨리 죽지 않는다 //
그것들(세포들)이 그러는(죽는) 것만큼 // 먹을 것을 구할 수 있을 때

[3] Contrary to what you might think, / a cell's health in this situation doesn't deteriorate.
여러분이 예상할 수 있는 것과는 반대로 / 이런 상황에서 세포의 건강은 악화되지 않는다

[4] The body, / (sensing deprivation), / seems to call all hands on deck / to conserve energy and prepare for the worst.
몸은 / (결핍을 감지하고는) / 온 힘을 모을 것을 요구하는 것으로 보인다 /
에너지를 아끼고 최악의 상황에 대비하기 위해

↓

(C) [5] In other words, / each cell grows tougher and more cautious.
다시 말해 / 각 세포는 더 강해지고 신중해진다

[6] This is thanks largely to a class of proteins called *sirtuins*, // which (some scientists suspect) reduce the rate of cell growth.
이것은 주로 시르투인이라는 일종의 단백질 덕분이다 //
그리고 그것이 (일부 과학자들이 추측하기로는) 세포의 생장 속도를 늦춘다

↓

(B) [7] Numerous studies back up this assumption.
수많은 연구가 이 가정을 뒷받침한다

[8] Reducing the normal diets of creatures (such as fruit flies, rats, and monkeys) / by 35 to 40 percent / has shown similar outcomes, / with lifespans increasing by as much as 30 percent.
동물들의 평소 식사량을 줄이는 것은 (초파리, 쥐, 원숭이와 같은) /
35~40%로 / 유사한 결과를 보여 왔다 / 수명이 30%까지 증가하며

해설

주어진 글의 내용 파악하기 ✿

어떤 동물이 만성적으로 먹을 것을 구하기 힘들 때 그것의 몸에서 무언가 흥미로운 일이 일어남.

단서로 정답 찾기 ✚

(A) Its는 주어진 글에서 언급된 '어떤 동물(an animal)'을 소유격으로 받으며(▶ **Point 1** 지시사/대명사), 먹을 것을 구할 수 없을 때 '동물의 몸에서 일어나는 흥미로운 일(something ~ level)'이 '노화가 느려지고 세포가 빨리 죽지 않는다(aging ~ quickly)'는 것임을 구체적으로 설명한다. 이어서 결핍이 있을 때 세포의 건강은 악화되지 않으며, 온 힘을 모은다고 부연 설명한다.

(C) In other words(다시 말해)로 세포는 더 강해지고 신중해진다고 앞 내용을 달리 바꾸어 말하는 내용이 이어진다.(▶ **Point 2 환언 연결어**) 이어서 이는 일부 과학자들이 추측하기로 세포의 생장 속도를 늦추는 시르투인 덕분이라고 부연 설명한다.

(B) this assumption은 (C)의 '일부 과학자들이 시르투인이 세포의 생장 속도를 늦춘다고 추측한다(some scientists suspect ~ growth)'는 내용을 받으며(▶ **Point 1** 지시사/대명사, 대용어), 이를 뒷받침하는 여러 연구의 결과를 제시한다.

어휘

all hands on deck 온 힘을 모으다　**assumption** 가정, 가설　**available** 구할[이용할] 수 있는　**back up** ~을 뒷받침하다; ~을 지지하다　**cautious** 신중한, 조심스러운　**chronically** 만성적으로, 고질적으로　**conserve** (에너지 등을) 아끼다; 보존하다　**deprivation** (필수적인 것의) 결핍, 부족　**deteriorate** 악화되다; (품질·가치가) 떨어지다　**intriguing** 아주 흥미로운, 호기심을 자극하는　**lifespan** 수명　**molecular** 분자의

구문 분석

[1] When an animal is **having a** chronically **difficult time filling** its belly, // ~.
<have a difficult time v-ing>: v하는 데 힘든 시간을 보내다

[6] This is thanks largely to a class of proteins called *sirtuins*, // which (**some scientists suspect**) reduce the rate of cell growth.
관계대명사 which와 관계사절의 동사 reduce 사이에 <S+V (some scientists suspect)>가 삽입된 구조임.

해석 [1] 어떤 동물이 배를 채우는 데 만성적으로 힘든 시간을 보낼 때, 그 동물의 몸에서는 분자 단위로 무언가 아주 흥미로운 일이 벌어진다. (A) [2] 그 동물의 노화 속도는 느려지고, 세포는 먹을 것을 구할 수 있을 때만큼 빨리 죽지 않는다. [3] 여러분이 예상할 수 있는 것과는 반대로, 이런 상황에서 세포의 건강은 악화되지 않는다. [4] 몸은 결핍을 감지하고는, 에너지를 아끼고 최악의 상황에 대비하기 위해 온 힘을 모을 것을 요구하는 것으로 보인다. (C) [5] 다시 말해, 각 세포는 더 강해지고 신중해진다. [6] 이것은 주로 시르투인이라는 일종의 단백질 덕분으로, 일부 과학자들이 추측하기로는 그것이 세포의 생장 속도를 늦춘다. (B) [7] 수많은 연구가 이 가정을 뒷받침한다. [8] 초파리, 쥐, 원숭이와 같은 동물들의 평소 식사량을 35~40%로 줄이는 것은 수명이 30%까지 증가하며 유사한 결과를 보여 왔다.

4 ③

> ¹There are many non-linear interactions / in ecology // and, as in the weather and the stock market, / a small disturbance can lead to a sudden and unpredictable change in state.
> 비선형적인 상호 작용이 많이 있다 / 생태계에는 // 그래서 날씨와 주식 시장에서처럼 /
> 작은 소란이 갑작스럽고 예측 불가능한 상태의 변화로 이어질 수 있다

↓

(B) ²An attempt to shoot foxes / to increase the number of red grouse prey, / for instance, / might have an undesirable effect, //
여우를 총으로 쏴서 죽이려는 시도는 / (여우의) 먹이인 붉은 뇌조의 수를 늘리기 위해 /
예를 들어 / 바람직하지 않은 결과를 가져올 수도 있다 //

for the predators normally catch / only *the birds* (most filled with parasites), //
왜냐하면 그 포식자들(여우)은 보통 잡기 때문이다 / 새(붉은 뇌조)만을 (기생충에 가장 많이 감염된) //

and once they are removed, // disease will spread and kill many more birds than before.
그리고 일단 그것들(여우)이 제거되면 // 질병이 퍼져서 전보다 더 많은 새들이 죽을 것이다

↓

(C) ³Such unforeseeable consequences / emphasize // that many of the connections among species (within a community) / are far from simple.
이러한 예측할 수 없는 결과는 / 강조한다 // 종(種)들 사이의 연관성 중 다수가 (한 군집 내에 있는) /
단순함과는 거리가 멀다는 것을

⁴In the intricate world beneath the soil, / as a case in point, / organisms differ wildly / from place to place / but somehow generate roughly the same mix of nutrients.
흙 밑의 복잡한 세계에서 / 이에 해당하는 예로 /
생물체들은 아주 다르다 / 장소마다 / 그러나 어떻게든 대략 똑같은 혼합비의 영양소를 생성한다

↓

(A) ⁵Each of those habitats / is filled with a chance group of *ecologically equivalent creatures*, // each of which arrived by accident.
그러한 서식지들 각각은 / 생태학적으로 동등한 생물들의 우연한 집합으로 가득 차 있다 //
(그것들은) 각기 어쩌다 (그곳에) 도착한

⁶Not only do such examples reveal our ignorance (of the laws behind ecosystems), // but they hint // that chaos and complexity may be the rule / rather than the exception.
이런 예들은 우리의 무지를 드러낼 뿐만 아니라 (생태계 이면에 있는 법칙에 대한) //
그것들(예)은 암시를 준다 // 혼돈과 복잡성이 (생태계의) 규칙일지도 모른다는 / 예외라기보다는

해설

주어진 글의 내용 파악하기 

> 생태계에서 일어나는 상호 작용은 비선형적이어서 사소한 일로 예측 불가능한 변화가 일어나기도 함.

≫

단서로 정답 찾기 ⊕

> **(B)** for instance(예를 들어)로 붉은 뇌조의 수를 늘리기 위해 포식자인 여우를 죽이면 오히려 더 많은 붉은 뇌조들이 질병으로 죽을 것이라는 예가 이어진다. (▶ **Point 2** 예시 연결어)
>
> **(C)** Such unforeseeable consequences는 여우들이 제거되면 오히려 붉은 뇌조들이 더 많이 죽는 예와 같은 바람직하지 않은 결과를 가리키며(▶ **Point 1** 지시사/대명사, 대용어), 한 군집 내의 종들 사이의 연관성은 단순하지 않다고 설명한다. 이어서 흙 밑에 존재하는 생물체들이 장소마다 달라도 비슷한 혼합비의 영양소를 생성한다는 또 다른 사례를 든다.
>
> ↓
>
> **(A)** those habitats는 (C)에서 언급한 흙 밑 생물체들의 다양한 서식지를 가리키며(▶ **Point 1** 지시사/대명사, 대용어), 생물학적으로 동등한 생물들이 우연히 각각의 서식지에 왔다고 설명한다. 이어서 이러한 예들은 혼돈과 복잡성이 생태계의 규칙일지도 모른다는 암시를 준다고 하며 글을 맺는다.

어휘

disturbance 소란, 소동; 방해   ecology 생태계; 생태학
cf. ecologically 생태학적으로   equivalent 동등한   ignorance 무지
in point ~에 해당하는, 적절한   intricate 복잡한, 정교한
non-linear 비선형의   parasite 기생충, 기생 동물[식물]
predator 포식자, 포식 동물   stock market 주식 시장
unforeseeable 예측할 수 없는

구문 분석

⁶**Not only do such examples reveal** our ignorance (of the laws behind ecosystems), // **but** they hint // ~.
<not only A but (also) B (A뿐 아니라 B도)>의 구조에서, 부정어인 not only가 문두에 와서 <조동사+S+V>의 어순으로 도치가 일어남.

해석 ¹생태계에는 비선형적인 상호 작용이 많이 있어서 날씨와 주식 시장에서처럼 작은 소란이 갑작스럽고 예측 불가능한 상태의 변화로 이어질 수 있다. (B) ²예를 들어, (여우의) 먹이인 붉은 뇌조의 수를 늘리기 위해 여우를 총으로 쏴서 죽이려는 시도는 바람직하지 않은 결과를 가져올 수도 있는데, 그 포식자들(여우)은 보통 기생충에 가장 많이 감염된 새(붉은 뇌조)만을 잡기 때문이며, 일단 여우들이 제거되면 질병이 퍼져서 전보다 더 많은 새들이 죽을 것이다. (C) ³이러한 예측할 수 없는 결과는 한 군집 내에 있는 종(種)들 사이의 연관성 중 다수가 단순함과는 거리가 멀다는 것을 강조한다. ⁴이에 해당하는 예로, 흙 밑의 복잡한 세계에서 생물체들은 장소마다 아주 다르지만, 어떻게든 대략 똑같은 혼합비의 영양소를 생성한다. (A) ⁵그러한 서식지들 각각은, 각기 어쩌다 (그곳에) 도착한, 생태학적으로 동등한 생물들의 우연한 집합으로 가득 차 있다. ⁶이런 예들은 생태계 이면에 있는 법칙에 대한 우리의 무지를 드러낼 뿐만 아니라, 혼돈과 복잡성이 예외라기보다는 (생태계의) 규칙일지도 모른다는 암시를 준다.

5 ⑤

> [1] When people try to control *situations* [that are essentially uncontrollable], // they are inclined to experience high levels of stress.
> 사람들이 상황을 통제하려 할 때 [근본적으로 통제할 수 없는] //
> 그들은 높은 수준의 스트레스를 경험하는 경향이 있다

↓

(C) [2] Thus, / suggesting // that they need to take active control / is bad advice / in those situations.
따라서 / 제안하는 것은 // 그들이 적극적 통제를 해야 할 필요가 있다고 /
잘못된 충고이다 / 그러한 상황에서

[3] Better advice would be to try to accept // that some things are beyond control.
더 좋은 충고는 받아들이도록 노력하라는 것일 것이다 // 어떤 일들은 통제할 수 없다는 것을

[4] Similarly, / teaching people to accept *a situation* [that could readily be changed] / could be bad advice.
마찬가지로 / 사람들에게 상황을 받아들이라고 가르치는 것은 [쉽사리 바뀔 수 있는] /
잘못된 충고가 될 수 있다

↓

(B) [5] And / that's because // sometimes *the only way* (to get what you want) / is to take active control.
그리고 / 그것은 ~이기 때문이다 // 때로로 유일한 방법은 (당신이 원하는 것을 얻는) /
적극적인 통제를 하는 것이(기 때문이다)

[6] This matters // because research has shown // that / when *people* [who feel helpless] / fail to take control, // they experience negative emotional states (such as anxiety and depression).
이는 중요하다 // 연구가 보여주었기 때문에 // (~라는) 것을 / 사람들이 ~할 때 [무력함을 느끼는] /
통제하는 데 실패(할 때) // 그들은 부정적인 감정 상태를 경험한다(는 것을) (불안과 우울증과 같은)

↓

(A) [7] Like stress, / these negative emotions can damage the immune response.
스트레스처럼 / 이런 부정적인 감정은 면역 반응을 손상할 수 있다

[8] We can see from this // that health is not linearly related to control.
우리는 이것으로부터 알 수 있다 // 건강이 통제와 직선으로 연결되어 있지 않다는 것을

[9] For optimum health, / people should be encouraged / to take control to a point / but to recognize // when further control is impossible.
최적의 건강을 위해 / 사람들은 권장되어야 한다 / 어느 정도까지 통제를 하도록 /
하지만 인식하도록 // 더 이상의 통제가 불가능한 때를

해설

주어진 글의 내용 파악하기 

사람들은 통제할 수 없는 상황을 통제하려 할 때 높은 스트레스를 받음.

⌄⌄

단서로 정답 찾기 ⊕

(C) those situations는 주어진 글에서 언급한 '근본적으로 통제할 수 없는 상황(situations that are essentially uncontrollable)'을 받는다.(▶ **Point 1** 지시사/대명사) 통제할 수 없기에 스트레스를 받는 것이므로 이때 통제의 필요성을 제안하는 것은 잘못되었다는 내용이 Thus(따라서)로 이어진다. (▶ **Point 2** 결과 연결어)

↓

(B) that's because(그것은 ~이기 때문이다)로 (C)에서 언급한 '사람들에게 쉽사리 바뀔 수 있는 상황을 받아들이라고 가르치는 것이 잘못된 충고가 될 수 있다(teaching ~ bad advice)'는 것의 원인에 대한 내용이 이어진다.(▶ **Point 1** 지시사/대명사, ▶ **Point 2** 원인 연결어)

↓

(A) these negative emotions는 (B)의 '부정적인 감정 상태(negative emotional states)'를 받으며(▶ **Point 1** 지시사/대명사, 대용어), 이것들이 면역 반응을 손상할 수 있다고 설명한다.

어휘

be inclined to-v v하는 경향이 있다　beyond control 통제[제어]할 수 없는, 불가항력의　depression 우울증　essentially 근본[본질]적으로　helpless 무력한　linearly 직선으로, 연속적으로　matter 중요하다; 문제, 일, 사안　optimum 최적의, 최고의　readily 쉽사리, 손쉽게　uncontrollable 통제할 수 없는

구문 분석

[9] For optimum health, / people should **be encouraged** / **to take** control to a point / but **to recognize** // when further control is impossible.
be encouraged 다음에 두 개의 to-v구가 but으로 연결되어 병렬 구조를 이룸.

해석 [1] 사람들이 근본적으로 통제할 수 없는 상황을 통제하려 할 때 그들은 높은 수준의 스트레스를 경험하는 경향이 있다. (C) [2] 따라서 그러한 상황에서 그들이 적극적 통제를 해야 할 필요가 있다고 제안하는 것은 잘못된 충고이다. [3] 더 좋은 충고는 어떤 일들은 통제할 수 없다는 것을 받아들이도록 노력하라는 것일 것이다. [4] 마찬가지로 사람들에게 쉽사리 바뀔 수 있는 상황을 받아들이라고 가르치는 것은 잘못된 충고가 될 수 있다. (B) [5] 그리고 그것은 때로로 당신이 원하는 것을 얻는 유일한 방법은 적극적인 통제를 하는 것이기 때문이다. [6] 무력함을 느끼는 사람들이 통제하는 데 실패할 때, 그들이 불안과 우울증과 같은 부정적인 감정 상태를 경험한다는 것을 연구가 보여주었기 때문에 이는 중요하다. (A) [7] 스트레스처럼, 이런 부정적인 감정은 면역 반응을 손상할 수 있다. [8] 우리는 이것으로부터 건강이 통제와 직선으로 연결되어 있지 않다는 것을 알 수 있다. [9] 최적의 건강을 위해, 사람들은 어느 정도까지 통제를 하지만, 더 이상의 통제가 불가능한 때를 인식하도록 권장되어야 한다.

1 ⑤

[1] In a series of experimental studies with young children, /
어린 자녀에 관한 일련의 실험 연구에서 /
feeding practices (commonly employed by parents) / were shown / to accidentally encourage *behaviors* (counter to their intentions).
밥을 먹이는 수법은 (부모들이 흔히 사용하는) / 보였다 /
뜻하지 않게 행동을 조장하는 것으로 (그들의 의도와 반대되는)

↓

(C) **[2]** For example, / limiting access to tasty foods / promotes children's preference for and intake of these "forbidden foods."
예를 들어 / 맛있는 음식에 대한 접근을 제한하는 것은 / 이러한 '금지된 음식'에 대한 자녀의 선호와 섭취를 촉진한다

[3] Forcing or pressuring children / to eat certain foods / decreases the preference for those foods.
자녀에게 강요하거나 압박하는 것은 / 특정한 음식을 먹도록 / 그 음식에 대한 선호도를 감소시킨다

[4] Rewarding children for eating a disliked food / resulted in a decline in the preference for that food.
싫어하는 음식을 먹은 것에 대해 자녀에게 보상하는 것은 / 그 음식에 대한 선호도 감소를 야기했다

↓

(B) **[5]** On the other hand, / if children are given both sweet and non-sweet foods / as rewards for encouraged behavior, // the preference for those foods is enhanced.
반면에 / 자녀가 단 음식과 달지 않은 음식 둘 다를 받게 되면 /
장려된 행동에 대한 보상으로서 // 그 음식들에 대한 선호도가 높아진다

↓

(A) **[6]** This reinforces the idea // that using a variety of rewards, / (including healthy options alongside occasional treats like sweets), /
이는 생각을 강화한다 // 다양한 보상을 사용하는 것이 ~라는 /
(단것과 같은 때때로의 특별한 선물과 함께 건강한 선택지를 포함한) /
can be an effective strategy (for encouraging positive behavior in children).
효과적인 전략이 될 수 있다(는) (자녀들의 긍정적인 행동을 장려하는 것에 대한)

해설

주어진 글의 내용 파악하기 ●

부모들이 흔히 사용하는 밥을 먹이는 수법은 그들의 의도와 반대되는 결과를 가져옴.

⌄⌄

단서로 정답 찾기 ●

(C) For example(예를 들어)로 자녀가 접근이 제한된 금지된 음식을 선호하고, 강요하는 음식에 대한 선호도가 감소하며, 싫어하는 음식의 섭취에 대해 보상하는 것이 그 음식에 대한 선호도 감소를 야기했다는, 부모들의 의도와 반대된 결과의 예시가 이어진다. (▶ **Point 2** 예시 연결어)

↓

(B) On the other hand(반면에)를 통해, 장려된 행동에 대한 보상으로 단 음식과 달지 않은 음식 둘 다를 받으면 그 음식들에 대한 선호도가 높아진다는, (C)의 예시와 상반되는 내용이 이어진다. (▶ **Point 2** 역접 연결어)

↓

(A) This는 (B)의 내용을 받으며(▶ **Point 1** 지시사/대명사), 이는 자녀들의 긍정적 행동을 장려하는 것에 단 것과 건강한 선택지를 포함한 다양한 보상이 효과적이라는 생각을 강화한다고 결론을 내린다.

어휘

accidentally 뜻하지 않게, 우연히   **counter** 반대의; (악영향에) 대응하다; 반박하다   **employ** (기술·방법을) 사용하다; 고용하다
enhance (정도·능력을) 높이다, 강화하다(= reinforce)
forbidden 금지된   **intake** 섭취(량)   **occasional** 때때로의, 가끔의
practice 수법, 책략; 연습(하다); 관례, 관행   **promote** 촉진[조장]하다; 승진시키다

구문 분석

[2] For example, / limiting access to tasty foods / promotes children's preference **for** and intake **of these "forbidden foods."**
these "forbidden foods"는 전치사 for와 of의 공통 목적어임.

해석 **[1]** 어린 자녀에 관한 일련의 실험 연구에서 부모들이 흔히 사용하는 밥을 먹이는 수법은, 뜻하지 않게 그들의 의도와 반대되는 행동을 조장하는 것으로 보였다. (C) **[2]** 예를 들어, 맛있는 음식에 대한 접근을 제한하는 것은 이러한 '금지된 음식'에 대한 자녀의 선호와 섭취를 촉진한다. **[3]** 자녀에게 특정한 음식을 먹도록 강요하거나 압박하는 것은 그 음식에 대한 선호도를 감소시킨다. **[4]** 싫어하는 음식을 먹은 것에 대해 자녀에게 보상하는 것은 그 음식에 대한 선호도 감소를 야기했다. (B) **[5]** 반면에, 장려된 행동에 대한 보상으로서 자녀가 단 음식과 달지 않은 음식 둘 다를 받게 되면, 그 음식들에 대한 선호도가 높아진다. (A) **[6]** 이는 단것과 같은 때때로의 특별한 선물과 함께 건강한 선택지를 포함한 다양한 보상을 사용하는 것이 자녀들의 긍정적인 행동을 장려하는 것에 대한 효과적인 전략이 될 수 있다는 생각을 강화한다.

2 ③

> [1] Most Americans firmly believe in the general goal (of equal opportunity for rich and poor children).
>
> 대부분의 미국인은 일반적인 목표가 옳다고 굳게 생각한다 (부유한 아이들과 가난한 아이들이 균등한 기회를 가져야 한다는)

↓

(B) [2] They also agree // that poor children should not suffer / from hunger, homelessness, or lack of medical care.

그들은 또한 동의한다 // 가난한 아이들이 고통받아서는 안 된다는 것에 / 배고픔, 집 없음, 또는 의료의 부족으로

[3] However, / there are differing opinions / on how to accomplish these goals.

그러나 / 다른 의견들이 있다 / 이러한 목표를 달성하는 방법에 대해서는

↓

(C) [4] This is nothing new: // Americans have always disagreed / about how to help their poorest citizens.

이것은 새삼스러운 일이 아니다 // 즉 미국인들은 항상 의견이 어긋나 왔다 / 그들의 가장 가난한 시민들을 어떻게 도와야 하는지에 대해서

[5] Every generation of reformers believes // that it can solve the problems of poor children / by implementing new and improved policies.

모든 개혁가의 세대는 믿는다 // 그것이 가난한 아이들의 문제를 해결할 수 있다고 / 새롭고 향상된 정책들을 시행함으로써

↓

(A) [6] In fact, / none of these policies has eliminated poverty / or closed the gap (between rich and poor children's prospects for success).

사실은 / 이 정책들 중 어느 것도 가난을 없애지 못했다 / 또는 격차를 좁히(지 못했다) (부유한 아이들과 가난한 아이들 간의 성공 가능성의)

[7] This suggests // that / addressing the complex and multifaceted challenges (of poverty) / requires *a comprehensive effort* [that goes beyond mere policy changes].

이는 암시한다 // ~라는 것을 / 복잡하고 광범위한 문제들을 다루는 것은 (가난의) / 종합적인 노력을 필요로 한다(는 것을) [단순한 정책 변화를 넘어서는]

해설

주어진 글의 내용 파악하기 ◉

> 대부분의 미국인은 부유한 아이들과 가난한 아이들이 균등한 기회를 가져야 한다고 생각함.

⌄

단서로 정답 찾기 ➕

> **(B)** They는 주어진 글의 '대부분의 미국인(Most Americans)'을 받아(▶ **Point 1 지시사/대명사**), 그들이 아이들이 고통받으면 안 된다는 다른 목표에도 동의하지만, 목표를 달성하는 방법에 대해서는 다른 의견들이 있다고 언급한다.
>
> ↓
>
> **(C)** This는 (B)의 '다른 의견들이 있다(there ~ opinions)'는 내용을 받아(▶ **Point 1 지시사/대명사**), 빈곤층을 돕는 목표를 달성하는 방법에 대한 의견은 항상 어긋나 왔다고 한다. 이어서 모든 개혁가의 세대는 새롭고 향상된 정책들로 문제를 해결할 수 있다고 믿는다고 설명한다.
>
> ↓
>
> **(A)** these polices는 (C)의 '새롭고 향상된 정책들(new and improved polices)'을 가리키며(▶ **Point 1 지시사/대명사**), In fact(사실은)로 모든 개혁가 세대의 믿음과 달리 새로운 정책으로 문제가 해결되지 않았다는 반대되는 내용이 강조된다.(▶ **Point 2 강조 연결어**) 마지막으로 빈곤 문제는 종합적인 노력이 필요하다는 것을 암시한다고 하며 글을 맺는다.

어휘

address (문제를) 다루다, 처리하다; (청중에게) 연설하다
believe in ~을 옳다고 생각하다; ~을 믿다   comprehensive 종합적인, 포괄적인   gap 격차, 차이; 틈, 간격   go beyond ~을 넘어서다
homelessness 집 없음; 노숙자임   implement 시행[실행]하다
mere 단순한, 그저 ~한   multifaceted 광범위한; 다면적인
prospect 가능성, 가망   reformer 개혁가

구문 분석

[5] **Every generation of reformers believes** // that it can solve the problems of poor children / by implementing new and improved policies.

Every generation은 단수 취급하므로 단수동사 believes가 쓰임.

해석 [1] 대부분의 미국인은 부유한 아이들과 가난한 아이들이 균등한 기회를 가져야 한다는 일반적인 목표가 옳다고 굳게 생각한다. (B) [2] 그들은 또한 가난한 아이들이 배고픔, 집 없음, 또는 의료의 부족으로 고통받아서는 안 된다는 것에 동의한다. [3] 그러나 이러한 목표를 달성하는 방법에 대해서는 다른 의견들이 있다. (C) [4] 이것은 새삼스러운 일이 아닌데, 즉 미국인들은 그들의 가장 가난한 시민들을 어떻게 도와야 하는지에 대해서 항상 의견이 어긋나 왔다. [5] 모든 개혁가의 세대는 새롭고 향상된 정책들을 시행함으로써 가난한 아이들의 문제를 해결할 수 있다고 믿는다. (A) [6] 사실은, 이 정책 중 어느 것도 가난을 없애거나 부유한 아이들과 가난한 아이들 간의 성공 가능성의 격차를 좁히지 못했다. [7] 이는 가난의 복잡하고 광범위한 문제들을 다루는 것은 단순한 정책 변화를 넘어서는 종합적인 노력을 필요로 한다는 것을 암시한다.

3 ④

¹In the early 1980s, / when personal computers were first made available, //
1980년대 초반 / 개인용 컴퓨터가 처음 이용 가능해졌을 때 //

software publishers were worried // that hackers might copy // what they considered to be their intellectual property: / the core code of their programs.
소프트웨어 발행자들은 우려했다 // 해커들이 복제할지도 모른다고 //
자신들의 지적 재산이라고 그들이 여기는 것을 / 즉, 그들의 프로그램의 핵심 코드

↓

(C) **²It was quite simple / to access the core code of a program, // and the laws against it weren't all that clear / at the time.**
(~은) 꽤 간단했다 / 프로그램의 핵심 코드에 접근하는 것은
// 그리고 그것을 규제하는 법이 그다지 명확하지 않았다 / 그 당시에는

³So / little undocumented features / were added // before applications were released.
그래서 / 문서로 기록되지 않은 소소한 기능이 / 추가되었다 // 응용 프로그램이 출시되기 전에

↓

(A) **⁴This way, / if the core code was stolen and adapted for another application, // the undocumented feature would also be incorporated / into the new program.**
이러한 방식으로 / 그 핵심 코드가 도난당하고 다른 응용 프로그램으로 개조되면 //
그 문서로 기록되지 않은 기능도 포함될 것이었다 / 그 새로운 프로그램에

⁵And / that would constitute proof of the theft.
그리고 / 그것은 절도의 증거를 구성할 것이었다

↓

(B) **⁶The practice continued to take off / later in the 1980s // when programmers were not always given official credit (for their work).**
그 관행은 계속해서 유행했다 / 1980년대 후반에 //
프로그래머들이 항상 공식적인 인정을 받지는 못했던 (자신들이 한 작업에 대해)

⁷To prove their involvement, / they'd bury a little something / in the code, / just to prove // (that) they were there in the beginning.
자신들이 참여했음을 증명하기 위해서 / 그들은 작은 무언가를 묻어 두곤 했다 /
코드 안에 / 단지 증명하기 위해 // 자신들이 처음에 거기에 있었음을

해설

주어진 글의 내용 파악하기 🔎

1980년대 초반에 소프트웨어 발행자들은 자신들이 만든 프로그램의 핵심 코드를 해커들이 복제할까 봐 우려함.

≫

단서로 정답 찾기 ➕

(C) 프로그램의 핵심 코드에 접근하는 것이 쉬웠고, 주어진 글에 언급된 '1980년대 초반(In the early 1980)'을 '그 당시에는(at the time)'으로 받아 당시 규제하는 법이 명확하지 않았다고 소프트웨어 발행자들의 우려를 부연 설명한다.(▶ Point 1 대용어) 이어서 이에 대한 대처로 응용 프로그램의 출시 전에 문서로 기록되지 않은 소소한 기능이 추가되었다고 언급한다.

↓

(A) This way는 (C)의 '응용 프로그램의 출시 전 문서로 기록되지 않은 소소한 기능이 추가되었다(little ~ released)'는 내용을 받으며(▶ Point 1 지시사/대명사, 대용어), 그 문서로 기록되지 않은 기능이 절도의 증거로 구성되는 방식임을 세부적으로 설명한다.

↓

(B) The practice는 앞에서 설명하고 있는 대처, 즉 응용 프로그램의 출시 전에 문서화되지 않은 기능을 추가하여 절도의 증거를 구성하는 것을 받는다.(▶ Point 1 대용어) 1980년대 후반에는 자신의 참여를 증명하기 위한 방안으로 그 관행이 계속해서 유행했다고 설명한다.

어휘

adapt (용도에 맞추어) 개조하다; 적응[조화]시키다 **bury** 묻어 두다, 묻다, 매장하다 **constitute** 구성하다; 설립[설치]하다 **core** 핵심; 속; 중심부; 핵심적인 **give credit** 공로를 인정하다 **take off** 유행하다, 급격히 인기를 얻다; (항공기 등이) 이륙하다 **incorporate** (일부로) 포함하다 **intellectual property** 지적 재산 **involvement** 참여, 관여; 몰두, 열중 **undocumented** 문서로 기록되지 않은; 증거가 없는

구문 분석

¹ ~, // software publishers were worried // that hackers might copy // **what** they **considered to be** their intellectual property ~.
<consider+O+to-v(O가 v라고 여기다)>의 구조로, 목적어는 선행사를 포함한 관계대명사 what임.

해석 **¹**1980년대 초반, 개인용 컴퓨터가 처음 이용 가능해졌을 때, 소프트웨어 발행자들은 자신들의 지적 재산이라고 그들이 여기는 것, 즉, 그들의 프로그램의 핵심 코드를 해커들이 복제할지도 모른다고 우려했다. (C) **²**프로그램의 핵심 코드에 접근하는 것은 꽤 간단했고, 그 당시에는 그것을 규제하는 법이 그다지 명확하지 않았다. **³**그래서 응용 프로그램이 출시되기 전에 문서로 기록되지 않은 소소한 기능(공식 안내서 등의 문서에 기록되어 있지 않아 사용자들에게 공개되지 않은 기능들)이 추가되었다. (A) **⁴**이러한 방식으로, 그 핵심 코드가 도난당하고 다른 응용 프로그램으로 개조되면, 그 문서로 기록되지 않은 기능도 그 새로운 프로그램에 포함될 것이었다. **⁵**그리고 그것은 절도의 증거를 구성할 것이었다. (B) **⁶**프로그래머들이 자신들이 한 작업에 대해 항상 공식적인 인정을 받지는 못했던 1980년대 후반에 그 관행은 계속해서 유행했다. **⁷**자신들이 참여했음을 증명하기 위해서, 단지 자신들이 처음에 거기에 있었음을 증명하기 위해, 그들은 코드 안에 작은 무언가를 묻어 두곤 했다.

4 ②

> [1] One of the dangers (of not choosing to spend a portion of your time / deliberately pursuing pleasure) / is //
> 위험 중 하나는 (당신의 시간의 일부를 사용하기로 선택하지 않는 것의 / 의도적으로 즐거움을 추구하는 데) / ~이다 //
> that you may allow yourself to simply drift through the day, / unwittingly contenting yourself by offsetting any negativity / with *periods of time* [that are just ordinary].
> 당신이 스스로를 그저 하루 종일 표류하게 할 수도 있다는 점 / 자기도 모르게 어떤 부정적인 성향을 상쇄하는 데 스스로 만족함으로써 / 시간으로 [단지 평범한]

↓

(B) [2] The short-term effects of this are minimal, // but long term / it can have a significant detrimental impact, //
이것의 단기적 영향은 아주 적다 // 그러나 장기적으로 / 이것은 상당히 해로운 영향을 가져올 수 있다 //
since ordinary routines are in themselves insufficient / to properly counter *any negativity* [(which[that]) you may experience].
평범한 일상은 그 자체로 불충분하기 때문에 / 어떤 부정적인 일에 적절히 대응하기에는 [당신이 경험할 수도 있는]

↓

(A) [3] Taking affirmative action / is the best solution (to creating a positive lifestyle structure, // one [that creates *pockets of time* (to spend doing whatever makes you happy)]).
적극적인 행동을 취하는 것이 / 최적의 해결책이다 (바람직한 생활 구조를 만드는 것에 관한 // 즉 (~한) 것 [시간을 만들어 내는 (무엇이든 당신을 행복하게 하는 것에 쓸)])

[4] The moment you stop doing everything else / and focus on doing whatever makes you happy, // you will feel yourself start to relax.
당신이 다른 모든 일을 멈추는 그 순간에 / 그리고 무엇이든 당신을 행복하게 하는 것에 집중하는 (그 순간에) // 당신은 스스로가 편안해지기 시작함을 느낄 것이다

↓

(C) [5] Continued application will result in a sustained increase in happiness, // and that will grow over time.
지속적인 적용은 행복감의 지속적인 증가를 불러올 것이다 // 그리고 그것은 시간이 흐를수록 커질 것이다

[6] So / make sure // that you don't simply wander aimlessly / without ever giving *sufficient pause* (to actively engage in making yourself happy).
그러므로 / 반드시 ~해라 // 당신이 그저 목적 없이 방황하지 않도록 / 충분한 휴식을 결코 취하지 않은 채 (당신 자신을 행복하게 만드는 일에 적극적으로 참여하는)

해설

주어진 글의 내용 파악하기 

즐거움을 추구하는 데 시간을 따로 할애하지 않으면 그저 평범한 시간으로 부정적인 성향을 상쇄하는 것에 만족하며 하루를 보내게 되는 위험이 있음.

단서로 정답 찾기 

(B) this는 주어진 글에서 언급한 문제점인 '단지 평범한 시간으로 어떤 부정적인 성향을 상쇄하면서 하루 종일 표류하는 것(simply drift ~ just ordinary)'을 지칭하며 (▶ **Point 1** 지시사/대명사), 평범한 일상은 부정적인 일에 대응하기에 불충분하므로 이는 장기적으로 해로울 수 있다고 설명한다.

(A) 앞에서 설명한 문제점에 대해 행복 추구에 시간을 할애하기 위해서는 적극적인 행동을 취해야 한다는 해결책을 제시한다. (▶ **Point 3** 문제 → 해결)

↓

(C) 적극적인 행동을 지속적으로 적용하면 행복감도 지속적으로 증가할 것이라는 결과로 (A)의 내용을 부연 설명한다. 이어서 자신을 행복하게 만드는 일에 적극적으로 참여해야 한다는 결론으로 글을 맺는다.

어휘

affirmative 적극적인, 긍정적인　aimlessly 목적 없이　application 적용, 응용; 지원　deliberately 의도[계획]적으로, 고의로　detrimental 해로운, 이롭지 못한　drift (확실한 목적 없이) 표류하다; (서서히 일어나는) 이동, 추이　insufficient 불충분한(↔ sufficient 충분한)　minimal 아주 적은, 최소의　negativity 부정적[비관적] 성향; 소극성　offset 상쇄[벌충]하다　portion 일부, 부분　sustained 지속적인, 한결같은　unwittingly 자기도 모르게

구문 분석

[1] ~, / unwittingly **contenting** yourself by offsetting any negativity / with *periods of time* [that are just ordinary].
contenting 이하는 부대상황을 나타내는 분사구문임.

[3] Taking affirmative action / is *the best solution* (**to creating a positive lifestyle structure**, // *one* [that creates *pockets of time* (to spend doing whatever makes you happy)]).
• creating은 전치사 to의 목적어 역할을 하는 동명사구를 이끎.
• a positive lifestyle structure와 one 이하는 동격 관계임.

해석 [1] 당신의 시간의 일부를 의도적으로 즐거움을 추구하는 데 사용하기로 선택하지 않는 것의 위험 중 하나는, 당신이 자기도 모르게 단지 평범한 시간으로 어떤 부정적인 성향을 상쇄하는 데 스스로 만족함으로써 스스로를 그저 하루 종일 표류하게 할 수도 있다는 점이다. (B) [2] 이것의 단기적 영향은 아주 적으나, 평범한 일상은 당신이 경험할 수도 있는 어떤 부정적인 일에 적절히 대응하기에는 그 자체로 불충분하기 때문에, 이것은 장기적으로 상당히 해로운 영향을 가져올 수 있다. (A) [3] 적극적인 행동을 취하는 것이 바람직한 생활 구조, 즉 무엇이든 당신을 행복하게 하는 것에 쓸 시간을 만들어 내는 것을 만드는 것에 관한 최적의 해결책이다. [4] 당신이 다른 모든 일을 멈추고 무엇이든 당신을 행복하게 하는 것에 집중하는 그 순간에 당신은 스스로가 편안해지기 시작함을 느낄 것이다. (C) [5] 지속적인 적용은 행복감의 지속적인 증가를 불러올 것이고, 그것은 시간이 흐를수록 커질 것이다. [6] 그러므로 반드시 당신 자신을 행복하게 만드는 일에 적극적으로 참여하는 충분한 휴식을 결코 취하지 않은 채 그저 목적 없이 방황하지 않도록 해라.

 **5** ②

> ¹Quite frequently, / we make mistakes / in our observations.
> 꽤 빈번히 / 우리는 실수를 한다 / 우리의 관찰에서
>
> ²For example, / what was your instructor wearing / on the first day of class?
> 예를 들어 / 당신의 강사가 무엇을 입고 있었는가 / 수업 첫날에
>
> ³If you have to guess, // it's because most of our daily observations are casual and semiconscious.
> 당신이 추측해야 한다면 // 그것은 우리의 일상적인 관찰의 대부분이 건성이고 반의식적이기 때문이다

↓

(B) ⁴If you'd gone to the first class / with a conscious plan (to observe and record // what your instructor was wearing), // you'd be far more likely / to be accurate.
당신이 첫 수업에 갔더라면 / 의식적 계획을 가지고 (관찰하고 기록하겠다는 // 당신의 강사가 무엇을 입고 있는지) // 당신은 가능성이 훨씬 더 있을 것이다 / 정확해질

⁵In many cases, / both simple and complex measurement devices / help guard against inaccurate observations.
많은 경우에 / 단순한 측정 장치와 복잡한 측정 장치 둘 다 / 부정확한 관찰이 생기지 않도록 조심하는 데 도움이 된다

↓

(A) ⁶Moreover, / they add a degree of precision (well beyond the capacity of the unassisted human senses).
게다가 / 그것들은 (~한) 정도의 정확성을 더해준다 (보조를 받지 않은 인간 감각의 능력을 훨쩍 넘어선 (정도의))

⁷Suppose, / for example, // that you'd taken color photographs of your instructor / that day.
가정해 보라 / 예를 들어 // 당신이 당신 강사의 컬러 사진을 찍었다고 / 그 날

↓

(C) ⁸In contrast to casual human inquiry, / scientific observation methods (like this one) / constitute a conscious activity.
인간의 무심코 하는 탐구와는 대조적으로 / 과학적 관찰 기법은 (이와 같은) / 의식적 활동이 된다

⁹They require you / to focus all of your attention / on a given subject.
그것들은(과학적 관찰 기법은) 당신에게 요구한다 / 당신의 모든 주의를 집중할 것을 / 특정한 주제에

해설

주어진 글의 내용 파악하기 

우리는 관찰에서 빈번히 실수를 한다고 하며, 한 예로 수업 첫날 강사가 입은 옷을 떠올리는 데 추측이 필요하다면 그것은 일상적 관찰 대부분이 건성이고 반의식적이기 때문이라고 설명함.

단서로 정답 찾기

(B) 첫 수업에 강사의 복장을 관찰하고 기록하려는 의식적 계획을 가지고 갔다면 정확해질 가능성이 더 있을 것이라고 주어진 글의 내용을 부연 설명한 다음, 측정 장치가 부정확한 관찰이 생기지 않도록 조심하는 데 도움이 된다고 설명한다.

↓

(A) they는 (B)의 '단순한 측정 장치와 복잡한 측정 장치 둘 다 (both simple and complex measurement devices)'를 받으며(▶ **Point 1** 지시사/대명사), Moreover(게다가)를 통해 그것들이 정확성을 더한다는 장점을 덧붙인다.(▶ **Point 2** 첨가 연결어) 이어서 그 예시로 강사의 컬러 사진을 찍었다고 가정해 보도록 한다.

↓

(C) this one은 (A)의 '컬러 사진을 찍은 것(taken color photographs)'을 의미한다.(▶ **Point 1** 지시사/대명사) 이 같은 과학적 관찰 기법은 의식적 활동이 되고, 그것은 특정 주제에 모든 주의를 집중하도록 한다고 설명한다.

어휘

casual 건성의, 무심코 한; 우연의   constitute ~이 되다, ~이 되는 것으로 여겨지다   given 특정한, 정해진   guard against A A가 생기지 않도록 조심[경계]하다   in contrast to A A와는 대조적으로   inquiry 탐구, 연구   instructor 강사   precision 정확(성), 정밀(성)   semiconscious 반의식적인, 반은 의식이 있는

구문 분석

⁴**If** you**'d gone** to the first class / with a conscious plan (to observe and record // what your instructor was wearing), // you**'d be** far more likely / to be accurate.
<If+S'+had p.p., S+would+동사원형> 형태의 혼합가정법 문장으로, '~했더라면 …할 텐데'의 뜻임.

[1]Misprints (in a book or in any written message) / usually have a negative impact on the content, / sometimes (literally) fatally.
오자는 (책이나 어떤 문자 메시지 속의) / 보통 내용에 부정적인 영향을 미친다 / 때로는 (문자 그대로) 치명적이게

[2](①) The displacement of a comma, / for instance, / may be a matter of life and death.
쉼표를 잘못된 곳에 배치한 것은 / 예를 들어 / (책의) 생사가 걸린 문제일 수 있다

[3](②) Similarly / most mutations have harmful consequences / for *the organism* [in which they occur], / meaning // that they reduce its reproductive fitness.
마찬가지로 / 대부분의 돌연변이는 해로운 결과를 가져온다 / 유기체에 [그것들(돌연변이)이 발생하는] / 그리고 이는 뜻한다 // 그것들(돌연변이)이 그것(유기체)의 생식 적합성을 감소시킨다는 것을

[4](③) Occasionally, / however, / *a mutation* may occur [that increases the fitness of the organism], //
때때로 / 그러나 / 돌연변이가 발생할 수 있다 [유기체의 적합성을 향상시키는] //

just as an accidental failure / to reproduce the text of the first edition / might provide more accurate or updated information.
꼭 (초판본의 오자를 수정한) 우연한 실수가 ~처럼 / 초판본의 원문을 다시 만들어 내는 데 / 더 정확하거나 최신의 정보를 제공할 수도 있는 것(처럼)

↓

> [5]④ At the next step in the argument, / however, / the analogy breaks down.
> 그 논거의 다음 단계에서 / 그러나 / 그 유사성은 깨진다

↓

[6]A favorable mutation is going to be more heavily represented / in the next generation, //
유리한 돌연변이는 더 많이 나타날 것이다 / 다음 세대에 //

since *the organism* [in which it occurred] / will have more offspring // and mutations are transmitted to the offspring.
유기체는 ~ 이기 때문에 [그것(유리한 돌연변이)이 발생한] / 더 많은 자손을 낳을 것(이기 때문에) // 그리고 돌연변이는 자손에게 유전되(기 때문에)

[7](⑤) By contrast, / there is no *mechanism* [by which *a book* [that accidentally corrects the mistakes of the first edition] / will tend to sell better].
대조적으로 / 메커니즘은 없다 [책이 [우연히 초판의 오류를 바로잡은] / 더 잘 팔리는 경향이 있는]

해설

주어진 문장의 내용 파악하기 ◎

'그러나(however)', '그 논거(the argument)'의 다음 단계에서 '그 유사성(the analogy)'이 깨짐.(▶ **Point 2** 역접 연결어, **Point 1** 정관사 the)
(앞부분에서 어떤 유사성을 설명하고 뒤에는 그 유사성이 깨진 것에 대한 설명이 나올 것을 예상할 수 있음.)

≫

단서로 정답 찾기 ➕

1 책이나 문자 메시지의 오자는 보통 부정적인 영향을 미침.
2 (①) for instance(예를 들어)로 쉼표를 잘못된 곳에 배치한 인쇄 오류는 치명적이라는 사례가 이어진다.
3 (②) Similarly(마찬가지로)로 대부분의 돌연변이가 유기체에 해롭다는 부정적 측면의 유사점이 이어진다.
4 (③) 초판본의 원문을 다시 만들 때 우연한 실수로 내용이 향상되듯이, 유기체의 적합성을 향상시키는 돌연변이가 발생할 수 있다는 긍정적 측면의 유사점이 however(그러나)로 이어진다.

↓

5 ④ 주어진 문장은 앞 내용 전체를 the argument, 앞의 인쇄 오류와 돌연변이의 유사성에 대한 내용을 the analogy로 받으며, however(그러나)로 이어져 다음 단계에서는 그 유사성이 깨진다는 대비되는 경우를 언급한다.

↓

6 유사성이 깨지는 것에 대한 설명으로, 유기체의 경우에는 유리한 돌연변이가 다음 세대에 더 많이 나타날 것이라고 설명한다.
7 (⑤) By contrast(대조적으로)로 초판의 오류를 바로잡은 책이 더 잘 팔리지는 않는다는 내용이 이어진다.

어휘

accidental 우연한, 돌발적인 *cf.* accidentally 우연히
displacement (제자리에서 쫓겨난) 이동   fatally 치명적으로
fitness 적합성; (신체적인) 건강   favorable 유리한; 호의적인
misprint 오자; 잘못 인쇄하다   offspring 자손; 자식; (동물의) 새끼
reproductive 생식[번식]의   transmit 유전시키다; 보내다; 전달하다

구문 분석

[4]Occasionally, / however, / ***a mutation*** may occur [**that** increases the fitness of the organism], // ~.
that이 이끄는 관계사절은 주어 a mutation을 수식함.

해석 [1]책이나 어떤 문자 메시지 속의 오자는 보통 내용에 부정적인 영향을 미치며, 때로는 (문자 그대로) 치명적이게 그러하다. [2]예를 들어, 쉼표를 잘못된 곳에 배치한 것은 책의 생사가 걸린 문제일 수 있다. [3]마찬가지로 대부분의 돌연변이는 그것들이 발생하는 유기체에 해로운 결과를 가져오는데, 이는 그것들(돌연변이)이 유기체의 생식 적합성을 감소시킨다는 것을 뜻한다. [4]그러나 때때로 꼭 초판본의 원문을 다시 만들어 내는 데 (초판본의 오자를 수정한) 우연한 실수가 더 정확하거나 최신의 정보를 제공할 수도 있는 것처럼, 유기체의 적합성을 향상시키는 돌연변이가 발생할 수 있다. [5]그러나 그 논거의 다음 단계에서 그 유사성은 깨진다. [6]유리한 돌연변이는 다음 세대에 더 많이 나타날 것인데, 그것이 발생한 유기체는 더 많은 자손을 낳을 것이고 돌연변이는 자손에게 유전되기 때문이다. [7]대조적으로, 우연히 초판의 오류를 바로잡은 책이 더 잘 팔리는 경향이 있는 메커니즘(어떤 대상의 작용 원리나 구조)은 없다.

Zoom 1

해석 잠의 분명한 보편성, 그리고 포유동물들이 한 번에 적어도 뇌의 한쪽에서는 잠을 유지하는 매우 고도로 복잡한 기제를 발전시켰다는 관찰 결과는 잠이 생명체에게 생명 유지에 필수적인 어떤 도움(들)을 제공한다는 것을 시사한다.
• **apparent** 분명한, 명백한   **universality** 보편성 *cf.* **universal** 보편적인
observation (관찰의) 결과; 관찰; 감시   **preserve** 유지하다; 보호하다; 보존하다
vital 생명 유지에 필수적인   **service** 도움; 제공하다
→ 잠의 한 가지 측면은 환경에 대한 감소된 반응성이기 때문에 이것은 특히 사실이다. • **responsiveness** 반응성
→ 이러한 잠재적인 대가가 치러져야 할 때조차도 잠이 보편적이라면, 그 함의는 조용한, 깨어있는 휴식만으로는 얻어질 수 없는 중요한 기능을 그것(잠)이 갖고 있다는 것일 수도 있다.
• **implication** 함의; 함축   **function** 기능(하다)   **wakeful** 깨어 있는

Zoom 2

해석 당신이 회의를 이끌고 있고 그곳에 있는 모든 사람이 의제에 관한 사본을 갖는 것을 당신이 확실히 하고 싶어 한다고 가정해 보라. 당신은 그 유인물의 각 사본에 참석한 사람들 각각의 이름의 첫 글자들을 차례로 적음으로써 이것을 처리할 수 있다.
• **conduct** 이끌다, 안내하다; 행동(하다)   **agenda** 의제, 안건
deal with ~을 처리하다; ~을 다루다   **label** (이름·라벨을) 적다, 붙이다; 분류하다
in turn 차례로; 결국   **initial** 이름의 첫 글자; 처음의
→ 이 과정을 마치기 전에 사본이 다 떨어지지 않는 한, 당신은 사람들에게 돌아갈 충분한 수의 사본이 있다는 것을 알 것이다.
• **run out of** ~이 다 떨어지다   **go around** (사람들에게 몫이) 돌아가다
→ 그렇다면 여러분은 산수에 의존하지 않고, 명시적인 계산 없이 이 문제를 해결한 것이다.
• **resort to A** A에 의존하다   **explicit** 명시적인, 명백한   **counting** 계산, 셈

Zoom 3

해석 미나마타병의 예방을 위해 산업 활동으로부터 나오는 수은의 직접적 방출에 대한 통제가 확실히 필요하다. 하지만 이제는 그런 어떤 산업적 방출과는 동떨어진 호수에서도 소량의 수은이 나타날 수 있다고 알려져 있다.
• **discharge** 방출[배출](하다); 해고하다   **trace** 소량; 흔적; 추적하다
far removed from ~와 동떨어진
→ 그러한 오염은 멀리 떨어진 발전소 혹은 지방 자치 단체의 소각로에서부터 공기를 통한 이동이 원인일 수 있다고 가정된다.
• **contamination** 오염   **result from** ~이 원인이다, ~에서 기인하다
airborne 공기로 운반되는; 비행 중인   **remote** 멀리 떨어진; 외진
municipal 지방 자치 단체의
→ 이 문제를 최소화하기 위해서 그러한 근원에 대한 엄격하게 통제된 배출 기준이 요구된다. • **emission** 배출(물)

Zoom 4

해석 몇몇 창의적인 회사들은 그들의 고객들이 거의 모든 것에 대한 소유권과 접근권을 공유하는 것을 가능하게 하고 있는데, 요트 공유 서비스에 참여함으로써, 회원들은 최대 7명의 다른 사람들과 요트 한 대를 공유함으로써 포르투갈인들의 꿈을 실현할 수 있다.
• **ownership** 소유(권)   **access** 접근(권); 접속하다

→ 그 서비스를 기술하면서, 최근의 한 신문 기사는 소비자들에게 요트를 공유하는 것은 '여러분이 원할 때 여러분이 그것을 항상 이용할 수 있을 것이라는 보장은 없다'는 것을 의미한다고 경고했다.
• **describe** 기술[서술]하다, 묘사하다   **guarantee** 보장(하다)
→ 이 제한처럼 보이는 것은 정확히 소비자들이 그것을 특별한 것으로 삼도록 돕는 것이다.
• **apparent** ~처럼 보이는, 겉보기의; 명백한   **limitation** 제한; 제약
precisely 정확히, 정밀하게   **treat** 특별한 것; 대하다

Focus & Practice p.78

1 ②   **2** ②   **3** ①   **4** ②   **5** ①   **6** ③

1 ②

해석 음파는 공기를 통해서뿐만 아니라 많은 고체 물질을 통해서 이동하는 것이 가능하다. (①) 예를 들어 나무처럼, 고체는 공기가 일반적으로 전달하는 것보다 음파를 훨씬 더 잘 전달하는데, 고체 물질의 분자들이 공기 중에 있는 것보다 훨씬 더 가깝고 더 빽빽이 서로 채워져 있기 때문이다. (② <u>이것은 고체가 그 파동을 더 쉽고 효율적으로 전달하게 하여, 결과적으로 더 큰 소리를 야기한다.</u>) 공기의 밀도 그 자체도 그것을 통과하는 음파의 세기에 대한 결정적인 요인으로 작용한다.
• **solid** 고체(의); 단단한   **sound wave** 음파   **material** 물질(적인); 재료
typically 일반적으로, 보통   **molecule** 분자   **substance** 물질; 본질, 실체
density 밀도, 농도   **determining factor** 결정적인 요인
해설 주어진 문장의 '이것(This)'은 고체가 '그 파동(the waves)'을 더 쉽고 효율적으로 전달하게 해서 그 결과 더 큰 소리가 난다고 설명한다. ② 앞 문장은 고체 물질의 분자들이 더 빽빽이 채워져 있기 때문이라는 원인에 대한 내용으로, 이를 This로 받아서 결과가 이어지는 흐름이 자연스럽고, the waves가 받는 대상은 sound waves가 된다. 따라서 주어진 문장이 들어가기에 가장 적절한 곳은 ②이다.

2 ②

해석 개들이 자신의 코를 쓰는 것을 너무나 잘하기 때문에, 우리는 그것들이 무엇이든, 언제든 냄새를 맡을 수 있다고 생각한다. 하지만 개들은 다른 감각들도 사용하며, 인간과 개 둘 다의 뇌는 한 번에 하나의 감각을 강화하는 경향이 있다. (①) 많은 주인들이 새로운 헤어스타일을 하거나 새 코트를 입고 집에 돌아갔을 때 그들의 개가 물려고 한 적이 있다. (② <u>익숙지 않은 실루엣이 그 집으로 밀고 들어오는 광경을 보고 놀라서, 이 개들은 그것들의 코 대신 눈을 사용하고 있었다.</u>) 그들의 코는 비범할 수 있지만, 항상 스위치가 켜진 것은 아니다.
• **vision** 광경; 시력; 시야   **unfamiliar** 익숙지 않은, 낯선   **silhouette** 실루엣, 윤곽[외형]   **assume** (사실일 것으로) 생각하다, 추정하다   **sense** 감각; (도덕적·지적) 의식, 관념; 느끼다   **intensify** 강화하다, 심화시키다; (정도·강도가) 격렬해지다

snap (동물이) 물려고 하다; 딱 부러뜨리다   hairdo 헤어스타일, 머리 모양
remarkable 비범한, 뛰어난; 주목할 만한   switch on 스위치를 켜다
해석 주어진 문장의 '이 개들(these dogs)'은 '그 집(the house)'에 익숙지
않은 실루엣이 들어오는 것을 보고 놀랐다고 했다. ② 앞 문장에서 많은 주인
들이 새로운 헤어스타일을 하거나 새 코트를 입고 집에 돌아갔을 때 개가 물려
고 한 적이 있다고 했으므로, 그 뒤에는 개들이 익숙하지 않아서 놀랐다고 이
유를 설명하는 흐름이 자연스럽다. 따라서 주어진 문장이 들어가기에 가장 적
절한 곳은 ②이다.

3 ①

해석 몇 년 전, Richard Lippa라는 이름의 심리학자는 내향적인 사람 한 집
단을 자신의 연구실에 부르고, 그들에게 수학 수업을 가르치는 척하는 동안 외
향적인 사람들처럼 행동하도록 요청했다. 그러고 나서 그와 그의 팀은 손에 비
디오 카메라를 들고 그들의 보폭, 그들의 '학생들'과 시선을 마주친 총 횟수, 그
들이 말하는 데 사용한 시간의 비율, 그리고 그들의 성량을 측정했다. (① 그들
은 또한 그들(가짜 외향적인 사람들)의 녹음된 목소리와 신체 언어에 기반을 두
어 그 가짜 외향적인 사람들이 전반적으로 얼마나 외향적으로 보이는지도 평
가했다.) 그다음, Lippa는 실제로 외향적인 사람들과 똑같은 것을 하고 결과를
비교했다. (②) 그는 후자의 집단이 더 외향적인 인상을 주기는 했지만, 가짜 외
향적인 사람들 중 몇몇은 놀랍도록 그럴듯했다는 것을 발견했다.
•rate 평가하다; 속도; 비율   extrovert 외향적인 (사람)   introvert 내향적인 (사람)
stride 보폭; 성큼성큼 걷다   latter 후자(의); 후반의   come across (특정한)
인상을 주다; 이해되다, 뜻이 통하다   convincing 그럴듯한; 설득력 있는
해설 주어진 문장의 '그들(They)'은 그 가짜 외향적인 사람들이 얼마나 외향적
으로 보이는지도 평가했다고 했으므로 ① 앞 문장에서 보폭, 시선을 마주친 횟
수, 말한 시간의 비율, 성량을 측정한 Lippa와 그의 팀을 받는다. '그 가짜 외향
적인 사람들(those fake extroverts)'이 받는 대상은 글 초반에 언급된 실험
에서 측정된 대상인 외향적인 척하는 내향적인 사람들이 된다. 따라서 주어진
문장이 들어가기에 가장 적절한 곳은 ①이다.

4 ②

해석 섬유 가공에서의 한 종류인 '실잣기'는 노즐의 하나 또는 그보다 많은 작
은 구멍들을 통해 액체를 짜고 그것이 굳어지게 함으로써 개개의 섬유를 만들
어 내는 것이다. (①) 거미와 누에는 수백만 년 동안 이러한 방식으로 섬유를 자
아 왔지만, 화학자들과 엔지니어들은 이 방법을 그것들로부터 겨우 한 세기 전
쯤에 배웠다. 다른 종류의 실잣기에서는 두 개 이상의 섬유가 서로 꼬아져서 실
을 만들어 낸다. (② 인간은 이 기술을 수천 년 전에 발견했고, 그들은 그것을 더
쉽고 더 빠르게 만들기 위해 몇몇 장치를 고안해 왔다.) 고대의 실을 감는 막대
와 추가 중세 시대에 물레에 의해 대체된 예이다.
•fiber 섬유(질)   process 가공하다; (만드는) 과정, 방법(= procedure)
harden 굳어지다, 단단해지다; 굳히다
해설 주어진 문장은 인간이 '이 기술(this art)'을 수천 년 전에 발견했고 그것
을 더 쉽고 빠르게 만들기 위해 몇몇 장치를 고안했다는 내용이다. ② 앞에서 두
개 이상의 섬유는 서로 꼬아져서 실을 만들어 낸다고 했으므로, 이를 this art
로 받아 더 쉽고 빠르게 하기 위해 몇몇 장치를 고안했다고 설명한 다음, 고안
된 장치의 예가 이어지는 흐름이 적절하다. ① 앞은 '실잣기'가 무엇인지 설명
하는 내용이며, 뒤는 거미와 누에가 섬유를 뽑는 절차를 인간은 늦게 알게 되
었다는 내용이므로, 인간이 수천 년 전에 발견했다는 주어진 문장은 그 사이에
들어갈 수 없다.

5 ①

해석 인간의 생체 리듬은 바깥에서 무슨 일이 일어나든, 한랭 전선(차가운 기단
이 따뜻한 기단을 밀어 올리고 이동하여 가는 곳에 나타나는 전선)이 다가오든,
또는 구름이 햇빛을 가리든, 대략 24시간 주기로 생리적 그리고 행동적 변화를
촉진한다. (① 그것이 사람들이 표준 시간대를 가로질러 여행할 때 시차증을 경
험하는 이유이다.) 그들의 체내 시계는 그들이 온 장소가 아니라 그들이 떠나온
장소에 맞춰 계속해서 작동하고, 그 둘을 재조정하는 데는 약간의 시간이 걸릴
수 있다. (②) 가장 놀라운 것은 우리의 체내 시계가 환경적 신호에 의해 재조
정될 수 있다는 것이다. (③) 우리는 지구 반대편에서 우리의 체내 시계에 매우
다른 낮밤 주기의 스케줄에 적응하라고 요구할 때 며칠 동안 시차증을 느낄 수
도 있지만, 그것(체내 시계)은 그것(적응)을 할 수 있다.
•jet lag 시차증 ((비행기를 이용한 장거리 여행 시 시차로 인한 피로감))
time zone 표준 시간대   facilitate 촉진하다; 용이하게 하다
physiological 생리적인; 생리학(상)의   roughly 대략; 거칠게   internal 체내의;
내부의   realign 재조정[변경]하다(= readjust); 재편성하다
해설 주어진 문장은 '그것(That)'이 사람들이 표준 시간대를 가로질러 여행할
때 시차증을 경험하는 이유라고 했다. ① 앞은 외부적 요인과 상관없이 생체 리
듬이 24시간 주기로 돌아간다는 내용이므로, 이를 That으로 받아 시차증의 이
유로 설명하는 흐름이 적절하다. 그다음의 Their internal clocks는 주어진
문장의 people, 즉 표준 시간대를 가로질러 여행하는 사람들과 연결된다. 지
문 초반에는 Their internal clocks와 연결되는 부분이 없어 흐름상 단절이
생기므로, 주어진 문장이 들어가기에 가장 적절한 곳은 ①이다.

6 ③

해석 경쟁의 정도가 특히 극심해지는 경우 시장에 있는 모두가 추가적인 비용
에 직면하게 된다는 점에서 제로섬 게임은 빠르게 네거티브섬 게임이 될 수 있
다. (①) 이에 대한 한 예로, 영국의 주요 시내 중심가 은행 중 하나가 토요일 오
전에 영업함으로써 경쟁 우위를 얻으려고 시도했을 때, 그것은 전통적인 월-금
은행 영업시간을 제약이라고 생각한 많은 신규 고객을 끌어 모았다. (②) 하지
만 고객 감소에 직면하자, 경쟁 상대 또한 토요일에 영업하는 것으로 대응했다.
(③ 이것의 순수 효과는 비록 고객들이 이득을 얻긴 했으나, 은행들은 그것들의
비용이 증가했지만 총 고객의 수는 여전히 같았으므로 손해를 보았다는 것이었
다.) 본질적으로, 이것은 네거티브섬 게임임이 드러났다.
•net effect 순수 효과, 최종 결과   lose out 손해를 보다; ~을 놓치다
intense (정도가) 극심한, 강렬한   high street 시내 중심가, 번화가
competitive advantage 경쟁 우위   constraint 제약; 제한
prove (~임이) 드러나다, 판명되다; 입증하다
해설 주어진 문장은 '이것(this)'의 순수 효과가 고객들은 이득을 얻었지만 은
행들은 손해를 본 것이라고 하는 내용이다. ③ 앞이 경쟁 상대 또한 토요일에
영업하는 것으로 대응했다는 내용이므로, 그 뒤에서 그에 대한 순수 효과를 설
명하는 흐름이 적절하다.

1 ③

1 The dynamics (of collective detection) / have an interesting feature.
역학은 (집단 탐지의) / 흥미로운 특징이 있다

2 Which cue(s) do individuals use / as evidence (of predator attack)?
개체들은 어느 단서를 사용하는가 / 증거로 (포식자 공격의)

3 In some cases, / when an individual detects a predator, // its best response is to seek shelter.
어떤 경우에는 / 개체가 포식자를 탐지할 때 // 그것(개체)의 최선의 반응은 피난처를 찾는 것이다

4 (①) Departure (from the group) / may signal danger / to nonvigilant animals / and (may) cause // what appears to be a coordinated flushing of prey / from the area.
이탈은 (무리로부터의) / 위험 신호를 보낼 수도 있다 / 경계하지 않는 동물들에게 / 그리고 야기할 수도 있다 // 먹잇감(동물)의 조직화된 날아오름으로 보이는 것을 / 그 구역에서

5 (②) Studies (on dark-eyed juncos (a type of bird)) / support the view // that nonvigilant animals attend / to departures (of individual group mates) //
연구는 (검은 눈을 가진 검은방울새(새의 한 종류)에 관한) / 견해를 뒷받침한다 // 경계하지 않는 동물들이 주목한다는 / 이탈에 (개별적인 무리 친구들의) //
but that / the departure (of multiple individuals) / causes a greater escape response / in the nonvigilant individuals.
그러나 ~라는 / 이탈은 (여러 개체의) / 더 큰 도망 반응을 일으킨다(는) / 경계하지 않는 개체에

↓

> **6** ③ This makes sense / from the perspective (of information reliability).
> 이것은 타당하다 / 관점에서 (정보 신뢰성의)

↓

7 If one group member departs, // it might have done so / for a *number of reasons* [that have little to do with predation threat].
무리 구성원 하나가 이탈한다면 // 그것은 그렇게 했을지도 모른다 / 여러 이유로
[포식 위협과 거의 관련이 없는]

8 (④) If nonvigilant animals escaped // each time a single member left the group, // they would frequently respond // when there was no predator (a false alarm).
경계하지 않는 동물들이 도망한다면 // 단 하나의 구성원이 무리를 떠날 때마다 // 그것들(경계하지 않는 동물들)은 자주 반응할 것이다 // 포식자가 전혀 없는 (거짓 경보인) 때에도

9 (⑤) On the other hand, / when several individuals depart the group at the same time, // a true threat is much more likely to be present.
반면에 / 여러 개체가 동시에 무리를 이탈할 때 // 진짜 위협이 존재할 가능성이 훨씬 더 크다

해설

주어진 문장의 내용 파악하기 ❷

'이것(This)'은 정보 신뢰성의 관점에서 타당함.(▶ **Zoom 1, 2, 3** 지시사/대명사)
(앞부분에 어떤 사실이 나오고, 뒤에 어떻게 타당한지 부연 설명이 이어질 것을 예상할 수 있음.)

≫

단서로 정답 찾기 ❸

1, 2, 3 집단 탐지의 역학은 흥미로운데, 어떤 경우에는 개체가 포식자를 발견했을 때 최선의 반응은 피난처를 찾는 것임.

4 (①) 피난처를 찾는다는 내용이 무리 이탈로 연결되며, 이는 위험 신호로 작용할 수 있다고 언급한다.

5 (②) 검은 눈을 가진 검은방울새를 예로 들어, 여러 개체의 무리 이탈이 개별적인 이탈보다 더 큰 도망 반응을 일으킨다고 설명한다.

↓

6 ③ 주어진 문장의 This는 앞 문장의 '여러 개체의 이탈은 경계하지 않는 개체에 더 큰 도망 반응을 일으킨다(the departure ~ individuals)'는 것을 가리키며, 이것이 정보 신뢰성 관점에서 타당하다고 언급한다.

↓

7 무리 구성원 하나가 이탈하는 것은 포식 위협과 관련이 없을 수 있다고 설명한다.

8 (④) 한 개체의 개별 이탈은 포식 위협과 관계가 거의 없는 거짓 경보일 수 있어서 경계하지 않는 동물들이 매번 도망하지 않는 것이라고 부연 설명한다.

9 (⑤) On the other hand(반면에)로 여러 개체가 동시에 이탈하는 경우에는 위험 가능성이 더 크다는 내용이 이어진다.

어휘

attend 주목[주의]하다; 참석하다   collective 집단의; 공동의
coordinate 조직화하다; 조화를 이루게 하다   departure 이탈; 출발
cf. depart 이탈하다; 출발하다   dynamics 역학; 원동력
make sense 타당하다; 이해가 되다

구문 분석

8 **If** nonvigilant animals **escaped** // each time a single member left the group, // they **would** frequently **respond** // ~.
가정법 과거 <If+S′+동사의 과거형, S+would+동사원형>으로 현재 사실의 반대를 가정함.

해석 **1** 집단 탐지의 역학은 흥미로운 특징이 있다. **2** 개체들은 어느 단서를 포식자 공격의 증거로 사용하는가? **3** 어떤 경우에는 개체가 포식자를 탐지할 때 그것(개체)의 최선의 반응은 피난처를 찾는 것이다. **4** 무리로부터의 이탈은 경계하지 않는 동물들에게 위험 신호를 보내서 먹잇감(동물)의 조직화된 날아오름으로 보이는 것을 그 구역에서 야기할 수도 있다. **5** 검은 눈을 가진 검은방울새(새의 한 종류)에 관한 연구는 경계하지 않는 동물들이 개별적인 무리 친구들의 이탈에 주목하지만 여러 개체의 이탈은 경계하지 않는 개체에 더 큰 도망 반응을 일으킨다는 견해를 뒷받침한다. **6** 이것은 정보 신뢰성의 관점에서 타당하다. **7** 무리 구성원 하나가 이탈한다면, 그것은 포식 위협과 거의 관련이 없는 여러 이유로 그렇게 했을지도 모른다. **8** 경계하지 않는 동물들이 단 하나의 구성원이 무리를 떠날 때마다 도망한다면, 그것들(경계하지 않는 동물들)은 포식자가 전혀 없는 (거짓 경보인) 때에도 자주 반응할 것이다.(한 개체가 이탈할 때마다 달아난다면 거짓 경보에 너무 자주 반응하는 것이 되어 정보 신뢰성은 떨어짐을 의미) **9** 반면에 여러 개체가 동시에 무리를 이탈할 때, 진짜 위협이 존재할 가능성이 훨씬 더 크다.

2 ④

[1] Coevolution is the concept // that two or more species of organisms can reciprocally influence / the evolutionary direction (of the other).
공진화는 개념이다 // 둘 혹은 그보다 많은 유기체가 상호적으로 영향을 미칠 수 있다는 / 진화 방향에 (다른 종의)

[2] In other words, / organisms affect the evolution (of other organisms).
다시 말해서 / 유기체는 영향을 미친다 (다른 유기체의 진화에)

[3] Since all organisms are influenced by other organisms, // this is a common pattern.
모든 유기체가 다른 유기체에 의해 영향을 받기 때문에 // 이는 흔한 패턴이다

[4] (①) For example, / grazing animals and *the grasses* [(which[that]) they consume] / have coevolved.
예를 들어 / 풀을 먹는 동물과 풀은 [그것들이 먹는] / 공진화해왔다

[5] (②) *Grasses* [that are eaten by grazing animals] / grow / from *the base of the plant* (near the ground) / rather than from the tips (of the branches) // as many plants do.
풀은 [풀을 먹는 동물에게 먹히는] / 자란다 /
식물의 맨 아래 부분에서부터 (땅과 가까운) / 끝에서부터 (자라지) 않고 (나뭇가지의) //
많은 식물이 그러하듯

[6] (③) Furthermore, / grasses have hard materials / in *their cell walls* [that make it difficult / for animals to crush the cell walls and digest them].
게다가 / 풀은 단단한 물질이 있다 / 그것들의 세포벽 안에
[(~을) 어렵게 만드는 / 동물이 그 세포벽을 부수고 소화시키는 것을]

↓

> [7] ④ Grazing animals / have different kinds of *adaptations* [that overcome these deterrents].
> 풀을 먹는 동물은 / 여러 종류의 적응 형태를 가지고 있다 [이러한 방해물들을 극복하는]

↓

[8] Many grazers / have *teeth* [that are very long or grow continuously / to compensate for *the wear* (associated with grinding hard cell walls)].
풀을 먹는 많은 동물은 / 이빨을 가지고 있다 [매우 길거나 계속해서 자라는 /
마모를 보완하기 위해 (단단한 세포벽을 씹어 으깨는 것과 관련이 있는)]

[9] (⑤) Others, (such as cattle), / have *complicated digestive tracts* [that allow microorganisms / to do most of the work of digestion].
다른 동물은 (소와 같은) / 복잡한 소화관을 가지고 있다 [미생물이 (~하게) 하는 / 대부분의 소화 작용을 하게]

해설

주어진 문장의 내용 파악하기 

풀을 먹는 동물은 '이러한 방해물들(these deterrents)'을 극복하는 여러 종류의 적응 형태를 가지고 있음.(▶ **Zoom 1, 2, 3** 지시사/대명사)

(앞부분에서 풀 먹는 동물들을 방해하는 것들이 나오고, 뒤에서 이에 대한 적응 형태를 설명할 것을 예상할 수 있음.)

⌄

단서로 정답 찾기 

1, 2, 3 유기체가 다른 종의 진화에 상호적으로 영향을 미치는 공진화라는 개념은 흔함.

4 (①) For example(예를 들어)로 풀을 먹는 동물과 풀이 공진화해왔다는 예가 이어진다.

5 (②) 풀을 먹는 동물에 의해 영향 받아 풀이 나뭇가지 끝에서부터 자라지 않고, 땅과 가까운 아래 부분에서부터 자란다고 설명한다.

6 (③) Furthermore(게다가)로 동물이 소화하기 어렵게 풀의 세포벽 안에 단단한 물질이 있다는 다른 특징이 추가로 제시된다.

↓

7 ④ 앞에서 언급한 풀을 먹는 동물에 의해 영향을 받아 풀이 진화한 두 가지 특징을 'these deterrents(이러한 방해물들)'로 바꾸어 표현하며, 풀을 먹는 동물이 이것들을 극복하는 여러 적응 형태를 가지고 있다고 언급한다.

↓

8 풀을 먹는 동물은 단단한 세포벽을 씹어 으깨는 것과 관련된 마모를 보완하기 위한 매우 길거나 계속 자라는 이빨을 가지고 있다는 하나의 적응 형태를 제시한다.

9 (⑤) 복잡한 소화관을 가지고 있는 동물도 있다고 하며 또 다른 적응 형태를 제시한다.

어휘

adaptation ((생물)) 적응 형태; 적응, 적합   consume 먹다, 마시다; 소모[소비]하다   deterrent 방해물; 방해하는, 제지하는   graze (동물이) 풀을 먹다; (가축을) 방목하다   grind 씹어 으깨다; (곡식을) 갈다, 빻다   organism 유기체; 생물   reciprocally 상호적으로   tip 끝 (부분); 꼭대기, 정점   wear 마모, 닳음; 착용

구문 분석

[5] *Grasses* [that are eaten by grazing animals] / grow / **from** *the base of the plant* (near the ground) / **rather than from** the tips (of the branches) // as many plants do.
from이 이끄는 두 개의 전치사구가 rather than으로 연결되어 병렬 구조를 이룸.

해석 [1] 공진화는 둘 혹은 그보다 많은 유기체가 다른 종의 진화 방향에 상호적으로 영향을 미칠 수 있다는 개념이다. [2] 다시 말해서, 유기체는 다른 유기체의 진화에 영향을 미친다. [3] 모든 유기체가 다른 유기체에 의해 영향을 받기 때문에, 이는 흔한 패턴이다. [4] 예를 들어, 풀을 먹는 동물과 그것들이 먹는 풀은 공진화해왔다. [5] 풀을 먹는 동물에게 먹히는 풀은 많은 식물이 그러하듯 나뭇가지의 끝에서부터 자라지 않고 땅과 가까운 식물의 맨 아래 부분에서부터 자란다. [6] 게다가, 풀은 그것들의 세포벽 안에 동물이 그 세포벽을 부수고 소화시키는 것을 어렵게 만드는 단단한 물질이 있다. [7] 풀을 먹는 동물은 이러한 방해물들을 극복하는 여러 종류의 적응 형태를 가지고 있다. [8] 풀을 먹는 많은 동물은 단단한 세포벽을 씹어 으깨는 것과 관련이 있는 마모를 보완하기 위해 매우 길거나 계속해서 자라는 이빨을 가지고 있다. [9] 소와 같은 다른 동물은 미생물이 대부분의 소화 작용을 하게 하는 복잡한 소화관을 가지고 있다.

3 ⑤

¹Parks take / *the shape* (demanded by the cultural concerns (of their time)).
공원은 취한다 / 형태를 (문화적 관심사에 의해 요구되는 (그 당대의))

²Once parks are in place, // they are no inert stage — // their purposes and meanings are made and (are) remade / by planners and by park users.
일단 공원이 마련되면 // 그것은 비활성화된 단계가 아니다 // 그것의 목적과 의미는 만들어지고 다시 만들어진다 / (공원) 계획자와 공원 이용자에 의해

³Moments (of park creation) / are particularly telling, / however, // for they reveal and actualize / ideas (about nature and its relationship to urban society).
순간들은 (공원 조성의) / 특히 인상적이다 / 그러나 // 그것들(공원 조성의 순간들)이 드러내고 실현하기 때문에 / 생각을 (자연과 그것(자연)이 도시 사회와 갖는 관계에 대한)

⁴(①) Indeed, / what distinguishes a park / from the broader category of public space / is the representation (of *nature* [that parks are meant to embody]).
실제로 / 공원을 구별하는 것은 / 더 넓은 범주인 공공 공간과 / 표현이다 (자연의 [공원이 구현하기로 되어 있는])

⁵(②) Public spaces include / parks, concrete plazas, sidewalks, even indoor atriums.
공공 공간은 포함한다 / 공원, 콘크리트 광장, 보도, 심지어 실내 아트리움도

⁶(③) Parks typically have trees, grass, and other plants / as their central features.
일반적으로 공원에는 나무, 풀, 그리고 다른 식물들이 있다 / 그것들(공원)의 중심적인 특색으로

⁷(④) When entering a city park, / people often imagine / a sharp separation (from streets, cars, and buildings).
도시 공원에 들어갈 때 / 사람들은 흔히 상상한다 / 뚜렷한 분리를 (거리, 자동차, 그리고 건물로부터의)

↓

⁸⑤ There's a reason for that: // traditionally, / park designers attempted to create such a feeling / by planting tall trees at park boundaries, / building stone walls, / and constructing other means of partition.
그것에는 이유가 있다 // 전통적으로 / 공원 설계자들은 그런 느낌을 만들어 내려고 했다 / 공원 경계에 큰 나무를 심음으로써 / 돌담을 쌓음으로써 / 그리고 다른 칸막이 수단을 세움으로써

↓

⁹What's behind this idea is / not only landscape architects' desire (to design aesthetically suggestive park spaces), / but a much longer history (of *Western thought* [that envisions cities and nature / as antithetical spaces and oppositional forces]).
이 생각의 뒤에 있는 것은 ~이다 / 조경가의 욕망뿐이 아니라 (미적으로 시사하는 바가 많은 공원 공간을 설계하려는) / 훨씬 더 오래된 역사 (서구 사상의 [도시와 자연을 상상하는 / 대조적인 공간과 대립적인 세력으로])

해설

주어진 문장의 내용 파악하기 

'그것(that)'의 이유는 공원 경계에 칸막이 수단을 세움으로써 공원 설계자들이 '그런 느낌(such a feeling)'을 만들려 했기 때문임.(▶ **Zoom 1, 2, 3** 지시사/대명사)

≫

단서로 정답 찾기 ⊕

1, 2, 3 공원은 당대의 문화적 관심사의 형태를 띠고 계획자와 이용자에 의해 목적과 의미가 만들어지는데, 특히 공원을 조성할 때 자연, 그리고 자연과 도시 사회의 관계에 대한 생각이 드러남.
4 (①) Indeed(실제로)로 공원과 공공 공간을 구별하는 것은 공원이 구현하려는 자연의 표현이라는 설명이 이어진다.
5 (②) 공공 공간이 포함하는 공간의 예를 제시한다.
6 (③) 공원에 있는 자연의 표현에 대한 예를 제시한다.
7 (④) 사람들은 도시 공원에 들어갈 때 흔히 도시와의 분리를 상상한다는 사실을 언급한다.

↓

8 ⑤ 주어진 문장의 that은 앞 문장 전체를, such a feeling은 앞 문장의 '뚜렷한 분리(a sharp ~ buildings)'를 받아서, 사람들이 공원에 들어갈 때 도시와의 분리를 상상하는 것은 공원 설계자들이 그런 분리감을 만들어 내려고 했기 때문이라고 설명한다.

↓

9 주어진 문장에서 언급된 '도시와 공원을 분리하려는 설계자의 생각'을 this idea로 받아, 이 생각의 배경을 설명한다.

어휘

attempt to-v v하려고 시도하다   be meant to-v v하기로 되어 있다; v할 생각[의도]이다   envision 상상하다   embody 구현[상징]하다   inert 비활성의; 기력이 없는   oppositional 대립적인; 반대의   partition 칸막이; 분할   telling 인상적인; 효과적인   suggestive 시사[암시]하는 바가 많은; 연상시키는

구문 분석

⁴Indeed, / what **distinguishes** a park / **from** the broader category of public space / ~.
<distinguish A from B>: A를 B와 구별하다

해석 ¹공원은 그 당대의 문화적 관심사에 의해 요구되는 형태를 취한다. ²일단 공원이 마련되면, 그것은 비활성화된 단계가 아니다. 즉 그것의 목적과 의미는 (공원) 계획자와 공원 이용자에 의해 만들어지고 다시 만들어진다. ³그러나 공원 조성의 순간들은 특히 인상적인데, 그것들(공원 조성의 순간들)이 자연과 그것(자연)이 도시 사회와 갖는 관계에 대한 생각을 드러내고 실현하기 때문이다. ⁴실제로 공원을 더 넓은 범주인 공공 공간과 구별하는 것은 공원이 구현하기로 되어 있는 자연의 표현이다. ⁵공공 공간은 공원, 콘크리트 광장, 보도, 심지어 실내 아트리움(현대식 건물 중앙 높은 곳에 유리로 지붕을 한 넓은 공간)도 포함한다. ⁶일반적으로 공원에는 그것들의 중심적인 특색으로 나무, 풀, 그리고 다른 식물들이 있다. ⁷도시 공원에 들어갈 때 사람들은 흔히 거리, 자동차, 그리고 건물로부터의 뚜렷한 분리를 상상한다. ⁸그것에는 이유가 있는데, 바로 전통적으로 공원 설계자들은 공원 경계에 큰 나무를 심고, 돌담을 쌓고, 다른 칸막이 수단을 세움으로써 그런 느낌을 만들어 내려고 했기 때문이다. ⁹이 생각의 뒤에 있는 것은 미적으로 시사하는 바가 많은 공원 공간을 설계하려는 조경가의 욕망뿐이 아니라 도시와 자연을 대조적인 공간과 대립적인 세력으로 상상하는 훨씬 더 오래된 서구 사상의 역사이다.

Zoom 1

해석 과학자들이 자기 학문 분야의 실질적인 내용에 대해서 훈련받긴 하지만, 그들은 '좋은 과학자가 되는 방법'에 대해서는 공식적으로 교육받지 않는다.
- **substantive** 실질[본질]적인　**discipline** 학문 (분야); 훈련, 단련
instruct 교육하다; 지시[명령]하다; 알리다
➔ 대신, 초보 과학자는 동료들로부터의 흡수, 즉 사회화를 통해 그 역할에 내재하는 도덕적 가치에 대한 자신의 이해를 얻는다.
- **apprentice** 초보자; 수습생　**moral** 도덕적인; 도덕과 관련된
inherent 내재하는　**absorption** 흡수; 병합; 전념, 몰두　**socialization** 사회화 (= socialising)
➔ 우리는 직업 자체의 가치가 위협받고 있는 것처럼, 이러한 가치(도덕적 가치)가 위협받고 있다고 생각한다. • **under threat** 위협[협박]을 받는

Zoom 2

해석 어떤 경우에는, 생존을 위한 최고의 기회를 제공하는 서식지가 최고의 번식 능력을 가능하게 하는 서식지와 같은 서식지가 아닐 수도 있다.
- **habitat** 서식지　**provide for** ~을 가능하게 하다; ~을 준비[대비]하다
reproductive 번식의, 생식의 *cf.* **reproduction** 번식, 생식; 복제
capacity 능력; 용량; 수용력
➔ 따라서, 많은 텃새 종의 개체들은 가장 높은 번식 성공이 일어나는 특정 서식지에 머물러 있음으로써 더 낮은 비번식기 생존율의 형태인 대가의 균형을 맞춰야 하게 될 수도 있다.
- **resident** 텃새의, 이동하지 않는; 거주자　**survivorship** 생존(율)
specific 특정한; 특수한, 특유한; 구체적인　**breeding** 번식의(↔ nonbreeding 비번식의)
➔ 그러나, 철새들은 비번식기 동안에는 생존을 위한 최적의 서식지를, 번식기 동안에는 번식을 위한 최적의 서식지를 자유롭게 선택한다.
- **migrant** 철새; 이주자　**optimal** 최적의

Zoom 3

해석 널리 효과가 있는 살충제가 유익한 곤충에 해로운 영향을 미칠 수 있다는 것이 분명해졌다 ....
- **pesticide** 살충제 *cf.* **pest** 해충　**beneficial** 유익한, 이로운
➔ 또한, 기업들이 새로운 살충제를 개발하는 것이 어려워졌는데, 주요한 이로운 효과가 있지만 부정적인 효과는 거의 없을 수 있는 것들조차 그러하다.
➔ 새로운 살충제에 대한 정부의 승인을 얻기 위해 필요한 모든 절차를 따르는 것에 매우 높은 비용이 수반된다. • **approval** 승인; 찬성, 동의

Zoom 4

해석 바빌로니아 천문학자들의 상세한 천체 기록, 즉 오늘날 우리가 과학적인 방법이라고 부르는 것의 씨앗의 중요성은 순조롭게 발전하지 않았다.
- **astronomer** 천문학자
➔ 사실, 유럽 중세 시대에, 손과 눈으로 계산하는 것은 다소 조잡한 지식, 즉 추상적 사고의 그것(지식)보다 열등한 것을 만드는 것으로 여겨졌다.
- **shabby** 조잡한, 보잘것없는; 초라한　**inferior** 열등한, 질 낮은; 하급의
abstract 추상적인, 관념적인
➔ 그 불신은 그 시대 스콜라 철학에의 고대 그리스인들의 영향에 기인했다.
- **suspicion** 불신, 의심; 혐의

Zoom 5

해석 문학은 매체들 가운데서도, 아이들의 삶에서 유일한 사회화 요인은 아니다.
- **agent** (어떤 사태를 일으키는) 요인, 동인; 대리인
➔ 예를 들어, 오늘날, 책의 영향력은 TV의 그것(영향력)에 의해 빛을 잃었다.
- **overshadow** 빛을 잃게 만들다; 그늘을 드리우다
➔ 하지만, 그 두 매체 사이에는 상당한 정도의 상호 작용이 있다.
- **considerable** 상당한; 많은　**interaction** 상호 작용

Focus & Practice

p.84

1 ②　**2** ②　**3** ①　**4** ③　**5** ②　**6** ③

1 ②

해석 혁신과 문화적 변화가 지구의 인간 수용력을 확장할 수 있다는 것은 가능성이 있다. (①) 세계 경제가 점점 더 태양 에너지와 수소 에너지 같은 '녹색의' 재생 가능한 산업을 검토하고 있으므로 우리는 이미 이를 보고 있다. (② 그러나, 많은 사람들이 우리가 결국 자원의 유한한 특성과의 충돌이 불가피한 지점에 도달할 것이라고 생각한다.) 그것은 생존이 궁극적으로 인구를 그것의 수용력 아래로 만드는 것에 달려 있을 수 있다는 것을 의미한다.
- **conflict** 충돌(하다), 상충(하다)　**inevitable** 불가피한　**innovation** 혁신
expand 확장하다, 팽창하다　**capacity** 수용력; 용량　**renewable** 재생 가능한
ultimately 궁극적으로

해설 주어진 문장은 역접 연결어 Still(그러나)이 이끌며, 결국 자원의 유한한 특성과의 충돌이 불가피한 지점에 도달할 것이라고 많은 사람들이 생각한다는 내용이다. ② 앞 문장에서 세계 경제가 점점 더 '녹색의' 재생 가능한 산업을 검토하고 있다고 했으므로, 이러한 지구의 인간 수용력 확장과는 반대되는, 자원의 유한한 특성과의 충돌이 불가피하다는 내용이 그 뒤에 이어지는 것이 자연스럽다. 또한 ② 뒤에서는 주어진 문장의 내용을 That으로 받아 그것은 생존이 인구를 지구의 수용력 아래로 만드는 것에 달려 있을 수 있다고 부연 설명하고 있다. 따라서 주어진 문장이 들어가기에 가장 적절한 곳은 ②이다.

2 ②

해석 한 전자 장치 회사의 서비스 담당 직원들에게, 판매하는 법을 배우는 것은 그들이 해 왔던 것과는 매우 다른 일이었다. (①) 그러나 그들은 자신들이 생각한 것보다 판매에 대해 이미 훨씬 더 많이 아는 것으로 밝혀졌다. (② 예를 들어, 장비를 점검하거나 설치하는 데(서비스 담당 직원들의 업무) 있어서 첫 단계는 고객들이 그 장비를 어떻게 사용했는지를 이해하기 위해 고객들과 대화하는 것이다.) 같은 것이 판매에도 적용된다.
- **service** 점검하다; 제공하다 *cf.* **service representative** 서비스 담당 직원
install 설치하다　**electronics** 전자 장치; 전자 공학　**turn out** ~인 것으로 밝혀지다[드러나다]

해설 주어진 문장은 예시 연결어 For example(예를 들어)이 이끌며, 장비 점검 혹은 설치 시 고객들과 대화하는 것이 첫 단계라고 설명한다. ② 앞 문장은 서비스 담당 직원들이 그들이 생각한 것보다 판매에 대해 훨씬 더 많이 안다는 내용이므로, 이에 대한 구체적 예로 그들의 업무 중 첫 단계가 고객들과 대화하는 것임을 드는 흐름은 자연스럽다. 또한 ② 뒤에서 '같은 것(The same)', 즉 첫 단계로 고객들과 대화하는 것이 판매에도 적용된다고 설명하며 이어지는 것을 확인할 수 있다. 따라서 주어진 문장이 들어가기에 가장 적절한 곳은 ②이다.

3 ①

해석 연구자들은 비꼼의 다양한 비언어적 특성들을 보고했다. 대부분은 비언어적 신호가 비꼼 또는 그것을 촉발하는 감정의 인지에 필수적인지에 관해 의견이 다르다. (① 그렇긴 하지만, 연구는 특히 언어적 신호와 비언어적 신호가 상충할 때, 비언어적 신호가 언어적 신호보다 더 믿을 만하다는 결과를 확증한다.) 또한, 비언어적 신호는 화자의 의도에 대한 더 나은 지표이다. (②) 비꼼의 본질이 의도와 메시지 사이의 모순을 암시하기 때문에, 속일 때 그러는 것처럼 비언어적 신호는 '샐'지도 모르며 화자의 실제 기분을 드러낼 수도 있다. (③) 표면상, 비꼬는 화자는 보통 듣는 사람이 그 비꼬는 의도를 알아차리기를 의도하지만, 반면에 속일 때는 화자가 보통 듣는 사람이 그 속이는 의도를 알아차리지 않기를 의도한다는 점에서 비꼼은 속임의 반대이다.

•**confirm** 확증하다, 확인해 주다 **nonverbal** 비언어적인, 말을 쓰지 않는 (↔ verbal 언어적인) **credible** 믿을 만한, 신뢰할 수 있는 **perception** 인지, 지각 **prompt** 촉발하다; 신속한, 재빠른 **indicator** 지표, 보여 주는 것 **intent** 의도, 의향 **contradiction** 모순; 반박, 부정 **leak** 새다, 새어 나오다 **deception** 속임, 기만; 사기 *cf.* **deceptive** 속이는, 현혹하는

해설 주어진 문장은 역접 연결어 Even so(그렇긴 하지만)가 이끌며, 비언어적 신호가 언어적 신호보다 더 믿을 만하다는 연구 결과를 설명한다. ① 앞 문장은 비언어적 신호가 비꼼 또는 그것을 촉발하는 감정의 인지에 필수적인지에 관해 연구자들의 의견이 다르다고 했으므로, 비언어적 신호의 신뢰성을 연구 결과가 확증한다는 내용이 역접 연결어로 이어지는 흐름은 자연스럽다. 또한 ① 뒤에서 비언어적 신호가 화자의 의도를 더 잘 보여준다는 내용이, 주어진 문장에 이어 첨가 연결어 Also(또한)로 이어지는 것이 자연스럽다. 따라서 주어진 문장이 들어가기에 가장 적절한 곳은 ①이다.

4 ③

해석 손발의 피부는 왜 목욕 후에 주름질까? 그것의 겉모습에도 불구하고, 당신의 피부는 사실 팽창하고 있다. 우리를 환경으로부터 보호하고 우리의 손과 발의 피부를 배나 얼굴의 것(피부)보다 더 단단하고 두껍게 만드는 두껍고 죽은 거친 피부층인 피부 각질층은 물을 빨아들이면 팽창한다. (①) 이 팽창은 주름지는 효과를 야기한다. (②) 그렇다면 왜 몸의 다른 부분의 피부 또한 물에 흠뻑 젖었을 때 주름지지 않을까? (③ 사실, 그것은 그러하지만(주름지지만), 이러한 덜 조밀하게 채워진 부분에는 그것(주름지는 것)이 드러나기 전에 수분이 흡수될 수 있는 공간이 더 있다.) 한 의사는 오랫동안 젖은 장화에 발이 잠긴 군인들은 그 덮인 부분 전체에 주름지는 것을 보일 것이라고 말했다.

•**moisture** 수분, 습기 **absorb** 흡수하다, 빨아들이다(= soak up) **densely** 조밀하게, 빽빽하게 **pack** 채우다, 꽉 메우다 **wrinkle** 주름지다; 주름, 구김살 **stratum corneum** 피부 각질층

해설 주어진 문장은 강조 연결어 Actually(사실)가 이끌며, 그것(it)이 그러하다(does)고 하고, 덜 조밀한 부분에는 그것이 드러나기 전에 수분이 흡수될 공간이 더 있다고 설명한다. ③ 앞에서는 손발의 피부가 물을 빨아들여 주름진다고 한 다음, 왜 손발이 아닌 다른 부분의 피부는 젖었을 때 주름지지 않는지 질문하고 있다. it이 the skin on other parts of the body를 받아 사실은 주름진다는 반대 내용을 강조하며 그렇게 보이지 않는 이유를 설명하는 흐름이

자연스럽다. 또한 ③ 뒤에서는 주어진 문장의 내용에 관한 예로 젖은 장화를 오래 신은 군인은 덮인 부분 전체가 주름질 것이라는 내용이 이어진다. 따라서 주어진 문장이 들어가기에 가장 적절한 곳은 ③이다.

5 ②

해석 대부분의 조직에서, 직원의 직속 관리자는 그 직원의 성과를 평가한다. (①) 이는 그 관리자가 감독을 제공하고, 업무를 나눠주고, 그 직원을 계발하면서, 그 직원의 성과를 책임지기 때문이다. (② 하지만, 문제는 관리자가 흔히 자신의 직원과 떨어진 위치에서 일해서 자신의 부하 직원들의 성과를 관찰할 수 없다는 것이다.) 관리자는 자신이 관찰할 수 없는 성과 범위에 대해 직원들을 평가해야 하는가? (③) 이 딜레마를 없애기 위해, 점점 더 많은 조직이 '다면 평가'라고 불리는 평가를 시행하고 있다.

•**supervisor** 관리자 *cf.* supervision 감독, 관리 **subordinate** 부하 (직원); 밑의; 아래에 두다 **immediate** 직속의; 직접적인; 즉각적인 **hand out** 나눠주다, 배포하다 **assignment** 업무; 과제; 배정 **dimension** 범위, 규모; 차원 **implement** 시행하다; 도구

해설 주어진 문장은 역접 연결어 however(하지만)가 이끌며, 관리자가 부하 직원과 떨어져 일하므로 성과를 관찰할 수 없는 것이 문제라고 제시한다. ② 앞에서는 관리자가 직원의 성과를 책임지기 때문에 관리자가 직원을 평가한다고 하고, 뒤에서는 관리자가 자신이 관찰할 수 없는 성과 범위에 대해 평가해야 하는지 의문을 제기하고 있다. 관리자가 직원을 평가하는 것에 대한 문제 제기는 그 사이에 들어가는 것이 자연스러우므로, 주어진 문장이 들어가기에 가장 적절한 곳은 ②이다.

6 ③

해석 지도 제작자들의 주된 문제는 집합적으로 '지형'이라고 불리는 산과 계곡, 경사지와 평지의 묘사이다. 이것(지형 묘사)은 여러 방법으로 행해질 수 있다. 하나는 햇빛과 그림자의 이미지를 만들어서, 땅 모양의 시각적 표현을 만들어 내는 것이다. (①) 또 다른 기술적으로 더 정확한 방법은 등고선을 그리는 것이다. (②) 등고선은 동일한 고도에 있는 모든 점을 연결한다. (③ 따라서 평야 위로 솟은 둥그런 산은 가장 큰 원이 맨 아랫부분에 그리고 가장 작은 원은 꼭대기 근처에 있는 일련의 동심원으로 지도에 나타날 것이다.) 등고선이 서로 가깝게 배치되면 산의 경사가 가파르고, 그것들이 더 멀리 떨어져 있으면 경사가 더 완만하다.

•**plain** 평야; 분명한; 보통의 **a set of** 일련의, 일습의 **challenge** 문제, 과제; 도전(하다) **depiction** 묘사 **valley** 계곡, 골짜기 **slope** 경사지; 경사면 **collectively** 집합적으로 **representation** 표현, 묘사; 대표, 대리 **contour line** ((지리)) 등고선 **lie** (위치해) 있다; 눕다; 거짓말(하다) **elevation** 고도, 높이; 증가 **steep** 가파른; 급격한 **gentle** 완만한; 온화한

해설 주어진 문장은 결과 연결어 therefore(따라서)가 이끌며, 평야 위로 솟은 산은 지도에 일련의 동심원으로 나타날 것이라고 설명한다. ③ 앞 문장은 등고선이 동일 고도에 있는 모든 점을 연결한다는 내용으로 그 이유가 되므로, 그 결과 지도에 산이 일련의 동심원으로 나타난다고 뒤에 이어지는 것이 자연스럽다. 또한 ③ 뒤에서는 주어진 문장의 A round hill을 the hill로 받아, 등고선의 간격이 그 산의 경사를 나타낸다고 부연 설명한다. 따라서 주어진 문장이 들어가기에 가장 적절한 곳은 ③이다.

1 ④

¹ Both the budget deficit and federal debt have soared / during the recent financial crisis and recession.
재정 적자와 연방 정부의 부채가 모두 치솟았다 / 최근의 재정 위기와 경기 침체 동안에

² (①) During 2009–2010, / nearly 40 percent of federal expenditures were financed / by borrowing.
2009년~2010년 동안에 / 연방 정부 지출의 거의 40퍼센트가 자금이 조달되었다 / 차입으로

³ (②) The huge recent federal deficits have pushed the federal debt / to *levels* (not seen / since the years (immediately following World War Ⅱ)).
최근의 막대한 연방 재정 적자는 연방 정부의 부채를 떠밀었다 /
수준까지 (보인 적이 없었던 / 기간 이후로 (제2차 세계 대전 바로 뒤에 이어진))

⁴ (③) The rapid growth (of baby-boomer retirees) / in the decade immediately ahead / will mean / higher spending levels and larger and larger deficits (for both Social Security and Medicare).
빠른 증가는 (베이비붐 세대 퇴직자의) / 임박한 향후 10년 동안 /
의미할 것이다 / 더 높은 지급 수준과 점점 더 커지는 적자를
(사회 보장 연금과 노인 의료 보험 제도 둘 다에 대한)

↓

> **⁵** ④ Moreover, / more than half of Americans age 18 and older derive benefits / from various transfer programs, / while paying little or no personal income tax.
> 더욱이 / 18세 이상의 미국인들 중 절반이 넘는 사람들이 보조금을 얻는다 /
> 다양한 (소득) 이전 지출 프로그램으로부터 / 개인 소득세를 거의 혹은 전혀 내지 않으면서

↓

⁶ All of these factors are going to make it extremely difficult / to slow the growth (of federal spending) / and (to) keep the debt from ballooning out of control.
이러한 모든 요인들은 (~을) 대단히 어렵게 만들 것이다 / 증가를 늦추는 것을 (연방 정부 지출의) /
그리고 부채가 통제할 수 없을 정도로 급증하지 못하게 막는 것을

⁷ (⑤) Projections indicate // that the net federal debt will rise / to 90 percent of GDP / by 2019, //
예측들이 보여 준다 // 연방 정부의 순부채가 증가하리라는 것을 /
국내 총생산의 90퍼센트까지 / 2019년쯤에는 //

and many believe // (that) it will be even higher // unless constructive action is taken soon.
그리고 많은 사람들은 생각한다 // 그것(연방 정부의 순부채)이 훨씬 더 높아질 것이라고 // 곧 건설적인 조치가 취해지지 않는 한

해설

주어진 문장의 내용 파악하기 ◉

'더욱이(Moreover)' 미국 성인의 절반이 넘는 사람들이 개인 소득세를 거의 혹은 전혀 내지 않으면서 정부 보조금을 얻음.(▶**Zoom 3** 첨가 연결어)
(앞에는 연결되는 유사한 내용이 나올 것임을 예상할 수 있음.)

⌄

단서로 정답 찾기 ⊕

1 최근의 재정 위기와 경기 침체 동안 재정 적자와 연방 정부 부채가 치솟았음.
2 (①) 2009년 ~ 2010년 연방 정부 지출의 거의 40%가 차입으로 조달되었다고 부연 설명한다.
3 (②) 연방 정부의 부채가 심각하다는 내용이 이어진다.
4 (③) 향후 베이비붐 세대 퇴직자의 빠른 증가로 인한 사회적 비용의 증가를 문제의 요인으로 제시한다.

↓

5 ④ Moreover(더욱이)로, 절반이 넘는 미국 성인이 소득세를 거의 혹은 전혀 내지 않고 보조금을 받는다는 다른 요인이 추가로 이어진다.

↓

6 앞서 언급한 두 가지 요인을 All of these factors로 받아, 이로 인해 연방 정부의 지출 및 부채를 막는 것이 어려울 것이라는 결과를 말한다.
7 (⑤) 어려운 전망에 대한 예측들을 말하고, 건설적 조치가 필요하다는 내용으로 글을 맺는다.

어휘

balloon 급증하다; 부풀다; 풍선   benefit (사회 보장 제도에 의한) 보조금; 혜택, 이득   derive A from B B에서 A를 얻다   expenditure 지출; 비용; 소비   finance 자금(을 조달[공급]하다)   income tax 소득세
net (돈의 액수에 대해) 순(純)-; 그물[망]   projection 예측, 추정; 투사(도)
recession 경기 침체, 불황; 후퇴   retiree 퇴직자, 은퇴자

구문 분석

² ~ nearly **40 percent of federal expenditures were financed** / by borrowing.
'부분'을 나타내는 표현에 이어지는 <of+명사>에서 명사의 수에 동사를 일치시킴.

해석 **¹** 최근의 재정 위기와 경기 침체 동안에 재정 적자(정부 재정 지출이 재정 수입을 초과)와 연방 정부의 부채가 모두 치솟았다. **²** 2009년~2010년 동안에 연방 정부 지출의 거의 40퍼센트가 차입으로 자금이 조달되었다. **³** 최근의 막대한 연방 재정 적자는 제2차 세계 대전 바로 뒤에 이어진 기간 이후로 보인 적이 없었던 수준까지 연방 정부의 부채를 떠밀었다. **⁴** 임박한 향후 10년 동안 베이비붐 세대 퇴직자의 빠른 증가는 사회 보장 연금과 노인 의료 보험 제도 둘 다에 대한 더 높은 지급 수준과 점점 더 커지는 적자를 의미할 것이다. **⁵** 더욱이, 18세 이상의 미국인들 중 절반이 넘는 사람들이 개인 소득세를 거의 혹은 전혀 내지 않으면서, 다양한 (소득) 이전 지출 (생산 활동과 무관하게 대가 없이 정부가 지급하는 소득의 이전) 프로그램으로부터 보조금을 얻는다. **⁶** 이러한 모든 요인들은 연방 정부 지출의 증가를 늦추는 것과 부채가 통제할 수 없을 정도로 급증하지 못하게 막는 것을 대단히 어렵게 만들 것이다. **⁷** 2019년쯤에는 연방 정부의 순부채가 국내 총생산의 90퍼센트까지 증가하리라는 것을 예측들이 보여주며, 많은 사람들은 곧 건설적인 조치가 취해지지 않는 한 그것(연방 정부의 순부채)이 훨씬 더 높아질 것이라고 생각한다.

2 ②

¹When trees grow together, // nutrients and water can be optimally divided / among them all //
나무들이 함께 자랄 때 // 영양분과 물이 최적으로 분배될 수 있다 / 그것들 모두 사이에서 //

so that each tree can grow / into *the best tree* [(that) it can be].
각 나무가 자랄 수 있도록 / 최고의 나무로 [그것이 될 수 있는]

²If you "help" individual trees / by getting rid of their supposed competition, // the remaining trees are bereft.
만약 여러분이 개별 나무를 '도와주면' / 그것들의 경쟁 상대로 여겨지는 나무를 제거함으로써 // 남은 나무들은 잃게 된다

³They send messages out to their neighbors unsuccessfully, // because nothing remains / but stumps.
그것들(남아 있는 나무들)은 이웃 나무들에게 메시지를 보내지만 성공하지 못한다 // 왜냐하면 아무것도 남아 있지 않기 때문이다 / 그루터기 외에는

⁴Every tree now grows on its own, / giving rise to great differences / in productivity.
이제 모든 나무가 독자적으로 자란다 / 그리고 이는 큰 차이를 낳는다 / 생산성에

⁵(①) Some individuals photosynthesize like mad // until sugar positively bubbles / along their trunk.
일부 개체들은 맹렬히 광합성을 한다 // 당분이 확실히 흐를 때까지 / 그것들의 나무줄기를 따라

↓

> ⁶② As a result, / they are fit and grow better, // but they aren't particularly long-lived.
> 그 결과 / 그것들은 건강하고 더 잘 자란다 // 하지만 그것들은 특별히 오래 살지는 않는다

↓

⁷This is // because a tree can be only as strong / as *the forest* [that surrounds it].
이는 ~이다 // 나무가 오직 강할 수 있기 때문 / 숲만큼만 [그것(나무)을 둘러싸고 있는]

⁸(③) And / there are now a lot of losers / in the forest.
그리고 / 이제 많은 패자가 있다 / 숲에는

⁹(④) *Weaker members*, // who would once have been supported / by the stronger ones, / suddenly fall behind.
더 약한 구성원들이 // 한때는 지원받았을 / 더 강한 것들(구성원)에 의해 / 갑자기 뒤처진다

¹⁰(⑤) Whether the reason (for their decline) / is their location and lack of nutrients, a passing sickness, or genetic makeup, // they now fall prey to insects and fungi.
원인이 (그것들(더 약한 구성원들)의 쇠약의) / 그것들의 위치 그리고 영양분 부족이든, 일시적인 질병이든, 혹은 유전적 구성이든 // 이제 그것들(더 약한 구성원들)은 곤충과 균류의 먹이가 된다

해설

주어진 문장의 내용 파악하기 

'그 결과(As a result)', '그것들(they)'이 건강하고 더 잘 자라지만, 특별히 오래 살지는 않음.(▶ **Zoom 2** 결과 연결어, **Point 1** 지시사/대명사)
(앞에는 'they'가 지칭하는 대상과 원인이 나오고, 뒤에는 특별히 오래 살지 못하는 이유가 이어질 것을 예상할 수 있음.)

≫

단서로 정답 찾기 +

1, 2, 3, 4 나무는 함께 자랄 때 영양분과 물이 최적으로 분배되어 잘 자라며, 만약 경쟁 상대로 여겨지는 나무를 자르면 남은 나무들은 혼자 자라는데, 이는 생산성에 큰 차이를 낳음.
5 (①) 일부 개체들은 맹렬히 광합성을 한다고 언급한다.

↓

6 ② they는 맹렬히 광합성을 하는 '일부 개체들(some individuals)'을 가리키며, As a result(그 결과)로 연결되어 이들이 건강하고 더 잘 자라지만 특별히 오래 살지는 않는다고 설명한다.

↓

7 이들이 특별히 오래 살지는 않는다는 주어진 문장의 내용을 This로 받아서, 나무는 자신을 둘러싼 숲만큼만 강할 수 있기 때문이라고 이유를 설명한다.
8 (③) 그래서 이제 숲에는 많은 패자가 있다고 결과를 말한다.
9 (④) 앞 문장의 패자를 Weaker members로 바꾸어 표현하며 약한 구성원들이 갑자기 뒤처진다고 부연 설명한다.
10 (⑤) 더 약한 구성원들이 뒤처진다는 앞의 내용을 their decline으로 받아, 그 원인이 무엇이든 간에 그것들은 곤충과 균류의 먹이가 된다고 결과를 설명한다.

어휘

bubble (졸졸) 흐르다; 거품(이 일다)   **decline** 쇠약; 거절하다; 감소(하다)   **fall behind** 뒤처지다   **fit** 건강한; 적합한, 알맞은   **fungus** (*pl.* fungi) 균류, 곰팡이류   **get rid of** ~을 제거하다   **makeup** 구성, 구조   **passing** 일시적인; 지나가는   **positively** 확실히, 분명히; 긍정적으로   **supposed** ~이라고 여겨지는, 가정의   **trunk** (나무)줄기; 몸통; 여행용 큰 가방

구문 분석

⁴~ / **giving rise to** great differences / in productivity.
<give rise to A>: A를 낳다[일으키다]

해석 ¹나무들이 함께 자랄 때, 각 나무가 그것이 될 수 있는 최고의 나무로 자랄 수 있도록 영양분과 물이 그것들 모두 사이에서 최적으로 분배될 수 있다. ²만약 여러분이 그것들의 경쟁 상대로 여겨지는 나무를 제거함으로써 개별 나무를 '도와주면', 남은 나무들은 잃게 된다. ³그것들은 이웃 나무들에게 메시지를 보내지만 성공하지 못하는데, 왜냐하면 그루터기 외에는 아무것도 남아 있지 않기 때문이다. ⁴이제 모든 나무가 독자적으로 자라고, 이는 생산성에 큰 차이를 낳는다. ⁵일부 개체들은 당분이 나무줄기를 따라 확실히 흐를 때까지 맹렬히 광합성을 한다. ⁶그 결과, 그것들은 건강하고 더 잘 자라지만 특별히 오래 살지는 않는다. ⁷이는 나무가 오직 그것을 둘러싸고 있는 숲만큼만 강할 수 있기 때문이다. ⁸그리고 이제 숲에는 많은 패자가 있다. ⁹한때는 더 강한 구성원들에 의해 지원받았을 더 약한 구성원들이 갑자기 뒤처진다. ¹⁰그것들의 쇠약의 원인이 그것들의 위치 그리고 영양분 부족이든, 일시적인 질병이든, 혹은 유전적 구성이든, 이제 그것들은 곤충과 균류의 먹이가 된다.

3 ④

¹ Film has no grammar.
영화에는 문법이 없다

² (①) There are, however, some vaguely defined rules (of usage in cinematic language), //
그러나 막연하게 정의된 몇 가지 규칙이 있다 (영화 언어 사용에 관한) //

and the syntax of film — / its systematic arrangement — / orders these rules / and indicates relationships among them.
그리고 영화의 문장 구조 / 그것(문장 구조)의 체계적인 (처리) 방식은 /
이러한 규칙을 정리한다 / 그리고 그것들(이러한 규칙) 사이의 관계를 보여준다

³ (②) As with written and spoken languages, / it is important to remember // that the syntax of film is a result of its usage, / not a determinant of it.
문어와 구어에서와 마찬가지로 / 기억하는 것이 중요하다 //
영화의 문장 구조는 그것(그 문장 구조)을 사용한 결과라는 것을 /
그것(그 문장 구조)의 결정 요인이 아니라

⁴ (③) There is *nothing* (preordained about film syntax).
(~인 것은) 아무것도 없다 (영화의 문장 구조에 관해 미리 정해진)

↓

> ⁵④ Rather, / it evolved naturally // as certain devices were found / in practice to be both workable and useful.
> 오히려 / 그것(영화의 문장 구조)은 자연스럽게 발전했다 // 특정 방법이 밝혀지면서 /
> 실제로 운용할 수 있고 유용하다는 것이

↓

⁶ Like the syntax of written and spoken language, / the syntax of film is an organic development, / (descriptive rather than prescriptive), //
문어와 구어의 문장 구조처럼 / 영화의 문장 구조는 자연스러운 발전의 결과이다 /
(규범적이기보다는 기술적이며) //

and it has changed considerably / over the years.
그리고 그것(영화의 문장 구조)은 상당히 변화해 왔다 / 여러 해에 걸쳐

⁷ (⑤) "Hollywood Grammar" may sound laughable now, // but during the thirties, forties, and early fifties / it was an accurate model (of *the way* [(that)] Hollywood films were constructed]).
'할리우드식 문법'은 이제 우습게 들릴지도 모른다 // 그러나 30년대, 40년대, 그리고 50년대 초반에 /
그것('할리우드식 문법')은 정확한 모델이었다 (방식의 [할리우드 영화가 구성되는])

해설

주어진 문장의 내용 파악하기 

'오히려(Rather)', '그것(it)'은 특정 방법이 실제로 운용할 수 있고 유용하다는 것이 밝혀지면서 자연스럽게 발전함.(▶ **Zoom 1** 역접 연결어, **Point 1** 지시사/대명사)
(앞에는 'it'이 지칭하는 대상이 나오고, 그것이 자연스럽게 발전했다는 주어진 문장과 반대되는 내용이 나올 것임을 예상할 수 있음.)

⌄

단서로 정답 찾기 

1 영화에는 문법이 없음.
2 (①) however(그러나)로, 영화 언어 사용에 관한 몇 가지 규칙이 있다는 상반되는 내용이 이어진다.
3 (②) 영화의 문장 구조는 그 구조의 결정 요인이 아니라 그 구조를 사용한 결과라고 설명한다.
4 (③) 영화의 문장 구조에 관해 미리 정해진 것은 없다고 앞 문장의 내용을 부연 설명한다.

↓

5 ④ Rather(오히려)로 이어지며 '영화의 문장 구조(film syntax)'를 it으로 받아, 그것이 자연스럽게 발전한 것이라고 설명한다.

↓

6 영화의 문장 구조는 자연스럽게 생긴 발전의 결과로 기술적이며, 여러 해에 걸쳐 변화해 왔다고 부연 설명한다.
7 (⑤) 영화의 문장 구조가 여러 해에 걸쳐 변화해 왔다는 앞 문장에 대한 예로 과거의 '할리우드식 문법'을 제시한다.

어휘

arrangement (처리) 방식; 준비; 배치; 정리　**determinant** 결정 요인　**device** 방법; 장치　**in practice** 실제로　**laughable** 우스운, 터무니없는　**organic** 자연스러운, 서서히 생기는; 유기농의　**syntax** 문장 구조, 구문 규칙　**systematic** 체계적인　**vaguely** 막연하게; 희미하게　**workable** 운용[실행]할 수 있는

구문 분석

⁵ ~ // as certain devices **were found** / in practice **to be both workable and useful**.
<find+O+(to be) C(O가 C임을 알게 되다)>의 수동형.

해석 ¹영화에는 문법이 없다. ²그러나 영화 언어(영화에서 의미, 감정, 이야기 등을 시청자에게 전달하기 위해 독특하게 사용되는 특별한 기술이나 요소들을 의미) 사용에 관한 막연하게 정의된 몇 가지 규칙이 있고, 영화의 문장 구조, 문장 구조의 체계적인 (처리) 방식은 이러한 규칙을 정리하고 그것들(이러한 규칙) 사이의 관계를 보여준다. ³문어와 구어에서와 마찬가지로, 영화의 문장 구조는 그 문장 구조의 결정 요인이 아니라 그것을 사용한 결과라는 것을 기억하는 것이 중요하다. ⁴영화의 문장 구조에 관해 미리 정해진 것은 아무것도 없다. ⁵오히려, 그것(영화의 문장 구조)은 특정 방법(영화를 찍는 기술, 도구, 장치 등을 의미)이 실제로 운용할 수 있고 유용하다는 것이 밝혀지면서 자연스럽게 발전했다. ⁶문어와 구어의 문장 구조처럼 영화의 문장 구조는 자연스러운 발전의 결과이고, 규범적(미리 설정된 규칙에 따르는 것)이기보다는 기술적(이미 사용된 것을 있는 그대로 설명하는 것)이며, 여러 해에 걸쳐 상당히 변화해 왔다. ⁷'할리우드식 문법'은 이제 우습게 들릴지도 모르지만, 30년대, 40년대, 그리고 50년대 초반에 그것은 할리우드 영화가 구성되는 방식의 정확한 모델이었다.

Zoom 1

해석 어둠 속에서 자라는 식물을 관찰해 온 과학자들은 그것들이 밝은 곳에서 자란 것들과 외형, 형태, 그리고 기능에서 매우 다르다는 것을 발견했다.

•**vastly** 매우, 대단히; 광대하게

어둠 속에서 자라는 실생 식물은 어둠 속에서 최대한의 역량으로 기능하지 않는, 떡잎과 뿌리와 같은 기관들에 가는 에너지의 양을 제한하고, 그 대신에 그 식물을 어둠 밖으로 나아가게 하기 위해 실생 식물 줄기의 연장에 착수한다.

•**seedling** 실생 식물((씨에서 싹이 나와 자라는 식물)) **capacity** 역량, 능력; 수용력
initiate (~에) 착수하다, 시작하다 **propel** 나아가게 하다, 몰다

아주 밝은 곳에서, 실생 식물은 그것들이 줄기 연장에 할당하는 에너지의 양을 줄인다.

•**allocate** 할당하다, 배분하다

에너지는 그것들의 잎을 넓히고 막대한 뿌리 체계를 발달시키는 것에 보내진다.

•**expand** 넓히다, 확장[확대]하다 **extensive** (수량·규모가) 막대한, 엄청난; 광범위한

Zoom 2

해석 문학 또는 영화와 대조적으로, 관광은 '실제적인', 감지할 수 있는 세계로 이어지는데, 반면에 그럼에도 불구하고 환상, 꿈, 소망, 즉 허구의 영역과 여전히 관련되어 있다. 그렇기 때문에 그것(관광)은 허구적 생각의 의식적 실행을 가능하게 한다.

•**tangible** 감지할[만질] 수 있는 **tie** 관련시키다; 묶다 **sphere** 영역; 구(체)
myth 허구; 신화 *cf.* **mythological** 허구적인; 신화적인 **ritual** 의식상의; 의례적인
enactment 실행; 법률 제정, 입법

➔ 사람들이 텔레비전에서 히말라야산맥에 대한 영화를 시청하고 장엄한 산봉우리의 '손대지 않은 자연'에 흥분하게 되는지, 또는 그들이 일어나서 네팔로 길고 고된 여행을 가는지에 관해서는 상당한 차이가 있다.

•**majestic** 장엄한, 웅장한 **trek** 길고 고된 여행; 트레킹하다

➔ 심지어 후자의 경우에도, 그들은 적어도 부분적으로는 가상의 세계에 머물러 있다. •**latter** 후자(의), 마지막의 **partly** 부분적으로, 어느 정도

Zoom 3

해석 사람과 쥐 모두 '단' 음식에 대한 맛의 선호를 진화시켜 왔는데, 이것(단 음식)은 풍부한 열량의 원천을 제공한다. 탄자니아의 Hadza 수렵 채집인 사이의 음식 선호에 관한 한 연구는 가장 높은 열량값을 가진 식품인 꿀이 가장 많이 선호되는 식품이었다는 것을 알아냈다. 인간의 갓난아기 또한 단 액체에 대한 강한 선호를 보인다. 사람과 쥐 모두 '쓰'고 '신' 음식을 싫어하는데, 이것들(쓰고 신 음식)은 독소를 포함하는 경향이 있다.

•**preference** 선호(도), 더 좋아함 **calorie** 열량, 칼로리 *cf.* **caloric** 열량의; 열의
hunter-gatherer 수렵 채집인 **newborn infant** 갓난아기, 신생아 **toxin** 독소

그들(사람과 쥐)은 또한 자신의 섭식 행동을 물, 열량, 소금의 부족에 대응하여 적응하도록 조정한다.

•**adaptively** 적응하도록, 적응하여 **adjust** 조정[조절]하다
deficit 부족; 결손, 적자 *cf.* **deficiency** 결핍, 부족

➔ 실험은 쥐가 소금 결핍을 처음 경험할 때 소금에 대한 즉각적인 기호를 보인다는 것을 보여준다. •**immediate** 즉각적인, 직계[직속]의 **liking** 기호, 좋아함

➔ 그것들은(쥐) 마찬가지로 에너지와 체액이 고갈된 경우에는 단것과 물 섭취를 늘린다.

•**intake** 섭취(량) **fluid** (동물의) 체액; 유동체; 부드러운
deplete 고갈[소모]시키다

Focus & Practice p.90

1 ② 2 ① 3 ③ 4 ② 5 ③

1 ②

해석 너무 많은 글쓴이들이 '논리적'이라는 용어가 연대순을 의미한다고 이해하고, 이전의 저작물에 대한 주의 깊은 재검토로 보고서와 논문을 시작하는 것이 습관적이게 되었다. (①) 보통, 이는 전술상 약하다. (② 대부분의 보고서와 논문의 독자들은 그들이 그 주제에 관심이 있고 그 주제에 대해 무언가를 알기 때문에 그 문서를 읽는다.) 따라서 그들에게 이전 저작물의 연구 결과를 되풀이하는 것은 그저 불필요한 상기로 그들을 지루하게 하는 것이다.

•**interpret** 이해[해석]하다; 통역하다 **term** 용어; 조건; 학기 **habitual** 습관적인, 버릇이 된 **review** 재검토(하다); 논평, 비평 **tactically** 전술상, 전략적으로
rehearse 되풀이하다; 예행연습[리허설]을 하다

해설 주어진 문장은 대부분의 보고서와 논문의 독자들은 그 주제에 관심이 있고 그 주제에 대해 알기 때문에 그 문서를 읽는다는 내용이다. ② 앞 문장의 this는 '이전의 저작물에 대한 주의 깊은 재검토로 보고서와 논문을 시작하는 것'을 가리키며, 이것이 전술상 약하다고 했으므로 이에 대한 구체적인 설명으로 주어진 문장이 이어지는 것이 자연스럽다. ② 뒤 문장의 them은 주어진 문장의 '대부분의 보고서와 논문의 독자들(Most readers ~ papers)'을 받아, 전술상 약하다는 것에 대한 설명을 이어간다. 따라서 주어진 문장이 들어가기에 가장 적절한 곳은 ②이다.

2 ①

해석 한 아이디어의 표현은 저작권에 의해 보호되며, 그 저작권을 침해하는 사람들은 법정에 소환되어 기소될 수 있다. (① 저작권은 아이디어의 표현을 보호하며, 아이디어 그 자체를 보호하지는 않는다는 것에 유의하라.) 이것은 예를 들어, 많은 스마트폰이 전부 유사한 기능을 가지고 있지만, 그 아이디어가 서로 다른 방식으로 표현되었고 저작권 보호를 받은 것은 바로 그 표현이기 때문에 이것이 저작권 침해를 나타내지 않는다는 것을 의미한다. (②) 저작권은 무료이며 저작자, 예를 들어 어떤 책의 저자나 프로그램을 개발하는 프로그래머에게 자동으로 부여되는데, 그들이 저작권을 다른 누군가에게 양도하지 않는 한 그러하다.

•**note** (~에) 유의하다 **cover** 보호하다; 덮다; 포함하다 **copyright** 저작권(을 보호하다) **court** 법정, 법원 **functionality** 기능 **represent** 나타내다; 대표[대신]하다 **invest** (권한 등을) 부여하다; 투자하다 **sign** (서명을 통해 권리 등을) 양도하다

해설 주어진 문장은 저작권이 아이디어 그 자체가 아닌 아이디어의 표현을 보호한다는 것에 유의하라는 내용이다. ① 뒤 문장은 예시 연결어 for example로 이어져, 기능이 유사한 스마트폰들이 많지만 그 표현 방식이 서로 다르기 때문에 '그것(This)'이 저작권 침해가 아니라는 것을 의미한다고 한다. 이는 주어진 문장의 내용을 This로 받아 부연 설명하는 예로 적절하므로 주어진 문장이 들어가기에 가장 적절한 곳은 ①이다.

3 ③

해석 Milica Milosavljevic과 그의 동료들은 시각적 두드러짐과 구매 결정 사이의 관계를 살펴보는 실험을 수행했다. 그들은 피실험자들에게 기능적 자기 공명 영상으로 막대 과자, 감자칩, 과일 맛이 나는 제품 등과 같은 15개의 각각 다른 식품 제품들을 보여주었다. (①) 이것들은 '가장 좋아하는 간식'에서 '전혀 좋아하지 않음'에 따라 1~15의 척도로 피실험자들에 의해 평가되었다. (②) 그 다음에 그것들은 가지각색의 밝기와 시간으로 제시되었으며, 피실험자들은 항상 두 가지 제품 중에 선택해야 했다. (③ 그 결과는 우리가 언제나 우리가 가장 좋아하는 것을 사는 것은 아니고, 일이 빨리 진행되어야 할 때, 우리는 우리의 눈을 가장 사로잡는 제품을 선호하는 경향이 있다는 것이었다.) 만약 우리가 또한 누군가랑 대화하거나, 통화 중이거나, 그때 우리의 생각이 다른 곳에 있어서 주의가 산만해지면, 어떤 제품에 대한 우리의 실제 선호는 이면으로 더 멀어지고 시각적으로 눈에 잘 띄는 것이 주목을 받게 된다.

•go for ~을 선호하다; ~을 얻으려고 애쓰다   subject 피실험자   distracted 주의가 산만해진   come to the fore 주목을 받게 되다; 중요한 역할을 하다

해설 주어진 문장은 우리가 언제나 가장 좋아하는 것을 사는 것은 아니고, 일이 빨리 진행되어야 할 때는 눈을 가장 사로잡는 제품을 선호한다는 결과를 제시하는 내용이다. ① 앞은 시각적 두드러짐과 구매 결정 사이의 관계를 살펴보는 실험에서 피실험자들에게 여러 식품 제품을 보여주었다는 내용이며, ② 앞 문장은 그 제품들의 선호도가 피실험자들에 의해 평가되었다는 내용이다. ③ 앞 문장은 그다음에 그 제품들이 가지각색의 밝기와 시간으로 제시되었고 피실험자들이 둘 중 하나를 선택해야 했다는 내용이므로, 그 뒤에 선택에 따른 이 실험의 결과를 제시하는 주어진 문장이 과정순으로 이어지는 것이 적절하다. ③ 다음의 문장은 우리가 또한 주의가 산만할 때 실제 선호는 이면으로 더 멀어진다고 덧붙이고 있다. 따라서 주어진 문장이 들어가기에 가장 적절한 곳은 ③이다.

4 ②

해석 뇌는 포도당의 고에너지 소비자인데, 포도당은 뇌의 연료이다. 그러나 당신의 뇌는 연료를 저장할 수 없으며, 그렇기 때문에 그것은 '활동하면서 대가를 지불'해야 한다. 당신의 뇌는 대단히 적응성이 있기 때문에, 그것은 연료 자원을 경제적으로 쓴다. (①) 따라서, 스트레스가 큰 기간에, 그것(뇌)은 상황의 미묘한 차이에 대한 분석에서 스트레스가 많은 가까운 상황에 대한 단일하고 고정된 초점으로 방향을 바꾼다.(② 당신은 스트레스를 받을 때 편안히 앉아서 삶의 의미에 대해 깊이 생각하지 않는다.) 그보다는, 당신은 무슨 행동을 해야 할지 알아내려 노력하는 것에 당신의 모든 에너지를 바친다. (③) 하지만, 때로는 뇌의 고차원적 사고 영역으로부터 자동적이고 반사적인 영역으로의 이러한 전환은 당신이 무언가를 생각 없이 너무 빠르게 하도록 이끌 수 있다.

•sit back 편안히 앉다; 가만히 있다   speculate 깊이 생각하다, 사색하다; 추측하다   adaptive 적응성 있는, 적응할 수 있는   economize 경제적으로 쓰다; 절약하다, 아끼다   shift (방향·방식·태도를) 바꾸다; 전환   nuance (음·의미 등의) 미묘한 차이, 뉘앙스   singular 단일의, 단독의; 뛰어난   at hand 가까운; 머지않아   devote (노력·시간 등을) 바치다, 쏟다   reflexive 반사적인

해설 주어진 문장은 당신이 스트레스를 받을 때 편안히 앉아 삶에 의미에 대해 깊이 생각하지 않는다는 내용이다. ② 앞 문장은 스트레스가 큰 기간에는 뇌가 상황의 미묘한 차이에 대한 분석에서 스트레스가 많은 가까운 상황에 대한 단일하고 고정된 초점으로 방향을 바꾼다는 내용이므로, 스트레스를 받을 때 상황의 미묘한 차이에 대한 분석을 하지 않는다는 내용을 주어진 문장이 구체적인 예로 먼저 부연 설명하는 것이 자연스럽다. ② 뒤 문장은 역접 연결어 Instead로 이어져, 단일하고 고정된 초점으로 방향을 바꾸는 것의 구체적인 예에 해당하는 내용이다. 따라서 주어진 문장이 들어가기에 가장 적절한 곳은 ②이다.

5 ③

해석 식품 선택을 결정하는 사회적 역학의 증가하는 복잡성은 마케팅 담당자와 광고주의 업무를 점점 더 어렵게 만든다. 과거에는 대량 생산이 제품에 대한 접근과 감당할 수 있는 비용을 가능하게 했으며, 발전의 신호로 받아들여졌다. (①) 오늘날 그것(대량 생산)은 개인의 선호를 반영하는 것으로 생각되는 점점 더 작은 부분들의 사이에서 소비자 파편화에 의해 점점 더 대체된다. (②) 현실에서, 개인적 선호라고 생각되는 이런 것들은 결국 문화적 감성, 사회적 일체감, 정치적 감성, 그리고 식이 요법과 건강에 관한 관심을 중심으로 확고해지는, 최근에 생겨나고, 일시적이며, 항상 바뀌고, 거의 부족적인 형성물들과 겹치게 된다. (③ 개인의 이야기는 더 큰 이야기와 연결되어, 결국 새로운 정체성을 만들어 낸다.) 이들 소비자 집단은 국가적 경계를 넘어 개념, 이미지, 관습의 전 세계적이고 널리 공유된 저장소 때문에 더 강해진다.

•dynamics 역학; 원동력; 활력   accessibility 접근 (가능성); 입수 가능함   affordability 감당할 수 있는 비용   segment 부분, 단편, 조각   overlap 겹쳐지다; 겹치다   tribal 부족의, 종족의   solidify 확고해지다, 굳어지다   sensibility 감성, 감수성   identification 일체감; 신원 확인   dietary 식이 요법의   boundary 경계(선)   feed on ~ 때문에 더 강해지다; ~을 먹다   practice 관습, 관례; 연습

해설 주어진 문장은 개인의 이야기가 더 큰 이야기와 연결되어 새로운 정체성을 만들어 낸다는 내용이다. ① 앞 문장은 과거에 대량 생산이 가졌던 장점을 언급한다. ② 앞 문장은 오늘날 대량 생산이 개인의 선호를 반영하는 것으로 생각되는 소비자 파편화에 의해 대체되고 있다고 과거와 대조하며, ③ 앞 문장은 그 개인적 선호(개인의 이야기)가 결국 여러 관심사를 중심으로 만들어진 부족적인 형성물(더 큰 이야기)과 겹치게 된다는 내용으로 생각되는 것과 상반되는 사실을 언급한다. 주어진 문장은 개인의 이야기와 더 큰 이야기의 연결이 새로운 정체성을 만들어 낸다는 결과로 앞에서 언급한 사실을 부연 설명한다. ③ 뒤 문장은 주어진 문장의 '새로운 정체성(new identities)'을 These consumer communities로 받아, 개인의 선호가 더해진 소비자 집단이 개념, 이미지, 관습을 공유하고 국가적 경계를 넘어 존재한다는 내용으로 글을 맺는다. 따라서 주어진 문장이 들어가기에 가장 적절한 곳은 ③이다.

1 ④

¹Negotiators should try to find *ways* (to slice a large issue / into smaller pieces), / (known as using *salami tactics*).
협상가들은 방법을 찾으려고 노력해야 한다 (큰 문제를 나누는 / 더 작은 조각들로) /
('살라미 전술'을 사용하는 것으로 알려진)

²(①) *Issues* [that can be expressed / in quantitative, measurable units] / are easy to slice.
문제들은 [표현될 수 있는 / 양적이고 측정 가능한 단위로] / 나누기 쉽다

³(②) For example, / compensation demands can be divided / into cents-per-hour increments // or lease rates can be quoted / as dollars per square foot.
예를 들어 / 보상금 요구는 나눠질 수 있다 /
시간당 센트 증가로 // 또는 임대료는 매겨질 수 있다 / 제곱 피트당 달러로

⁴(③) When working / to fractionate issues (of principle or precedent), /
작업할 때 / 쟁점을 세분하기 위해 (원칙이나 전례의) /
parties may use the time horizon / (when the principle goes into effect // or how long it will last) / as *a way* (to fractionate the issue).
당사자들은 시간 지평을 사용할 수 있다 / (언제 원칙이 발효하는지 //
또는 얼마나 오래 지속될지(와 같은)) / 방법으로 (그 쟁점을 세분하는)

↓

> ⁵④ It may be easier / to reach an agreement //
> when settlement terms don't have to be implemented /
> until months in the future.
> (~은) 더 쉬워지도 모른다 / 합의에 이르는 것은 //
> 합의 조건이 이행될 필요가 없을 때 / 이후의 몇 달까지

↓

⁶Another approach is to vary / the number of *ways* [that the principle may be applied].
또 다른 접근법은 다양화하는 것이다 / 방법의 수를 [원칙이 적용될 수 있는]

⁷(⑤) For example, / a company may devise / *a family emergency leave plan* [that allows employees the opportunity (to be away from the company / for a period (of no longer than three hours, / and no more than once a month), / for illness in the employee's immediate family)].
예를 들어 / 기업은 고안할 수 있다 / 가족 긴급 휴가 계획을
[직원들에게 기회를 주는 (회사로부터 떠나 있을 / 기간 동안 (세 시간 이내의 / 그리고 한 달에 한 번 이내의) / 직원의 직계 가족의 질병에 대해)]

해설

주어진 문장의 내용 파악하기 

합의 조건 이행까지 시간이 더 있다면 (당장 이행되어야 할 때보다) 합의에 이르기가 더 쉬울 수 있음.

≫

단서로 정답 찾기 ⊕

1 협상가는 문제를 작게 나누려고 노력해야 함.
2 (①) 양적이고 측정 가능한 단위로 표현될 수 있는 문제들이 나누기 쉽다고 설명한다.
3 (②) For example(예를 들어)로 보상금 요구와 임대료는 단위당 금액으로 나눠질 수 있다는 예가 이어진다.
4 (③) 쟁점을 세분하는 다른 방법으로 시간 지평을 사용하는 것을 제시한다.

↓

5 ④ 합의 조건을 당장 이행할 필요가 없는 쟁점은 합의에 이르기 더 쉬울 수 있다는, 시간 지평을 사용하는 것에 대한 부연 설명이 이어진다.(▶ **Zoom 2, 3 구체적/세부적 진술**)

6 문제를 작게 나누는 또 다른 방법으로 원칙이 적용될 수 있는 방법의 수를 다양화하는 것을 제시한다.
7 (⑤) For example(예를 들어)로 기업이 기간, 빈도, 사유, 가족 범위 등으로 세분화한 가족 긴급 휴가 계획을 고안할 수 있다는 구체적인 예가 이어진다.

어휘

compensation 보상(금)　devise 고안하다　go into effect 발효하다, 실시되다　implement (계약 등을) 이행[시행]하다　lease 임대(하다)　negotiator 협상가　precedent 전례; 관례　quantitative 양적인　quote 시세를 매기다; 인용하다　settlement 합의; 해결

구문 분석

⁷For example, / a company may devise / *a family emergency leave plan* [that allows employees **the opportunity** (**to be** away from the company / for a period ~)].
the opportunity와 to be 이하는 동격 관계임.

해석 ¹협상가들은 '살라미 전술(협상에서 한 번에 목표를 달성하는 것이 아니라 문제를 부분별로 세분하고 쟁점화하여 각각에 대한 대가를 받아 냄으로써 이익을 극대화하는 전술)'을 사용하는 것으로 알려진, 큰 문제를 더 작은 조각들로 나누는 방법을 찾으려고 노력해야 한다. ²양적이고 측정 가능한 단위로 표현될 수 있는 문제들은 나누기 쉽다. ³예를 들어, 보상금 요구는 시간당 센트 증가로 나눠지거나 임대료는 제곱 피트당 달러로 매겨질 수 있다. ⁴원칙이나 전례의 쟁점을 세분하기 위해 작업할 때, 당사자들은 그 쟁점을 세분하는 방법으로 (언제 원칙이 발효하는지 또는 얼마나 오래 지속될지와 같은) 시간 지평을 사용할 수 있다. ⁵합의 조건이 이후의 몇 달까지 이행될 필요가 없을 때 합의에 이르는 것은 더 쉬울지도 모른다. ⁶또 다른 접근법은 원칙이 적용될 수 있는 방법의 수를 다양화하는 것이다. ⁷예를 들어, 기업은 직원들에게 직원의 직계 가족의 질병에 대해 세 시간 이내의 그리고 한 달에 한 번 이내의 기간 동안 회사로부터 떠나 있을 기회를 주는 가족 긴급 휴가 계획을 고안할 수 있다.

2 ③

[1] Acknowledging the making of artworks does not require / a detailed, technical knowledge (of, (say), how painters mix different kinds of paint, / or how an image editing tool works).
예술품의 제작을 인정하는 것은 필요로 하지 않는다 /
자세하고 기술적인 지식을 ((예를 들어) 화가가 다양한 종류의 물감을 섞는 방법에 관한 /
또는 이미지 편집 도구가 작동하는 방식(에 관한))

[2] (①) *All* [that is required] / is a general sense (of a significant difference (between working with paints and working with an imaging application)).
전부는 [필요한] / 일반적인 감각이다 (중요한 차이에 대한
(물감으로 작업하는 것과 이미징 응용 프로그램을 사용하는 것 사이의))

[3] (②) This sense might involve / a basic familiarity (with paints and paintbrushes) / as well as a basic familiarity (with how we use computers, / perhaps including how we use consumer imaging apps).
이러한 감각은 포함할 수도 있다 / 기본적인 숙지를 (물감과 그림붓에 대한) /
기본적인 숙지뿐만 아니라 (컴퓨터를 사용하는 방법에 대한 /
아마도 우리가 소비자 이미징 응용 프로그램을 사용하는 방법을 포함하여)

↓

[4] ③ In the case of specialists (such as art critics), / a deeper familiarity (with materials and techniques) / is often useful / in reaching an informed judgement (about a work).
전문가의 경우에는 (예술 비평가와 같은) / 더 깊은 숙지가
(재료와 기법에 대한) / 흔히 유용하다 /
정통한 판단에 도달하는 데 (작품에 대한)

↓

[5] This is // because every kind of artistic material or tool comes / with its own challenges and affordances (for artistic creation).
이것은 ~이다 // 모든 종류의 예술 재료나 도구가 함께 오기 때문 /
그것의 고유한 도전 그리고 행위 유발성과 (예술 창작을 위한)

[6] (④) Critics are often interested / in *the ways* [(that) artists exploit different kinds of materials and tools / for particular artistic effect].
비평가들은 흔히 관심이 있다 / 방식에 [예술가들이 다양한 종류의 재료와 도구를 활용하는 /
특정한 예술적 효과를 위해]

[7] (⑤) They are also interested / in the success of *an artist's attempt* — / (embodied in the artwork itself) — / (to push the limits (of what can be achieved / with certain materials and tools)).
그들(비평가들)은 또한 관심이 있다 / 예술가의 시도가 성공하는 것에 /
(예술품 그 자체로 구현된) / (한계를 밀어붙이려는 (달성될 수 있는 것의 / 특정 재료와 도구로))

해설

주어진 문장의 내용 파악하기 🅟

전문가들이 작품에 대한 정통한 판단을 하는 데는 예술 재료와 기법을 더 깊이 숙지하는 것이 유용함.
(뒤에는 더 깊은 숙지가 유용하다는 것에 대한 논거나 부연 설명이 이어질 것을 예상할 수 있음.)

≫

단서로 정답 찾기 ➕

1 예술품의 제작을 인정하는 것은 자세한 기술적인 지식을 필요로 하지 않음.

2 (①) 예술품의 제작을 인정하는 데 필요한 것은 서로 다른 작업 간의 차이를 아는 일반적인 감각이라고 설명한다.

3 (②) This sense는 앞 문장의 '일반적인 감각(a general sense)'을 받아, 우리(일반인들)는 재료와 프로그램 사용에 대한 기본적인 숙지를 포함하여 서로 다른 작업 간의 차이를 알기만 하면 된다고 부연 설명한다.

↓

4 ③ 전문가의 경우에는 더 깊은 숙지가 유용하다는 대조되는 내용을 제시한다.(▸ **Zoom 1** 일반적/추상적 진술)

↓

5 주어진 문장을 This로 받아, 모든 종류의 예술 재료나 도구에는 고유한 도전과 행위 유발성이 따르기 때문이라고 이유를 설명한다.

6 (④) 앞에서 언급된 '모든 종류의 예술 재료나 도구(every kind of artistic material or tool)'가 different kinds of materials and tools로 연결되어, 비평가들은 그것들의 활용 방식에 관심을 둔다는 결과가 이어진다.

7 (⑤) '비평가들(Critics)'을 They로 받아, 그들이 특정 재료와 도구로 한계를 넘으려는 시도에도 관심이 있다고 하며, 비평가들의 관심을 추가로 제시한다.

어휘

acknowledge 인정하다, 동의하다 application 응용 프로그램(app); 지원(서); 적용 critic 비평가, 평론가 embody 구현하다; 포함하다 familiarity 숙지, 잘 앎; 친숙(함) informed 정통한, 잘 아는; 정보에 근거한

구문 분석

[5] This is // **because** every kind of artistic material or tool comes / with its own challenges and affordances (for artistic creation).
because는 명사절을 이끌어 문장의 주어나 보어로 쓰일 수 있음.

해석 [1]예술품의 제작을 인정하는 것은 예를 들어, 화가가 다양한 종류의 물감을 섞는 방법이나 이미지 편집 도구가 작동하는 방식에 관한 자세하고 기술적인 지식을 필요로 하지 않는다. [2]필요한 전부는 물감으로 작업하는 것과 이미징(시각적으로 인식할 수 있는 형태로 정보를 표현하는 것) 응용 프로그램을 사용하는 것 사이의 중요한 차이에 대한 일반적인 감각이다. [3]이러한 감각은 아마도 우리가 소비자 이미징 응용 프로그램을 사용하는 방법을 포함하여, 컴퓨터를 사용하는 방법에 대한 기본적인 숙지뿐만 아니라 물감과 그림붓에 대한 기본적인 숙지를 포함할 수도 있다. [4]예술 비평가와 같은 전문가의 경우에는 재료와 기법에 대한 더 깊은 숙지가 작품에 대한 정통한 판단에 도달하는 데 흔히 유용하다. [5]이것은 모든 종류의 예술 재료나 도구가 예술 창작을 위한 그것의 고유한 도전 그리고 행위 유발성과 함께 오기 때문이다. [6]비평가들은 흔히 예술가들이 특정한 예술적 효과를 위해 다양한 종류의 재료와 도구를 활용하는 방식에 관심이 있다. [7]그들(비평가들)은 또한 예술품 그 자체로 구현된, 특정 재료와 도구로 달성될 수 있는 것의 한계를 밀어붙이려는 예술가의 시도가 성공하는 것에 관심이 있다.

3 ⑤

[1] Erikson believes // that when we reach the adult years, // several physical, social, and psychological stimuli / trigger a sense (of *generativity*).
Erikson은 믿는다 // 우리가 성년에 이를 때 //
몇 가지 신체적, 사회적, 그리고 심리적 자극이 / 인식을 유발한다고 ('생산성'에 대한)

[2] A central component (of this attitude) / is the desire (to care for others).
한 가지 중심 구성 요소는 (이러한 태도의) / 욕구이다 (다른 사람들을 돌보고자 하는)

[3] (①) For the majority of people, / parenthood is perhaps the most obvious and convenient opportunity (to fulfill this desire).
대다수 사람들에게 / 부모 되기는 아마 가장 분명하고 편리한 기회일 것이다 (이러한 욕구를 충족시킬)

[4] (②) Erikson believes // that / another distinguishing feature (of adulthood) / is the emergence (of an inborn desire (to teach)).
Erikson은 믿는다 // ~라고 / 또 다른 독특한 특징이 (성인기의) /
출현이(라고) (타고난 욕구의 (가르치고자 하는))

[5] (③) We become aware of this desire // when the event (of being physically capable of reproducing) / is joined /
우리는 이 욕구(가르치고자 하는 타고난 욕구)를 인식하게 된다 // 일이 (~할) 때 (신체적으로 번식하는 것이 가능해지는) / 결합될 (때) /
with the events (of participating / in a committed relationship, the establishment of an adult pattern of living, and the assumption of job responsibilities).
일들과 (참여하는 / 헌신적인 관계, 성인 생활 패턴의 확립, 그리고 업무 책임 떠맡기에)

[6] (④) According to Erikson, / by becoming parents / we learn // that we have the need (to be needed / by *others* [who depend on our knowledge, protection, and guidance]).
Erikson에 따르면 / 부모가 됨으로써 / 우리는 알게 된다 //
우리가 욕구가 있음을 (필요해지고 싶은 / 다른 사람들에게 [우리의 지식, 보호, 그리고 지도에 의존하는])

↓

[7] ⑤ We become entrusted / to teach culturally appropriate behaviors, values, attitudes, skills, and information about the world.
우리는 위임받게 된다 / 문화적으로 적절한 행동, 가치, 태도, 기술, 그리고 세상에 대한 정보를 가르치는 것을

↓

[8] By assuming the responsibilities (of being primary caregivers to children) / through their long years of physical and social growth, / we concretely express // what Erikson believes / to be an inborn desire (to teach).
책임을 떠맡음으로써 (아이들에게 일차적인 보호자가 되는) /
신체적, 사회적으로 성장하는 긴 세월 동안 /
우리는 명확하게 표현한다 / Erikson이 믿는 것을 / 타고난 욕구라고 (가르치고자 하는)

해설

주어진 문장의 내용 파악하기 

우리는 문화적으로 적절한 행동, 가치, 태도, 기술 그리고 세상에 대한 정보를 가르치는 것을 위임받게 됨.

⌄

단서로 정답 찾기 ➕

1, 2 Erikson에 의하면, 성년에 이를 때 생산성에 대한 인식이 유발되며 생산성의 한 중심 요소는 타인을 돌보고자 하는 욕구임.

3 (①) 타인을 돌보려는 욕구를 this desire로 받아, 부모 되기가 그 욕구를 충족시킬 가장 분명하고 편리한 기회일 것이라고 언급한다.

4 (②) 성인기의 또 다른 특징이 가르치고자 하는 타고난 욕구의 출현이라고 제시한다.

5 (③) 가르치고자 하는 타고난 욕구를 this desire로 받아 신체적으로 번식이 가능해짐과 사회적 책임이 결합될 때 이를 인식하게 된다고 부연 설명한다.

6 (④) 부모가 됨으로써 우리의 지식, 보호, 지도에 의존하는 다른 사람들, 즉 자식에게 필요해지고 싶은 욕구가 있음을 알게 된다고 이어서 설명한다.

↓

7 ⑤ 문화적으로 적절한 행동, 가치, 태도, 기술, 세상에 대한 정보를 예로 들어, 자식에게 어떤 것을 가르치게 되는지를 구체적으로 설명한다.(▶ **Zoom 2, 3** 구체적/세부적 진술)

↓

8 아이들의 일차적 보호자인 부모가 되어 가르치고자 하는 타고난 욕구를 표현한다는 내용으로 글을 맺는다.

어휘

assumption (임무·책임을)떠맡기; 추정   committed 헌신적인, 열성적인   component (구성) 요소   concretely 명확하게, 구체적으로   emergence 출현; 발생   entrust 위임하다, 맡기다   establishment 확립, 확정; 설립   fulfill (조건·요구를) 충족시키다; (의무·약속을) 이행하다; 달성하다   inborn 타고난, 선천적인   primary 일차적인; 주요한; 초기의   reproduce 번식하다; 복사[복제]하다

구문 분석

[5] ~ the events (of participating / in **a committed relationship, the establishment of an adult pattern of living,** ⏢and⏢ **the assumption of job responsibilities**).
전치사 in의 목적어인 세 개의 명사구가 콤마(,)와 and로 병렬 연결됨.

해석 [1] Erikson은 우리가 성년에 이를 때, 몇 가지 신체적, 사회적, 그리고 심리적 자극이 '생산성'에 대한 인식을 유발한다고 믿는다. [2] 이러한 태도(생산성)의 한 가지 중심 구성 요소는 다른 사람들을 돌보고자 하는 욕구이다. [3] 대다수 사람들에게, 부모 되기는 아마 이러한 욕구를 충족할 가장 분명하고 편리한 기회일 것이다. [4] Erikson은 성인기의 또 다른 독특한 특징이 가르치고자 하는 타고난 욕구의 출현이라고 믿는다. [5] 신체적으로 번식하는 것이 가능해지는 일이 헌신적인 관계, 성인 생활 패턴의 확립, 그리고 업무 책임 떠맡기에 참여하는 일들과 결합될 때 우리는 이 욕구(가르치고자 하는 타고난 욕구)를 인식하게 된다. [6] Erikson에 따르면, 부모가 됨으로써, 우리는 우리의 지식, 보호, 그리고 지도에 의존하는 다른 사람들에게 필요해지고 싶은 욕구가 있음을 알게 된다. [7] 우리는 문화적으로 적절한 행동, 가치, 태도, 기술, 그리고 세상에 대한 정보를 가르치는 것을 위임받게 된다. [8] 신체적, 사회적으로 성장하는 긴 세월 동안 아이들에게 일차적인 보호자가 되는 책임을 떠맡음으로써, 우리는 Erikson이 가르치고자 하는 타고난 욕구라고 믿는 것을 명확하게 표현한다.

1 ④

1 The true force behind life / lies in *tiny cellular factories of energy*, (called mitochondria), // which burn *almost all the oxygen* [(that) we breathe in].
생명의 이면에 있는 참된 원동력은 / 작은 에너지 세포 공장에 있다 (미토콘드리아라고 불리는) //
그런데 이것은 거의 모든 산소를 태운다 [우리가 들이마시는]

2 But / breathing has a price.
하지만 / 호흡에는 대가가 있다

3 (①) *The burning of oxygen* [that keeps us alive and active] / generates *by-products* (called oxygen free radicals).
산소의 연소는 [우리를 살아 활동력 있게 하는] / 부산물을 만들어 낸다 (활성 산소라는)

4 (②) They serve as / both guardians and destroyers / in our system.
그것들(활성 산소)은 ~의 역할을 한다 / 수호자와 파괴자 둘 다 / 우리의 몸에서

5 (③) On the one hand, / they help ensure our survival.
한편으로 / 그것들은 우리의 생존 보장을 돕는다

↓

6 ④ For example, / when the body gears up / to combat infectious agents, // it creates a burst of oxygen free radicals / to destroy the invaders very efficiently.
예를 들어 / 신체가 준비를 갖출 때 / 감염의 요인과 싸우기 위해 //
그것(신체)은 활성 산소를 폭발적으로 만들어 낸다 / 침입자를 아주 효율적으로 파괴하기 위해

↓

7 On the other hand, / oxygen free radicals bounce randomly through the body, /
다른 한편으로 / 활성 산소는 신체를 닥치는 대로 돌아다닌다 /

attacking cells, / turning their fats rancid, / rusting their proteins, / piercing their membranes / and corrupting their genetic code // until the cells become dysfunctional or just give up and die.
세포를 공격하면서 / 그것들(세포)의 지방을 산패시키면서 / 그것들의 단백질을 부식시키면서 /
그것들의 세포막을 뚫으면서 / 그리고 그것들의 유전 암호를 변질시키면서 //
그 세포가 제대로 기능을 하지 못하게 되거나 그저 포기하여 죽어버릴 때까지

8 (⑤) These fierce radicals are also the potent agents of aging.
이런 사나운 활성 산소는 또한 노화의 강력한 요인이다

해설

주어진 문장의 내용 파악하기 🅟

'예를 들어(For example)', 감염의 요인과 싸우기 위해 준비를 갖출 때 신체는 침입자를 효율적으로 파괴하기 위해 활성 산소를 폭발적으로 만들어 냄.(▶ **Point 2** 예시 연결어)

⌄

단서로 정답 찾기 ➕

1,2 생명의 원동력을 지닌 미토콘드리아는 우리가 들이마시는 거의 모든 산소를 태우는데, 호흡에는 대가가 있음.
3 (①) 산소의 연소가 활성 산소라는 부산물을 만들어 낸다고 앞 문장에서 말한 대가를 구체적으로 설명한다.
4 (②) They는 '활성 산소(oxygen free radicals)'를 받으며 이것이 수호자와 파괴자의 역할을 한다고 언급한다.
5 (③) 한편으로는 이 활성 산소가 우리의 생존 보장을 돕는다고 하며 그것의 긍정적 역할을 언급한다.

↓

6 ④ For example(예를 들어)로 감염의 요인과 싸우기 위해 신체가 활성 산소를 폭발적으로 만들어 낸다는 활성 산소의 긍정적 역할을 설명하는 예가 이어진다.

↓

7 On the other hand(다른 한편으로)로 앞 내용과 대조되는, 신체 내에서 활성 산소가 행하는 부정적 역할을 나열한다.
8 (⑤) 활성 산소를 These fierce radicals로 받아, 이것이 노화의 강력한 요인이라는 부정적 역할을 추가적으로 제시한다.

어휘

agent 요인, 동인; 대리인; 중개인   by-product 부산물; 부작용
combat ~와 싸우다; 전투, 싸움   corrupt 변질시키다; 부패하게 만들다; 부패한; 타락한   dysfunctional 제대로 기능을 하지 않는, 고장 난
fierce 사나운, 맹렬한; 극심한   gear up 준비를 갖추다
pierce 뚫다, 찌르다   potent 강력한; 효능 있는   rust 부식시키다; 부식하다; (금속 등의) 녹

구문 분석

7 ~ / **oxygen free radicals** bounce randomly through the body, / **attacking** cells, / **turning** their fats rancid, / **rusting** their proteins, / **piercing** their membranes / and **corrupting** their genetic code // ~.
다섯 개의 분사구문이 콤마(,)와 and로 병렬 연결되었으며, 이들의 의미상 주어는 oxygen free radicals임.

해석 **1**생명의 이면에 있는 참된 원동력은 미토콘드리아라고 불리는 작은 에너지 세포 공장에 있는데, 이것은 우리가 들이마시는 거의 모든 산소를 태운다. **2**하지만 호흡에는 대가가 있다. **3**우리를 살아 활동력 있게 하는 산소의 연소는 활성 산소라는 부산물을 만들어 낸다. **4**그것들(활성 산소)은 우리의 몸에서 수호자와 파괴자 둘 다의 역할을 한다. **5**한편으로, 그것들은 우리의 생존 보장을 돕는다. **6**예를 들어, 감염의 요인과 싸우기 위해 신체가 준비를 갖출 때, 신체는 침입자를 아주 효율적으로 파괴하기 위해 활성 산소를 폭발적으로 만들어 낸다. **7**다른 한편으로, 활성 산소는 신체를 닥치는 대로 돌아다니면서 세포가 제대로 기능을 하지 못하게 되거나 그저 포기하여 죽어버릴 때까지 세포를 공격하고, 세포의 지방을 산패시키고, 세포의 단백질을 부식시키고, 세포의 세포막을 뚫고 그것들의 유전 암호를 변질시킨다. **8**이런 사나운 활성 산소는 또한 노화의 강력한 요인이다.

2 ②

¹ By teaching people / to identify their negative thoughts / and (to) replace them with more positive ones, /
사람들에게 가르침으로써 / 자신의 부정적 사고를 찾도록 / 그리고 그것을 보다 긍정적인 것들(사고)로 대치하도록 /

cognitive therapists hope to help / patients overcome dysfunctional thinking / by becoming masters of their own emotions.
인지 치료사들은 돕기를 바란다 / 환자들이 역기능적인 사고를 극복할 수 있도록 / 자신의 감정의 주인이 됨으로써

² (①) By training ourselves / to eliminate *thoughts* [that provoke bad moods] / and to encourage *thoughts* [that foster pleasant emotions], /
우리 자신을 훈련시킴으로써 / 생각을 제거하도록 [나쁜 감정을 일으키는] / 그리고 생각을 북돋울 수 있도록 [유쾌한 감정을 불러 일으키는] /

we may be able to gain some measure of control (over our emotional state) / and (may be able to) lift ourselves out of the blues / by willpower alone.
우리는 어느 정도의 통제력을 얻을 수 있을지 모른다 (우리의 감정 상태에 대한) / 그리고 우울에서 우리 자신을 구해낼 수 있을지 모른다 / 오직 의지력 하나만으로

↓

> **³** ② But / this may not always be possible.
> 그러나 / 이것이 언제나 가능한 것은 아닐지도 모른다

↓

⁴ Sometimes, / the intensity of the emotion / may not permit alternative thoughts to be entertained, // which is why cognitive therapy does not always work.
때로 / 감정의 강도가 / 대안적 사고가 품어지도록 허용하지 않을 수 있다 // 그리고 이것이 인지 치료가 항상 효과가 있는 것은 아닌 이유이다

⁵ (③) For *someone* [who is slightly blue], / it may help / to suggest alternative ways (of looking at his situation).
누군가에게는 [조금 우울한] / (~이) 도움이 될 수 있다 / 대안적인 방식을 제안하는 것이 (자신의 상황을 바라보는)

⁶ (④) But / for someone (in the grip of a severe depression), / such suggestions may appear rather insensitive.
그러나 / 누군가에게는 (심각한 우울증에 시달리는) / 그러한 제안이 다소 무신경하게 느껴질 수 있다

⁷ (⑤) Telling a severely discouraged person to think positively / is not *a very effective way* (to cheer him up).
심하게 낙담한 사람에게 긍정적으로 사고하라고 말하는 것은 / 그다지 효과적인 방법이 아니다 (그에게 힘을 불어넣어 주는)

해설

주어진 문장의 내용 파악하기 

'그러나(But)', '이것(this)'이 언제나 가능한 것은 아닐지도 모름.
(▶ **Point 2** 역접 연결어, **Point 1** 지시사/대명사)
(앞부분에는 this가 무엇인지 언급될 것이고, 뒤에는 왜 가능하지 않은지에 대한 이유가 나올 것을 예상할 수 있음.)

단서로 정답 찾기

1 인지 치료사들은 환자들이 부정적 사고를 찾고 그것을 긍정적으로 바꿈으로써 감정의 주인이 되어 역기능적 사고를 극복하도록 도우려 함.
2 (①) 유쾌한 감정을 불러일으키는 생각을 하도록 훈련함으로써 감정 상태에 대한 통제력을 얻어, 의지력으로 우울에서 벗어날 수 있을지 모른다고 앞 내용을 부연 설명한다.

↓

3 ② 앞 문장의 내용을 this로 받아, 이것이 언제나 가능한 것은 아닐 수 있다는 내용이 But(그러나)으로 이어진다.

↓

4 주어진 문장의 내용에 대한 이유로 감정의 강도가 대안적 사고를 못하게 할 수 있음을 든다.
5 (③) 조금 우울한 사람에게는 상황을 보는 대안적 방식을 제안하는 것이 도움이 될 수 있다고 한다.
6 (④) 심각한 우울증이 있는 사람에게는 그것이 무신경하게 느껴질 수 있다는 반대의 예가 But(그러나)으로 이어진다.
7 (⑤) 심하게 낙담한 사람에게는 긍정적으로 사고하라는 말이 힘을 주는 데 효과적이지 않다는 내용으로 글을 맺는다.

어휘

alternative 대안(적인)　cognitive 인지의, 인식의
discouraged 낙담한; 의욕을 잃어버린　insensitive 무신경한, 냉담한; 무감각한　intensity 강도; 강렬함　in the grip of ~에 시달리는
permit 허용[허락]하다; 가능하게 하다　provoke 일으키다, 생기게 하다

구문 분석

⁵ For *someone* [who is slightly blue], / **it** may help / **to suggest** alternative ways (of looking at her situation).
to suggest ~ her situation이 진주어, it은 가주어임.

해석 **¹** 사람들에게 자신의 부정적 사고를 찾고 그것을 보다 긍정적인 사고로 대치하도록 가르침으로써, 인지 치료사들은 환자들이 자신의 감정의 주인이 됨으로써 역기능적인 사고를 극복할 수 있도록 돕기를 바란다. **²** 나쁜 감정을 일으키는 생각을 제거하도록, 그리고 유쾌한 감정을 불러일으키는 생각을 북돋울 수 있도록 우리 자신을 훈련시킴으로써, 우리는 우리의 감정 상태에 대한 어느 정도의 통제력을 얻고 오직 의지력 하나만으로 우울에서 우리 자신을 구해낼 수 있을지 모른다. **³** 그러나 이것이 언제나 가능한 것은 아닐지도 모른다. **⁴** 때로 감정의 강도가 대안적 사고가 품어지도록 허용하지 않을 수 있는데, 이것이 인지 치료가 항상 효과가 있는 것은 아닌 이유이다. **⁵** 조금 우울한 누군가에게는 자신의 상황을 바라보는 대안적인 방식을 제안하는 것이 도움이 될 수 있다. **⁶** 그러나 심각한 우울증에 시달리는 누군가에게는 그러한 제안이 다소 무신경하게 느껴질 수 있다. **⁷** 심하게 낙담한 사람에게 긍정적으로 사고하라고 말하는 것은 그에게 힘을 불어넣어 주는 그다지 효과적인 방법이 아니다.

3 ⑤

[1]Consider // how a four-year-old boy takes justice into his own hands.
생각해 보라 // 네 살짜리 소년이 어떻게 정의를 직접 처리하는지

[2]The boy has just seen / *a puppet show* [in which one puppet played with a ball / while interacting with two other puppets].
그 소년은 방금 막 보았다 / 인형극을 [한 인형이 공을 가지고 논 / 다른 두 인형과 상호 작용을 하면서]

[3](①) The center puppet would slide the ball / to *the puppet on the right*, // who would always pass it back.
중앙에 있는 인형은 공을 미끄러뜨려 보내곤 했다 / 오른쪽에 있는 인형에게 // 그리고 그것(오른쪽에 있는 인형)은 항상 그것(공)을 다시 건네주곤 했다

[4](②) And the center puppet would slide the ball / to *the puppet on the left*, // who would always run away with it.
그리고 중앙에 있는 인형이 공을 미끄러뜨려 보내곤 했다 / 왼쪽에 있는 인형에게 // 그리고 그것(왼쪽에 있는 인형)은 항상 그것(공)을 가지고 달아나곤 했다

[5](③) After the play / the two puppets on the ends were brought down from the stage / and set before the boy.
인형극이 끝난 후 / 양쪽 끝에 있던 두 인형이 무대에서 내려졌다 / 그리고 소년 앞에 놓였다

[6](④) Each was placed next to a pile of treats // and the boy was asked / to take one away from one puppet.
각각은 선물 더미 옆에 놓였다 // 그리고 소년은 요청받았다 / 한 인형에게서 그것(선물 더미)을 빼앗으라고

↓

> [7]⑤ Of course, / the "naughty" puppet, // who had been on the left, / had it taken away.
> 당연히 / '못된' 인형이 // 왼쪽에 있던 / 그것(선물 더미)을 빼앗겼다

↓

[8]But / this wasn't enough — // he then leaned over / and hit the puppet!
그러나 / 이것은 충분하지 않았다 // 그는 몸을 기울였다 / 그리고 그 인형을 때렸다

해설

주어진 문장의 내용 파악하기 ⊙

> 당연히 왼쪽에 있던 '못된' 인형이 '그것(it)'을 빼앗김.(▶ Point 1 지시사/대명사)
> (앞에는 it이 가리키는 대상, 빼앗긴 원인 등이 나올 것을 예상할 수 있음.)

⌄

단서로 정답 찾기 ➕

1, 2 세 인형이 공을 가지고 노는 인형극을 본 소년이 정의를 처리하는 방식에 대해 생각해 보도록 함.

3 (①) 오른쪽에 있는 인형은 중앙에 있는 인형과 서로 공을 주고받았다고 설명한다.

4 (②) 그리고 왼쪽에 있는 인형은 중앙에 있는 인형에게 공을 받으면 가지고 달아났다는 내용을 덧붙인다.

5 (③) 왼쪽에 있는 인형과 오른쪽에 있는 인형을 the two puppets on the ends로 받아, 인형극이 끝난 후 소년 앞에 그 두 인형이 놓였다고 한다.

6 (④) 소년 앞에 놓인 각 인형을 each로 받으며, 소년이 둘 중 한 인형에게서 선물 더미를 빼앗으라고 요청받는 상황이 주어진다.

↓

7 ⑤ 주어진 문장의 it은 앞 문장의 '그것[선물 더미(one[a pile of treats])]'을 지칭하고, 소년이 (항상 공을 가지고 달아난) 왼쪽에 있던 '못된' 인형에게서 선물 더미를 빼앗았다는 내용이 이어진다.

↓

8 소년이 '못된' 인형에게서 선물 더미를 빼앗았다는 주어진 문장의 내용을 this로 받아 이것이 충분하지 않았다고 하고, 소년이 그 인형을 때렸다는 사실을 덧붙인다.

어휘

a pile of ~ 더미, ~한 무더기 interact 상호 작용을 하다; 소통하다
lean over 몸을 기울이다 naughty 못된, 버릇없는
puppet 인형, 꼭두각시 slide 미끄러지게 하다; 미끄러지다
take A into one's own hands A를 직접 처리하다
treat (대접하여 주는) 선물, 특별한 것; 대접

구문 분석

[3]The center puppet **would slide** the ball / to *the puppet on the right*, // who **would** always **pass** it back.
<would+동사원형>: ~하곤 했다 ((과거의 습관))

해석 [1]네 살짜리 소년이 어떻게 정의를 직접 처리하는지 생각해 보라. [2]그 소년은 한 인형이 다른 두 인형과 상호 작용을 하면서 공을 가지고 논 인형극을 방금 막 보았다. [3]중앙에 있는 인형이 오른쪽에 있는 인형에게 공을 미끄러뜨려 보내면, 오른쪽에 있는 인형은 항상 공을 다시 건네주곤 했다. [4]그리고 중앙에 있는 인형이 왼쪽에 있는 인형에게 공을 미끄러뜨려 보내면, 왼쪽에 있는 인형은 항상 공을 가지고 달아나곤 했다. [5]인형극이 끝난 후, 양쪽 끝에 있던 두 인형이 무대에서 내려졌고 소년 앞에 놓였다. [6]각각은 선물 더미 옆에 놓였고 소년은 한 인형에게서 선물 더미를 빼앗으라고 요청받았다. [7]당연히 왼쪽에 있던 '못된' 인형이 선물 더미를 빼앗겼다. [8]그러나 이것은 충분하지 않았는데, 그는 몸을 기울였고 그 인형을 때렸다!

4 ④

1 Deontologists are often criticized / for arguing // that moral rules are absolute and cannot conflict.
의무론자들은 종종 비판받는다 / 주장하는 것에 대해 // 도덕적 원칙은 절대적이고 상충할 수 없다고

2 Consider / the case of *Dutch fishermen* (smuggling Jewish refugees to England / during World War Ⅱ).
생각해 보라 / 네덜란드 어부들의 경우를 (유대인 난민들을 영국으로 밀입국시키는 /
제2차 세계 대전 동안)

3 (①) They were sometimes stopped by *Nazis*, // who inquired / as to who was on board / and where the boat was headed.
때때로 그들(네덜란드 어부들)은 나치에 의해 멈춰 세워졌다 // 그리고 그들(나치)은 물었다 /
누가 배에 타고 있는지에 관해 / 그리고 배가 어디로 향하는지(에 관해)

4 (②) The fishermen had a choice: / lie or allow the passengers (and themselves) to be captured.
어부들은 선택권이 있었다 / 거짓말하기 또는 승객들(그리고 자신들)이 포로로 붙잡히게 하기

5 (③) Here / two absolute rules / ("it is wrong to lie" / and "it is wrong to let innocent people be captured") / conflict.
여기에서 / 두 가지 절대적 원칙이 / ('거짓말하는 것은 나쁘다' / 그리고 '무고한 사람들이 포로로 잡히게 하는 것은 나쁘다') / 충돌한다

↓

> **6** ④ To account for situations like these, / W. D. Ross argued // that moral duties are not universal constraints.
> 이와 같은 상황을 설명하기 위해 / W. D. Ross는 주장했다 //
> 도덕적 의무는 보편적 제약이 아니라고

↓

7 Rather, / they are *conditional obligations* (to act) [that result from the specifics of a situation].
오히려 / 그것들(도덕적 의무)은 조건적 의무이다 (행해야 할) [상황의 세부 사항에서 기인하는]

8 (⑤) One must judge / in a given case // which duties apply / and which duties are of more importance.
사람은 판단해야 한다 / 주어진 상황에서 // 어느 의무가 적용되는지를 /
그리고 어느 의무가 더욱 중요한지를

해설

주어진 문장의 내용 파악하기 ✐

'이와 같은 상황(situations like these)'을 설명하기 위해 W. D. Ross는 도덕적 의무는 보편적 제약이 아니라고 주장함.(▶ **Point 1** 지시사/대명사)
(앞부분에는 특정한 상황이 언급될 것을 예상할 수 있음.)

☰

단서로 정답 찾기 ✚

1, 2 도덕적 원칙이 절대적이고 상충할 수 없다는 주장을 비판하는 예로 유대인 난민의 밀입국을 돕는 네덜란드 어부들의 경우를 제시함.

3 (①) 네덜란드 어부들을 They로 받아, 나치가 그들을 때때로 멈춰 세우고 배의 탑승자와 도착지를 질문했다고 한다.

4 (②) 어부들은 거짓말하거나 승객과 함께 포로로 붙잡히는 선택권을 가졌다고 이어서 설명한다.

5 (③) 앞의 예에서 두 가지 절대적 원칙이 충돌한다는 사실을 지적한다.

↓

6 ④ 절대적 원칙이 충돌하는 상황을 situations like these로 받아, 이런 상황에 대한 설명으로 도덕적 의무는 보편적 제약이 아니라는 주장을 제시한다.

↓

7 도덕적 의무를 they로 받아, 이것들은 상황의 세부 사항에서 기인하는 조건적인 의무라는 내용이 Rather(오히려)로 이어진다.

8 (⑤) 주어진 상황에서 어느 의무가 적용되고 더 중요한지 판단해야 한다는 결론으로 글을 맺는다.

어휘

absolute 절대적인; 완전한, 철저한   **capture** 포로로 잡다; (마음·관심을) 사로잡다   **conflict** 상충하다, 충돌하다; 갈등   **constraint** 제약; 제한, 통제   **innocent** 무고한, 무죄인; 순수한   **inquire** 묻다, 질문을 하다   **obligation** (법적·도의적) 의무, 책무   **refugee** 난민, 망명자

구문 분석

8 One must judge / in a given case // **which duties apply** / [and] **which duties are of more importance**.

- must judge의 목적어인 which duties ~ apply와 which duties ~ importance가 and로 병렬 연결됨.
- 목적어가 길고 부사구가 상대적으로 짧을 때는 <S+V+O+부사구> 형태의 문장이 <S+V+부사구+O>의 어순으로 쓰일 수 있음.

해석 **1** 의무론자들은 도덕적 원칙은 절대적이고 상충할 수 없다고 주장하는 것에 대해 종종 비판받는다. **2** 제2차 세계 대전 동안 유대인 난민들을 영국으로 밀입국시키는 네덜란드 어부들의 경우를 생각해 보라. **3** 때때로 그들은 나치에 의해 멈춰 세워졌는데, 그들(나치)은 누가 배에 타고 있는지, 그리고 배가 어디로 향하는지에 관해 물었다. **4** 어부들은 거짓말하거나 승객들(그리고 자신들)이 포로로 붙잡히게 하는 선택권이 있었다. **5** 여기에서 두 가지 절대적 원칙('거짓말을 하는 것은 나쁘다', 그리고 '무고한 사람들이 포로로 잡히게 하는 것은 나쁘다')이 충돌한다. **6** 이와 같은 상황을 설명하기 위해, W. D. Ross는 도덕적 의무는 보편적 제약이 아니라고 주장했다. **7** 오히려, 그것들(도덕적 의무)은 상황의 세부 사항에서 기인하는, 행해야 할 조건적 의무이다. **8** 사람은 주어진 상황에서 어느 의무가 적용되는지, 그리고 어느 의무가 더욱 중요한지를 판단해야 한다.

5 ⑤

[1] Instead of metal coinage or paper money, / the natives of the Pacific island of Yap traditionally traded / huge, doughnut-shaped, limestone discs.
금속 주화나 지폐 대신 / 태평양의 야프섬의 원주민들은 전통적으로 교환했다 / 커다란 도넛 모양의 석회암 원반을

[2] (①) These are called *rai*, // and their value is based on size and weight.
그것들은 '라이'라고 불린다 // 그리고 그것들의 가치는 크기와 무게에 기반을 둔다

[3] (②) *Rai* stones may be used / for social transactions (such as marriages, inheritances, and political deals), / or just in exchange for food.
'라이' 돌은 쓰일 수 있다 / 사회적 거래에 (결혼, 상속, 정치적 거래 같은) / 또는 단순히 음식과의 교환에

[4] (③) Of course, / carrying a large stone around instead of money / is not always possible.
물론 / 화폐 대신 커다란 돌을 가지고 다니는 것은 / 항상 가능한 일은 아니다

[5] (④) Instead, / many of them are placed / in front of meeting houses or specific pathways, // so / though the ownership of a particular stone changes, // the stone itself is rarely moved.
대신 / 그것(라이)들 중 다수는 놓여 있다 / 예배당이나 특정한 길 앞에 // 그래서 / 특정한 돌의 소유권이 바뀌더라도 // 그 돌 자체는 거의 옮겨지지 않는다

↓

---

[6] ⑤ As it is far more convenient to carry and to use, // modern money has largely replaced the *rai* / as everyday currency.
그것(현대의 돈)이 소지하고 이용하기 훨씬 더 편리하기 때문에 // 현대의 돈은 '라이'를 대부분 대체했다 / 일상적인 통화로서

↓

[7] It is true, / though, // that it is still a unit of exchange / for the islanders, / according to their tradition.
(~이) 사실이다 / 그렇지만 // 그것(라이)이 여전히 교환 단위인 것이 / 섬사람들 사이에서는 / 그들의 전통에 따라

주어진 문장의 내용 파악하기 🔎

현대의 돈이 소지하고 이용하기 훨씬 더 편리하기 때문에, 일상적인 통화로서 '라이'를 대부분 대체함.
(앞에는 '라이'가 무엇인지 설명되었을 것이고, 이것이 화폐 역할을 했지만 소지나 이용이 불편했을 것을 예상할 수 있음.)

⟱

단서로 정답 찾기 ➕

[1] 야프섬의 원주민들은 전통적으로 동전이나 지폐 대신 커다란 도넛 모양의 석회암 원반을 교환함.

[2] (①) These는 앞에 언급된 '커다란 도넛 모양의 석회암 원반 (huge ~ discs)'을 받아 이것이 라이이며, 가치는 크기와 무게에 기반을 둔다고 설명한다.

[3] (②) 라이는 사회적 거래나 단순히 음식과의 교환에 쓰일 수 있다고 하며, 라이의 역할을 부연 설명한다.

[4] (③) 항상 큰 돌을 가지고 다니는 것이 가능하지는 않다는 문제를 제시한다.

[5] (④) Instead(대신)로 이어져, 라이는 소유권이 바뀌더라도 거의 옮겨지지 않는다고 설명한다.

↓

[6] ⑤ 소지와 이용이 더 편리한 현대의 돈이 일상적 통화로서 라이를 대부분 대체했다고 설명한다.(▶ **Point 3** 원인 → 결과)

↓

[7] though(그렇지만)로 내용이 전환되고 '라이(the *rai*)'를 it으로 받아, 그것이 섬사람들 사이에서는 여전히 교환 단위라고 언급하며 글을 끝맺는다.

어휘

coinage 주화   currency 통화; 통용, 유통   disc 원반 (모양의 물건); 음반
inheritance 상속, 유산   islander 섬사람   limestone 석회암
meeting house 예배당   ownership 소유권   transaction 거래, 매매

구문 분석

[4] Of course, / carrying a large stone around instead of money / is **not always** possible.
부정어와 always가 함께 쓰이면 부분 부정을 나타내며 '항상[언제나] ~인[하는] 것은 아니다'라는 뜻임.

해석 [1] 금속 주화나 지폐 대신, 태평양의 야프섬의 원주민들은 전통적으로 커다란 도넛 모양의 석회암 원반을 교환했다. [2] 그것들은 '라이'라고 불리고, 그것들의 가치는 크기와 무게에 기반을 둔다. [3] '라이' 돌은 결혼, 상속, 정치적 거래 같은 사회적 거래 또는 단순히 음식과의 교환에 쓰일 수 있다. [4] 물론, 화폐 대신 커다란 돌을 가지고 다니는 것은 항상 가능한 일은 아니다. [5] 대신, 그것들 중 다수는 예배당이나 특정한 길 앞에 놓여 있고, 그래서 특정한 돌의 소유권이 바뀌더라도 그 돌 자체는 거의 옮겨지지 않는다. [6] 현대의 돈이 소지하고 이용하기 훨씬 더 편리하기 때문에, 그것은 일상적인 통화로서 '라이'를 대부분 대체했다. [7] 그렇지만 전통에 따라 섬사람들 사이에서는 '라이'가 여전히 교환 단위인 것이 사실이다.

1 ④

[1] Studies demonstrate // that motorists are more likely to yield / to pedestrians / in marked crosswalks.
연구들은 입증한다 // 운전자들이 양보할 가능성이 더 높다는 것을 / 보행자들에게 / 표시가 있는 건널목에서

[2] But / as researchers have discovered, // that does not necessarily make things safer.
그러나 / 연구자들이 발견했듯이 // 그것이 반드시 상황을 더 안전하게 해주지는 않는다

[3] (①) When they compared *the way* [(that) pedestrians crossed streets], //
그들이 방식을 비교했을 때 [보행자들이 길을 건너는] //
they found // that / people (at unmarked crosswalks) tended / to look both ways more often / and (to) cross the road more quickly.
그들은 알아냈다 // (~라는) 것을 / 사람들이 (표시가 없는 건널목에 있는) / 경향이 있다는 / 양쪽을 더 자주 쳐다보는 / 그리고 길을 더 빨리 건너는

[4] (②) Researchers suspect // that both drivers and pedestrians are more aware // that drivers are supposed to yield / in marked crosswalks.
연구자들은 추측한다 // 운전자와 보행자 모두 더 잘 인지하고 있다고 // 운전자가 양보해야 한다는 것을 / 표시가 있는 건널목에서는

[5] (③) But / neither are aware of this fact / when it comes to unmarked crosswalks.
하지만 / 둘 중 어느 쪽도 이 사실을 알지 못한다 / 표시가 없는 건널목에서라면

↓

[6] ④ Due to the uncertainty // whether cars are supposed to stop — // or if they will (stop) — // pedestrians act more cautiously.
그 불확실성 때문에 // 자동차가 멈춰야 하는지 // 또는 그것들이 멈출 것인지(에 대한) // 보행자들은 더 조심스럽게 행동한다

↓

[7] Marked crosswalks, / by contrast, / may give pedestrians / a false sense of security.
표시가 있는 건널목은 / 대조적으로 / 보행자들에게 줄 수도 있다 / 거짓된 안전감을

[8] (⑤) It turns out // (that) the lack of clear traffic expectations is / actually a good thing for pedestrians.
(~인 것으로) 드러난다 // 교통에 대한 명확한 예상이 없는 것이 ~인 / 실제로는 보행자에게 좋은 것

해설

주어진 문장의 내용 파악하기 

'자동차가 멈춰야 하는지 또는 멈출 것인지에 대한 그 불확실성 (the uncertainty ~ will (stop))' 때문에 보행자들은 더 조심스럽게 행동함. (▶ **Point 1** 정관사 the)

≫

단서로 정답 찾기 ➕

1, 2 표시가 있는 건널목에서 운전자들이 보행자들에게 양보할 가능성이 더 높다는 것이 입증됐지만, 연구자들이 발견했듯이, 표시가 있는 건널목이 반드시 더 안전한 것은 아님.
3 (①) they는 앞 문장의 '연구자들(researchers)'을 받으며, 보행자들이 표시가 없는 건널목에서 양쪽을 더 자주 쳐다보고 더 빨리 건넌다는 구체적인 연구 내용이 이어진다.
4 (②) 표시가 있는 건널목에서는 운전자가 양보해야 한다는 것을 운전자와 보행자 모두 더 잘 인지하고 있다고 설명한다.
5 (③) But(하지만)으로 표시가 있는 건널목과는 달리, 표시가 없는 건널목에서는 운전자도 보행자도 어느 쪽이 양보해야 하는지 알 수 없다는 내용이 이어진다.

↓

6 ④ the uncertainty ~ will (stop)은 운전자와 보행자 둘 다 앞에서 언급된 사실을 알지 못하는 것을 받으며, 이로 인해 보행자은 더 조심스럽게 행동한다고 설명한다.

↓

7 by contrast(대조적으로)로, 표시가 있는 건널목은 보행자들에게 거짓된 안전감을 줄 수도 있다고 표시가 없는 건널목과 대조한다.
8 (⑤) 교통에 대한 명확한 예상이 없는 것이 보행자들에게 좋은 것이라는 결론으로 글을 끝맺는다.

어휘

be supposed to-v v해야 한다, 하기로 되어 있다
cautiously 조심스럽게   crosswalk 건널목, 횡단보도
demonstrate 입증하다; 보여주다   motorist (승용차) 운전자
pedestrian 보행자   suspect 추측하다; 용의자; 의심하다
yield (길을) 양보하다; 생산하다; 항복하다

구문 분석

[3] ~ people (at unmarked crosswalks) / tended / **to look** both ways more often / and (to) **cross** the road more quickly.
tended 뒤에 나오는 to look과 (to) cross가 and로 병렬 연결된 구조임.

해석 [1]연구들은 운전자들이 표시가 있는 건널목에서 보행자들에게 양보할 가능성이 더 높다는 것을 입증한다. [2]그러나 연구자들이 발견했듯이, 그것이 반드시 상황을 더 안전하게 해주지는 않는다. [3]그들이 보행자들이 길을 건너는 방식을 비교했을 때, 표시가 없는 건널목에 있는 사람들이 양쪽을 더 자주 쳐다보고, 길을 더 빨리 건너는 경향이 있다는 것을 알아냈다. [4]연구자들은 표시가 있는 건널목에서는 운전자가 양보해야 한다는 것을 운전자와 보행자 모두 더 잘 인지하고 있다고 추측한다. [5]하지만 표시가 없는 건널목에서라면 둘 중 어느 쪽도 이 사실을 알지 못한다. [6]자동차가 멈춰야 하는지 또는 멈출 것인지에 대한 그 불확실성 때문에 보행자들은 더 조심스럽게 행동한다. [7]대조적으로, 표시가 있는 건널목은 보행자들에게 거짓된 안전감을 줄 수도 있다. [8]교통에 대한 명확한 예상이 없는 것이 실제로는 보행자에게 좋은 것으로 드러난다.

2 ④

¹Fishing vessels are trawling / thousands of feet below the ocean surface.
어선들이 저인망 어업을 하고 있다 / 수천 피트 해수면 아래에서

²(①) They may be wiping out life (at the ocean depths) / even faster // than scientists can discover it.
그것들은 생물들을 완전히 없애고 있는지도 모른다 (바다 깊은 곳의) / 더 빠르게 // 과학자들이 그것들을 발견할 수 있는 것보다

³(②) Recently, / stronger nets, cable, and engines have allowed / fishing companies to extend their reach / to depths of 3,000 feet and beyond.
최근에는 / 더 강력한 그물, 케이블, 그리고 엔진이 (~할 수 있도록) 했다 / 어업 회사들이 그들의 구역을 확장할 수 있도록 / 수심 3,000피트 이상의 깊이까지

⁴(③) At those depths, / growth is so slow // that harvested fish can take decades / to be replaced.
그렇게 깊은 곳에서는 / 성장이 너무 느리다 // 그래서 포획된 물고기가 수십 년이 걸릴 수도 있다 / 대체되는 데

↓

> ⁵④ Also, / like the fish, / coral at those depths grows extremely slowly, / and may never recover from damage from trawling.
> 또한 / 물고기처럼 / 그렇게 깊은 곳에 있는 산호도 매우 천천히 자란다 / 그리고 저인망 어업에 의해 입은 피해로부터 결코 회복하지 못할 수도 있다

↓

⁶A recent study found // that 95 percent (of the trawled ocean bottom) (in deep water) (off Tasmania) / is bare rock.
최근 한 연구는 발견했다 // 95퍼센트가 (저인망 어업을 하는 바다 밑바닥의) ((수심이) 깊은) (태즈메이니아섬에서 떨어진) / 아무것도 안 덮인 바위라는 것을

⁷(⑤) In contrast, / coral covers almost 100 percent of *untrawled areas*, // which also contain many sponges and sea fans.
대조적으로 / 산호가 저인망 어업을 하지 않은 지역의 거의 100퍼센트를 덮고 있다 // 그리고 그것(저인망 어업을 하지 않은 지역)은 또한 많은 해면동물과 산호충을 포함한다

해설

주어진 문장의 내용 파악하기 

'또한(Also)', '물고기(the fish)'처럼, 그렇게 깊은 곳에 있는 산호도 매우 천천히 자라고, 저인망 어업에 의한 산호의 피해는 결코 회복하지 못할 수도 있음.(▶ **Point 2** 첨가 연결어, **Point 1** 정관사 the)
(앞부분에서 깊은 곳에서는 물고기가 천천히 자란다는 내용이 나올 것을 예상할 수 있음.)

⌄⌄

단서로 정답 찾기 

1 어선들이 수천 피트 해수면 아래에서 저인망 어업을 함.
2 (①) They는 앞 문장의 '어선들(Fishing vessels)'을 받으며, 그것들이 바닷속 생물들을 빠르게 없애고 있을지 모른다고 한다.
3 (②) 최근에는 더 강력한 장비들로 어업 회사들이 수심 3,000피트 이상의 깊이까지 어업 구역을 확장하고 있다고 설명한다.
4 (③) 앞 문장의 '수심 3,000피트 이상의 깊이(depths of ~ beyond)'를 those depths로 받으며, 그곳에서는 물고기의 성장이 느려서 포획된 물고기의 수가 대체되는 데 시간이 많이 걸린다고 언급한다.

↓

5 ④ Also(또한)로 앞에서 언급한 물고기의 경우와 같이 그렇게 깊은 곳에 있는 산호도 너무 천천히 자라서 저인망 어업에 의한 피해를 회복하지 못할 수도 있다고 덧붙인다.

↓

6 저인망 어업을 하는 바다 밑바닥의 95퍼센트가 아무것도 안 덮인 바위라는 한 예시로 피해 회복이 어렵다는 것을 부연 설명한다.
7 (⑤) In contrast(대조적으로)로 저인망 어업을 하지 않은 지역은 산호가 거의 100퍼센트를 덮고 있으며, 많은 해면동물과 산호충도 있다는 반대의 경우가 이어진다.

어휘

bare 아무것도 안 덮인; 벌거벗은   **coral** 산호   **harvest** 포획하다, 사냥하다; 수확하다   **life** 생물(체); 삶, 생명   **reach** 구역; 미치는 범위; ~에 닿다   **vessel** (대형) 배, 선박   **wipe out** ~을 완전히 없애다[파괴하다]

구문 분석

⁴At those depths, / growth is so slow // that harvested fish can take decades / **to be replaced**.
의미상 주어인 harvested fish가 '대체되는' 수동의 의미이므로, to-v의 수동태가 사용됨.

해석 ¹어선들이 수천 피트 해수면 아래에서 저인망 어업(그물을 배 뒤로 늘어뜨려 밑바닥까지 끌고 다니면서 깊은 바닷속의 물고기를 잡는 것)을 하고 있다. ²그것들은 과학자들이 발견할 수 있는 것보다 더 빠르게 바다 깊은 곳의 생물들을 완전히 없애고 있는지도 모른다. ³최근에는 더 강력한 그물, 케이블, 그리고 엔진이 어업 회사들이 그들의 구역을 수심 3,000피트 이상의 깊이까지 확장할 수 있도록 했다. ⁴그렇게 깊은 곳에서는 성장이 매우 느려서 포획된 물고기가 대체되는 데 수십 년이 걸릴 수도 있다. ⁵또한 물고기처럼, 그렇게 깊은 곳에 있는 산호도 매우 천천히 자라고, 저인망 어업에 의해 입은 피해로부터 결코 회복하지 못할 수도 있다. ⁶최근 한 연구는 태즈메이니아섬에서 떨어진 저인망 어업을 하는 수심이 깊은 바다 밑바닥의 95퍼센트가 아무것도 안 덮인 바위라는 것을 발견했다. ⁷대조적으로, 산호가 저인망 어업을 하지 않은 지역의 거의 100퍼센트를 덮고 있고, 그것은 또한 많은 해면동물과 산호충을 포함한다.

3 ③

1 Most liquids, / (when chilled), / contract by about 10 percent, // and water does too, / but only down to a point.
대부분 액체는 / (차가워지면) / 10퍼센트 정도 수축한다 //
그리고 물도 마찬가지이다 / 그러나 어느 정도까지만 (그렇다)

2 Once it nears its freezing point, // it begins to expand / in an unexpected manner.
일단 그것(물)이 어느점에 아주 가까워지면 // 그것은 팽창하기 시작한다 / 예기치 않은 방식으로

3 (①) By the time it is solid, // it is almost a tenth more voluminous // than it was before.
그것이 고체가 될 때쯤에는 // 그것은 부피가 거의 10분의 1이 더 크다 // 그것이 전에 그랬던 것보다

4 (②) Because it expands, // ice floats on water — / "an utterly bizarre property," / according to John Gribbin.
그것(얼음)은 팽창하기 때문에 // 얼음은 물에 뜬다 / 이는 '완전히 기묘한 성질'이다 / John Gribbin에 따르면

↓

5 ③ If water lacked its extraordinary qualities, // ice would sink, // and lakes and oceans would freeze / from the bottom up.
만약 물이 기이한 성질을 가지고 있지 않다면 // 얼음은 가라앉을 것이다 //
그리고 호수와 바다는 얼어붙을 것이다 / 바닥부터

↓

6 Without *surface ice* (to hold heat in), / the water's warmth would radiate away, // which would leave it even chillier / and create yet more ice.
수면 위의 얼음이 없다면 (안에 열을 유지할) / 물의 온기는 방출될 것이다 //
그리고 이는 그것(물)을 훨씬 더 차가워지게 할 것이다 / 그리고 더 많은 얼음을 만들어 낼 것이다

7 (④) Soon even the oceans would freeze / and almost certainly stay that way / for a very long time, probably forever — / hardly *the conditions* (to nurture life).
심지어 바다도 곧 얼어버릴 것이다 / 그리고 거의 확실히 그 상태로 지속될 것이다 /
아주 오랫동안, 어쩌면 영원히 / 조건이 결코 아닐 (생명체를 육성할)

8 (⑤) Thankfully for us, / water seems unaware / of the rules of chemistry or laws of physics.
우리에게는 다행스럽게도 / 물은 (~을) 모르는 것 같다 / 화학 규칙이나 물리 법칙을

해설

주어진 문장의 내용 파악하기 ✎

물의 '기이한 성질(extraordinary qualities)'이 없다면 얼음이 가라앉고 호수와 바다가 바닥부터 얼어붙을 것임.
(앞이나 뒤에 물의 기이한 성질에 대한 설명이 제시될 것을 예상할 수 있음.)

⌄⌄

단서로 정답 찾기 ✚

1, 2 대부분 액체는 차가우면 수축하지만, 물은 어느 정도까지만 수축하고 어는점에 가까워지면 팽창함.
3 (①) 물을 it으로 받아, 그것이 얼음이 될 때쯤에는 전보다 부피가 더 크다는 사실을 부연 설명한다.
4 (②) 얼음은 팽창하므로 물에 뜨는데, 이를 기묘한 성질이라고 언급한다.

↓

5 ③ extraordinary qualities는 어는점에 가까워지면 팽창하여 물에 뜨는 기묘한 성질을 받는다. 이러한 성질이 없으면 얼음은 가라앉고 호수와 바다는 바닥부터 얼어붙을 것이라고 얼음이 물에 뜨는 기묘한 성질에 대해 덧붙여 설명한다. (▶ **Point 3** 구체적/세부적 진술)

↓

6 얼음이 가라앉고 호수와 바다가 바닥부터 얼 것이라는 가정에 대해 수면 위의 얼음이 없다면 물이 더 차가워져 얼음이 더 많아질 것이라고 부연 설명한다.
7 (④) 바다도 곧 얼어버릴 것이고 그 상태가 오래 지속되어 생명체가 살아갈 조건이 결코 아닐 것이라고 이어서 설명한다.
8 (⑤) 물이 과학 법칙을 따르지 않음이 우리에게는 좋은 일이라는 내용으로 글을 마무리한다.

어휘

bizarre 기묘한, 특이한   contract 수축하다; 계약(서)
extraordinary 기이한; 비범한   freezing point 어는점, 빙점
manner 방식; 태도   nurture 육성[양성]하다; 영양물을 공급하다
radiate (열·빛 등이)방출되다; 퍼지다; 방출하다   utterly 완전히, 순전히
voluminous (부피가) 큰, (양이) 방대한

구문 분석

1 Most liquids, / (**when chilled**), / contract by about 10 percent, // and water does too, / but only down to a point.
주어와 동사 사이에 when chilled가 삽입된 구조임.

해석 **1** 대부분 액체는 차가워지면 10퍼센트 정도 수축하고, 물도 마찬가지이지만 어느 정도까지만 그렇다. **2** 일단 물이 어느점에 아주 가까워지면, 그것은 예기치 않은 방식으로 (부피가) 팽창하기 시작한다. **3** 그것(물)이 고체(얼음)가 될 때쯤에는, (얼음이 되기) 전보다 부피가 거의 10분의 1이 더 크다. **4** 얼음은 팽창하기 때문에 물에 뜨는데, John Gribbin에 따르면 이는 '완전히 기묘한 성질'이다. **5** 만약 물이 기이한 성질을 가지고 있지 않다면 얼음은 가라앉고 호수와 바다는 바닥부터 얼어붙을 것이다. **6** (물) 안에 열을 유지할 수면 위의 얼음이 없다면, 물의 온기는 방출될 것이고, 이는 그것(물)을 훨씬 더 차가워지게 하여 더 많은 얼음을 만들어 낼 것이다. **7** 심지어 바다도 곧 얼어버릴 것이고 거의 확실히 아주 오랫동안, 어쩌면 영원히 그 상태로 지속되어 생명체를 육성할 조건이 결코 아닐 것이다. **8** 우리에게는 다행스럽게도, 물은 화학 규칙이나 물리 법칙을 모르는 것 같다.

4 ③

¹Espresso is *strong coffee* (made by forcing high-pressure steam / through finely ground coffee beans); // it is served / in a tiny cup.
에스프레소는 진한 커피이다 (높은 압력의 증기를 가함으로써 만들어지는 /
곱게 간 커피콩에) // 그것은 제공된다 / 작은 컵에

²(①) When steamed milk is added to espresso, // it becomes caffe latte — / Italian for "milk coffee."
데운 우유가 에스프레소에 더해지면 // 그것은 카페 라테가 된다 / '밀크 커피'를 뜻하는 이탈리아어인

³(②) But / when an espresso is mixed / with steamed milk and foamed milk, // it's called a cappuccino.
하지만 / 에스프레소가 섞이면 / 데운 우유와 우유 거품과 // 그것은 카푸치노라고 불린다

↓

> ⁴③ The precise proportions (of the ingredients) / and *the way* [in which the drink is served] / depend on *the person* [who makes it].
> 정확한 비율 (그 재료들의) / 그리고 방식은
> [그 음료가 제공되는] / 사람에게 달려 있다 [그것(음료)을 만드는]

↓

⁵For instance, / some people think // that an authentic Italian cappuccino should be / about one part espresso, one part steamed milk, and two parts foamed milk.
예를 들어 / 어떤 사람들은 생각한다 // 진정한 이탈리아 카푸치노는 (~이) 되어야 한다고 /
약 에스프레소 비율 1, 데운 우유 비율 1, 그리고 우유 거품 비율 2

⁶(④) However, / others say // (that) it should be made / with equal parts espresso, steamed milk, and foamed milk.
하지만 / 다른 사람들은 말한다 // 그것(진정한 이탈리아 카푸치노)은 만들어져야 한다고 / 동등한 비율의 에스프레소, 데운 우유, 그리고 우유 거품으로

⁷(⑤) There are many non-traditional variations (of these drinks), / including mocha latte / and *cappuccino* (sprinkled with chocolate powder).
많은 비전통적인 변형들이 있다 (이 음료들의) /
모카 라테를 포함하여 / 그리고 카푸치노를 (초콜릿 가루가 뿌려진)

해설

주어진 문장의 내용 파악하기

'그 재료들(the ingredients)'의 정확한 비율과 '그 음료(the drink)'가 제공되는 방식은 그것을 만드는 사람에게 달려 있음.
(▶ **Point 1** 정관사 the)
(앞에는 어떤 음료와 재료들이 언급되었을 것임을 예상할 수 있음.)

⌄⌄

단서로 정답 찾기

1 에스프레소는 작은 컵에 제공되는 곱게 간 커피콩에 고압 증기를 가해 만드는 진한 커피임.

2 (①) 에스프레소에 데운 우유를 더하면 카페 라테가 된다고 한다.

3 (②) But(하지만)으로 이어져 에스프레소가 데운 우유와 우유 거품과 섞이면 카푸치노가 된다고 다른 재료가 더해지는 경우를 설명한다.

↓

4 ③ 에스프레소, 데운 우유, 우유 거품을 the ingredients로, 카푸치노를 the drink로 받으며, 음료의 재료 비율과 제공 방식은 만드는 사람에게 달려 있다고 한다.

↓

5 For instance(예를 들어)로 '어떤 사람들(some people)'이 생각하는 진정한 이탈리아 카푸치노 재료의 비율에 대한 설명이 이어진다.

6 (④) However(하지만)가 이끌며, 앞 문장의 '어떤 사람들'과는 대조되는 '다른 사람들(others)'이 생각하는 카푸치노 재료의 비율을 제시한다.

7 (⑤) 앞서 소개한 음료들을 these drinks로 받아, 이 음료들의 비전통적 변형이 많음을 언급하며 글을 끝맺는다.

어휘

authentic 진정한, 진짜의   finely 곱게, 잘게; 멋있게; 섬세하게
ground 간, 가루로 만든; 빻은   part (혼합 등의) 비율; 부분, 일부
precise 정확한, 정밀한   proportion (전체에서 차지하는) 비율, 부분
sprinkle 뿌리다, 끼얹다   strong (술·음료가) 진한, 독한
variation 변형; 변화

구문 분석

⁴~ / and *the way* [**in which** the drink is served] / depend on *the person* ~.
the way를 수식하는 관계사절을 이끄는 <전치사+관계대명사> 형태의 in which는 관계부사 that으로 바꿔 쓸 수 있음.

해석 ¹에스프레소는 곱게 간 커피콩에 높은 압력의 증기를 가함으로써 만들어지는 진한 커피로, 작은 컵에 제공된다. ²데운 우유가 에스프레소에 더해지면, 그것은 '밀크 커피'를 뜻하는 이탈리아어인 카페 라테가 된다. ³하지만 에스프레소가 데운 우유와 우유 거품과 섞이면, 그것은 카푸치노라고 불린다. ⁴그 재료들의 정확한 비율과 그 음료가 제공되는 방식은 그것(음료)을 만드는 사람에게 달려 있다. ⁵예를 들어, 어떤 사람들은 진정한 이탈리아 카푸치노는 에스프레소, 데운 우유, 그리고 우유 거품의 비율이 약 1 : 1 : 2가 되어야 한다고 생각한다. ⁶하지만, 다른 사람들은 진정한 이탈리아 카푸치노는 동등한 비율의 에스프레소, 데운 우유, 그리고 우유 거품으로 만들어져야 한다고 말한다. ⁷모카 라테와 초콜릿 가루가 뿌려진 카푸치노를 포함하여 이 음료들의 많은 비전통적인 변형들이 있다.

 **5** ④

¹The "cargo cult" is an example (of *observed patterns* [that have no basis / in an underlying cause]).
'화물 숭배'는 한 예이다 (관찰된 패턴의 [기초를 두지 않는 / 근본적인 원인에])

²The phrase originally described *practices* (developed / by the native inhabitants (of islands in the South West Pacific)) / after the Second World War.
그 말은 원래 풍습을 설명했다 (발전된 / 원주민들에 의해 (남서태평양에 있는 섬의)) / 제2차 세계 대전 이후에

³(①) They'd observed / first the Japanese and then the Allied soldiers / building airstrips, marching, directing landing aircraft, and wearing certain styles of dress.
그들(남서태평양에 있는 섬의 원주민들)은 관찰했다 / 처음에는 일본군이, 그다음에는 연합군이 / 임시 활주로를 건설하고, 행진하고, 착륙하는 비행기의 방향을 유도하고, 특정한 스타일의 옷을 입고 있는 것을

⁴(②) Associated with these curious behaviors was /
이러한 특이한 행동들과 연관되어 있었다 /
the arrival (of *giant flying machines* (carrying vast quantities of *exotic material goods* — / canned food, clothes, vehicles, guns, radios, and so on — / (called "cargo" by the newcomers))).
출현은 (거대한 하늘을 나는 기계들의 (엄청난 양의 이국적인 물건들을 운반하는 / 즉 통조림, 의복, 차량, 총, 라디오 등 / (새로 온 사람들에 의해 '화물'이라고 불리는)))

⁵(③) When the war ended and the visitors left, // the natives reasoned // that if they carried out the same sort of activities, // the planes would return.
전쟁이 끝나고 방문자들이 떠났을 때 // 원주민들은 추론했다 // 만약 그들이 같은 종류의 행동들을 수행한다면 // 비행기들이 돌아올 것이라고

↓

> ⁶④ So / they built airstrips out of straw and coconuts, // and dressed themselves / to resemble *the military personnel* [(whom[that]) they'd encountered].
> 그래서 / 그들은 지푸라기와 코코넛으로 임시 활주로를 건설했다 // 그리고 자신들을 꾸몄다 / 군인들과 닮도록 [그들이 만났던]

↓

⁷They reproduced the waved landing signals / from their "runways."
그들은 손을 흔드는 착륙 신호를 재현했다 / 자신들의 '활주로'에서

⁸(⑤) They'd observed a pattern — / *the curious behavior of the visitors* (followed by the arrival of rich rewards) — / and concluded // that there was a connection.
그들은 패턴을 관찰했다 / 즉 방문자들의 특이한 행동 (많은 보상의 등장이 이어지는) / 그리고 결론을 내렸다 // 관련성이 있다고

⁹But / the inferred relationship / was not actually a causal one.
하지만 / 그 추론된 관계는 / 사실 원인이 되는 것이 아니었다

주어진 문장의 내용 파악하기 

> '그래서(So)' '그들(they)'은 임시 활주로를 건설하고 그들이 만났던 군인들과 닮게 꾸몄음.(▶ **Point 1** 지시사/대명사, **Point 2** 결과 연결어)
> (앞에는 they가 지칭하는 대상과 임시 활주로를 건설한 원인, 군인들을 만났던 경험이 나올 것임을 예상할 수 있음.)

≫

단서로 정답 찾기 ➕

1, 2 '화물 숭배'는 근본적 원인에 기초를 두지 않는 관찰된 패턴의 한 예이며, 이 말은 원래 제2차 세계 대전 이후 남서태평양 섬 원주민들의 풍습을 설명함.

3 (①) 섬의 원주민들을 They로 받아, 그들이 일본군과 연합군의 행동을 관찰했다고 한다.

4 (②) 일본군과 연합군의 행동을 these curious behaviors로 받아, 이는 화물 운송 비행기의 출현과 연관되어 있었다고 설명한다.

5 (③) 전쟁이 끝나 방문자들(일본군과 연합군)이 떠났을 때 원주민들은 군인들이 했던 것과 같은 행동을 하면 비행기가 돌아올 것이라고 추론했다고 한다.

↓

6 ④ they는 '원주민들(the natives)'을 받으며, 앞 문장에서 언급된 추론의 결과 그들이 활주로를 건설하고 스스로 군인들과 닮도록 꾸몄다는 내용이 So(그래서)로 이어진다.

↓

7 원주민들이 자신들이 만든 활주로에서 착륙 신호를 재현했다는 내용을 덧붙인다.

8 (⑤) 그들이 방문자들의 특이한 행동 뒤에 엄청난 양의 화물을 운반하는 비행기의 출현이라는 보상이 이어지는 패턴을 관찰해 관련성이 있다는 결론을 내렸다고 설명한다.

9 But(하지만)이 이끌며 앞 문장에서 설명한 패턴을 the inferred relationship으로 받아, 사실은 특이한 행동이 원인은 아니었다는 내용으로 글을 끝맺는다.

어휘

carry out ~을 수행[이행]하다   causal 원인이 되는, 인과 관계의
curious 특이한; 호기심이 강한   cult 숭배   direct (방향을) 유도하다; 지휘하다; 감독[연출]하다   exotic 이국적인; 외국의
personnel (조직·군대의) 인원[직원들]   practice (*pl.*) 풍습; 관행; 연습
underlying 근본적인, 기초적인

구문 분석

⁴**Associated with these curious behaviors was / the arrival** (of *giant flying machines* (carrying ~ newcomers))).
보어가 문장 맨 앞으로 오면서 <V+S> 어순으로 도치가 일어남.

해석 ¹'화물 숭배'는 근본적인 원인에 기초를 두지 않는 관찰된 패턴의 한 예이다. ²그 말은 원래 제2차 세계 대전 이후에 남서태평양에 있는 섬의 원주민들에 의해 발전된 풍습을 설명했다. ³그들은 처음에는 일본군이, 그다음에는 연합군이 임시 활주로를 건설하고, 행진하고, 착륙하는 비행기의 방향을 유도하고, 특정한 스타일의 옷을 입고 있는 것을 관찰했다. ⁴새로 온 사람들에 의해 '화물'이라고 불리는 엄청난 양의 이국적인 물건들, 즉 통조림, 의복, 차량, 총, 라디오 등을 운반하는 거대한 하늘을 나는 기계들의 출현은 이러한 특이한 행동들과 연관되어 있었다. ⁵전쟁이 끝나고 방문자들이 떠났을 때, 원주민들은 만약 그들이 같은 종류의 행동들을 수행한다면 비행기들이 돌아올 것이라고 추론했다. ⁶그래서 그들은 지푸라기와 코코넛으로 임시 활주로를 건설했고 그들이 만났던 군인들과 닮도록 자신들을 꾸몄다. ⁷그들은 자신들의 '활주로'에서 손을 흔드는 착륙 신호를 재현했다. ⁸그들은 패턴, 즉 많은 보상의 등장이 이어지는 방문자들의 특이한 행동을 관찰했고 관련성이 있다고 결론을 내렸다. ⁹하지만 그 추론된 관계는 사실 원인이 되는 것이 아니었다.

[1] How you focus your attention / plays a critical role / in how you deal with stress.
여러분이 여러분의 주의를 집중시키는 방식은 / 중요한 역할을 한다 / 여러분이 스트레스를 다루는 방식에

[2] Scattered attention harms your ability (to let go of stress), // because even though your attention is scattered, // it is narrowly focused, //
흩어진 주의력은 여러분의 능력을 손상시킨다 (스트레스를 푸는) //
왜냐하면 여러분의 주의력이 흩어지더라도 // 그것(여러분의 주의력)이 좁게 집중되기 때문이다 //

for you are able to fixate / only on the stressful parts (of your experience).
여러분은 집착할 수 있으므로 / 스트레스가 많은 부분에만 (여러분의 경험 중)

[3] When your attentional spotlight is widened, // you can more easily let go of stress.
여러분의 주의의 초점이 넓어지면 // 여러분은 스트레스를 더 쉽게 풀 수 있다

[4] You can put in perspective many more aspects of any situation / and (can) not get locked / into *one part* [that ties you down / to superficial and anxiety-provoking levels of attention].
여러분은 어떤 상황이라도 그 상황의 더 많은 측면을 균형 잡힌 시각으로 볼 수 있다 /
그리고 갇히지 않을 수 있다 / 한 부분에 [여러분을 옭아매는 / 피상적이고 불안을 유발하는 주의력 수준에]

[5] A narrow focus heightens the stress level (of each experience), // but a widened focus turns down the stress level //
좁은 초점은 스트레스 수준을 높인다 (각 경험의) / 그러나 넓은 초점은 스트레스 수준을 낮춘다 //

because you're better able to put each situation / into a broader perspective.
여러분이 각 상황을 더 잘 볼 수 있기 때문에 / 더 넓은 시각으로

[6] One anxiety-provoking detail is less important / than the bigger picture.
불안감을 유발하는 하나의 세부 사항은 덜 중요하다 / 더 큰 전체적인 상황보다

[7] It's like transforming yourself / into a nonstick frying pan.
그것은 여러분 자신을 변형시키는 것과 같다 / 들러붙지 않는 프라이팬으로

[8] You can still fry an egg, // but the egg won't stick to the pan.
여러분은 여전히 달걀을 부칠 수 있다 // 그러나 그 달걀은 팬에 들러붙지 않을 것이다

해설

밑줄 문장 확인하기 ⓟ

[7] 그것은 여러분 자신을 '들러붙지 않는 프라이팬'으로 변형시키는 것과 같음.

추론 근거로 정답 찾기 ⊕

[3] 주의의 초점이 넓어지면 스트레스를 푸는 것이 더 쉬움.
[4, 5] 초점이 넓으면 문제가 되는 한 부분에 갇히지 않을 수 있고, 스트레스 수준이 낮아짐.
[6] 불안감을 유발하는 한 세부 사항보다 전체적인 상황이 중요함.

주의의 초점을 넓게 하면 상황을 균형 잡힌 시각으로 보게 되어 스트레스가 낮아진다고 했다. 따라서 넓게 봄으로써 스트레스를 주는 경험에 집착하지 않게 된다는 것임을 추론할 수 있다.
→ ④ having a larger view of an experience beyond its stressful aspects(스트레스를 주는 측면을 넘어 경험을 더 넓은 시각으로 바라보는 것)

오답 확인

① never being confronted with any stressful experiences in daily life
일상생활에서 스트레스가 많은 어떤 경험에도 결코 직면하지 않는 것
② broadening one's perspective to identify the cause of stress 스트레스의 원인을 찾기 위해 시각을 넓히는 것
*①, ② → 언급되지 않은 내용.
③ rarely confining one's attention to positive aspects of an experience
경험의 긍정적인 측면에 주의를 좀처럼 국한시키지 않는 것
→ 긍정적인 측면이 아니라 부정적인 부분에 집중하지 않아야 함.
⑤ taking stress into account as the source of developing a wide view 넓은 시각을 기르는 원천으로 스트레스를 고려하는 것
→ 넓은 시각으로 스트레스를 기르는 것이 아니라 스트레스에 얽매이지 않을 수 있음.

어휘

fixate 집착하다; 정착[고정]시키다   let go of ~을 풀다[놓아주다]
scattered 흩어진, 산재한   superficial 피상[표면]적인; 깊이 없는, 얄팍한
[선택지] confine 국한시키다; 가두다   confront 직면하다

구문 분석

[4] You can **put in perspective** many more aspects ~.
<put A in(to) perspective>: A를 균형 잡힌 시각으로[넓게] 보다

해석 [1] 여러분이 여러분의 주의를 집중시키는 방식은 여러분이 스트레스를 다루는 방식에 중요한 역할을 한다. [2] 흩어진 주의력은 여러분의 스트레스를 푸는 능력을 손상시키는데, 왜냐하면 여러분의 주의력이 흩어지더라도, 여러분은 여러분의 경험 중 스트레스가 많은 부분에만 집착할 수 있으므로, 그것(여러분의 주의력)이 좁게 집중되기 때문이다. [3] 여러분의 주의의 초점이 넓어지면, 여러분은 스트레스를 더 쉽게 풀 수 있다. [4] 여러분은 어떤 상황이라도 그 상황의 더 많은 측면을 균형 잡힌 시각으로 볼 수 있으며, 피상적이고 불안을 유발하는 주의력 수준에 여러분을 옭아매는 한 부분에 갇히지 않을 수 있다. [5] 좁은 초점은 각 경험의 스트레스 수준을 높이지만, 넓은 초점은 여러분이 각 상황을 더 넓은 시각으로 더 잘 볼 수 있기 때문에 스트레스 수준을 낮춘다. [6] 불안감을 유발하는 하나의 세부 사항은 더 큰 전체적인 상황보다 덜 중요하다. [7] 그것은 여러분 자신을 들러붙지 않는 프라이팬으로 변형시키는 것과 같다. [8] 여러분은 여전히 달걀을 부칠 수 있지만, 그 달걀은 팬에 들러붙지 않을 것이다.

Zoom 1

해석 (이전 생략) 우리는 세계를 '정말 있는 그대로'가 아니라, 그것이 우리에게 보이는 대로만 볼 수 있는데, 왜냐하면 세계에 형태를 부여하는 관점이 없다면 '정말 있는 그대로'는 없기 때문이다. 철학자 Thomas Nagel은 '아무것도 아닌 곳에서 나온 관점'은 없다고 주장했는데, 왜냐하면 우리는 특정 관점에서 보는 것 외에는 세계를 볼 수 없고, 그 관점이 우리가 보는 것에 영향을 미치기 때문이다. •perspective 관점, 시각

우리가 세계를 이해할 수 있게 만드는 인간의 렌즈를 통해서만 우리는 세계를 경험할 수 있다. •intelligible (쉽게) 이해할 수 있는

➔ 밑줄 의미 = 편견 없고 객관적인 세계관
•unbiased 편견 없는   objective 객관적인

Zoom 2

해석 인간은 잡식성으로, 이는 그들이 주변 환경에서 발견되는 다양한 식물과 동물을 먹고 소화할 수 있다는 것을 의미한다. (중간 생략) 이 딜레마, 즉 보수성에 대한 필요와 결합된 실험의 필요는 잡식성의 역설로 알려져 있다.
•omnivorous 잡식성의   conservatism 보수성, 보수적 경향

그것은 음식과 관련된 두 가지의 모순되는 심리적인 충동을 야기한다. 첫 번째는 새로운 음식에 대한 끌림이며, 두 번째는 익숙한 음식에 대한 선호이다.
•contradictory 모순되는, 상반된   impulse 충동, 욕구; 충격

➔ 밑줄 의미 = 음식에 대해 융통성 있고도 조심스러워야 할 필요
•flexible 융통성 있는, 유연한   cautious 조심스러운, 신중한

Zoom 3

해석 오늘날 거의 핵심인 것처럼 보이는 많은 보조 사업들이 한때는 여정의 가장자리로서 시작했다.

예를 들어, 소매상들은 흔히 조립이나 설치 서비스와 같은 수반하는 지원으로 매출을 끌어올린다. 조립되지 않은 야외 그릴을 부품 상자로 판매해서 고객의 임무를 미완성 상태로 두는 가정용품 소매상을 생각해 보라.(바로 사용이 불가능해서 고객이 제품으로 하려던 일을 하지 못함을 의미) 그 소매상이 또한 조립과 배달도 판매할 때, 그것은 자신의 뒤뜰에서 요리하기라는 그 고객의 진정한 임무를 향해 여정에서 또 다른 한 걸음을 나아간다. (중간 생략) 유지 관리, 설치, 교육, 배달, 손수 하는 것을 나를 위해 해주는 해결책으로 바꿔주는 무엇이든 핵심 제품이 고객의 여정과 교차하는 곳의 가장자리를 탐구하는 것에서 원래 비롯되었다.
•edge 가장자리, 모서리; (칼 등의) 날   retailer 소매상, 소매업자
boost 끌어 올리다; 신장시키다, 북돋우다   accompanying 수반하는
assembly (기계 부품의) 조립; 집회   installation 설치, 설비
home goods 가정용품   mission 임무, 사명   maintenance 유지 (관리); 지속

➔ 밑줄 의미 = 고객의 기본적인 구매를 넘어 추가 서비스를 제공하는 것
•primary 기본적인; 최초의

Focus & Practice

p.106

1 ① **2** ② **3** ③ **4** ③

1 ①

해석 ... 관광업은 발전을 의미할 수 있지만, 대부분은 흔히 전통과 문화적 독특성의 상실을 의미하기도 한다. 그리고 물론 '문화 오염', '상스럽게 함(저속화)', '가짜 민속 문화'와 같은 예들이 있다. 그러한 특징들의 배경은 흔히 다소 낭만적이고, 이전의 혹은 (현재) 지배적인 진짜(문화)에 대해 규정하는 생각이다. (관광객의 구미에 맞추기 위해 가짜 문화가 생겨났다는 의미) 이상적으로 (일부 사람들에게는) 현대 소비자들이 여행이나 휴가 동안에 바라보거나 혹은 심지어 잠시라도 들어가 볼 수 있는 고대 문화가 존재해야 한다. 이것은 토착민이든 아니든 우리 모두가 같은 사회 구조의 일부인 지구촌 세계에서 지키기 어려운 우리 모델이다.
•phony-folk-culture 가짜 민속 문화   more or less 다소; 거의
normative 규정하는; 규범적인   prevailing 지배적인, 우세한
authenticity 진짜임; 진정성, 진실성   gaze at ~을 바라보다[응시하다]
cage 우리, 새장   fabric 구조; 직물, 천
① 소비를 위해 과거 문화를 그것의 원래 형태로 보존하는 것
② 보존을 위해 선사시대 유적지에 대한 일반인의 접근을 제한하는 것
③ 문화 정책 및 규정에 대한 예산을 유지하는 것
•conservation 보존, 보호   regulation 규정; 규제

해설 밑줄 문장은 '이것(This)'이 모두가 같은 사회 구조의 일부인 지구촌 세계에서 지키기 어려운 '우리 모델'이라는 내용이므로 지구촌 세계에서 지키기 어려운 것이 무엇인지를 확인해야 한다. 직전 문장은 관광하면서 볼 수 있는 고대 문화가 있어야 한다고 일부 사람들이 생각한다는 내용이다. 이것이 밑줄 문장의 This로 이어지므로, 밑줄 문장은 관광을 위해 과거 문화를 있는 그대로 보존하는 게 어렵다는 의미임을 추론할 수 있다. 앞에서부터 살펴보면, 관광업으로 전통과 문화적 독특성이 상실된다고 하고 문화 오염, 저속화 등의 예를 들었으므로, 밑줄 문장은 전통 문화를 그대로 보존하는 것이 이상적이지만 어렵다는 의미임을 확인할 수 있다. 따라서 밑줄 친 부분이 의미하는 바로 가장 적절한 것은 ① 'preserving a past culture in its original form for consumption (소비를 위해 과거 문화를 그것의 원래 형태로 보존하는 것)'이다. 보존된 문화에 관광객이 방문할 수 있어야 한다고 했으므로 보존을 위해 접근을 제한한다는 ②는 적절하지 않으며, 예산에 대한 내용은 언급되지 않았으므로 ③도 적절하지 않다.

2 ②

해석 나는 균류가 그것들의 더 큰 상대보다 조금 더 앞서 '생각한다'고 추측한다. 나무들 사이에서, 각각의 종들은 다른 종들과 싸운다. 중부 유럽 토종의 너도밤나무가 그곳 대부분의 숲에서 승리를 거둔다고 가정해 보자. ... 만약 너도밤나무의 대부분을 감염시키고 그것들을 죽이는 새로운 병원균이 생기면 무슨 일이 일어날까? 그런 경우에는, 계속해서 자라며 어린 너도밤나무들이 발아하고 자라기 위해 필요한 그늘을 제공할 ... 일정 수의 다른 종들이 주위에 있으면 더 이롭지 않을까? 다양성은 아주 오래된 숲에 안전을 제공한다. 균류 또한 안정적인 환경에 매우 의존적이기 때문에, 그들은 한 종의 나무가 우위를 차지해 내지 않도록 확실히 하기 위하여 지하의 다른 종을 지원하고 그것들을 완전한

붕괴로부터 보호한다.
• **emerge victorious** 승리를 거두다 **come along** 생기다, 나타나다; 도착하다
infect 감염시키다; 오염시키다 **sprout** 발아하다; 자라기 시작하다; 새싹
stable 안정적인, 안정된 **collapse** 붕괴(되다) **ensure** 확실히 하다; 보증하다
manage to-v (용케[어떻게든]) v 해내다 **dominate** 우위를 차지하다; 지배하다
① 한 종의 우세를 지원하는 데 열심인
② 다양성이 숲의 안정으로 이어진다는 것을 알고 있는
③ 숲이 붕괴 이후 재생하는 것을 돕는 것에 무관심한
• **eager** 열심인; 열망하는 **indifferent** 무관심한
regenerate (생물체의 손상된 부분을) 재생시키다; 재건하다

해설 밑줄 문장은 균류가 더 큰 상대보다 더 '앞서 '생각한다''는 내용이다. 균류
가 더 큰 상대에 비해 어떻게 생각하는지를 확인하기 위해 글을 읽어 내려간다.
나무 종은 서로 싸워서 우위를 차지하려고 하는데, 숲에서는 다양성이 안전을
제공한다고 한 다음, 균류는 안정적인 환경을 위해 한 나무 종이 우세해지지 않
도록 다른 종을 지원하고 보호한다고 했다. 이는 균류가 서로 싸우는 더 큰 상
대인 나무와 달리, 다양성이 중요하다는 것을 알고 있는 것을 의미한다. 따라서
밑줄 친 부분이 의미하는 바로 가장 적절한 것은 ② 'aware that diversity
leads to the stability of forests(다양성이 숲의 안정으로 이어진다는 것
을 알고 있는)'이다. 균류가 한 종의 나무가 우세하지 않도록 한다는 내용과 반
대되므로 ①은 적절하지 않으며, 숲이 붕괴된 후의 재생에 관한 내용이 아니므
로 ③도 적절하지 않다.

3 ③

해석 예술과 미학은 다양한 인간 경험에 대한 감정적인 연결을 제공한다. "예
술은 단순한 혀에 있는 설탕 이상이 될 수 있다,"고 펜실베이니아 대학의 교수
인 Anjan Chatterjee는 말한다. "예술에서, 도전적인 무언가가 있을 때, 그리
고 그것이 또한 불편할 수 있을 때, 이 불편함은, 우리가 만약 기꺼이 그것과 교
전하려 한다면, 어떤 변화, 어떤 변형의 가능성을 제공한다. 그것은 또한 강렬
한 미적 경험이 될 수 있다." 예술은, 이런 식으로, 다른 상황에서는 어렵고 불
편한 생각 및 개념과 싸우는 매개체가 된다. Picasso가 1937년에 그의 걸작
인 Guernica를 그렸을 때, 그는 전쟁의 가슴 아프고 잔혹한 본질을 포착했
고, 세계에 스페인 내전으로 인한 전반적인 고통을 고찰할 방법을 제공했다. …
• **aesthetics** 미학 *cf.* **aesthetic** 미적인; 심미적, 미학적 **engage** 교전하다;
관계를 맺다 **vehicle** 매개체, 수단; 차량 **contend with** ~와 싸우다, 씨름하다
masterpiece 걸작, 명작
① 심리적 불안을 완화시키는 것에 한몫을 하다
② 우리에게 미의 절대성에 대해 가르치다
③ 즐거움 이상의 여러 가지 경험들을 포괄하다
• **anxiety** 불안(감), 염려 **enlighten** 가르치다; 계몽하다 **absoluteness** 절대성;
완전함; 확실함 **embrace** 포괄하다; 받아들이다

해설 밑줄 문장은 예술이 '단순한 혀에 있는 설탕 이상이 될 수 있다'는 내용이
므로, 예술이 단순한 어떤 것을 넘어서 어떤 기능을 하는지를 확인한다. 먼저 첫
문장인 직전 문장은 예술과 미학이 다양한 인간 경험에 대한 감정적 연결을 준
다고 했다. 이어서 살펴보면, 예술에서 불편하고 도전적인 것은 변화의 가능성
을 제공하고 강렬한 미적 경험이 될 수 있다고 했다. 또한 예술은 어렵고 불편
한 생각 및 개념과 싸우는 매개체가 된다고 하며 전쟁의 본질을 그린 Picasso
의 작품을 예로 들고 있으므로, 예술이 '단순히 즐겁거나 아름다운 것 이상을 포
함할 수 있음'을 추론할 수 있다. 따라서 밑줄 친 부분이 의미하는 바로 가장 적
절한 것은 ③ 'embrace a variety of experiences beyond pleasure
(즐거움 이상의 여러 가지 경험들을 포괄하다)'이다. 심리적 불안을 완화시키는
예술의 기능을 설명한 것이 아니라 예술이 어렵고 불편한 생각 및 개념과 싸우
는 매개체가 된다고 했으므로 ①은 적절하지 않으며, 미의 절대성은 언급되지
않았으므로 ②도 적절하지 않다.

 4 ③

해석 … 고객 중심 기업은 경쟁사들에 비해 높은 고객 만족을 전하기를 추구
하지만, 그것은 고객 만족을 '최대화'하려고 시도하지는 않는다. 기업은 언제
나 가격을 내리거나 서비스를 확대하여 고객 만족을 증대시킬 수 있다. 그러
나 이는 더 낮은 수익으로 이어질 수 있다. 그러므로 마케팅의 목적은 고객 가
치를 수익이 있게 만들어 내는 것이다. 이것은 몹시 까다로운 균형을 요구하는
데, 즉 마케팅 담당자는 더 큰 고객 가치와 만족을 만들어 내야 하지만 '집을 거
저 주어서는' 안 된다.
• **profit** 수익, 이익, 이윤 *cf.* **profitably** 수익이 있게; 유리하게
cf. **profitability** 수익성 **delicate** 까다로운; 섬세한 **give away** 거저 주다
① 경쟁사의 강점을 간과하다
② 회사의 평판을 해치다
③ 회사의 수익성을 위태롭게 하다
• **complaint** 불만, 불평, 항의 **reputation** 평판, 명성
risk 위태롭게 하다; 위험(을 무릅쓰다)

해설 밑줄 문장은 '이것(This)'이 까다로운 균형을 요구한다고 하며, 마케팅 담
당자는 고객 가치와 만족을 더 크게 만들어 내야 하지만 '집을 거저 주어서는'
안 된다는 부연 설명이 이어진다. 마케팅 담당자가 어떤 것에 유의하며 균형을
맞춰야 하는지를 확인한다. 직전 문장은 마케팅의 목적이 수익성 있게 고객 가
치를 만들어 내는 것이라고 했으므로, 밑줄 문장은 고객 가치를 만들어 내면서
'기업의 이익이 침해당하면 안 된다'는 의미일 것을 유추할 수 있다. 앞에서부터
살펴보면, 고객 중심 기업은 고객 만족을 추구하지만 최대화하려 하지는 않으
며, 고객 만족 증대를 위한 방안이 수익을 감소시킬 수 있다고 했다. 고객의 만
족을 위하면서 낮은 수익은 피해야 한다는 내용이므로, 밑줄 친 부분이 의미하
는 바로 가장 적절한 것은 ③ 'risk the company's profitability(회사의 수
익성을 위태롭게 하다)'이다. 경쟁사의 강점에 대한 언급은 없고 경쟁사보다는
높은 고객 만족을 추구한다고만 했으므로 ①은 적절하지 않으며, 평판에 대한
내용이 아니므로 ②도 적절하지 않다.

1 ①

¹Coming of age in the 18th and 19th centuries, / the personal diary became a centerpiece (in *the construction of a modern subjectivity*), //
18세기와 19세기에 충분히 발달함에 따라 / 개인 일기는 중심이 되었다 (근대적 주체성 구축의) //
at the heart of which is *the application* (of reason and critique) / (to the understanding of world and self), // which allowed the creation (of a new kind of knowledge).
그것(근대적 주체성 구축)의 중심에는 적용이 있다 (이성과 비판의) /
(세계와 자아에 대한 이해에의) // 이는 창조를 가능하게 했다 (새로운 종류의 지식의)

²Diaries were *central media* [through which enlightened and free subjects could be constructed].
일기는 중심 매체였다 [그것을 통해 계몽된 자유로운 주체가 만들어질 수 있는]

³They provided *a space* [where one could write daily / about her whereabouts, feelings, and thoughts].
그것은 공간을 제공했다 [사람들이 매일 쓸 수 있는 / 자신의 행방, 감정, 그리고 생각에 대해]

⁴Over time and with rereading, / disparate entries, events, and happenstances / could be rendered into insights and narratives (about the self), / and allowed for the formation (of subjectivity).
시간이 지남에 따라 그리고 다시 읽음으로써 / 이질적인 내용, 사건 및 우연이 /
통찰과 이야기로 만들어질 수 있었다 (자신에 관한) / 그리고 형성을 가능하게 만들었다 (주체성의)

⁵It is in that context // that the idea of "the self [as] both made and explored with words" emerges.
바로 그러한 맥락에서다 // '말로 만들어지고 탐구되는 (것으로서의) 자아'라는 개념이 나타나는 것은

⁶Diaries were personal and private; // one would write for oneself, // or, in Habermas's formulation, / one would make oneself public to oneself.
일기는 개인적이고 사적인 것이었다 // 사람들은 자신을 위해 쓰곤 했다 //
Habermas의 명확한 표현으로 다시 말하면 / 사람들은 자신을 자신에게 공개적으로 만들곤 했다

⁷By making the self public in a private sphere, / the self also became an object (for self-inspection and self-critique).
자아를 사적 영역에서 공개함으로써 / 자아는 또한 대상이 되었다 (자기 점검과 자기비판의)

해설

밑줄 문장 확인하기 

> **6** 일기는 개인적이고 사적인 것으로 자신을 위해 쓰곤 했는데, 즉 사람들은 '자신을 자신에게 공개적으로 만들곤' 했음.

추론 근거로 정답 찾기 

> **4, 5** 일기를 통해 자신을 통찰하고 주체성을 형성하며, 말로 만들어지고 탐구되는 자아 개념이 발생함.
> **7** 일기를 쓰며 스스로를 점검하고 비판함.
>
> 밑줄 문장 뒤에서 자아를 사적 영역에 공개하여 자기 점검과 자기 비판을 한다고 했고, 앞에서는 일기로 주체성을 형성하고, 자아라는 개념이 나타난다고 했다. 따라서 일기로 자신을 자신에게 공개하는 것은 '자신을 되돌아보기 위한 것'임을 추론할 수 있다.
> → ① use writing as a means of reflecting on oneself
> (글을 자신을 되돌아보는 수단으로 사용하다)

오답 확인

② build one's identity by reading others' diaries
타인의 일기를 읽음으로써 자신의 정체성을 확립하다
③ exchange feedback in the process of writing
글쓰기 과정에서 의견을 교환하다 → 일기는 개인적이고 사적인 것이며 의견 교환을 하는 것이 아님.
④ create an alternate ego to present to others
다른 사람들에게 제시하기 위한 대체 자아를 창조하다
⑤ develop topics for writing about selfhood
자아에 관한 글을 쓰기 위한 주제를 개발하다
*②, ④, ⑤ → 언급되지 않은 내용.

어휘

centerpiece 중심(적 존재); 중앙 장식물   come of age (무엇이) 충분히 발달한 상태가 되다   entry (일기 등의 개별) 내용, 항목; 들어감[옴]
formulation 명확한 표현; 공식화   happenstance 우연
whereabouts 행방, 소재

구문 분석

¹~ / the personal diary became a centerpiece (in *the construction of a modern subjectivity*), // at the heart of **which** is *the application* (of reason and critique) / ~.
여기서 which는 the construction ~ subjectivity를 보충 설명하는 절을 이끌며, 장소 부사구가 앞으로 오면서 도치가 일어남.

해석 ¹18세기와 19세기에 충분히 발달함에 따라(대중화되었다는 의미) 개인 일기는 근대적 주체성 구축의 중심이 되었는데, 그것의 중심에는 세계와 자아에 대한 이해에의 이성과 비판의 적용이 있고 이는 새로운 종류의 지식의 창조를 가능하게 했다. ²일기는 그것을 통해 계몽된 자유로운 주체가 만들어질 수 있는 중심 매체였다. ³그것은 사람들이 자신의 행방, 감정, 그리고 생각에 대해 매일 쓸 수 있는 공간을 제공했다. ⁴시간이 지남에 따라 그리고 다시 읽음으로써, 이질적인 내용, 사건 및 우연이 자신에 관한 통찰과 이야기로 만들어질 수 있었으며, 주체성의 형성을 가능하게 만들었다. ⁵'말로 만들어지고 또한 탐구되는 (것으로서의) 자아'라는 개념이 나타나는 것은 바로 그러한 맥락에서다. ⁶일기는 개인적이고 사적인 것으로 사람들은 자신을 위해 쓰곤 했는데, Habermas의 명확한 표현으로 다시 말하면, 사람들은 자신을 자신에게 공개적으로 만들곤 했다. ⁷자아를 사적 영역에서 공개함으로써 자아는 또한 자기 점검과 자기비판의 대상이 되었다.

2 ②

[1] *The single most important change* [(which[that]) you can make / in your working habits] / is to switch to creative work first, reactive work second.
단 한 가지 가장 중요한 변화는 [여러분이 만들어 낼 수 있는 / 여러분의 일하는 습관에서] /
창조적인 일 먼저, 대응적인 일은 그다음으로 전환하는 것이다

[2] This means / blocking off a large chunk of time every day / for creative work / on your own priorities, / with the phone and e-mail off.
이것은 의미한다 / 매일 상당히 많은 시간을 차단하는 것을 /
창조적인 일을 위해 / 여러분 자신의 우선순위에 따라 / 전화기와 이메일을 끈 채

[3] I used to be a frustrated writer. // Making this switch / turned me into a productive writer.
나는 예전에는 좌절감을 느끼는 작가였다 // 이런 전환을 하는 것이 / 나를 생산적인 작가가 되게 했다

[4] Yet / there wasn't *a single day* [when I sat down / to write an article, blog post, or book chapter / without a string of people waiting for me to get back to them].
하지만 / 단 하루도 없었다 [내가 앉아 있던 날은 / 기사나 블로그 게시글 혹은 책의 한 챕터를 쓰기 위해 / 일련의 사람들이 내가 그들에게 나중에 다시 연락하기를 기다리는 것 없이]

[5] It wasn't easy, // and it still isn't (easy), // particularly when I get *phone messages* (beginning "I sent you an e-mail *two hours ago*...!")
그것은 쉽지 않았다 // 그리고 그것은 아직도 쉽지 않다 // 특히 내가 전화 메시지를 받을 때는
("'2시간 전에' 이메일을 보냈어요…!"라고 시작하는)

[6] By definition, / this approach goes against the grain / of others' expectations and *the pressures* [(which[that]) they put on you].
당연히 / 이러한 접근 방식은 맞지 않는다 / 다른 사람들의 기대와 압박에 [그들이 여러분에게 가하는]

[7] It takes willpower / to switch off the world, / even for an hour.
(~은) 의지가 필요하다 / 세상에 대해 신경을 끄는 것에는 / 단 한 시간 동안이라도

[8] It feels uncomfortable, // and sometimes people get upset.
그것은 불편한 느낌이 든다 // 그리고 때로 사람들이 화가 나기도 한다

[9] But / it's better / to disappoint a few people over small things, / than to abandon your dreams / for <u>an empty inbox</u>.
그러나 / (~이) 낫다 / 사소한 것에 대해 소수의 사람들을 실망시키는 것이 /
여러분의 꿈을 포기하는 것보다 / 빈 수신함을 위해

[10] Otherwise, / you're sacrificing your potential / for the illusion of professionalism.
그렇게 하지 않으면 / 여러분은 자신의 잠재력을 희생하고 있는 것이다 / 전문성이라는 환상을 위해

밑줄 문장 확인하기 

[9] 그러나 '빈 수신함'을 위해 꿈을 포기하는 것보다 사소한 것에 대해 소수의 사람들을 실망시키는 것이 나음.

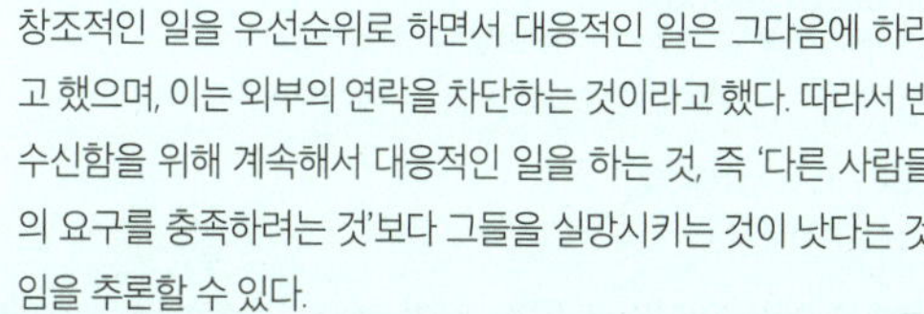

추론 근거로 정답 찾기 ⊕

[1] 창조적인 일을 먼저 하고, 대응적인 일을 나중에 해야 함.
[2] 우선순위인 창조적인 일을 위해 외부와의 연락을 차단한다는 의미임.

↓

창조적인 일을 우선순위로 하면서 대응적인 일은 그다음에 하라고 했으며, 이는 외부의 연락을 차단하는 것이라고 했다. 따라서 빈 수신함을 위해 계속해서 대응적인 일을 하는 것, 즉 '다른 사람들의 요구를 충족하려는 것'보다 그들을 실망시키는 것이 낫다는 것임을 추론할 수 있다.

→ ② attempting to satisfy other people's demands
(다른 사람들의 요구를 충족하려고 시도하는 것)

오답 확인

① following an innovative course of action
혁신적인 행동 방침을 따르는 것
③ completing challenging work without mistakes
실수 없이 도전적인 일을 완수하는 것
*①, ③ → 언급되지 않은 내용.
④ removing social ties to maintain a mental balance
정신적 균형을 유지하기 위해 사회적 유대를 제거하는 것 → 곧바로 답하여 수신함을 비우는 것은 사회적 유대를 제거하기보다 유지하는 것을 의미하며, 정신적 균형은 언급되지 않음.
⑤ securing enough opportunities for social networking
소셜 네트워킹을 위한 충분한 기회를 확보하는 것 → 소셜 네트워킹을 위해 기회를 확보하라는 내용은 없으며 외부와의 연락을 차단하라고 했음.

어휘

abandon 포기하다, 버리다   block off ~을 차단하다[막다]
by definition 당연히, 분명히; 정의상, 의미상   chunk 상당히 많은 양; 덩어리   go against the grain 맞지 않다, 거스르다
professionalism 전문성   reactive 대응적인; 반응을 나타내는
switch 전환(하다) *cf.* switch off 신경을 끄다; 스위치를 끄다
willpower 의지(력)

구문 분석

[9] But / it's better / **to disappoint** a few people over small things, / **than to abandon** your dreams / ~.
진주어에서 두 개의 to-v구가 비교됨.

해석 [1] 여러분이 일하는 습관에서 만들어 낼 수 있는 단 한 가지 가장 중요한 변화는 창조적인 일 먼저, 대응적인 일은 그다음으로 전환하는 것이다. [2] 이것은 전화기와 이메일을 끈 채, 여러분 자신의 우선순위에 따라 창조적인 일을 위해 매일 상당히 많은 시간을 차단하는 것을 의미한다. [3] 나는 예전에는 좌절감을 느끼는 작가였다. 이런 전환을 하는 것이 나를 생산적인 작가가 되게 했다. [4] 하지만 일련의 사람들이 내가 그들에게 나중에 다시 연락하기를 기다리는 것 없이 기사나 블로그 게시글 혹은 책의 한 챕터를 쓰기 위해 내가 앉아 있던 날은 단 하루도 없었다. [5] 그것은 쉽지 않았고, 특히 내가 "'2시간 전에' 이메일을 보냈어요…!"라고 시작하는 전화 메시지를 받을 때는 아직도 쉽지 않다. [6] 당연히, 이러한 접근 방식은 다른 사람들의 기대와 그들이 여러분에게 가하는 압박에 맞지 않는다. [7] 단 한 시간 동안이라도 세상에 대해 신경을 끄는 것에는 의지가 필요하다. [8] 그것은 불편한 느낌이 들고, 때로 사람들이 화가 나기도 한다. [9] 그러나 빈 수신함을 위해 여러분의 꿈을 포기하는 것보다, 사소한 것에 대해 소수의 사람들을 실망시키는 것이 낫다. [10] 그렇게 하지 않으면, 여러분은 전문성이라는 환상을 위해 자신의 잠재력을 희생하고 있는 것이다.

3 ①

¹Although (it is) not the explicit goal, // the best science can really be seen / as refining ignorance.
비록 명시적인 목표는 아니지만 // 최고의 과학은 실제로 여겨질 수 있다 / 무지를 정제하는 것으로

²Scientists, / (especially young ones), / can get too obsessed with results. // Society helps them along / in this mad chase.
과학자들은 / (특히 젊은 과학자들) / 결과에 너무 집착하게 될 수 있다 //
사회는 그들(과학자들)을 도와서 하게 한다 / 이 어리석은 추구를

³Big discoveries are covered in the press, / show up on the university's home page, / help get grants, / and make the case (for promotions).
큰 발견들이 언론에 보도된다 / 대학의 홈페이지에 등장한다 /
보조금을 받는 데 도움을 준다 / 그리고 근거를 만든다 (승진을 위한)

⁴But / it's wrong.
그러나 / 그것(결과에 너무 집착하는 것)은 잘못된 것이다

⁵Great scientists, / (*the pioneers* [that we admire]), / are not concerned with results but (concerned) with the next questions.
위대한 과학자들은 / (선구자들인 [우리가 존경하는]) / 결과가 아니라 그다음 질문들에 관심이 있다

⁶The highly respected physicist Enrico Fermi told his students //
아주 존경받는 물리학자인 Enrico Fermi는 자신의 학생들에게 말했다 //
that / *an experiment* [that successfully proves a hypothesis] / is a measurement; // *one* [that doesn't (successfully prove a hypothesis)] / is discovery.
~라고 / 실험은 [가설을 성공적으로 입증하는] /
측정이(라고) // 그리고 (~한) 것(실험)은 / [그렇지 않은] / 발견이(라고)

⁷A discovery, an uncovering — / of new ignorance.
발견, 즉 드러내는 것 / 새로운 무지를

⁸The Nobel Prize, the pinnacle of scientific accomplishment, / is awarded, / not for a lifetime of scientific achievement, / but for a single discovery, a result.
과학적 성취의 정점인 노벨상은 /
수여된다 / 평생의 과학적인 업적에 대해서가 아니라 / 하나의 발견, 즉 결과에 대해

⁹Even the Nobel committee realizes / in some way // that this is not really in the scientific spirit, //
노벨상 위원회조차도 인식하고 있다 / 어떤 점에서는 // 이것이 실제로 과학의 진정한 의미 속에 있는 것이 아니라는 것을 //
and their award citations commonly honor the discovery (for having "opened a field up," / "transformed a field," / or "taken a field in new and unexpected directions.")
그래서 그들(노벨상 위원회)의 상에 쓰인 문구들은 흔히 발견을 기린다 ('한 분야를 연' / '한 분야를 변화시킨' / 혹은 '한 분야를 새롭고 예상치 못한 방향으로 이끈')

해설

밑줄 문장 확인하기 

> 1 명시적인 목표는 아니지만 최고의 과학은 '무지를 정제하는 것'으로 여겨질 수 있음.

⌄

추론 근거로 정답 찾기 ➕

> 5 위대한 과학자는 결과가 아니라 아직 모르는 것에 관심이 있음.
> 6, 7 가설을 입증하지 못하는 실험은 새로운 무지를 드러내는 발견임.
> 9 노벨상의 문구는 무지를 드러낸 발견을 기림.

↓

결과 지향적인 과학을 비판하며, 무지를 드러내는 발견이 가치 있고 위대한 과학자들은 결과 이후의 질문에 관심을 가진다고 했다. 따라서 최고의 과학이 무지를 정제하는 것은 '알려진 결과를 넘어 그다음을 보는 것'임을 추론할 수 있다.

→ ① looking beyond what is known towards what is left unknown(알려진 것을 넘어서 알려지지 않은 채로 있는 것을 향해 보는 것)

오답 확인

② offering an ultimate account of what has been discovered 발견된 것에 대한 궁극적인 설명을 제공하는 것
③ analyzing existing knowledge with an objective mindset 객관적인 사고방식을 가지고 기존의 지식을 분석하는 것
④ inspiring scientists to publicize significant discoveries 과학자들이 중요한 발견을 발표하도록 고무시키는 것
*②, ③, ④ → 글의 내용과 반대됨.
⑤ informing students of a new field of science 과학의 새로운 분야에 대해 학생들에게 알려주는 것
→ 언급되지 않은 내용.

어휘

citation 인용(구) committee 위원회 grant 보조금; 승인[허락]하다; 수여하다 hypothesis 가설 ignorance 무지, 무식 pioneer 선구자, 개척자
[선택지] account 설명; (예금) 계좌 publicize 발표하다; 홍보하다

구문 분석

⁹~ // and their award citations commonly honor the discovery (for **having** "**opened** a field up," / "**transformed** a field," / or "**taken** a field in new and unexpected directions.")
동명사의 완료형(having p.p.)을 써서 문장의 동사 honor보다 이전 일임을 나타냄.

---

^{해석} ¹비록 명시적인 목표는 아니지만, 최고의 과학은 실제로 무지를 정제하는 것으로 여겨질 수 있다. ²과학자들, 특히 젊은 과학자들은 결과에 너무 집착하게 될 수 있다. 사회는 그들을 도와서 이 어리석은 추구를 하게 한다. ³큰 발견들이 언론에 보도되고, 대학의 홈페이지에 등장하고, 보조금을 받는 데 도움을 주고, 승진을 위한 근거를 만든다. ⁴그러나 그것은 잘못된 것이다. ⁵우리가 존경하는 선구자들인 위대한 과학자들은 결과가 아니라 그다음 질문들에 관심이 있다. ⁶아주 존경받는 물리학자인 Enrico Fermi는 자신의 학생들에게 가설을 성공적으로 입증하는 실험은 측정이며, 그렇지 않은 것은 발견이라고 말했다. ⁷새로운 무지의 발견, 즉 (새로운 무지를) 드러내는 것이라고 ⁸과학적 성취의 정점인 노벨상은 평생의 과학적인 업적에 대해서가 아니라 하나의 발견, 즉 결과에 대해 수여된다. ⁹노벨상 위원회조차도 어떤 점에서는 이것이 실제로 과학의 진정한 의미 속에 있는 것이 아니라는 것을 인식하고 있으며, 그들의 상에 쓰인 문구들은 흔히 '한 분야를 연', '한 분야를 변화시킨', 혹은 '한 분야를 새롭고 예상치 못한 방향으로 이끈' 발견을 기린다.

"

Point 2 · 글의 주제로 정답 찾기

Zoom 1

해석 (이전 생략) 그러므로 음식점 종업원이 여러분에게 메뉴를 제공하는 경우는 놀랄 일이 아니다. 그녀가 여러분에게 안에 투명한 액체가 담긴 유리잔을 가져다줄 때, 여러분은 그것이 물인지 물을 필요가 없다. 식사를 한 후에, 여러분은 왜 더 이상 배가 고프지 않은지 알아낼 필요가 없다. 이 모든 것들은 예상되며 따라서 해결해야 할 문제가 아니다. (중간 생략) 매일, 기능의 고정성은 저주가 아니라 안도가 되는 것이다. 그것이 여러분의 모든 선택지와 가능성을 고려하기를 시도조차 해서는 안 되는 이유이다. 여러분은 그럴 수도 없다. 여러분이 그렇게 하려고 한다면, 여러분은 절대 아무것도 완수할 수 없을 것이다. 그러므로 상자를 부수지 마라. 역설적으로, 그것이 여러분의 사고를 제한하기는 하지만, 그것은 여러분을 똑똑하게 만들어 주기도 한다. 그것은 현실보다 한발 앞서 있도록 여러분을 도와준다.

• **fluid** 액체, 유동체 **functional** 기능의, 기능적인 **relief** 안도(가 되는 것) **curse** 저주(하다) **attempt** 시도(하다) **ironically** 역설적으로, 반어적으로

➜ 밑줄 의미 = 늘 하는 예상을 바탕으로 문제를 처리하라.

• **deal with** ~을 처리하다, ~을 다루다 **habitual** 늘 하는, 습관적인; 상습적인

Zoom 2

해석 구직은 수동적인 일이 아니다. (중간 생략) 만일 당신이 목적을 가지고 행동한다면, … 그렇다면 당신은 직접적이어야 하고, 집중해야 하며 가능한 한 언제든 영리해야 한다. 직업을 구하는 다른 모두가 같은 목표를 가지며, 같은 일자리를 위해 경쟁한다. 당신은 그 무리의 나머지보다 더 많은 것을 해야만 한다. 당신이 원하는 일자리를 찾아 얻기까지 얼마나 오래 걸리는지에 관계없이, 적극적인 것은 당신이 온라인 구인란을 훑어보고 가끔 이력서를 이메일로 보내는 것에만 의존할 때보다 논리적으로 당신에게 결과를 더 빨리 가져다 줄 것이다. 그런 활동들은 나머지 양들에게 남겨라.

• **herd** 무리, 떼 **proactive** 적극적인, 상황을 앞서서 주도하는 **browse** 훑어보다, 둘러보다; 대강 읽다 **occasional** 가끔의 **resume** 이력서

➜ 밑줄 의미 = 다른 구직자들보다 두드러지기 위해 더 적극적으로 행동하라.

• **job-seeker** 구직자

Zoom 3

해석 작가 Elizabeth Gilbert는 명상을 하면서 추종자들을 이끌었던 위대한 성인의 우화를 이야기한다. 추종자들이 자신들의 선의 순간에 빠지고 있을 때, 그들은 야옹 하고 울고 모두를 신경 쓰이게 하면서 사원을 걸어 다니는 고양이에 의해 방해받곤 했다. 성인은 간단한 해결책을 제시했는데, 그는 명상 시간 동안 고양이를 기둥에 묶기 시작했다. 이 해결책은 빠르게 의례로 발전했는데, 즉 먼저 기둥에 고양이를 묶고, 다음으로 명상을 하라는 것이었다. 그 고양이가 결국 자연사했을 때, 종교적인 위기가 뒤따랐다. 추종자들은 무엇을 해야 했는가? 고양이를 기둥에 묶지 않고 그들이 도대체 어떻게 명상을 할 수 있었는가? 이 이야기는 내가 보이지 않는 규칙이라고 일컫는 것을 분명히 보여 준다. 이것들은 불필요하게 규칙으로 굳어진 습관과 행동들이다. 글로 쓰인 규칙들이 변화에 저항할 수는 있으나, 보이지 않는 것들은 더욱 완강하다. 그들은 조용한 살인자들이다.

• **fable** 우화, 꾸며낸 이야기 **meditation** 명상, 묵상; 심사숙고 cf. **meditate** 명상하다 **disrupt** 방해하다, 지장을 주다 **come up with** (해결책을) 제시하다 **ritual** 의례, 의식 **crisis** 위기, 최악의 고비

---

resistant 저항하는 **stubborn** 완강한, 완고한, 고집스러운

➜ 밑줄 의미 = 우리의 행동을 무의식적으로 지배하는 보이지 않는 규칙들

• **govern** 지배하다; 통치하다

Focus & Practice

p.112

1 ③ **2** ② **3** ③ **4** ②

1 ③

해석 우리의 언어는 우리의 더 깊은 가정을 드러내는 것을 돕는다. (더 깊은 가정을) 드러내는 이 구절들을 생각해 보라. 우리가 무언가 중요한 것을 성취할 때, 우리는 그것에 '피, 땀, 눈물'이 들었다고 말한다. 우리는 중요한 성취는 '애써서 얻은' 것이라고 말한다. … 우리가 '쉽게 번 돈'이라는 표현을 쓸 때, 우리는 그것이 불법적이거나 미심쩍은 수단을 통해 획득되었음을 암시한다. 우리는 '당신이 그렇게 말하긴 쉽다'는 구절을 비판으로 사용하는데, 대개 우리가 누군가의 의견이 틀렸음을 입증하려 할 때 그러하다. 이는 우리가 '옳은' 방식은 필연적으로 더 힘든 것이라고 자동적으로 받아들이는 것과 같다. 내 경험상 이것은 거의 의심되지 않는다. 당신이 정말 이 신성한 소에 맞선다면 무슨 일이 생길까? 우리는 중요하고 가치 있는 무언가가 쉽게 달성될 수 있다는 것을 잠시도 멈춰 고려하지 않는다. 우리가 중요한 것을 하지 못하게 하는 가장 큰 것이 그것에 큰 노력이 들어가야 한다는 잘못된 가정이라면 어떨까?

• **assumption** 가정; 전제; 추정 **revealing** (흥미로운 사실을) 드러내는, 보여 주는; (옷이) 살을 드러내는, 노출이 심한 **easy money** 쉽게 번 돈 **obtain** 획득하다; 얻다; 달성하다 **questionable** 미심쩍은, 의심스러운 **inevitably** 필연적으로, 불가피하게 **sacred cow** 신성한 소, 성우 ((지나치게 신성시되어 비판·의심이 허용되지 않는 관습·제도 등))

① 어떤 어려움이든 피하려는 경향에 저항하다

② 격식을 차린 언어를 사용하는 것의 압박으로부터 벗어나다

③ 힘든 일만이 가치 있다는 굳은 믿음을 의심하다

• **tendency** 경향; 성향; 동향 **hardship** 어려움

해설 밑줄 문장은 당신이 정말 '이 신성한 소에 맞선다'면 무슨 일이 생기는지를 묻는다. 밑줄 문장 앞에서는 옳은 방식이 더 힘들다는 생각이 거의 의심되지 않는다고 했으며, 뒤에서는 중요한 것에는 큰 노력이 들어가야 한다는 잘못된 가정이 우리가 중요한 것을 하지 못하게 하는 것인지 의문을 제기했다. 따라서 가치 있는 것은 힘든 방식으로만 얻을 수 있다는 생각에 맞서는 것과 연결됨을 추론할 수 있다. 앞에서부터 살펴보면, 중요하고 가치 있는 것은 힘들다는 우리의 믿음이 언어에 반영된 것을 설명한다. 따라서 밑줄 친 부분이 의미하는 바로 가장 적절한 것은 ③ 'doubt the solid belief that only hard work is worthy (힘든 일만이 가치 있다는 굳은 믿음을 의심하다)'이다. 어려움을 피하려는 경향에 저항하는 것이 아니라 가치 있는 것은 무조건 어려움을 수반한다는 생각에 맞서는 것이므로 ①은 적절하지 않으며, 격식을 차린 언어를 사용하는 것의 압박감에 대한 내용이 아니므로 ②도 적절하지 않다.

2 ②

해석 폭(다들 조금은 번아웃되었다고 느낀다)과 깊이(몇몇은 너무 번아웃되어서 더는 그들의 일을 할 수 없다)에 대한 필요의 균형을 맞추기 위해 우리는 번아웃을 '상태'가 아니라 '스펙트럼'으로 생각해야 한다. 번아웃에 대한 대부분의 대중적인 논의에서 우리는 '번아웃된' 근로자들에 대해, 마치 그 현상이 흑백이 분명한 것처럼 얘기한다. … 전구의 경우에서처럼, 번아웃된 것과 안 된 것 사이의 명확한 경계가 있다면, 그렇다면 우리는 자신이 번아웃되었다고 말하지만 여전히 자신의 일을 능숙하게 해내는 사람들을 분류할 좋은 방법이 없다. 번아웃을 스펙트럼으로 생각하는 것이 이 문제를 해결하는데, 번아웃을 주장하지만 그것에 의해 쇠약해지지 않는 사람들은 그저 부분적이거나 덜 심한 형태의 번아웃에 대처하고 있는 것이다. 그들은 번아웃'되고 있지' 않으면서 번아웃을 겪는다. 번아웃은 마지막 진술을 하지 않았다.

• **breadth** 폭, 너비 **depth** 깊이 **spectrum** 스펙트럼, (변하는) 범위
black and white (논리 등이) 흑백이 분명한 **categorize** 분류하다
competently 능숙하게, 유능하게 **partial** 부분적인
① 번아웃에 대한 대중적인 논의는 끝나지 않았다.
② 더 심한 정도의 지침의 여지가 여전히 있다.
③ 지침의 정도는 개개인의 인식에 의해 형성된다.
• **perception** 인식, 인지; 지각

해설 밑줄 문장은 '번아웃은 마지막 진술을 하지 않았다'고 했다. 앞 문장부터 보면, 그저 부분적이거나 덜 심한 형태의 번아웃에 대처하고 있는 사람들은 번아웃되고 있지 않으면서 번아웃을 겪는다고 했다. 따라서 번아웃은 다양하게 경험될 수 있음을 유추할 수 있다. 글 전반을 살펴보면 번아웃은 어떤 상태나 흑백이 분명한 것이 아니라 명확한 경계가 없는 스펙트럼으로 생각해야 하며, 번아웃을 겪지만 여전히 능숙하게 해내는 사람들이 있다고 설명한다. 이 경우는 번아웃이 부분적이거나 덜 심한 경우로서, 더 심한 형태의 번아웃이 있다는 것을 추론할 수 있다. 따라서 밑줄 친 부분이 의미하는 바로 가장 적절한 것은 ② 'There still exists room for a greater degree of exhaustion.(더 심한 정도의 지침의 여지가 여전히 있다.)'이다.

3 ③

해석 만약 당신이 '자율 주행' 자동차를 1950년대에 만들길 원했다면, 당신의 최선의 선택은 가속 장치에 벽돌을 끈으로 묶는 것이었을지도 모른다. 물론, 그 차가 스스로 앞으로 움직일 수는 있었겠지만, 그것은 속도를 늦추거나 멈추거나 장애물을 피하기 위해 방향을 돌릴 수는 없었다. … 그러나 그것이 자율 주행 자동차라는 전체 개념이 추구할 가치가 없다는 것을 의미하는가? 아니다, 그것은 우리가 지금은 가지고 있는, 자동차가 자율적일 뿐만 아니라 안전하게도 작동하게 할 수 있도록 하는 도구를 그 당시에는 아직 가지고 있지 않았음을 의미할 뿐이다. 이 한때는 멀었던 꿈이 이제는 우리의 범위 안에 있는 것 같다. 이것은 의학에서도 마찬가지이다. 20년 전에, 우리는 여전히 가속 장치에 벽돌을 끈으로 묶고 있었다. 오늘날, 우리는 환자를 유일무이한 개인으로 우리가 이해하는 것을 향상하는 방식으로 적절한 기술을 집중하기 시작할 수 있는 지점에 가까워지고 있다. 실제로, 많은 환자들이 이미 그들의 상태를 실시간으로 추적 관찰하는 장치를 착용하고 있다 ….

• **self-driving** 자율 주행; 자율 주행의 **strap** 끈으로 묶다(= tape); 끈
accelerator (자동차의) 가속 장치 **vehicle** 차, 수송 수단 **barrier** 장애물, 장벽
pursue 추구하다 **bring ~ to bear** (에너지·영향력 등을) 집중하다; 쏟다
advance 향상하다; 촉진하다; 진보하다 **unique** 유일무이한; 독특한
① 의학 교육의 중요성이 간과되었다
② 안전한 운전을 위한 장치는 그 당시에 이용할 수 없었다
③ 진보된 도구의 부족이 환자를 이해하는 데 문제를 야기했다

• **overlook** 간과하다, 못 보고 넘어가다 **pose** (위협·문제 등을) 야기[제기]하다; ~인 체하다

해설 밑줄 문장은 20년 전에 '우리는 여전히 가속 장치에 벽돌을 끈으로 묶고 있었다'는 내용이다. 직전 문장은 이것이 의학에서도 마찬가지라고 했고, 뒤에서는 우리가 환자를 유일무이한 개인으로 이해하는 것을 향상시키는 적절한 기술을 집중하기 시작할 수 있는 지점에 가까워지고 있다고 했다. 앞에서부터 살펴보면 과거에는 자율 주행 자동차를 만들려면 가속 장치에 벽돌을 끈으로 묶는 것이 최선이었는데, 당시에는 적절한 도구가 없었고 오늘날에는 멀었던 꿈이 가까워졌다고 했다. 의학에서도 과거에는 적절한 도구나 기술이 부재하여 문제가 있었다는 내용으로 대조될 것을 추론할 수 있으므로, 밑줄 친 부분이 의미하는 바로 가장 적절한 것은 ③ 'lack of advanced tools posed a challenge in understanding patients(진보된 도구의 부족이 환자를 이해하는 데 문제를 제기했다)'이다. 의학 교육의 중요성에 대한 내용은 언급되지 않았으므로 ①은 적절하지 않으며, 안전 운전을 위한 장치가 의학 분야와 관련된 것이 아니므로 ②도 적절하지 않다.

4 ②

해석 최상의 수행과 동기 부여에 관한 과학 연구는 각각의 업무가 우리의 에너지 수준에 이상적으로 맞춰져야 한다는 사실을 지적한다. 예를 들어, 분석적인 업무는 우리의 에너지가 높고 우리가 집중을 방해하는 것으로부터 자유롭고 집중할 수 있을 때 가장 잘 성취된다. 나는 주로 활기 있는 상태로 일어난다. 몇 년간, 나는 지속적으로 '아침 식사로 나의 문제를 먹는' 습관을 지켜 왔다. 나는 아직 발생하지 않은 각각의 시나리오와 대화를 과하게 생각하는 경향이 있는 사람이다. 내가 불만족스러운 고객과 대화하는 것이나 불쾌한 이메일을 처리하는 것을 미룰 때, 나는 내가 하루에 너무 많은 감정적 에너지를 낭비한다는 것을 깨닫는다. … 그래서 나에게, 그것은 언제나 내가 첫 번째로 끝내는 일이 될 것이다. 만약 당신이 자신이 아침형 인간이 아닌 것을 안다면, 당신의 어려운 일을 더 늦은 단계로 예정하는 것에 있어 전략적이도록 하라.

• **peak** 최상의, 최고의; 절정 **motivation** 동기 부여 **analytical** 분석적인
distraction 집중을 방해하는 것; 오락 **energize** 활기를 북돋우다; 열정을 돋우다
stick to A A를 지키다[고수하다]; A를 계속하다 **strategic** 전략적인
schedule 예정하다, 일정을 잡다; 일정 **late in the day** 늦은 단계에서, 늦게
① 어제의 즐거운 일들을 회상하도록 노력하는
② 가장 부담이 큰 업무들을 에너지가 가득할 때 처리하는
③ 아침에 의사 결정을 하는 것을 피하기 위해 밤에 준비하는
• **handle** 처리하다, 다루다 **demanding** 부담이 큰, 힘든; 요구가 많은

해설 밑줄 문장은 화자가 지속적으로 '아침 식사로 자신의 문제를 먹는' 습관을 지켜 왔다는 내용이다. 앞뒤의 문장을 보면 화자는 활기찬 상태로 일어나며, 발생하지 않은 일을 과하게 생각하는 경향이 있는 사람이라고 했다. 앞에서부터 살펴보면 업무는 에너지 수준에 맞춰져야 하는데, 화자는 감정적 에너지를 낭비하지 않기 위해 불쾌한 일들을 우선적으로 처리한다고 했다. 또, 만약 아침형 인간이 아니라면 어려운 일을 전략적으로 늦게 하라고 했으므로, 화자는 자신의 에너지가 높은 아침에 어려운 일을 처리함을 추론할 수 있다. 따라서 밑줄 친 부분이 의미하는 바로 가장 적절한 것은 ② 'handling the most demanding tasks while full of energy(가장 부담이 큰 업무들을 에너지가 가득할 때 처리하는)'이다. 즐거운 일을 회상하는 내용은 언급되지 않았으므로 ①은 적절하지 않고, 아침에 의사 결정을 피하는 것이 아니라 어려운 일을 처리하는 것이므로 ③도 적절하지 않다.

1 ③

¹Lawyers sometimes describe ownership / as a *bundle of sticks*.
변호사들은 때때로 소유권을 묘사한다 / '막대 묶음'으로

²This metaphor was introduced / about a century ago, // and it has dramatically transformed the teaching and practice of law.
이 비유는 도입되었다 / 약 한 세기 전에 // 그리고 이것(이 비유)은 법률 교육과 실무를 극적으로 변화시켰다

³The metaphor is useful // because it helps us see ownership / as *a grouping of interpersonal rights* [that can be separated and (can be) put back together].
그 비유는 유용하다 // 그것(그 비유)이 우리가 소유권을 간주하도록 돕기 때문에 /
개인 간의 권리들의 모음으로 [분리될 수 있고 다시 합쳐질 수 있는]

⁴When you say *It's mine* / in reference to a resource, // often that means // (that) you own / *a lot of the sticks* [that make up the full bundle]: /
여러분이 '그것은 내 것이다.'라고 말할 때 / 어떤 자원에 관해 // 흔히 이는 의미한다 //
여러분이 소유한다는 것을 / 많은 막대를 [그 묶음 전체를 구성하는] /

the sell stick, the rent stick, *the right* (to mortgage, license, give away, even destroy the thing).
즉 판매 막대, 임대 막대, 권리 (그것(자원)을 저당 잡히고, 허가하고, 증여하며, 심지어 파괴할 수 있는)

⁵Often, though, / we split the sticks up, / as for a piece of land: //
그러나 흔히 / 우리는 그 막대들을 분할한다 / 토지 한 구획에 대해 //

there may be / a landowner, / a bank (with a mortgage), / a tenant (with a lease), / a plumber (with a license (to enter the land)), / an oil company (with mineral rights).
즉 (~이) 있을 수 있다 / 토지 소유자 / 은행 (저당권을 가진) / 세입자 (임대차 계약을 맺은) / 배관공 (허가를 받은 (토지에 들어갈)) / 석유 회사 (채굴권이 있는)

⁶Each (of these parties) / owns / a stick (in the bundle).
각각은 (이러한 당사자들의) / 소유한다 / 막대 하나를 (그 묶음의)

해설

밑줄 문장 확인하기 🔎

> 6 '이러한 당사자들(these parties)' 각각은 '그 묶음의 막대 하나'를 소유함.

추론 근거로 정답 찾기 ➕

> 1 변호사들이 소유권을 막대 묶음으로 묘사함.
> 3 그 비유는 소유권을 분리하고 합칠 수 있는 권리들로 나타냄.
> 4, 5 '자원을 소유함'은 막대 묶음을 구성하는 많은 막대를 소유하는 것인데, 흔히 각 막대, 즉 권리는 분할됨.
>
> ↓
>
> 밑줄 문장의 these parties는 직전 문장에 나열된 토지 한 구획에 대한 권리를 가진 여러 당사자들을 받는다. 앞에서부터 살펴보면, 변호사들은 소유권을 분리되고 합쳐질 수 있는 막대 묶음으로 비유하는데, 자원의 소유는 묶음 전체를 구성하는 막대를 가지는 것이라고 했다. 이어서 토지 구획에 대한 권리를 예로 들어 흔히 권리를 분할한다고 설명했으므로, 막대 하나를 소유하는 것은 소유권의 일부를 가지는 것임을 추론할 수 있다.
> → ③ a right to use one aspect of the property(그 재산의 한 측면을 사용할 수 있는 권리)

오답 확인

① a legal obligation to develop the resource
그 자원을 개발할 법률상의 의무
② a priority to legally claim the real estate
법적으로 그 부동산을 차지할 우선권
*①, ② → 언급되지 않은 내용.

④ a building to be shared equally by tenants
임차인들에 의해 동등하게 공유되는 건물
→ 임차인에 한정되지 않으며, 모두가 같은 권리를 동등하게 공유하는 것이 아님.

⑤ a piece of land nobody can claim as their own
아무도 자신의 것으로 주장할 수 없는 토지의 한 구획
→ 소유권을 나눠 가지므로 각자가 권리를 주장할 수 있음.

어휘

interpersonal 개인 간의; 대인 관계의   **lease** 임대차 계약; 임대하다
license 허가(하다); 면허(증)   **metaphor** 비유, 은유   **party** 당사자; 정당
[선택지] claim 차지하다, 얻다; (권리를) 주장하다   **real estate** 부동산

구문 분석

³The metaphor is useful // because it helps us **see** ownership / **as** *a grouping of interpersonal rights* ~.
<see A as B>: A를 B로 간주하다

해석 ¹변호사들은 때때로 소유권을 '막대 묶음'으로 묘사한다. ²이 비유는 약 한 세기 전에 도입되었고, 이것은 법률 교육과 실무를 극적으로 변화시켰다. ³그 비유는 그것이 우리가 소유권을 분리될 수 있고 다시 합쳐질 수 있는, 개인 간의 권리들의 모음으로 간주하도록 돕기 때문에 유용하다. ⁴여러분이 어떤 자원에 관해 '그것은 내 것이다.'라고 말할 때, 흔히 이는 여러분이 그 묶음 전체를 구성하는 많은 막대, 즉 판매 막대, 임대 막대, 그것(자원)을 저당 잡히고, 허가하고, 증여하며, 심지어 파괴할 수 있는 권리를 소유한다는 것을 의미한다. ⁵그러나 흔히 우리는 토지 한 구획에 대해 그 막대들을 분할하는데, 즉 토지 소유자, 저당권을 가진 은행, 임대차 계약을 맺은 세입자, 토지에 들어갈 허가를 받은 배관공, 채굴권이 있는 석유 회사가 있을 수 있다. ⁶이러한 당사자들 각각은 그 묶음의 막대 하나를 소유한다.

2 ⑤

[1] *Any learning environment* [that deals with only the database instincts or only the improvisatory instincts] / ignores one half (of our ability). // It is bound to fail.
어떤 학습 환경이든 [데이터베이스 직감만을 혹은 즉흥적인 직감만을 다루는] / 절반을 무시한다 (우리 능력의) / 그것은 반드시 실패한다

[2] It makes me think of jazz guitarists: // They're not going to make it // if they know a lot about music theory / but don't know / how to jam in a live concert.
그것은 내게 재즈 기타리스트를 생각나게 한다 // 그들은 성공하지 못할 것이다 // 그들이 음악 이론에 대해 많이 알고 있다면 / 그러나 모른다(면) / 라이브 콘서트에서 즉흥 연주하는 법을

[3] Some schools and workplaces emphasize / a stable, rote-learned database.
어떤 학교와 직장은 강조한다 / 안정적이고 기계적으로 암기한 데이터베이스를

[4] They ignore *the improvisatory instincts* (drilled into us / for millions of years). // Creativity suffers.
그들은 즉흥적인 직감을 무시한다 (우리에게 주입된 / 수백만 년 동안) // 창의력은 악화된다

[5] Others emphasize creative usage (of a database), / without installing a fund of knowledge / in the first place.
다른 곳들은(다른 학교와 직장은) 창의적인 사용을 강조한다 (데이터베이스의) / 지식의 축적을 자리 잡게 하지 않고 / 애초에

[6] They ignore *our need* (to obtain a deep understanding of a subject), // which includes / memorizing and storing a richly structured database.
그들은 우리의 욕구를 무시한다 (어떤 주제에 대한 깊은 이해를 얻고자 하는) // 그리고 그것은 포함한다 / 풍부하게 구조화된 데이터베이스를 암기하고 저장하는 것을

[7] You get *people* [who are great improvisers / but don't have depth of knowledge].
여러분은 사람들을 얻게 된다 [훌륭한 즉흥 연주자인 / 그러나 지식의 깊이는 없는]

[8] You may know someone like this // where you work.
여러분은 이런 누군가를 알지도 모른다 // 여러분이 일하는 곳에서

[9] They may look like jazz musicians / and have the appearance of jamming, // but in the end / they know nothing.
그들은 재즈 음악가처럼 보일지 모른다 / 그리고 즉흥 연주를 하는 모습을 지니고 있을지 모른다 // 그러나 결국 / 그들은 아무것도 모른다

[10] They're playing intellectual air guitar.
그들은 지적인 기타 연주 흉내를 내고 있다

해설

밑줄 문장 확인하기 

10 '그들(They)'은 '지적인 기타 연주 흉내를 내고' 있음.

⌄

추론 근거로 정답 찾기 ⊕

1 데이터베이스(지식)나 즉흥적인 직감 중 하나만 쓰는 학습은 반드시 실패함.
7 창의성만 강조하면 지식의 깊이가 없어짐.
9 즉흥적 직감은 있고 깊은 지식은 없는 사람들은 재즈 음악가로 보이지만 사실 아무것도 모름.

↓

밑줄 문장의 They는 바로 앞 문장의 '즉흥 연주를 하는 재즈 음악가로 보이지만 아무것도 모르는 사람들'을 받는다. 앞에서부터 살펴보면 지식이나 창의력 둘 중 하나만 쓰는 학습은 실패하며, 창의력만 중시하면 지식의 깊이는 없어진다고 했다. 따라서 그들(They)은 지식 없이 겉보기에만 창의성을 보이고 있음을 추론할 수 있다.

→ ⑤ displaying seemingly creative ability not rooted in firm knowledge(확실한 지식에 뿌리를 두지 않은 겉보기에만 창의적인 능력을 보여주고 있는)

오답 확인

① acquiring necessary experience to enhance their creativity
자신들의 창의력을 향상시키기 위해 필요한 경험을 습득하고 있는
→ 즉흥적 직감이 있는 사람들은 창의력을 이미 가지고 있으므로 창의력을 향상시키고자 하는 것이 아님.

② exhibiting artistic talent coupled with solid knowledge of music 탄탄한 음악 지식과 결합된 예술적 재능을 보이고 있는

③ posing as experts by demonstrating their in-depth knowledge
자신들의 깊이 있는 지식을 보여줌으로써 전문가인 체하고 있는
*②, ③ → 글의 내용과 반대됨.

④ performing musical pieces to attract a highly educated audience
고학력 청중을 끌어들이기 위해 음악 작품을 공연하고 있는
→ 언급되지 않은 내용.

어휘

air guitar 기타 연주 흉내   fund (지식 등의) 축적; 자금(을 대다)
improvisatory 즉흥적인, 즉석의 *cf.* improviser 즉흥 연주자

구문 분석

[1] ~ // It **is bound to fail**.
<be bound to-v>: 반드시 v하다

해석 [1]데이터베이스(에 기반을 둔) 직감만을 혹은 즉흥적인 직감만을 다루는 어떤 학습 환경이든 우리 능력의 절반을 무시한다. 그것은 반드시 실패한다. [2]그것은 내게 재즈 기타리스트를 생각나게 하는데, 그들이 음악 이론에 대해 많이 알고 있지만 라이브 콘서트에서 즉흥 연주하는 법을 모른다면, 그들은 성공하지 못할 것이다. [3]어떤 학교와 직장은 안정적이고, 기계적으로 암기한 데이터베이스를 강조한다. [4]그들은 수백만 년 동안 우리에게 주입된 즉흥적인 직감을 무시한다. 창의력은 악화된다. [5]다른 곳들은(다른 학교와 직장)은 애초에 지식의 축적을 자리 잡게 하지 않고 데이터베이스의 창의적인 사용을 강조한다. [6]그들은 풍부하게 구조화된 데이터베이스를 암기하고 저장하는 것을 포함하는, 어떤 주제에 대한 깊은 이해를 얻고자 하는 우리의 욕구를 무시한다. [7](그 결과) 여러분은 훌륭한 즉흥 연주자이지만 지식의 깊이는 없는 사람들을 얻게 된다. [8]여러분은 여러분이 일하는 곳에서 이런 누군가를 알지도 모른다. [9]그들은 재즈 음악가처럼 보이고 즉흥 연주를 하는 모습을 지니고 있을지 모르지만, 결국 그들은 아무것도 모른다. [10]그들은 지적인 기타 연주 흉내를 내고 있다.

3 ②

[1] Gold plating (in the project) / means needlessly enhancing the expected results, / namely, adding *characteristics* [that are costly, not required], / and [that have low added value / with respect to the targets] — /
금도금은 (프로젝트에서의) / 예상되는 결과를 불필요하게 향상시키는 것을 의미한다 /
즉 특성을 추가하는 것 [값비싸지만 필요하지는 않은] /
그리고 [낮은 부가 가치를 갖는 / 목표에 관하여] /

in other words, / giving more / with no real justification / other than to demonstrate one's own talent.
다시 말해 / 더 많은 것을 쏟는 것 / 실질적인 명분 없이 / 자신의 기량을 보여주는 것 외에

[2] Gold plating is especially interesting / for project team members, // as it is typical / of projects (with a marked professional component) — /
금도금은 특히 흥미롭다 / 프로젝트 팀원들에게 //
그것이 일반적이기 때문이다 / 프로젝트에서 (뚜렷한 전문 요소를 갖춘) /

in other words, / *projects* [that involve specialists (with proven experience and extensive professional autonomy)].
다시 말해 / 프로젝트 [전문가들을 수반하는 (입증된 경험과 폭넓은 전문적 자율성을 갖춘)]

[3] In these environments / specialists often see the project / as an opportunity (to test and (to) enrich their skill sets).
이러한 환경에서 / 전문가들은 종종 프로젝트를 여긴다 /
기회로 (자신의 다양한 능력을 시험하고 향상시킬)

[4] There is therefore *a strong temptation*, / (in all good faith), / (to engage in gold plating), /
따라서 강한 유혹이 있다 / (오로지 선의로) / (금도금을 하려는) /

namely, (to achieve / *more or higher-quality work* [that gratifies the professional / but does not add value to the client's requests, / and at the same time removes valuable resources / from the project]).
즉 (달성하려는 / 더 많은 또는 더 높은 품질의 성과를 [전문가를 만족시키는 / 하지만 고객의 요구 사항에 가치를 더하지 않는 / 그리고 동시에 귀중한 자원을 없애는 / 프로젝트에서])

[5] As the saying goes, // "The best is the enemy (of the good)."
속담에도 이르듯이 // '최고는 적이다 (좋은 것의)'

추론 근거로 정답 찾기 ➕

[1] 프로젝트에서 '금도금(gold plating)'은 자신의 기량을 보여주기 위해 불필요하게 예상되는 결과를 향상시키는 것을 의미함.
[4] 고객의 요구에 맞지 않고, 자원을 없애면서 고품질을 달성하려는 금도금에 대한 강한 유혹이 생김.

↓

밑줄 문장에 인용문이 바로 소개되었고, 직전 문장에서 불필요하게 고품질의 성과를 내려는 금도금을 부정적으로 언급했다. 첫 문장에서도 금도금은 기량을 보이기 위해 결과를 불필요하게 향상시키는 것을 의미한다고 했으므로, 자신의 기량을 보이기 위한 금도금이 옳지 않음을 의미함을 추론할 수 있다.
→ ② Raising work quality only to prove oneself is not desirable.(오로지 자신을 증명하기 위해 성과의 질을 올리는 것은 바람직하지 않다.)

오답 확인

① Pursuing perfection at work causes conflicts among team members.
일에서 완벽을 추구하는 것은 팀원 간 갈등을 유발한다.
③ Inviting overqualified specialists to a project leads to bad ends.
프로젝트에 필요 이상의 자격을 갖춘 전문가를 초청하는 것은 나쁜 결과로 이어진다. → 전문가의 자격이 필요 이상인 것이 아니라 전문가가 종종 불필요하게 성과의 질을 높이려는 것이 문제라고 했음.
④ Responding to the changing needs of clients is unnecessary. 고객의 변화하는 요구에 대응하는 것은 불필요하다.
⑤ Acquiring a range of skills for a project does not ensure success.
프로젝트를 위한 다양한 기술을 습득하는 것이 성공을 보장하지는 않는다.
*①, ④, ⑤ → 언급되지 않은 내용.

어휘

added value 부가 가치   component (구성) 요소, 성분
in good faith 선의로; 옳다고 믿고   justification 명분; 정당화

구문 분석

[1] ~ / means needlessly **enhancing** the expected results, / namely, **adding** characteristics ~, / in other words, / **giving** more / with no real justification ~.
세 개의 동명사구가 동격으로 이어짐.

해석 [1] 프로젝트에서의 금도금은 예상되는 결과를 불필요하게 향상시키는 것, 즉 값비싸지만 필요하지는 않으며 목표에 관하여 낮은 부가 가치를 갖는 특성을 추가하는 것으로, 다시 말해 자신의 기량을 보여주는 것 외에 실질적인 명분 없이 더 많은 것을 쏟는 것을 의미한다. [2] 금도금은 특히 프로젝트 팀원들에게 흥미로운데, 그것이 뚜렷한 전문 요소를 갖춘 프로젝트, 다시 말해 입증된 경험과 폭넓은 전문적 자율성을 갖춘 전문가들을 수반하는 프로젝트에서 일반적이기 때문이다. [3] 이러한 환경에서 전문가들은 종종 프로젝트를 자신의 다양한 능력을 시험하고 향상시킬 기회로 여긴다. [4] 따라서 오로지 선의로 금도금을 하려는, 즉 전문가를 만족시키지만, 고객의 요구 사항에 가치를 더하지 않는 동시에 프로젝트에서 귀중한 자원을 없애는 더 많은 또는 더 높은 품질의 성과를 달성하려는 강한 유혹이 있다. [5] 속담에도 이르듯이, '최고는 좋은 것의 적이다.'

1 ⑤

[1]The practice (of risk-sharing) / is one of the most widespread and well-established activities / in human societies all over the world, //
관행은 (위험 분담이라는) / 가장 널리 퍼져 있고 잘 정착된 활동 중 하나이다 / 전 세계 인류 사회에 //
and for evidence (of just how important a practice it is), / one need look no further / than our highly institutionalized insurance industry.
그리고 증거를 위해 (그것이 얼마나 중요한 관행인가에 관한) / 더 멀리서 찾을 필요가 없다 / 우리의 고도로 제도화된 보험 산업보다

[2]People pay for insurance, // because it offers them *a means* (to protect against *unexpected and rare events* [that they would otherwise be unable to prepare for]).
사람들은 보험에 돈을 낸다 // 그것이 그들에게 수단을 제공하기 때문에 (예상치 못한 드문 사건에 대비할 [그렇지 않으면 그들이 대비할 수 없을])

[3]This concept dates as far back as *ancient Greece*, // when people teamed up in funeral societies / to make *small annual contributions* (to pay for the funeral (of *any member* [who happened to die])).
이 개념은 고대 그리스까지 거슬러 올라간다 // 사람들이 장례 협회를 구성하여 협력했던 / 작은 연간 부담금을 만들기 위해 (장례를 위해 지불하기 위한 (어느 회원의 것이든 [사망하게 된]))

[4]As a means (of insuring individuals / against the financial risk of untimely death), / the forward-thinking Athenians embraced the concept (of cooperative protection).
수단으로 (개인을 지키는 / 때 이른 죽음의 재정적 위험으로부터) / 장래를 고려하는 아테네인들은 개념을 받아들였다 (협동적인 보호라는)

[5]Building upon the ancient concept (of shared security), / the principle of risk-sharing is not only preserved / but has also evolved into diverse forms.
고대 개념을 바탕으로 (공유된 안전이라는) / 위험 분담의 원칙은 보존되었을 뿐만 아니라 / 또한 다양한 형태로 진화해 왔다

[6]Investors and entrepreneurs have crafted numerous "funeral societies" / to address a wide range of challenges.
투자자와 기업가들은 수많은 '장례 협회'를 조성해 왔다 / 다양한 위험에 대처하기 위해

해설

밑줄 문장 확인하기 

6 투자자와 기업가들은 다양한 위험에 대처하기 위해 수많은 '장례 협회'를 조성해 옴.

추론 근거로 정답 찾기 ➕

1 위험 분담 관행은 인류 사회에 널리 퍼져있고 잘 정착됨.
3, 4 위험 분담 관행은 사망한 사람의 장례를 위한 부담금을 만들기 위해 장례 협회를 구성했던 고대 그리스 때까지 거슬러 올라가며, 이때 협동적 보호라는 개념이 받아들여짐.
5 고대의 공유된 안전 개념으로부터 위험 분담의 원칙이 보존되고 다양하게 진화해 옴.

협동적 보호, 공유된 안전이라는 고대 개념으로부터 위험 분담의 원칙이 다양하게 진화했고, 오늘날에 잘 정착되어 있다고 했다. 따라서 투자자와 기업가들은 위험에 대비한 보험, 즉 상호 위험 완화를 위한 협력 네트워크를 만들어 왔을 것임을 추론할 수 있다.
→ ⑤ collaborative networks for mutual risk mitigation
(상호 위험 완화를 위한 협력 네트워크)

오답 확인

① balances between high risk and high reward
고위험과 고수익 사이의 균형 → 관련 없는 내용.
② adaptations for inevitable personal challenges
피할 수 없는 개인적인 위험에 대한 적응 → 다양한 위험에 대응하기 위해 조성한 것이라고 했으므로 틀림.
③ strategic risk distributions based on virtue
미덕에 기반을 둔 전략적 위험 분배 → 미덕에 기반을 둔 것인지는 알 수 없음.
④ step-by-step plans for unforeseen circumstances
예상치 못한 상황에 대한 단계적인 계획 → 위험을 분담하는 것이지만 위험 상황에 대비한 단계적인 계획을 세우는 것은 아님.

어휘

contribution 부담금; 기여 forward-thinking 장래를 고려[대비]하는; 진보적인 insurance 보험 *cf.* insure (위험 등에서) 지키다; 보험에 들다
untimely 때 이른
[선택지] mitigation 완화, 진정; (형벌 등의) 경감

구문 분석

[1]~ // and for evidence (**of** just **how important a practice it is**), / one need look no further ~.
전치사 of의 목적어로 의문사 how가 이끄는 <의문사+형+명+S´+V´> 어순의 명사절이 사용됨.

해석 [1]위험 분담이라는 관행은 전 세계 인류 사회에 가장 널리 퍼져 있고 잘 정착된 활동 중 하나이며, 그것이 얼마나 중요한 관행인가에 관한 증거를 위해, 우리의 고도로 제도화된 보험 산업보다 더 멀리서 찾을 필요가 없다. [2]사람들은 보험이 그들에게 그렇지(보험에 들지) 않으면 그들이 대비할 수 없을 예상치 못한 드문 사건에 대비할 수단을 제공하기 때문에 보험에 돈을 낸다. [3]이 개념은 사망하게 된 어느 회원의 것이든 그의 장례를 위해 지불하기 위한 작은 연간 부담금을 만들기 위해 사람들이 장례 협회를 구성하여 협력했던 고대 그리스까지 거슬러 올라간다. [4]장래를 고려하는 아테네인들은 때 이른 죽음의 재정적 위험으로부터 개인을 지키는 수단으로 협동적인 보호라는 개념을 받아들였다. [5]공유된 안전이라는 고대 개념을 바탕으로, 위험 분담의 원칙은 보존되었을 뿐만 아니라 다양한 형태로 진화해 왔다. [6]투자자와 기업가들은 다양한 위험에 대처하기 위해 수많은 '장례 협회'를 조성해 왔다.

2 ②

¹Indecision is one of the most damaging (of all time-wasters).
우유부단은 가장 큰 피해를 주는 것 중 하나이다 (시간을 낭비하게 하는 모든 것 중에서도)

²Don't get caught / in the endless loop (of / "Should I wash the dishes first / or tidy the living room?" // or "Is it more important to call a client / or finish this report?")
잡히지 말라 / 끝없는 고리에 (~라는 / '먼저 설거지를 해야 할까 / 아니면 거실을 정돈해야 할까?' // 혹은 '고객에게 전화하는 것이 더 중요할까 / 아니면 이 보고서를 마치는 게 (더 중요할까)?')

³This internal struggle can leave you immobilized, / consuming precious moments / and hindering productivity.
이러한 내적 갈등은 당신이 움직이지 못하게 만들 수 있다 / 소중한 순간을 소모하며 / 그리고 생산성을 저해하며

⁴Breaking free from this cycle is crucial, // as / when you're involved or in motion, // you travel on momentum — // you'll get something done.
이 순환에서 벗어나는 것이 중요하다 // (~이기) 때문에 / 여러분이 관여하거나 움직인다면 // 여러분은 가속도가 붙어 이동하게 되기 / 그리고 여러분은 무언가를 끝내게 될 것이기

⁵I believe // that most procrastination is due to the fear (of making a wrong decision), // but you're far better off making mistakes / than not making decisions.
나는 믿는다 // 미루는 버릇 대부분이 두려움에서 기인한다고 (잘못된 결정을 내리는 것에 대한) // 그러나 여러분이 실수를 하는 것이 훨씬 낫다 / 결정을 내리지 않는 것보다

⁶Think of it / like organizing a messy desk.
그것을 생각하라 / 엉망인 책상을 정리하는 것처럼

⁷Your goal is to create / a clear and functional work environment.
여러분의 목표는 만들어 내는 것이다 / 방해가 없고 실용적인 업무 환경을

⁸Avoid investing excessive time / picturing an ideal layout.
과도한 시간을 투자하는 것을 피하라 / 이상적인 배치를 상상하며

⁹Once you start and clear the chaos, // a few misplaced items won't bother you.
여러분이 일단 시작해서 혼돈을 치우면 // 약간의 잘못 놓인 물품들은 여러분을 신경 쓰이게 하지 않을 것이다

¹⁰Remember, / progress holds far greater power / than perfection.
기억하라 / 진척은 훨씬 더 대단한 힘을 가진다 / 완벽보다

해석 ¹우유부단은 시간을 낭비하게 하는 모든 것 중에서도 가장 큰 피해를 주는 것 중 하나이다. ²'먼저 설거지를 해야 할까 아니면 거실을 정돈해야 할까?' 혹은 '고객에게 전화하는 것이 더 중요할까, 아니면 이 보고서를 마치는 게 더 중요할까?'라는 끝없는 고리에 잡히지 말라. ³이러한 내적 갈등은 당신이 소중한 순간을 소모하고 생산성을 저해하며 움직이지 못하게 만들 수 있다. ⁴이 순환에서 벗어나는 것이 중요한데, 여러분이 관여하거나 움직인다면, 가속도가 붙어 이동하게 되고, 무언가를 끝내게 될 것이기 때문이다. ⁵나는 미루는 버릇 대부분이 잘못된 결정을 내리는 것에 대한 두려움에서 기인한다고 믿는데, 여러분이 실수를 하는 것이 결정을 내리지 않는 것보다 훨씬 낫다. ⁶그것을 엉망인 책상을 정리하는 것처럼 생각하라. ⁷여러분의 목표는 방해가 없고 실용적인 업무 환경을 만들어 내는 것이다. ⁸이상적인 배치를 상상하며 과도한 시간을 투자하는 것을 피하라. ⁹여러분이 일단 시작해서 혼돈을 치우면, 약간의 잘못 놓인 물품들은 여러분을 신경 쓰이게 하지 않을 것이다. ¹⁰기억하라, 진척은 완벽보다 훨씬 더 대단한 힘을 가진다.

3 ③

¹In today's interconnected world, / we frequently shift / from one trend to another / and effortlessly explore the world around us.
오늘날의 상호 연결된 세계에서 / 우리는 자주 이동한다 / 하나의 유행으로부터 다른 것으로 / 그리고 쉽게 우리 주변의 세계를 탐구한다

²Exposure to diverse experiences / keeps us mentally stimulated, / broadening our horizons / and prompting us / to acquire new skills and knowledge.
다양한 경험에의 노출은 / 우리를 정신적으로 활성화된 상태로 계속 있게 한다 / 우리의 지평선을 넓히면서 / 그리고 우리를 자극하면서 / 새로운 기술과 지식을 습득하도록

³Yet, / while external experiences enrich our lives, // it is within our own thoughts, emotions, and reflections // that we discover the true essence (of who we are).
하지만 / 외부의 경험이 우리의 삶을 풍요롭게 하는 반면 // 바로 우리의 생각, 감정, 그리고 성찰 안에 있다 // 우리가 진정한 본질을 발견하는 것은 (우리가 누구인지에 대한)

⁴Just as we follow the outside world, // we need to carve out time / to decipher *the underlying patterns* (shaping our perspectives).
우리가 바깥세상을 따르는 것처럼 // 우리는 시간을 할애해야 한다 / 근본적인 양식을 해독하기 위해 (우리의 관점을 형성하는)

⁵Through contemplation and self-analysis, / we chart *the contours of our inner world*, // which enables us to move through life / with intention and deliberation.
사색과 자기 분석을 통해 / 우리는 우리의 내면세계의 윤곽을 지도로 만든다 // 그리고 이는 우리가 삶을 헤쳐 나갈 수 있게 한다 / 목적과 신중함을 가지고

⁶In essence, / the process (of understanding and extracting meaning / from external experiences / through internal exploration) is //
본질적으로 / 과정은 (의미를 이해하고 끌어내는 것의 / 외부 경험으로부터 / 내적 탐구를 통해) / ~이다 //

what molds the fundamental structure (of our being), / defining // who we are and who we aspire to be.
근본적인 구조를 형성하는 것 (우리 존재의) / 규정하며 // 우리가 누구이고 우리가 누가 되기를 열망하는지를

⁷As it is often said, // "The only journey is the one within."
흔히 말하듯이 // '유일한 여정은 마음속에 있는 것이다.'

오답 확인

① The society one belongs influences one's self-perception. 개인이 속한 사회는 개인의 자아 인식에 영향을 준다.
→ 사회, 외부 경험보다는 내적 탐구가 영향을 준다고 함.

② External influences tend to amplify personal vulnerability. 외부 영향은 개인적 취약성을 증폭시키는 경향이 있다.
→ 외부 경험은 삶을 풍요롭게 하며 그것에서 의미를 이끌어낸다고 했음.

④ The true self emerges from a lifetime's experiences. 진정한 자아는 평생의 경험으로부터 생겨난다. → 자아를 발견하는 것이 생각, 감정, 성찰 안에 있다고만 함.

⑤ Following inner voice earns the respect of others. 내면의 목소리를 따르는 것은 타인의 존경을 얻는다.
→ 언급되지 않은 내용.

어휘

aspire 열망[염원]하다   carve out (시간을) 할애하다; 잘라내다; (노력하여) 얻다   contemplation 사색, 명상; 응시   contour 윤곽(을 그리다); 등고선   decipher 해독[판독]하다   deliberation 신중함; 숙고, 숙의   mold 형성하다; 주조하다; 주형   prompt 자극하다; (사상·감정을) 불어넣다; 즉각적인
[선택지] amplify 증폭시키다, 확대하다   conscious 의도적인, 의식적인

구문 분석

³~ // **it** is within our own thoughts, emotions, and reflections // **that** we discover ~.
<it is ~ that ...> 강조구문이 부사구인 within ~ reflections를 강조함.

해석 ¹오늘날의 상호 연결된 세계에서, 우리는 하나의 유행으로부터 다른 것으로 자주 이동하고, 쉽게 우리 주변의 세계를 탐구한다. ²다양한 경험에의 노출은 우리의 지평선을 넓히고 우리를 새로운 기술과 지식을 습득하도록 자극하면서 우리를 정신적으로 활성화된 상태로 계속 있게 한다. ³하지만, 외부의 경험이 우리의 삶을 풍요롭게 하는 반면, 우리가 누구인지에 대한 진정한 본질을 발견하는 것은 바로 우리의 생각, 감정, 그리고 성찰 안에 있다. ⁴우리가 바깥세상을 따르는 것처럼, 우리의 관점을 형성하는 근본적인 양식을 해독하기 위해 우리는 시간을 할애해야 한다. ⁵우리는 사색과 자기 분석을 통해 우리의 내면세계의 윤곽을 지도로 만들고, 이는 우리가 목적과 신중함을 가지고 삶을 헤쳐 나갈 수 있게 한다. ⁶본질적으로, 내적 탐구를 통해 외부 경험으로부터 의미를 이해하고 끌어내는 것의 과정은 우리가 누구이고 우리가 누가 되기를 열망하는지를 규정하며 우리 존재의 근본적인 구조를 형성하는 것이다. ⁷흔히 말하듯이, '유일한 여정은 마음속에 있는 것이다.'

4 ④

1 Scores of Hollywood horror movies / portray full-moon nights / as peak times (of creepy occurrences (such as murders and psychotic behaviors)).
많은 할리우드 공포영화들은 / 보름달이 뜨는 밤을 묘사한다 /
피크타임으로 (오싹한 일들의 (살인과 정신 이상 행동과 같은))

2 With regard to this lunar effect, / some researchers have argued // that people generally fall prey / to *a phenomenon* (called "illusory correlation") — / the perception of an association // when one does not in fact exist.
이러한 달의 영향과 관련하여 / 일부 연구자들은 주장해 왔다 //
사람들이 일반적으로 희생물이 된다고 / 현상의
('착각적 상관'이라고 불리는) / 즉 연계 지각 // 실제로는 그것(연계)이 존재하지 않을 때의

3 Such illusory correlations result in part / from *our mind's inclination* (to recall unusual events better / than ordinary ones).
그러한 착각적 상관은 부분적으로 기인한다 / 우리 정신의 경향에
(특이한 사건들을 더 잘 기억하는 / 평범한 것들보다는)

4 When there is a full moon // and something decidedly odd happens, // we usually notice it, tell others about it, and remember it.
보름달이 뜨면 // 그리고 확실히 이상한 일이 발생하(면) //
우리는 보통 그것을 알아차리고, 다른 사람들에게 그것에 대해 말하고, 그것을 기억한다

5 We do so // because such co-occurrences are rare and thus memorable.
우리는 그렇게 한다 // 그렇게 동시에 발생하는 일들이 드물고 그래서 기억할 만하기 때문에

6 In contrast, / when there is a full moon // and nothing odd happens, // this night without incident quickly fades from our memory.
이와 대조적으로 / 보름달이 뜨면 // 그런데도 이상한 일이 아무것도 발생하지 않는다(면) //
이 사건 없는 밤은 우리의 기억에서 빨리 사라진다

7 Due to selective recall, / links (between mutually unrelated events) / are made.
선택적인 기억으로 인해 / 연관성이 (서로 무관한 사건들 사이의) / 만들어진다

8 Only by stepping out of the moon's shadow / can we see <u>the true constellations above</u>.
달의 그림자 밖으로 나가야만 / 우리는 위에 있는 진정한 별자리를 볼 수 있다

해설

밑줄 문장 확인하기 🔎

8 달의 그림자 밖으로 나가야만 우리는 '위에 있는 진정한 별자리'를 볼 수 있음.

추론 근거로 정답 찾기 ➕

3 착각적 상관은 특이한 사건을 더 잘 기억하는 우리의 경향 때문에 발생함.
4, 6 보름달이 뜨고 특이한 사건이 발생하면 우리가 알아차리고 기억하며, 사건이 없을 때는 빨리 잊음.
7 선택적인 기억 때문에 무관한 사건 간의 연관성이 생김.

↓

우리는 특이한 사건을 선택적으로 더 잘 기억하여 무관한 사건 간의 연관성을 만들어 낸다는 내용이다. 따라서 보름달이 뜨면 오싹한 일이 일어난다는 착각에 불과한 연관성에서 벗어나야 현실을 객관적으로 볼 수 있음을 추론할 수 있다.

→ ④ an objective and unbiased understanding of reality(현실에 대한 객관적이고 편파적이지 않은 이해)

오답 확인

① the hidden truth beyond our current knowledge
우리의 현재 지식을 넘어서는 숨겨진 진실
② a sound decision uninfluenced by past experiences
과거 경험에 영향을 받지 않은 타당한 결정
③ a diverse perspective that defeat a singular viewpoint
하나의 관점을 이기는 다양한 관점
*①, ②, ③ → 언급되지 않은 내용.
⑤ an independence from commonly held beliefs
흔히 갖고 있는 믿음으로부터의 독립 → 흔한 믿음이 아니라 무관한 사건 간의 연관성을 만드는 개인의 정신 경향에 대한 내용임.

어휘

constellation 별자리   correlation 상관 (관계), 연관성
decidedly 확실히, 분명히   illusory 착각에 의한; 가공의, 실체가 없는
inclination 경향, 기질; 기울어짐   mutually 서로, 상호간에
score (*pl.* scores) 많음, 다수
[선택지] sound 타당한; 건강한; 음, 소리

구문 분석

8 Only by stepping out of the moon's shadow / **can we see** the true constellations above.
준부정어(Only) 포함 어구가 문두에 위치해 <조동사+S+V> 어순으로 도치됨.

해석 **1** 많은 할리우드 공포영화들은 보름달이 뜨는 밤을 살인과 정신 이상 행동과 같은 오싹한 일들의 피크타임으로 묘사한다. **2** 이러한 달의 영향과 관련하여, 일부 연구자들은 사람들이 일반적으로 '착각적 상관'이라고 불리는 현상, 즉 실제로는 연계가 존재하지 않을 때의 연계 지각의 희생물이 된다고 주장해 왔다. **3** 그러한 착각적 상관은 평범한 것들보다는 특이한 사건들을 더 잘 기억하는 우리 정신의 경향에 부분적으로 기인한다. **4** 보름달이 뜨고 확실히 이상한 일이 발생하면, 우리는 보통 그것을 알아차리고, 다른 사람들에게 그것에 대해 말하고, 그것을 기억한다. **5** 우리는 그렇게 동시에 발생하는 일들이 드물고 그래서 기억할 만하기 때문에 그렇게 한다. **6** 이와 대조적으로, 보름달이 떴는데도 이상한 일이 아무것도 발생하지 않으면, 이 사건 없는 밤은 우리의 기억에서 빨리 사라진다. **7** 선택적인 기억으로 인해, 서로 무관한 사건들 사이의 연관성이 만들어진다. **8** 달의 그림자 밖으로 나가야만 우리는 <u>위에 있는 진정한 별자리</u>를 볼 수 있다.

5 ⑤

[1] A researcher (at a sleep clinic in Boston) / wondered //
whether drinking coffee may not, / (in the long run), / make
people sleepier.
한 연구자는 (보스턴에 있는 수면 클리닉의) / 궁금했다 //
커피를 마시는 것이 (~하지) 않을 수도 있는지 / (장기적으로) / 사람들을 더 졸리게 하지

[2] He did a survey / and found // that / *people* [who drank coffee]
/ generally described themselves / as sleepy in the mornings.
그는 설문조사를 했다 / 그리고 발견했다 / ~임을 / 사람들이 [커피를 마신] /
일반적으로 자신들을 설명했(음을) / 아침에 졸리다고

[3] Ordinarily, / *people* [who give up coffee] / say // that /
the clear stimulus [(which[that]) they used to feel] / is no longer
there, // but that the average productivity of their day improves.
대개 / 사람들은 [커피를 끊는] / 말한다 / ~라고 /
분명한 자극은 [그들이 (커피를 마셨을 때) 느끼곤 했던] / 더 이상 없다(고) //
그러나 그들의 하루의 평균 생산성은 향상된다(고)

[4] *Some people* [who drink coffee / to "reset" their body clocks /
each morning] / end up having difficulty going to bed on time,
// which in turn makes the need for coffee greater.
일부 사람들은 [커피를 마시는 / 그들의 신체 시계를 '다시 맞추려고' /
아침마다] / 결국 제시간에 잠자리에 드는 것이 더 어렵게 된다 //
이는 결과적으로 커피에 대한 욕구를 더 크게 만든다

[5] Continual consumption of caffeine / causes a biochemical
imbalance in the body / by boosting production of counter-
caffeine chemicals.
카페인의 지속적인 섭취는 / 신체의 생화학적 불균형을 초래한다 /
카페인과 반대로 작용하는 화학 물질의 생산을 증대시켜

[6] This may also lead to side effects (such as headaches).
이것은 또한 부작용으로 이어질 수 있다 (두통과 같은)

[7] Ultimately, / coffee drinkers / become like perpetual travelers, /
constantly seeking alertness / while in <u>a never-ending state of
jet lag</u>.
결국 / 커피를 마시는 사람들은 / 영원한 여행자처럼 된다 /
끊임없이 각성을 추구하는 / 끝없는 시차증 상태에 있으면서

해설

밑줄 문장 확인하기 

> **7** 결국 커피를 마시는 사람들은 '끝없는 시차증 상태'에 있으면서
> 끊임없이 각성을 추구하는 영원한 여행자처럼 됨.

⌄

추론 근거로 정답 찾기 ⊕

> **2** 커피를 마시는 사람들이 아침에 졸리다고 느낌.
> **4, 5** 아침마다 커피를 마시면 제시간에 잠들기 어려워서 커피를
> 더 찾게 되고, 카페인을 지속적으로 섭취하면 생화학적으로 불균
> 형해짐.

↓

카페인을 계속 섭취하는 것이 오히려 제시간의 수면을 방해해서
피곤하게 만들고 신체의 생화학적 불균형을 초래한다는 내용이
다. 따라서 커피를 마시는 사람들은 몸의 자연스러운 수면 리듬이
만성적으로 방해받음을 추론할 수 있다.
→ ⑤ a chronic disruption to the body's natural sleep
rhythm(몸의 자연스러운 수면 리듬에 대한 만성적 붕괴)

오답 확인

① an imbalance between emotions and surroundings
감정과 환경 간의 불균형
② a mismatch of personal commitments and sleep
cycles 개인적 책무와 수면 주기의 부조화
③ an irregular work schedule due to fluctuating
deadlines 변동을 거듭하는 마감일로 인한 불규칙한 업무 일정
④ an ongoing conflict of managing sleep and work
demands 수면과 업무 요구 간의 관리에 있어서의 지속적인 충돌
*①, ②, ③, ④ → 언급되지 않은 내용.

어휘

alertness 각성; 빈틈없음　biochemical 생화학적　boost 증대시키다,
돋우다; 밀어 올리다　jet-lag 시차증　perpetual 영원한; 끊임없는;
종신의
[선택지] chronic 만성적인　commitment 책무; 전념
disruption 붕괴; 분열　fluctuating 변동을 거듭하는

구문 분석

[3] Ordinarily, / *people* [who give up coffee] / say // **that** /
the clear stimulus [(which[that]) they used to feel] / is no
longer there, // 　but　 **that** the average productivity of their
day improves.
say의 목적어로 that이 이끄는 두 개의 명사절이 but으로 병렬 연
결됨.

해석 **[1]** 보스턴에 있는 수면 클리닉의 한 연구자는 커피를 마시는 것이 장기적으로 사람들을 더 졸리게 하지 않을 수도 있는지 궁금했다. **[2]** 그는 설문조사를 했고 커피를 마신 사람
들이 일반적으로 자신들이 아침에 졸리다고 설명했음을 발견했다. **[3]** 대개, 커피를 끊는 사람들은 그들이 (커피를 마셨을 때) 느끼곤 했던 분명한 자극은 더 이상 없으나 그들의 하루
의 평균 생산성은 향상된다고 말한다. **[4]** 그들의 신체 시계를 '다시 맞추려고' 아침마다 커피를 마시는 일부 사람들은 결국 제시간에 잠자리에 드는 것이 더 어렵게 되고, 이는 결과적
으로 커피에 대한 욕구를 더 크게 만든다. **[5]** 카페인의 지속적인 섭취는 카페인과 반대로 작용하는 화학 물질의 생산을 증대시켜 신체의 생화학적 불균형을 초래한다. **[6]** 이것은 또한
두통과 같은 부작용으로 이어질 수 있다. **[7]** 결국, 커피를 마시는 사람들은 <u>끝없는 시차증</u> 상태에 있으면서 끊임없이 각성을 추구하는 영원한 여행자처럼 된다.

1 ④

[1] Language has two interrelated benefits: // one is that it is social, //
언어에는 서로 밀접한 연관을 갖는 이점이 두 가지 있다 // 하나는 그것이 사교적이라는 것이다 //

and the other is // that it supplies *expressions* (to make *thoughts* public [that would otherwise remain private]).
그리고 다른 하나는 ~이다 // 그것이 표현들을 제공한다는 점 (생각들을 공공연하게 만들 수 있는 [그렇지 않으면 사적인 것으로 남아 있을])

[2] When we see or hear *something* [that a companion is not looking at or listening to], //
무언가를 우리가 보거나 들을 때 [친구가 보거나 듣고 있지 않은] //

we can usually make him or her aware of it / by saying, "look," or "listen," / or even by a simple gesture.
우리는 보통 그나 그녀가 그것을 알아차리게 할 수 있다 / "봐" 또는 "들어봐"라고 말함으로써 / 혹은 심지어 간단한 몸짓으로도

[3] But / if we saw a fox, / (for example), "yesterday," // it wouldn't be possible without language / to communicate this fact / to *anyone* [who wasn't present with us at that moment].
그러나 / 우리가 여우를 봤다면 / (예를 들어) '어제' // (~은) 언어 없이 가능하지 않을 것이다 / 이 사실을 전달하는 것은 / 누군가에게 [그때 우리와 같이 있지 않았던]

[4] This depends upon the fact // that the word "fox" applies equally / to *a fox* (seen) / or *a fox* (remembered), // so that we can make a memory or thought known to others.
이것은 사실에 달렸다 // '여우'라는 단어가 똑같이 적용된다는 / 여우에 (목격된) / 또는 여우(에) (기억되는) // 그래서 우리는 기억이나 생각을 다른 이들에게 알릴 수 있다

[5] Language unlocks the past experience, / transforming "yesterday's fox" / into *a story* [(which[that]) others can see].
언어는 과거의 경험을 해제한다 / 그리고 '어제의 여우'를 변형시킨다 / 이야기로 [다른 사람들이 볼 수 있는]

[6] Without its unique ability, / we can only see *the canvas* (devoid of color).
그것의 독특한 능력이 없다면 / 우리는 캔버스만을 볼 수 있다 (색채가 없는)

해설

밑줄 문장 확인하기 ⊙

6 '그것의 독특한 능력(its unique ability)'이 없다면 우리는 '색채가 없는 캔버스'만을 볼 수 있음.

추론 근거로 정답 찾기 ⊙

1 표현하지 않으면 개인에게만 남을 수 있는 생각들을 언어를 통해 드러낼 수 있음.
4 언어 사용을 통해 타인에게 기억이나 생각 전달이 가능함.
5 언어는 개인적 과거 경험을 타인이 볼 수 있게 변형함.

its unique ability는 앞 문장에 언급된 개인적 과거 경험을 타인이 볼 수 있게 변형하는 언어의 능력을 의미한다. 또한 앞에서 언어는 개인적인 생각이나 기억을 타인에게 전달 가능하게 한다고 했다. 따라서 이 능력이 없다면 이미 널리 알려진 세상의 인식이나 이해(대중의 의식 속 기존 개념)만을 언급할 수 있을 것임을 추론할 수 있다.

→ ④ preexisting notions within the public consciousness(대중의 의식 속 기존 개념)

오답 확인

① distorted reality constructed by individual bias
개인적 편향에 의해 구성된 왜곡된 현실
② a limited amount of nuance in emotional depth
감정적 깊이에서 제한된 양의 뉘앙스
③ direct experience independent from past interpretations
과거의 해석으로부터 독립적인 직접적 경험
⑤ a loss of connection with personal authenticity
개인적인 진정성과의 연결 손실
*①, ②, ③, ⑤ → 언급되지 않은 내용.

어휘

companion 친구, 동료　devoid of ~이 없는
interrelate 밀접한 연관을 갖다[갖게 하다]
[선택지] authenticity 진정성; 확실성, 신뢰성　distort 왜곡하다; 비틀다
interpretation 해석, 이해; 통역

구문 분석

[4] This depends upon the fact ~, // **so that** we can make a memory or thought known to others.
<~(,) so that>: ((결과)) 그래서 ~하다

해석 [1] 언어에는 서로 밀접한 연관을 갖는 이점이 두 가지 있는데, 하나는 그것이 사교적이라는 것이고 다른 하나는 그렇지(표현하지) 않으면 사적인 것으로 남아 있을 생각들을 공공연하게 만들 수 있는 표현들을 제공한다는 점이다. [2] 친구가 보거나 듣고 있지 않은 무언가를 우리가 보거나 들을 때, 보통 "봐" 또는 "들어봐"라고 말함으로써, 혹은 심지어 간단한 몸짓으로도 우리는 그나 그녀가 그것을 알아차리게 할 수 있다. [3] 그러나, 예를 들어 '어제' 우리가 여우를 봤다면, 그때 우리와 같이 있지 않았던 누군가에게 이 사실을 전달하는 것은 언어 없이 가능하지 않을 것이다. [4] 이것은 '여우'라는 단어가 목격된 여우나 기억되는 여우에 똑같이 적용된다는 사실에 달렸고, 그래서 우리는 기억이나 생각을 다른 이들에게 알릴 수 있다. [5] 언어는 과거의 경험을 해제하고, '어제의 여우'를 다른 사람들이 볼 수 있는 이야기로 변형시킨다. [6] 그것의 독특한 능력이 없다면, 우리는 색채가 없는 캔버스만을 볼 수 있다.

2 ③

[1] Many political scientists used to assume // that people vote selfishly, / choosing *the candidate* [that will benefit them the most].
많은 정치학자들은 가정하곤 했다 // 사람들이 이기적으로 투표한다고 / 후보를 선택하여 [그들에게 가장 많은 이익을 가져다줄]

[2] But / research on public opinion has led to the conclusion // that self-interest is a weak indicator (of policy preferences).
그러나 / 여론에 관한 연구는 결론에 이르렀다 // 이기주의는 약한 지표라는 (정책 선호에 대한)

[3] In fact, / political opinions function as <u>matching uniforms of team sports</u>.
사실 / 정치적 의견은 팀 스포츠의 공통적인 유니폼의 역할을 한다

[4] Parents of children in public school / are not more supportive of government aid to schools / than other citizens; //
공립학교 학생의 부모가 / 정부의 학교 지원을 더 지지하는 것은 아니다 / 다른 시민들에 비해 //
people [who lack health insurance] / are not more likely to support government-issued health insurance / than *people* (already covered by insurance).
사람들이 [건강 보험이 없는] / 정부에서 발급하는 건강 보험을 더 지지할 것으로 예상되지는 않는다 / 사람들보다 (이미 보험으로 보장받는)

[5] Rather, / people care about their *groups*, // whether those be racial, regional, political, or religious.
오히려 / 사람들은 그들의 '집단'을 신경 쓴다 // 그것들이 인종적이든, 지역적이든, 정치적이든, 혹은 종교적이든

[6] In matters of public opinion, / citizens seem to be asking themselves not "What's in it for me?" / but rather "What's in it for us?"
여론에 있어서 / 시민들은 스스로에게 '이것이 나한테 무슨 이익이 되지?'라고 묻는 것이 아닌 듯하다 / 그러나 오히려 '이것이 우리에게 무슨 이익이 되지?'라고 (묻는 듯하다)

[7] In essence, / political beliefs act as a way (to identify with and represent / *the groups* [(which[that]) we belong to]).
본질적으로 / 정치적 믿음은 방법의 역할을 한다 (동일시하고 대표하는 / 집단을 [우리가 속하는])

해설

밑줄 문장 확인하기 

[3] 사실, 정치적 의견은 '팀 스포츠의 공통적인 유니폼'의 역할을 함.

추론 근거로 정답 찾기

[2] 정책 선호에 있어서 이기주의의 영향은 크지 않음.
[5] 사람들은 자신이 속한 집단을 의식함.
[7] 정치적 믿음을 통해 자신의 집단을 동일시하고 대표함.

사람들은 개인의 이익보다는 자신이 속한 집단의 이익을 의식하며, 정치적 믿음을 통해 집단을 동일시하고 대표한다고 했다. 따라서 정치적 의견은 개인을 집단과 연결하는 역할을 한다는 것을 추론할 수 있다.

→ ③ personal connections to a larger group(더 큰 집단과의 개인적 연결)

오답 확인

① expressions of universal moral values
보편적인 도덕적 가치의 표현
② reflections of prevailing cultural norms
우세한 문화적 규범의 반영 → 우세한 문화가 아닌 자신이 속한 집단을 반영함.
④ significant divisions between different groups
서로 다른 집단 간의 상당한 분열 → 자신이 속한 집단을 동일시하고 대표하는 방법이라고 했을 뿐, 다른 집단들 간의 분열에 대해서는 언급되지 않음.
⑤ competitive advantages against current regulations
현재의 규정에 대한 경쟁 우위
*①, ⑤ → 언급되지 않은 내용.

어휘

candidate 후보(자); 지원자   cover (보험으로) 보장하다; 씌우다; 다루다
identify with ~와 동일시하다   insurance 보험; 보험금; 보험료
regional 지역의; 지방적인   self-interest 이기주의, 이기심; 사리사욕
[선택지] norm 규범; 표준; 기준   prevailing 우세한, 지배적인
regulation 규정; 제한; 규제, 통제

구문 분석

[2] But / research on public opinion has led to **the conclusion** // **that** self-interest is a weak indicator (of policy preferences).
that은 the conclusion과 동격인 명사절을 이끎.

해석

[1] 많은 정치학자들은 사람들이 그들에게 가장 많은 이익을 가져다줄 후보를 선택하여 이기적으로 투표한다고 가정하곤 했다. **[2]** 그러나 여론에 관한 연구는 이기주의는 정책 선호에 대한 약한 지표라는 결론에 이르렀다. **[3]** 사실, 정치적 의견은 팀 스포츠의 공통적인 유니폼의 역할을 한다. **[4]** 공립학교 학생의 부모가 다른 시민들에 비해 정부의 학교 지원을 더 지지하는 것은 아니며, 건강 보험이 없는 사람들이 이미 보험으로 보장받는 사람들보다 정부에서 발급하는 건강 보험을 더 지지할 것으로 예상되지는 않는다. **[5]** 오히려, 사람들은 그것들이 인종적이든, 지역적이든, 정치적이든, 혹은 종교적이든 그들의 '집단'을 신경 쓴다. **[6]** 여론에 있어서, 시민들은 스스로에게 '이것이 나한테 무슨 이익이 되지?'라고 묻는 것이 아니라, 오히려 '이것이 우리에게 무슨 이익이 되지?'라고 묻는 듯하다. **[7]** 본질적으로, 정치적 믿음은 우리가 속하는 집단을 동일시하고 대표하는 방법의 역할을 한다.

3 ⑤

¹The adage "practice makes perfect" / needs qualification.
'연습이 완벽을 낳는다.'라는 속담은 / 조건을 필요로 한다

²It would indeed be more correct to say // that "practice makes permanent," // for it is *practice* [that is of the right kind] // which leads to the highest levels (of skilled performance).
사실 말하는 것이 더 정확할 것이다 // '연습이 영속성을 만든다.'라고 //
왜냐하면 바로 연습이기 때문이다 [올바른 종류의] //
숙련된 수행 능력에 이르게 하는 것은 (가장 높은 수준의)

³To give an example from tennis, / imagine *a tennis player* [who had poured countless hours / into mastering the two-handed backhand / for increased power and consistency on the court].
테니스에서의 예를 들어 / 테니스 선수를 상상해보라 [수많은 시간을 쏟아 부은 /
두 손을 사용하는 백핸드를 숙달하는 것에 / 코트에서의 향상된 힘과 일관성을 위해]

⁴While it served him well early on, // this technique revealed its weaknesses // as he progressed against more skilled opponents.
그것(두 손을 사용하는 백핸드)은 초기에는 그의 요구를 잘 충족시켰지만 // 이 기술은 그것의 약점을
드러냈다 // 그가 더 숙련된 상대와 맞붙어 나아가면서

⁵Recognizing the necessity (of altering the old approach), / the player attempted to switch his swinging pattern / to a one-handed backhand.
필요성을 인식하여 (과거의 방식을 변경할) / 그 선수는 자신의 스윙 패턴을 바꾸려고 시도했다 /
한 손만 사용하는 백핸드로

⁶However, / despite the awareness (of the need for change), / ingrained muscle memory and the comforting familiarity of the old swing / kept creeping back.
그러나 / 인식에도 불구하고 (변화의 필요에 대한) /
깊이 밴 근육 기억과 이전 스윙의 안심이 되는 익숙함이 / 계속해서 살며시 돌아왔다

⁷Even when he managed to execute that stroke, // his performance became even worse // than it was / with his well-established backhand.
심지어 그가 그 타법을 실행해낼 수 있을 때에도 // 그의 동작은 심지어 더 나빠졌다 //
그것이 그랬던(나빴던) 것보다 / 그의 잘 확립된 예전 백핸드로

⁸Brick by brick, / the player had built <u>a solid fortress around himself</u>.
벽돌을 쌓듯이 차곡차곡 / 그 선수는 자신을 둘러싼 단단한 요새를 세웠다

해설

밑줄 문장 확인하기 ◉

8 벽돌을 쌓듯이 차곡차곡, 그 선수는 '자신을 둘러싼 단단한 요새'를 세움.

추론 근거로 정답 찾기 ◉

2 올바른 연습만이 완벽으로 이어지며, 연습은 영속성을 만든다고 말하는 것이 정확함.
6, 7 테니스 선수가 스윙 패턴을 바꾸려고 해도 익숙한 옛 방식이 계속 돌아오고, 바꾸더라도 옛 동작보다 나쁨.
↓
연습으로 인해 영속성이 생겨 더 좋은 방식으로의 변화가 쉽지 않고, 변화하더라도 익숙했던 것보다 좋지 못하다고 했다. 따라서 반복에 의해 최적이 아닌 습관이 굳어졌음을 추론할 수 있다.
→ ⑤ a suboptimal habit cemented by blind repetition
(기계적인 반복에 의해 굳어진 최적이 아닌 습관)

오답 확인

① a strong desire to acquire new knowledge
새로운 지식을 습득하고 싶은 강한 욕망 → 새로운 것을 습득하려는 욕망이 점점 강해진다는 내용이 아님.

② a mental stability achieved through persistence
끈기를 통해 이루어진 정신적 안정 → 끈기로 정신적 안정을 얻은 것이 아니라 안 좋은 습관이 굳었다는 내용이므로 틀림.

③ a conviction that goes beyond mere imitation
단순한 모방을 넘어선 확고한 신념

④ a defensive stance blocking meaningful competition
의미 있는 경쟁을 막는 방어적 태도

*③, ④ → 언급되지 않은 내용.

어휘

adage 속담, 격언   brick by brick (벽돌을 쌓듯이) 차곡차곡
creep 살며시 다가가다; 기다; 살금살금 걷다   execute 실행[수행]하다; 처형하다   fortress 요새; 안전한 곳   ingrained 깊이 밴; 뿌리 깊은
opponent (게임·대회·논쟁 등의) 상대   qualification 조건, 제한; 자격; 자질   serve ~의 요구를 충족시키다; 제공하다
[선택지] blind 기계적인, 맹목적인   cement 굳(히)다; 접합하다
suboptimal 최적이 아닌

구문 분석

²~ // for **it** is *practice* [that is of the right kind] // **which** leads to the highest levels (of skilled performance).
부사절 접속사 for가 이끄는 절에 <It ~ which> 강조구문이 쓰여, practice ~ the right kind를 강조함.

해석 ¹'연습이 완벽을 낳는다.'라는 속담은 조건을 필요로 한다. ²사실 '연습이 영속성을 만든다.'라고 말하는 것이 더 정확할 것인데, 왜냐하면 가장 높은 수준의 숙련된 수행 능력에 이르게 하는 것은 바로 올바른 종류의 연습이기 때문이다. ³테니스에서의 예를 들어, 코트에서의 향상된 힘과 일관성을 위해 두 손을 사용하는 백핸드를 숙달하는 것에 수많은 시간을 쏟아 부은 테니스 선수를 상상해보라. ⁴그것(두 손을 사용하는 백핸드)은 초기에는 그의 요구를 잘 충족시켰지만, 그가 더 숙련된 상대와 맞붙어 나아가면서 이 기술은 약점을 드러냈다. ⁵과거의 방식을 변경할 필요성을 인식하여, 그 선수는 자신의 스윙 패턴을 한 손만 사용하는 백핸드로 바꾸려고 시도했다. ⁶그러나, 변화의 필요에 대한 인식에도 불구하고, 깊이 밴 근육 기억과 이전 스윙의 안심이 되는 익숙함이 계속해서 살며시 돌아왔다. ⁷심지어 그가 그 타법을 실행해낼 수 있을 때에도, 그의 잘 확립된 예전 백핸드로 그의 동작이 나빴던 것보다 심지어 더 나빠졌다. ⁸벽돌을 쌓듯이 차곡차곡, 그 선수는 <u>자신을</u> 둘러싼 단단한 요새를 세웠다.

4 ②

[1]Unlike the Mesopotamian cultures, / the early Greeks paid less attention to astronomy / and more to cosmology.
메소포타미아 문화와 달리 / 고대 그리스인들은 천문학에는 더 적은 관심을 쏟았다 / 그리고 우주론에 더 (관심을 쏟았다)

[2]Their gaze was not on the precise steps of the stars, / but on *the grand stage* [upon which Earth and its cosmic companions performed].
그들의 시선은 별의 정확한 움직임에 있지 않았다 / 그러나 거대한 무대에 (있었다) [지구와 그것의 우주의 동료들이 공연하는]

[3]Because of this, / their astronomical observations were not accurate.
이로 인하여 / 그들의 천문 관측은 정확하지 않았다

[4]Time was not marked / by the strict notes (of astronomical precision).
시간은 표시되지 않았다 / 엄격한 기호로 (천문학적 정밀도의)

[5]In fact, / during the Greek times, / most dates were given / in terms of the rhythmic beats of the Olympiads, / the four-year intervals between Olympic Games.
사실 / 그리스 시대 동안 / 대부분의 날짜는 주어졌다 / 올림피아드의 주기적인 박자 관점에서 / 올림픽 대회 사이의 4년 간격인

[6]If something happened during the 10th Olympiad, // it meant the event occurred / within a four-year span.
만약 어떤 일이 열 번째 올림피아드 도중에 발생했다면 // 그것은 그 사건이 발생한 것을 의미했다 / 4년의 기간 내에

[7]Pinpointing the exact year / within those four years / proved difficult / due to this broad time frame.
정확한 연도를 특정하는 것은 / 그 4년(의 범위) 안에서 / 어렵다고 판명되었다 / 이 넓은 기간 때문에

[8]Such notations created headaches for *historians*, // who ended up <u>conducting *a symphony*</u> (guided only by a vague rhythm).
이러한 표기법은 역사학자들에게 두통을 불러일으켰다 // 결국 교향곡을 지휘하게 된 (모호한 리듬에 의해서만 인도되는)

[9]A common practice was to make educated guesses / as to the actual dates of Greek events.
어느 정도 지식을 가지고 하는 추측이 일반적 관행이었다 / (고대) 그리스 사건의 실제 날짜에 관해서는

오답 확인

① focusing more on the cultural impact of events on society
사건이 사회에 미치는 문화적 영향에 더 중점을 두는
③ documenting only significant events based on personal judgment
개인적 판단에 기반을 두어 중요한 사건만을 기록하는
④ struggling with identifying biases from factual information
사실적 정보에서 편견을 식별하려고 고심하는 → 편견을 식별하는 것이 아니라 정확한 연도 특정에 어려움을 겪는다고 했음.
⑤ taking an excessively long time to make any progress
어떠한 진전을 이루는 데 과도하게 오랜 시간이 걸리는
*①, ③, ⑤ → 언급되지 않은 내용.

어휘

akin to A A와 유사한   astronomy 천문학   educated guess 어느 정도 지식을 가지고[알고] 하는 추측   interval 간격; 사이   notation 표기[표시]법 *cf.* note 기호; 기록; 주의   time frame 기간, 시간   vague 모호한; 어렴풋한
[선택지] chronological 연대순의

구문 분석

[2]Their gaze was **not** on the precise steps of the stars, / **but** on *the grand stage* ~.
<not A but B>: A가 아니라 B

해석 [1]메소포타미아 문화와 달리, 고대 그리스인들은 천문학에는 더 적은 관심을 쏟았고 우주론에 더 관심을 쏟았다. [2]그들의 시선은 별의 정확한 움직임에 있지 않았고, 지구와 그것의 우주의 동료들이 공연하는 거대한 무대에 있었다. [3]이로 인하여, 그들의 천문 관측은 정확하지 않았다. [4]시간은 천문학적 정밀도의 엄격한 기호로 표시되지 않았다. [5]사실, 그리스 시대 동안 대부분의 날짜는 올림픽 대회 사이의 4년 간격인 올림피아드의 주기적인 박자 관점에서 주어졌다. [6]만약 어떤 일이 열 번째 올림피아드 도중에 발생했다면, 그것은 그 사건이 4년의 기간 내에 발생한 것을 의미했다. [7]그 4년(의 범위) 안에서 정확한 연도를 특정하는 것은 이 넓은 기간 때문에 어렵다고 판명되었다. [8]이러한 표기법은 결국 <u>모호한 리듬에 의해서만 인도되는 교향곡을 지휘하게</u> 된 역사학자들에게 두통을 불러일으켰다. [9](고대) 그리스 사건의 실제 날짜에 관해서는 어느 정도 지식을 가지고 하는 추측이 일반적 관행이었다.

5 ⑤

[1] If you went on an African safari / but traveled around only during daylight hours / to see animals, // you would miss out on a whole lot of action in the bush.
만약 당신이 아프리카 사파리 여행을 간다면 / 그러나 낮 시간 동안에만 돌아다닌다면 / 동물들을 보러 // 당신은 숲 속의 전반적인 많은 활동을 놓칠 것이다

[2] This is due to the fact // that a significant percentage of wildlife is active at night, / fostering a dynamic ecosystem after sunset.
이것은 사실 때문이다 // 상당한 비율의 야생 동물들이 밤에 활동적이라는 / 그래서 일몰 후에 역동적인 생태계를 조성한다

[3] By way of analogy, / we can see a similar problem / in the business world //
이를 통해 유추할 때 / (이와) 유사한 문제를 볼 수 있다 / 기업 세계에서 //

when managers are only attuned to the strongest, brightest signals (such as *highly-promoted big-ticket projects* [that carry little risk]).
관리자들이 가장 강하고 밝은 신호에만 적절히 대응할 때 (홍보가 많이 되고 주요한 계획과 같은 [위험 부담이 거의 없는])

[4] They fail to perceive / the weaker signals, / *the bolder experiments* (led by *individuals or small teams* [who prefer to stay out of the corporate spotlight]).
그들(관리자들)은 인식하지 못한다 / 더 약한 신호를 / 즉 더 과감한 실험들을 (개인이나 소규모 팀에 의해 이끌어지는 [기업의 관심에서 벗어나 있길 선호하는])

[5] Yet, / as these hidden innovators may hold / the key (to unlocking unforeseen opportunities and breakthroughs), //
그러나 / 이 숨겨진 혁신자들은 가지고 있을지도 모르므로 / 열쇠를 (예측하지 못한 기회와 돌파구를 여는 것에 이르는) //

the manager [who can pick up the "weaker signals"] / will reap big rewards.
관리자는 ['더 작은 신호'를 알아볼 수 있는] / 큰 보상을 거둘 것이다

[6] What managers need / is not just a sharper eye, / but <u>a set of night vision binoculars</u>.
관리자가 필요로 하는 것은 / 단지 더 날카로운 눈이 아니다 / 야간 투시 쌍안경 세트(이다)

해설

밑줄 문장 확인하기 🔎

6 관리자가 필요로 하는 것은 단지 더 날카로운 눈이 아니라 '야간 투시 쌍안경 세트'임.

추론 근거로 정답 찾기 ➕

1 사파리를 낮 시간에만 보면 숲 속의 많은 활동을 놓칠 것임.

3, 4 기업 세계에서도 관리자들이 크고 위험 부담이 적은 계획에만 대응하면 비슷한 문제가 발생하여, 작지만 더 과감한 것들을 놓칠 수 있음.

5 기회나 돌파구를 열 작은 신호를 알아보는 관리자들이 큰 보상을 얻을 수 있음.

↓

관리자들이 눈에 띄는 계획에만 대응하면, 더 큰 보상을 얻을 수 있는 작은 신호들을 놓칠 수 있다는 내용이다. 따라서 관리자에게 필요한 것은 기업의 관심에서 벗어나 있으면서 더 과감한 실험들을 인식할 수 있는 것임을 추론할 수 있다.

→ ⑤ directing attention to where it matters the most (가장 중요한 것에 관심을 돌리는 것)

오답 확인

① decreasing reliance on established methods
확립된 방법에의 의존을 줄이는 것
② applying information verified by specialized experts
전문가들에 의해 확인받은 정보를 적용하는 것
③ identifying the personal weaknesses of individuals
개개인의 개인적 약점을 인식하는 것
*①, ②, ③ → 관련 없는 내용.
④ looking more closely at details of challenging situations
어려운 상황의 세부 사항을 더욱 가까이 보는 것 → 어려운 상황은 언급되지 않음.

어휘

analogy 유추; 유사(점)　attuned 적절히 대응하는
big-ticket 주요한; 비싼 가격표가 붙은　binocular 쌍안경
bold 과감한, 용감한; 선명한　breakthrough 돌파구
corporate 기업의, 법인의　foster 조성하다, 발전시키다; 기르다, 양육하다
reap (성과 등을) 거두다, 얻다　unforeseen 예측하지 못한

구문 분석

[1] **If you went on** an African safari / but **traveled around** only during daylight hours / ~, // **you would miss out** on a whole lot of action in the bush.
<If+S´+동사의 과거형 ~, S+would+동사원형 …>: 만약 ~라면, …할 텐데

해석 [1] 만약 당신이 아프리카 사파리 여행을 가지만 동물들을 보러 낮 시간 동안에만 돌아다닌다면, 당신은 숲 속의 전반적인 많은 활동을 놓칠 것이다. [2] 이것은 상당한 비율의 야생 동물들이 밤에 활동적이어서 일몰 후에 역동적인 생태계를 조성한다는 사실 때문이다. [3] 이를 통해 유추할 때, 기업 세계에서 (이와) 유사한 문제를 볼 수 있는데 관리자들이 위험 부담이 거의 없는 홍보가 많이 되고 주요한 계획과 같은 가장 강하고 밝은 신호에만 적절히 대응할 때 그렇다. [4] 그들(관리자들)은 더 약한 신호, 즉 기업의 관심에서 벗어나 있길 선호하는 개인이나 소규모 팀에 의해 이끌어지는 더 과감한 실험들을 인식하지 못한다. [5] 그러나, 이 숨겨진 혁신자들은 예측하지 못한 기회와 돌파구를 여는 것에 이르는 열쇠를 가지고 있을지도 모르므로, '더 작은 신호'를 알아볼 수 있는 관리자는 큰 보상을 거둘 것이다. [6] 관리자가 필요로 하는 것은 단지 더 날카로운 눈이 아니라 <u>야간 투시 쌍안경 세트</u>이다.

1 ①

¹Surprisingly, / caffeine is not a typical stimulant; // it does not push brain cells / to become alert / and (to) perform better.
놀랍게도 / 카페인은 일반적인 각성제가 아니다 // 그것은 뇌세포가 (~하도록) 밀어붙이지 않는다 /
기민하게 되도록 / 그리고 더 잘 수행하도록

²Caffeine, / rather, / works in a roundabout way.
카페인은 / 오히려 / 간접적인 방식으로 작용한다

³Instead of triggering the release (of "up" chemicals), / it blocks the action of *the neurotransmitter, adenosine,* [that ordinarily tells the brain / to quiet down / and (to) go to sleep].
방출을 촉진하는 대신 ('기분을 북돋우는' 화학 물질의) / 그것(카페인)은 신경 전달 물질인 아데노신의
활동을 억제한다 [대개 뇌가 (~하도록) 하는 / 진정하도록 / 그리고 잠이 들도록]

⁴Since the caffeine molecule chemically resembles adenosine, // it can occupy brain cell receptor sites, / displacing adenosine.
카페인 분자는 화학적으로 아데노신과 닮았기 때문에 //
그것은 뇌세포의 수용체 영역을 차지할 수 있다 / 아데노신을 대신하여

⁵This prevents adenosine from suppressing / *the alertness* (caused by "upper" neurotransmitters, (such as dopamine)).
이것은 아데노신이 억압하는 것을 막는다 / 각성 상태를
('기분을 더 북돋우는' 신경 전달 물질에 의해 야기되는 (도파민과 같은))

⁶Thus, / caffeine, / (by disguising itself as adenosine), / fools brain cells / into remaining in a persistent state of excitability.
이렇게 / 카페인은 / 그 자체를 아데노신으로 위장함으로써) / 뇌세포를 속인다 /
지속적인 흥분 상태에 머물도록

⁷A little caffeine goes a long way.
소량의 카페인이라도 효과가 크다

⁸Experts say // that / the caffeine (in a couple of cups of coffee) / can knock out half the brain's adenosine receptors / for a couple of hours, / keeping your brain on high alert.
전문가들은 말한다 // ~라고 / 카페인이 (커피 두어 잔의) /
뇌의 아데노신 수용체의 절반을 잠들게 할 수 있다(고) / 두어 시간 동안 /
그래서 당신의 뇌가 계속해서 높은 각성 상태에 있도록 한다(고)

해설

빈칸 문장 확인하기 ❷

2 카페인은 오히려 '무엇을 함'.

추론 근거로 정답 찾기 ❶

1 카페인은 뇌세포가 기민하게 되고 더 잘 수행하게 하는 일반적인 각성제가 아님.
3 카페인은 기분을 북돋우는 화학 물질을 방출하도록 하지 않고, 뇌가 진정하고 잠들도록 하는 아데노신의 활동을 억제함.
5, 6 카페인은 아데노신이 뇌의 각성 상태를 막지 못하게 하고, 아데노신으로 위장해서 뇌세포가 계속 흥분 상태에 머물게 함.

빈칸 문장 앞에서 카페인은 일반적인 각성제가 아니라고 하고, 바로 뒤에서는 그것이 뇌가 진정하고 잠들게 하는 아데노신의 활동을 억제한다고 했다. 또한 아데노신의 각성 상태 억압을 막고 뇌를 흥분 상태로 유지한다고 했으므로, 카페인이 간접적인 방식으로 각성 효과를 낸다는 것을 추론할 수 있다.

→ ① works in a roundabout way(간접적인 방식으로 작용하다)

오답 확인

② performs with other stimulants
다른 각성제와 함께 기능하다
③ takes part in many brain functions
뇌의 많은 기능에 참여하다
④ fosters various effects of chemicals
화학 물질의 여러 가지 효과를 촉진하다 → 촉진하기보다는 오히려 신경 전달 물질인 아데노신의 활동을 억제한다고 했음.
⑤ functions differently according to its type
그것의 종류에 따라 다르게 기능하다
*②, ③, ⑤ → 언급되지 않은 내용.

어휘

disguise 위장하다; 변장(하다)　displace 대신하다, 대체하다
excitability 흥분; 격하기 쉬운 성질　go a long way 효과가 크다; 크게
도움이 되다　persistent 지속적인, 끊임없는　stimulant 각성제; 자극(물)
suppress 억압[억제]하다　trigger 촉진하다; 유발하다; (총의) 방아쇠
[선택지] roundabout 간접적인, 우회적인; 빙 도는

구문 분석

⁸Experts say // that / the caffeine ~ a couple of hours, / keeping your brain on high alert.
keeping 이하는 '결과'를 나타내는 분사구문임.

해석 ¹놀랍게도, 카페인은 일반적인 각성제가 아니며, 그것은 뇌세포가 기민하게 되고 더 잘 수행하도록 밀어붙이지 않는다. ²오히려 카페인은 간접적인 방식으로 작용한다. ³'기분을 북돋우는' 화학 물질의 방출을 촉진하는 대신, 그것(카페인)은 대개 뇌가 진정하고 잠이 들도록 하는 신경 전달 물질인 아데노신의 활동을 억제한다. ⁴카페인 분자는 화학적으로 아데노신과 닮았기 때문에, 그것은 아데노신을 대신하여 뇌세포의 수용체 영역을 차지할 수 있다. ⁵이것은 아데노신이 도파민과 같은 '기분을 더 북돋우는' 신경 전달 물질에 의해 야기되는 각성 상태를 억압하는 것을 막는다. ⁶이렇게, 카페인은 그 자체를 아데노신으로 위장함으로써 지속적인 흥분 상태에 머물도록 뇌세포를 속인다. ⁷소량의 카페인이라도 효과가 크다. ⁸전문가들은 커피 두어 잔의 카페인이 두어 시간 동안 뇌의 아데노신 수용체의 절반을 잠들게 할 수 있어 당신의 뇌가 계속해서 높은 각성 상태에 있도록 한다고 말한다.

2 ②

> [1] Throughout history, / auroral displays (in the skies at high latitudes) / have been a source of wonder, //
> 역사를 통틀어 / 오로라의 시각적 발현은 (고위도 지방 하늘의) / 경이의 원천이었다 //
> but not until the twentieth century were they understood / to be caused / by *particles* (emitted from the sun).
> 그러나 20세기가 되어서야 비로소 그것들이 이해되었다 / 유발된 것으로 / 입자에 의해 (태양에서 방출된)

↓

(B) [2] The electrically charged particles form *the solar wind* [that constantly bathes the earth] //
대전 입자는 태양풍을 형성한다 [지구를 항상 휩싸는] //
and [that, (due to interaction with the earth's magnetic field), reaches further into the atmosphere (near the poles)].
그리고 [(지구 자기장과의 상호 작용으로 인해) 대기 속으로 더 멀리 도달하는 (극지 근처의)]

[3] Variations in the solar wind are produced / by *solar storms and particle ejections*, // which tend to be more frequent // when the sun approaches the peak of its 11-year sunspot cycle.
태양풍의 변화는 야기된다 / 태양 폭풍과 입자 방출에 의해 //
그런데 이것들은 더 빈번해지는 경향이 있다 // 태양이 그것의 11년의 흑점 주기의 절정기에 다다를 때

↓

(A) [4] Such events exert *various impacts* / on the earth's environment, // which are generally called space weather.
그러한 사건들은 다양한 영향을 미친다 / 지구 환경에 //
그런데 이것들은 일반적으로 우주 기상이라고 불린다

[5] At the surface / they cause *changes in the earth's magnetic field*, // which brings about variations (in the direction of compass needles).
표면적으로 보면 / 그것들(태양 폭풍과 입자 방출)은 지구 자기장의 변화를 유발한다 //
그리고 이는 변화를 야기한다 (나침반 바늘 방향의)

↓

(C) [6] The shifts in the magnetic field / also influence *electrical currents* (flowing in the upper atmosphere) / and thereby impact on the transmission (of long-distance radio signals).
자기장의 변환은 / 또한 전류에도 영향을 미친다
(대기 윗부분에 흐르는) / 그리고 그로 인해 전송에 영향을 준다 (장거리 전파 신호의)

[7] Pilots and astronauts are subject to enhanced radiation hazard // while variations in solar heating affect atmospheric drag / and thus spacecraft orbits.
조종사들과 우주 비행사들은 높아진 방사능 위험을 겪는다 //
태양 열기의 변화가 대기 장애물에 영향을 미치는 동안 /
그리고 따라서 우주선 궤도(에 영향을 미치는 동안)

해설

주어진 글의 내용 파악하기

20세기가 되어서야 오로라의 시각적 발현이 태양에서 방출된 입자로 유발된 것으로 이해됨.

단서로 정답 찾기

(B) '대전 입자(The electrically charged particles)'는 주어진 글의 '태양에서 방출된 입자(particles emitted from the sun)'를 받아(▶ **Point 1** 대용어), 이것이 태양풍을 형성한다고 설명한다. 또한 태양풍의 변화를 일으키는 태양 폭풍과 입자 방출은 흑점 주기의 절정기에 다다를 때 빈번해진다고 설명한다.

↓

(A) Such events는 (B)에서 언급한 '태양 폭풍과 입자 방출(solar ~ ejections)'을 받으며(▶ **Point 1** 지시사/대명사, 대용어), 이것들이 지구 자기장의 변화를 야기하는 등 지구 환경에 다양한 영향을 미친다고 설명한다.

↓

(C) '자기장의 변환(The shifts in the magnetic field)'은 (A)에서 언급한 '지구 자기장의 변화(changes in the earth's magnetic field)'를 받으며(▶ **Point 1** 대용어), 이로 인한 연쇄적인 영향들을 설명하며 글을 맺는다.

어휘

bathe 휩싸다   compass 나침반   electrical current 전류
exert (영향 등을) 미치다; (권력 등을) 행사하다, 가하다   latitude 위도
particle 입자   pilot 조종사; 시험[견본]용 프로그램
pole 극지; (전체의) 극   radio signal 전파 신호   solar storm 태양 폭풍
cf. solar wind 태양풍   space weather 우주 기상   subject (~을) 겪는, 당하는; 영향을 받는; 주제   sunspot 태양의 흑점   transmission 전송, 전달

구문 분석

[1] ~, // but **not until** the twentieth century **were they understood** / to be caused / ~.
부정어구를 포함한 <not until+명사구>가 문두로 나가며 <조동사+S+V> 어순으로 도치가 일어남.

[2] The electrically charged particles form ***the solar wind*** [**that** constantly bathes the earth] // and [**that**, ~, reaches further into the atmosphere (near the poles)].
that이 이끄는 두 개의 관계대명사절이 and로 병렬 연결되어 선행사 the solar wind를 수식하는 구조임.

해석 [1] 역사를 통틀어, 고위도 지방 하늘의 오로라의 시각적 발현은 경이의 원천이었지만, 20세기가 되어서야 비로소 그것들이 태양에서 방출된 입자에 의해 유발된 것으로 이해되었다. (B) [2] 대전 입자(전기를 띠고 있는 입자)는 지구를 항상 휩싸고 지구 자기장과의 상호 작용으로 인해 극지 근처의 대기 속으로 더 멀리 도달하는 태양풍을 형성한다. [3] 태양풍의 변화는 태양 폭풍과 입자 방출에 의해 야기되는데, 이것들은 태양이 그것의 11년의 흑점 주기의 절정기에 다다를 때 더 빈번해지는 경향이 있다. (A) [4] 그러한 사건들은 지구 환경에 다양한 영향을 미치는데, 이것들은 일반적으로 우주 기상이라고 불린다. [5] 표면적으로 보면, 그것들은 지구 자기장의 변화를 유발하고, 이는 나침반 바늘 방향의 변화를 야기한다. (C) [6] 자기장의 변환은 또한 대기 윗부분에 흐르는 전류에도 영향을 미치고, 그로 인해 장거리 전파 신호의 전송에 영향을 준다. [7] 태양 열기의 변화가 대기 장애물에 영향을 미치고 따라서 우주선 궤도에 영향을 미치는 동안 조종사들과 우주 비행사들은 높아진 방사능 위험을 겪는다.

3 ②

¹In the yard of a Tennessee prison, / every movement of the inmates is tracked / by *six hidden cameras* [whose software recognizes / facial expressions, physical gestures, and group behavior patterns].
테네시주 교도소의 마당에서는 / 수감자들의 모든 움직임이 추적된다 / 여섯 대의 숨겨진 카메라에 의해 [그것의 소프트웨어가 인식하는 / 얼굴의 표정, 신체 동작, 그리고 집단행동 유형을]

²(①) Unlike *prison guards*, // who are subject to distractions and fatigue, /
교도관들과는 달리 // 주의 산만과 피로의 영향을 받는 /

the computer-vision system / is continuously alert to potentially dangerous incidents / and instantly warns prison officers // when danger is detected.
컴퓨터 비전 시스템은 / 위험해질 가능성이 있는 상황을 지속적으로 경계한다 / 그리고 즉시 교도관들에게 알린다 // 위험이 탐지되면

↓

³② The potential applications (for such artificial intelligence systems) / extend well beyond the high-security confines of U.S. state penitentiaries.
적용 가능성은 (이러한 인공 지능 시스템의) / 미국 주(州) 교도소의 엄중한 경비 영역을 훨씬 넘어서까지 확대된다

↓

⁴Computer-vision systems in hospitals / can remind staff / to wash their hands / before and after touching patients, /
병원의 컴퓨터 비전 시스템은 / 직원들에게 알려줄 수 있다 / 그들의 손을 씻을 것을 / 환자와 접촉하기 전후에 /

or (can) send alerts // when a restless patient is at the risk (of falling out of bed).
또는 경보를 보낼 수 있다 // 가만히 있지 못하는 환자가 위험에 처할 때 (침대에서 떨어질)

⁵(③) They can analyze the faces (of *people* (watching pilot TV shows or movie trailers)), // and studios can tailor their offerings / according to the data.
그것들은[컴퓨터 비전 시스템은] 표정을 분석할 수 있다 (사람들의 (시험용 TV 프로그램이나 영화 예고편을 보는)) // 그리고 스튜디오는 그것들의 작품을 조정할 수 있다 / 그 정보에 따라

⁶(④) Computers are definitely getting better / at observing and understanding / human behavior and emotions.
컴퓨터는 분명히 더욱 발전해 가고 있다 / 관찰하고 이해하는 데 있어 / 사람의 행동과 감정을

⁷(⑤) Where the proliferation (of such watchful artificial intelligence) / will lead us // remains to be seen.
확산이 어디로 ~할지는 (이러한 지켜보는 인공 지능의) / 우리를 이끌(지는) // 지켜봐야 하는 상태로 남는다

해설

주어진 문장의 내용 파악하기 

단서로 정답 찾기

1 테네시주 교도소 마당에서는 숨겨진 카메라가 수감자들의 움직임을 추적함.

2(①) 교도관들과는 달리 지속적으로 경계하고 알릴 수 있다는 컴퓨터 비전 시스템의 기능적 장점을 제시한다.
↓
3 ② '컴퓨터 비전 시스템(the computer-vision system)'을 such artificial intelligence systems로 받아, 그것의 적용 가능성이 주 교도소 경비 영역을 넘어서까지 확대된다고 언급한다.
↓
4 적용 가능성이 확대된 예로 병원에서의 컴퓨터 비전 시스템의 적용을 제시한다.

5(③) 컴퓨터 비전 시스템을 They로 받아 TV 프로그램이나 영화 스튜디오에서의 적용 가능성을 다른 예로 든다.

6(④) 컴퓨터가 사람의 행동과 감정을 관찰하고 이해하는 데 있어 발전하고 있음을 언급한다.

7 (⑤) 컴퓨터 비전 시스템을 such watchful artificial intelligence로 받아 이것이 우리를 어디로 이끌지는 지켜봐야 한다는 내용으로 글을 맺는다.

어휘

application 적용; 신청, 지원   confine 영역, 범위; 한정하다
distraction 주의 산만, 정신이 흐트러짐; 기분 전환
inmate (교도소·병원 등의) 수감자, 입소자   proliferation 확산, 급증
restless 가만히 있지 못하는; 제대로 쉬지 못하는; 끊임없는
tailor (특정한 목적·사람 등에) 조정하다[맞추다]; 재봉사
trailer 예고편; (자동차 등의) 트레일러
watchful 지켜보는; 주의 깊은; 빈틈없는

구문 분석

⁷**Where** the proliferation (of such watchful artificial intelligence) / will lead us // remains to be seen.
의문사 where가 이끄는 명사절이 문장 전체의 주어임.

해석 ¹테네시주 교도소의 마당에서는, (카메라의) 소프트웨어가 얼굴의 표정, 신체 동작, 그리고 집단행동 유형을 인식하는 여섯 대의 숨겨진 카메라에 의해 수감자들의 모든 움직임이 추적된다. ²주의 산만과 피로의 영향을 받는 교도관들과는 달리, 컴퓨터 비전 시스템은 위험해질 가능성이 있는 상황을 지속적으로 경계하고, 위험이 탐지되면 즉시 교도관들에게 알린다. ³이러한 인공 지능 시스템의 적용 가능성은 미국 주(州) 교도소의 엄중한 경비 영역을 훨씬 넘어서까지 확대된다. ⁴병원의 컴퓨터 비전 시스템은 직원들에게 환자와 접촉하기 전후에 그들의 손을 씻을 것을 알려줄 수 있거나, 또는 가만히 있지 못하는 환자가 침대에서 떨어질 위험에 처할 때 경보를 보낼 수 있다. ⁵그것들은 시험용 TV 프로그램이나 영화 예고편을 보는 사람들의 표정을 분석할 수 있고, 스튜디오는 그 정보에 따라 그것들의 작품을 조정할 수 있다. ⁶컴퓨터는 사람의 행동과 감정을 관찰하고 이해하는 데 있어 분명히 더욱 발전해 가고 있다. ⁷이러한 지켜보는 인공 지능의 확산이 우리를 어디로 이끌지는 지켜봐야 하는 상태로 남는다.

4 ③

[1] Stephen Bertman, / (in *Hyperculture: The Human Cost of Speed*), / contends // that America's addiction to speed / has transformed its values.

Stephen Bertman은 / (<하이퍼 컬처: 속도에 대해 인간이 치르는 비용>이라는 책에서) / 주장한다 // 미국의 속도 중독이 / 그것(미국)의 가치관을 바꿔 왔다고

[2] More and more information is presented / in shorter and shorter statements, // which are broadcast on radio or TV.

점점 더 많은 정보가 제시된다 / 점점 더 짧은 표현법으로 // 그리고 그것들이 라디오나 텔레비전에 방송된다

[3] A typical hour of prime-time television / has as many as thirty-six commercials, // and individual images seldom remain on screen long.

황금 시간대 텔레비전의 보통의 한 시간은 / 36개나 되는 광고를 포함한다 // 그리고 개별 이미지들이 화면에 오래 머무는 경우도 거의 없다

[4] At prime-time hours, / viewers face the dilemma (of whether they should wait for the commercials to end / or (should) start flipping the channels).

황금 시간대에 / 시청자들은 딜레마에 당면한다 (그들이 광고가 끝나기를 기다려야 할지 / 또는 채널을 돌리기 시작해야 할지의)

[5] This extends to other forms of media as well.

이것은 또한 다른 형태의 매체까지 확장된다

[6] Social media posts often have limited word counts // and news is delivered / in short, attention-grabbing headlines.

소셜 미디어 게시물은 주로 제한된 단어 총계를 가진다 // 그리고 뉴스는 보도된다 / 짧고 주의를 끄는 헤드라인으로

[7] Such short-lived impressions / lead people to expect impermanence / in all aspects of their lives, / even important principles and beliefs — /

그러한 일시적인 인상은 / 사람들이 일시성을 기대하도록 이끈다 / 그들의 삶의 모든 면에서 / 심지어는 중요한 원칙과 신념(에 있어서까지) /

persistence to be replaced by the temporary, / memory (to be replaced) by sensation, / and intellect (to be replaced) by impulse.

즉 지속성이 일시적인 것으로 대체되도록 / 기억이 (현재의) 느낌으로 (대체되도록) / 그리고 지성이 충동으로 (대체되도록)

[8] The "power of now" has immersed us / in the symphony of staccatos.

'현재의 힘'은 우리를 빠져들게 해 왔다 / 스타카토 교향곡에

추론 근거로 정답 찾기 

[1] 미국의 속도 중독이 가치관을 바꿔 왔다는 주장을 제시함.
[2] 정보는 점점 짧은 표현법으로 라디오와 텔레비전에 방송됨.
[5] 다른 형태의 매체에까지 짧은 표현법의 사용이 확장됨.
[7] 사람들이 삶의 모든 면에서 일시성을 기대하게 됨.

속도 중독이 가치관을 바꿨다는 주장을 인용하고, 정보가 짧은 표현법으로 라디오와 텔레비전에 제시되고 방송되며, 다른 매체도 마찬가지라고 했다. 또한 이는 사람들이 삶에서 일시성을 기대하게 한다고 했으므로, 현재의 순간을 중시하고 순간적인 것을 선호하는 현재의 힘은 우리가 계속해서 짧은 자극을 추구하게 해 왔음을 추론할 수 있다.

→ ③ an ongoing chase for fleeting stimuli(잠깐의 자극에 대한 지속적인 추구)

오답 확인

① an intense real-world engagement
열정적인 현실 세계 참여
② a deepening connection with the past
과거와의 깊어지는 연결
*①, ② → 관련 없는 내용.
④ a constant change for personal advancement
개인적 발전을 위한 지속적 변화
⑤ an ambition to achieve more and push boundaries
더 많은 것을 이루고 경계를 넓히려는 야망
*④, ⑤ → 개인의 발전이나 야망에 관한 내용은 언급되지 않음.

어휘

commercial 광고; 상업의, 상업적인   contend 주장하다; 겨루다
immerse 빠져들게 하다; (액체 속에) 담그다   impermanence 일시성, 비영구성   impulse 충동; 자극, 충격   prime-time (방송) 황금 시간대
sensation 느낌, 기분; 감각   staccato 스타카토, 단음; (소리가) 짧고 날카로운
[선택지] ambition 야망, 야심   engagement 참여; 약혼; 약속
fleeting 잠깐의, 순식간의; 덧없는   ongoing 지속적인, 진행 중인; 전진(하는)

구문 분석

[3] A typical hour of prime-time television / has **as many as** thirty-six commercials, // ~.
<as many/much as>: ~나 되는, ~만큼 많은

해석 [1] <하이퍼 컬처: 속도에 대해 인간이 치르는 비용>이라는 책에서 Stephen Bertman은 미국의 속도 중독이 그것(미국)의 가치관을 바꿔 왔다고 주장한다. [2] 점점 더 많은 정보가 점점 더 짧은 표현법으로 제시되고, 그것들이 라디오나 텔레비전에 방송된다. [3] 황금 시간대 텔레비전의 보통의 한 시간은 36개나 되는 광고를 포함하며, 개별 이미지들이 화면에 오래 머무는 경우도 거의 없다. [4] 황금 시간대에, 시청자들은 그들이 광고가 끝나기를 기다려야 할지 또는 채널을 돌리기 시작해야 할지의 딜레마에 당면한다. [5] 이것은 또한 다른 형태의 매체까지 확장된다. [6] 소셜 미디어 게시물은 주로 제한된 단어 총계를 가지며, 뉴스는 짧고 주의를 끄는 헤드라인으로 보도된다. [7] 그러한 일시적인 인상은 사람들이 그들의 삶의 모든 면에서, 심지어는 중요한 원칙과 신념에 있어서까지 일시성을 기대하도록, 즉 지속성이 일시적인 것으로, 기억이 (현재의) 느낌으로, 지성이 충동으로 대체되도록 이끈다. [8] '현재의 힘'은 우리를 스타카토 교향곡에 빠져들게 해 왔다.

1 ⑤

[1] It is common / for *those* [who have glimpsed something beautiful] / to express regret / at not having been able to photograph it.
(~은) 흔하다 / (~한) 사람들이 [아름다운 무언가를 언뜻 봤던] /
유감을 나타내는 일은 / 그것의 사진을 찍지 못했던 것에 대해

[2] So successful has been / the camera's role (in defining beauty) // that photographs, / (rather than the real world), / have become the standard of the beautiful.
매우 성공적이었다 / 카메라의 역할이 (아름다움을 규정하는 데 있어) //
그래서 사진이 / (실제 세계가 아니라) / 아름다움의 기준이 되었다

[3] Except for *those situations* [in which the camera is used to document commemorative events], / what moves people to take photographs / is finding something beautiful.
그러한 상황들을 제외하고 [기념행사들을 기록하기 위해 카메라가 사용되는] /
사람들로 하여금 사진을 찍게 하는 것은 / 아름다운 무언가를 발견하는 것이다

[4] Just to demonstrate // how truly beautiful their dwelling is, / house-proud hosts may well pull out home photographs / instead of showing someone around the house itself.
단지 증명하기 위해 // 자신이 사는 집이 정말이지 얼마나 아름다운지 /
자신의 집을 뿌듯해하는 주인들은 아마 집 사진을 꺼내 보일 것이다 /
누군가에게 집 자체를 둘러보도록 안내하는 대신

[5] We, too, regard ourselves as attractive / at precisely *those times* [that we believe // (that) we would look good in a photograph].
우리 역시도 우리 자신을 매력적으로 여긴다 / 바로 그때에
[우리가 믿는 // 사진 속에서 우리가 멋져 보일 것이라고]

[6] After all, / nobody exclaims, // "Isn't that ugly! I must take a photograph of it."
결국 / 누구도 외치지 않는다 // "저것 참 못생기지 않았나! 내가 사진을 찍어야겠어"라고

[7] And / even if someone did say that, // all it would mean is: // "I find that ugly thing ... beautiful."
그리고 / 설령 누군가가 그런 말을 하더라도 // 그건 다만 의미일 것이다 //
"나는 저 못생긴 것을 … 아름답다고 생각해"라는

해설
빈칸 문장 확인하기 🔎

2 아름다움을 규정하는 데 있어 카메라의 역할이 매우 성공적이어서, 실제 세계가 아니라 사진이 '무엇을 함'.

⌄

추론 근거로 정답 찾기 ➕

3 사람들은 아름다운 것을 발견하면 사진을 찍음.

↓

빈칸 문장에서 아름다움을 규정하는 데 카메라의 역할이 성공적이라고 했고, 이어서 사람들은 아름다운 것을 발견하면 사진을 찍는다고 했다. 뒤에서는 여러 예를 들어 이를 뒷받침하므로 사진이 아름다움의 기준이 되었음을 추론할 수 있다.
→ ⑤ become the standard of the beautiful(아름다움의 기준이 되었다)

오답 확인

① inspired us to create beauty in our lives
우리가 삶에서 아름다움을 창조하도록 영감을 주었다
② changed our impressions of the beautiful
아름다움에 대한 우리의 느낌을 바꾸었다
③ allowed us to remember the very moment
우리로 하여금 바로 그 순간을 기억하게 해주었다
→ 빈칸 다음 문장에 카메라의 기록이 언급되지만 글의 중심 내용과 무관함.
④ led us to search for beauty in nature
자연에서 아름다움을 찾도록 우리를 이끌었다
*①, ②, ④ → 언급되지 않은 내용.

어휘

commemorative 기념의, 기념적인   demonstrate 증명하다, 입증하다; (반대하여) 시위하다   document 기록하다; 문서, 서류
dwelling 집; 주거; 거주   exclaim 외치다, 소리치다
glimpse 언뜻 보다; 흘끗 봄   may well 아마 ~일 것이다; ~하는 것도 당연하다   precisely 바로, 정확히

구문 분석

[2] **So successful** has been / the camera's role (in defining beauty) // **that** photographs, / (rather than the real world), / have become ~.
<so ~ that …(매우 ~해서 …하다)>의 구조에서 보어인 So successful이 문두에 위치하면서 주어와 동사가 도치된 구조임.

해석 [1] 아름다운 무언가를 언뜻 봤던 사람들이 그것의 사진을 찍지 못했던 것에 대해 유감을 나타내는 일은 흔하다. [2] 아름다움을 규정하는 데 있어 카메라의 역할이 매우 성공적이어서, 실제 세계가 아니라 사진이 아름다움의 기준이 되었다. [3] 기념행사들을 기록하기 위해 카메라가 사용되는 그러한 상황들을 제외하고, 사람들로 하여금 사진을 찍게 하는 것은 아름다운 무언가를 발견하는 것이다. [4] 단지 자신이 사는 집이 정말이지 얼마나 아름다운지 증명하기 위해, 자신의 집을 뿌듯해하는 주인들은 아마 누군가에게 집 자체를 둘러보도록 안내하는 대신 집 사진을 꺼내 보일 것이다. [5] 우리 역시도 우리가 사진 속에서 멋져 보일 것이라고 믿는 바로 그때에 우리 자신을 매력적으로 여긴다. [6] 결국, 누구도 "저것 참 못생기지 않았나! 내가 사진을 찍어야겠어"라고 외치지 않는다. [7] 그리고 설령 누군가가 그런 말을 하더라도, 그건 다만 "나는 저 못생긴 것을 … 아름답다고 생각해"라는 의미일 것이다.

> [1]Most researchers agree // that short-term memory is anchored and translated into long-term memory // when we sleep.
> 연구원 대부분은 동의한다 // 단기 기억이 고정되어 장기 기억으로 바뀐다는 것에 // 우리가 잘 때

↓

(B) [2]*The process* (called memory consolidation) / appears to involve two simultaneous procedures: //
이 과정은 (기억 강화라고 불리는) / 동시에 일어나는 두 가지 절차를 포함하는 것으로 보인다 //
weakening rarely used neural connections / and strengthening the patterns of newly formed memories / by replaying them.
즉 거의 사용되지 않는 신경 연결을 약화하는 것 / 그리고 새롭게 형성된 기억들의 패턴을 강화하는 것 / 그것들을 재생함으로써

↓

(A) [3]Neuroscientist Mayank Mehta likened it / to erasing the chalkboard // so new messages do not overlap and get confused with old ones.
신경과학자 Mayank Mehta는 이것을 비유했다 / 칠판을 지우는 것에 //
새로운 메시지가 예전의 것들(메시지)과 겹쳐 혼동되지 않도록

[4]Giulio Tononi and his colleague propose // that / *the large, slow brain waves* [that dominate deep sleep] / wash the board clean / by reducing the number of active connections, //
Giulio Tononi와 그의 동료는 말한다 // ~라고 / 크고 느린 뇌파가 [숙면의 두드러지는 특징이 되는]
/ (신경) 칠판을 깨끗이 닦는(다) / 활동적인 연결의 수를 줄임으로써
while the brief bursts of faster activity / inscribe new learning.
더 빠른 활동의 짧은 (신경) 격발은 (~하는) 반면에 / 새로운 학습을 쓰는

↓

(C) [5]The wonderful result of this brain-wave activity is // that new memories are allowed to stand out clearly.
이러한 뇌파 활동의 놀라운 결과는 ~이다 // 새로운 기억이 명확히 두드러지도록 한다는 점

[6]It seems that we forget / in order to remember, // and we do this best // when we are deeply asleep, all is quiet, our breathing is slow, and the slate is clean.
우리는 잊는 것처럼 보인다 // 기억하기 위해 / 그리고 우리는 이것(기억하기 위해 잊는 것)을 가장 잘한다 // 우리가 깊이 잠들고, 모든 것이 조용하고, 우리의 숨결이 느리고, 석판이 깨끗할 때

해설

주어진 글의 내용 파악하기 

대부분의 연구원들이 자는 동안 단기 기억이 장기 기억으로 바뀐다는 것에 동의함.

⌄

단서로 정답 찾기 ➕

(B) The process는 주어진 글에서 언급한 '잘 때 단기 기억이 고정되어 장기 기억으로 바뀌는(short-term ~ we sleep)' 과정을 받으며, 이러한 기억 강화 과정에는 잘 안 쓰이는 신경 연결을 약화하고 새롭게 형성된 기억 패턴을 강화하는 두 가지 절차가 포함된다고 설명한다.(▶ **Point 1** 대용어)

↓

(A) it으로 주어진 글과 (B)에서 언급한 기억 강화 과정을 받아, 과학자들이 이를 칠판을 지우는 것에 비유한 내용을 제시한다. 느린 뇌파는 칠판을 지우는 것처럼 뇌의 신경 연결을 줄이고 빠른 뇌파는 칠판에 쓰는 것처럼 새로운 학습을 한다는 것이다.(▶ **Point 1** 지시사/대명사)

↓

(C) this brain-wave activity는 (A)에서 설명한 뇌파의 활동을 가리키며, 이를 통해 새로운 기억이 두드러진다는 결과를 제시한다.(▶ **Point 1** 지시사/대명사) 그리고 우리는 잠들었을 때 새로운 것을 기억하기 위해 잊는 것을 잘한다는 결론으로 글을 맺는다.

어휘

anchor 고정시키다; 닻(을 내리다)　burst 격발; 폭발, 파열
consolidation 강화; 통합, 합병　dominate ~의 두드러지는 특징이 되다; 지배하다　inscribe (이름 등을) 쓰다[새기다]
liken A to B A를 B에 비유하다[비기다]　neural 신경의
neuroscientist 신경과학자　overlap 겹치다; 겹치게 하다
propose 말하다, 제시하다; 제안하다　simultaneous 동시에 일어나는, 동시의　stand out 두드러지다, 눈에 띄다

구문 분석

[6]~ // **when** we are deeply asleep, all is quiet, our breathing is slow, **and** the slate is clean.
부사절 접속사 when이 이끄는 절에 we are deeply asleep, all is quiet, our breathing is slow, the slate is clean이 콤마(,)와 and로 병렬 연결된 구조임.

해석 [1]연구원 대부분은 우리가 잘 때 단기 기억이 고정되어 장기 기억으로 바뀐다는 것에 동의한다. (B) [2]기억 강화라고 불리는 이 과정은 동시에 일어나는 두 가지 절차, 즉 거의 사용되지 않는 신경 연결을 약화하는 것, 그리고 새롭게 형성된 기억들의 패턴을 그것들을 재생함으로써 강화하는 것을 포함하는 것으로 보인다. (A) [3]신경과학자 Mayank Mehta는 이것을 새로운 메시지가 예전의 메시지와 겹쳐 혼동되지 않도록 칠판을 지우는 것에 비유했다. [4]Giulio Tononi와 그의 동료는 더 빠른 활동의 짧은 (신경) 격발은 새로운 학습을 쓰는 반면에, 숙면의 두드러지는 특징이 되는 크고 느린 뇌파가 활동적인 연결의 수를 줄임으로써 (신경) 칠판을 깨끗이 닦는다고 말한다. (C) [5]이러한 뇌파 활동의 놀라운 결과는 새로운 기억이 명확히 두드러지도록 한다는 점이다. [6]우리는 기억하기 위해 잊는 것처럼 보이고, 우리는 이것(기억하기 위해 잊는 것)을 우리가 깊이 잠들고, 모든 것이 조용하고, 우리의 숨결이 느리고, 석판이 깨끗할 때 가장 잘한다.

3 ⑤

[1] It's instructive / to compare and contrast two greeting rituals: /
(~은) 유익하다 / 두 가지 인사 의식을 비교하고 대조하는 것은 /

the *handshake*, / currently the predominant greeting ritual in Western countries, / and *the handkiss*, // which was popular among European aristocrats / in the 18th and 19th centuries // (but which has since fallen out of fashion).
즉 '악수' / 현재 서구 국가에서 널리 퍼진 인사 의식인 / 그리고 '손등에 하는 키스' // 유럽의 귀족들 사이에서 인기 있었던 / 18, 19세기에 // (하지만 그 이후 유행이 지난)

[2] Both are gestures (of trust and friendship), // but they differ / in their political implications.
둘 다 몸짓이다 (신뢰와 우정의) // 그러나 그것들은 다르다 / 그것들의 정치적인 암시에서

[3] (①) Shaking hands is symmetric / and fundamentally represents equality; // it's a ritual (between supposed equals).
악수하는 것은 균형이 잡힌 것이다 / 그리고 근본적으로 평등을 나타낸다 // 그것은 의식이다 (동등하다고 여겨지는 사람들 사이의)

[4] (②) Hand-kissing, / however, / is inherently asymmetric, / setting the kisser / apart from, / and subordinate to, / the recipient of the kiss.
손등에 하는 키스는 / 하지만 / 본질적으로 불균형적이다 / 키스하는 사람을 만들어서 / ~와 다르게 / 그리고 ~에게 종속되게 / 키스를 받는 사람

[5] (③) The kisser must press his lips / on another person's (potentially germ-ridden) hands, / while simultaneously lowering his head / and possibly kneeling.
키스하는 사람은 그의 입술을 눌러야 한다 / 다른 사람의 (어쩌면 세균이 들끓는) 손에 / 동시에 그의 머리를 낮추며 / 그리고 아마 무릎을 꿇으며

[6] (④) This gesture is submissive, // and when it's performed freely, // it's an implicit promise of loyalty.
이 몸짓은 복종적이다 // 그리고 그것이 자발적으로 행해질 때 // 그것은 암묵적인 충성의 약속이다

↓

[7] ⑤ What is more, / even when the ritual is somewhat forced, // it can send a powerful political message.
게다가 / 심지어 그 의식이 다소 강요될 때조차 // 그것은 강력한 정치적 메시지를 보낼 수 있다

↓

[8] Kings and popes, / for example, / would often "invite" their subjects / to line up for public kiss-the-ring ceremonies, /
왕과 교황들은 / 예를 들어 / 흔히 자신들의 신하들을 '초대한다' / 공개적인, 반지에 키스하는 의식을 위해 줄 서도록 /

putting everyone's loyalty and submission on conspicuous display / and thereby creating common knowledge (of the leader's dominance).
모두의 충성과 복종을 눈에 잘 띄게 과시하며 / 그리고 그렇게 함으로써 누구나 아는 사실을 만들며 (지도자의 우월함에 대한)

해설

주어진 문장의 내용 파악하기 🔎

'게다가(what is more)', 심지어 '그 의식(the ritual)'이 다소 강조될 때조차 그것은 강력한 정치적 메시지를 보낼 수 있음.
(▶ **Point 2** 첨가 연결어, **Point 1** 정관사 the)
(앞에는 유사한 내용이 나오고 어떤 의식이 언급될 것을 예측할 수 있음.)

≫

단서로 정답 찾기 ➕

1, 2 악수와 손등에 하는 키스라는 두 인사 의식은 모두 신뢰와 우정의 몸짓이지만, 정치적인 암시에 있어 서로 다름.

3 (①) 악수는 평등을 나타내며 동등하다고 여겨지는 사람들 사이의 의식이라고 설명한다.

4 (②) however(하지만)로 연결되어 악수와 달리 손등에 하는 키스는 하는 사람과 받는 사람을 구분하고 종속 관계로 만드는 불균형한 것이라고 설명한다.

5 (③) 손등에 하는 키스를 하며 취하는 동작을 설명한다.

6 (④) 앞 문장의 동작을 This gesture로 받아 이것이 복종적이고, 자발적으로 행해진다면 암묵적 충성의 약속이라고 설명한다.

↓

7 ⑤ the ritual은 앞 문장의 '이 몸짓(This gesture)'을 받으며, What is more(게다가)로 이어져 강조될 때조차도 그 의식이 강력한 정치적 메시지를 보낼 수 있다고 덧붙인다.

↓

8 for example(예를 들어)로, 사실상 신하들에게 강요된 반지에 키스하는 의식으로 왕과 교황들이 강력한 정치적 메시지를 보내는 예를 든다.

어휘

asymmetric 불균형적인, 비대칭적인   conspicuous 눈에 잘 띄는, 두드러진   fall out of fashion 유행이 지나다   germ-ridden 세균이 들끓는   implicit 암묵적인, 함축적인   inherently 본질적으로; 내재적으로   instructive 유익한, 교육적인   predominant 널리 퍼진; 지배적인, 우세한   subject 신하; 과목; 주제   submissive 복종적인, 순종하는 *cf.* submission 복종; 항복; 제출   subordinate 종속된; 부차적인; 부하

구문 분석

[1] ~ / **the *handshake*,** / **currently the predominant greeting ritual in Western countries,** / ~.
the handshake와 currently ~ countries는 동격 관계임.

해석 [1] 두 가지 인사 의식, 즉 현재 서구 국가에서 널리 퍼진 인사 의식인 '악수', 그리고 18, 19세기에 유럽의 귀족들 사이에서 인기 있었던 (하지만 그 이후 유행이 지난) '손등에 하는 키스'를 비교하고 대조하는 것은 유익하다. [2] 둘 다 신뢰와 우정의 몸짓이나, 그것들은 정치적인 암시에서 다르다. [3] 악수하는 것은 균형이 잡힌 것이고, 근본적으로 평등을 나타내는데, 즉 그것은 동등하다고 여겨지는 사람들 사이의 의식이다. [4] 하지만 손등에 하는 키스는 키스하는 사람을 키스를 받는 사람과 다르게, 그리고 키스를 받는 사람에게 종속되게 만들어서 본질적으로 불균형적이다. [5] 키스하는 사람은 그의 머리를 낮추고 아마 무릎을 꿇는 동시에, 그의 입술을 다른 사람의 (어쩌면 세균이 들끓는) 손에 눌러야 한다. [6] 이 몸짓은 복종적이고, 그것이 자발적으로 행해질 때 그것은 암묵적인 충성의 약속이다. [7] 게다가, 심지어 그 의식이 다소 강요될 때조차, 그것은 강력한 정치적 메시지를 보낼 수 있다. [8] 예를 들어, 왕과 교황들은 흔히 자신들의 신하들을 '초대하여' 공개적인, 반지에 키스하는 의식을 위해 줄 서도록 하며, 모두의 충성과 복종을 눈에 잘 띄게 과시하고 그렇게 함으로써 지도자의 우월함에 대한 누구나 아는 사실을 만든다.

4 ①

¹ Imagine *a company* (asking customers // what features they want to see in their product).
회사를 상상해보라 (고객들에게 물어보는 // 그들이 자신들의 제품에서 어떤 특징을 보길 원하는지)

² Unfortunately for the company, / it is a fatal mistake / to change the product / to deliver those requested features.
그 회사에는 불행하게도 / (~은) 치명적인 실수이다 /
그 제품을 바꾸는 것은 / 그렇게 요구된 특징들을 내주기 위해

³ What is crucial / is *the forethought* (to reinvent its product and make the product better / in *a way* [that customers could never have imagined // until they saw the product]).
매우 중대한 것은 / 사전 계획이다 (그것(회사)의 제품을 재발명하고 더 좋게 만들기 위한 /
방식으로 [고객들이 절대 상상하지 못했으며 // 그들이 그 제품을 보기 전까지는])

⁴ Customers can only talk / about *the things* [that are broken] / and how they want them to be fixed.
고객들은 오직 말해줄 수 있다 / 물건들에 대해서 [고장 난] /
그리고 그들이 그것들(고장 난 물건들)이 어떻게 수리되길 원하는지(에 대해서)

⁵ An entrepreneur needs to keep in mind // that / while fulfilling customers' needs is a part of the job description, // there are other goals.
기업가는 명심해야 한다 // ~라는 것을 / 고객의 요구를 만족시키는 것이 직무 내용의 일부이긴 하지만 // 다른 목표들이 있다(는)

⁶ Part of the entrepreneur's job / is to invent the future.
기업가들의 직무 중 일부는 / 미래를 발명하는 것이다

⁷ Successful entrepreneurs understand // that the greatest satisfaction comes / not from fixing the present, / but from inventing the future.
성공한 기업가들은 이해한다 // 가장 큰 만족감이 온다는 것을 /
현재를 고치는 데서가 아니라 / 미래를 발명하는 데서

⁸ When customers seek a brighter candle, // entrepreneurs don't just pour more wax.
고객들이 더 밝은 양초를 찾을 때 // 기업가들은 그저 더 많은 왁스를 붓지 않는다

⁹ They flip the light switch.
그들은 전등 스위치를 찰칵 누른다

해설

밑줄 문장 확인하기 

9 '그들(They)'은 '전등 스위치를 찰칵 누름'.

추론 근거로 정답 찾기 ⊕

3 고객이 상상하지 못한 더 좋은 방식으로 제품을 재발명하고 개선할 사전 계획이 중요함.

6, 7 미래를 발명하는 것도 기업가의 직무에 해당하며, 성공한 기업가는 미래를 발명하는 일에서 가장 큰 만족감을 얻음.

↓

기업은 고객이 상상하지 못한 방식으로 발명하는 것이 중요하며, 성공한 기업가는 현재를 고치는 것보다 미래를 발명하는 데서 만족감이 오는 것을 안다고 했다. 밑줄 문장의 They는 앞 문장의 '기업가들'을 받으며, 이들이 당장의 고객의 요구를 넘어 새로운 것을 제시함, 즉 현재의 상황에 도전함을 추론할 수 있다.

→ ① challenge the status quo to go beyond desires
(요구를 넘어서기 위해 현재의 상황에 도전하다)

오답 확인

② adapt to changing demands and market conditions
변화하는 요구와 시장 조건에 적응하다
③ build loyal customer base through active communication
활발한 소통을 통해 충성스러운 고객층을 만들다
④ determine customer preferences based on data
데이터에 기반을 두어 고객 선호를 알아내다
⑤ gather information to navigate uncertainties
불확실성을 다루기 위해 정보를 모으다
*②, ③, ④, ⑤ → 언급되지 않은 내용.

어휘

deliver (원하는 서비스·결과 등을) 내주다, 내놓다; 배달하다
entrepreneur 기업가, 사업가   fatal 치명적인; 죽음을 초래하는
forethought (사전의) 계획, 고려; 신중, 조심   job description 직무 내용
keep A in mind A를 명심하다
[선택지] navigate (복잡한 상황을) 다루다, 처리하다; 길을 찾다
status quo 현재의 상황

구문 분석

⁷ ~ // that the greatest satisfaction comes / **not** from fixing the present, / **but** from inventing the future.
<not A but B>: A가 아니라 B

해석 ¹ 고객들에게 자신들의 제품에서 어떤 특징을 보길 원하는지 물어보는 회사를 상상해보라. ² 그 회사에는 불행하게도, 그렇게 요구된 특징들을 내주기 위해 그 제품을 바꾸는 것은 치명적인 실수이다. ³ 매우 중대한 것은 고객들이 그 제품을 보기 전까지는 절대 상상하지 못했을 방식으로 그것(회사)의 제품을 재발명하고 더 좋게 만들기 위한 사전 계획이다. ⁴ 고객들은 오직 고장 난 물건들과 그들이 그것들이 어떻게 수리되길 원하는지에 대해서 말해줄 수 있다. ⁵ 기업가는 고객의 요구를 만족시키는 것이 직무 내용의 일부이긴 하지만 다른 목표들이 있다는 것을 명심해야 한다. ⁶ 기업가들의 직무 중 일부는 미래를 발명하는 것이다. ⁷ 성공한 기업가들은 현재를 고치는 데서가 아니라 미래를 발명하는 데서 가장 큰 만족감이 온다는 것을 이해한다. ⁸ 고객들이 더 밝은 양초를 찾을 때, 기업가들은 그저 더 많은 왁스를 붓지 않는다. ⁹ 그들은 전등 스위치를 찰칵 누른다.

1 ②

1 Once upon a time, / status was bestowed upon people / by their class and birth.
옛날에는 / 사람들에게 지위가 부여되었다 / 그들의 계급과 가문에 의해

2 Nowadays, / immersed in a consumer culture of overwhelming choice, / we define our social circle / by style and aesthetics.
지금은 / 압도적인 선택의 소비문화에 빠져서 /
우리는 우리가 속한 사회적 집단을 정한다 / 스타일과 미학으로

3 As Virginia Postrel explains / in *The Substance of Style*, // our surface is our entire identity.
Virginia Postrel이 설명하는 것처럼 / <스타일이라는 실체>에서 //
우리의 외양은 우리의 정체성 전체이다

4 Before we say anything with words, // we declare ourselves / through look and feel.
우리가 무언가를 말로 이야기하기 전에 // 우리는 우리 자신을 나타낸다 / 외모와 느낌으로

5 *Here I am.* // *I'm like this.* // *I'm not like that.*
'내가 여기 있어요 // 나는 이런 사람이에요 // 나는 저런 사람이 아니에요'

6 Aesthetic identity is an expression (of <u>with whom we want, or expect, to be grouped</u>).
미적 정체성은 표현이다 (우리가 누구와 함께 분류되기를 원하거나 기대하는지의)

7 Do you want to be thought of / as *a practical, frugal person* [who sees fashion accessories as foolish and vain]?
당신은 여겨지고 싶은가 / 실용적이고 검소한 사람으로
[패션 액세서리를 어리석고 헛된 것으로 보는]

8 Or / do you prefer to seem / like *those* [who pay attention to every detail, / including personal appearance]?
아니면 / 당신은 보이기를 더 선호하는가 / (~한) 사람처럼 [모든 세세한 것들에 주의를 기울이는 /
개인의 외모를 포함한]

9 No matter what, / you'll tend to attract the like-minded / while alienating *those* [who disagree].
무엇이든 간에 / 당신은 생각이 비슷한 사람들을 끌어당기는 성향을 보일 것이다 /
(~한) 사람들을 멀리하는 동시에 [((당신과) 생각이 다른]

10 Because others make similar selections, / for similar reasons, // *I like this* becomes *I'm like this*.
다른 사람들도 비슷한 선택을 내리기 때문에 / 비슷한 이유로 //
'나는 이것을 좋아해요'는 곧 '나는 이런 사람이에요'가 된다

해설

빈칸 문장 확인하기 ⊙

6 미적 정체성은 '무엇'의 표현임.

추론 근거로 정답 찾기 ⊙

2 우리는 스타일과 미학으로 자신의 사회적 집단을 정함.
7, 8, 9 당신이 어떤 성향의 사람으로 보이기를 선호하든, 당신은 생각이 다른 사람들은 멀리하고, 생각이 비슷한 사람들을 끌어당기게 될 것임.

우리가 스타일과 미학으로 우리가 속한 사회적 집단을 정한다고 했으며, 빈칸 문장 뒤에서는 어떻게 보이길 원하든, 비슷한 사람들끼리 끌어당기는 성향을 보일 것이라고 했다. 따라서 미적 정체성은 누구와 함께 분류되기를 원하거나 기대하는지의 표현과 관련 있음을 추론할 수 있다.

→ ② with whom we want, or expect, to be grouped
(우리가 누구와 함께 분류되기를 원하거나 기대하는지)

오답 확인

① why style has become more significant than before
왜 스타일이 예전보다 더 중요해졌는지 → 지금은 스타일이 사회적 집단을 정한다고는 했지만, 미적 정체성의 표현과는 관련 없음.

③ how you dress and act in the way you like most
당신이 어떻게 가장 좋아하는 방식대로 옷을 입고 행동하는지

④ why you judge others more harshly than yourself
왜 당신이 자신보다 타인을 더 가혹하게 평가하는지

⑤ how you have been influenced by the media
당신이 대중 매체로부터 어떻게 영향을 받아왔는지
*③, ④, ⑤ → 언급되지 않은 내용.

어휘

aesthetics 미학 *cf.* aesthetic 미적인; 심미적   alienate 멀리하다; 멀어지게 만들다; 소외감을 느끼게 하다   bestow 부여[수여]하다   declare 나타내다, 보이다; 선언[선포]하다   frugal 검소한, 절약하는   substance 실체, 실질; 물질   vain 헛된, 무익한

구문 분석

2 Nowadays, / **immersed** in a consumer culture of overwhelming choice, / we define our social circle / ~.
immersed ~ choice는 '이유'를 나타내는 분사구문임.

해석 **1** 옛날에는 계급과 가문에 의해 사람들에게 지위가 부여되었다. **2** 지금은, 압도적인 선택의 소비문화에 빠져서, 우리는 스타일과 미학으로 우리가 속한 사회적 집단을 정한다. **3** Virginia Postrel이 <스타일이라는 실체>에서 설명하는 것처럼, 우리의 외양은 우리의 정체성 전체이다. **4** 우리가 무언가를 말로 이야기하기 전에 우리는 외모와 느낌으로 우리 자신을 나타낸다. **5** '내가 여기 있어요. 나는 이런 사람이에요. 나는 저런 사람이 아니에요'라고. **6** 미적 정체성은 <u>우리가 누구와 함께 분류되기를 원하거나 기대하는지</u>의 표현이다. **7** 당신은 패션 액세서리를 어리석고 헛된 것으로 보는 실용적이고 검소한 사람으로 여겨지고 싶은가? **8** 아니면 당신은 개인의 외모를 포함한 모든 세세한 것들에 주의를 기울이는 사람처럼 보이기를 더 선호하는가? **9** 무엇이든 간에, 당신은 (당신과) 생각이 다른 사람들을 멀리하는 동시에, 생각이 비슷한 사람들을 끌어당기는 성향을 갖게 될 것이다. **10** 다른 사람들도 비슷한 이유로 비슷한 선택을 내리기 때문에 '나는 이것을 좋아해요'는 곧 '나는 이런 사람이에요'가 된다.

> [1] In Madagascar, / botanists have discovered a species of tree / so big // that it can be identified in satellite images.
> 마다가스카르에서 / 식물학자들은 나무 종(種)을 발견했다 /
> (그 크기가) 너무 커서 // 인공위성 이미지로도 그것이 확인될 수 있는
>
> [2] The species is unique to Madagascar; //
> nothing like this tree has ever been seen before.
> 이 종은 마다가스카르에서만 볼 수 있다 //
> 이전에 이 나무와 비슷한 것이 발견된 적은 한 번도 없었다

↓

(C) [3] Madagascar islanders knew of its existence, // but none had seen it flower until recently, // when it flowered in an extraordinary way.
마다가스카르 섬사람들은 그것(그 나무)의 존재를 알고 있었다 // 그러나 최근에서야 비로소 그 나무가 꽃을 피우는 것을 보게 되었다 // 그런데 그때 그것은 특이한 방식으로 개화했다

[4] Botanists from England's Kew Gardens, / hearing of the event, / traveled to the island to see it for themselves.
영국 큐 식물원의 식물학자들은 / 그 사건에 대한 소식을 듣고 /
그것을 직접 보기 위해 그 섬으로 떠났다

↓

(A) [5] *Those* [who witnessed the flowering] / were amazed.
(~한) 사람들(식물학자)은 [개화를 목격한] / 매우 놀랐다

[6] They reported // that initially one very long shoot emerged alone / from the treetop.
그들은 보고했다 // 처음에 매우 긴 어린 가지가 하나 돋아났다고 / 나무 꼭대기에서

[7] Then, a few weeks later, / this single shoot began to change and (to) spread.
그런 다음 몇 주 후 / 이 한 개의 어린 가지가 (모양이) 변하면서 뻗어 나가기 시작했다

[8] They said // that in the end the thing resembled a Christmas tree.
그들은 말했다 // 결국에는 그것(가지)이 크리스마스트리를 닮게 되었다고

↓

(B) [9] Hundreds of tiny flowers then / blossomed on the branches.
그런 다음 수백 개의 작은 꽃들이 / 그 가지에서 피어났다

[10] After pollination, / the tiny flowers turn into fruit, //
수분 작용 다음에는 / 그 작은 꽃들이 열매로 바뀐다 //
but since a massive amount of energy is spent / on this reproductive cycle, // the tree cannot but collapse and die after flowering.
그러나 대량의 에너지가 소모되기 때문에 / 이런 생식 주기에 //
그 나무는 꽃을 피운 다음 쓰러져 죽지 않을 수 없다

해설

주어진 글의 내용 파악하기

식물학자들이 마다가스카르에서만 볼 수 있는 희귀한 나무 종을 발견함.

⌄

단서로 정답 찾기

(C) its는 주어진 글의 '나무 종(a species of tree[this tree])'을 소유격으로 받는다. (▶ **Point 1** 지시사/대명사) 마다가스카르 섬사람들은 그 나무의 존재를 알았지만 특이한 개화 방식은 최근에서야 봤으며, 이를 보기 위해 영국 식물학자들이 그 섬으로 떠났다는 내용이 이어진다.

↓

(A) Those ~ the flowering은 (C)의 개화를 직접 보기 위해 떠난 '영국 큐 식물원의 식물학자들(Botanists from England's Kew Gardens)'을 받아 (▶ **Point 1** 지시사/대명사) 그들이 관찰한 구체적인 개화 과정을 설명한다. 한 개의 어린 가지가 돋아나 모양이 변하며 뻗어 나가기 시작했다는 것이다.

↓

(B) the branches는 모양이 변하며 뻗어 나간 가지를 받아 (▶ **Point 1** 대용어), 그 가지에서 꽃들이 피어나고 열매로 바뀐다고 순차적 개화 과정을 설명한다.

어휘

botanist 식물학자 cannot but v v하지 않을 수 없다
collapse 쓰러지다, 무너지다 extraordinary 특이한, 비정상적인
initially 처음에, 시초에 pollination ((식물)) 수분(受粉) 작용
reproductive 생식의, 번식의 see for oneself 자신이 직접 보다,
스스로 확인하다 shoot 어린 가지, 순; 식물의 발아; 사격
witness 목격하다, 보다; 목격자; 증거(물)

구문 분석

[1] In Madagascar, / botanists have discovered a species of tree / **so** big // **that** it can be identified in satellite images.
<so ~ that ...>: 너무[아주] ~해서 …하다

3 ④

[1] Scientists construct their understanding of nature / through logical reasoning, // in which they follow *a sequence of statements* [that are true to their conclusion].
과학자들은 자연에 대한 그들의 이해를 구성한다 / 논리적인 추론을 통해 // 그리고 그 안에서 그들은 일련의 진술을 따른다 [그들의 결론에 적용되는]

[2] There are two types of logical reasoning: / inductive and deductive.
논리 추론에는 두 가지 유형이 있다 / 귀납적 (추론) 그리고 연역적 (추론)

[3] (①) Inductive reasoning begins / with a detailed truth about something / at first.
귀납적 추론은 시작한다 / 어떤 것에 대한 상세한 사실에서 / 처음에

[4] (②) Then it uses that truth / to construct a generalized understanding (of how the greater system or phenomenon functions).
그다음에 그것(귀납적 추론)은 그 사실을 이용한다 / 일반화된 이해를 구축하기 위해 (더 큰 시스템이나 현상이 어떻게 기능하는지에 대한)

[5] (③) Using this approach / to understand complex systems / can be tricky // because a few small details may not accurately represent / the entirety of the system.
이 접근법을 이용하는 것은 / 복잡한 시스템을 이해하는 데 / 까다로울 수 있다 // 몇 가지 사소한 세부 사항들이 정확하게 나타내지 못할 수도 있기 때문에 / 시스템 전체를

↓

> [6] ④ Deductive reasoning, / on the other hand, / starts with broad generalizations / and gradually focuses in / on a specific statement (of assumed truth).
> 연역적 추론은 / 반면에 / 광범위한 일반화에서 시작한다 / 그리고 점진적으로 초점을 맞춘다 / 특정 진술에 (가정된 사실에 대한)

↓

[7] The approach is most useful // when you don't properly understand the details of something, // but you can observe some of its outcomes.
이 접근법은 가장 유용하다 // 여러분이 어떤 것에 대한 세부 사항을 제대로 이해하지는 못할 때 // 하지만 여러분이 그것의 결과들 중 일부를 관찰할 수 있을 (때)

[8] (⑤) A scientist rules out one option after another, / by means of it, // until he or she has narrowed the field of truth down / to just one or a few reasonable explanations.
과학자는 선택지를 차례차례 배제한다 / 이를 사용해서 // 그 사람이 사실의 범위를 좁힐 때까지 / 단 하나 또는 몇 개의 합리적인 설명들까지

단서로 정답 찾기

1, 2 과학자들은 귀납적 추론과 연역적 추론이라는 두 유형의 논리 추론을 통해 자연을 이해한다고 언급함.

3 (①) 앞 문장에 제시된 두 유형 중 귀납적 추론은 처음에 상세한 사실에서 시작한다고 설명한다.

4 (②) 귀납적 추론을 it으로, 상세한 사실을 that truth로 받아, 귀납적 추론은 상세한 사실을 통해 일반화된 이해를 구축한다는 부연 설명이 Then(그다음에)으로 이어진다.

5 (③) 귀납적 추론을 this approach로 받아, 이 접근법으로는 복잡한 시스템을 이해하기 어려울 수 있다는 한계를 제시한다.

↓

6 ④ 연역적 추론은 넓은 일반화로 시작해 점진적으로 특정한 진술, 즉 세부 사항에 초점을 맞춘다는 구체적 내용으로, 앞서 설명한 귀납적 추론의 순서와 반대되는 내용이 on the other hand (반면에)로 이어진다.

↓

7 연역적 추론을 The approach로 받아, 이 접근법이 유용한 경우를 제시한다.

8 (⑤) 연역적 추론을 다시 it으로 받아, 그것으로 과학자가 선택지의 범위를 좁힌다고 부연 설명한다.

어휘

assume 가정하다; 추정하다   complex 복잡한; 복합의; 복합 빌딩   deductive 연역적인, 추론적인   generalized 일반화된, 일반적인   *cf.* generalization 일반화, 보편화   inductive 귀납적인, 귀납의   outcome 결과, 성과; 결론   phenomenon 현상   reasoning 추론, 추리   rule out 배제하다, 제외시키다

구문 분석

[7] The approach is most useful // **when** you don't properly understand the details of something, // [but] you can observe some of its outcomes.
when이 이끄는 부사절 안에서 두 개의 절이 but으로 병렬 연결됨.

해석 [1] 과학자들은 논리적인 추론을 통해 자연에 대한 그들의 이해를 구성하고, 그 안에서 그들은 그들의 결론에 적용되는 일련의 진술을 따른다. [2] 논리 추론에는 두 가지 유형이 있는데, 귀납적 추론과 연역적 추론이다. [3] 귀납적 추론은 처음에 어떤 것에 대한 상세한 사실에서 시작한다. [4] 그다음에 귀납적 추론은 더 큰 시스템이나 현상이 어떻게 기능하는지에 대한 일반화된 이해를 구축하기 위해 그 사실을 이용한다. [5] 몇 가지 사소한 세부 사항들이 시스템 전체를 정확하게 나타내지 못할 수도 있기 때문에, 복잡한 시스템을 이해하는 데 이 접근법을 이용하는 것은 까다로울 수 있다. [6] 반면에, 연역적 추론은 광범위한 일반화에서 시작하고 가정된 사실에 대한 특정 진술에 점진적으로 초점을 맞춘다. [7] 이 접근법은 여러분이 어떤 것에 대한 세부 사항을 제대로 이해하지는 못하지만, 그것의 결과들 중 일부를 관찰할 수 있을 때 가장 유용하다. [8] 이를 사용해서 과학자는 단 하나 또는 몇 개의 합리적인 설명들까지 사실의 범위를 좁힐 때까지 선택지를 차례차례 배제한다.

4 ④

1 We turn to *our surroundings* (to mirror and remind us of / *the moods and ideas* [(which[that]) we respect]).
우리는 우리의 주변 환경에 의지한다 (반영하고 우리에게 일깨워 줄 / 분위기와 관념을 [우리가 중요시하는])

2 Wallpaper, benches, paintings, and streets / help us / combat *the feeling* [that our true selves are disappearing].
벽지, 벤치, 그림, 거리가 / 우리를 돕는다 / 감정과 싸우도록 [우리의 진정한 자아가 사라지고 있다는]

3 In this way, / we honor / *that place* [whose outlook most matches our own] / with the word *home*.
이런 식으로 / 우리는 명예를 준다 / 그 장소에 [조망이 우리의 것과 가장 일치하는] / '집'이라는 단어로

4 To speak of a building as a home / is simply to recognize // that it's in harmony with our hearts.
한 건물을 집이라고 말하는 것은 / 그저 인식하는 것이다 // 그것이 우리의 마음과 조화를 이룬다는 것을

5 Our love of a home / is an acknowledgement // that our identity is not entirely self-determined.
집에 대한 우리의 사랑은 / 인정이다 // 우리의 정체성이 전적으로 스스로 결정되지는 않는다는

6 Just as our moods and ideas are reflected / in our environment, // so too are they shaped by it.
우리의 감정과 생각이 반영되는 것처럼 / 우리의 환경에 // 그것들(우리의 감정과 생각) 또한 그것(우리의 환경)에 의해 형성된다

7 In a sense, / our homes become physical manifestations of our inner selves, / sculpted from the very essence of who we are.
어느 정도 / 우리의 집은 우리 내적 자아의 물리적 표명이 된다 / 우리가 누구인지에 대한 바로 그 본질로부터 형상이 만들어진

8 Yet, / as our inner selves shift over time, // our homes often become outdated versions.
그러나 / 우리의 내적 자아가 시간이 흐르면서 바뀌듯이 // 우리의 집도 종종 구식의 형태가 된다

9 This is // when we step into the role of the architect.
이는 ~이다 // 우리가 건축가의 역할을 시작할 때

10 In the process of reconstruction, / we bridge the gap (between the old and the new).
재건축 과정에서 / 우리는 간극을 메운다 (옛것과 새로운 것 사이의)

해설

밑줄 문장 확인하기 ⊙

9 '이(This)'는 우리가 '건축가의 역할을 시작할' 때임.

추론 근거로 정답 찾기 ⊕

6, 7 우리의 감정과 생각이 환경에 반영되듯, 우리의 감정과 생각도 환경의 영향을 받아 형성되므로, 우리의 집은 어느 정도 우리의 내적 자아를 물리적으로 보여주는 것임.
8 내적 자아가 바뀌듯이 우리의 집도 종종 구식의 형태가 됨.
10 우리는 재건축으로 옛것과 새로운 것의 간극을 메움.

↓

인간의 정체성과 집은 서로 영향을 주고받으며 형성된다는 내용이다. 빈칸 문장의 This는 우리의 내적 자아가 바뀌듯이 우리의 집도 종종 구식의 형태가 된다는 앞 문장의 내용을 받으므로, 내적 자아(정체성)가 바뀌면 그것의 물리적 표명인 우리의 집(환경)도 바꿔서 차이를 줄이고 조화시켜야 함을 추론할 수 있다.
→ ④ harmonize our environments with our evolving identities(우리의 환경을 우리의 점진적으로 변화하는 정체성과 조화시키다)

오답 확인

① reorganize our places to discover our potential
우리의 잠재력을 발견하기 위해 우리의 장소를 개조하다
② transform ourselves to break free from old habits
오래된 습관을 떨치도록 우리 자신을 바꾸다
③ explore new experiences to broaden our perspective
우리의 관점을 넓히기 위해 새로운 경험을 탐구하다
⑤ give weight to long-lasting consequences and sustainability 오래 지속되는 결과와 지속 가능성을 중요시하다
*①, ②, ③, ⑤ → 언급되지 않은 내용.

어휘

acknowledgement 인정; 감사   combat 싸우다; 전투
manifestation 표명; 징후   mirror 반영하다; 비추다
outdated 구식의   outlook 조망, 경치; 관점   respect 중요시하다; 존경(하다)   sculpt 형상을 만들다; 조각하다   step into ~을 시작하다
turn to A A에 의지하다
[선택지] give weight to A A를 중요시하다   reorganize 개조하다, 개편하다; 재편성하다   sustainability 지속 가능성

구문 분석

3 In this way, / we honor / ***that place*** [**whose** outlook most matches our own] / with the word *home*.
소유격 관계대명사 whose가 이끄는 절이 that place를 수식함.

해석 **1** 우리는 우리가 중요시하는 분위기와 관념을 반영하고 우리에게 일깨워 줄 우리의 주변 환경에 의지한다. **2** 벽지, 벤치, 그림, 거리가 우리의 진정한 자아가 사라지고 있다는 감정과 싸우도록 우리를 돕는다. **3** 이런 식으로, 우리는 조망이 우리의 것과 가장 일치하는 그 장소에 '집'이라는 단어로 명예를 준다. **4** 한 건물을 집이라고 말하는 것은 그저 그것이 우리의 마음과 조화를 이룬다는 것을 인식하는 것이다. **5** 집에 대한 우리의 사랑은 우리의 정체성이 전적으로 스스로 결정되지는 않는다는 인정이다. **6** 우리의 감정과 생각이 우리의 환경에 반영되는 것처럼, 그것들(우리의 감정과 생각) 또한 그것(우리의 환경)에 의해 형성된다. **7** 어느 정도, 우리의 집은 우리 내적 자아의 물리적 표명이 되며, 우리가 누구인지에 대한 바로 그 본질로부터 형상이 만들어진 것이다. **8** 그러나, 우리의 내적 자아가 시간이 흐르면서 바뀌듯이 우리의 집도 종종 구식의 형태가 된다. **9** 이는 우리가 건축가의 역할을 시작할 때이다. **10** 재건축 과정에서, 우리는 옛것과 새로운 것 사이의 간극을 메운다.

MEMO

쎄듀 초·중등 커리큘럼

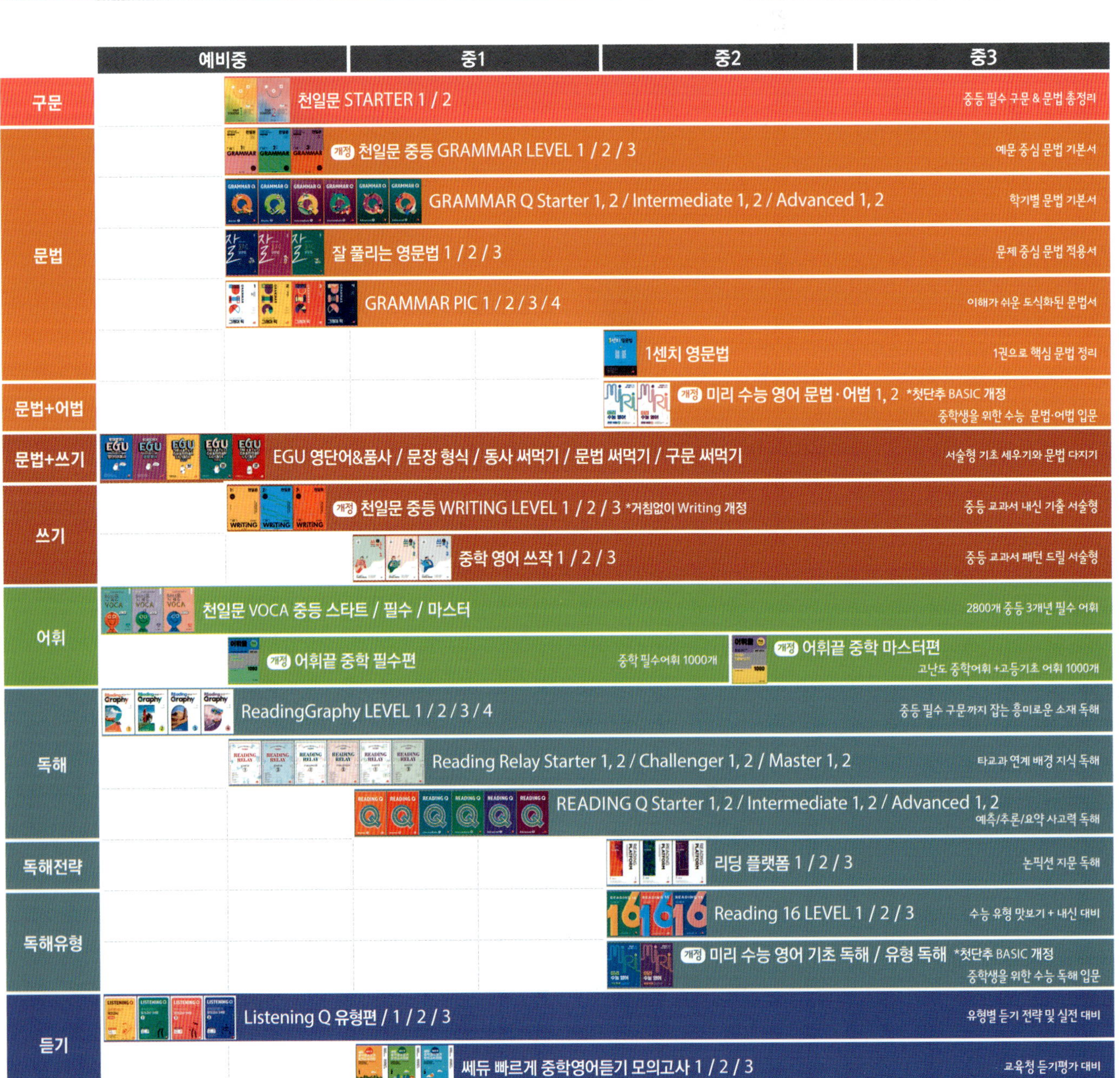

초등

	예비초	초1	초2	초3	초4	초5	초6
구문		천일문 365 일력 |초1-3| 교육부 지정 초등 필수 영어 문장		초등코치 천일문 SENTENCE 1001개 통문장 암기로 완성하는 초등 영어의 기초			
문법				초등코치 천일문 GRAMMAR 1001개 예문으로 배우는 초등 영문법			
		왓츠 Grammar			Start (초등 기초 영문법) / Plus (초등 영문법 마무리)		
독해		왓츠 리딩 30|40 / 50 / 60 / 70 / 80 / 90 / 100			쉽고 재미있게 완성되는 영어 독해력		
어휘				초등코치 천일문 VOCA&STORY 1001개의 초등 필수 어휘와 짧은 스토리			
		패턴으로 말하는 초등 필수 영단어 1 / 2		문장 패턴으로 완성하는 초등 필수 영단어			
ELT	Oh! My PHONICS 1 / 2 / 3 / 4			유·초등학생을 위한 첫 영어 파닉스			
		Oh! My SPEAKING 1 / 2 / 3 / 4 / 5 / 6 핵심 문장 패턴으로 더욱 쉬운 영어 말하기					
		Oh! My GRAMMAR 1 / 2 / 3 쓰기로 완성하는 첫 초등 영문법					

중등

	예비중	중1	중2	중3
구문		천일문 STARTER 1 / 2		중등 필수 구문 & 문법 총정리
문법		개정 천일문 중등 GRAMMAR LEVEL 1 / 2 / 3		예문 중심 문법 기본서
		GRAMMAR Q Starter 1, 2 / Intermediate 1, 2 / Advanced 1, 2		학기별 문법 기본서
		잘 풀리는 영문법 1 / 2 / 3		문제 중심 문법 적용서
		GRAMMAR PIC 1 / 2 / 3 / 4		이해가 쉬운 도식화된 문법서
			1센치 영문법	1권으로 핵심 문법 정리
문법+어법			개정 미리 수능 영어 문법·어법 1, 2 *첫단추 BASIC 개정 중학생을 위한 수능 문법·어법 입문	
문법+쓰기	EGU 영단어&품사 / 문장 형식 / 동사 써먹기 / 문법 써먹기 / 구문 써먹기			서술형 기초 세우기와 문법 다지기
쓰기		개정 천일문 중등 WRITING LEVEL 1 / 2 / 3 *거침없이 Writing 개정		중등 교과서 내신 기출 서술형
		중학 영어 쓰작 1 / 2 / 3		중등 교과서 패턴 드릴 서술형
어휘	천일문 VOCA 중등 스타트 / 필수 / 마스터			2800개 중등 3개년 필수 어휘
		개정 어휘끝 중학 필수편	중학 필수어휘 1000개 · 개정 어휘끝 중학 마스터편	고난도 중학어휘 +고등기초 어휘 1000개
독해	ReadingGraphy LEVEL 1 / 2 / 3 / 4			중등 필수 구문까지 잡는 흥미로운 소재 독해
		Reading Relay Starter 1, 2 / Challenger 1, 2 / Master 1, 2		타교과 연계 배경 지식 독해
		READING Q Starter 1, 2 / Intermediate 1, 2 / Advanced 1, 2		예측/추론/요약 사고력 독해
독해전략			리딩 플랫폼 1 / 2 / 3	논픽션 지문 독해
독해유형			Reading 16 LEVEL 1 / 2 / 3	수능 유형 맛보기 + 내신 대비
			개정 미리 수능 영어 기초 독해 / 유형 독해 *첫단추 BASIC 개정	중학생을 위한 수능 독해 입문
듣기	Listening Q 유형편 / 1 / 2 / 3			유형별 듣기 전략 및 실전 대비
		쎄듀 빠르게 중학영어듣기 모의고사 1 / 2 / 3		교육청 듣기평가 대비

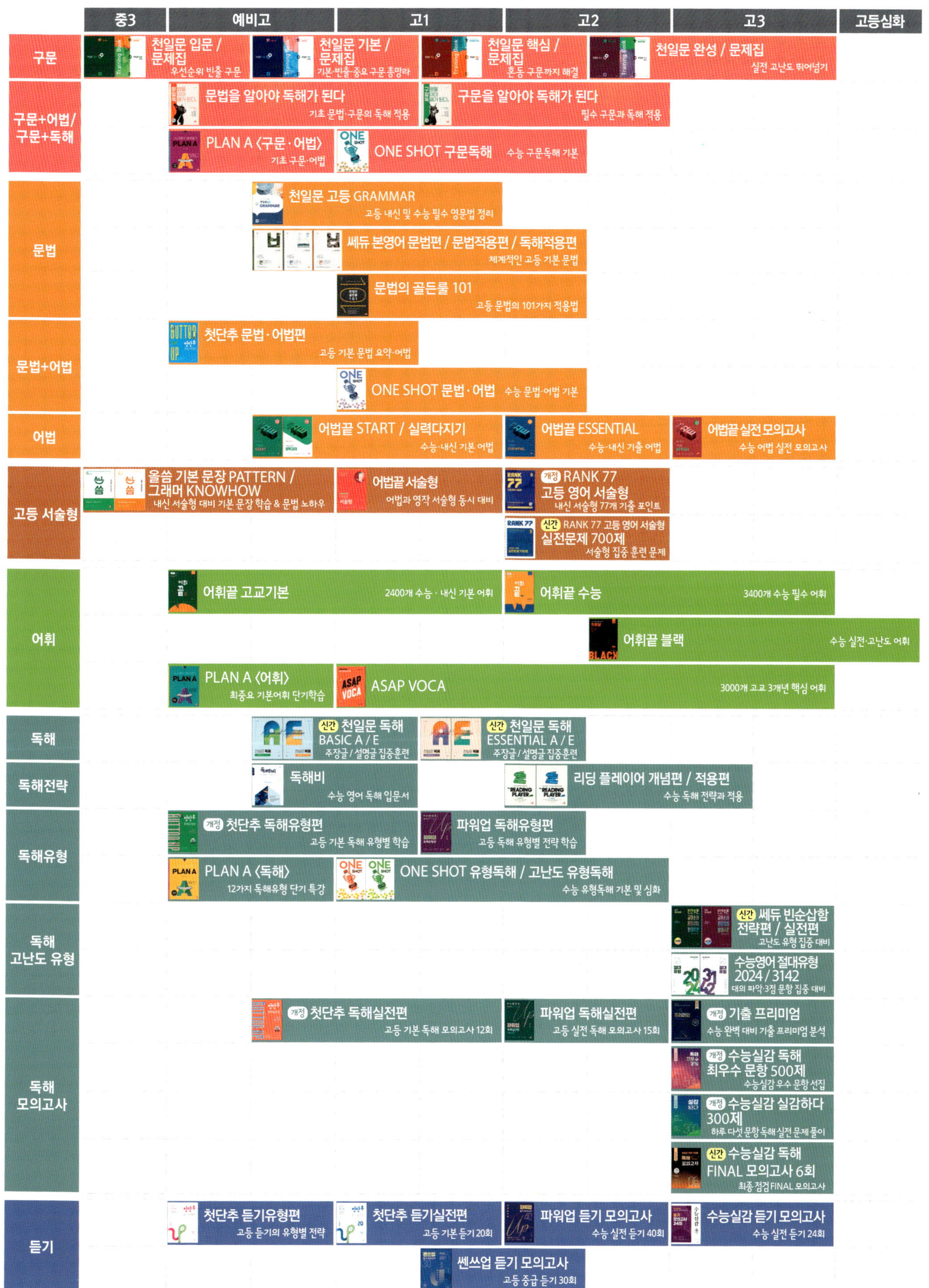

쎄듀 고등 커리큘럼

중3 | 예비고 | 고1 | 고2 | 고3 | 고등심화

구문
천일문 입문 / 문제집
우선순위 빈출 구문
천일문 기본 / 문제집
기본·빈출·중요 구문 총망라
천일문 핵심 / 문제집
혼동 구문까지 해결
천일문 완성 / 문제집
실전 고난도 뛰어넘기

구문+어법 / 구문+독해
문법을 알아야 독해가 된다
기초 문법·구문의 독해 적용
구문을 알아야 독해가 된다
필수 구문과 독해 적용
PLAN A 〈구문·어법〉
기초 구문·어법
ONE SHOT 구문독해
수능 구문독해 기본

문법
천일문 고등 GRAMMAR
고등 내신 및 수능 필수 영문법 정리
쎄듀 본영어 문법편 / 문법적용편 / 독해적용편
체계적인 고등 기본 문법
문법의 골든룰 101
고등 문법의 101가지 적용법

문법+어법
첫단추 문법·어법편
고등 기본 문법 요약·어법
ONE SHOT 문법·어법 수능 문법·어법 기본

어법
어법끝 START / 실력다지기
수능·내신 기본 어법
어법끝 ESSENTIAL
수능·내신 기출 어법
어법끝 실전 모의고사
수능 어법 실전 모의고사

고등 서술형
올쏨 기본 문장 PATTERN / 그래머 KNOWHOW
내신 서술형 대비 기본 문장 학습 & 문법 노하우
어법끝 서술형
어법과 영작 서술형 동시 대비
개정 RANK 77 고등 영어 서술형
내신 서술형 77개 기출 포인트
신간 RANK 77 고등 영어 서술형
실전문제 700제
서술형 집중 훈련 문제

어휘
어휘끝 고교기본 2400개 수능·내신 기본 어휘
어휘끝 수능 3400개 수능 필수 어휘
어휘끝 블랙 수능 실전·고난도 어휘
PLAN A 〈어휘〉
최중요 기본어휘 단기학습
ASAP VOCA 3000개 고교 3개년 핵심 어휘

독해
신간 천일문 독해 BASIC A / E 주장글 / 설명글 집중훈련
신간 천일문 독해 ESSENTIAL A / E 주장글 / 설명글 집중훈련

독해전략
독해비 수능 영어 독해 입문서
리딩 플레이어 개념편 / 적용편 수능 독해 전략과 적용

독해유형
개정 첫단추 독해유형편 고등 기본 독해 유형별 학습
파워업 독해유형편 고등 독해 유형별 전략 학습
PLAN A 〈독해〉 12가지 독해유형 단기 특강
ONE SHOT 유형독해 / 고난도 유형독해 수능 유형독해 기본 및 심화

독해 고난도 유형
신간 쎄듀 빈순삽함 전략편 / 실전편 고난도 유형 집중 대비
수능영어 절대유형 2024 / 3142 대의 파악·3점 문항 집중 대비

독해 모의고사
개정 첫단추 독해실전편 고등 기본 독해 모의고사 12회
파워업 독해실전편 고등 실전 독해 모의고사 15회
개정 기출 프리미엄 수능 완벽 대비 기출 프리미엄 분석
개정 수능실감 독해 최우수 문항 500제 수능실감 우수 문항 선집
개정 수능실감 실감하다 300제 하루 다섯 문항 독해실전 문제 풀이
신간 수능실감 독해 FINAL 모의고사 6회 최종 점검 FINAL 모의고사

듣기
첫단추 듣기유형편 고등 듣기의 유형별 전략
첫단추 듣기실전편 고등 기본 듣기 20회
파워업 듣기 모의고사 수능 실전 듣기 40회
수능실감 듣기 모의고사 수능 실전 듣기 24회
쎈쓰업 듣기 모의고사 고등 중급 듣기 30회